A Guide to the IBA Rules on the Taking of Evidence in International Arbitration

A Guide to the IBA Rules on the Taking of Evidence in International Arbitration

ROMAN KHODYKIN

Partner, Bryan Cave Leighton Paisner LLP, Visiting Professor in the Centre for Commercial Law at Queen Mary University of London

CAROL MULCAHY

Chartered Arbitrator, Partner, Bryan Cave Leighton Paisner LLP

NICHOLAS FLETCHER QC

4 New Square, London

OXFORD
UNIVERSITY PRESS

OXFORD
UNIVERSITY PRESS

Great Clarendon Street, Oxford, OX2 6DP,
United Kingdom

Oxford University Press is a department of the University of Oxford.
It furthers the University's objective of excellence in research, scholarship,
and education by publishing worldwide. Oxford is a registered trade mark of
Oxford University Press in the UK and in certain other countries

First Edition published in 2019

Published in the United States of America by Oxford University Press
198 Madison Avenue, New York, NY 10016, United States of America

British Library Cataloguing in Publication Data

Data available

Library of Congress Control Number: 2019936392

ISBN 978–0–19–881834–2

Preface

The IBA Rules on the Taking of Evidence in International Arbitration have their genesis in the 1983 IBA Supplementary Rules Governing the Presentation and Reception of Evidence in International Commercial Arbitration. At the instigation of the Arbitration Committee of the IBA, these earlier rules were replaced in 1999 by the IBA Rules on the Taking of Evidence in International Arbitration ('1999 Rules'). The 1999 Rules were drawn up, after extensive consultation, by a working party comprising eminent arbitrators and arbitration counsel drawn from all parts of the world and, importantly, from differing legal traditions. The 1999 Rules were widely adopted and their success was such that, in 2008, a subcommittee was established by the IBA Arbitration Committee to review the operation of those rules and to consider the extent to which revisions and amendments were appropriate. As with the original working party, the IBA Rules of Evidence Review Subcommittee comprised distinguished practitioners from a variety of common law and civil law backgrounds. It also had the benefit of input from members of the original working party.

Revised rules were approved by the IBA Council on 29 May 2010. It is those rules (the 'Rules', or the 'IBA Rules') that are the subject of this book, although changes from the text of the 1999 Rules are analysed, and we have endeavoured in such situations to explain the rationale for the change and, where possible, the mischief that it was intended to address.

One of the great strengths of the IBA Rules, in each of their incarnations, has been their flexibility and that they have proved popular with both common law and civil law practitioners alike. In recognition of this, and to make this guide as useful as possible, we have therefore sought to cast a wide net in our analysis of the IBA Rules and the manner in which they have been interpreted, utilized, and deployed throughout the international arbitration community. Together, we represent both common law and civil law traditions and have sought to reflect that experience in our commentary. We have also been assisted in this by friends and colleagues in arbitration practices throughout the world, for which assistance we are most grateful. It is our hope that, from whatever legal tradition they come, all international arbitration practitioners will find this book to be of assistance.

In their latest incarnation, the Rules are almost ubiquitous. Early procedural orders, whether proposed by arbitrators or drafted by counsel, almost invariably make reference to the Rules. Frequently, the Rules are adopted as a guide, rather than on a mandatory basis. We examine the reasons for that in the text.

The book follows the structure of the Rules themselves, starting with the Preamble and then tracking from Article 1 all the way through to Article 9. Each chapter sets out the text of the full Article before examining the individual provisions in more detail. Many practitioners will be most familiar with the wording and application of Article 3, 'Documents', and Article 9, 'Admissibility and Assessment of Evidence'. It is these two articles that most often exercise parties in their application to the process of document production. We thoroughly examine the operation of these provisions and the manner in which they are applied. However, we pay equally close attention to those elements of the Rules that are often neglected or glossed over by the parties. These include the need for consultation on evidentiary issues, increasingly important, given the time and costs challenges faced by parties and counsel, the rules applicable to witnesses of fact and to experts (whether appointed by the parties or by the tribunal), and to the running of the hearing itself.

The background and experience of counsel participating in international arbitration varies enormously. In the course of our careers we have encountered very many eminent and knowledgeable arbitration practitioners who will be alive to many of the questions raised in this book. We hope that those individuals will nonetheless find issues of interest within the commentary and analysis that we have included. For those practitioners with less extensive experience of international arbitration, we have included material explaining the background and context for many of the provisions contained within the Rules. Lastly, to be useful to practitioners, a guide needs above all to be practical. In addition to our commentary on the text of the Rules, we have, wherever appropriate, sought to include practical examples and to provide checklists in relation to specific Articles that may assist some readers. We welcome feedback on these, as well as upon the text as a whole.

We hope that readers find this book a timely addition to the learning on the application and scope of the IBA Rules. At the time of writing, a new set of rules on the conduct of proceedings in international arbitration has been produced. The Prague Rules on the Efficient Conduct of Proceedings in International Arbitration were published on 14 December 2018. The promoters of the Prague Rules believe that these rules, which are said to be based on the inquisitorial model of procedure, will encourage a more active role by arbitral tribunals and will contribute to increasing efficiency in international arbitration. We will watch with interest the extent to which the Prague Rules are taken up by practitioners, or whether more flexible use is made of the IBA Rules to achieve the same outcomes sought by the promoters of the Prague Rules. What is clear today is that the IBA Rules have a firm and fast place in the conduct of international arbitration and we trust this text will assist practitioners in understanding and applying the IBA Rules for many years to come.

As Consultant Editor, I extend my thanks first of all to Carol Mulcahy and Roman Khodykin of Bryan Cave Leighton Paisner. This book was their idea and it is they who have done the hardest work of all. Together, we thank Victoria Clark of Bryan Cave

Leighton Paisner, who has been tireless in tracking down sources for the book and without whom it could not have been completed, the many law firms around the globe who have responded to our questionnaire on use of the IBA Rules (and to whom we express individual thanks elsewhere in this book), the IBA for permitting us to reprint the rules, the invaluable Commentary on those rules written by the IBA Rules of Evidence Review Subcommittee and, last but by no means least, Oxford University Press for their support for our endeavours.

Nicholas Fletcher QC
4 New Square, Lincoln's Inn
May 2019

Acknowledgements

Over the period 2017 to 2018 the authors conducted a survey on use of the IBA Rules on the Taking of Evidence in International Arbitration among a number of law firms in various jurisdictions (referred to in the text as BCLP Survey on use of the IBA Rules). We wish to thank the many firms who contributed to that survey. In particular, we thank Gonzalo García Delatour and Alejandro Markous of Beccar Varela (Argentina); Scott Chesterman of Minter Ellison (Australia); Kent Thomson and Sean Campbell of Davies Ward Phillips & Vineberg LLP (Canada); Xuehua Wang of Beijing Huanzhong & Partners (China); Athina Fouchard Papaefstratiou of Eversheds Sutherland (formerly with Lazareff Le Bars) (France); Dr Inka Hanefeld of Hanefeld Rechtsanwälte (Germany); Sharon Daly of Matheson (Ireland); Filippo Corsini of Chiomenti Studio Legale with the assistance of Camera Arbitrale di Milano (Italy); Krushchev Ekwueme of Olaniwun Ajayi LP (Nigeria); Alberto Fortun and Rita Gouveia of Cuatrecasas (Spain and Portugal); James Hope of Advokatfirman Vinge KB (Sweden); and James Hosking of Chaffetz Lindsey LLP (US). Last, but not least, our thanks go to our colleagues in the Bryan Cave Leighton Paisner offices in Moscow, Paris, Hong Kong, Singapore, and the UAE.

The extracts from the IBA Rules on the Taking of Evidence in International Arbitration that appear at the beginning of each chapter of this book, and the Commentary on the Revised Text of the 2010 IBA Rules on the Taking of Evidence in International Arbitration, are reproduced by kind permission of the International Bar Association, London, UK, and are available at: www.ibanet.org/Publications/publications_IBA_guides_and_free_materials.aspx

Contents

Table of Cases

INTERNATIONAL

European Court Reports

International Centre for Settlement of Investment Disputes (ICSID)

International Chamber of Commerce

International Court of Justice (ICJ)

North American Free Trade Agreement (NAFTA)

Permanent Court of Arbitration (PCA)

NATIONAL COURTS

Argentina

Australia

Canada

China

France

Holland

Hong Kong

India

Iran-US Claims Tribunal

Ireland

Russia

Scotland

Singapore

Sweden

Switzerland

United Kingdom

United States

Table of Legislation and other Legal Instruments

UK STATUTES

ENGLISH CIVILP ROCEDURE RULES 1998 (SI 1998/3132)

OTHER LEGISLATION

Australia

Belgium

Brazil

Canada

EC SECONDARY LEGISLATION

INSTITUTIONAL ARBITRATION RULES

INTERNATIONAL INSTRUMENTS

Conventions

Model Laws

Protocols, Guidance and Optional Rules for Use in Arbitration

1

Provenance and Development of the IBA Rules on Evidence

A. Provenance of the IBA Rules

The IBA Rules on the Taking of Evidence in International Arbitration (the 'IBA Rules') are internationally recognized and widely used in the practice of international arbitration. Although the first edition of the IBA Rules adopted in 1983 is materially different in a number of respects from the most recent edition adopted in 2010, the fundamental objective underlying each version of the rules remains the same: to provide some common ground for the production of evidence in the significant number of international arbitrations that take place globally every year, and to provide a bridge between the different legal traditions and domestic practices with which individual arbitration practitioners are familiar. 1.1

The IBA Rules derive from the work product of IBA Committee D (Procedures for Settling Disputes).[1] When the first edition of the rules was produced in 1983, Committee D comprised approximately 380 lawyers from many different countries around the world. In an article on the drafting of the 1983 Rules,[2] David Shenton, then Chair of that committee, explains that Committee D seemed a useful forum for discussion of the problems that can arise when lawyers and arbitrators from countries with different procedural rules come to present and address claims in international arbitration. 1.2

The task with which a subcommittee of Committee D was then charged was clear, but challenging. Shenton explains that the intention was not to draft a uniform set of rules to govern arbitration proceedings. There were existing institutional and ad hoc rules 1.3

[1] Committee D (Procedures for Settling Disputes) of the International Bar Association's Section on Business Law.

[2] DW Shenton, 'An Introduction to the IBA Rules of Evidence' [1985] Arbitration International 118 (hereafter 'Shenton').

that provided such frameworks. Instead, the rules to be drafted were to be confined to procedures for production of evidence, a subject that was—to a great extent—avoided by the more general arbitration rules. Shenton's view was that those other rules did not 'face up to the difficult decisions of detail that have to be made or agreed between those advising the parties or, failing them, the arbitrators, in circumstances where the parties, their counsel, and the tribunal may come from a mixture of common law and civil law jurisdictions.

1.4 Thus, it was decided that the work of the subcommittee should be directed to 'the mechanics of presenting or receiving evidence'. Shenton goes on to describe how, in undertaking its work, the subcommittee:

> [T]ried to go through the sort of negotiations that would be carried out in practice if lawyers and arbitrators from common law and civil law systems actually had to sit down and agree upon a procedure for an actual arbitration between parties of a civil law and of a common law country.

1.5 One of the most significant problems the subcommittee had to deal with was the differences that exist between the common law adversarial approach to the laying out of a case for judicial consideration, and the civil law's inquisitorial system. The subcommittee had available to it the reports of a symposium held by the Institute of Arbitrators[3] in February 1974 on presenting evidence in proceedings and arbitrations in civil law and common law countries.[4] At that symposium, eminent practitioners[5] (principally from Western and Eastern Europe and the United States) explained, in turn, the approach to presentation of evidence generally adopted in international commercial arbitration conducted in their home jurisdictions, and the expectations around that subject that practitioners derive from their domestic legal regime. Speakers explained the process adopted in some detail, by reference to a hypothetical case. . Common themes, as well as significant differences, were identified. A key difference was the manner of presenting evidence through witnesses, and the relative value of evidence obtained under 'destructive' cross-examination compared with that contained in documents.

1.6 Shenton's description of the problems the subcommittee faced in trying to draft the 1983 Rules reflects the differences expressed at the symposium, and provides background context as to why it was desirable to find a workable middle ground for users of international arbitration:

> In the adversarial system, the burden lies with the parties, or more accurately their legal advisers, to allege their case, to deploy and lay out the evidence they propose

[3] Now the Chartered Institute of Arbitrators.

[4] Symposium held in London on 14–16 February 1974 on the theme '*Analysis of Differences in the Way of Presenting Evidence in Arbitrations under Civil and Common Law Systems*' published in Arbitration (The Journal of the Chartered Institute of Arbitrators) April 1974 (Special Issue).

[5] Well-known participating practitioners from the field of international arbitration included Yves Derains, Pierre Lalive, Arthur Marriott, Alan Redfern, Pieter Sanders, Hans van Houtte, Bernado Cremades, Howard Holtzmann and Sergei Lebedev, to name but a few.

to put before the arbitrators in order to prove their allegations and to test and, as far as possible, to discredit the evidence called in support of the allegations of the other side by the process which common law lawyers call cross-examination. The tribunal's role is to examine the evidence and arguments deployed on behalf of the parties, to rule on its admissibility or otherwise, to decide on the weight to be attached to it, to act as a kind of referee ensuring that the rules of the game are fairly observed, and, finally, to decide the merits on the basis of the evidence and arguments presented by the two sides.

[...]

It is an integral requirement of this system that the parties disclose to each other in advance the documentation comprising the written part of the evidence. It is also fundamental that each party disclose to the other side all the relevant written material, whether such material is supportive of that party's case or not. This is the procedure known as discovery, and under the common law system it is regarded as of paramount importance. It is a cornerstone of the system that the basic evidence is called in the form of verbal testimony of witnesses, including the testimony of the parties to the dispute. It is equally fundamental that such evidence be tested by cross-examination. As Mr Robert Goff QC, stated in his presentation at the Symposium, '[i]t is a strong conviction of English practising lawyers that, on a contested question of fact, the most satisfactory way to get to the bottom of the matter is, if possible, to see and hear the actual witnesses and to test their evidence by cross-examination in the light of all relevant matters, including contemporary documents . . . '

In civil law systems, whether arbitrators are expected to apply the rules of evidence and procedure of their national courts, or whether they are themselves left to determine the procedure for examining and taking evidence, the approach is inquisitorial. Lawyers having presented written arguments, allegations and documents in advance, it is for the judge or arbitrator adjudicating on the matter to determine how the testimony will be received, how evidentiary matters that remain unclear will be investigated, and where or whether verbal testimony is required. It is the tribunal that questions the witness of its own motion or, at best, at the instance of the lawyers of one or other of the parties. As Professor Roger Perrot put it; '[t]he technique of "direct examination" and of "cross-examination" of the parties, witnesses or experts is totally unknown in our legal systems in Continental Europe. The arbitrator is the person in charge of the investigation. It is he who conducts the hearing of witnesses, who puts questions to them and who challenges them if necessary in order to obtain further details . . . '

It is said that the civil law system does not have 'discovery' as understood in common law systems. However, in exercising its functions, any tribunal, be it a court or arbitrators, has the power to require the parties to produce documents which are considered to be conclusive for the resolving of the dispute . . . a refusal by a party to accede to the invitation of the arbitrator would be met by the well-known formula that the arbitrator may 'draw all legal consequences', ie accept submissions of fact by the opposing party which, it is suggested, could have been proved by the documents that the other party refuses to produce upon the arbitrator's order. There is undoubtedly a strong feeling among civil lawyers that documentary evidence is more reliable than oral testimony.[6]

B. Publication of the IBA Rules on Evidence

1.7 The first edition of the IBA Rules was adopted on 28 May 1983.[7] The full title given to those rules (*Supplementary Rules Governing the Presentation and Reception of Evidence in International Commercial Arbitration*) reflects the subcommittee's decision that the new rules should provide practical procedures for the reception of evidence that would *supplement* the procedural framework provided by existing institutional and ad hoc arbitration rules.[8] Importantly, the introduction to the 1983 Rules suggested that, even if not specifically adopted by agreement between the parties, the rules could still serve as a guide to arbitrators 'when the parties in contention come from law areas[9] having rules of procedures derived from different systems'.

1.8 The subcommittee responsible for producing the 1983 Rules remained as a standing committee to consider revisions to those rules. Despite the wide geographical membership of IBA Committee D, members of the subcommittee were principally lawyers from England, France, Germany, and the United States. The composition of the Working Party responsible for production of a revised set of rules in 1999 had a very similar composition.[10] Importantly, by the time that work on the current 2010 Rules was undertaken, the composition of the drafting subcommittee had a much wider global representation, including representatives from the United States, Canada, Colombia, Argentina, New Zealand, the United Kingdom, France, Spain, Germany, Switzerland, Greece, the UAE, China, Korea, and Japan.[11]

1.9 The IBA Rules have been a significant success and are generally regarded as representing best practice in international arbitration. In particular, where the participants

[6] Shenton (n 2) 120–22.

[7] IBA Supplementary Rules Governing the Presentation and Reception of Evidence in International Commercial Arbitration 1983 (hereafter '1983 IBA Rules').

[8] ibid Article 1.1, states expressly that '[t]hese are procedural rules governing the presentation of evidence ... *intended to supplement any other rules applicable to the arbitration* ...' (emphasis added).

[9] The Introduction to the 1983 IBA Rules (n 7) uses the phrase 'law areas having rules of procedures derived from different systems'. There is no commentary on this particular choice of words in the 1983 Rules, but we believe it may be reasonably inferred from the phraseology used in subsequent iterations of the rules and commentary that it is intended to refer to jurisdictions with different legal traditions (ie in broad terms common law systems or civil law systems) and therefore different procedural rules. The Introduction to the 1999 IBA Rules and to the 2010 Rules uses the phrase 'parties from different legal traditions'. The Commentary on the revised text of the 2010 Rules refers to the procedural issues that can arise 'when the parties come from different legal backgrounds and cultures'. It also references the adoption of the 1983 Rules and the fact that they 'were frequently discussed at arbitration conferences as an example of the harmonization procedures that can occur in international arbitrations'.

[10] The Working Party charged with drafting the 1999 IBA Rules was made up of representatives from Italy, Sweden, England, France, Spain, The Netherlands, Switzerland, Germany, Belgium, the United States, and Hong Kong.

[11] The IBA Rules of Evidence Review Subcommittee, led by Richard Kreindler of the United States/Germany.

to an arbitration are from different jurisdictions, the IBA Rules provide a workable regime sensitive to the differences in perception and practice around presentation of evidence. However, this success has not happened overnight. Use and acceptance of the IBA Rules has evolved over time in tandem with the various iterations of those rules.

1. The 1983 IBA Rules

The 1983 IBA Rules had only seven articles compared with the nine articles contained in the (current) 2010 Rules. 1.10

In addition to Article 1 (*Scope of Application*) and Article 2 (*Definitions*), the 1983 IBA Rules contained (in summary) five articles that together covered written submissions, production of documents, witnesses, and tribunal powers. Article 3 (*Introductory Submissions*) is interesting because it does not appear in any of the later iterations of the rules; it is also very short. It simply provides that any *Introductory Submission* (defined broadly to include any form of pleading or submissions) should contain 'the means by which the facts relevant to the dispute are intended to be provided by that party, including, for each of such facts, the names of witnesses and references to documents'.[12] For parties from common law jurisdictions this would have been a novel requirement. 1.11

Article 4 of the 1983 IBA Rules (*Production of Documents*) was important because it represented a first attempt at compromise between common law and civil law approaches to disclosure of documents. Under Article 4, following the conclusion of pre-hearing written submissions, each party was required to produce to the other party a list of the documents upon which it wished to rely. In addition, as a concession to the common law approach of 'complete' disclosure or discovery of relevant documents (including adverse documents), Article 4(4) provided that a party could make a request for a document not listed by its opponent but that was 'relevant to the dispute'. However, for common law lawyers, the provision came with an impediment in the form of a requirement that the requested document must (a) have passed to/from the opponent party from/to a third party and (b) be capable of identification with reasonable particularity. Thus (as Shenton notes) documents generated entirely within a corporate body would not fall within the disclosure mechanism provided for in the rule. 1.12

Article 5 (*Witnesses*) also represented a compromise between legal traditions. Under this article, witness evidence was to be produced in the form of written statements to be delivered to the tribunal only. The tribunal would then circulate the witness evidence to the parties simultaneously.[13] The right to request the attendance of a witness 1.13

[12] 1983 IBA Rules (n 7), Article 3. Article 6 (*Scope of Proceedings*) also provides that whenever terms of reference are drawn up they shall contain a list of the witnesses who will be called upon to give evidence at the hearing, and the issues upon which each witness will testify.

[13] 1983 IBA Rules (n 7), Articles 5.1 and 5.3. Each party had the right to deliver further or supplementary witness evidence.

for cross-examination (regarded as an essential tool in common law court process) was permitted, but more tightly controlled than would be the case today.[14] Witnesses attending for examination were to be questioned first by the tribunal before being handed over to counsel for examination in chief and cross-examination.

1.14 Article 7 (*Arbitrator's Powers*) set out express powers of the arbitrator in relation to management and assessment of evidence. These included the power to call witnesses to give evidence orally, or to rule that evidence from a witness should be ignored if the witness failed to appear. The tribunal was also empowered to appoint experts to assist the tribunal or to present evidence, and to rely on the tribunal's own expert knowledge.[15] In addition, in what appears to be a 'sweep up' provision, Article 7 provided for the tribunal to have power to 'exercise all powers it deems necessary to make the arbitration effective and its conduct efficient as regards the taking of evidence'.

2. The 1999 IBA Rules

1.15 In 1997, a Working Party was established to update and review the 1983 IBA Rules. A revised set of rules was published in 1999.[16] The commentary on those new rules noted that in the sixteen years that had elapsed since the 1983 IBA Rules:

> [T]he nature of international arbitration has changed significantly. New procedures have developed; different norms as to appropriate procedures have taken root; and the scope of international arbitration has grown considerably, as many regions of the world formerly inhospitable to international arbitration have now embraced it.[17]

1.16 The 1999 IBA Rules made a number of changes. Some of these were refinements to existing provisions and others introduced more fundamental changes.

1.17 The important phrase 'relevant and material to outcome' appeared for the first time in expanded provision for document production. The revised provisions removed the restriction in the 1983 IBA Rules that limited requests for documents to documents passing between the opponent party and a third party. A party was permitted to address a request to the tribunal for an order requiring production of *any* document believed to be held by the other party, subject to a requirement that the request identify

[14] 1983 IBA Rules (n 7), Articles 4.5–4.8. Following receipt of witness evidence, each party had the right to deliver a notice requesting the right to give oral evidence, or for any of its witnesses to give oral evidence at the hearing, or to request that the witnesses of the other party give oral evidence. The notice had to stipulate the issues to which that oral evidence related. If the other party objected to the request, the question of whether the witness should attend, and the scope of the evidence to be given orally, was to be determined by the tribunal. The tribunal could also itself require witnesses to attend for examination.

[15] The parties were entitled to deliver statements from an expert. See 1983 IBA Rules (n 7), Article 5.2 dealing with witness statements.

[16] IBA Rules on the Taking of Evidence in International Commercial Arbitration 1999 (hereafter '1999 IBA Rules').

[17] IBA Working Party, 'Commentary on the New IBA Rules of Evidence in International Commercial Arbitration' (2000) 2 Business Law International 16 (hereafter 'Commentary on the 1999 IBA Rules').

the document with precision and include an explanation as to how the document was 'relevant and material to the outcome of the case'.[18] Thus, access to a party's internal documents—something that most common law lawyers regarded as a necessary right—was to be permitted but with the safeguard of a stringent test of 'materiality to outcome', designed to keep the expanded access under tight control and within boundaries that recognized the concerns of civil lawyers about encroachment of common law discovery practices.

A second protective measure also introduced by the 1999 IBA Rules was the right of a party to raise an objection to a document production request on one of a number of grounds expressly provided for in the rules as setting the boundaries for evidence to be used in the arbitration.[19] These grounds for excluding evidence and denying requests for production—relevance and materiality, privilege, unreasonable burden, loss or destruction, commercial or technical confidentiality, political or institutional sensitivity, and considerations of fairness or equality—were the foundation for the current provisions in Article 9.2 of the 2010 IBA Rules. A more detailed analysis of these mechanisms—what the Working Party described as a 'well-balanced compromise between the broader view generally taken in common law countries and the more narrow view generally held in civil law countries'—appears later in this text in respect of the current formulation contained in the 2010 IBA Rules. **1.18**

The revisions introduced by the 1999 IBA Rules also included the addition of a Preamble, which set out a number of general principles considered important in 'illustrating both what the Rules hope to accomplish and what they do not intend to do'.[20] Some of the principles were a restatement of matters mentioned in the Introduction to the 1983 IBA Rules, but additions included an express statement that: **1.19**

> The taking of evidence shall be conducted on the principle that each Party shall be entitled to know, reasonably in advance of any Evidentiary Hearing, the evidence on which the other parties rely.

The commentary on the 1999 IBA Rules describes this statement as 'the overriding principle' of the 1999 IBA Rules. In addition, the Preamble introduced a statement encouraging early identification by the tribunal of the issues it regarded as being relevant and material to the outcome of the case, including issues suitable for preliminary determination.[21] The commentary attributed this guidance to a desire for an effective and cost-efficient process.[22]

Clear and detailed provisions relating to the use of expert evidence that accommodated both the common law practice of party-appointed experts (Article 5) and the civilian **1.20**

[18] 1999 IBA Rules (n 16), Article 3.3.
[19] 1999 IBA Rules (n 16), Article 9.2.
[20] Commentary on the 1999 IBA Rules (n 17) 3.
[21] 1999 IBA Rules (n 16), Preamble.
[22] Commentary on the 1999 IBA Rules (n 17) 18.

approach of tribunal-appointed experts (Article 6) were introduced with related provisions intended to preserve the integrity and fairness of the process, and to provide a degree of comfort for those practitioners unfamiliar with one or other of these ways of managing expert evidence. For example, a party-appointed expert had to disclose in the expert report any pre-existing relationship with the instructing party. In relation to tribunal-appointed experts, the tribunal was required to consult with the parties before making the appointment, the parties were entitled to respond to the expert's report by way of submissions, and the expert was required to attend the evidentiary hearing for examination by the parties.

3. The 2010 IBA Rules

1.21 In 2008, the IBA Arbitration Committee established the IBA Rules of Evidence Review Subcommittee and tasked it to review and, as needed, to update the 1999 IBA Rules. The subcommittee held many meetings, and discussed the rules at open fora of the IBA in Buenos Aires in October 2008, in Dubai in February 2009, and in Madrid in October 2009. The subcommittee also conducted an online survey of Arbitration Committee members and others in 2008. In early 2010, the Arbitration Committee circulated a draft for public comment. The contemplated revisions were discussed at numerous arbitration conferences, and the comments received were considered during the review process. Revised IBA Rules were adopted by the IBA Council on 29 May 2010. It is this (latest) version of the IBA Rules that will be examined in this text.

1.22 Some five years later, in June 2015, the Arbitration Committee organized a subcommittee to conduct a worldwide survey on the use of IBA arbitration practice guidelines and rules, including the IBA Rules.[23] The committee received 845 responses from around the world, including from every region. The committee also solicited and received fifty-five country reports containing analysis of the survey responses received from that individual country, and the use of the IBA Rules as reflected in its arbitral jurisprudence and doctrine.[24] Based on that information, the committee found that:[25]

- Nearly half (48 per cent) of the arbitrations known to the survey respondents referenced the IBA Rules on Evidence.
- Save for Latin America and Africa,[26] reference is made to the IBA Rules in more than 50 per cent of arbitrations in all regions.
- The IBA Rules are treated as binding in 20 per cent of arbitrations known to the respondents. However, they are followed in 93.43 per cent of the remaining 80 per

23 The IBA Arbitration Guidelines and Rules Subcommittee.

24 The IBA Arbitration Guidelines and Rules Subcommittee, 'Report on the Reception of the IBA Arbitration Soft Law Products' (International Bar Association 2016) paras 6–9, 40, 49, and 59 <www.ibanet.org/Document/Default.aspx?DocumentUid=105d29a3-6261-4437-84e2-1c8637844beb>accessed 27 November 2018 (hereafter '2016 IBA Report').

25 2016 IBA Report (n 24) paras 12–18.

26 References in Latin America and Africa were 30 per cent and 25 per cent, respectively.

cent of cases where they are consulted as guidelines only, ie only in 6.57 per cent of cases in which they are used as guidelines are they are not followed.

- The survey results did not indicate any significant difference in relation to the frequency with which the IBA Rules on Evidence are referenced in common and civil law jurisdictions.[27]
- There appears to be general consensus that the use of the IBA Rules will grow.[28]

Although there was also found to be a minority view that the IBA Rules are 'too American',[29] these findings indicate the important role that the IBA Rules have come to play in the practice of international arbitration, and speak to the growing acceptance and application of those rules over the four decades since they were introduced. **1.23**

Significantly, other responses to the survey suggest that the IBA Rules should be regarded as an evolving project with possible scope for additional refinement as engagement with the rules increases. The committee noted that the jurisdictions where the rules are most used seem to support most strongly the position that they do not need to be reviewed or revised. In contrast, jurisdictions where the rules are not ordinarily used had a much higher number of respondents in favour of amendment. The committee concluded that jurisdictions such as Africa (where the IBA rules are not commonly used) may want those rules changed in order to reflect a regional compromise, rather than the practices of those currently using them.[30] Further evolution of the IBA Rules may be one route forward. However, if awareness and application of the current rules increases in those jurisdictions, it may be that users will become more comfortable with application of the existing provisions, or that the flexibility inherent in the rules themselves will be fully utilized to accommodate different ways of doing things. **1.24**

[27] An example given in the report is that a relatively high number of English arbitrations referenced the IBA Rules (72 per cent), while a lower number of US arbitrations (56 per cent) did so. The frequency of such references in France was said to lie somewhere between the two (62 per cent). 2016 IBA Report (n 24) para 39.

[28] In circumstances identified by respondents where the IBA Rules were not referenced, respondents cited lack of awareness of the IBA Rules and/or the availability of local or institutional rules on evidence that made reference to the IBA Rules unnecessary.

[29] Interestingly, this view was expressed by respondents from both civil law and common law jurisdictions, being Italy, Brazil, Germany, Finland, Switzerland, Japan, New Zealand, Canada, England, and Ireland. 2016 IBA Report (n 24) para 87. .

[30] 2016 IBA Report (n 24) paras 79–86.

2

Preamble

1. These IBA Rules on the Taking of Evidence in International Arbitration are intended to provide an efficient, economical and fair process for the taking of evidence in international arbitrations, particularly those between Parties from different legal traditions. They are designed to supplement the legal provisions and the institutional, ad hoc or other rules that apply to the conduct of the arbitration.

2. Parties and Arbitral Tribunals may adopt the IBA Rules of Evidence, in whole or in part, to govern arbitration proceedings, or they may vary them or use them as guidelines in developing their own procedures. The Rules are not intended to limit the flexibility that is inherent in, and an advantage of, international arbitration, and Parties and Arbitral Tribunals are free to adapt them to the particular circumstances of each arbitration.

3. The taking of evidence shall be conducted on the principles that each Party shall act in good faith and be entitled to know, reasonably in advance of any Evidentiary Hearing or any fact or merits determination, the evidence on which the other Parties rely.

A. Introduction

2.1 The IBA Rules provide procedures for the taking of evidence that take into account differences of approach in different legal traditions, adopt various forms of procedural compromise, and introduce new models of practice. The Preamble to the IBA Rules comprises three short paragraphs (referred to in this text as Preamble 1 to 3). Those paragraphs explain what the IBA Rules are intended to accomplish, and express two general principles underlying the drafting and application of those rules.

2.2 The principles and objectives set out in the Preamble are important in aiding interpretation of the IBA Rules. While noting the need to apply the rules in a manner appropriate to an individual arbitration, Article 1.4 of the IBA Rules makes clear that a purposive approach to interpretation of the rules is to be adopted. This necessarily involves having regard to the objectives set out Preamble 1 and Preamble 2.[1]

The principles contained in the Preamble also inform the approach to be adopted by a tribunal where both the IBA Rules and the General Rules[2] are silent on a matter affecting the taking of evidence and the parties have been unable to reach agreement on how that matter is to be addressed. Article 1.5 provides that, in such a case, the tribunal is to determine the steps to be taken by reference to the 'general principles of the IBA Rules'.[3] **2.3**

It seems likely that the reference at Article 1.5 to general principles of the IBA Rules is intended primarily as a reference to the principles described in the Preamble. The 1983 Rules did not contain a preamble. When the IBA Working Party reviewed the 1983 Rules in the period leading to publication of the 1999 Rules, they concluded that it would be desirable to include a statement of general principles 'so that parties and arbitral tribunals could best understand how to apply them'.[4] A preamble containing a statement of principles and objectives was introduced in the 1999 Rules,[5] and has been developed in the current 2010 Rules.[6] However, the wording of Article 1.5 does not shut out consideration of other general principles found elsewhere in the IBA Rules, where appropriate, eg the principle set out at Article 1.3.[7] **2.4**

B. Preamble 1: Efficient, Economical, and Fair

1. These IBA Rules on the Taking of Evidence in International Arbitration are intended to provide an efficient, economical and fair process for the taking of evidence in international arbitrations, particularly those between Parties from

[1] Preamble 1 makes clear that the purpose of the IBA Rules on the Taking of Evidence in International Arbitration 2010 (hereafter 'IBA Rules') is (a) to provide an efficient, economical and fair process for the taking of evidence in international arbitration, particularly between parties from different legal traditions and (b) to supplement the legal provisions and arbitration rules applicable to a particular arbitration. Preamble 2 indicates that the rules are not intended to limit the flexibility inherent in international arbitration. They may be adopted in whole or in part, may be used as guidance only, or may be adapted to suit the needs of a particular case. In practice, the IBA Rules are rarely adopted in part, and are predominantly adopted as guidance only. See further paras 2.5–2.31 on Preamble 1, and paras 2.32–2.39 on Preamble 2.

[2] 'General Rules' are defined under the IBA Rules (n 1) to mean the institutional, ad hoc, or other rules that apply to the conduct of the arbitration. See the 'Definitions' section of the IBA Rules (n 1) following the Preamble.

[3] IBA Rules (n 1), Article 1.5 (emphasis added).

[4] IBA Working Party, 'Commentary on the New IBA Rules of Evidence in International Commercial Arbitration' (2000) 2 Business Law International 16 (hereafter 'Commentary on the 1999 IBA Rules').

[5] The Preamble introduced by the IBA Rules on the Taking of Evidence in International Commercial Arbitration 1999 (hereafter '1999 IBA Rules') referred to the principle of an 'efficient and economical' process and to the principle that each party should have reasonable notice of the evidence relied on by the other party to the dispute.

[6] The current (2010) IBA Rules (n 1) introduced express reference to the principle of a fair process and the expectation of good faith conduct by the parties.

[7] This provides that, in case of conflict between any provisions of the IBA Rules (n 1) and the General Rules, the Arbitral Tribunal shall apply the IBA Rules in the manner that it determines best in order to accomplish the purposes of both the General Rules and the IBA Rules, unless the Parties agree to the contrary.

different legal traditions. They are designed to supplement the legal provisions and the institutional, ad hoc or other rules that apply to the conduct of the arbitration.

2.5 Preamble 1 confirms the overall purpose behind the IBA Rules. Namely:

(a) to provide an *efficient, economical and fair process* for taking evidence that will meet, so far as reasonably possible, the expectations of parties from different legal traditions; and

(b) to deliver a set of provisions designed to *supplement* other legal provisions and rules applicable to the arbitration (the content of which will often lack detail on procedures for the taking and presentation of evidence).

1. Nature of the Process: Efficient, Economical, and Fair

2.6 The goal of an 'efficient, economical and fair process' can be found in many arbitration laws, and in institutional rules.[8] This objective informs the provisions contained within the IBA Rules[9] and should be a key focus point when those rules are applied in a particular arbitration. One commentator suggests that, whenever a tribunal has doubts about whether to make a particular form of order, it should ask itself whether making the order would be efficient, economical and fair.[10] We endorse that approach.

[8] There are many examples of national arbitration laws that contain reference to these concepts. For example, the English Arbitration Act 1996 imposes an obligation on a tribunal to: 'adopt procedures suitable to the circumstances of the particular case, avoiding *unnecessary delay or expense, so as to provide a fair means for the resolution of the matters falling to be determined*' (emphasis added). The Hong Kong Arbitration Ordinance provides at Section 46 that the arbitral tribunal is required: '. . . (b) to act fairly and impartially as between the parties, giving them a reasonable opportunity to present their cases and to deal with the cases of their opponents; and (c) *to use procedures that are appropriate to the particular case, avoiding unnecessary delay or expense, so as to provide a fair means for resolving the dispute to which the arbitral proceedings relate*' (emphasis added). In the United States, the Revised Uniform Arbitration Act states that an 'arbitrator may conduct an arbitration in such manner as the arbitrator considers appropriate for *a fair and expeditious disposition of the proceeding* . . . ' (emphasis added). Similar provisions can be found in institutional rules. For example, Article 14 of the LCIA Rules provides that the tribunal has a duty to 'act fairly and impartially between all parties' and shall 'adopt procedures suitable to the circumstances of the arbitration, avoiding unnecessary delay and expense, so as to provide a *fair, efficient and expeditious means for the final resolution of the parties' dispute*' (emphasis added). Article 23(2) of the SCC Rules states that in 'all cases, the Arbitral Tribunal shall conduct the arbitration in an *impartial, efficient and expeditious manner, giving each party an equal and reasonable opportunity to present its case*' (emphasis added). Article 13.1 of the HKIAC Rules states that '[s]ubject to these Rules, the arbitral tribunal shall adopt suitable procedures for the conduct of the arbitration in order to *avoid unnecessary delay or expense*, having regard to the complexity of the issues, the amount in dispute and the effective use of technology, and provided that such procedures *ensure equal treatment of the parties and afford the parties a reasonable opportunity to present their case*' (emphasis added).

[9] 1999 IBA Working Party and 2010 IBA Rules of Evidence Review Subcommittee, 'Commentary on the Revised Text of the 2010 IBA Rules on the Taking of Evidence in International Arbitration' (International Bar Association) <www.ibanet.org/Document/Default.aspx?DocumentUid=DD240932-0E08-40D4-9866-309A635487C0> accessed 27 November 2018 (hereafter 'Commentary on the IBA Rules'). This is a revised and expanded version of the Commentary on the 1999 IBA Rules (n 4).

[10] Peter Ashford, *The IBA Rules on the Taking of Evidence in International Arbitration* (CUP 2013) 11 (hereafter 'Ashford').

Preamble 1

- **the procedure used for taking and presenting evidence should be efficient, economical and fair**
- **the rules are intended to supplement arbitration laws/rules that apply to the arbitration – the rules add detailed procedures for the taking of evidence**

a. Provenance and practical application of 'efficient, economical and fair'

The principle of an 'efficient, economical and fair process' contained in Preamble 1 has its provenance in Article 7(h) of the 1983 Rules, which provided that the arbitrator shall have the power to 'exercise all the powers he deems necessary to make the arbitration effective *and its conduct efficient* as regards the taking of evidence'.[11] **2.7**

The Preamble introduced by the 1999 IBA Rules made no mention of a 'fair' process but did include express reference to an intention that those rules should 'govern in an *efficient and economical* manner the taking of evidence in international commercial arbitrations'.[12] **2.8**

The word 'fair' was introduced into Preamble 1 in the current (2010) version of the IBA Rules. This was done deliberately and in tandem with the introduction in Preamble 3 of the principle that each Party should act in good faith in relation to the taking of evidence.[13] The Commentary to the IBA Rules confirms that: **2.9**

> '[T]he IBA Rules of Evidence are intended to provide an '*efficient, economical and fair process*' for the taking of evidence in international arbitration . . . The Review Subcommittee revised this sentence to include expressly the principle of fairness. This change goes hand in hand with the revision to paragraph 3 of the Preamble, which now includes a requirement that each Party shall act 'in good faith' in the taking of evidence pursuant to the IBA Rules.[14]

The requirement of a 'fair' process is a simple confirmation of a rule of natural justice reflected elsewhere in national arbitration laws and arbitration rules.[15] In an article on the 1983 Rules written by the then-Chairman of the IBA drafting committee, the differences between common law and civil law approaches to the taking of evidence were described in some detail. However, the author also noted that, despite these differences, in each system there existed protections intended to preserve the right of a party to **2.10**

[11] Emphasis added.
[12] Emphasis added. Commentary on the 1999 Rules (n 4), Preamble 3 states that this principle influenced the drafting of all of the rules. The Working Party responsible for drafting those rules placed emphasis on the need for parties and tribunals to find ways of resolving disputes in the least costly way: '[t]he Working Party believed that as international arbitration grows more complex and the size of cases increases, it is important for parties and arbitral tribunals to find methods to resolve their disputes in the most cost effective and least costly manner'.
[13] See paras 2.40–2.99.
[14] Commentary on the IBA Rules (n 9) (emphasis added).
[15] See Chapter 4, paras 4.39–4.42 and 4.77.

understand and answer evidence submitted by the opposing party.[16] It follows that a common concept of fairness existed.

2.11 Within reasonable limits and unhindered by domestic court rules that may lay down specific requirements in relation to the form and order of evidence,[17] a tribunal has the flexibility and discretion to assess what form of process is 'fair' in an individual arbitration. For example, a fundamental element of a fair process is that each party should be able to see documents held by its opponent that meet the test for production under the IBA Rules.[18] Each party should also have reasonable notice of the evidence that will be advanced by its opponent and an opportunity to respond to that evidence. Thus, in aid of a fair process under Preamble 1, the obligation to act in good faith when discharging obligations relating to evidence, and the principle of 'no surprises', are given prominence in Preamble 3 to the IBA Rules (see paragraphs 2.43–2.107). Efficiency also has a part to play. Where one party to an arbitration has limited resources, and the arbitration is not conducted in a cost-efficient way, any resulting loss of opportunity for that party to present its case may also give rise to issues of fairness (see paragraphs 2.18–2.24).

2.12 Other provisions of the IBA Rules contain mechanisms that assist in achieving efficiency. One, applicable to the introduction of evidence, is the 'relevant and material to outcome' test that is present as a consistent theme throughout the IBA Rules. In using this benchmark, the introduction of evidence is limited to that which is truly necessary for a proper determination of the issues before the tribunal. It is a fundamental requirement to be met when a party makes a request for production of documents under Article 3[19] and is a key test under Article 9 in relation to the exclusion by the tribunal of evidence that it does not consider appropriate for admission into the arbitration.[20]

2.13 Other changes to the IBA Rules introduced in 2010 are also relevant to controlling the costs of an arbitration. For example, in relation to the production of electronic documents, the power of the tribunal to order a party to specify search terms that will facilitate an efficient search for such documents (Article 3.3(a)(ii)) and, more significantly, the power of the tribunal to exclude evidence on the basis of procedural economy (Article 9.2(g)). These provisions are dealt with in more detail in Chapter 6 and Chapter 12, respectively.[21]

16 DW Shenton, 'An Introduction to the IBA Rules of Evidence' (1985) Arbitration International 118 (hereafter 'Shenton').

17 For example, Merkin and Flannery note that, by contrast with standard English litigation procedures, there is no unfairness if the tribunal gives the last word to the Respondent, rather than to the Claimant. Robert Merkin and Louis Flannery, *Arbitration Act 1996* (5th edn, Informa Law Routledge 2014) 129 citing *Margulead Ltd v Exide Technologies* [2005] 1 Lloyd's Rep 324 [29]–[30].

18 IBA Rules (n 1), Article 3.

19 See the requirement at IBA Rules (n 1) Article 3.3(b) that, in its request, the requesting Party includes 'a statement as to how the Documents requested are relevant to the case and material to its outcome'.

20 IBA Rules (n 1) Article 9.2(a) provides that the 'Arbitral Tribunal shall, at the request of a Party or on its own motion, exclude from evidence or production any Document, statement, oral testimony or inspection for . . . lack of sufficient relevance to the case or materiality to its outcome'.

21 See also Christopher Newmark, '"Efficient, Economical and Fair": The Mantra of the New IBA Rules' (2010) International Arbitration Law Review 165 (hereafter 'Newmark'), which provides an analysis of amendments introduced by IBA Rules (n 1) aimed at improving the efficiency of the arbitral process.

b. Potential for tension between the Preamble 1 objectives of efficiency, economy and fairness

The potential in some cases for tension between the requirements of efficiency, economy and fairness is inevitable. Subject to any agreement between the parties, it is the role of the tribunal to try to guide the arbitral process in a way that achieves a reasonable balance between any competing considerations. **2.14**

As a matter of principle, any clearly unnecessary steps and associated costs should be avoided. In the event of disagreement between the parties on the appropriate process to be followed, the tribunal must hear the competing arguments and then take the lead in navigating a reasonable course through the available procedural options that neither offends due process nor results in unwarranted or disproportionate costs being expended. This requires some form of cost/benefit assessment in relation to all aspects of the proposed procedure in a particular case. **2.15**

In the authors' view, absent any prior agreement on cost-capping, where a particular procedural step is costly but, after careful assessment, considered to be the only means of achieving fairness in the taking and/or presentation of evidence, the requirement of fairness should generally override considerations of cost. **2.16**

If the parties have deep pockets and are intent upon 'throwing money' at the arbitration process, then the tribunal may be tempted simply to ensure fair play in the deployment of resources. A 'no expense spared' process, where each side has the opportunity to air its case ad nauseam and to respond to all aspects of the other party's case, may be the result, giving rise to little tension between resources and fair process. However, such an approach may give insufficient weight to the requirement of an efficient process set out in Preamble 1. It may also ignore a similar obligation to ensure efficiency contained in many institutional rules and/or domestic arbitration laws that may be applicable to the arbitration.[22] Whatever the available resources, the tribunal must do what it can to ensure that the procedure adopted avoids unnecessary or disproportionate costs being incurred. **2.17**

An even more difficult situation is where one of the parties has limited resources. In such cases, the party with the greater resources may use them to obstruct pursuit of the other party's claim or defence. The means by which they may do so will be familiar to regular users of international arbitration. They include over-complicating the claim (eg raising peripheral issues of expert evidence that necessitate the instruction of several experts), advocating costly and protracted procedures (several rounds of evidence rather than just one or two), extensive document requests/production, or the use of successive interim applications that eat away at the available resources of the other party and may divert the tribunal's time away from the core issues. **2.18**

[22] For example, the LCIA Rules, Article 14, and the English Arbitration Act 1996, s 33.

2.19 In considering the appropriate procedure to adopt in an arbitration, most tribunals will have regard to the *value of the claims* in dispute. It is widely accepted that proportionality is a proper matter to take into account when tailoring procedures to the needs of a case. In contrast, the authors have been unable to find any evidence to suggest that the *relative resources of the parties* is a factor routinely taken into account in the early stages of formulating the procedure to be adopted, although it may well form the basis for party objection to specific proposals in a particular case. However, as the arbitration progresses and the tribunal sees that one party is using its deep pockets to browbeat its opponent, the resourcing of particular procedural steps may become conflated with issues of fairness.

2.20 This is dangerous ground for a tribunal as it must not take procedural shortcuts in order to alleviate the position of the less well-resourced party. An illustration of a tribunal going too far is the English case of *Norbrook Laboratories Ltd v Tank*,[23] conducted under the Short Procedure Rules of the Institution of Chemical Engineers (SPR), where the tribunal wished to impose 'an orderly and economical procedure' designed to ensure a speedy award. On notice to the parties, the arbitrator made direct unilateral contact with three potential witnesses on the basis of his power under Rule 7(e) of the SPR to 'himself take the initiative in ascertaining the facts and the law . . . '. The arbitrator regarded this step as being appropriate by reason of the parties' inequality of resources.

2.21 In a judgment setting aside the arbitrator's award, the English Court stated that the arbitrator, although entitled to discover facts relevant to the substantive issues by his own initiative,[24] must do so in a way that meets the requirement of fairness. That requirement had not been properly observed in this case. There was a risk that the arbitrator might have been influenced by what was said to him during the course of his contact with the potential witnesses. In turn, this led to a failure of objective impartiality. However, the Court also found that the arbitrator's desire for an orderly and economical procedure driven by 'his perception that this was generally desirable by reason in particular of [one party's] more limited resources' was 'not an inappropriate consideration'.[25]

2.22 While taking account of the lessons that might be learned from such cases, when dealing with the taking of evidence under the IBA Rules a tribunal should, as mentioned earlier, use its powers appropriately to monitor and rein in any procedural excesses that may be legitimately curtailed without compromising any party's ability to put its case, eg by calling a limit to proposed steps relating to evidence that is clearly

[23] [2006] APP LR 05/12.

[24] The tribunal's power to do this is widely accepted and reflected in a number of provisions contained in the IBA Rules. It is also illustrated by the remarks made by the Administrative Council of ICSID in relation to a proposal to disqualify members of an ICSID tribunal on grounds of alleged partiality based on questions put to the parties: '[t]he Tribunal's efforts to complete gaps in the evidentiary record and to ascertain the Parties' positions on additional points do not provide a basis for speculation as to a biased motive . . . I note that arbitrators routinely propose their own analysis of facts and law to disputing parties, and then allow the parties a fair opportunity to present their views . . . '. *Vattenfall AB and others v Federal Republic of Germany* (ICSID Case No. ARB/12/12).

[25] *Norbrook Laboratories Ltd v Tank*, [2006] APP LR 05/12 [84]–[85], [138]–[141], and [151]–[157].

not relevant and material to outcome, or where the desired outcome may be achieved by more efficient means. This may necessitate a rigorous analysis of voluminous document production requests in order to determine whether the issues to which the documents are said to relate are actually on the critical path to a determination of the dispute. Another example relates to the use of information technology. A recent report by the ICC on *Information Technology in International Arbitration*,[26] while recognizing and endorsing the role that IT can play in saving time and costs, cautions that this is not always the case, and that tribunals should be careful about authorizing the use of expensive IT solutions where this may put a party with scarce resources under pressure.[27]

Even where the opposing party does not adopt a strategy of actively oppressing the less well-resourced party, the latter may struggle to present its case in the most advantageous or comprehensive way. A Practice Guideline issued by the Chartered Institute of Arbitrators provides guidance in relation to the challenge facing a tribunal trying to achieve a balance between the obligation to do justice between the parties and the requirement to treat each party equally.[28] In relation to the taking of evidence, the Practice Guideline suggests that the tribunal may take a more active role in the examination of witnesses than might otherwise be the case in order to better draw out aspects of the ill-resourced party's case, saying: **2.23**

> [T]he arbitrator can provide some assistance by asking questions of witnesses and of the weaker party which will enable it to present its case equally and fairly. The arbitrator should be at least as accommodating to a weaker party as a court would be under similar circumstances. As with all these observations, though, the arbitrator must be extremely careful not to show bias towards one of the parties. As with all matters of procedure, the attitude of the arbitrator must be one of listening and attempting to seek out the truth and reach the correct decision rather than promoting either side's case.

This suggested approach can be considered against the arbitrator's conduct in *Norbrook*, where the tribunal was found to have overstepped the mark. **2.24**

2. The IBA Rules as Supplementary Provisions

Preamble 1 makes clear that the IBA Rules are intended to supplement—not replace—the institutional or ad hoc arbitration rules, or national arbitration laws, that apply to the conduct of an arbitration. **2.25**

[26] ICC Arbitration Commission Report on Information Technology in International Arbitration (International Chamber of Commerce 2017).

[27] ibid 6.

[28] Chartered Institute of Arbitrators, Practice Guideline 17: Guidelines for arbitrators dealing with cases involving consumers and parties with significant differences of resources.

2.26 As explained in Chapter 1, the subcommittee charged with drafting the original 1983 IBA Rules was not charged with drafting a uniform set of rules to govern arbitration proceedings. Instead, the proposed IBA Rules were to be confined to procedures for production of evidence in commercial arbitration, a subject that was, to a great extent, avoided by most arbitration rules,[29] but which was often a minefield to navigate in an international arbitration involving parties from different legal traditions. Thus, it was decided that the work of the subcommittee should focus on the 'the mechanics of presenting or receiving evidence'.[30]

2.27 The Commentary to the IBA Rules explains that parties who adopt or use the IBA Rules must still select a set of institutional or ad hoc arbitration rules, or design their own rules, to establish the overall procedural framework for the arbitration. It reiterates that the IBA Rules 'fill in gaps intentionally left in those procedural framework rules with respect to the taking of evidence'.[31]

3. The IBA Rules Applicable to All Forms of International Arbitration

2.28 The title of the 2010 IBA Rules does not contain the word 'commercial', which appeared in the previous version of the rules. This deletion is reflected in Preamble 1, which now states that the IBA Rules are intended to provide an efficient, economical and fair process for the taking of evidence in 'international arbitration' rather than (as previously) limiting their application to 'international commercial arbitration'.

2.29 The Commentary to the 2010 IBA Rules explains that the word 'commercial' was deleted in acknowledgment of the fact that the IBA Rules may be, and are, used both in commercial and investment arbitration.

2.30 A 2016 report prepared by the IBA following a survey on the use of IBA Arbitration Soft Law Products[32] indicates that, in those arbitrations known to the respondents to the survey in which the Rules on Evidence were referenced, 91 per cent were commercial arbitrations, while only 9 per cent were investment arbitrations.[33] Interestingly, the

[29] These generally deal with the overarching infrastructure of an arbitral process: initiation of process, formation of the tribunal, default timing/manner of presentation of pleadings and evidence, arbitrator powers, challenges, language and seat, allocation of costs, etc. The IBA Rules (n 1) are concerned only with matters relating to the taking of evidence. They therefore complement other rules applicable to the arbitration by providing a relatively detailed starting point procedure for the taking and presentation of evidence that can supplement those other rules.

[30] Shenton (n 16) 119.

[31] Commentary on the IBA Rules (n 9) 3.

[32] The IBA Arbitration Guidelines and Rules Subcommittee, 'Report on the Reception of the IBA Arbitration Soft Law Products' (International Bar Association 2016), <www.ibanet.org/Document/Default.aspx?DocumentUid=105D29A3-6261-4437-84E2-1C8637844BEB> accessed 27 November 2018 (hereafter '2016 IBA Report'). That report was based on the results of a worldwide survey conducted by the subcommittee to which there were 845 responses covering every region across the globe.

[33] The report goes on to point out that it does not necessarily follow from this that the IBA Rules (n 1) are necessarily referenced more frequently to this extent in commercial arbitrations, since the survey results may have been influenced by the particular practice areas of individual respondents.

report also indicates that the frequency with which the IBA Rules are referenced in investment treaty arbitrations varies among regions, ranging from 20 per cent (North America) to 3 per cent (Asia–Pacific).

The Commentary on the IBA Rules draws attention to the fact that those rules do not contain any specialized rules for investment arbitration and thus, for example, where the arbitration involves the participation of an amicus curiae,[34] the IBA Rules provide no detailed guidance on the presentation of evidence by such a party. **2.31**

C. Preamble 2: Flexibility

2. **Parties and Arbitral Tribunals may adopt the IBA Rules of Evidence, in whole or in part, to govern arbitration proceedings, or they may vary them or use them as guidelines in developing their own procedures. The Rules are not intended to limit the flexibility that is inherent in, and an advantage of, international arbitration, and Parties and Arbitral Tribunals are free to adapt them to the particular circumstances of each arbitration.**

Preamble 2 states in terms that the IBA Rules are not intended to restrict the inherent flexibility of international arbitration, regarded by many users of arbitration to be one of its greatest advantages. This provision makes clear that parties and/or the tribunal may: **2.32**

(a) adopt all, or only part, of the rules;
(b) adapt or vary the rules before application; and
(c) use the rules merely as guidelines in developing their own procedures.

The Commentary to the 1999 IBA Rules notes that there is not a single best way to conduct all international arbitrations. The rules should be used by parties and tribunals in the manner that suits them best, according to the needs of the case.[35]

In practice, the terms of the IBA Rules are rarely adapted by parties before being applied in a particular arbitration. Likewise, it is rare to see only part of the IBA Rules adopted except where occasionally parties make express reference to application of the rules in connection with document production only. When considering use of the IBA Rules, the principal choice that participants in an arbitration have to make is between formally adopting the IBA Rules and using them as guidelines only. The ICCA **2.33**

[34] Latin for 'friend of the court'. A non-party with an interest in the outcome of a pending lawsuit who argues or presents information in support of or against one of the parties to the lawsuit. In many instances, the amicus curiae attempts to draw the court's attention to arguments or information that the parties may not have presented, such as the effects of a particular court ruling on the interests of certain third parties. Rule 37(2) of the ICSID Arbitration Rules was amended in 2006 to make express provision for tribunals, in particular circumstances, to accept amicus briefs with or without the consent of the parties. One of those circumstances is where the amicus submission would assist the tribunal to determine a factual or legal issue in the proceedings. Rule 37 of the ICSID Arbitration Rules (Visits and Inquiries; Submissions of Non-Disputing Parties).

[35] Commentary on the 1999 IBA Rules (n 4) 17–18.

Drafting Sourcebook for Logistical Matters in Procedural Orders contains a number of template provisions recording an agreement to adopt the IBA Rules or to use them as Guidelines.[36]

2.34 Where the IBA Rules are formally adopted then, subject to certain exceptions, those rules will govern the taking of evidence in the arbitration.[37]

2.35 The 2016 IBA Report shows that in nearly half (48 per cent) of the arbitrations considered, reference was made to the IBA Rules.[38] However, in around 80 per cent of those arbitrations, the tribunal consulted the rules on the basis that they represented *non-binding* guidelines. A provision adopting the IBA Rules as guidelines only is often found in the draft PO1 circulated by a tribunal at commencement of an arbitration.

Preamble 2

- **the rules (or part of them) may be formally adopted or used only as guidelines**
- **the rules are not intended to limit the flexibility of the arbitration process**

2.36 There are many reasons why parties and tribunals use the IBA Rules as guidelines rather than formally adopting them. In the experience of the authors, reference to use of the IBA Rules is rarely included in an arbitration agreement embedded in a commercial contract. The IBA Rules contain a level of detail on the arbitration process about which contracting parties, in the first flush of a successful commercial negotiation, have little interest. When a dispute first arises it can be difficult for parties to agree anything and a proposal to adopt the IBA Rules may be viewed with suspicion as giving the proposing party some form of advantage. It may be easier for a tribunal to propose, or for the parties to agree, that the rules should be used as guidance only.

2.37 Another reason that participants to an arbitration may prefer to use the IBA Rules as guidance only is a perception that formal adoption of those rules may restrict or provide a basis for challenge in respect of management of evidence.

2.38 A primary function of the IBA Rules is the provision of detailed procedures not present in other arbitration rules around the taking of evidence. However, this same level of detail may, in certain cases, be exploited for strategic reasons by parties and counsel who will claim that the procedures laid down in the IBA Rules were formally adopted, are binding, but have not been properly observed. The ICC recently published a collection

[36] International Council for Commercial Arbitration, *The ICCA Drafting Sourcebook for Logistical Matters in Procedural Orders* (International Council for Commercial Arbitration 2015) 3.

[37] IBA Rules (n 1), Article 1.1. Even when the IBA Rules are silent on a particular situation concerning the taking of evidence, the tribunal is to deal with the matter in accordance with the general principles of the IBA Rules (Article 1.5). In case of conflict between the General Rules and the IBA Rules, the tribunal is to have regard to the purposes of both sets of rules; IBA Rules, Article 1.3. Only if the IBA Rules are in conflict with a mandatory provision of law applicable to the case will the IBA Rules yield to the conflicting provision. See Chapter 4.

[38] 2016 IBA Report (n 32) 36.

of case materials that refer to the IBA Rules. The commentary to that collection states that 'arbitrators have been particularly insistent on their freedom not to be bound by the IBA Rules', and later in the text that the 'insistence is intended to protect the flexibility of the arbitration proceedings and . . . to guard against attempts to set aside awards on the grounds that the tribunal failed to follow the Rules'. The ICC collection includes an extract from an award in which communications from a tribunal to the parties on this point are described. That text states:

> [T]he President wrote to the Parties stating that the Arbitral Tribunal would prefer to retain some flexibility as regards the application of the [IBA Rules]. The Tribunal's concern stemmed from a number of US court decisions where arbitral awards have been set aside on the basis that the Arbitral Tribunal, despite having declared to be bound by the IBA Rules, had not strictly applied them. The Tribunal explained that the Preamble to the Rules specifically states that they are not intended to limit the flexibility that is inherent in, and an advantage of, international arbitration, and Parties and Arbitral Tribunals are therefore free to adapt them to the particular circumstances of each arbitration. The Arbitral Tribunal therefore suggested that Article 3.6 and Article 5.3 of P01 should state that the Tribunal shall be 'guided but shall not be bound' by the IBA Rules.

Interestingly, and perhaps consistent with a position where parties and arbitrators are happy with the IBA Rules but do not want to be legally bound to them, the IBA report mentions that even where the rules were adopted only as guidelines, they were followed in 90 per cent of such cases. All of the statistics contained in that report confirm the important role that the IBA Rules have in providing soft boundaries in relation to the taking and presentation of evidence in arbitration. **2.39**

D. Preamble 3: Good Faith and Reasonable Notice of Evidence

> **3. The taking of evidence shall be conducted on the principles that each Party shall act in good faith and be entitled to know, reasonably in advance of any Evidentiary Hearing or any fact or merits determination, the evidence on which the other Parties rely.**

1. The IBA General Principles

Preamble 3 expresses two key principles on which the taking of evidence is to be conducted under the IBA Rules. Those principles are that: **2.40**

1. each party shall act in good faith (sometimes referred to in this text as the 'First Principle'); and

2. each party shall be entitled to know reasonably in advance of any evidentiary hearing or facts/merits determination, the evidence on which the other party relies (referred to in this text as the 'Second Principle').

2.41 The First Principle imposes an express obligation upon the parties to the arbitration. The Second Principle stipulates a core requirement of the rules that underpins its provisions. Both principles address the requirement for a fair process.

2.42 The use of the word 'shall' in Preamble 3 is significant. It suggests that, notwithstanding the exhortation to flexible application of the IBA Rules contained in Preamble 2, there should be no deviation from these core underlying principles in relation to the taking of evidence under the rules.

Preamble 3

- **parties must act in good faith in taking and presenting evidence**
- **each party has a right to know about the evidence relied on by another party a reasonable time before the hearing**

2. The First Principle: Good Faith

a. Introduction of an express obligation of good faith

2.43 The First Principle does not refer expressly to the imposition on the parties of a duty of good faith. The language used might be read as merely aspirational, were it not for Article 9.7 of the IBA Rules (introduced at the same time as the First Principle). That provision provides a sanction for breach of the First Principle, and therefore makes clear that an *obligation* of good faith does exist under the rules.[39] Article 9.7 enables a tribunal to take a party's failure to act in good faith into account when allocating costs of the arbitration.[40]

2.44 The Commentary to the IBA Rules confirms that position. It describes the First Principle as constituting a requirement that each Party shall act in good faith and that breaches of that obligation may be addressed under various provisions of the IBA Rules. The Commentary says as follows:

> [P]aragraph 3 of the Preamble . . . includes a *requirement* that each Party shall act 'in good faith' in the taking of evidence pursuant to the IBA Rules. At the discretion of the arbitral tribunal, *violation of the good faith requirement* can result in the consequences set out in Articles 9.5, 9.6 and 9.7.[41]

[39] This analysis is consistent with the view taken by other commentators. For example, one commentator states 'Whilst there is . . . no express reference to a duty of good faith, any doubt that such a duty arises is removed by the new provision at Article 9.7'. Ashford (n 10) 13. Also see Newmark (n 21) 166.

[40] See Chapter 12, paras 12.385–12.401.

[41] Commentary on the IBA Rules (n 9) 3 (emphasis added).

A question has been raised as to whom the duty is owed.[42] We submit that it must be a duty first and foremost owed to the counterparty to the arbitration agreement or arbitration proceedings into which the IBA Rules have been adopted. However, as the tribunal is the entity charged with implementation of the parties' agreement, the duty must, by extension, also be owed to the tribunal. 2.45

b. Does the IBA obligation of good faith add anything to existing obligations and practice?

It is suggested that an obligation to act in good faith is created by the parties' agreement to arbitrate—no express provision to this effect is necessary.[43] In one of the leading texts on international commercial arbitration, Gary Born puts forward an unequivocal statement of the obligation in these terms: 2.46

> The most fundamental objective and effect of an international arbitration agreement are to obligate the parties to participate cooperatively and in good faith in the resolution of their disputes by arbitration pursuant to that agreement. As discussed above, this obligation is a sui generis one—requiring parties whose underlying commercial or other relations have deteriorated to the point of litigation to cooperate together, in good faith, in an adjudicatory procedure that will finally resolve their disputes, either for or against one of the parties.[44]

Similar views have been expressed by some tribunals. In one ICSID decision the requirement of good faith was discussed in the context of the alleged interception and 2.47

[42] Peter J Rees, 'The Revised IBA Rules of Evidence' (2010) 76 Arbitration 514 (hereafter 'Rees').

[43] Gary B Born, *International Commercial Arbitration* (2nd edn, Kluwer Law International 2014) 1253 ff (hereafter 'Born'); Abba Kolo, 'Witness Intimidation, Tampering and Other Related Abuses of Process in Investment Arbitration: Possible Remedies Available to the Arbitral Tribunal' (2010) Arbitration International 46, 53–54. See also VV Veeder, 'The 2001 Goff Lecture: The Lawyer's Duty to Arbitrate in Good Faith' (2002) Arbitration International 431 (hereafter 'Veeder'). Assuming such an obligation were to exist, it may give rise to some interesting conflict of laws questions. The proper law of the host contract is not always the same as the law governing the arbitration agreement contained within it. In the absence of express provision, the latter may be found to be the law of the seat. If a duty of good faith is implied into the underlying contract under its applicable law, does it have any relevance in relation to obligations arising under the arbitration agreement governed by a different law? It might be argued that it is the law governing the arbitration agreement that must determine the scope of any duty of good faith said to exist in respect of the arbitration process.

[44] Born (n 43). See also the references in Veeder (n 43) 439, to the conclusions of Professor Bernard Hanotiau that it is a 'basic principle of international commercial arbitration that the parties have the duty to co-operate in good faith in the performance of their agreement as well as in the arbitral proceedings'. Veeder also quotes a decision of the Hong Kong High Court (Mr Justice Kaplan) in which the grant of leave to enforce a CIETAC award on the ground that the losing defendant was estopped from relying on the improper constitution of the arbitration tribunal formed in Beijing (rather than Shenzhen as was required by the arbitration agreement) because a party's general obligation to arbitrate in good faith required the defendant promptly to bring to the notice of the arbitral tribunal or CIETAC its objection to the tribunal's formation rather than wait two years after losing to do so. *China Nanhai Oil Joint Services Corporation v Gee Tai Holdings Limited* (1995) ICCA Yearbook Commercial Arbitration 671. After reviewing various decisions of the US courts, another commentator concludes that: 'in an arbitration context the covenant of good faith and/or the duty to co-operate imputes to each party a sub silentio commitment to abide by the rules and orders contemplated by their arbitrat[ion] contract. Otherwise, their common purpose—a fair, less costly and speedier alternative to litigation—can be defeated [. . .] . Applying this old doctrine to the modern power issue satisfies the sine qua non of an arbitrator's authority – contractual intent'. Gary V McGowen, 'Sanctions in US and International Arbitrations: Old Law In Modern Context' (Kluwer Arbitration Blog, 10 October 2013) <https://arbitrationblog.kluwerarbitration.com/2013/10/10/sanctions-in-us-and-international-arbitrations-old-law-in-modern-context/> accessed 26 November 2018.

surveillance by Turkish police of legally privileged communications between the claimant, its counsel, and witnesses. In addressing the parties' submissions on the issue, the tribunal said as follows:

> Nor does the Tribunal doubt for a moment that, like any other international tribunal, it must be regarded as endowed with the inherent powers required to preserve the integrity of its own processes—even if the remedies open to it are necessarily different from those that might be available to a domestic court of law in an ICSID Member State. The tribunal would express the principle as being that parties have an obligation to arbitrate fairly and in good faith and that an arbitral tribunal has the inherent jurisdiction to ensure that this obligation is complied with; this principle applies in all arbitration, including investment arbitration, and to all parties, including States (even in the exercise of their sovereign powers).[45]

2.48 Even if not 'built-in' to an arbitration agreement, an expectation of good faith conduct generally exists among parties to international arbitration. One member of the committee responsible for drafting the IBA Rules suggests that the express requirement of good faith introduced into those rules merely mirrors accepted good practice:

> [A]s with all general principles, ad hoc solution by parties and arbitrators in particular cases must still be found and the 'good faith' rule does no more and not more and not less than what is already reflected in the practice as applied by experienced international arbitrators. The fact, however, that good arbitrators are always capable of spotting a party acting in bad faith cannot be a valid reason for avoiding a stipulation of the rule . . . [46]

2.49 The existence of an automatic and mutual obligation on disputing parties to conduct arbitration proceedings in good faith remains a matter of debate, but the express reference to good faith in Preamble 3 serves to remove any doubt as to the standard of conduct expected under the IBA Rules.[47]

[45] *Libananco Holdings Co. Limited v Republic of Turkey* (Decision on Preliminary Issues, 23 June 2008) ICSID Case No. ARB/06/8. On the back of this decision, a further interesting question has been posed: namely, on the basis that there is an obligation to arbitrate fairly and in good faith, does that duty also apply to the making of a claim, or does it apply only to the procedural obligations that come with an agreement to arbitrate (ie cooperation and conduct in the proceedings)? In particular, does it extend to an obligation that the underlying claims themselves are made in good faith? See Andrew Newcombe, 'The Obligation to Arbitrate Fairly and in Good Faith in Investment Arbitration' (Kluwer Arbitration Blog, 19 April 2010) <https://arbitrationblog.kluwerarbitration.com/2010/04/19/the-obligation-to-arbitrate-fairly-and-in-good-faith-in-investment-treaty-arbitration/> accessed 26 November 2018, where reference is made both to the *Libananco* decision and *Phoenix Action, Ltd. v The Czech Republic* (Award, 15 April 2009) ICSID Case No. ARB/06/5. Of course, such a question is unlikely to arise under the IBA Rules, which deal predominantly with the procedure for presentation of evidence.

[46] Georg von Segesser, 'The IBA Rules on the Taking of Evidence in International Arbitration' (2010) 28 ASA Bulletin 735, 740 (hereafter 'Segesser'). Rules available for download at www.ibanet.org. This view is mirrored by other commentators, one of whom has suggested that the introduction of the good faith provision in Preamble 3 'reflects a current trend in international arbitration, whereby the parties' conduct in proceedings with regard to fairness and good faith is more strictly scrutinized and sanctioned'. He attributes this to the desire of tribunals to reduce time and costs and thereby address the single greatest criticism levelled against arbitration proceedings. Detlev Kühner, 'The Revised IBA Rules on the Taking of Evidence in International Arbitration' (2010) Journal of International Arbitration 667.

[47] A member of the drafting subcommittee has explained that the committee was of the view that, given the different approaches in adversarial and inquisitorial proceedings, embedding the principle of good faith in the

The additional express reference at Article 9.7 to the possible imposition of cost sanctions where there is a failure to meet that standard, gives the provision additional force.[48] In practice, where the rules are used as guidelines only, the extent to which a tribunal may penalize parties for failing to act in good faith by reference to the terms of the IBA Rules alone may be in doubt and, to that extent, may undermine the effectiveness of this provision.[49] 2.50

c. Operation of the obligation of good faith

Preamble 3 puts the concept of good faith at the heart of performance of procedures for the taking of evidence under the IBA Rules. It provides the tribunal with a fact-sensitive benchmark against which it may measure and guide performance. However, it also raises a number of questions. These include: 2.51

- What does 'good faith' mean?
- How is a duty of good faith to be applied to the taking of evidence under the IBA Rules?
- What sanctions are available to a tribunal under the IBA Rules in the event that a party fails to act in good faith?

d. What does 'good faith' mean?

i. *'Good faith' is not defined in the IBA Rules*

The IBA Rules do not contain a definition of good faith, although one member of the drafting committee has suggested that, as a general rule, it implies a 'duty for the parties to conduct their case without improper means'.[50] This is a description that few practitioners would challenge, but what exactly does it mean in practice? 2.52

One suggested approach to determining the standard of conduct expected of parties is to consider the 'transparency' requirements of the IBA Rules—for example, in relation to document production, the requirement that a requesting party already in possession of the requested documents should explain why it would be unreasonably burdensome for the requesting party to produce them,[51] the requirement to present original documents for inspection upon request,[52] or the requirement to provide details of any past or present relationship between a party and its party-appointed expert.[53] It is argued that these provisions contain an indication of what is meant by good faith conduct.[54] 2.53

IBA Rules would be particularly helpful for those parties that had no, or less, experience with international arbitration, and that it would also provide the tribunal with a yardstick to conduct the evidentiary proceedings. See Segesser (n 46) 740.

[48] This is in addition to any other sanctions available to the tribunal under the IBA Rules. For example, the use of adverse inferences. See Chapter 12, paras 12.357–12.386.

[49] The tribunal may still have the power to sanction parties for a lack of good faith conduct under its general discretionary, or other, powers.

[50] Segesser (n 46) 740.

[51] IBA Rules (n 1), Article 3.3(c)(i).

[52] ibid Article 3.12(a).

[53] ibid Article 5.2(a).

[54] Pedro J Martinez-Fraga, 'King or Arbitrator: Exploring the Inherent Authority of Arbitrators to Impose Sanction within the Framework of the 2010 IBA Rules on the Taking of Evidence in International Arbitration'

We agree that these provisions—aimed at ensuring a fair and efficient process in which no party is taken by surprise—provide valuable context for expected standards of conduct, but they do not provide a complete answer to issues around good faith that may arise in practice.

2.54 The absence of a definition of good faith is considered by some to be a negative feature of the IBA Rules, particularly in light of the express link between the duty to act in good faith and the later allocation of costs under Article 9.7.[55] It is suggested that, as a result, costs apportionment will become even more complex and contentious as allegations of bad faith are advanced.[56] In response to this criticism, a member of the drafting subcommittee has made the legitimate point that such allegations are frequently advanced in any event.[57] That may be so, but perhaps in order to observe or apply an obligation of good faith in arbitration conducted under the IBA Rules, and to impose (costs or other) sanctions for breach of that obligation, participants need a workable understanding of what the obligation entails and how far it extends. A lack of definition may lead to a level of uncertainty that participants in the arbitral process find unsatisfactory.[58] Where delay, obstruction, and obfuscation is in one party's best commercial interests, and where those objectives can (at least ostensibly) be achieved within the boundaries of any applicable arbitration rules without obvious 'dishonest' conduct, it can be difficult to pinpoint a basis of complaint to take to the tribunal, As Veeder puts it when speaking of procedural unfairness, such situations often concern 'ambiguous acts short of deliberate dishonesty which cross the line of procedural unfairness because no-one really knows quite where that line is now drawn at the international level'.[59]

2.55 On the other hand, a fixed definition might make the concept of good faith conduct less adaptable to developing practices and party tactics. Once defined, parties may become more confident engaging in conduct that they feel they can demonstrate falls outside of the definition. Tribunals will have less discretion to decide whether a breach of the requirement of good faith has occurred on the basis of the individual facts and circumstances of the particular arbitration.

2.56 Those charged with drafting the next iteration of the IBA Rules will no doubt consider whether it is desirable to give any further definition of good faith conduct in relation to the taking of evidence, or to perhaps provide a list of examples of conduct that would

(2011) 12 Spain Arbitration Review 57 (hereafter 'Martinez-Fraga').The author goes on to say that '[w]hile transparency as a criteria (sic) is hardly a substitute for a substantive definition of the term "good faith" within the context of the Rules, it does provide for some uniformity and universality concerning the affirmative exercise of good faith as well as acts and omissions that may only be construed as wanting in good faith to the extent that such conduct obstructs or hampers the disclosure and exchange of information. The emergence of the principle of transparency as a conceptual rubric towards a substantive understanding of good faith is but a modest point of departure'. ibid 74.

[55] Ashford (n 10) 14.
[56] Rees (n 42) 516.
[57] Segesser (n 46) 740.
[58] This is a subject of debate among commentators. See Martinez-Fraga (n 54); Rees (n 42); Newmark (n 21).
[59] Veeder (n 43) 118.

generally be regarded as having breached the obligation. In the meantime, it is useful to consider briefly whether guidance on the relevant standard of conduct expected may be derived from national laws or other arbitration rules.

ii. No universal definition of 'good faith' across national laws

While there may be relatively wide acceptance across jurisdictions of a concept of good faith in commercial and contractual relationships, recognition of its existence is not universal and, where it is recognized, complex variations exist in its application. These factors will be reflected in the differing experience of individual counsel and arbitrators. **2.57**

To many lawyers from a civil law tradition, a requirement to act in good faith in performance of a contractual obligation will be a familiar concept. In a number of jurisdictions domestic law may even import an obligation of good faith. For example, such provisions can be found in the Civil Codes of France, Germany, and Italy.[60] Common law countries have been more resistant to the idea of an inherent obligation of good faith existing between contracting parties,[61] although generally recognizing an obligation of good faith if expressly agreed to by the parties, and in some circumstances willing to imply such a duty. While there are some indications that traditional resistance is softening,[62] this is not universal, and developments in different jurisdictions are not all the same. Within legal systems the concept of good faith may be understood differently in different contexts.[63] Even when arising out of a contractual relationship (which, of course, is what an arbitration agreement is), the notion of 'good faith' is still capable of embracing a spectrum of unacceptable conduct. Various possibilities have **2.58**

[60] French Civil Code as amended by Order No. 2016-131 of 10 February 2016. New Article 1104 provides that contracts must be negotiated, formed, and performed in good faith. German Civil Code Article 242 requires performance according to good faith. The Italian Civil Code incorporates the duty of good faith in a number of its provisions. For example, Article 1175 provides that 'the debtor and the creditor shall behave according to rules of fairness' and Article 1375 provides that a 'contract must be executed in good faith'. See further Duarte Gorjão Henriques, 'The Role of Good Faith in Arbitration: Are Arbitrators and Arbitral Institutions Bound to Act in Good Faith?' (2015) ASA Bulletin 514, which contains a comparative analysis of codification of the idea of good faith in civil law jurisdictions.

[61] In 1992, the then-House of Lords found that a contractual obligation to negotiate in good faith (broadly analogous with an agreement to resolve a dispute by arbitration in good faith) was unworkable. Lord Ackner stated that: '... the concept of a duty to carry on negotiations in good faith is inherently repugnant to the adversarial position of the parties when involved in negotiations'. *Walford and Others v Miles and Another* [1992] 2 WLR 174 [138].

[62] For example, in Canada, Australia, and New Zealand. See [127]–[131] of the judgment of Leggett J in the English case of *Yam Seng Pte Ltd v International Trade Corp Ltd* [2013] EWHC 111 (hereafter *Yam Seng*) where the Judge refers to decisions in those jurisdictions. In *Yam Seng*, the Judge took the opportunity to express his views on the desirability of the doctrine of good faith. However, any suggestion that such a doctrine might emerge or exist in English contract law was very quickly quashed in a number of judgments that followed *Yam Seng* (see, for example, the decision of the Court of Appeal in *Mid Essex Hospital Services NHS Trust v Compass Group UK and Ireland Ltd (Trading As Medirest)* [2013] EWCA Civ 200 at [104] and [105]), although it has subsequently been suggested that there is a growing recognition that a duty of good faith may be readily implied into relational contracts. See *Sheikh Tahnoon Bin Saeed Bin Shakhboot Al Nehayan v Ioannis Kent (AKA John Kent)* [2018] EWHC 333 (Comm) [168], [173]–[174] (hereafter '*Tahoon*').

[63] For example, within the US common law tradition, good faith varies in scope, application, and meaning depending upon whether it is used in a commercial context within the ambit of the Uniform Commercial Code, as an element of fiduciary duty, as a factor to be weighed in evaluating a standard of care, or as conduct required in relation to the disclosure of documents. In relation to the latter, the required conduct may vary according to whether it is being applied (for example) to the designation of documents as confidential, the disclosure of the identity of parties who may have disclosable information, or in exercising self-disclosure requirements. See further Martinez-Fraga (n 54) 59.

been mentioned in English case law. In one decision, where the idea of a general obligation of good faith was rejected, the Court nonetheless went on to find that it could readily accept an implied term not to do anything to frustrate the purpose of the contract.[64] The observance of standards that exclude 'improper', 'commercially unacceptable', or 'unconscionable' conduct are other commercial expectations mentioned in *Yam Seng*,[65] and 'conduct which in the relevant context would be regarded as commercially unacceptable by reasonable and honest people' is referred to in *Tahnoon*.[66] In *Bristol Groundschool Ltd v Intelligent Data Capture Ltd.*, when the commercial relationship between two contracting parties started to break down, one party improperly accessed the other party's computer systems and downloaded various files to protect its position. This action was found to be commercially unacceptable and a breach of an implied duty to act in good faith, including a duty to act honestly.[67] Such conduct would almost certainly be found to be unacceptable in an arbitration context.

2.59 Similar duties are recognized in other jurisdictions. For example, in *Bhasin v Hrynew*, the Canadian Supreme Court recognized a common law duty of honest performance. This was said to 'impose on contracting parties an obligation not to lie or otherwise knowingly mislead about matters directly linked to the performance of the contract'.[68] Again, this standard of conduct is likely to be expected from parties to an arbitration.

2.60 While helpful in providing illustrations of the type of conduct that most people would regard as reprehensible when they come across it, the points of view and authorities described in these cases do little to remove the difficulty in defining good faith in the abstract and without reference to a specific set of facts. As a result, available 'general' principles offer little tangible assistance in relation to interpretation of the IBA Rules requirement of good faith, or how it should be applied between parties from different legal traditions.

iii. Lack of guidance in other arbitration rules

2.61 Likewise, there is little guidance on the meaning of good faith conduct to be derived from other arbitration rules. The majority of institutional rules make no mention of such a duty. Exceptions to this position include the LCIA Rules, the Swiss Rules, and the rules of arbitration of the Belgian Centre for Arbitration and Mediation (CEPANI), which make express reference to good faith conduct on the part of the parties, albeit directed at an efficiency of process and enforceability of the award, rather than the more restricted 'taking of evidence' as appears in the IBA Rules.[69]

[64] *Hamsard 3147 Limited Trading as 'Mini Mode Childrenswear', J S Childrenswear (in liquidation) v Boots UK Ltd* [2013] EWHC 3251 [86].

[65] *Yam Seng* (n 62).

[66] *Tahoon* (n 62) [175].

[67] *Bristol Groundschool Ltd v Intelligent Data Capture Ltd* [2014] EWHC 2145 (Ch) [136]–[137].

[68] *Bhasin v Hrynew* 2014 SCC 71 [73]. See further Martinez-Fraga (n 54) 57.

[69] Another example the authors have identified is Article 20.5 of the Rules of Arbitration of the Court of Arbitration of Madrid, which provides that '[a]ll persons participating in the arbitration proceedings shall act in accordance with the principle of good faith and will ensure that the arbitration is carried out efficiently and without

Article 14.5 of the LCIA Rules (Conduct of the Proceedings) provides that: 2.62

> The Arbitral Tribunal shall have the widest discretion to discharge these general duties, subject to such mandatory law(s) or rules of law as the Arbitral Tribunal may decide to be applicable; and at all times *the parties shall do everything necessary in good faith for the fair, efficient and expeditious conduct of the arbitration, including the Arbitral Tribunal's discharge of its general duties.*[70]

Article 32.2 of the LCIA Rules (General Rules) provides that:

> For all matters not expressly provided in the Arbitration Agreement, the LCIA Court, the LCIA, the Registrar, the Arbitral Tribunal and each of the parties *shall act at all times in good faith, respecting the spirit of the Arbitration Agreement*, and shall make every reasonable effort to ensure that any award is legally recognised and enforceable at the arbitral seat.[71]

However, available commentaries on the LCIA Rules provide little guidance on what 2.63 the good faith requirement means. Referring to Article 32.2, one commentary queries whether the reference to principles of good faith, and the objective of an enforceable award, will be of any practical usefulness for the purposes of filling gaps left open by the parties' arbitration agreement. While it concludes that, properly construed, reference to good faith 'imposes a free standing obligation of good faith on the parties, the Tribunal and the LCIA' it questions the value of this provision. It observes that 'the spirit' of the arbitration agreement and the notion of good faith appear on their own to be too vague to offer genuinely effective guidance to a tribunal or the parties. It also suggests that there are no known instances where the LCIA Court or LCIA Secretariat have made express reference to the equivalent provision under the previous (1998) version of the LCIA Rules.[72]

Article 18.1 of the CEPANI Rules states that: 2.64

> In the conduct of the proceedings the Arbitrator and the parties shall act in a timely manner and *in good faith*. In particular, the parties shall abstain from any dilatory acts as well as from any other action having the object or effect of delaying the proceedings.[73]

Article 15.7 of the Swiss Rules states that: 2.65

> *All participants in the arbitral proceedings shall act in good faith*, and make every effort to contribute to the efficient conduct of the proceedings and to avoid unnecessary

delay'. The authors have been unable to find any reported cases addressing the meaning of good faith in that provision, or the other rules mentioned.

---

[70] Emphasis added.
[71] Emphasis added.
[72] Maxi Scherer, Lisa Richman, and Rémy Gerbay, *Arbitrating under the 2014 LCIA Rules: A User's Guide* (Kluwer Law International 2015). Also see Shai Wade, Phillip Clifford, and James Clanchy, *Commentary on the LCIA Arbitration Rules 2014* (Sweet and Maxwell 2015), which says 'Article 41 of the 2012 ICC Rules is in similar terms to Article 32.2 of the LCIA rules and again lacks any explanation as to what the "spirit" of the ICC rules is . . .'.
[73] Emphasis added.

costs and delays. The parties undertake to comply with any award or order made by the arbitral tribunal or emergency arbitrator without delay.[74]

2.66 A commentary on the Swiss Rules provides a little more substance in relation to the reference to 'good faith' and provides examples of how the stated obligation of good faith translates into performance in the conduct of the arbitration:

> Good faith is regarded as one of the fundamental principles in arbitration. The principle of good faith is part of the substantial and procedural public policy. It applies to both the arbitral tribunal and the parties. It includes, among other things, the participants' duty to actively make 'every effort to [conduct] efficient proceedings without unnecessary costs and delays'; the parties' duty to 'carry out any award and order made by the arbitral tribunal or emergency arbitrator without delay'; the parties' duty to pay their share of the advance on costs; the parties' duty to raise formal complaints without delay instead of waiting until the arbitral award has been rendered and the arbitral tribunal's duty to give the parties notice of possible peremptory consequences in cases where the parties fail to pay the advance on costs promptly, if such consequences are not clearly apparent from the applicable procedural rule. The duty to act in good faith and to make every effort to efficient proceedings also includes the parties' obligation to refrain from any improper conduct.[75]

The authors can find no reported cases concerning application of the Swiss Rules requirement of good faith.

2.67 Other institutional rules, while not containing reference to an obligation of good faith, make provision for the parties to act 'in the spirit' of the relevant rules in matters not expressly provided for in the relevant rules and (in broad terms) with the objective of ensuring that the award is enforceable and/or that the conduct of the arbitration is fair. For example, the SCC Rules provide that:

> In all matters not expressly provided for in these Rules, the SCC, the Arbitral Tribunal and the parties shall act in the spirit of these Rules and shall make every reasonable effort to ensure that any award is legally enforceable.[76]

[74] Emphasis added.

[75] Michael Lazopoulos, 'Chapter 3, Part II: Commentary on the Swiss Rules, Article 15 [General Provisions]' in Manuel Arroyo (ed), *Arbitration in Switzerland: The Practitioner's Guide* (2nd edn, Kluwer Law International 2018) 601–16.

[76] SCC Rules, Article 2(2). See also the HKIAC Rules, Article 13.9: 'In all matters not expressly provided for in these Rules, HKIAC, the arbitral tribunal, emergency arbitrator and the parties shall act in the spirit of these Rules'. Other institutional rules provide that the tribunal shall act within the spirit of the relevant rules. See the ICC Rules, Article 42: 'In all matters not expressly provided for in the Rules, the Court and the arbitral tribunal shall act in the spirit of the Rules and shall make every effort to make sure that the award is enforceable at law'; and the SIAC Rules, Rule 41.2: 'In all matters not expressly provided for in these Rules, the President, the Court, the Registrar and the Tribunal shall act in the spirit of these Rules and shall make every reasonable effort to ensure the fair, expeditious and economical conclusion of the arbitration and the enforceability of any Award'.

The authors have been unable to find any decisions on what the 'spirit of the rules' means under these rules.

iv. Conclusion

Given the absence of any definition of good faith in the IBA Rules, and the possibility that parties may differ in their understanding of what it means, it may be helpful for a tribunal to make clear at the start of the proceedings what sort of conduct it will consider to be a breach of the duty of good faith.[77] This may cause the parties to reflect on the manner in which they conduct the arbitration. However, some caution should be exercised. There are dangers in laying down in advance detail of the type of conduct that the tribunal considers would, or would not, breach the obligation of good faith—the facts and circumstances of subsequent party conduct may reveal such guidance to be a hostage to fortune. As with a definition of good faith, an obvious danger is that the parties may view the listed items of unacceptable behaviour as exhaustive. Even where such a discussion does take place, participants in an international arbitration will inevitably bring to the proceedings their own individual understanding of what good faith means. If it comes to argument on this issue, parties will, of course, defend their position as best they can. From a tribunal's perspective, given that there is very little material available to guide consistent practical dealings with specific incidents of questionable conduct, it is inevitable that different standards will be applied by different tribunals sitting in different types of case in different parts of the world.[78] 2.68

e. Practical application of the duty of good faith to performance under the IBA Rules

Here we address three specific areas in which the application and scope of the duty of good faith may need to be considered. These are: 2.69

1. performance of positive obligations under the IBA Rules;
2. party conduct that has the effect of undermining the general objectives and principles underpinning the IBA Rules; and
3. the relevance of the good faith obligation to circumstances falling within Article 1.5 of the IBA Rules.[79]

[77] Newmark (n 21) 166.

[78] ibid. See also Ashford (n 10) 14. It has also been suggested that because the term 'good faith' is not defined in IBA Rules (n 1), the tribunal has much greater power than would otherwise be the case and, as a result, the principle of party autonomy is diminished. Although the parties may have expressly agreed to application of IBA Rules, the lack of predictability in application of the good faith provision, and the potential for imposition of sanctions, remove control from the parties. Martinez-Fraga (n 54) 58. However, against these criticisms it might be said that we have to start somewhere. As Veeder (n 43) 123 puts it: '[a] formulation based only on good faith could be too vague to be of practical use [but] . . . in default of any other available legal principle, it is the necessary starting point'.

[79] That is to say matters on which the IBA Rules (n 1) and the General Rules (ie the ad hoc, institutional, or other rules applicable to the arbitration) are silent, and the parties are unable to reach agreement.

i. Party conduct relating to performance of positive obligations

2.70 In the authors' view, the obligation to act in good faith expressed in Preamble 3 must extend to positive obligations contained in the IBA Rules.[80] For example, it must apply to the obligation to produce documents in accordance with the provisions of Article 3.4 and the obligation under Article 4.1 to identify all witnesses upon whose testimony a party intends to rely.

2.71 Likewise, a bad faith violation of an express positive obligation must amount to a breach of the corresponding obligation of good faith.[81] For example, the failure to identify all expert witnesses on whose testimony the party intends to rely with the intention to ambush or surprise the other party at a later date, raising objections to produce documents under Article 3.5 without a reasonable and good faith basis for doing so, and deliberately withholding production of documents that are known to exist and that fall within an order for production by a tribunal. Any other interpretation would undermine effective application of the good faith principle. Indeed, it has been rightly pointed out that the duty of good faith is perhaps most easily expressed in the negative.[82]

2.72 A more general question is whether the obligation to act in good faith should be interpreted as setting a benchmark for the level of cooperation required in respect of the Article 2 provision for early consultation on evidential issues. There appears to be a measure of consensus that the language used in Article 2 ('the Arbitral Tribunal shall consult the Parties at the earliest appropriate time . . . and *invite them to consult* with each other *with a view to agreeing on* an efficient, economical and fair process . . .'[83]) is sufficient to indicate that the suggested cooperation is voluntary and that the parties are not under an increased burden to reach agreement by reason of the good faith obligation imposed upon them under Preamble 3.[84] We agree with that interpretation of Article 2 with the caveat that bad faith conduct designed to thwart agreement on 'an efficient, economical and fair process' may nonetheless, for the reasons given here, still fall within the good faith obligation.

ii. Party conduct that has the effect of undermining the objectives and principles underpinning the IBA Rules

2.73 A more difficult question is whether the duty of good faith at Preamble 3 extends to all conduct by which parties implement the procedures for presentation of evidence laid down under the IBA Rules. In our view, there is a strong case for saying that it does. The IBA Rules are concerned with 'the taking of evidence in international arbitration'. This

[80] See further Ashford (n 10) 17–18. (Amy Cohen Klasener, 'The Duty of Good Faith in the 2010 IBA Rules on the Taking of Evidence in International Arbitration' (2010) International Arbitration Law Review 160, 161(hereafter 'Klasener').

[81] This position is agreed by other commentators. See ibid 161; Ashford (n 10) 17–18.

[82] Klasener (n 80) 161. Other commentators agree that an act of bad faith is a much more tangible thing than 'an act not in good faith'. Rees (n 41) 515.

[83] Emphasis added.

[84] Klasener (n 80) 163; Ashford (n 10) 18–19.

is the *raison d'être* of the rules. Preamble 3 states expressly that 'the taking of evidence *shall be conducted* on the principles that each Party shall act in good faith . . .'.[85]

However, establishing the practical boundaries of this wider obligation is problematic and likely to accentuate differences in understanding of what good faith means. For example, on one view, such an overarching duty of good faith might be interpreted to require voluntary submission of key documents that would be adverse to the party's case in circumstances where a positive obligation to produce them has not arisen either under Article 3.1 (because the party does not intend to rely on them) or under Article 3.3 (because the documents have not been properly requested under Article 3, perhaps because the opposing party does not have sufficient information to know or suspect that they exist).[86] This might be said to be consistent with an objective of ensuring that all relevant and material documents are available to the tribunal, as illustrated by the power of the tribunal under Article 8.1 to call for documents on its own initiative. Another possible scenario is that the duty of good faith gives rise to an affirmative duty to preserve evidence or prevent destruction of potentially relevant and material evidence when a dispute appears likely, even though the IBA Rules do not impose such an express obligation.[87] There is unlikely to be practitioner consensus on such matters and certain steps (for example, voluntary production of adverse materials) may, in some cases, present a conflict with the professional conduct rules applicable to counsel in the case.[88] 2.74

On this wider interpretation, the obligation of good faith might also extend to the prohibition of conduct that undermines effective operation of the IBA Rules in achieving the provision of an 'efficient, economical and fair process' as required by Preamble 1. For example, where a party, with the intention of delay or of increasing the other party's costs, submits document requests that are intentionally burdensome, or produces a significant volume of documents with only peripheral relevance to the matters in dispute but which an under-resourced receiving party will have to review in order to establish this fact. 2.75

85 Emphasis added.

86 This issue remains a matter of debate. In relation to the example cited, one member of the committee responsible for drafting the IBA Rules (n 1) has suggested that the obligation of good faith may include an obligation to produce a document manifestly helpful to its opponent's case or even harmful to its own case. See Segesser (n 46) 740. In an article written shortly before publication of the IBA Rules, Veeder appears to take the same view and raises concerns about the implications of such an obligation. See VV Veeder 'Chapter 6. Are the IBA Rules Perfectible?' in Teresa Giovannini and Alexis Mourre (eds), *Written Evidence and Discovery in International Arbitration: New Issues and Tendencies* (vol 6, Kluwer Law International 2009) 322 (hereafter 'Veeder 'Are the IBA Rules Perfectible?'').

87 Of course, if the parties or the tribunal agree on data preservation measures under the consultation procedure provided for in IBA Rules (n 1), Article 2, a duty to comply in good faith with that measure would then arise. See further Klasener (n 80) 161. See also Ashford (n 10) 16. See further discussion on this topic at Chapter 12 paras 12.267–12.274.

88 For example, see German Civil and Criminal Procedure Code: 'The relationship between a lawyer and his client is protected by a number of professional confidentiality regulations. In the absence of the consent of the client, a lawyer is prohibited from divulging any confidential information or documents obtained in the course of his professional activities (Section 203(1), Criminal Code). This obligation to preserve confidentiality is mirrored by the right of the lawyer to refuse to divulge such information (Sections 383 and 142(2), Civil Procedure Code, and Section 53 of the Criminal Procedure Code)'.

2.76 Other suggested violations of an implicit duty of good faith include adducing perjured evidence or 'coaching' a witness.[89] In relation to the latter, we discuss in Chapter 7 at paras 7.30–7.57 comparative ethical norms around witness preparation. Provided that the preparation does not involve distortion of the witness evidence we think it very unlikely that preparing a witness to give evidence would, of itself (and absent any agreement between the parties to the contrary), breach an obligation of good faith.

iii. Matters concerning the taking of evidence on which the IBA Rules are silent

2.77 Lastly, Article 1.5 (Scope of Application) contains an express requirement that the *tribunal* should conduct the taking of evidence by reference to the general principles of the IBA Rules. This will include the principle of good faith conduct. Article 1.5 applies only where the IBA Rules and General Rules (ie in most cases, the chosen institutional rules) are silent on any matter concerning the taking of evidence and the parties have not been able to agree how that matter should be addressed.[90]

2.78 In practice, when the tribunal comes to determine the most appropriate way in which to deal with a matter in dispute on which the IBA Rules are silent, the principle that each party is to receive reasonable notice of its opponent's evidence will generally play a much more significant role than considerations of good faith. Article 1.5 concerns the future conduct of the arbitration. Save that the tribunal may make an assumption that the parties will act in good faith when complying with whatever order the tribunal decides to make, it is difficult to see how issues of good or bad faith conduct can arise, because that order has yet to be implemented.[91]

2.79 However, it has been suggested that the terms of Article 1.5 can be used to import a required standard of good faith conduct whenever the IBA Rules do not specifically prescribe another standard for party behaviour. The example is given of a situation in which a party wishes to rely on the exception to the confidentiality that, under Article 3.13, would otherwise attach to a document submitted or produced in the arbitration—namely, that disclosure by that Party is required 'to fulfil a legal duty, protect or pursue a legal right, or enforce or challenge an award in bona fide legal proceedings'. On this basis, even absent the qualifying reference to bona fide legal proceedings, a duty of good faith could be implied so as to exclude from the exception at Article 3.13 bad faith acts having the primary purpose of disclosure to a third party rather than the protection of a legal right.[92] We take the view that the same outcome is more appropriately arrived at by direct application of the duty of good faith as discussed at paragraphs 2.73– 2.76.

89 Ashford (n 10) 17.

90 Article 1.5 is dealt with in more detail in Chapter 4, paras 4.106–4.119.

91 A tribunal may wish to take earlier reprehensible conduct into account in deciding how to deal with a later issue in relation to the taking of evidence but the ability to do so would arise as a matter of the general discretion afforded to the tribunal under Article 1.5 rather than by reference to the principle of good faith expressed in Preamble 3. Under Article 1.5, in the absence of agreement between the parties in relation to a matter on which the rules are silent 'the Arbitral Tribunal shall conduct the taking of evidence *as it deems appropriate*, in accordance with the general principles of the IBA Rules of Evidence' (emphasis added).

92 Ashford (n 10) 12.

iv. Conclusion

Regardless of whether the obligation of good faith referred to at Preamble 3 is given a narrow or wider interpretation, there are many different types of conduct that might be said to breach such an obligation. Anyone experienced in the practice of international arbitration will recognize what these are. A tribunal in a particular case will have to decide whether conduct should be categorized as bad faith conduct or as routine tactics that parties expect to be able to use and to have deployed against them as part of the 'cut and thrust' of any dispute. The answer is likely to lie in the facts of the case. It is the tribunal who, knowing the procedural history, and having heard the 'defaulting' party's explanation for what has occurred, will determine on which side of the line a particular action may fall. **2.80**

f. Who is responsible for the breach of the obligation of good faith?

A related question is who bears responsibility for any breach of the duty of good faith? **2.81**

Preamble 3 states that '*each Party* shall act in good faith'.[93] However, in most instances a party's legal team will have implemented, if not initiated, the conduct in question. Counsel can have a very significant influence on the manner in which a party conducts an arbitration and the nature of the tactics that may be deployed. In that sense counsel may, in certain cases, be regarded as the primary protagonist. **2.82**

There does not appear to be any clear view on whether the duty of good faith attaches to counsel as well as to the parties in any meaningful way. To the extent that counsel is acting as agent and representative of a party (the position in all but an exceptional case), it is reasonable to assume that acts of counsel will be attributed to the relevant party and that the tribunal should exercise sanctions in an appropriate fashion on that basis. **2.83**

In addition, there will, of course, be situations where bad faith conduct by a party may be unknown to counsel, for example, where a party deliberately conceals or destroys documents adverse to its case that are subject to production. This has been raised as a problem in relation to the proper policing of a good faith obligation and the professional awkwardness that may result from obliging legal practitioners to effectively police their own clients.[94] **2.84**

Equally, there may be circumstances where the conduct is more reasonably laid at the door of counsel—for example, where counsel pleads facts that are inconsistent with undisclosed documents. Provided such conduct can be established as having a sufficient connection with the taking of evidence under the IBA Rules, a breach of the obligation of good faith may arise under those rules. In each case, counsel will still be acting as agent or representative of his or her instructing party and the question of whether the conduct was driven by the client or by counsel will be irrelevant to the issue of whether **2.85**

[93] Emphasis added.
[94] Veeder 'Are the IBA Rules Perfectible?' (n 86) 322.

a breach has arisen, although the tribunal may consider it a relevant factor in deciding whether and how to sanction the conduct.

2.86 The lack of an internationally acceptable code of conduct, and limitations on a tribunal's ability to censure counsel, makes an obligation of good faith difficult to enforce against counsel separately from any sanctions imposed on the instructing party. Depending on the facts, and if applicable to the particular arbitration proceedings, some remedy may exist under one of the more general provisions governing counsel conduct that are emerging as part of the 'soft law' of international arbitration.[95]

3. Available Sanctions for a Breach of the IBA Obligation of Good Faith Conduct

2.87 A number of sanctions are available under the IBA Rules in the event that a party fails to act in good faith in relation to the taking of evidence. Only Article 9.7 is expressly linked to a party's failure to conduct itself in good faith.[96]

a. Assignment of costs

2.88 Article 9.7 of the IBA Rules makes express provision for a tribunal to impose costs sanctions where a party fails to conduct itself in good faith in the taking of evidence. That provision states:

> If the Arbitral Tribunal determines that a Party has failed to conduct itself in good faith *in the taking of evidence*, the Arbitral Tribunal may, in addition to any other measures available under these Rules, *take such failure into account in its assignment of the costs of the arbitration, including* costs arising out of or in connection with the taking of evidence.[97]

The scope and application of this provision is addressed in Chapter 12.

b. Non-costs sanctions under the IBA Rules

2.89 Assignment of costs against the defaulting party is not the only sanction permitted under the IBA Rules where a tribunal is satisfied that a party has failed to act in good faith. Article 9.7 contains an express statement that the power to assign costs may be used '*in addition* to any other measures available under these Rules'. Therefore, it is clear that the imposition of a costs sanction does not affect the ability of a tribunal to also

[95] For example, see IBA Guidelines on Party Representation in International Arbitration (International Bar Association 2013) Guideline 27, which says in 'addressing issues of misconduct, the Arbitral Tribunal should take into account . . . (d) the good faith of the Party Representative'. See also Article 18.5 and Article 18.6 of the LCIA Rules.

[96] However, the Commentary on the IBA Rules (n 9) notes that violation of the good faith requirement can result in the consequences set out in IBA Rules (n 1), Articles 9.5 and 9.6 (adverse inferences), as well as that indicated in Article 9.7 (costs allocation).

[97] Emphasis added.

impose or exercise other measures available to it under the IBA Rules. The nature of the measures that it is appropriate to apply will depend upon the facts of the case and the nature of the conduct under scrutiny.

i. Tribunal initiatives

If a party has tried to suppress evidence, or has presented a case that is suspected (on reasonable grounds) of being inconsistent with evidence not available to the opposing party, a tribunal may itself require the production of the 'hidden' evidence by making a request for documents (Article 3.10), the appearance of a person to give testimony (Article 4.10), or the appointment of a tribunal-appointed expert (Article 6.1). Where a tribunal suspects that documents required to be produced exist but have not been properly searched for, the tribunal may require an affidavit or witness statement from the relevant party, or one of its officers, reporting on the extent and results of the search that has been undertaken. **2.90**

In some cases, a further practical response to bad faith conduct may be for the tribunal to review the procedural timetable and make appropriate adjustments that will mitigate the consequences of that conduct. The power to do this exists under most institutional rules, and (arguably) also under the IBA Rules in pursuit of the IBA Principle of a 'fair process' contained in Preamble 1. **2.91**

One ICC case provides an interesting example of where a tribunal was asked to make significant changes to the procedural timetable, although, on the facts of the case, it declined to do so. In that case, the claimant tried to persuade the tribunal that there had been irregularities in the preparation by the respondent of statements in English from Korean witnesses.[98] Lawyers for the respondent had prepared English language versions of witness statements for witnesses of limited English proficiency. After the statements had been filed, the English language version was translated into the Korean language for review by the witnesses. The claimant argued that this demonstrated that the taking of evidence had not been conducted in good faith. In doing so, the claimant relied on the IBA Rules and Article 18 of the UNCITRAL Model Law as requiring the taking of evidence to be conducted in good faith with each party entitled to know in advance of the hearing the evidence on which the other party relied. The claimant also cited a number of legal authorities concerning the denial of a fair hearing. **2.92**

The claimant's core complaint was that the process by which the evidence was collected and presented remained undisclosed by the respondent until discrepancies between the English and Korean versions of the statements emerged at the hearing. The claimant applied for an order that there be an oral rehearing of all evidence—such rehearing to be without reliance on the witness statements and to include evidence-in-chief, cross-examination, re-examination, and tribunal questions. The tribunal's decision suggests **2.93**

[98] Procedural Order, August 2014 in 'Extracts from ICC Case Materials on the Taking of Evidence with References to the IBA Rules' (2016) ICC Dispute Resolution Bulletin No. 1 127.

that it accepted there had been a breach of obligation on the part of the respondent, but took the view that the remedy must be proportionate to the breach. The delay and costs occasioned by the requested rehearing would be disproportionate. The tribunal appears to have been satisfied that the Korean witnesses had produced evidence to the tribunal that each had approved.[99]

ii. Assessment of the evidence

2.94 Another appropriate response may be for the tribunal to take such matters into account in its assessment of the evidence.[100] If a witness who has provided a statement refuses to attend for cross-examination, or is simply 'unavailable' without good reason, then, if the IBA Rules have been formally adopted in the arbitration, the witness statement must be disregarded altogether by the tribunal.[101] This sanction may be fitting when the non-attendance of the witness is an obvious strategy adopted by the party ostensibly tendering the witness. However, if the IBA Rules are being used as guidance only, the tribunal has open to it the option of taking the statement into account, but adjusting the weight that the tribunal attaches to it. The fact that the evidence of the witness was not tested in cross-examination is likely to result in it being given significantly less weight. However, the weighing of evidence is a subjective exercise and the overall value attributed to the statement (if any) will depend in part on the tribunal's view of why the witness did not attend, including whether this was a manifestation of bad faith conduct.

2.95 The drawing of adverse inferences is another option that may be appropriate where a party has improperly failed to produce relevant evidence. Both Article 9.5 (documents) and Article 9.6 (other relevant evidence, including testimony) empower the tribunal to 'infer that such [document or other relevant evidence, including testimony] would be adverse to the interests of [the non-producing] Party'. Under both of those provisions, the recalcitrant party must either have failed to provide a satisfactory explanation for non-production of evidence properly requested by the other party under the IBA Rules, or the evidence must have been ordered to be produced by the tribunal. Whether an explanation for non-production is regarded as 'satisfactory', or the non-producing party is to be regarded as acting in bad faith, will be a matter for assessment by the tribunal in an individual case.[102]

2.96 Looking at more extreme situations, some ICSID tribunals have been prepared to consider drawing adverse inferences where an injunction to restrain a potential witness

[99] Interestingly, the tribunal noted that a viva voce re-run of the respondent's evidence without reliance on witness statements would be contrary to the IBA Rules which contemplate the provision of witness statements in advance of the evidentiary hearing. However, the tribunal also made clear that it did not approve of the method of evidence-gathering undertaken by the respondent. It said that a Korean (not English) version of the witness statements should have been presented first to each witness. In addition, as the IBA Rules suggest, each witness should have stated in his or her statement the language in which the statement had been prepared.

[100] See Chapter 12 paras 12.31–12.34.

[101] IBA Rules (n 1) Article 4.7. This is subject to the exceptions stated in that article.

[102] Nigel Blackaby and others, *Redfern and Hunter on International Arbitration* (6th edn, OUP 2016) paras 6.112–6.115. Commentary on the IBA Rules (n 9) indicates that the use of adverse inferences under IBA Rules (n 1), Articles 9.5 and 9.6 may be an appropriate sanction for violation of the requirement of good faith.

from giving evidence is seen as a tactical act on the part of the restraining party.[103] It is suggested that, in these circumstances, a tribunal may properly infer that the party obtaining the injunction had something to hide and, provided the other party has made out a prima facie case, the tribunal is entitled to shift the burden of proof to the guilty party.[104] It seems to us that this is going too far. Likewise, where evidence before the tribunal has been obtained by coercion, it will be more appropriate for the tribunal to attach no weight to it than to infer that the 'real' evidence of the witness would have confirmed or substantiated the other party's case.

The use of adverse inference under the IBA Rules is dealt with in more detail in Chapter 12. However, one helpful illustration of the difficulty of formulating an appropriate adverse inference given elsewhere is the example of a dispute involving a construction delay claim, where the contractor refuses to produce all construction schedules. The question that arises is whether it is reasonable for the tribunal to draw an adverse inference that the contractor breached the scheduling requirements or, alternatively, if it would be fair for the tribunal to infer that the contractor concealed from the owner the fact that the project would be delayed.[105] In practice, given these constraints, the possible use of adverse inference may be most effective as a deterrent. **2.97**

c. Other general remedies existing outside of the IBA Rules

Parties at the receiving end of bad faith conduct in connection with the taking of evidence under the IBA Rules may also wish to consider what remedies may be granted by the tribunal under its general discretionary powers or specific provisions of applicable arbitration rules or laws. Monetary penalties are one possibility, for example, an order for immediate payment of interim costs or a requirement that a party underwrite the costs of future steps made necessary by a party's bad faith conduct. Furthermore, the seeking of a peremptory order[106] from the tribunal may, in certain circumstances, be of some practical assistance - for example, where a party is deliberately trying to obstruct progress in the proceedings. None of these remedies is a sanction provided for under the IBA Rules. In relation to the first remedy, Article 9.7 provides for an adjustment of costs, but only at the end of the proceedings.[107] The other two remedies mentioned **2.98**

[103] *Enron Corporation and Ponderosa Assets, L.P. v Argentine Republic* (Award, 22 May 2007) ICSID Case No. ARB/01/3, and *Sempra Energy International v The Argentine Republic* (Award, 28 September 2007) ICSID Case No. ARB/02/16. See further Kolo (n 42) 77.

[104] Kolo (n 42) 78.

[105] See Nadia Darwazeh, 'Document Discovery and the IBA Rules on Evidence: A Practitioner's View' (2002) International Arbitration Law Review 101.

[106] A peremptory order is an order requiring a party to comply with an earlier order, failing which specific stated consequences will follow. For example, if a party fails to file expert evidence within a deadline stipulated by a tribunal, the defaulting party may be debarred from relying on expert evidence. Non-escalation orders by which parties are directed by a tribunal not to do anything that will serve to escalate or increase the matters in dispute can be effective if the need to keep the tribunal 'on-side' is seen by both parties as a strategic objective. However, a party already suspected of serious bad faith conduct may pay little heed to such an order.

[107] This view appears to be shared by other commentators. Newmark (n 21) states that 'a tool that the new Rules does not make use of is the making of interim costs orders'. See also Ashford (n 10) 15. This may be something that will be considered in the new review of the rules. As noted by Newmark 'requiring the parties to pay as they go has been shown in commercial litigation to have a dramatic effect in discouraging unmeritorious interim applications . . . and

would also require the exercise of tribunal powers derived from sources other than the IBA Rules.

2.99 In principle, another possibility is for the non-defaulting party to seek contractual remedies from the tribunal in relation to its opponent's breach of an obligation to conduct the arbitration in good faith. If parties to an arbitration formally adopt the IBA Rules (as opposed to using them as guidelines only) those rules form part of the contract to arbitrate made between the parties. An argument may be made that traditional remedies for breach of contract should be available to the non-defaulting party. However, those remedies—specific performance, damages, and contract termination—are, in practice, rarely adequate to address bad faith conduct.[108]

4. The Second Principle: Reasonable Notice of Evidence Relied on by the Other Parties

2.100 The Second Principle contained in Preamble 3 requires that the taking of evidence be conducted on the principle that each party is entitled to know, reasonably in advance of any evidentiary hearing or any fact or merits determination, the evidence on which the other parties rely.

2.101 This principle was present in the 1999 Rules. The reference to a fact or merits determination (in addition to an evidentiary hearing) was introduced by the current (2010) version of the IBA Rules. It appears to make little difference to the substance of the provision, but the change may have been considered desirable so as to remove any doubt that the principle applies to *any* hearing leading to a determination that may be evidence based.

2.102 The principle that each party should have reasonable notice of the evidence on which its opponent intends to rely is uncontroversial, but important. Advance notice of an opponent's evidence is essential if the other party is to have a reasonable opportunity to

excessive document production requests'. However, he also notes that the use of interim costs order in international arbitration is complicated by the fact that they are likely to require the making of interim awards.

[108] *Specific performance* has limited practical application. An application to court to stay proceedings brought in breach of an arbitration agreement, if granted, is easily enforced. An award or order that a party take positive steps in the arbitration in compliance with its duty of good faith is a very different matter. *Termination of the agreement* is another possibility—like any other contract, and subject to the requirements of its governing law, an arbitration agreement (or reference) is generally capable of being terminated for repudiatory breach (eg see the English case of *Downing v Al Tameer Establishment* [2002] EWCA Civ 721 [25]). Whether obstructive bad faith conduct, for example, a persistent refusal to submit evidence or produce key documents in accordance with a tribunal's order, could be regarded as a breach justifying termination of the arbitration reference is a matter for debate. The writers are not aware of any case in which this argument has been run. Damages may also be awarded for breach of an arbitration agreement (see the English case of *Mantovani v Caparelli SpA* [1980] 1 Lloyd's Rep 375, and the 'Chinese case' described in an article by Jane Wessel and Sherri North Cohen, 'In Tune with Mantovani: The "Novel" Case of Damages for Breach of an Arbitration Agreement' (2001) International Arbitration Law Review 65). However, in the majority of cases, even if a clear breach of the obligation of good faith could be established, there will be obvious difficulties in identifying the precise consequences of that conduct needed to advance and support a claim to financial loss.

prepare its arguments and/or to challenge that evidence. A denial of these rights would call into question the fairness of the arbitration process and possibly expose the award to challenge. Article V of the New York Convention provides that enforcement of an award may be refused if the party against whom the award is invoked was unable to present its case.[109] The same principle is found in the majority of institutional rules.[110]

The Second Principle is reflected in many provisions of the IBA Rules—the Commentary describes it as 'infus[ing] all of the provisions of those rules'.[111] For example, the requirement that each party provide to the other party the documents upon which it relies (Article 3.1), early identification of the witnesses of fact/expert witnesses upon whose testimony a party intends to rely, and provision for the delivery of a witness statement/expert report in advance of the evidential hearing (Articles 4.1–4.4 and Article 5.1). **2.103**

Under the IBA Rules the tribunal will lay down a procedural timetable after consultation with the parties. This will include deadlines by which evidence is to be produced. If any party believes that the deadlines stipulated will compromise its ability to deal with the evidence, it can raise those concerns during the consultation process. However, as the proceedings develop, new issues of facts may emerge that cause parties to introduce new evidence late or at short notice. It is in relation to these situations that a tribunal must be careful to observe the requirements of the Second Principle. **2.104**

The question of what constitutes a reasonable period for receipt of evidence in advance of a hearing will depend on a blend of factors, such as the nature and complexity of the evidence, the availability of the receiving party's witnesses and experts to deal with it, and whether relevant deadlines can be extended without an immoveable hearing date being compromised. **2.105**

There are numerous examples of challenges to an award on grounds that the losing party did not have a fair opportunity to put its case because it had insufficient notice of evidence submitted by the other party. For example, *Netherlands No. 24, Rice Trading (Guyana) Ltd. v Nidera Handelscompagnie BV, Gerechtshof*[112] concerned an award made in a commodity arbitration sought to be enforced in the Netherlands. It was found by the Dutch court that enforcement should be refused because the party against whom the award was made had not been permitted to comment on new evidence submitted **2.106**

[109] The New York Convention on the Recognition and Enforcement of Foreign Arbitral Awards 1958, Article V 1.(b).

[110] For example, see Article 22(4) of the ICC Rules; Article 23(2) of the SCC Rules; and Article 13.1 of the HKIAC Rules. The LCIA Rules go one step further by making express reference to a party's right to a reasonable opportunity to deal with its *opponent's* case. LCIA Rules Article 14.4 provides that: 'Under the Arbitration Agreement, the Arbitral Tribunal's general duties at all times during the arbitration shall include: (i) a duty to act fairly and impartially as between all parties, *giving each a reasonable opportunity of putting its case and dealing with that of its opponent(s)*...' (emphasis added).

[111] Commentary on the IBA Rules (n 9).

[112] 'Netherlands No. 24, *Rice Trading (Guyana) Ltd. v Nidera Handelscompagnie BV, Gerechtshof*, The Hague, 28 April 1998 and President, Arrondissementsrechtbank, Rotterdam, 2 October 1997' in Albert Jan van den Berg (ed), *Yearbook Commercial Arbitration* (vol 23, Kluwer Law International 1998) 731–34.

after an oral hearing had taken place. In *Paklito Investment Ltd. v Klockner East Asia Ltd. [1993] HKLR 39*,[113] a case involving a CIETAC award, the Supreme Court of Hong Kong held that Paklito should be refused permission to enforce the award in Hong Kong because the tribunal had issued its award *before* giving Klockner an opportunity to comment on expert evidence commissioned by the tribunal under its discretionary powers.[114]

2.107 It is clear that both of these examples would breach the Second Principle. Whether the fault for denial of due process in such cases as these can be attributed to the tribunal and/or lies with one of the parties will depend on the facts of the case, and the steps taken by the tribunal to ensure a fair procedure.

[113] '*Paklito Investment Ltd. v Klockner East Asia Ltd. [1993] HKLR 39*' in Albert Jan van den Berg (ed), *Yearbook Commercial Arbitration* (vol 19, Kluwer Law International 1994) 664–74.

[114] ibid [39]–[40]; the Court found that: 'It is clear that the Tribunal relied on these reports and that the defendants were given no chance to deal with this very different case which suddenly presented itself. The defendants should have been given an opportunity to deal with this new evidence. They asked for such an opportunity but the award came too soon and they never received an answer to their request [. . .]. Taking all the matters canvassed by both sides into account I have come to the very clear conclusion that the defendants were prevented from presenting their case and they have thus made out the grounds set out in Sect. 44(2)(c) of the Arbitration Ordinance. The defendants were denied a fair and equal opportunity of being heard'.

3

Definitions Used in the IBA Rules on Evidence

A. Introduction

The Commentary to the IBA Rules explains that the definitions section of those rules sets out basic definitions to be applied when using the IBA Rules on Evidence, and that these are 'generally straightforward, with commonly understood meanings'. The Commentary also confirms that the definitions themselves do not provide any substantive rules of conduct or evidence.[1] **3.1**

B. Definitions

Each of the definitions provided in the Definitions section of the IBA Rules is described below. **3.2**

1. 'Arbitral Tribunal' Means a Sole Arbitrator or a Panel of Arbitrators

The definition of 'arbitral tribunal' is straightforward and unambiguous. Additional wording included in earlier iterations of the rules ('or the majority of them as the case **3.3**

[1] 1999 IBA Working Party and 2010 IBA Rules of Evidence Review Subcommittee, 'Commentary on the Revised Text of the 2010 IBA Rules on the Taking of Evidence in International Arbitration' (International Bar Association) 4 <www.ibanet.org/Document/Default.aspx?DocumentUid=DD240932-OE08-40D4-9866-309A635487CO> accessed 27 November 2018 (hereafter 'Commentary on the IBA Rules').

may be and shall include an umpire'[2] and 'validly deciding by majority or otherwise')[3] have wisely been removed from the 2010 version of the rules.

2. 'Claimant' means the Party or Parties who Commenced the Arbitration and Any Party Who, through Joinder or Otherwise, Becomes Aligned with Such Party or Parties

3.4 This definition of 'Claimant' is the same as appears in the 1999 IBA Rules. It extends the definition contained in the 1983 Rules by addition of the words 'who, through joinder or otherwise, becomes aligned with such Party or Parties'. We assume that this addition was considered desirable in light of the increased frequency with which joinder and consolidation occur in current practice and in the light of revisions to a number of institutional rules in the period post-1983 to permit joinder and consolidation.[4]

3. 'Document' Means a Writing, Communication, Picture, Drawing, Program, or Data of any Kind, Whether Recorded or Maintained on Paper or by Electronic, Audio, Visual, or any Other Means

3.5 Although the definition of 'Document' in the 1999 IBA Rules[5] was considered by the drafting committee to be broad enough to include most forms of electronic evidence, minor changes were nonetheless introduced in the 2010 IBA Rules. The Commentary on the 2010 IBA Rules explains that the Review Subcommittee wanted to be sure that all forms of evidence, including electronic evidence, are subject to the IBA Rules and may be requested, subject to the requirements of Article 3.3 (including satisfaction of the relevance and materiality standard) and Article 9 (grounds for objection to production).[6] In line with that objective, the definition was reworded to its present form. However, consideration of the previous definition in the 1999 IBA Rules ('a writing of any kind, whether recorded on paper, electronic means, audio or visual recordings or

[2] IBA Supplementary Rules Governing the Presentation and Reception of Evidence in International Commercial Arbitration 1983, Article 2 (hereafter '1983 IBA Rules').

[3] IBA Rules on the Taking of Evidence in International Commercial Arbitration 1999, Article 1 (hereafter '1999 IBA Rules').

[4] For example, in relation to joinder, see the LCIA Rules 1998 and 2014, which give the tribunal the power to join third parties to the arbitration, at the request of a party, provided that the third party and the applicant party consent in writing (LCIA Rules 1998, Article 22.1(h); LCIA Rules 2014, Article 22.1(viii)); the SIAC Rules 2013 give the tribunal the power to allow one or more third parties to be joined in the arbitration, provided that they are a party to the arbitration agreement and with the written consent of the third party (SIAC Rules 2013, Rule 24.1(b)). See also the ICC Rules 2012 and 2017, Article 7, and the HKIAC Administered Arbitration Rules 2013 and 2018, Article 27.

[5] 'Document' means a writing of any kind, whether recorded on paper, electronic means, audio or visual recordings, or other mechanical or electronic means of storing or recording information. 1999 IBA Rules (n 3), Article 1.

[6] Commentary on the IBA Rules (n 1) 4.

other mechanical or electronic means of storing or recording information') confirms that this was largely an updating exercise, rather than the introduction of any material change.

In substance, under the IBA Rules, electronic documents are treated in the same way as paper documents, although there is an acknowledgement in Article 3 that some discussion around identification of file names and search terms may be necessary in relation to a request for electronic documents. There is no additional express provision for issues generated by the nature and volume of electronic documents—for example, data preservation. A recent IBA report on the results of a survey on the IBA Rules noted that a number of respondents advocated for revisions 'aimed at facilitating the exchange of e-documents between the parties and providing guidance on the use of electronic evidence'.[7] **3.6**

4. 'Evidentiary Hearing' Means any Hearing, Whether or Not Held on Consecutive Days, at which the Arbitral Tribunal, Whether in Person, by Teleconference, Videoconference, or Other Method, Receives Oral or Other Evidence

The definition of 'Evidentiary Hearing' is straightforward. Given technological advances, and the more frequent use of virtual hearings, the previous definition of evidentiary hearing contained in the 1999 Rules has been updated to include express reference to hearings 'by teleconference, video conference or other method'. **3.7**

5. 'Expert Report' Means a Written Statement by a Tribunal-Appointed Expert or a Party-Appointed Expert

The definition of 'expert report' is straightforward and, importantly, includes both a report from a party-appointed expert as provided for in Article 5, and a report from a tribunal-appointed expert as provided for in Article 6. **3.8**

The previous definition of expert report contained in the 1999 IBA Rules included a requirement for the report to be 'submitted pursuant to the IBA Rules of Evidence'. In practice, this wording appears to add little and has been deleted from the current version of the IBA Rules. **3.9**

[7] The IBA Arbitration Guidelines and Rules Subcommittee, 'Report on the Reception of the IBA Arbitration Soft Law Products' (International Bar Association 2016) 91 www.ibanet.org/Document/Default.aspx?DocumentUid=105d29a3-6261-4437-84e2-1c8637844beb accessed 27 November 2018.

6. 'General Rules' Means the Institutional, ad hoc, or Other Rules that Apply to the Conduct of the Arbitration

3.10 'General Rules' is a term not commonly used elsewhere. As defined in the IBA Rules, it refers to institutional, ad hoc, or other rules that apply to the arbitration, eg institutional rules such as the ICC Rules, the LCIA Rules, and the SIAC Rules, and ad hoc rules such as the UNCITRAL Rules. We assume that the inclusion of 'other rules' is a 'sweep up provision intended to catch any other set of rules that may apply'.[8] For example, the parties may have agreed to adopt the IBA Guidelines on Party Representation in International Arbitration.[9]

3.11 The definition of General Rules in the 1999 Rules referred to the rules 'according to which the Parties are conducting their arbitration'. The current description—rules 'that apply to the conduct of the arbitration'—is arguably more accurate in circumstances where application of the relevant rules has been agreed in a binding arbitration agreement.

3.12 Interestingly, the corresponding definition in the 1983 IBA Rules referred to 'the specific rules of Arbitration agreed upon by the parties except *in so far as evidence is concerned*'.[10] This formulation—suggesting that the provisions of the IBA Rules would take precedence over the General Rules in relation to matters of evidence—reflected the express wording to this effect contained in the Introduction to the 1983 IBA Rules.[11] A more nuanced approach to issues of conflict was adopted in the 1999 IBA Rules, and followed in the 2010 IBA Rules, under which a tribunal is required to apply the IBA Rules in a manner that best accomplishes the purposes of both the IBA Rules and the General Rules. This may account for the original definition being abandoned. It is in Article 1.3 (where this new approach is stipulated) and in Article 1.5 (dealing with a situation where both the IBA Rules and the General Rules are silent) that the term 'General Rules' is used.

[8] In our view, the definition of General Rules does not extend to rules not intended to apply specifically to the conduct of the arbitration as a whole, or that the parties to the arbitration have not agreed to adopt in relation to the arbitration. For example, in our view, professional conduct rules applicable to individual counsel involved in the arbitration would not fall within the definition of General Rules. There may, of course, be mandatory provisions of law that may apply to the arbitration (eg mandatory provisions of law at the seat of arbitration). However, under the IBA Rules, these are treated as a different category of provision. See, for example, IBA Rules (n 8), Article 1.1 of the IBA Rules, which makes express provision for circumstances of conflict between the IBA Rules and a mandatory provision of law. See also IBA Rules (n 8), Article 1.3 which addresses a conflict between the IBA Rules and the General Rules.

[9] Although those provisions are entitled 'guidelines', they make clear that their terms may be adopted as a matter of contract by agreement between the parties. International Bar Association, *IBA Guidelines on Party Representation in International Arbitration* (International Bar Association 2013) 2. It appears to us that, in such circumstances, they may be regarded as rules falling within the definition of 'General Rules'.

[10] Emphasis added.

[11] The Introduction to 1983 IBA Rules (n 2) stated that 'where [the IBA Rules] are inconsistent with the [. . .] General Rules, these I.B.A. Rules of Evidence shall prevail but solely as regards the presentation and reception of evidence'.

7. 'IBA Rules on Evidence' or 'Rules' Means these IBA Rules on the Taking of Evidence in International Arbitration, as They May Be Revised or Amended from Time to Time

This is a new definition introduced in the 2010 Rules. The definition suggests that any reference to the IBA Rules should be treated as a reference to the current version of those rules. In this respect, the terms of Article 1.2 of the IBA should be borne in mind. This provision is discussed in more detail in Chapter 4 but, in summary, it provides that where parties have agreed to apply the IBA Rules, they are deemed to have agreed to the version current *on the date of such agreement*, ie not the version current on the date the arbitration commences. **3.13**

8. 'Party' Means a Party to the Arbitration

For the purposes of the IBA Rules, we believe this definition to be straightforward and unambiguous. **3.14**

9. 'Party-Appointed Expert' Means a Person or Organization Appointed by a Party in Order to Report on Specific Issues Determined by the Party

This definition refers to an expert appointed within the umbrella of Article 5 of the IBA Rules (*Party-Appointed Experts*). **3.15**

The definition in the 1999 IBA Rules did not include reference to an organization. The expanded wording makes clear that the expert appointed by a party can be an organization as well as an individual. This more accurately reflects the common position where expert evidence is prepared by, and credited to, several individuals within an organization, even though only one of them may ultimately give oral evidence. The new definition also describes the purpose of the expert appointment as being 'to report on specific issues'. It is not clear, but this wording may have been intended to emphasize that the expert evidence produced should be focused and address the particular issues in the case on which expert evidence may assist the tribunal. **3.16**

10 'Request to Produce' Means a Written Request by a Party that Another Party Produce Documents

The definition of 'Request to Produce' is different to that contained in the 1999 IBA Rules.[12] The change is a consequence of a substantive change to the rules themselves, by which a **3.17**

[12] The definition in 1999 IBA Rules (n 3) was 'a request by a Party for a procedural order by which the arbitral tribunal would direct another Party to produce documents'.

party is now permitted to make a written request to produce direct to another party, rather than delivering a request to produce to the tribunal, as was the previous position.[13]

11. 'Respondent' Means the Party or Parties against whom the Claimant Made Its Claim, and any Party who, through Joinder or Otherwise, Becomes Aligned with such Party or Parties, and Includes a Respondent Making a Counter-Claim

3.18 This definition is in similar terms to that given for 'Claimant'. It also makes clear that references to 'Respondent' in the IBA Rules will 'capture' a respondent for all purposes, ie a counter-claiming respondent will not be treated as being a 'Claimant' in relation to the counter-claim.

12. 'Tribunal-Appointed Expert' Means a Person or Organization Appointed by the Arbitral Tribunal in Order to Report to It on Specific Issues Determined by the Arbitral Tribunal

3.19 This definition refers to an expert appointed within the umbrella of Article 6 of the IBA Rules (*Tribunal-Appointed Experts*). As with party-appointed experts (see 9. 'Party-Appointed Expert') the definition now extends to the appointment of an organization and not just an individual.

13. 'Witness Statement' Means a Written Statement of Testimony by a Witness of Fact

3.20 The 1983 IBA Rules contained a definition of witness statement ('a written statement complying with the provisions of Article 5(2) [as to content]') but extended to statements from both a witness of fact and an expert.[14] The definition was dropped in the 1999 IBA Rules but reappears in the current IBA Rules. It is confined to statements 'by a witness of fact', with expert evidence produced by tribunal- or party-appointed experts having their own separate definition.

[13] 1999 IBA Rules (n 3), Article 3.2. Compare this with the current IBA Rules (n 8), Article 3.2, which provides for delivery to both the tribunal, and to the other party. In both cases the tribunal has to stipulate the date by which production is to be given and, where objection is raised by the 'producing' party, the tribunal has to make an order for production.

[14] 1983 IBA Rules (n 2), Article 5.2 required the statement to reflect 'whether the witness is a witness of fact or an expert . . .'.

4

Article 1: Scope of Application

Article 1

1. **Whenever the Parties have agreed or the Arbitral Tribunal has determined to apply the IBA Rules of Evidence, the Rules shall govern the taking of evidence, except to the extent that any specific provision of them may be found to be in conflict with any mandatory provision of law determined to be applicable to the case by the Parties or by the Arbitral Tribunal.**
2. **Where the Parties have agreed to apply the IBA Rules of Evidence, they shall be deemed to have agreed, in the absence of a contrary indication, to the version as current on the date of such agreement.**
3. **In case of conflict between any provisions of the IBA Rules of Evidence and the General Rules, the Arbitral Tribunal shall apply the IBA Rules of Evidence in the manner that it determines best in order to accomplish the purposes of both the General Rules and the IBA Rules of Evidence, unless the Parties agree to the contrary.**
4. **In the event of any dispute regarding the meaning of the IBA Rules of Evidence, the Arbitral Tribunal shall interpret them according to their purpose and in the manner most appropriate for the particular arbitration.**
5. **Insofar as the IBA Rules of Evidence and the General Rules are silent on any matter concerning the taking of evidence and the Parties have not agreed otherwise, the**

Arbitral Tribunal shall conduct the taking of evidence as it deems appropriate, in accordance with the general principles of the IBA Rules of Evidence.

A. Purpose

4.1 Article 1 addresses the interaction between the IBA Rules and the various other rules that may apply in an individual arbitration.

4.2 Many arbitrations will be conducted pursuant to a set of institutional rules. In addition, parties may elect to adopt the IBA Rules. There may also be related party agreements and applicable national laws/international treaty obligations that operate on the arbitration proceedings.

4.3 Necessary interaction between the IBA Rules and these other categories of provision creates the potential for inconsistency or conflict, as well as exposing gaps in the procedural framework. Article 1 of the IBA Rules lays down a number of basic principles by reference to which inconsistencies, conflicts, gaps, and uncertainties in the arbitration infrastructure affecting the taking of evidence are to be resolved.

4.4 Article 1 does not deal with a conflict between application of the IBA Rules and the professional conduct/ethical rules applicable to counsel in a particular arbitration.[1] Nor could it. This is a matter for individual counsel to address in the particular circumstances of the case. The ongoing development of internationally recognized norms of practice in international arbitration may in any event assist in reducing the potential for such conflicts to arise.

4.5 There is little commentary on the operation of Article 1, but this should not detract from the important role its provisions play in effective application of the IBA Rules.

4.6 Firstly, Article 1 sets out a number of principles that are to be applied in addressing a conflict between the IBA Rules and (a) any applicable mandatory provisions of law or (b) the institutional, ad hoc or other rules that have been chosen to apply to the arbitration (defined in the IBA Rules as the 'General Rules').

4.7 Secondly, it lays down the principles to be applied in the event of a dispute regarding interpretation of the IBA Rules, or where the parties are unable to agree what to do when those rules are silent on a particular matter concerning the taking of evidence.

4.8 Lastly, Article 1 stipulates which version of the IBA Rules is to apply to a particular arbitration.

[1] For example, where it would be contrary to the professional conduct rules applicable to an individual lawyer for that lawyer to comply with an order to produce on behalf of their client a particular document that, for reasons of privilege, confidentiality, etc., (s)he is not permitted to disclose.

Subject to one addition and a number of refinements, the terms of Article 1 of the IBA Rules follow very closely the wording of its predecessor provision in the 1999 IBA Rules.[2] **4.9**

B. Conflict with a Mandatory Provision of Law

> **1.1. Whenever the Parties have agreed or the Arbitral Tribunal has determined to apply the IBA Rules of Evidence, the Rules shall govern the taking of evidence, except to the extent that any specific provision of them may be found to be in conflict with any mandatory provision of law determined to be applicable to the case by the Parties or by the Arbitral Tribunal.**

1. Introduction

Article 1.1 is concerned with potential conflict between the IBA Rules and applicable mandatory provisions of law. **4.10**

2. Application of the IBA Rules Pursuant to Article 1.1

The use of the word 'shall' in Article 1.1 means that, where the IBA Rules apply, the provisions of those rules will govern all matters relating to the taking of evidence in the arbitration. **4.11**

Before considering the effect of Article 1.1, it is therefore necessary to decide if the IBA Rules apply. The opening words of Article 1.1 provide that the IBA Rules shall apply when 'the parties have agreed' or 'the Arbitral Tribunal has determined' to apply them. **4.12**

a. Formal adoption of the IBA Rules or use as guidelines only?

An important distinction exists between formal adoption of the IBA Rules as binding rules operating on the arbitration, and an agreement to use them as guidelines only. The mandatory application of the IBA Rules contemplated by the opening words of Article 1.1 will apply in the former situation, but not in the latter. **4.13**

Available data indicates that use of the IBA Rules as guidelines is much more common than formal adoption of the rules. A 2016 IBA Report suggests that nearly half (48 per cent) of the arbitrations considered in the survey referenced the IBA Rules on Evidence. However, in around 80 per cent of those arbitrations, the tribunal consulted the rules as **4.14**

[2] IBA Rules on the Taking of Evidence in International Commercial Arbitration 1999, Article 2 (hereafter '1999 IBA Rules').

guidelines only.[3] In the 20 per cent of arbitrations where there was agreement that the IBA Rules were to be binding, that agreement was reached *after* commencement of the arbitration in over 90 per cent of cases.[4]

4.15 In the majority of cases where the IBA Rules have been formally adopted into the arbitration proceedings, this will have been done by express agreement of the parties. The agreement may be contained in the parties' arbitration clause or may have been made during post-dispute negotiations on procedural directions and timetable.

4.16 The IBA Rules also contemplate application of the rules at the election of the tribunal,[5] and, where a clear direction has been given that the IBA Rules are to apply, the opening statement in Article 1.1 will take effect. In practice, this will generally be done with express or tacit agreement from the parties. In the authors' experience, even if it wishes to do so, a tribunal is often reluctant to take a unilateral decision to apply the IBA Rules in the face of opposition from the parties. In addition, despite the express statement at Preamble 2 that the IBA Rules are not intended to limit the flexibility inherent in the arbitration process, arbitrators may feel more comfortable exercising such flexibility without obligatory application of the IBA Rules.[6]

4.17 Where there is disagreement—for example, where one party is keen to apply the rules and the other party is not, each seeing a particular disadvantage or advantage relative to their position in the particular dispute—the tribunal may decide or prefer to apply the IBA Rules as non-binding guidelines.[7] In this case, the opening lines of Article 1.1 do not apply.

b. Adaptation of the IBA Rules to be applied under Article 1.1

4.18 The second sentence of Preamble 2 of the IBA Rules makes clear that the rules are intended to be used flexibly and may be adapted to suit the particular needs of an individual arbitration. Consistent with the principle of party autonomy, it is the adapted version of the IBA Rules that will apply to the arbitration.

[3] The IBA Arbitration Guidelines and Rules Subcommittee, 'Report on the Reception of the IBA Arbitration Soft Law Products' (International Bar Association 2016) paras 12–18 <www.ibanet.org/Document/Default.aspx?DocumentUid=105d29a3-6261-4437-84e2-1c8637844beb> accessed 27 November 2018 (hereafter '2016 IBA Report').

[4] ibid. See also Chapter 2, paras 2.33–2.39.

[5] IBA Rules on the Taking of Evidence in International Arbitration 2010, Preamble 2 (hereafter 'IBA Rules').

[6] There is some evidence to suggest that some tribunals are reluctant to give binding force to the IBA Rules for fear of challenge to an award on grounds that the tribunal has failed to follow the precise letter of those rules. See also: 'Extracts from ICC Case Material on the Taking of Evidence with References to the IBA Rules' (2016) 1 ICC Dispute Resolution Bulletin 127. See further Chapter 2, paras 2.35–2.39. Tribunals may also be nervous about mandatory application of certain provisions without express agreement from the parties. For example, the provision at IBA Rules (n 5), Article 4.7 stipulates that, in the event a witness requested to attend for cross-examination at an evidentiary hearing fails to do so, the witness statement of that witness is to be disregarded. There is some criticism of this provision as being too draconian notwithstanding the express exceptions to its application. See Chapter 7, paras 7.137–7.167.

[7] The 2016 IBA Report (n 3) mentions that even where the IBA Rules were adopted only as guidelines they were followed in 90 per cent of such cases.

Although not expressly stated in Preamble 2, it seems sensible that, where parties wish to adapt the IBA Rules, this should be done consensually at the time of adopting the IBA Rules or at commencement of the arbitration, if later. It would be unfair (as well as difficult) for one party to seek to adapt the IBA Rules in the face of disagreement from the other party after an agreement to apply the IBA Rules as they stand has already been made. **4.19**

If an irreconcilable disagreement about proposed adaptations emerges during negotiations on whether to apply the IBA Rules, then the parties will have to choose whether to adopt the IBA Rules unadapted, abandon use of those rules altogether, or agree that they may be used as guidelines only. **4.20**

3. Resolution of Conflict between an IBA Rule and a Mandatory Provision of Law

Article 1.1 contains a proviso to the general position that, where adopted, the provisions of the IBA Rules shall apply to the taking of evidence. The proviso concerns the relationship between the IBA Rules and mandatory provisions of law. Article 1.1 says that the IBA Rules shall govern **4.21**

> except to the extent that any specific provision of [the IBA Rules] may be found to be in conflict with any mandatory provision of law . . . (emphasis added).

A mandatory provision of law is one that must be observed and cannot be departed from as a matter of contract. The effect of Article 1.1 is that a mandatory law provision will take precedence over a specific provision of the IBA Rules with which it is in conflict. In this way the conflict is resolved and the integrity of the IBA Rules is preserved without offending the relevant system of law containing the mandatory provision. **4.22**

It is not expressly stated in the IBA Rules, but the natural consequence of Article 1.1 is that the mandatory law provision will, where appropriate, be given effect to in the arbitration proceedings. **4.23**

The inclusion of the phrase 'to the extent' in Article 1.1 indicates that the relevant provision of the IBA Rules should be displaced only to the extent necessary to remove conflict with the relevant mandatory provision of law. The reference to a 'specific provision' of the IBA Rules supports this interpretation. **4.24**

4. Sources of Potential Conflict between the IBA Rules and Mandatory Provisions of Law

The taking of evidence is a critical component in the arbitration process and the IBA Rules have wide reach in relation to that aspect of the proceedings. Thus, the scope **4.25** of subject matter within the IBA Rules to which a conflict may attach is, in principle, relatively wide.

4.26 However, while there are also many potential sources of mandatory law operating in an international arbitration, those mandatory provisions will very often apply to substantive issues between the parties.[8] The sources of mandatory provisions of law that touch on 'procedural' aspects (eg, the process of taking evidence and, in turn, on many of the matters covered by the IBA Rules) will be more limited. Nonetheless, they may arise from time to time.

4.27 Save in relation to investment arbitrations under the ICSID regime governed directly by international law,[9] the law of the seat of arbitration is the most likely source of a mandatory law provision affecting procedural aspects of an international arbitration with which the IBA Rules are concerned. Indeed, it has been suggested that the reference to mandatory applicable law in Article 1.1 of the IBA Rules is best understood as a reference to the law of the seat.[10] Some support for that view is found in the Commentary to the IBA Rules, which states in the introduction to Article 1 that international arbitrations are 'subject to . . . mandatory law relating to arbitration procedure at the seat of the arbitration', although the Commentary does go on to refer to '*any* mandatory legal provisions'.[11]

4.28 Unlike institutional rules which, for the most part, have many common themes reflecting accepted practice in international arbitration, the arbitration law within a particular national jurisdiction may vary significantly from that in other jurisdictions. As a result, it was impossible for those drafting the IBA Rules to anticipate or take into account all of the specific provisions of local law that might conflict with the procedures

[8] For example, even where the arbitration concerns a dispute under a contract subject to an express choice of governing law, mandatory provisions of another law may apply. The law of the domicile of a signatory party to a disputed contract may play a part in determining whether that party had capacity to make the agreement, and therefore whether the agreement is binding; the law of the seat concerning money laundering and/or the proceeds of crime may, in certain circumstances, have an impact on the enforceability of obligations contained in the contract. See further examples in Nigel Blackaby and others, *Redfern and Hunter on International Arbitration* (6th edn, OUP 2016) para 3.129 (hereafter 'Redfern and Hunter').

[9] The ICSID Convention nominates Washington DC as the seat, but an ICSID arbitration is governed solely by the ICSID Convention and the ICSID Arbitration Rules. ICSID Convention, Article 2 provides that 'The seat of the Centre shall be at the principal office of the International Bank for Reconstruction and Development (hereinafter called the Bank) . . . '. ICSID Convention, Article 44 states: 'Any arbitration proceeding shall be conducted in accordance with the provisions of this Section and, except as the parties otherwise agree, in accordance with the Arbitration Rules in effect on the date on which the parties consented to arbitration. If any question of procedure arises which is not covered by this Section or the Arbitration Rules or any rules agreed by the parties, the Tribunal shall decide the question.' There is no seat of arbitration in the conventional sense. The unique character of ICSID arbitration derives from the fact that, unlike international commercial arbitrations, ICSID proceedings are, for the most part, detached from national legal systems. In particular, they are not subject to supervision by the courts at the seat of the arbitration.

[10] Amy F Cohen, 'Chapter 13. Options for Approaching Evidentiary Privilege in International Arbitration' in Teresa Giovannini and Alexis Mourre (eds), *Written Evidence and Discovery in International Arbitration: New Issues and Tendencies* (Kluwer Law International 2009) 433.

[11] 1999 IBA Working Party and 2010 IBA Rules of Evidence Review Subcommittee, 'Commentary on the Revised Text of the 2010 IBA Rules on the Taking of Evidence in International Arbitration' (2010) International Bar Association 4 <www.ibanet.org/Document/Default.aspx?DocumentUid=DD240932-0E08-40D4-9866-309A635487C0> accessed 28 November 2018 (hereafter 'Commentary on the IBA Rules') (emphasis added).

laid down in the IBA Rules. Article 1.1 of the IBA Rules provides the manner of resolution of any conflict that may arise: namely, that the mandatory provision of law will prevail. This express provision reflects the most likely outcome on application of general principles. Redfern and Hunter confirm that '... once a place of arbitration has been chosen, it brings with it its own law. If that law contains provisions that are mandatory as far as arbitrations are concerned, those provisions must be obeyed'.[12] On one view, Article 1.1 of the IBA Rules simply acknowledges that position.

However, the mandatory provisions of law engaged by Article 1.1 are not limited to mandatory provisions of the seat of arbitration. As mentioned, Article 1.1 refers to '*any* mandatory provisions of law determined to be applicable to the case'.[13] Although the Commentary to the IBA Rules suggests that this provision is directed at the law of the seat of arbitration, there is no limitation to that effect in the rules and, as a matter of principle, it is difficult to see why there should be. **4.29**

a. Mandatory provisions at the seat of arbitration

The law of the seat or 'legal home' of an international arbitration can play an important role in the arbitration proceedings, sometimes most significantly by not facilitating unnecessary intervention in the conduct of the arbitration. **4.30**

When parties select a seat for their arbitration they often make a conscious choice of seat based not only on considerations of geographical or other factors of practical convenience, but also by reference to the framework of arbitration law existing in that jurisdiction. The arbitration law of the seat will, in nearly all cases, constitute the law governing the arbitration proceedings (the *lex arbitri*).[14] The law of the seat is likely to include express mandatory and supervisory powers—most importantly, the power to set aside an award and thereby affect the successful party's ability to enforce that award elsewhere under the New York Convention as well as at the seat.[15] It may also involve application of less tangible but equally important 'mandatory norms' concerning the conduct of arbitration. **4.31**

i. Mandatory provisions of law at the seat

As mentioned, the potential for conflict between the detailed provisions of the IBA Rules and mandatory provisions of law at the seat of arbitration covering the same subject matter is likely to be relatively limited. In the majority of arbitrations, the seat chosen by the parties, or that arrived at under the default provisions of most popular **4.32**

[12] Redfern and Hunter (n 8) para 3.64. See also Jeffrey Waincymer, *Procedure and Evidence in International Arbitration* (Kluwer Law International 2012) 127–216, para 3.7.1 (hereafter 'Waincymer').

[13] Emphasis added.

[14] It is theoretically possible for the parties to select the law of another jurisdiction as the *lex arbitri*. See paragraph 4.50 and (n 41).

[15] The New York Convention on the Recognition and Enforcement of Foreign Arbitral Awards 1958 (hereafter 'New York Convention'). Under the New York Convention, Article V(1)(e), recognition and enforcement of an award may be refused if the award has been set aside or suspended by the Courts of the country in which the award was made.

institutional rules, is likely to result in one of a number of seats of arbitration generally regarded as 'arbitration friendly' or, at the very least, a seat that both parties can 'live with' as part of the overall commercial negotiation.[16]

4.33 In addition to having the necessary infrastructure (for example, a pool of experienced arbitrators, purpose-built arbitration hearing facilities, easy international access and entry requirements, transcription services, etc) and being a party to the New York Convention,[17] the key characteristic of these jurisdictions is that their arbitration laws will support, rather than interfere with, the arbitration process.

4.34 Countries seeking to support and encourage international arbitration within their territory will generally enact legislation providing an appropriate framework. The UNITRAL Model Law on International Commercial Arbitration has been adopted or has formed the basis for arbitration laws in a significant number of jurisdictions.[18] Other jurisdictions maintain a discrete statute (eg the English Arbitration Act)[19] or include the arbitration law as part of their Civil Code (see the Belgian Judicial Code,[20] the German Code of Civil Procedure,[21] and the Swiss Private International Law Statute).[22]

4.35 Consistent with a 'light touch' approach to the conduct of arbitrations adopted in many such jurisdictions, the arbitration law at a seat of arbitration is unlikely to deal in any

[16] The Queen Mary 2015 International Arbitration Survey found that the five most preferred seats of arbitration are London, Paris, Hong Kong, Singapore and Geneva. Queen Mary University of London, '2015 International Arbitration Survey: Improvements and Innovations in International Arbitration' (White & Case 2015) <www.arbitration.qmul.ac.uk/media/arbitration/docs/2015_International_Arbitration_Survey.pdf> accessed 6 December 2018.

[17] New York Convention (n 15). The principal reasons why a party will wish to bring the arbitration under the umbrella of a contracting state relate to enforcement of the arbitration agreement and of any award obtained. Subject to certain conditions laid down in the Convention being satisfied, contracting parties to the New York Convention agree to recognize and give effect to (a) an arbitration agreement and (b) an award made in another state. The Convention contains a reciprocity reservation permitting a contracting state to limit its enforcement obligation to awards made in the territory of another contracting state. See New York Convention (n 15), Article I(3).

[18] UNCITRAL Model Law on International Commercial Arbitration (as adopted by UNCITRAL on 21 June 1985 and as amended by UNCITRAL on 7 July 2006) (hereafter 'UNCITRAL Model Law'). For list of jurisdictions that have based their legislation on the Model Law, see <www.uncitral.org/uncitral/en/uncitral_texts/arbitration/1985Model_arbitration_status.html> accessed 29 November 2018. The number of jurisdictions that have adopted the UNCITRAL Model Law is in excess of 70.

[19] English Arbitration Act 1996.

[20] Arbitrations with a seat in Belgium are governed by the Belgium Law on Arbitration, which is set out in Part VI of the Belgian Judicial Code (hereafter 'BJC').

[21] The core of the German arbitration law is integrated in the German Code of Civil Procedure (Zivilprozessordung, hereafter 'ZPO'), where it constitutes its 10th Book. It is supplemented by a number of arbitration-specific provisions in other statutes relating primarily to the non-arbitrability of certain disputes. Some of the other provisions of the ZPO may become applicable in arbitration-related court proceedings in support or in supervision of the arbitration.

[22] Chapter 12 of the Swiss Private International Law Statute (hereafter 'PILS') which entered into force on 1 January 1989. Chapter 12 of PILS is not based on the UNCITRAL Model Law (n 18), but does not differ fundamentally from that law. Rather, it comprises 19 articles (Articles 176–194). By contrast, the ZPO (n 21), which governs domestic arbitration in Switzerland, is much more detailed and contains 47 articles (Articles 353–399). Other relevant provisions are however found in PILS ch 1 (Article 7) or in other federal statutes. PILS Article 7 governs the effects of the arbitration agreement when Swiss courts are seized on the merits in respect of a dispute covered by such arbitration agreement. Federal Statute on the Swiss Federal Supreme Court, Article 77 provides, in conjunction with PILS Article 191, the legal basis for the action for setting aside awards rendered in Switzerland. Finally, the provisions of the Swiss Code of Civil Procedure (hereafter 'Swiss ZPO') concerning 'the nomination, revocation or replacement of the arbitrators' apply 'by analogy' in international arbitration because PILS Article 179(2) refers to the Swiss ZPO for these issues.

detail (if at all) with the particular procedures to be adopted in an individual arbitration in relation to the taking of evidence.[23] This will be left to the agreement of the parties and/or the discretion of the tribunal (a position that is entirely consistent with the terms and manner of application of the IBA Rules). At least one jurisdiction has gone as far as to enact express statutory provision to the effect that rules of arbitration agreed to be adopted by the parties shall apply and be given effect unless inconsistent with a mandatory provision of that jurisdiction's arbitration law.[24] This position reduces significantly the risk of direct conflict between matters of detail in the IBA Rules and the law of the seat.

A different position may exist in relation to those jurisdictions that have unique or unusual features contained within their laws—whether matters of principle or detail. There may be occasions where a specific mandatory provision of the law of the seat will conflict with a provision contained in the IBA Rules. One such example relates to the law of the United Arab Emirates (UAE). Under UAE law, in arbitrations conducted 'on shore'[25] in the UAE (whether involving domestic or international parties), fact and expert witnesses must give testimony under oath. When making the oath these witnesses must also use the specific language stipulated in the UAE Evidence Law.[26] Article 8.4 of the IBA Rules is less prescriptive on this point and does not require the giving of evidence on oath.[27] **4.36**

Any conflict between the two provisions is resolved by the terms of Article 1.1 of the IBA Rules. In an arbitration having its seat 'onshore' in the UAE in which the parties have adopted the IBA Rules, the provision contained in Article 8.4 would not apply **4.37**

[23] The arbitration laws of such jurisdictions are likely to provide a default mechanism enabling the appointment of a tribunal, provide for the local court to have express powers in support of arbitration proceedings (eg the power to make interim orders preserving property pending the outcome of the proceedings, or the power to order witnesses to attend the arbitration hearing to provide testimony), and procedures by which the tribunal or its award may be challenged in the event that fundamental requirements of natural justice are not observed in the conduct of the arbitration. For example, English Arbitration Act 1996, s 68 provides a mechanism by which a party may challenge an award on grounds that there has been a serious irregularity affecting the proceedings. See also BJC (n 20), Article 171 s 3 (grounds for setting aside an award) and ZPO (n 21), ss 1059 et seq dealing with the setting aside of awards that are successfully challenged and approval of the enforcement of awards that are upheld.

[24] Singaporean International Arbitration Act Chapter 143A, s 15A(1) (hereafter 'SIA') states that: 'It is hereby declared for the avoidance of doubt that a provision of rules of arbitration agreed to or adopted by the parties, whether before or after the commencement of the arbitration, shall apply and be given effect to the extent that such provision is not inconsistent with a provision of the Model Law of this Part [of the statute] from which the parties cannot derogate'. The SIA also provides guidance as to circumstances that are not to be regarded as giving rise to a conflict. For example, SIA s 15A(3) provides that rules of arbitration are not inconsistent with provisions of the Singapore legislation merely because the rules are silent on a matter covered by the legislation.

[25] In the UAE an arbitration may be classed as 'onshore' or 'offshore'. 'Onshore' arbitrations are those that take place in the UAE proper. Regardless of whether these arbitrations involve domestic or international parties, they are governed by the Federal Civil Procedure Code No. 11 of 1992 (hereafter 'CPC'). 'Offshore' arbitrations are those that take place in one of the UAE's free zones benefiting from a distinct arbitration regime and, whether involving domestic or international parties, will be governed by the arbitration law applicable in such zone. The two free zones that have enacted arbitration legislation are the Dubai International Financial Centre (DIFC) and the Abu Dhabi Global Market (ADGM).

[26] Federal Civil Procedure Code No. 11 of 1992 and the UAE Evidence Law. See also Sami Tannous, Samantha Lord Hill, and Sarah-Jane Fick, 'National Report for the United Arab Emirates (2018)' in Jan Paulsson and Lise Bosman (eds), *ICCA International Handbook on Commercial Arbitration* (Supplement No. 101, Kluwer Law International 2018).

[27] IBA Rules (n 5), Article 8.4. See Chapter 11, paras 11.78–11.85.

and, in practice, the mandatory requirements of UAE law requiring witness and experts to give evidence under oath in a manner complying with the relevant provisions of UAE law would prevail. The practical operation of Article 1.1 of the IBA Rules may therefore be significant. In the example given, a failure of the witnesses to give testimony under oath in the manner prescribed could result in the award being set aside by the local courts.

ii Mandatory norms at the seat

4.38 The 'mandatory provision of law' giving rise to a conflict with the IBA Rules may not be limited to discrete provisions of national law directed at specific matters. In our view a conflict may also arise in connection with more general mandatory norms at the seat of arbitration concerned with the operation and conduct of arbitration proceedings. Therefore, it may be necessary to examine what mandatory norms may apply.

4.39 The arbitration laws of most favoured seats of arbitration will lay down what should be the overall objective of an international arbitration conducted within that jurisdiction. Those laws may also set out the guiding principles to be applied in such arbitrations. For example, the Hong Kong Arbitration Ordinance CAP 609 provides at Section 46 that:

> . . . (2) The parties must be *treated with equality*.
>
> (3) When conducting arbitral proceedings or exercising any of the powers conferred on an arbitral tribunal by this Ordinance or by the parties to any of those arbitral proceedings, the arbitral tribunal is required:
>
> [. . .]
>
> (b) to act fairly and impartially as between the parties, giving them a *reasonable opportunity to present their cases* and to deal with the cases of their opponents; and
>
> (c) *to use procedures that are appropriate to the particular case, avoiding unnecessary delay or expense, so as to provide a fair means for resolving the dispute to which the arbitral proceedings relate.*[28]

4.40 Having identified procedural norms contained in national arbitration laws we must then ask whether or not such norms are mandatory.

4.41 Mandatory norms have been described as those that the relevant legislature wishes to apply, regardless of the will of the parties or any discretion otherwise given to the tribunal. Participants in international arbitration will, for the most part, recognize that some mandatory norms may operate to constrain party autonomy and arbitral discretion.[29]

[28] Emphasis added. See also section 33 of the English Arbitration Act 1996 and section 15(a) of the United States Revised Uniform Arbitration Act. English Arbitration Act 1996, s 33(1)(ii). Revised Uniform Arbitration Act, s 15(a), as adopted by 18 states and the District of Columbia.

[29] Waincymer (n 12) 183.

In some instances, the relevant system of law will make clear whether a procedural norm is mandatory. For example, the English Arbitration Act states which provisions of that legislation are mandatory. Those mandatory provisions include Section 33, which requires the tribunal to 'act fairly and impartially between the parties', and to give 'each party a reasonable opportunity of putting its case and dealing with that of its opponent' and to 'adopt procedures suitable to the circumstances of the particular case, avoiding unnecessary delay or expense . . . '. Section 33(2) provides that those duties apply to all of the tribunal's decisions on matters of procedure and evidence, and in the exercise of all powers conferred on it.[30] 4.42

However, some commentators suggest that even when not expressly stated to be mandatory, the terms or nature of certain national provisions may indicate that they are to be treated as such, ie they must be applied by a tribunal regardless of the (express or implied) contrary intention of the parties. One cited example is Article 18 of the UNCITRAL Model Law, which requires that parties are to be 'treated with equality and each party shall be given a full opportunity of presenting his case'. Article 19 of the Model Law goes on to provide that the parties are free to agree on the procedure to be followed by the arbitral tribunal in conducting the proceedings, but that article contains the caveat 'Subject to the provisions of this Law', thereby making party autonomy subject to the principles contained in Article 18. The second part of Article 19 contains a similar proviso in relation to the power of the tribunal to determine the procedure in the event that the parties cannot agree on the steps to be taken.[31] 4.43

Similar analysis and evidence of legislators' intentions can be found elsewhere. For example, Article 1699 of the BJC contains the following provision relating to arbitrations which have their seat in Belgium: 4.44

> *Notwithstanding any agreement to the contrary*, the parties shall be treated with equality and each party shall be given a full opportunity of presenting his case, pleas in law and arguments in conformity with the [right to be heard]. *The arbitral tribunal shall ensure that this requirement as well as the principle of fairness of the debates is respected.*[32]

Although Article 1699 is not included in the list of mandatory provisions referred to in Article 1676 of the BJC, it is treated as being mandatory in nature by the inclusion of the 4.45

[30] English Arbitration Act 1996, s 4 states that the mandatory provisions of the Act are to have effect notwithstanding any agreement to the contrary. The mandatory provisions are listed in Schedule 1 to the Act. Article 1676 of the BJC (n 20) also sets out a list of mandatory provisions. See also the French New Code of Civil Procedure published on 13 January 2011 and introduced by Décret No. 2011-48. Article 1464 provides that the principles of procedure set out in Articles 4–10, 11.1, and 13–21, 22, and 23.1 of the CPC applicable to court process shall at all times apply to arbitration procedure.

[31] UNCITRAL Model Law (n 18) Article 19 (Determination of rules of procedure) states that '(1) Subject to the provisions of this Law, the parties are free to agree on the procedure to be followed by the arbitral tribunal in conducting the proceedings; and (2) Failing such agreement, the arbitral tribunal may, subject to the provisions of this Law, conduct the arbitration in such manner as it considers appropriate . . . '. See further Waincymer (n 12) 182.

[32] Emphasis added.

phrase 'notwithstanding any agreement to the contrary'. As a result, neither the parties nor the arbitrators may deviate from this provision.[33]

4.46 It may be that the potential for conflict with mandatory norms is more apparent than real. The procedural norms contained in the international arbitration laws of many chosen seats of arbitration will be broadly consistent both with the detailed provisions of the IBA Rules, and with the objectives and general principles set out in the Preamble to the IBA Rules that govern other steps in connection with the taking of evidence not covered by the express provisions[34]—namely, (in general terms) to provide an efficient, economical, and fair process,[35] a reasonable opportunity for each party to put its case, and an expectation of good faith conduct by the parties.[36]

4.47 However, there may exist differences of emphasis and degree. Will such differences engage Article 1.1? For example, in an international arbitration with a seat in Singapore, the provisions of the UNCITRAL Model Law will apply, including the principle at Article 18 that each party shall be given a 'full' opportunity of presenting its case.[37] Preamble 1 to the IBA Rules states the intention of the IBA Rules as being the provision of an 'efficient, economical and fair' process. Under that umbrella, Article 8.2 of the IBA Rules provides that the tribunal may exclude the appearance of a witness at the evidentiary hearing if it considers such appearance to be 'irrelevant, immaterial, unreasonably burdensome, duplicative or otherwise covered by a ground of objection set forth in Article 9.2'. If the tribunal were to exercise its discretion to exclude evidence under Article 8.2 of the IBA Rules, would this be in conflict with the mandatory provisions of Article 18 of the Model Law because it will restrict the right of a party to present one of its witnesses, even though the process as a whole will have been a fair one?

4.48 This particular conflict may be capable of resolution. A similar dichotomy arises when comparing the UNCITRAL Model Law requirement of a 'full opportunity' of presenting a case with the provision in the 2012 ICC Arbitration Rules (renewed in Article 22(4) of the 2017 ICC Rules)[38] that parties have a 'reasonable opportunity' to present

[33] Caroline Verbruggen, 'Commentary on Part VI of the Belgian Judicial Code, Chapter V: Article 1699' in Niuscha Bassiri and Maarten Draye (eds), *Arbitration in Belgium* (Kluwer Law Commentary to similar effect on the mandatory nature of procedural norms contained in national arbitration laws can be found elsewhere. For example, in relation to the Swiss Private International Law Statute see Sébastien Besson, 'Chapter 2, Part I: Salient Features and Amenities of Chapter 12 PILS' in Manuel Arroyo (ed), *Arbitration in Switzerland: The Practitioner's Guide* (2nd edn, Kluwer Law International 2018); and in connection with the German Code of Civil Procedure, Klaus Sachs and Torsten Lörcher, 'Part II: Commentary on the German Arbitration Law (10th Book of the German Code of Civil Procedure), Chapter V: Conduct of the Arbitral Proceeding, § 1042—General Rules of Procedure' in Patricia Nacimiento, Stefan Michael Kroll, and Karl-Heinz Bockstiegel (eds), *Arbitration in Germany: The Model Law in Practice* (2nd edn, Kluwer Law International 2015).

[34] IBA Rules (n 5), Article 1.5.

[35] ibid Preamble 1. See Chapter 2.

[36] ibid Preamble 3. See Chapter 2.

[37] SIA (n 24) s 3(1) provides that: 'Subject to this Act, the Model Law, with the exception of Chapter VIII thereof [dealing with Recognition and Enforcement of Awards], shall have the force of law in Singapore'. UNCITRAL Model Law (n 18) Article 18 provides that: 'The parties shall be treated with equality and each party shall be given a full opportunity of presenting his case'.

[38] ICC Rules, effective 1 March 2017. ICC Rules Article 22(4) provides that: 'In all cases, the arbitral tribunal shall act fairly and impartially and ensure that each party has a reasonable opportunity to present its case'.

their case. Although on a literal reading a 'full' opportunity might go further than a 'reasonable' opportunity, it could fairly be said that each is concerned with fairness and due process. On this basis, it has been argued that legislators who use the terms 'reasonable' or 'adequate' are not seeking to limit the due process obligation. They are merely trying to prevent its abuse—for example, by a party seeking to argue that a 'full' opportunity to present its case means that it should be the sole arbiter of how many witnesses it may present.[39]

Despite such decisions, it is possible that, to suit their own ends, parties may draw attention to apparent conflicts between procedural norms laid down in the applicable arbitration law and provisions or principles of the IBA Rules.[40] In the absence of guidance or case law on the meaning of a particular provision, a tribunal faced with an alleged conflict between the IBA Rules and a 'mandatory norm' embedded in the laws of the seat may have to interpret the domestic provision as best it can and no doubt taking into account arguments of the nature articulated here. **4.49**

b. Applicable mandatory provisions of law other than those at the seat

Applicable mandatory provisions may derive from sources other than the law of the seat. For example, in theory, parties may agree to subject their arbitration to another procedural law of their choice.[41] Experienced practitioners will rightly question why parties would wish to complicate the conduct of an arbitration in this way,[42] but where another procedural law has been chosen it is equally possible for that law to be in conflict with a provision of the IBA Rules. We have not found a practical example of such a situation, but an interesting issue around how to proceed might arise where a mandatory provision of the law of the seat and a mandatory provision of the chosen procedural law are in conflict with each other, whether or not they are also in conflict with a provision of the IBA Rules. **4.50**

[39] Waincymer (n 12) 184. This analysis is consistent with that adopted by some national courts. For example, in *Triulzi Cesare SRL v Xinyi Group (Glass) Co Ltd*, the Singapore Court considered the terms of Article 18 of the Model Law, adopted into national law by the Singapore International Arbitration Act 2002 (as revised). *Triulzi Cesare SRL v Xinyi Group (Glass) Co Ltd* [2014] SGHC 220. With particular reference to 'equality' the court said that 'the term "equality" must be "interpreted reasonably in regulating the procedural aspects of the arbitration" . . . Article 18 does not require the arbitral tribunal to ensure that both parties are treated identically. Notably, the principle of equality in Art 18 is about applying similar standards to all parties throughout the arbitral process . . . '. [2014] SGHC 220 [112].

[40] IBA Rules (n 5) Preamble.

[41] As a matter of English law there has been clear judicial recognition of the validity of such an arrangement. See *Naviera Amazonica Peruana SA v Campania International de Siguros del Peru* [1988] 1 Lloyd's Rep 116. In that case the English Court of Appeal said (at Conclusion E) that '[t]here is equally no reason in theory which precludes parties to agree that an arbitration shall be held at a place or in a country X but subject to the procedural laws of Y. The limits and implications of any such agreement have been much discussed in the literature but apart from the decision in the instant case there appears to be no reported case where this has happened. This is not surprising when one considers the complexities and inconveniences which such an agreement would involve'. English Arbitration Act 1996, s 4(5) confirms the right of the parties to adopt a foreign procedural law in relation to matters covered by the non-mandatory aspects of that legislation, saying that '[t]he choice of a law other than the law of England and Wales . . . as the applicable law in respect of a matter provided for by a non-mandatory provisions of this Part is equivalent to an agreement making provision about that matter'.

[42] See further Redfern and Hunter (n 8) 177.

4.51 It is also possible that the substantive law applicable to the dispute (in most cases the governing law of a contract) may contain mandatory rules that touch on the taking of evidence. For example, questions concerning the introduction of extrinsic evidence as an aid to interpretation of a contract are sometimes regarded as being governed by its applicable law.[43] In some national law systems this may result in documents being inadmissible, eg the exclusionary rule in English law restricts the use of evidence of pre-contract negotiations.[44] A party to the arbitration may argue that this is in conflict with the tribunal's power under Article 9.1 to determine issues of admissibility.[45] Similar issues may arise in relation to burden of proof.[46]

4.52 Further possibilities are likely to exist on a case-by-case basis. For example, it has been suggested that, in Europe at least, tribunals may be obliged under EU law to address issues of European competition law even where they have not been raised by the parties themselves.[47] Investigation of the issue will still require due process to be observed and the tribunal may need to hear evidence on the matter. The tribunal may exercise its right under Article 4.10 to request testimony but if this is met by permitted objection from one of the parties under Article 9.2 (a) (*a lack of sufficient relevance to the case or materiality to its outcome*) there may be a stalemate. There is no definition of 'case' in the IBA Rules, but on a narrow interpretation it could mean only the issues between the parties on the claims/counterclaims (ie not including the additional matter sought to be investigated by the tribunal). The reference in Article 1.1 to the mandatory law provision being 'applicable to the case' does not, on a literal reading, appear to defeat such an interpretation of Article 9.2. Despite this, we think it unlikely that a tribunal would, on this basis, abandon its request for testimony. In our view, in the circumstances described, the EU requirement should be

[43] See further Lord Collins of Mapesbury and others (eds), *Dicey, Morris and Collins on The Conflict of Laws* (15th edn, Sweet & Maxwell 2012) paras 32-143–32-145 (hereafter 'Dicey and Morris').

[44] See *Investors Compensation Scheme v West Bromwich Society* [1998] 1 All ER 98. The exclusionary rule is driven in part by the common law approach of looking for the objective intention of the parties in contrast to the approach adopted in many civil law jurisdictions of seeking the subjective intention. Pre-contract negotiations are seen to be more relevant to the latter than to the former, although in *Chartbrook Ltd v Persimmon Homes* [2009] UKHL 38 [33] and [41], Lord Hoffmann acknowledged that it would not be inconsistent with the English objective theory of contractual interpretation to admit evidence of previous communications between the parties. Interestingly, he also admitted that application of the exclusionary rule may lead to injustice on the basis that parties to a dispute may be 'held bound by a contract in terms which, upon a full investigation of the course of negotiations, a reasonable observer would not have taken them to have intended'.

[45] See *BQP v BQQ* [2018] SGHC 55, where the issue was addressed by the Singapore High Court in relation to a SIAC arbitration and against the background of the Singapore Evidence Act. There is data to suggest that, in practice, tribunals do not always comply strictly with the requirements of the relevant substantive law in this respect. See further Carol Mulcahy, 'What Does it Mean? Contractual Interpretation in International Commercial Arbitration' [2015] Dispute Resolution International 15.

[46] The case for dealing with questions relating to the burden of proof under the applicable substantive law in appropriate cases is dealt with in Dicey and Morris (n 43) para 7-034. For an interesting examination of the relationship between substantive law provisions on burden of proof and document production under best practice in international arbitration, see Rolf Trittmann, 'The Interplay between Procedural and Substantive Law in International Arbitration' (2016) SchiedsVZ 7.

[47] Redfern and Hunter (n 8) 196.

treated as over-riding the possible restriction created by Article 4.10 and Article 9.2. Similar considerations may arise in relation to such matters as economic or political sanctions.

It is sometimes suggested that the mandatory provisions of national law of the jurisdictions in which an award is likely to be enforced should also be reviewed for potential conflicts with the intended applicable arbitration rules. Given the possibility that such provisions may have a material impact on the ability to enforce the award, this may be prudent. However, there does not appear to be any theoretical justification for doing so in the context of Article 1.1, unless 'applicable to the case'[48] has a wider meaning than 'applicable to the arbitration'.[49] **4.53**

5. Who Determines Whether the Mandatory Provision of Law Is Applicable to the Case?

Under Article 1.1 determination of whether the mandatory provision of law potentially creating the conflict is actually applicable to the case (and therefore attracts the application of Article 1.1) is a matter for determination 'by the Parties or by the Arbitral Tribunal'. **4.54**

Having regard to the principle of party autonomy, there is a strong case for saying that, if the parties agree that a provision of mandatory law inconsistent with a particular provision of the IBA Rules is applicable to the case, that view should prevail, even in the face of disagreement from the tribunal. However, it is worthwhile considering the issue from the opposite perspective, ie a situation in which it is the parties, rather than the tribunal, that believe the mandatory provision of law does not apply to the case. The tribunal has an obligation to produce an enforceable award and, if the tribunal believes that ignoring the mandatory provision might place the award in jeopardy, it might be said that the tribunal's view on the application of the mandatory provision should prevail. **4.55**

The nature of the submissions (if any) that the tribunal may seek from the parties on this issue will vary according to the particular circumstances of the case. It has been suggested that, where a party asserts that a mandatory law external to the law of the seat applies, it will need to satisfy the tribunal 'why the law is mandatory, why it applies to the arbitration and why it is not otherwise dealt with or overruled by the lex arbitri or procedural rule selected'.[50] We agree with that approach. **4.56**

[48] Article 1.1 is concerned with mandatory provisions of law 'applicable to the case'.
[49] See also Waincymer (n 12) 186.
[50] Waincymer (n 12) 186.

C. Version of the IBA Rules to Be Applied

1.2. Where the Parties have agreed to apply the IBA Rules of Evidence, they shall be deemed to have agreed, in the absence of a contrary indication, to the version as current on the date of such agreement.

4.57 Article 1.2 contains a clear statement as to which version of the IBA Rules should apply to an arbitration in which the parties have agreed to apply those rules.

4.58 Article 1.2 refers to the parties' agreement to 'apply' the IBA Rules. This suggests an agreement to formally adopt the IBA Rules as binding on the parties. However, in our view, the rule set out in Article 1.2 should, as a matter of principle, apply in the same way to an agreement to use the IBA Rules as guidance only. It would nonetheless be prudent for the tribunal to confirm in its first procedural order whether the IBA Rules have been formally adopted or whether they are to be used as guidance only, and the version applicable to the arbitration.

1. Default Position: Version in Force on the Date of Agreement

4.59 The original 1983 IBA Rules have been revised on two occasions to produce the 1999 IBA Rules and the current IBA Rules. Given the success of the IBA Rules it appears likely that they will continue to be used extensively in international arbitration and therefore that they will be subject to review at an appropriate point in the future.

4.60 Under Article 1.2, in the absence of a contrary indication from the parties, the version of the IBA Rules current on the date of the parties' agreement to apply the rules, *not* the version current at the time of commencement of the arbitration (if different), will apply. This is in contrast to the position under many institutional rules where, unless the parties agree otherwise, the version of the rules in force at the date of commencement of the arbitration will apply.[51] Thus, the practical position under the IBA Rules is that, in relation to all agreements to apply the IBA Rules made after 29 May 2010 (the effective date of the 2010 Rules), the current IBA Rules will apply.

2. Party Agreement to the Contrary

4.61 Where the Parties agree to apply the IBA Rules after the dispute has arisen, the version of the rules that they have in mind is likely to be the (then) current version in any event.

4.62 If the parties' agreement to apply the IBA Rules is contained in an arbitration clause in a commercial contract it is possible that there may be a significant time lapse

[51] For example, see the ICC Rules, Article 6.1, and the LCIA Rules, Preamble.

between the date of the agreement and the date on which a dispute actually arises. If, at the time of negotiating that agreement, the parties wish to ensure that the version of the IBA Rules that will apply to any later dispute is that in force at the date the arbitration commences, they would be wise to make express provision for this in their arbitration agreement. This approach is recommended in the Commentary to the IBA Rules.[52] However, if this not done, when the dispute is referred to arbitration there is nothing to prevent the parties from agreeing to apply the current version of the IBA Rules.

The following is one possible formulation of such an express agreement (dealing both with formal adoption of the IBA Rules and their use as guidance only): **4.63**

> In addition to the [institutional or ad hoc rules chosen by the parties] the parties agree that the arbitration shall be conducted [in accordance with] [taking guidance from] the IBA Rules on the Taking of Evidence in International Arbitration as current on the date of commencement of the arbitration].[53]

D. Conflict with a Provision of the General Rules

> **1.3. In case of conflict between any provisions of the IBA Rules of Evidence and the General Rules, the Arbitral Tribunal shall apply the IBA Rules of Evidence in the manner that it determines best in order to accomplish the purpose of both the General Rules and the IBA Rules of Evidence, unless the Parties agree to the contrary.**

1. Introduction

Article 1.3 deals with the issue of conflict between the IBA Rules and the General Rules. The General Rules are defined by the IBA Rules as the institutional, ad hoc, or other rules that apply to the conduct of the arbitration.[54] **4.64**

The IBA Rules do not provide a complete framework for the conduct of an arbitration. As Preamble 1 makes clear, the IBA Rules are intended to introduce practical procedures around the reception of evidence that flesh out and supplement the infrastructure provided by the applicable General Rules. **4.65**

[52] Commentary on the IBA Rules (n 11) 5, which states that '[a]s the IBA Rules could be potentially subject to further updates, parties wishing to apply the version of the IBA Rules current at the time of the arbitration should consider including this in the arbitration clause'.

[53] This draft adopts a combination of drafting used in the recommended clauses contained in IBA Rules (n 5) Foreword, and in *IBA Guidelines for Drafting International Arbitration Clauses* (International Bar Association 2010).

[54] IBA Rules (n 5) Definitions.

4.66 In a perfect world the General Rules and the IBA Rules would always work in harmony together to provide a unified framework for the conduct of the arbitration. However, while those responsible for drafting the IBA Rules made every effort to ensure that those rules were drafted to conform with the principal institutional and ad hoc rules used by parties, the Commentary to the IBA Rules,[55] and the terms of Article 1.3, acknowledge that conflicts may nonetheless arise.

2. Party Autonomy

4.67 Party autonomy is central to any international arbitration and this is acknowledged by the closing words of Article 1.3, 'unless the parties agree to the contrary'. If the parties to the arbitration are able to agree how a conflict between the IBA Rules and the General Rules is to be dealt with, that choice will be effective. The position agreed by the parties will generally apply, regardless of what view the tribunal may take or has expressed to the parties in relation to the conflict. In practice, any agreement reached between the parties is likely to be a pragmatic position specific to the particular circumstances of the conflict.

3. Where the Parties Cannot Agree

4.68 If the parties cannot agree how a conflict between the IBA Rules and the General Rules is to be resolved, Article 1.3 is triggered and provides guidance as to how the tribunal is to deal with the conflict.

4.69 The 1983 IBA Rules simply provided that, absent party agreement, in the event of a conflict between the General Rules and the IBA Rules, the IBA Rules should prevail. That provision was revised on introduction of the 1999 IBA Rules and the revised provision remains effective under the current IBA Rules. The relevant wording of the current Article 1.3 provides that

> the Arbitral Tribunal shall apply the IBA Rules of Evidence *in the manner that it determines best in order to accomplish the purposes of both the General Rules and the IBA Rules of Evidence.*[56]

4.70 The commentary to the 1999 IBA Rules does not provide an explanation for this change, but it is to be assumed that the more nuanced approach provided for in the current version of the rules—designed, as far as possible, to give effect to both sets of rules—was considered a more attractive option. In the commentary to the 1999 Rules, and restated in the commentary accompanying the current IBA Rules, the drafters of this revision

[55] Commentary on the IBA Rules (n 11) 5.
[56] Emphasis added.

state that 'the arbitral tribunal shall try to *harmonise the two sets of rules* to the greatest extent possible'.[57] This more sophisticated approach to the issue than that contained in the 1983 IBA Rules grants the tribunal greater flexibility in its application of the particular IBA rule affected by the conflict.

Although it is not entirely clear from the wording of Article 1.3 that the discretion granted to the tribunal extends to ignoring the particular provision of the IBA Rules altogether where it is appropriate to do so, this would appear to be in keeping with the overall intent behind Article 1.3. **4.71**

Although many arbitrators will favour an intuitive approach over a forensic one, in principle, Article 1.3 provides for a two-stage process. **4.72**

a. Identifying the 'purpose' of the two sets of rules

In order to decide how best to achieve the purposes of both sets of rules as required by Article 1.3, the tribunal must first consider the purpose/s of each and the degree of consistency or inconsistency in purpose that may exist. **4.73**

i. The IBA Rules

In relation to the IBA Rules themselves, a tribunal should have regard to the general purpose behind those rules as set out in Preamble 1 and 2, and the general principles upon which the taking of evidence is to be conducted set out in Preamble 3. These matters are dealt with in more detail in Chapter 2. While a theoretical distinction might be drawn between the objectives of the IBA Rules set out in Preamble 1 and 2 and the underlying general principles stated in Preamble 3, such a distinction would be an entirely artificial one. Each of the provisions in the Preamble is an expression of what the IBA Rules are intended to achieve. **4.74**

In summary, for the purposes of Article 1.3, the key provisions are: **4.75**

Preamble 1: to provide an *efficient, economical, and fair process* for the taking of evidence that will meet, so far as reasonably possible, the expectations of parties from different legal traditions;

Preamble 2: to supplement other applicable arbitration rules but *not to impede the flexibility of the arbitration process to meet the needs of the case*; and

Preamble 3: the taking of evidence is to be conducted on the principles that:

- each party shall act in *good faith*; and
- each party shall be *entitled to know reasonably in advance* of any evidentiary hearing or fact/merits determination, *the evidence on which the other party relies.*

[57] Commentary on the IBA Rules (n 11) 5 (emphasis added).

ii. The General Rules

4.76 The tribunal must then also consider the 'purpose' of the General Rules with which the IBA Rules are in conflict. This will involve looking beyond the precise wording of the individual provision giving rise to the conflict, to the broader purpose behind the rules as derived from related provisions and any statement of underlying purpose included within those rules.

4.77 Although frequently couched in terms of tribunal responsibility, many institutional and other arbitration rules contain express provisions indicating the overall objectives and procedural norms expected by application of the rules—the equivalent of the procedural norms contained in domestic arbitration laws mentioned earlier. For the most part, these are likely to be expressed in very similar terms to those that appear in the Preamble to the IBA Rules. They will frequently refer to such matters as providing a fair and efficient process, granting a reasonable opportunity for each side to present its case, avoiding unnecessary expense, and securing an enforceable award.[58]

4.78 Some institutional rules may go further and make express reference to additional considerations. For example, Article 6 of the Arbitration Rules of The Vilnius Court of Commercial Arbitration (Principles of the Arbitration Proceedings) states that:

> The Arbitral Tribunal, the Chair of the VCCA and the Secretariat shall examine and resolve the issues attributed to their competence in accordance with the *principles of the parties' autonomy, procedural equality of arms, disposition, the adversarial principle, the principles of confidentiality*, economy, *cooperation* and expedition of the arbitration proceedings.[59]

4.79 Other sets of rules, although containing similar aspirations, may contain some modification to the more usual provisions because they are designed for a specific purpose, eg expedition or low cost. A number of arbitral institutions offer expedited or fast-track procedures.[60] Generally speaking, expedited procedures shorten time limits for rendering a final award. For example, several rules provide for an award to be rendered within six months of either the case management conference[61] or from the constitution of the tribunal.[62] Other measures include provisions on whether the tribunal may decide the case on a documents-only basis or whether a hearing will be held.[63] Examples of low-cost arbitration rules include the Chartered Institute of Arbitrators' Cost Controlled Arbitration Rules and the ARIAS Fast Track Arbitration Rules.

[58] For example, see ICC Rules Articles 22.1 and 22.4; LCIA Rules Article 14.4, 14.5, and 32.2; SIAC Rules Rule 19.1 and 41.2; and UNCITRAL Rules Article 17.1.

[59] Arbitration Rules of The Vilnius Court of Commercial Arbitration Article 6 (emphasis added). However, it is possible that in some cases apparent differences may be due to issues of translation between language versions, rather than reflecting a difference of substance.

[60] Institutions offering expedited procedures include the ICC, SCC, ICDR, HKIAC, SIAC, and CIETAC.

[61] For example ICC Rules Article 4(1) Appendix VI.

[62] For example, SIAC Rules Rule 5.2(d).

[63] For example, ICC Rules Article 3(5) Appendix VI; SCC Expedited Arbitration Rules Article 33; ICDR Rules Article 1(4); HKIAC Rules Article 42(2)(e), and SIAC Rules Rule 5.2(c).

b. How best to accomplish the purpose of both sets of rules?

Having determined what each set of rules is intended to accomplish, the tribunal must then apply the IBA Rules to the matter in issue in the 'manner that it determines best' in order to accomplish the purposes of both sets of rules.[64] **4.80**

In practice, the broad objectives of the IBA Rules and the relevant General Rules are likely to be closely aligned. The approach ultimately taken will depend very much on the view of the particular tribunal whether, on the facts of the case, it is best to apply the provisions of the IBA Rules giving rise to the conflict, to adopt the position under the relevant General Rule, or to adopt some other course permitted within the IBA Rules. However, where the General Rules have a special objective (such as expedition) the tribunal may wish to tailor the approach taken to meet that objective, provided such tailoring does not compromise observance of the underlying principles upon which the IBA Rules operate. **4.81**

c. Illustrations

The authors have been unable to find any reported examples of how Article 1.3 has been applied in circumstances of conflict. The following scenarios illustrate the sorts of issue that could arise. **4.82**

i. Scenario 1

An arbitration is being conducted under the SIAC Arbitration Rules 2016 and the IBA Rules. Both sets of rules provide that a party may request the attendance at the evidentiary hearing of any witness whose witness statement is relied upon by its opponent.[65] **4.83**

There is a potential conflict between those two sets of rules in the event that the witness fails to attend the hearing in accordance with such request. **4.84**

SIAC Rule 25.4 states that where a witness fails to attend 'the Tribunal may place such weight on the written testimony as it thinks fit, disregard such written testimony, or exclude such written testimony altogether'. **4.85**

In contrast IBA Article 4.7 provides that '[absent] a valid reason [for such non-attendance] . . . the Arbitral Tribunal *shall* disregard any Witness Statement related to that Evidentiary Hearing by that witness, unless in exceptional circumstances the Arbitral Tribunal decides otherwise'.[66] **4.86**

If in the arbitration a witness were to fail to attend the evidentiary hearing for cross-examination the tribunal will have to decide whether to simply exclude the witness statement of that witness altogether (as contemplated by the IBA Rules) or deal with the **4.87**

[64] The Commentary on the IBA Rules (n 11) states that 'the arbitral tribunal shall try to harmonise the two sets of rules to the greatest extent possible'.
[65] SIAC Rules Rule 25.4, and IBA Rules (n 5) Article 8.1.
[66] Emphasis added.

evidence as a matter of weight—to decide in due course what weight (if any) it will place upon the evidence contained in the witness statement (the SIAC position).

4.88 There is no obvious dichotomy in the objectives of the two sets of rules. They appear on their face to be broadly the same. At the most basic level the IBA Rules require an 'efficient, economical and fair process for the taking of evidence'. The SIAC Rules require the tribunal to conduct the arbitration to ensure 'the fair, expeditious, economical and final resolution of the dispute'.[67] The approach of the two provisions dealing with witness evidence (Article 4 of the IBA Rules and SIAC Rule 25) appears to have a similar purpose, namely, transparency as to the witness testimony to be relied upon and the opportunity to test that evidence.

4.89 In practice, a tribunal faced with this situation might be reluctant to adopt the IBA position. That position has attracted some criticism for being too rigid[68] and the exit route provided by Article 1.3 might be used to adopt a more flexible approach. On the other hand, the SIAC formulation permits a total disregard of the witness statement as another option open to the tribunal and this response might therefore be seen as at least sharing common ground with the IBA position.

4.90 A more nuanced approach might be to invite submissions from the parties on which of the three possibilities under the SIAC Rules the tribunal should adopt: (a) disregard the evidence (as in the IBA Rules); (b) exclude the evidence; or (c) place such weight on the evidence as it thinks fit. Under the IBA Rules, it is likely that the tribunal would, in any event, hear submissions on the question of whether 'valid reasons' or 'exceptional circumstances' existed under IBA Article 4.7 that justified a departure from the default position of disregarding the evidence. Whether the tribunal ultimately adopted a pragmatic approach of admitting the statement (but perhaps attributing little or no weight to it) or disregarding/excluding it altogether, both parties would have had an opportunity to present their arguments on the issue and the need for transparency and party perceptions of 'fairness' underlying both sets of rules would have been satisfied in a reasonably efficient way.

ii. Scenario 2

4.91 An arbitration is being conducted under the SCC Rules for Expedited Arbitration 2017 (the 'SCC Expedited Arbitration Rules') and the IBA Rules. Both sets of rules provide that, at the request of one of the parties to the arbitration, the tribunal may order the production of documents held by the other party.[69] However, there is a potential conflict between those rules in relation to the required degree of proximity that such documents should have to the issues in the case.

[67] SIAC Rules, Rule 19.1.
[68] See Chapter 7, paras 7.153–7.159.
[69] SCC Expedited Arbitration Rules 2017 Article 32(3). IBA Rules (n 5) Article 3.7.

Article 3 of the IBA Rules sets out a procedure by which parties to the arbitration may make requests for production of documents, and the conditions for doing so that must be satisfied as part of that process. If those conditions are met then, absent the existence of one or more of a number of grounds for objection set out in Article 9, the tribunal 'may order the Party to whom such Request is addressed to produce any requested documents in its possession'. One of the conditions for a request for production of documents is that it explains how the requested documents 'are relevant to the case and material to its outcome'. Conversely, a ground for objection to the request is that there is a 'lack of sufficient relevance to the case or materiality to its outcome'. 4.92

Article 32(3) of the SCC Expedited Arbitration Rules states that 'at the request of a party . . . the Arbitrator may order a party to produce any documents . . . that may be relevant to the case and material to its outcome'. 4.93

It is by reference to small differences like this that parties intent on resisting an order for production may seek to build a case. In the event of a request to produce a contested document, what test should the tribunal apply before making an order for production? If challenged on the test it intends to apply, how should a tribunal respond? 4.94

Should the tribunal be satisfied that the requested document '*is* relevant to the case and material to its outcome' (an arguable position under the IBA Rules debate) or only that it '*may*' be so relevant and material (the position under the SCC Expedited Arbitration Rules)? Is there a significant difference between the two tests given that, until an individual document is actually produced, it is impossible to know how relevant/material it is? 4.95

This issue might be thought to be a distinction without a difference, but academic writing suggests that it is not. It has been argued that 'potential and prima facie relevance and materiality are two different standards that should not be confused', and that the prevailing view of scholars is that prima facie relevance and materiality is the applicable threshold under the IBA Rules.[70] 4.96

There is no fundamental difference in the objectives of the two sets of rules. They are very similar. The IBA Rules seek an 'efficient, economical and fair process for the taking of evidence'. The SCC Rules require the tribunal to conduct the arbitration in an 'impartial, efficient and expeditious manner giving each party an equal and reasonable opportunity to present its case'. However, the SCC provision goes on to provide 'considering at all times the expedited nature of the proceedings'.[71] The approach of the two provisions dealing with document production (SCC Expedited Arbitration Rules Article 32 (3) and IBA Rules Article 3) have the common purpose of providing a mechanism by 4.97

[70] Reto Marghitola, *Document Production in International Arbitration* (Kluwer Law International 2015) 53 (hereafter 'Marghitola') describes prima facie as meaning a degree of probability of over 50 per cent. See Chapter 6, paras 6.125–6.129.

[71] SCC Expedited Arbitration Rules 2017 Article 24(2). See also the SCC Expedited Arbitration Rules 2017 Article 29(3).

which parties may obtain limited document production that will assist the tribunal in a determination of the issues in the case.

4.98 A tribunal faced with this issue could approach the question in a number of ways depending on the facts and procedural history of the particular case. The more onerous requirement in the IBA Rules might be seen as enhancing achievement of the objective of speedy resolution underlying the SCC Expedited Arbitration Rules. On the other hand, the SCC rules require that each party has 'an equal' as well as 'a reasonable' opportunity to present its case. If it is a case where all of the documents are in the hands of one party (eg as sometimes happens in a construction dispute) the tribunal may feel that application of the less onerous standard of test better meets the overall combined purposes of the two sets of rules.

E. Interpretation of the IBA Rules

1.4. In the event of any dispute regarding the meaning of the IBA Rules of Evidence, the Arbitral Tribunal shall interpret them according to their purpose and in the manner most appropriate for the particular arbitration.

1. Introduction

4.99 Article 1.4 addresses disputes on the interpretation of the IBA Rules.

4.100 The IBA Rules are the product of considered analysis and expert drafting. However, differences of interpretation are bound to arise. There may be ambiguities that come to light in the course of proceedings, parties may adopt different positions for tactical reasons in order to suit their case, or new developments in technology or practice may occur to which the proper manner of application of the IBA Rules as drafted may be unclear.

4.101 There are two limbs to the guidance given in Article 1.4. The Arbitral Tribunal is to interpret the IBA Rules (a) 'according to their purpose' *and* (b) 'in a manner most appropriate for the particular arbitration'.

2. The First Limb: According to Their Purpose

4.102 A purposive approach to construction of the IBA Rules is to be adopted that takes into account the stated objective of the IBA Rules as set out in Preamble 1 and Preamble 2[72]

[72] IBA Rules (n 5) Preambles 1 and 2.

(namely, an efficient, economical, and fair process, and flexibility of procedures; see Chapter 2). In the event of a dispute about the interpretation of a particular provision of the IBA Rules, the Arbitral Tribunal will need to consider the meaning of the provision under scrutiny in the context of these underlying objectives.

However, when considering issues of interpretation, the tribunal should also have regard to the general principles of the IBA Rules set out in Preamble 3.[73] An interpretation that gives effect to those principles should be preferred over one that does not. **4.103**

A further and legitimate point is that the IBA Rules build a bridge between civil law and common law practices and a 'one-sided' interpretation of those rules should be rejected.[74] We agree with that view. The Preamble to the IBA Rules states expressly that the rules are intended, in particular, for use 'between Parties from different legal traditions'. Absent particular circumstances justifying such an approach (eg where both the tribunal and all parties to the dispute are from the same legal tradition), an interpretation reflecting a middle ground between the two traditions is generally to be preferred. **4.104**

3. The Second Limb: Appropriate for the Particular Arbitration

In addition to looking at the underlying purpose of the IBA Rules, the tribunal must consider what interpretation is appropriate for the particular arbitration. In essence, the tribunal must decide which of the possible/competing interpretations will work best to attain the objectives of the IBA Rules in 'this arbitration', with 'these parties', and in the 'actual circumstances of this case'. Furthermore, the second limb of Article 1.4, by which an interpretation 'most appropriate for the particular arbitration' is to be sought, suggests that there is no 'correct' answer on issues of interpretation. In the event of two conflicting interpretations resting (respectively) on the first and second limbs of Article 1.4, the latter is likely to be preferred. This would be consistent with the intended flexibility of the IBA Rules[75] and the requirement found in many institutional rules to adopt procedures suitable for the particular dispute,[76] subject always to requirements of due process. **4.105**

[73] IBA Rules (n 5) Preamble 3. In summary, these are that the taking of evidence is to be conducted on the principles that each party shall act in good faith, and that each party is entitled to have reasonable notice of the evidence upon which its opponent intends to rely.

[74] Marghitola (n 70) 35.

[75] See IBA Rules (n 5) Preamble 2.

[76] See, for example, the HKIAC Rules Article 13.1 ('Subject to these Rules, the arbitral tribunal shall adopt suitable procedures for the conduct of the arbitration in order to avoid unnecessary delay or expense, having regard to the complexity of the issues, the amount in dispute and the effective use of technology, and provided that such procedures ensure equal treatment of the parties and afford the parties a reasonable opportunity to present their case.') and LCIA Rules Article 14.4(ii) ('[the Tribunal's duties shall include] . . . a duty to adopt procedures suitable to the circumstances of the arbitration . . . ').

F. Matters upon which the IBA Rules Are Silent

1.5. Insofar as the IBA Rules of Evidence and the General Rules are silent on any matter concerning the taking of evidence and the Parties have not agreed otherwise, the Arbitral Tribunal shall conduct the taking of evidence as it deems appropriate, in accordance with the general principles of the IBA Rules of Evidence.

1. Introduction

4.106 Article 1.5 addresses a situation where both the IBA Rules and the General Rules[77] are *silent* on a matter affecting the taking of evidence, and the parties have been unable to reach an agreement concerning that matter. This provision, in contrast to other parts of Article 1, is not dealing with a situation of conflict between two competing or inconsistent provisions, but rather with an absence of provision.

2. Pre-Conditions to the Application of Article 1.5

4.107 Because the IBA Rules are, and are intended to be, relatively detailed in relation to matters affecting the taking of evidence, it should be fairly easy to identify whether a matter arising is or is not addressed in the IBA Rules. If there is disagreement on this point, the issue will have to be decided by the tribunal under its general powers.

a. IBA and General Rules both silent on the matter

4.108 Article 1.5 will apply only where, *and to the extent*, both the IBA Rules and the General Rules are silent on a particular matter affecting the taking of evidence. The opening words of Article 1.5 ('insofar as' rather than 'if' or 'when') appear to contemplate situations where the IBA Rules (or indeed the applicable General Rules) make some relevant provision, but are not sufficient to deal with the entirety of the matter to be addressed.

4.109 Given the general nature of most institutional and other arbitration rules it will not be surprising to find that the General Rules are silent on a number of matters of detail affecting the taking of evidence.

4.110 In contrast, the IBA Rules aim to lay down practical procedures around the reception of evidence—to provide detail to supplement the General Rules. As a result, the identification of gaps in the available guidance afforded by the IBA Rules is likely to occur

[77] 'General Rules' are defined to mean the institutional, ad hoc, or other rules that apply to the conduct of the arbitration. See IBA Rules (n 5) Definitions, following the Preamble.

in a limited number of cases. However, no set of rules can be drafted to deal with every eventuality; if they could, they would be too inflexible.

b. No party agreement

In recognition of the principle of party autonomy, if the parties are able to reach agreement on how they wish to deal with the issue on which the General Rules and the IBA Rules are silent, that agreement will prevail. **4.111**

3. Application of Article 1.5 Guidance

When both the IBA Rules and the General Rules are silent on a matter affecting the taking of evidence, and the parties have been *unable* to reach agreement on that matter, Article 1.5 provides that the tribunal should deal with the matter as it deems appropriate in accordance with the general principles of the IBA Rules. **4.112**

Unlike Article 1.3 and Article 1.4, which both refer to a consideration of the 'purpose/s' of the IBA Rules, Article 1.5 refers to the 'general principles' of the IBA Rules. The change in terminology from 'purpose' to 'principles' suggests that, in exercising its discretion to make a decision on an issue on which both the IBA Rules and the General Rules are silent, the tribunal's focus should be to give effect to the general principles set out in Preamble 3 to the IBA Rules, ie that the parties shall act in good faith in the taking of evidence, and (in particular) each party shall have reasonable advance notice of the evidence upon which its opponent intends to rely.[78] **4.113**

Subject to this requirement, in practice the tribunal is also likely to take into account the Preamble 1 objective of an 'efficient, economical and fair process'. **4.114**

a. Illustrations

Given the idiosyncrasies of individual arbitrations, it is possible that situations may occur for which there may be no express provision in either the IBA Rules or the General Rules. However, by having regard to the factors mentioned in Article 1.5, the tribunal should be able to arrive at a reasonable and workable solution. **4.115**

i. Scenario 1

For example, in an arbitration under the LCIA/IBA Rules, one party may turn up at an evidentiary hearing brandishing a number of material new documents and witness evidence obtained from a new witness. Neither set of rules makes express provision for this situation and the tribunal should therefore have regard to the guidance in Article 1.5. **4.116**

Provided the tribunal is satisfied that there is no deliberate bad faith on the part of the party producing the evidence from the new witness, the tribunal may be loath to **4.117**

[78] IBA Rules (n 5) Preamble 3.

exclude material that will assist in its determination of the dispute. However, the tribunal must conduct the arbitration on the principle that the other party is entitled to know about the new evidence reasonably in advance of the evidentiary hearing. There will be any number of ways in which a tribunal may seek to reconcile the competing interests of the parties in relation to the presentation of the new evidence, depending upon the demands of the hearing timetable. In order to give the other party an opportunity to consider the new material, it might order an adjournment of the hearing until the following day or, if practical, it might reorganize the timetable so that issues to which the new material relates are postponed until later in the hearing schedule. Following an opportunity to consider the materials, the tribunal must hear from the receiving party as to what time and further directions it feels it needs, consider the producing party's answers to the points made, and then make a decision as to whether or not a longer adjournment of the hearing is necessary. The process will be fact-specific, but a balance will have to be struck between minimizing disruption to the timetable and ensuring that the non-producing party has an adequate opportunity to address the new evidence.

ii. Scenario 2

4.118 Another example might be an arbitration under the ICC/IBA Rules, where a party serves an important witness statement in the language of the arbitration (English) together with a notice (as required under Article 4.1(c) of the IBA Rules) that the witness statement was originally prepared in another language (Lithuanian). The witness statement is served with a copy of the original statement in the Lithuanian language. The other party subsequently contends that the English language version of the witness statement is not an accurate translation of the original statement.

4.119 The serving party may argue that the point raised by its opponent is a matter that can be ironed out during cross-examination of the witness, at which an interpreter will be present. However, once again, under Article 1.5 of the IBA Rules the tribunal must have regard to the principle that a party is entitled to know in advance of an evidentiary hearing the nature of the evidence that will be relied on by the other side. In the circumstances described, it is important that the receiving party has a clear understanding of the evidence that is being presented. The tribunal could direct that a translator for each side should confer to agree a definitive English language version of the original statement a reasonable period in advance of the hearing.

5

Article 2: Consultation on Evidentiary Issues

Article 2 Consultation on Evidentiary Issues

1. The Arbitral Tribunal shall consult the Parties at the earliest appropriate time in the proceedings and invite them to consult each other with a view to agreeing on an efficient, economical and fair process for the taking of evidence.
2. The consultation on evidentiary issues may address the scope, timing and manner of the taking of evidence, including:
   (a) the preparation and submission of Witness Statements and Expert Reports;
   (b) the taking of oral testimony at any Evidentiary Hearing;
   (c) the requirements, procedure and format applicable to the production of Documents;
   (d) the level of confidentiality protection to be afforded to evidence in the arbitration; and
   (e) the promotion of efficiency, economy and conservation of resources in connection with the taking of evidence.
3. The Arbitral Tribunal is encouraged to identify to the Parties, as soon as it considers it to be appropriate, any issues:
   (a) that the Arbitral Tribunal may regard as relevant to the case and material to its outcome; and/or
   (b) for which a preliminary determination may be appropriate.

A. Introduction

Article 2 addresses the active role that a tribunal is encouraged to play in ensuring that **5.1**
the taking of evidence is handled in an efficient and economic manner, while at the same time making sure that the process is fair to both sides. It requires the tribunal to

initiate and to participate in discussions with the parties on evidentiary issues. It also encourages the tribunal to identify issues that are important to a determination of the dispute, or the early determination of which may lead to a quicker or more efficient resolution.

5.2 Article 2 is a new provision introduced by the current IBA Rules. The IBA Commentary[1] reveals that the drafting subcommittee considered whether and how the IBA Rules could be adapted in light of the increased size and complexity of arbitrations and the evidentiary issues associated with them. After careful consideration and a review of various domestic and international arbitration rules and procedures, the subcommittee decided to adopt what they describe as a 'meet and consult' approach.[2]

5.3 Article 2 consists of 3 parts:

(a) Article 2.1 provides for a mandatory consultation between the tribunal and the parties at the earliest appropriate time in the proceedings with the objective of agreeing on an 'efficient, economical and fair process for the taking of evidence'.
(b) Article 2.2 provides a framework for discussing evidentiary issues. It sets out a non-exhaustive list of evidentiary matters that the tribunal and parties may wish to consider during the mandatory consultation.
(c) Article 2.3 encourages, but does not require, the tribunal to identify to the parties, as soon as it considers it to be appropriate, any issues: (i) that the tribunal may regard as relevant to the case and material to its outcome; and/or (ii) for which a preliminary determination may be appropriate.

5.4 A similar approach is adopted in a number of institutional rules that also contain express provision for the parties and the tribunal to make early contact to discuss and agree proposals for the conduct of the arbitration.[3] Similarly, soft law guides, including the UNCITRAL Notes on Organizing Arbitral Proceedings and the ICC Guide to the Effective Management of Arbitration, emphasize the benefits of early consultation between the parties.[4]

5.5 What distinguishes Article 2 from other provisions is that it encourages the tribunal and the parties to focus on evidentiary issues—something that is largely overlooked in institutional rules, but which may be particularly important where parties are from

[1] 1999 IBA Working Party and 2010 IBA Rules of Evidence Review Subcommittee, 'Commentary on the Revised Text of the 2010 IBA Rules on the Taking of Evidence in International Arbitration' (International Bar Association) 22 <www.ibanet.org/Document/Default.aspx?DocumentUid=DD240932-0E08-40D4-9866-309A635487C0> accessed 27 November 2018 (hereafter 'Commentary on the IBA Rules').

[2] ibid 5.

[3] Examples include ICC Rules Article 24; LCIA Rules Article 14; SCC Rules Article 28(1); SIAC Rules Rule 19; HKIAC Rules Article 13; and UNCITRAL Rules Article 17.2.

[4] UNCITRAL Notes on Organizing Arbitral Proceedings (United Nations Commission on International Trade Law 2016) para 1(a) (hereafter 'UNCITRAL Notes') sets out the general principle of consultation between the parties and the arbitral tribunal. *Effective Management of Arbitration: A Guide for In-House Counsel and Other Party Representatives* (International Chamber of Commerce 2014) 13 (hereafter 'ICC Guide to Effective Management of Arbitration').

different legal traditions and have different expectations. The consultation process under Article 2 provides a forum where these different views may be aired.

In most arbitrations, early consultation between the tribunal and the parties will result in a first procedural order dealing with a wide variety of issues including, but not limited to, the process by which evidence will be taken. However, because such discussions tend to deal with all procedural aspects of the arbitration, the process for the taking of evidence may not be addressed in as much detail as when guided by the provisions of Article 2.2. This may mean that opportunities to improve the efficiency of the process are missed. **5.6**

Articles 2.1 and 2.2 are entirely new provisions. However, they very much reflect the overarching objective found in Preamble 1 to the IBA Rules that the IBA Rules are to provide an 'efficient, economical and fair process' for the taking of evidence in international arbitration. The provenance and practical application of this principle is discussed in detail in Chapter 2. The relationship between Preamble 1 and Article 2 should not be overlooked. Preamble 1 provides context and additional weight to the Article 2.1 requirement that parties and the tribunal must consult early on matters of evidence. **5.7**

Article 2.3, which deals with identification of issues relevant to the case and material to its outcome and/or potential preliminary issues, is a development of what was paragraph 3 of the Preamble to the 1999 IBA Rules. The only material difference is that, in those earlier rules, issues appropriate for preliminary determination were expressed as a subset of issues that the tribunal regarded as being relevant and material to outcome.[5] **5.8**

An IBA Report indicates that Article 2 has been referenced in only 8 per cent of cases in which the IBA Rules were applied.[6] However, this does not mean that tribunals will not have engaged in consultation with the parties at an early stage of the proceedings, either because they are required to by applicable institutional rules or as an exercise of their general case management powers. **5.9**

Limited application of Article 2.3 may be due to a concern on the part of some arbitrators that early identification of issues by the tribunal could lead to allegations of prejudging the dispute and result in a challenge to the tribunal and/or the award. As one commentator puts it: **5.10**

> The focus on the decisive issues probably has the largest potential for improving costs control and efficiency in international arbitration . . . On the other hand, some

[5] IBA Rules on the Taking of Evidence in International Commercial Arbitration 1999, Preamble 3 (hereafter '1999 IBA Rules') states that: 'Each Arbitral Tribunal is encouraged to identify to the Parties, as soon as it considers it to be appropriate, the issues that it may regard as relevant and material to the outcome of the case, including issues where a preliminary determination may be appropriate.' IBA Rules on the Taking of Evidence in International Arbitration 2010, Article 2.3 (hereafter 'IBA Rules') contains a stand-alone reference to issues suitable for preliminary determination.

[6] The IBA Arbitration Guidelines and Rules Subcommittee, 'Report on the Reception of the IBA Arbitration Soft Law Products' (International Bar Association 2016) <www.ibanet.org/Document/Default.aspx?DocumentUid=105d29a3-6261-4437-84e2-1c8637844beb> accessed 27 November 2018.

arbitrators might feel uncomfortable telling the parties at the outset of the proceedings which issues they consider to be important. They might be concerned that this is premature and improper and could even lead to accusations of partiality.[7]

5.11 There have indeed been attempts to set aside awards on the basis that the tribunal prejudged the case or predetermined the outcome of the dispute by raising matters similar to those articulated in Article 2.3. However, if the tribunal exercises its powers prudently, the prospects of success of such challenge should be limited. For example, during proceedings to challenge an award brought before the Swedish Svea Court of Appeal,[8] an argument of prejudgement or bias was raised in relation to comments made by the chairman of the tribunal during a pre-hearing conference. Those comments were directed at identifying for the parties issues that the parties should focus on during the hearing. It was alleged that the comments were directed at one party more than the other and that, as a result, the chairman was helping the former party to prepare its case. The court rejected the claim of lack of impartiality or bias.

5.12 In our view, proper use of Article 2.3 should be encouraged. Tribunals should not fear challenges based on allegations of prejudging the dispute. Case law shows that the courts are slow to make any findings against arbitrators exercising their powers in the interests of efficiency, provided the tribunal complies with its duties to the parties—in particular, giving each party a reasonable opportunity to present its case and properly considering the arguments on each side.

B. Consultation: Party/Party and Tribunal/Party

2.1. The Arbitral Tribunal shall consult the Parties at the earliest appropriate time in the proceedings and invite them to consult each other with a view to agreeing on an efficient, economical and fair process for the taking of evidence.

1. Overview of the Consultation Process

5.13 Article 2.1 addresses the initiation and purpose of the consultation process.

5.14 The proposed consultation has two elements. It requires the tribunal to (a) consult the parties and (b) invite the parties to consult with each other. These two elements are two sides of the same coin, although there are some differences.

[7] Tobias Zuberbühler and others, *IBA Rules of Evidence: Commentary on the IBA Rules on the Taking of Evidence in International Arbitration* (Sellier European Law Publishers 2012) 18 (hereafter 'Zuberbühler'; internal references are omitted).

[8] *Cypress Oilfield Holdings Limited v China Petrochemical International Company Limited* Case T-5296-14 (Swedish Svea Court of Appeal, 19 February 2016).

The *first element* (consulting the parties) means that the tribunal should seek the views of the parties on evidentiary matters. 5.15

As mentioned, this is consistent with a general recognition that early consultation between the tribunal and the parties is a key factor in ensuring efficiency of time and costs. Early consultation may enable a timetable and date for an evidentiary hearing to be fixed. It may also flush out issues that might otherwise adversely affect the efficiency and fairness of the process if raised later in the proceedings. In addition, it may alert the tribunal to differences in approach between parties from different legal traditions. 5.16

The *second element* (inviting the parties to consult with each other) appears to put the onus on the parties to consult with each other with the aim of agreeing a process for the taking of evidence. However, it is not clear whether the words 'with a view to agreeing' apply solely to the consultation between the parties, or whether they refer also to the suggested consultation between the parties *and* the tribunal. In other words, it is not clear whether Article 2.1 puts the onus on the parties to reach an agreement or whether it is a consultation between the parties and the tribunal that is intended to lead to an agreement. The first interpretation may acknowledge the fact that, in the early stages of an arbitration, the parties may be better placed than the tribunal to understand the issues in the case and to tailor an appropriate procedure. The second interpretation recognizes the important role that the tribunal may play in mediating between the parties and, as necessary, imposing a procedure that balances their competing interests and gives effect to the tribunal's obligation to organize the arbitration as efficiently as possible. In practice, the distinction may be of little relevance. Parties will generally explore what measure of agreement can be reached and will then lay that provisional agreement before the tribunal. The tribunal will stress test and raise questions on what is proposed before moving on to explore with the parties whether any middle ground can be reached in relation to the remaining disputed matters. 5.17

2. Timing of the Consultation

Article 2.1 requires the tribunal to consult the parties 'at the earliest appropriate time in the proceedings' but no time limit is set. This is in contrast to some institutional rules that do set a time limit.[9] 5.18

The focus of Article 2 is consultation on 'evidentiary issues' as opposed to more general procedural issues; this may have an impact on when the 'earliest appropriate time' for consultation on those issues may arise. 5.19

[9] For example, LCIA Rules Article 14.1 requires the parties to make contact as soon as practicable but no later than twenty-one days from the date of the formation of the arbitral tribunal.

5.20 In some cases, not all evidentiary issues will have crystallized in the initial stages of an arbitration and it may be appropriate to postpone some elements of the consultation to a later date. This point is addressed in the IBA Commentary:[10]

> Under normal circumstances, this consultation would coincide with a procedural conference or exchange of views early in the proceedings. Early timing allows the participants to organise the taking of evidence in an efficient, economical and fair manner. Where evidentiary issues are not considered to be sufficiently clear at an early stage in the arbitration, the arbitral tribunal might postpone such conference or exchange.

5.21 By way of example, US respondents to a survey on use of the IBA Rules[11] indicated that, in their experience, consultation on evidentiary issues usually comes at a later stage of the arbitration and that parties may be less willing to discuss evidentiary issues before written submissions have been exchanged and the matters in issue are clear.

5.22 However, this does not mean that the entirety of the consultation should be left for many weeks or months after commencement of the arbitration. It may be important to address some issues early. For example, in the context of document production, where parties intend to use computer technology to retrieve potentially relevant documents by use of parameters based on key word searches, date ranges, custodian, or location, early consultation between the parties to agree those parameters may be very important. If the parties do not discuss and agree a consistent approach, complaints about the scope of retrieval may be made by one side or the other at a later stage. If those complaints are justified, the document retrieval exercise may have to be repeated with a consequential waste of time and costs.

5.23 Thus, in most cases, it will be appropriate to conduct consultation early in the proceedings in order to address those evidentiary issues that can or must be addressed at that stage, leaving others to be dealt with at a later stage or as they arise. Where potentially relevant matters are postponed for later discussion there should be transparency between the tribunal and the parties about the nature of the matters deferred. Those matters should be kept under careful review. In all cases where new issues arise during the course of the arbitration proceedings, further consultation on evidence may be required.

5.24 In the majority of arbitrations, tribunals will wish to issue a first procedural order setting out a timetable for the arbitration. In most cases, this will be an appropriate time for a first round of consultation on the matters described in Article 2. Many arbitrators have a standard first procedural order that they will circulate in draft to the parties following their appointment under cover of a request for comments/proposals. This approach often provides a useful starting point when the IBA Rules are being applied.

[10] Commentary on the IBA Rules (n 1) 5.

[11] BCLP Survey on the use of the IBA Rules.

When circulating the draft the tribunal can ask the parties to give particular consideration to the matters identified in Article 2.2.

Another way of encouraging parties to actively engage in consultation is for the tribunal to send them a questionnaire inviting their comments on topics identified in that document. Reported ICC cases provide examples of this.[12] In similar vein, the Practice Guidelines issued by the Chartered Institute of Arbitrators recommend that arbitrators should prepare a draft agenda for a case management conference with the parties and circulate this to them for comment.[13] **5.25**

In all of these scenarios, the tribunal will wish to issue a procedural order at the relevant time recording the process agreed on or determined by the tribunal in respect of the matters discussed. **5.26**

3. Achieving a Process that Is Efficient, Economical, and Fair

Article 2.1 envisages the agreement of an efficient, economical and fair process for the taking of evidence. The provenance, development and practical application of the principle of an 'efficient, economical and fair process' is considered in detail in Chapter 2. As discussed, there is potential for tension between the objectives of efficiency, economy and fairness. For example, considerations of efficiency may favour avoiding unnecessary steps in the process, but this approach may conflict with fairness in the sense of allowing party a reasonable opportunity to put its case. At one extreme, options for improving efficiency could—in theory—include limited (or no) document production and/or fact or expert evidence, and deciding the case solely on the basis of written submissions without an oral hearing. In relation to each of these possibilities, there is a cost/benefit analysis to be conducted, albeit sometimes an unconscious one. The evidentiary value of each step to a party's case (and the tribunal's determination) needs to be balanced against the time and expense required to present it.[14] In the event of disagreement between the parties on the appropriate process to be adopted, the tribunal must hear the competing arguments and then take the lead in navigating a reasonable course through the available options that neither offends due process nor results in unnecessary or disproportionate costs being expended. **5.27**

A further consideration that the tribunal may have to take into account in certain cases is how best to achieve efficient and fair resolution when one party has greater financial resources at its disposal than the other.[15] This issue is discussed further in Chapter 2. **5.28**

12 See, for example, Order 7170 of 1991 in Dominique Hascher, *The Collection of Procedural Decisions in ICC Arbitration 1993–1996* (2nd edn, Kluwer Law International 1998) 24.

13 Chartered Institute of Arbitrators, *International Arbitration Practice Guidelines: Managing Arbitrations and Procedural Orders* 5.

14 For a more detailed discussion of the advantages and disadvantages of the different options see ICC Guide to Effective Management of Arbitration (n 4).

15 'Practice Guideline 17: Guidelines for Arbitrators Dealing with Cases Involving Consumers and Parties with Significant Differences of Resources' (Chartered Institute of Arbitrators 2011).

5.29 The necessity of resolving these tensions highlights the important role the tribunal plays in the consultation process.

a. Role of the tribunal where parties agree on a process

5.30 Where the parties themselves are able to agree on a procedure for the taking of evidence, does the tribunal still have a part to play in the consultation process provided for by Article 2? In particular, should the tribunal intervene if it feels that the process agreed by the parties is not efficient, economical or fair?

5.31 The lack of clarity around whether successful application of Article 2.1 can be achieved by an agreement between the parties alone, or whether it must necessarily involve agreement by the tribunal (see para 5.17), may have some theoretical relevance to this question. However, in reality, a tribunal may be presented at any time with party agreement on a matter of procedure or evidence either within a consultation process conducted pursuant to Article 2 or outside of it. For this reason, even if under the Article 2.1 consultation process the agreement of the tribunal was determined to be a requirement, and this were to give rise to a conflict between Article 2.1 and a provision of applicable institutional rules (eg Article 22.2 of the ICC Rules), the guidance at Article 1 of the IBA Rules on how to deal with such conflicts would be of limited assistance.

5.32 There are differing views on the more general question of whether an agreement of the parties, or the views of the tribunal, should prevail where there is a difference between the two. One view is that, subject to public policy and applicable mandatory provisions of the law, party autonomy is of fundamental importance and must be respected. This view has been expressed by one commentator in the following terms:

> Given the importance of party autonomy as a fundamental principle of arbitration, the arbitral tribunal would do well to follow the parties' agreement on evidentiary issues unless it violates international public policy or mandatory provisions of the procedural law of juridical seat of the arbitration (*lex arbitri*).[16]

5.33 An alternative view, expressed by another commentator, is that the tribunal has an active role to play in the consultation process and should not just accept whatever the parties may agree:

> While much can be said in favor of letting the parties prescribe the procedure, it would appear preferable to grant the primary authority to prescribe the applicable procedures to the arbitral tribunal. If arbitration is to maintain its reputation for efficient and effective adjudication, the tribunal must retain control of the arbitral proceedings. The responsibility for ensuring the kind of adjudication arbitration

[16] Nassib G Ziadé, 'Taking of Evidence in Arbitration: The Arab Experience' in Andrea Carlevaris and others (eds), *International Arbitration Under Review. Essays in Honour of John Beechey* (ICC Publication No. 772E, International Chamber of Commerce 2015) 442. Ziadé goes on to make the point that '[i]n the end, irrespective of the evidentiary rules chosen by the parties, the tribunal retains full discretion to determine the relevance, materiality and weight of the evidence presented'.

> purports to offer rests ultimately with the tribunal which sees to it that the parties obtain what has been promised them. In arbitral practice, the tribunal can obtain the requisite authority by adoption of a procedural order right at the beginning of the arbitration, agreed upon between the parties and the tribunal, granting the tribunal the authority to prescribe the procedural rules that will be observed. Once this order has been adopted, the parties cannot change it without the concurrence of the arbitrators. It also provides the authority for deviating from institutional and other rules the parties may have agreed upon.[17]

The CIArb Guidelines suggest a middle ground to the effect that intervention by the tribunal should not be limited to cases where public policy and/or mandatory law provisions are engaged, but should extend to situations where inefficiency, or the incurring of unnecessary costs, would otherwise be the result: **5.34**

> If the parties have reached an agreement as to the procedure to be followed, the arbitrators should respect the parties' agreement provided that it is not contrary to any overriding mandatory laws and/or principles of public policy at the place of arbitration *and/or would cause the proceedings to be conducted in a manner which is inefficient and unnecessarily costly.* In these circumstances, arbitrators should consider encouraging the parties to adopt a more suitable procedure and, if appropriate, make a procedural order to that effect.[18]

We agree with the latter approach. While acknowledging party autonomy, the tribunal should not accept something it considers would be unproductive and/or would contradict the tribunal's general duty to conduct the proceedings in a fair, efficient and economic manner.[19] In our experience, much may be achieved by means of gentle coercion from the tribunal. In many cases, neither party will wish to antagonize the tribunal in the early stages of the proceedings. However, where (despite the tribunal's best efforts) there remains a direct conflict between what the parties have agreed and what the tribunal believes is the best way of managing the evidence, the tribunal may sometimes face a dilemma. **5.35**

The IBA Rules operate within the legal infrastructure of the arbitration created by the arbitration agreement, the law of the seat, and any applicable institutional rules. These instruments may contain provisions relevant to the position faced by the tribunal. For example, different institutional rules may place more or less emphasis on the tribunal's role as final arbiter. Article 14.2 of the LCIA Rules provides that parties may agree on joint proposals 'for consideration' by the tribunal. In contrast, Article 22 of the ICC Rules states that, following consultation with the parties, the tribunal may adopt such **5.36**

[17] Hans Smit, 'Roles of the Arbitral Tribunal in Civil Law and Common Law Systems with Respect to Presentation of Evidence' in Albert Jan van den Berg (ed), *Planning Efficient Arbitration Proceedings: The Law Applicable in International Arbitration* (Kluwer Law International 1996) 161–72, 164 (hereafter 'Smit').

[18] Chartered Institute of Arbitrators (n 13) 3 (emphasis added).

[19] Such duty may be a mandatory requirement of the law of the seat. For example, see the English Arbitration Act 1996, s 33; the Swedish Arbitration Act 1999, s 21.

procedural measures as it considers appropriate, 'provided that they are not contrary to the agreement of the parties'.[20] However, in the final analysis, whatever powers the tribunal may have under the applicable institutional rules, the arbitration and the arbitrators are a product of an agreement made between the parties and any authority granted to the tribunal must, as a matter of principle, be subject to the right of the parties to override or vary that position.[21]

5.37 Mandatory provisions of law at the seat may also have some application to this situation, but again these will not necessarily provide a final resolution of any conflict between the wishes of the parties and the view of the tribunal. This can be illustrated by reference to the provisions of the English Arbitration Act 1996. Section 33 of the Act imposes a mandatory obligation on the tribunal to adopt procedures suitable to the circumstances of the particular case, and to avoid unnecessary delay and expense. Section 34(1) provides that the tribunal shall decide all procedural and evidential matters 'subject to the right of the parties to agree any matter'. It has been suggested that, in circumstances where, against the wishes of the tribunal, the parties agree to adopt disproportionately expensive procedural steps, there is little the tribunal can do and that discharge of its obligations under Section 33 may be limited to pointing out the consequences of the parties' agreement.[22] Where the tribunal does not feel that it can continue the proceedings in light of the steps agreed between the parties, the only other course open to it may be to resign.[23]

5.38 The possibility that a tribunal may face such a dilemma was recognized during the drafting of the English Arbitration Act 1996. In comments relating to Section 25(3) of that legislation (providing that where an arbitrator resigns from an arbitration s/he may apply to the English court to be relieved from any liability incurred as a result of that resignation and/or for payment of fees), the relevant government advisory committee responsible for the legislation noted that one situation where it would be reasonable to grant such relief might be where 'the arbitrator may (reasonably) not be prepared to adopt a procedure agreed by the parties (i.e. pursuant to [Section] 34) during the course of an arbitration, taking the view that his duty under [Section] 33 conflicts with their suggestions'.[24] The advisory committee went on to say that:

> 157. In our view it is neither desirable nor practicable to stipulate that the tribunal can override the agreement of the parties. It is not desirable because the type of arbitration we are discussing is a consensual process which depends on the agreement of the

[20] LCIA Rules Article 14.2, and ICC Rules Article 22. See also ICC Rules Article 19.

[21] One manifestation of this in extreme circumstances is the right (subject to any applicable mandatory provisions of law) of the parties by agreement to remove the arbitrator/s. For example, the English Arbitration Act 1996, s 23 (3)(a) expressly recognises the right of the parties jointly to revoke the authority of an arbitrator. In practice, the consequences of such action in wasted time and costs will militate against it. See further Robert Merkin and Louis Flannery, *Arbitration Act 1996* (5th edn, Informa Law from Routledge 2014) 82.

[22] ibid 132.

[23] ibid 134 and fn 1.

[24] Lord Justice Saville, 'Departmental Advisory Committee on Arbitration Law 1996 Report on the Arbitration Bill' (1997) Arbitration International 275 para 113.

> parties who are surely entitled (if they can agree) to have the final say on how they wish their dispute to be resolved. It is not practicable, since there is no way in which the parties can be forced to adopt a manner of proceeding if they are agreed that this is not the way they wish to proceed. The latter is the case even if it could be established that their agreement was ineffective since it undermined or prevented performance of the duty made mandatory by [Section] 33.
>
> [...]
>
> 159. In circumstances such as these, the tribunal (assuming it has failed to persuade the parties to take a different course) has the choice of adopting the course preferred by the parties or of resigning.[25]

b. Role of the tribunal where parties are unable to agree a process

In the event of disagreement between the parties on any aspect of the appropriate process to be adopted, the tribunal must hear the competing arguments and then take the lead in navigating and, if necessary, making a unilateral decision on the best of the available procedural options. **5.39**

If only one party (or neither) engages with the consultation process, the tribunal may have to proceed with issuing the procedural order it believes appropriate in the circumstances. However, it is advisable that the tribunal should first share a draft order with the parties to give the recalcitrant party/parties a further opportunity to raise any particular objections to what is proposed. **5.40**

From a party perspective, there is a risk in leaving determination of the procedure for presentation of evidence in the hands of the tribunal. In an attempt to find middle ground, the tribunal may come up with a compromise that is not ideal for either party. For this reason parties will generally attempt to agree on steps for the taking of evidence.[26] At least in a negotiation they will have a degree of control over the concessions and compromises that are made. **5.41**

Under Article 2.1, the tribunal has an obligation both to 'consult the parties' and to 'invite the parties to agree'. These steps are interconnected and the scope of discussions should be similar in each case. **5.42**

C. The Matters to Be Considered during Consultation

> **2.2. The consultation on evidentiary issues may address the scope, timing and manner of the taking of evidence, including:**
>
> **(a) the preparation and submission of Witness Statements and Expert Reports;**

[25] ibid paras 154–59.

[26] Julio César Rivera, *Arbitraje comercial, internacional y doméstico* (2nd edn, Actualizada Abeledoperrot 2014) 603.

(b) the taking of oral testimony at any Evidentiary Hearing;

(c) the requirements, procedure and format applicable to the production of Documents;

(d) the level of confidentiality protection to be afforded to evidence in the arbitration; and

(e) the promotion of efficiency, economy and conservation of resources in connection with the taking of evidence.

1. Overview

5.43 Article 2.2 sets out a non-exhaustive list of the issues that may be considered by the parties and the tribunal as part of the consultation process described in Article 2.1.

5.44 The use of the words 'may' and 'including' in Article 2.2 makes it clear that the list of topics included there is neither mandatory, nor exhaustive. However, it is a good indication of issues that the parties and the tribunal should consider and, if appropriate, decide at the beginning of an arbitration.

5.45 Article 2.2 suggests that, in relation to each element of the process of taking evidence being discussed, consideration should be given to three distinct aspects: 'scope', 'timing', and 'manner'.

5.46 *Scope* is the identification of the type and breadth of evidence likely to be necessary for the tribunal to determine the issues in the case, eg the topics on which fact and documentary evidence will be required, and what disciplines of expert (if any) will be needed. It may also involve consideration of whether or not a particular step is necessary. For example, in the context of document production, it prompts the parties to consider whether the non-voluntary production of documents (ie production of documents additional to those that each party intends to volunteer in support of its case case) is needed.

5.47 *Timing* is the setting of a sequence and dates for the relevant steps to be taken within the procedural timetable. For example, in the context of document production, timing determines whether document production requests should be made before, during, or after delivery of written submissions.

5.48 *Manner* is the identification of how best to present the desired evidence, taking account of the need to do so efficiently and economically while also observing fairness to each party to the dispute.

5.49 The specific issues relevant in a particular arbitration will vary from case to case. The commentary in the next section highlights some of the more common issues that the parties and the tribunal are likely to consider. A more comprehensive checklist of points to consider at the consultation can be found at Appendix 3.

2. Particular Matters to Be Considered

a. Witness/expert evidence

Article 2.2(a) prompts the parties to consider issues relating to the scope, timing, and manner of taking witness and expert evidence. **5.50**

Articles 4, 5, and 6 of the IBA Rules contain specific provisions dealing with witnesses of fact and party-appointed and tribunal-appointed experts. These provisions are considered in detail in Chapters 7, 8, and 9. Parties and the tribunal need to consider these articles when agreeing proposals under Article 2. **5.51**

A number of questions may be considered as part of an Article 2 consultation process relating to witness/expert evidence. **5.52**

i. Preliminary considerations—is the evidence necessary or desirable?

Firstly, is there a genuine need for witnesses of fact and/or experts and, if there is, what should it cover? Preparation of witness/expert evidence is time and cost intensive and, to the extent practicably possible, should be limited to that which is needed to determine the dispute. **5.53**

In the majority of cases, fact witnesses and/or expert witnesses will be necessary to prove disputed facts and/or to present opinion evidence on technical issues. However, this is not always the case. For example, if the dispute between the parties turns on a question of law, with no dispute as to the facts, there is little need or advantage in calling fact or expert witnesses to testify. If the claimant claims an unpaid debt under a contract, the tribunal will not need a quantum expert to prove the amount to be awarded where the issue between the parties is limited to liability and there is no dispute about the sum due if liability is established.[27] **5.54**

Even if the parties agree that witness evidence is necessary, the tribunal has the power to limit or exclude such evidence.[28] This is consistent with provisions found in a number of institutional rules that empower the tribunal to limit the scope of witness evidence.[29] The tribunal may also request the provision of witness evidence not volunteered by the parties,[30] or may appoint an expert itself under Article 6.[31] **5.55**

[27] The practice of producing multiple expert reports where one or none were necessary was one of the reasons for reforms in civil litigation in the English Courts. See: Doug Jones, 'Party Appointed Expert Witnesses in International Arbitration: A Protocol at Last' Arbitration International (2006) 24(1) 138.

[28] IBA Rules (n 5) Article 9.2.

[29] See for example: LCIA Rules, Article 20.3; SIAC Rules, Rule 25.2; and ICDR Arbitration Rules, Article 20.3. ICC Rules, Article 3(4) of Appendix VI (Expedited Procedure Rules) provides: 'The arbitral tribunal shall have discretion to adopt such procedural measures as it considers appropriate. In particular, the arbitral tribunal may, after consultation with the parties, decide not to allow requests for document production or to limit the number, length and scope of written submissions and written witness evidence (both fact witnesses and experts)'. Interestingly, the UNCITRAL Rules and SCC Rules do not explicitly give the Arbitral Tribunal a right to exclude witness or expert evidence. See further Chapter 7.

[30] IBA Rules (n 5) Article 4.10.

[31] See Chapter 9.

ii. Scope of witness/expert evidence

5.56 In cases where evidence from fact witnesses and/or experts is required, Article 2.2(a) prompts the parties and the tribunal to consider early identification of the issues on which witness testimony/expert evidence is desirable; who the witnesses/experts should be; and how many witnesses/experts are genuinely necessary. The tribunal should endeavour to find the right balance between such matters as the time and cost of the proposed evidence, the extent to which it will contribute to establishing the facts in the issue, and whether those facts are on the critical path to a determination of the dispute. Similar considerations may arise in relation to expert evidence.

5.57 For various reasons, parties will often wish to introduce fact evidence from witnesses that may have had only a peripheral part to play in the events that have occurred. The tribunal should endeavour to bring focus to the exercise of identifying the relevant issues of fact to be addressed in witness evidence. This may assist in cutting down the pool of potential witnesses only to those who will add value. For example, a lengthy witness statement that does nothing more than walk the tribunal though the documentary evidence without adding anything of value may be considered a waste of time.

5.58 Articles 4.1 and 5.1 require each party to identify (by a date ordered by the tribunal) the witnesses and/or experts whose evidence it wishes to rely on, and the subject matter of their testimony. These are matters that a tribunal may wish to discuss during an initial consultation. If the parties are not at that stage in a position to express an informed view, the tribunal may impose a date by which the information required by Articles 4.1 and 5.1 is to be provided and defer further detailed discussion on these matters.

5.59 However, even where during initial discussions the parties are unable to name witnesses and/or experts, counsel for the parties are often capable of forming a provisional view as to whether witnesses of fact are needed, and if so, on which issues, as well as what disciplines of expert may be desirable. This information may help to inform the initial timetable agreed during a first consultation.

5.60 At whatever time the information required by Articles 4.1 and 5.1 is provided, it is open to the tribunal to question whether the proposed subject matter of the evidence is necessary for determination of the dispute. If the tribunal is not satisfied by the explanation justifying the evidence, it is, in theory, open to the tribunal to make an order excluding such evidence pursuant to Article 9.2(a) and/or Article 9.2(g).

5.61 As far as expert evidence is concerned, the tribunal will wish to understand the nature, extent, and importance of any technical issues that exist, or are likely to arise between the parties. At as early a stage as possible, the tribunal will wish to gain a preliminary appreciation of the scope and discipline of expert evidence necessary to assist the tribunal in determining the dispute.

iii. The manner in which evidence is to be presented

Fact evidence Fact evidence will be required in most cases. Article 2.2(a) refers to but does not require the tribunal to order the submission of witness statements. However, the commentary to Article 4.4 suggests that the use of witness statements is desirable in the interests of procedural efficiency.[32] An alternative is the provision of witness summaries, a brief document containing a summary of the intended scope of witness evidence. Another, but little used, alternative is simply for the witness to turn up at the oral hearing and present his or her evidence 'live'.[33] **5.62**

Where witness statements are to be submitted, consideration should be given to whether it is desirable and feasible to impose a limit on length. A coherent and well-structured witness statement can be a valuable tool in helping the tribunal to understand the case. Lengthy unfocused witness statements may merely consume time and cost. **5.63**

Other points to consider will include whether the witness statements should be organized by reference to issue or phase, the number of rounds of witness statements, and whether parties should have the opportunity to submit rebuttal evidence.[34] **5.64**

Expert evidence Consultation on expert evidence should extend to whether any expert evidence required on particular issues is best presented by party-appointed experts or by a tribunal-appointed expert.[35] **5.65**

In the majority of cases there will be a consensus, or even an assumption, that the expert evidence should be presented by way of written report with an opportunity for questions or cross-examination during the evidential hearing. **5.66**

Another matter often discussed and agreed during consultation on expert evidence is the need for a mechanism by which party-appointed experts may narrow the issues between them, with consequential savings in costs and hearing time. As a result, the procedural timetable will often contain provision for a meeting between experts of the same discipline to explore what can be agreed and, where this is not possible, what their points of disagreement are on the particular issue. Depending on the stage at which the meeting takes place, the experts may then only need to prepare reply reports on the points of disagreement. At the hearing, the cross-examination of the experts may also be more limited. IBA Rules Article 5.4 makes express provision for the tribunal to order such a meeting between experts. **5.67**

Issues of foreign law Additionally, a question sometimes arises as to whether issues of foreign law should be addressed by means of expert evidence or in submissions. It is not uncommon in international arbitration for foreign law to be dealt with as part of submissions—initially in written submissions (with attachment of the relevant **5.68**

[32] See Chapter 7, paras 7.62–7.67.

[33] The disadvantages of this approach in all but the most exceptional cases are dealt with in more detail in Chapter 7.

[34] See Chapter 7, paras 7.68–7.75 and 7.127–7.136.

[35] The advantages and implications of each approach are addressed at Chapters 8 and 9.

authorities) and, if necessary, by supplementary oral submissions—rather than to prove it by expert evidence. Presenting evidence in this way can result in time and costs savings. This is an issue that is best discussed and agreed at an early stage.[36]

5.69 If the legal team on each side of the dispute includes counsel qualified in the relevant jurisdiction who are able to deal with any question from the tribunal at the evidentiary hearing, then no issue may arise. If the relevant foreign law has similarities with a legal system familiar to members of the tribunal, the tribunal may still be content to proceed without expert evidence where all parties wish to deal with foreign law by way of submissions. In some instances, the parties may insist on appointing expert witnesses to deal with issues of law even though the tribunal does not feel it is necessary. This sometimes happens in investment arbitration cases where the parties wish to adduce expert evidence on international law even though the tribunal may consider itself expert in, and perfectly capable of, applying that law.[37]

5.70 In the event of dispute the tribunal should decide what is efficient and fair having in mind the parties' wishes, the likely cost of the expert evidence, and the tribunal's degree of familiarity with the relevant legal system. In a situation where only one party-appointed member of a three-arbitrator tribunal is familiar with the relevant law, fairness often dictates that, rather than the tribunal simply relying on that one party appointed arbitrator, expert evidence on foreign law should be permitted.[38]

iv. Timing of witness/expert evidence

5.71 The timing of delivery of witness/expert evidence will be a key consideration for discussion. In the interests of efficiency, it will be important that the tribunal and the parties are able to fix a date in their diaries for the evidentiary hearing. In order to do this, they will need to agree a timetable for the principal steps leading up to that hearing.

5.72 To this end, thought will need to be given to how much time the parties need to prepare the evidence and whether delivery of the witness evidence should be simultaneous or consecutive.

5.73 The date for delivery will generally be an issue for negotiation between the parties in the context of the overall timetable. The timing of delivery within the procedural timetable

[36] See Chapter 8, paras 8.22–8.24. This practice is adopted in some courts, for example, there is provision for the Singapore International Commercial Court to order that any question of foreign law be dealt with by way of submission. See: para 110 of the Singapore Commercial Court Practice Directions. See also David Foxton, 'Foreign Law in Domestic Courts' 2017 29 SAcLG 194 for an interesting discussion of domestic court practice.

[37] See, for example: Christopher Harris, 'Expert evidence: the 2010 revisions to the IBA Rules on the Taking of Evidence in International Arbitration' [2010] International Arbitration Law Review 212, 215.

[38] '*International Arbitration Practice Guidelines: Party-Appointed and Tribunal-Appointed Experts*' (Chartered Institute of Arbitrators 2016) 4 suggests that the following factors are relevant when considering the benefits of adducing expert opinion on law: (a) the degree of familiarity of the arbitrators with the applicable law and/or similar system(s) of law; (b) the degree of counsel's competence in and familiarity with the applicable law and/or similar system(s) of law; (c) the extent to which the application of the law will impact on that issue and the likely effect this will have on the case; and (d) whether it involves general legal principles or some unique aspects of the applicable law.

may depend to an extent on whether a memorial or common law style approach to submissions/pleadings is to be adopted.

The memorial style approach derives from the practice of civil law courts where witnesses are normally identified in written submissions, and a summary of their respective testimony is included in those submissions.[39] The modern memorial approach adopted in international arbitration generally involves each party submitting an extended pleading incorporating legal argument and reference to the material facts, and accompanied by all documentary evidence relied on and, in many cases, by witness and expert evidence. **5.74**

In contrast, the pleadings approach (also known as the conventional or common law approach) requires each party to submit pleadings with only the most relevant documents, and for witness statements and expert reports to be delivered at a later date. One perceived advantage of this approach is that, at the beginning of the arbitration, the parties may not have identified all of the fact and expert witnesses whose evidence they wish to rely on in the proceedings. **5.75**

Both approaches are used in international arbitration, with growing acceptance on the part of both civil lawyers and common law lawyers of the other tradition's approach. This means that the tribunal's focus can be on determining which is the best approach in an individual arbitration. **5.76**

b. Oral testimony

Article 2.2(b) prompts the parties to consider issues relating to the taking of oral testimony at any evidentiary hearing. This may be a discussion that is deferred to a later stage of the process when there is a clearer understanding of the precise issues in dispute, the identity of the potential witnesses/experts, and the scope of their evidence. **5.77**

Article 8 of the IBA Rules contains specific provisions relating to the evidentiary hearing, including the taking of oral testimony. These provisions are considered in detail in Chapter 11. Parties and the tribunal should consider the provisions of Article 8 when discussing proposals under Article 2.2(b). **5.78**

Points to consider include: **5.79**

(a) Early identification of witnesses whose appearance is requested at the hearing. Consideration should be given to setting a deadline under Article 8.1 for the parties to identify the fact witnesses/experts whose presence is required. This will promote efficiency by allowing those witnesses to make travel arrangements and to obtain any necessary visas well in advance of the hearing date (see Chapter 11, paras 11.7–11.9).

[39] Smit (n 17) 161.

(b) The weight that will be accorded to witness testimony in circumstances where (1) appearance of the witness is not requested and (2) appearance is requested but the witness fails to attend.[40]
(c) Whether physical appearance of the fact/expert witness is necessary or whether oral testimony can be given by telephone, video conference or some other technology. If video conferencing or other technology is to be used, arrangements should be put in place to ensure that the technology and connections are adequate and the procedure followed is a fair one.[41]
(d) Scheduling of witnesses and experts and the allocation of time. There will often be agreement as to how the hearing should be divided up between submissions and presentation of evidence, and how much time each party should have for cross-examination of witnesses.[42] This imposes a degree of discipline and may be relevant to considerations of fairness. However, it will generally be difficult for the parties and tribunal to have an informed discussion on such matters until a fairly advanced stage in the proceedings when they know how many witnesses and experts they will be presenting for cross-examination, or the number and breadth of the matters in issue between the parties. For this reason, precise scheduling and allocation of time is an issue that the parties and the tribunal may wish to defer to a later, pre-hearing conference (see further discussion of this topic in Chapter 8).
(e) Whether interpreters will be required and, if so, the impact of this on the allocation of time between the parties (see for more detail Chapter 7, paras 7.116–7.117, Chapter 11, paras 11.108–11.110).
(f) Whether a witness should give oral evidence under oath (for more detail, see Chapter 11, paras 11.78–11.85).
(g) The use of witness conferencing, or 'hot-tubbing' (see for more detail Chapter 11, paras 11.72–11.74).

For example, is this something the tribunal thinks it will find useful and do the parties have any objection? It is useful to flush this out early, as very often a compromise is possible that will satisfy everyone. For example, a party may have no objection to hot-tubbing provided that it also has the opportunity to cross examine the other party's witness/expert.

5.80 Parties are well advised to discuss and agree the date and length of any evidentiary hearing as soon as possible. Where there is a lack of clarity on the number of witnesses and experts, a possible solution may be to book a one-week hearing with a second week

[40] If the IBA Rules (n 5) are adopted as binding rules, rather than being used as guidance only, the provisions of IBA Rules Article 4.7 will determine this issue unless excluded by agreement between the parties. See Chapter 7, paras 7.137–7.167.
[41] Further guidance can be found in the *ICC Arbitration Commission Report on Information Technology in International Arbitration* (International Chamber of Commerce 2017) (hereafter 'ICC Report on Information Technology').
[42] See further Zuberbühler (n 7) 17.

being held in reserve, if needed. Arbitrators' diaries are filled very quickly. If time is not booked well in advance, it may be impossible to add another week; however, it will be much easier to release a second week should that prove to no longer be required. This may be an expensive approach for the parties given that reservation/cancellation fees are often charged by arbitrators. However, in disputes where the value of the claim is substantial and/or an early determination may be critical, it will frequently be justified. If the decision is kept under review it may well be possible to release additional dates before the tribunal's cancellation policy comes into effect. The tribunal should be prepared to tell the parties if they think the time estimate is too long or too short.

c. The process for the production of documents

Article 2.2(c) prompts the parties to consider issues relating to production of documents—both documents to be produced on a voluntary basis and those that may be requested by another party and/or ordered to be produced by the tribunal. Those matters may include consideration of the subject matter of documents potentially relevant to the dispute, the source and manner of collection of such documents, the format in which they are to be retrieved and produced, and whether document production should include electronic documents.[43] **5.81**

Article 3 of the IBA Rules contains comprehensive provisions setting out a process for voluntary and non-voluntary production of documents (see Chapter 6). Unless the parties wish to vary or depart from those provisions, there may be few issues between them concerning the procedure by which document production is to be completed. The parties may simply agree that document production will be conducted in accordance with Article 3. However, even if this is the case, there will still need to be discussion on the timing of those steps—for example, in relation to delivery of requests for production. In addition, there may be questions around the manner in which soft copy documents are to be collected, and the form in which they are to be provided to the other party. Article 2.2 does not expressly address electronic disclosure, but it should be read in conjunction with Article 3.3(a)(ii) and Article 3.12.[44] **5.82**

Other points to consider include early identification of the computer systems, electronic devices, storage systems and media on which the electronic documents are held; how the search is to be conducted; whether the parties are willing to consult on the use of search parameters; and the format and methods for the production of documents. Techniques and guidance for managing electronic document production include the Chartered Institute of Arbitrators' Protocol for E-Disclosure in International Arbitration and the ICC Commission Report on Techniques for **5.83**

[43] The Commentary on the IBA Rules (n 1) notes that, should the circumstances of the case make this appropriate, the tribunal and the parties may decide not to require disclosure of electronic evidence.

[44] These provisions address the requirement of a sufficiently detailed description of the document/category of document requested by the other party, and address the format in which the document/category of document is to be provided. See Chapter 6.

Managing Electronic Document Production.[45] See also the more detailed discussion of this topic in Chapter 6.[46]

5.84 An increasingly common trend is for parties to use special electronic document management platforms to search and select documents. Searching by reference to agreed words or phrases has become a matter of routine. More recently, various electronic platforms have been developed to carry out what is known as 'predictive coding'. Predictive coding is machine-learning technology driven by human tuition. A senior lawyer reviews a small 'seed set' of documents, which is then analysed by the software programme and used to generate a further sample of documents for review. Through a process of iterative refinement, an algorithm in the software used to harvest relevant documents can reach a level of review accuracy that can be applied across the entire dataset, identifying relevant documents in a manner that is far more efficient and scalable than a traditional document review. A series of sample reviews, privilege sweeps, and other human interventions can then be used to verify the results and finalize the documents prior to production. In England, the courts have allowed the use of predictive coding for a review of electronic documents even when that approach was opposed by the other party, who wanted a more traditional keyword search to be used.[47]

5.85 The use of predictive coding is likely to grow in international arbitration and it may be prudent for the parties to discuss it as part of a consultation agenda, if only to obtain transparency around any party's intended use of such technology. There is also evidence that the results of a predictive coding review are statistically superior to a traditional manual review.[48] Although there remains a risk that the platform can miss potentially relevant material because use of different words was not programmed for retrieval, given the volume of electronic documents being created on a daily basis, parties are becoming more willing to accept the risk that the platform may miss a small number of documents. Nonetheless, there may be cases where the use of the predictive coding is not appropriate due to the limited number of documents to be searched or because it is considered important to find each and every relevant document. The cost of predictive coding can also be very expensive, which may deter some parties from using it where to do so would be disproportionate.

5.86 Another issue around document production often discussed at an early stage and incorporated into a first procedural order is whether the parties wish to use what is

[45] *ICC Arbitration Commission Report on Managing E-Document Production* (International Chamber of Commerce 2012).

[46] Chapter 6, paras 6.24–6.25, 6.68–6.75, and 6.366–6.373.

[47] *Brown v BCA Trading Ltd* [2016] EWHC 1464 (Ch) endorsing the approach adopted in *Pyrrho Investments Ltd v MWB Property Ltd* [2016] EWHC 256 (Ch). In the latter case, the majority of the documents were held by the party wishing to use predictive coding. One of the factors that the court took into account when approving the use of predictive coding was cost. It was estimated that using predictive coding would cost around £130,000 compared to a possible cost of £250,000–£338,000 if search terms were used. For discussion on the use of search terms see Chapter 6, paras 6.68–6.75.

[48] *Moore v Publicis Groupe* 11 Civ 1279 (ALC) (AJP) (US District Court SDNY, 24 February 2012).

known as a 'Redfern Schedule' for their document production requests. A Redfern Schedule is a table with different columns in which the requesting party sets out its request and supporting explanation for why the documents are needed. The parties exchange Redfern Schedules and complete their opponent's table with confirmation of whether the opponent's request is accepted and, if it is not, on what grounds objection to production is made. Any outstanding disputed items can then be adjudicated upon by the tribunal looking at the Redfern Schedules and then entering its decision in the final column of the table. Chapter 6 provides an example of a Redfern Schedule,[49] and sample Redfern Schedules are located in Appendix 4 and Appendix 5.[50]

Deadlines for delivery of requests for documents will need to be put in place, and consideration given as to whether there should be a second round of requests following delivery of subsequent submissions or evidence. **5.87**

Other issues regarding the format of document production include:[51] **5.88**

- whether documents should be produced in hard copy and/or electronically and, if the latter, in what file type;
- if electronically, whether documents should be produced in native format; and
- whether metadata should be produced.

These issues are expressly addressed in the IBA Rules—in particular, by Article 3. If a party wants to depart from the provisions of the IBA Rules governing a particular issue they should raise this during the consultation stage.

Another question that sometimes arises concerns translation of foreign language documents. In international arbitration there will generally be an agreement or direction that the proceedings will be conducted in a particular language. However, given the types of dispute referred to international arbitration, there will often be documents relevant to the dispute that contain content in a language other than the language of the arbitration. Depending on volume, the burden of preparing a translation of those documents may be significant both in terms of cost and time. Article 3.12 of the IBA Rules makes reference to the use of translations but only to say that any translations introduced in the proceedings should be accompanied by a copy of the original language document.[52] However, the IBA Rules do not govern whether translations are required in individual arbitral proceedings, whether particular documents may be translated in part only, or the resolution of disputes regarding translations or the timing of submissions of translations.[53] **5.89**

[49] Chapter 6, para 6.205.
[50] See also further discussion on the use of Redfern Schedules at paras 6.199–6.207.
[51] For more detail see paras 6.366–6.373; see also discussion on rights to production of metadata in paras 6.120–6.124.
[52] See paras 6.379–6.385.
[53] Commentary to the IBA Rules (n 1).

5.90 The absence of clear agreement on these issues may lead to disagreements between the parties later in the process. Issues around translation of documents were mentioned by a number of respondents to a survey on the use of the IBA rules.[54] A law firm respondent in Italy mentioned a case where a party submitted a document without a translation. The opponent party asked the tribunal to declare the document inadmissible due to it not being submitted in the language of the arbitration (English). The tribunal held that the lack of an English translation constituted 'a curable procedural defect which can be repaired'. On that basis, the tribunal declined to declare the document inadmissible but ordered the party to produce a translation.[55] An American respondent reported that, in one arbitration seated in the United States, a party complained that the documents produced were all in a language other than English. The tribunal accepted the opponent party's argument that the documents need only be produced in the form in which they are kept in the ordinary course of business.[56]

5.91 In these circumstances it is sensible for the parties to try to reach an agreement early on about the general approach to be adopted with regard to translation of documents and which party will bear the burden (practical and economic) of preparing any translations to be provided. It is sensible for power to be reserved to the tribunal to deal with any issues that may arise during the course of the proceedings regarding specific documents.

5.92 In relation to documents upon which the parties wish to rely, they may consider it sensible to agree that a translation should be provided at the same time as the original document so that the full import of that document is clear to the other party and to the tribunal, regardless of language skills. It may be relatively easy to obtain agreement that the relying party will bear the burden of obtaining a translation as part of the costs of preparing and presenting its case. The position in relation to document production may be more problematic. In many arbitrations a great number of documents are produced but a relatively small number are included in the hearing bundles or are relied on before the tribunal. Given this factor, the early provision of a professional third-party translation with each document may not be the most efficient approach. In some cases, counsel on both sides may have someone in their team who has a good command of the relevant language/s and the parties may be content for documents to be produced without a translation. When the parties later identify the documents (if any) that they wish to refer to before the tribunal, that document, or the relevant section of it, can be translated. In many cases, a tailored approach meeting the individual facts of the case may be required. For example, if there is a dispute about the relevance and materiality of the requested document, but the party in possession is prepared to produce them

[54] BCLP Survey on the use of the IBA Rules.
[55] ibid.
[56] ibid.

provided it does not have to bear the burden of providing translations, then a possible compromise (or tribunal direction) may be that the requesting party carry the burden of translation. In either case, if the party preparing the translation is successful in the dispute it will be able to seek recovery of its costs of translation as part of its costs of the arbitration in the normal way.

d. Confidentiality

Article 2.2(d) prompts the parties to consider issues relating to the level of confidentiality protection to be attached to evidence in the arbitration. 5.93

The IBA Rules deal with confidentiality at Article 3.13 and Article 9.4.[57] Article 3.13 sets out an express obligation of confidentiality in relation to documents introduced into the arbitration and suggests that a tribunal may wish to issue an order setting out the terms of that confidentiality. Article 9.4 provides that a tribunal may, where appropriate, make arrangements for evidence to be presented subject to suitable and tailored confidentiality protection. 5.94

The tribunal's power under Article 9.4 is most commonly exercised when a party has been requested/ordered to produce documents it claims are subject to some special commercial or technical confidentiality.[58] However, this is not always the case. The nature of the industry in which the parties operate, or the nature of the dispute itself, may be such as to make it apparent from the outset that confidential material is likely introduced into evidence. In such circumstances it may be desirable for the parties, and the tribunal, to discuss as early as possible the confidentiality measures that may be appropriate.[59] 5.95

In all cases, the issue of confidentiality is something that should appear on a consultation agenda even if only to be dismissed by the parties as unnecessary. If an order addressing confidentiality in general terms is made early in the proceedings as part of the Article 2 consultation, it can be built upon by specific orders later made under Article 9.4 of the IBA Rules, as required. Points to consider at the outset of proceedings when the precise nature of the confidential documents likely to be introduced may not be known include: 5.96

(a) How confidential material introduced into the arbitration is to be identified;
(b) To whom the documents identified as confidential should be distributed in the first instance; and
(c) What provisional restrictions on access/copying should be put in place.

[57] See Chapter 6, paras 6.386–6.394 and Chapter 12, paras 12.317–12.356.

[58] This is a ground of objection to production under IBA Rules (n 5) Article 9.2(e). If the tribunal does not find the grounds of objection compelling but recognizes the sensitive nature of the documents it may impose confidentiality safeguards. See Chapter 12, paras 12.317–12.356.

[59] The nature and range of confidentiality protections that may be put in place is discussed in more detail in Chapter 12.

5.97 Where the introduction of confidential material is considered likely, but the precise nature of that material is not yet known, there are dangers in being too prescriptive. The key points are:

(a) that the material should be clearly identified as confidential; and
(b) dissemination/copying should be restricted on a provisional basis while the case for, and nature of, confidentiality safeguards are worked out between the parties and tribunal.

Of course, in practice, many parties will prefer to withhold the material altogether until a tailored application under Article 9.4 has been made.

5.98 Additional confidentiality and data security issues may arise from the use of IT in the arbitration and additional levels of protection may be required to ensure that neither the parties nor any third parties (deliberately or inadvertently) misuse any data transmitted to/stored by them. For example, it is important to consider how the confidentiality and security of evidence will be maintained where that material is distributed to third parties in the normal course of the arbitration.[60]

5.99 A further point may sometimes arise where the parties are involved in multiple parallel disputes before different courts and/or tribunals, but the same underlying facts apply in each case. The parties may wish to agree that the confidentiality regime in the arbitration[61] should not prevent the parties from using documents obtained in the arbitration in the parallel proceedings. For clarity, such proceedings can be defined precisely by case number and names of the parties.

e. Efficiency, economy and conservation of resources

5.100 The purpose of the IBA Rules is to provide an efficient and economical process for the taking of evidence;[62] thus, it is not surprising to see these words repeated in Article 2.2(e).

5.101 The point has been made that Article 2.2(e) adds very little to the opening words of Article 2.1, which expresses the whole objective of the consultation process as being to arrive at an efficient and economic (and fair) process.[63] However, if Article 2.2 is to serve as a 'default' agenda for the consultation mentioned in Article 2.1, it seems to us that it does no harm to include express reference to considerations of cost and efficiency as an agenda item.

5.102 The inclusion of the phrase 'conservation of resources' in Article 2.2(e) is an interesting addition and the phrase is not seen elsewhere in the IBA Rules. It appears to be directed

60 ICC Report on Information Technology (n 41). See also 'Draft Cybersecurity Protocol for International Arbitration' (Consultation Draft, ICCA/CPR/New York City Bar Association Working Group on Cybersecurity in Arbitration, 10 April 2018) <www.arbitration-icca.org/media/10/43322709923070/draft_cybersecurity_protocol_final_10_april.pdf> accessed 28 November 2018.

61 Even if a tailored regime has not been put in place pursuant to the IBA Rules (n 5) Article 9.4, the provisions of Article 3.13 will apply.

62 IBA Rules (n 5) Preamble.

63 Christopher Newmark, '"Efficient, Economical and Fair": The Mantra of the New IBA Rules' (2010) 13 International Arbitration Law Review 164, 167 (hereafter 'Newmark').

at conservation in the ecological sense.[64] Examples of techniques that might be used to conserve resources include:

(a) exclusive use of electronic documents and electronic hearing bundles to prevent waste of paper, eg a decision that no letters or documents should be sent in paper form, and
(b) use of video conferencing for the examination of witnesses/experts if those individuals would otherwise have to travel by air to the hearing.

D. Tribunal Identification of Material Issues and/or Discrete Issues Suitable for Preliminary Determination

2.3. The Arbitral Tribunal is encouraged to identify to the Parties, as soon as it considers it to be appropriate, any issues:
(a) that the Arbitral Tribunal may regard as relevant to the case and material to its outcome; and/or
(b) for which a preliminary determination may be appropriate.

1. Overview

Article 2.3 encourages the tribunal to identify for the parties any key issues for the presentation of evidence, or for preliminary determination, that the parties should consider in the context of procedural efficiency. However, in contrast with Article 2.1, Article 2.3 is not mandatory and leaves it to the discretion of the tribunal whether to implement its terms. As mentioned, there appears to be an inherent reluctance on the part of many tribunals to do so (see paras 5.10–5.12). **5.103**

There are two elements to Article 2.3. **5.104**

Article 2.3(a) is about the identification of issues that the tribunal may regard as relevant to the case and material to its outcome (see Chapter 6 for a discussion of what these terms mean). Equally importantly, the Tribunal may identify those issues that it does not consider to be relevant to the case or material to its outcome. The exercise is about identifying issues that the tribunal regards as being on the critical path to deciding the outcome of the case. The tribunal may want to encourage the parties to focus their resources on those aspects of the dispute and indicate that expenditure of time and costs on other aspects of the dispute may be wasteful of time and costs. The **5.105**

[64] This is supported by the Commentary on the IBA Rules (n 1), which confirms that it refers to conservation of resources 'which could include, by way of example, the economic and environmental costs of travel or document production . . . '. See further Newmark (n 63) 167.

tribunal will wish to ensure that all of the evidence it will need to determine the dispute is available to it.

5.106 Article 2.3(b) is about the identification of issues that may be appropriate for preliminary determination. In substance, it encourages the tribunal to consider whether there may be threshold issues that could be dispositive of the entire arbitration or discrete issues that could usefully be addressed early in order to narrow or simplify other issues in dispute.

2. Issues to Be Identified by the Tribunal

a. Identification of issues relevant to the case and material to outcome

5.107 Article 2.3(a) encourages the tribunal to take a pro-active role in the identification of issues that it may regard as relevant to the case and material to the outcome. The term 'issues' is not defined but, in the authors' view, the term is wide enough to encompass not only matters that have been pleaded by the parties in written submissions, but also any issues that the tribunal would need to consider when deciding the case, ie to flag for the parties where it expects the focus of their evidence to be. In practice, identification of these issues may be an iterative process.

5.108 Not all issues between the parties will be relevant and material to outcome. However, some tribunals may nonetheless look to identify as soon as possible issues between the parties that can be identified from the Request for Arbitration and Response to the Request. If requested, counsel for the parties should be prepared to draw up a list of those issues they believe to exist between the parties. From such beginnings, it is generally possible to reach a degree of consensus on the key issues that emerge. In other cases, it may not be appropriate to have this sort of dialogue until after detailed submissions have been exchanged. In all cases, the list of identified issues may need to be updated as the case progresses and new issues emerge, or as concessions are made on points previously in dispute.

5.109 The approach encouraged by the terms of Article 2.3 is accepted good practice in international arbitration. The UNCITRAL Notes on Organizing Arbitral Proceedings highlight the benefit of preparing a list of points in issue between the parties:

> It is often considered helpful for the arbitral tribunal to prepare in consultation with the parties an indicative list of points at issue (as opposed to those that are undisputed) based on the parties' submissions. Such a list, when prepared at an appropriate stage of the arbitral proceedings and updated as necessary, can assist the parties in focusing their arguments on the issues identified as critical by the arbitral tribunal, thereby improving the efficiency of the arbitral proceedings and reducing costs.[65]

[65] UNCITRAL Notes (n 4) paras 57, 58, and 68. A recent recommendation of the PCA Secretary General in ICSID case *Vattenfall AB and others v. Federal Republic of Germany* (ICSID Case No. ARB/12/12) emphasises that a tribunal may legitimately seek to complete gaps in the evidentiary records, and to ascertain the parties' positions on particular points.

As mentioned, Article 2.3 allows the tribunal to direct the parties' attention to any issues that the tribunal regards as relevant to the case and material to its outcome. In many cases, the parties will welcome this sort of indication from the tribunal as it allows them to address the issues directly in submissions or in evidence. In addition, relevance to the case and materiality to its outcome are the main tests for a tribunal when deciding whether or not a particular document or statement should be admitted into evidence.[66] For parties who wish to seek non-voluntary document production, it is not easy to predict whether a tribunal will share their view of what documents are relevant to the case and material to its outcome. An early indication of these matters by the tribunal may provide greater clarity. 5.110

b. Determination of preliminary issues

Article 2.3 also encourages the tribunal to identify possible issues for preliminary determination. If there is an issue that may have an impact on the overall claim or defence, it may be more efficient and economical to deal with it at an early stage in the proceedings – perhaps as a preliminary issue in relation to which the tribunal may issue a partial final award.[67] Another example is a jurisdictional dispute which may warrant a preliminary hearing because if the tribunal finds it does not have jurisdiction, the time and expense of arguing the case on the merits will be avoided. 5.111

Another further example where early determination may be found appropriate is where a party raises a limitation defence. If, in a complex and significant dispute, the respondent pleads that the claims are time-barred, the entire proceedings may be an exercise in futility if the claim is ultimately dismissed on that ground. In the same way, issues of liability and quantum may be bifurcated. If liability has not been established, the tribunal will be relieved of the need to receive evidence on quantum. 5.112

Having identified a potential preliminary issue or the possibility of bifurcation, the tribunal will then need to consider whether a determination on that basis is the most efficient and economical way of proceeding. Matters that the tribunal may wish to consider 5.113

66 See, for example, the IBA Rules (n 5) Articles 3.3(b), 3.7, and 9.2(a).

67 Many national laws provide expressly that an arbitral tribunal has the power to make partial awards unless the parties agree otherwise. Examples include the English Arbitration Act 1996 s 47; Swedish Arbitration Act s 29; and Swiss Private International Law Statute Article 188. Most institutional rules also provide that the tribunal may make separate awards on different issues at different time. Examples include the LCIA Rules Article 26(1); ICC Rules Article 2(v); and SIAC Rules Rule 32.5. If the parties' arbitration agreement were to expressly exclude partial awards and require a single award disposing of the entire dispute, that agreement must be given effect by the tribunal; otherwise, any award may be subject to annulment and non-recognition under the New York Convention on the Recognition and Enforcement of Foreign Arbitral Awards 1958 Article V(1)(d). See, for example, *Assoc'd Corset & Brassiere Mfrs v Corset & Brassiere Workers* 16 NYS2d 736, 736 (NY Sup Ct 1939), where the award of the arbitrator was void in that he failed to rule on all the matters submitted to him for determination and there was no consent to a partial award. In practice, it is rare for parties to exclude the possibility of partial awards in their arbitration agreements. However, from a practical perspective, it should be noted that some jurisdictions (eg Dubai) impose time restrictions on the arbitral process. This may make it impossible or inadvisable for a tribunal to deal first with a preliminary issue. Federal Arbitration Law Article 42(1) states that the arbitral tribunal shall issue the award by the date agreed by the parties and that if no date is agreed, the award shall be issued within six months from the date of holding the first hearing of the arbitration procedures. The six-month time limit can be extended with the agreement of the parties. The award can be annulled pursuant to Federal Arbitration Law Article 53(1)(g) if the time limit for rendering the award is not met.

include those usefully identified by (the then) Mr Justice Neuberger in *Steele v Steele*[68] in the English commercial court. Those factors are:

(a) Whether the determination of the issue would dispose of the case or any aspect of the case;
(b) Whether the cost and time involved in pre-trial preparation would be significantly reduced;
(c) If the issue was an issue of law, what effort would be involved in identifying the relevant material;
(d) If an issue of law, how far it was to be determined on agreed facts, given that if there were numerous disputes the issue could probably not be safely resolved until the disputes were resolved;
(e) Whether the issue's determination could unreasonably fetter the parties or the court in achieving a fair result at trial;
(f) The extent to which there was a risk that determining the issue would delay and increase the costs of the trial;
(g) How far the determination of the issue was relevant and the likelihood of it having to be determined by the court;
(h) The risk of the determination of the issue leading to an application for the amendment of pleadings in a bid to avoid the consequences of the determination; and
(i) Whether the determination was just and right.

5.114 Although Article 2.3 does not refer specifically to efficiency, economy, or fairness, as explained earlier, that is the underlying rationale for the whole of Article 2. As a result, the tribunal will need to consider very carefully whether carving out issues for early determination will actually save time and costs. Unfortunately, in some cases, the cost/benefit review required to assess these matters will be made difficult because, at an early stage, the tribunal may not have enough information about the dispute to be able to assess whether hiving off an issue will achieve greater efficiency.

3. Timing of Identification of Issues by the Tribunal

5.115 Article 2.3 of the IBA Rules specifically requires the Tribunal to identify the issues mentioned there 'as soon as it considers it appropriate'. Early discussion may be very important. For example, if a decision to bifurcate liability and quantum is not made early, the opportunity to do so efficiently may be lost. On the other hand—particularly in relation to identification of issues relevant and material to outcome—a tribunal may not wish to express a position too early for fear of being perceived as prejudging those matters. In other cases, the tribunal may not be in a position to actively participate in a discussion on determinative or preliminary issues because, until the parties have exchanged at least one round of written submissions, the tribunal is often in the dark as to the case

[68] [2001] 4 WLUK 500.

before it and what issues are joined, or admitted. One commentary suggests that identification of relevant and material issues is best done later in the process:

> The fact that the provision on identification of relevant and material issues is positioned within an article focused on early case management conferences gives the impression that such identification by the arbitral tribunal should happen very early in the case. In practice, however, it will often be better to identify the relevant and material issues *later in the proceedings*, at a time when the arbitrators know more about the case (e.g. before the hearing).[69]

In ICC arbitrations, unless the tribunal considers it inappropriate, the terms of reference to be drawn up must include a list of issues to be determined.[70] While differing from the requirements of Article 2.3 in necessarily being done in the initial stages of the arbitration (rather than when 'appropriate'), the Guidance on the ICC Rules acknowledges that the parties should identify questions of fact and law which, at the time of drafting the Terms of Reference, appear to be relevant and material to determining the parties' respective claims. The tribunal and the parties are thus encouraged to single out the issues on which the case is likely to hinge, so as to give a greater focus to the arbitration proceedings.[71] Despite this encouragement, and although the list of issues is not intended to be binding or exhaustive, in many cases the preparation of an agreed list of issues proves too controversial and so is not included.[72] This may highlight the wisdom of the provision made at Article 2.3, which allows the tribunal to judge the right moment to identify issues for the parties to consider. **5.116**

In our view, a tribunal should seek to strike the right balance between caution and proactivity. If identification of discrete issues suitable for preliminary determination is overly delayed, the opportunity to deal with the matter effectively may be lost. As to issues that the tribunal considers to be relevant and material, if the tribunal is not able/willing to identify such issues at the outset, it should nonetheless monitor the direction being taken by the parties in connection with the substance of document production and witness evidence in case some redirecting of that evidence is required. **5.117**

69 Zuberbühler (n 7) 19 (emphasis added).

70 ICC Rules Article 23(1)(d).

71 Jason Fry, Simon Greenberg, and Francesca Mazza, *The Secretariat's Guide to ICC Arbitration* (International Chamber of Commerce 2012) para 3-849.

72 For more detail see ibid paras 3-850–3-851.

6

Article 3: Documents

Article 3 Documents

1. **Within the time ordered by the Arbitral Tribunal, each Party shall submit to the Arbitral Tribunal and to the other Parties all Documents available to it on which**

it relies, including public Documents and those in the public domain, except for any Documents that have already been submitted by another Party.

2. Within the time ordered by the Arbitral Tribunal, any Party may submit to the Arbitral Tribunal and to the other Parties a Request to Produce.
3. A Request to Produce shall contain:
   (a) (i) a description of each requested Document sufficient to identify it, or
   (ii) a description in sufficient detail (including subject matter) of a narrow and specific requested category of Documents that are reasonably believed to exist; in the case of Documents maintained in electronic form, the requesting Party may, or the Arbitral Tribunal may order that it shall be required to, identify specific files, search terms, individuals or other means of searching for such Documents in an efficient and economical manner;
   (b) a statement as to how the Documents requested are relevant to the case and material to its outcome; and
   (c) (i) a statement that the Documents requested are not in the possession, custody or control of the requesting Party or a statement of the reasons why it would be unreasonably burdensome for the requesting Party to produce such Documents, and
   (ii) a statement of the reasons why the requesting Party assumes the Documents requested are in the possession, custody or control of another Party.
4. Within the time ordered by the Arbitral Tribunal, the Party to whom the Request to Produce is addressed shall produce to the other Parties and, if the Arbitral Tribunal so orders, to it, all the Documents requested in its possession, custody or control as to which it makes no objection.
5. If the Party to whom the Request to Produce is addressed has an objection to some or all of the Documents requested, it shall state the objection in writing to the Arbitral Tribunal and the other Parties within the time ordered by the Arbitral Tribunal. The reasons for such objection shall be any of those set forth in Article 9.2 or a failure to satisfy any of the requirements of Article 3.3.
6. Upon receipt of any such objection, the Arbitral Tribunal may invite the relevant Parties to consult with each other with a view to resolving the objection.
7. Either Party may, within the time ordered by the Arbitral Tribunal, request the Arbitral Tribunal to rule on the objection. The Arbitral Tribunal shall then, in consultation with the Parties and in timely fashion, consider the Request to Produce and the objection. The Arbitral Tribunal may order the Party to whom such Request is addressed to produce any requested Document in its possession, custody or control as to which the Arbitral Tribunal determines that (i) the issues that the requesting Party wishes to prove are relevant to the case and material to its outcome; (ii) none of the reasons for objection set forth in Article 9.2 applies; and (iii) the requirements of Article 3.3 have been satisfied. Any such Document shall be produced to the other Parties and, if the Arbitral Tribunal so orders, to it.

8. In exceptional circumstances, if the propriety of an objection can be determined only by review of the Document, the Arbitral Tribunal may determine that it should not review the Document. In that event, the Arbitral Tribunal may, after consultation with the Parties, appoint an independent and impartial expert, bound to confidentiality, to review any such Document and to report on the objection. To the extent that the objection is upheld by the Arbitral Tribunal, the expert shall not disclose to the Arbitral Tribunal and to the other Parties the contents of the Document reviewed.
9. If a Party wishes to obtain the production of Documents from a person or organisation who is not a Party to the arbitration and from whom the Party cannot obtain the Documents on its own, the Party may, within the time ordered by the Arbitral Tribunal, ask it to take whatever steps are legally available to obtain the requested Documents, or seek leave from the Arbitral Tribunal to take such steps itself. The Party shall submit such request to the Arbitral Tribunal and to the other Parties in writing, and the request shall contain the particulars set forth in Article 3.3, as applicable. The Arbitral Tribunal shall decide on this request and shall take, authorize the requesting Party to take, or order any other Party to take, such steps as the Arbitral Tribunal considers appropriate if, in its discretion, it determines that (i) the Documents would be relevant to the case and material to its outcome, (ii) the requirements of Article 3.3, as applicable, have been satisfied and (iii) none of the reasons for objection set forth in Article 9.2 applies.
10. At any time before the arbitration is concluded, the Arbitral Tribunal may (i) request any Party to produce Documents, (ii) request any Party to use its best efforts to take or (iii) itself take, any step that it considers appropriate to obtain Documents from any person or organisation. A Party to whom such a request for Documents is addressed may object to the request for any of the reasons set forth in Article 9.2. In such cases, Article 3.4 to Article 3.8 shall apply correspondingly.
11. Within the time ordered by the Arbitral Tribunal, the Parties may submit to the Arbitral Tribunal and to the other Parties any additional Documents on which they intend to rely or which they believe have become relevant to the case and material to its outcome as a consequence of the issues raised in Documents, Witness Statements or Expert Reports submitted or produced, or in other submissions of the Parties.
12. With respect to the form of submission or production of Documents:
    (a) copies of Documents shall conform to the originals and, at the request of the Arbitral Tribunal, any original shall be presented for inspection;
    (b) Documents that a Party maintains in electronic form shall be submitted or produced in the form most convenient or economical to it that is reasonably usable by the recipients, unless the Parties agree otherwise or, in the absence of such agreement, the Arbitral Tribunal decides otherwise;

(c) a Party is not obligated to produce multiple copies of Documents which are essentially identical unless the Arbitral Tribunal decides otherwise; and
(d) translations of Documents shall be submitted together with the originals and marked as translations with the original language identified.

13. Any Document submitted or produced by a Party or non-Party in the arbitration and not otherwise in the public domain shall be kept confidential by the Arbitral Tribunal and the other Parties, and shall be used only in connection with the arbitration. This requirement shall apply except and to the extent that disclosure may be required of a Party to fulfil a legal duty, protect or pursue a legal right, or enforce or challenge an award in bona fide legal proceedings before a state court or other judicial authority. The Arbitral Tribunal may issue orders to set forth the terms of this confidentiality. This requirement shall be without prejudice to all other obligations of confidentiality in the arbitration.
14. If the arbitration is organised into separate issues or phases (such as jurisdiction, preliminary determinations, liability or damages), the Arbitral Tribunal may, after consultation with the Parties, schedule the submission of Documents and Requests to Produce separately for each issue or phase.

A. Introduction

Article 3 deals with documents. Most importantly, it addresses requests to produce documents made by one party to another, objections to such requests, and the process by which disputes around requests for production are to be determined. It also deals with the introduction of documents relied on by a party and requests for documents by the tribunal, as well as a number of other issues connected with access to documents and the form in which documents are to be produced. **6.1**

Documents play a very important role in the arbitration process. Tribunals attach significant weight to documentary evidence that is (save in the case of fraud) often regarded as a more reliable source of fact evidence than that provided by a witness whose memory may be unreliable and/or whose recollection of events may have been influenced by their employer or legal team. However, the approach to document production in civil law and common law jurisdictions is very different. While the precise rules for obtaining documents may vary between common law jurisdictions, most common law lawyers will generally regard document production—in particular, the right to access all relevant documents held by an opponent—as an essential tool in the fact-finding exercise necessary to the preparation of a client's case. The underlying principle is that all documents relevant to the disputes must be disclosed to the other party. **6.2**

In contrast, the approach to document production adopted in civil law jurisdictions is much more restricted and the right to request documents of an opponent may be **6.3** limited to those documents that prove an already pleaded fact.[1] Marghitola gives the example of a Request to Produce the original of a contract of which the requesting party has only an unsigned copy.[2]

6.4 Article 3 of the IBA Rules represents a compromise between the two legal traditions and, as such, it is invaluable for use by parties to international arbitration. Given the importance of documentary evidence, it is logical that Article 3 should be a fundamental provision of the IBA Rules. It may also explain why Article 3 is the longest and most detailed provision.

6.5 The results of an IBA survey show that Article 3 is by far the provision most frequently referred to of the IBA Rules. Approximately 21 per cent of references to the IBA Rules were references to Article 3.[3]

1. The Scope of Article 3

6.6 The term 'Documents' is widely defined in the IBA Rules as 'a writing, communication, picture, drawing, program or data of any kind, whether recorded or maintained on paper or by electronic, audio, visual or any other means'.[4] The breadth of this definition is unsurprising. The IBA Rules are concerned with the taking of evidence. It is important that the provisions relating to 'Documents' pick up all forms of evidence that are not witness evidence or expert opinion evidence.

6.7 The Commentary to the IBA Rules helpfully summarizes the categories of documents with which Article 3 is concerned:

> Article 3 refers to three groups of documents: (1) documents that are at the party's own disposal; (2) documents that the party wants to use as evidence for its submissions but cannot produce on its own, because they are either in the possession of the other party in the arbitral proceedings or in the possession of a third party outside of the arbitration; and (3) documents that neither party has introduced or wants to introduce as evidence into the arbitral proceedings, but which are seen as relevant and material by the arbitral tribunal.[5]

[1] Reto Marghitola, *Document Production in International Arbitration* (Kluwer Law International 2015) 11 (hereafter 'Marghitola').

[2] ibid 15.

[3] See The IBA Arbitration Guidelines and Rules Subcommittee, 'Report on the Reception of the IBA Arbitration Soft Law Products' (International Bar Association 2016) <www.ibanet.org/Document/Default.aspx?DocumentUid=105D29A3-6261-4437-84E2-1C8637844BEB> accessed 27 November 2018 (hereafter '2016 IBA Report').

[4] See Chapter 3 (Definitions).

[5] 1999 IBA Working Party and 2010 IBA Rules of Evidence Review Subcommittee, Commentary on the Revised Text of the 2010 IBA Rules on the Taking of Evidence in International Arbitration' (International Bar Association 2010) <www.ibanet.org/Document/Default.aspx?DocumentUid=DD240932-0E08-40D4-9866-309A635487C0> accessed 6 August 2018 (hereafter 'Commentary on the IBA Rules').

Article 3 contains discrete procedural mechanisms dealing with each of these three categories:[6] 6.8

(a) Article 3.1 and Article 3.11 deal with documents accessible to a party and upon which it wishes to rely;
(b) Articles 3.2–3.9 address documents that a party believes to be relevant and material to the case, but which it cannot produce/access because they are in the possession, custody, or control of another party to the arbitration, or a third party; and
(c) Article 3.10 concerns documents that neither party has introduced nor wants to introduce as evidence, but that are regarded as relevant and material by the tribunal.

The provisions of Article 3 dealing with voluntary production of documents in support of a party's own case are relatively uncontroversial. These provisions are addressed in further detail at 6.26-6.36 and 6.341-6.349. The position in relation to a request for production of documents made by an opponent party, or by the tribunal, is more complex and invites some further introduction before being addressed in more detail later in this chapter. 6.9

2. The Need for Provisions Relating to Document Production

It is rare to see detailed provisions covering the process of document production. It is relatively uncommon for the parties' arbitration agreement to contain any reference or detailed provision about production of documents. In addition, although express provision empowering the tribunal to order document production—either pursuant to its general powers or by means of a specific reference to document production—is often found in applicable national arbitration legislation,[7] and in arbitration rules,[8] such provisions are often silent as to the criteria to be applied by the tribunal when exercising that power. Even published guidelines on managing the conduct of arbitration proceedings say very little about this topic. 6.10

[6] See further Hilmar Raeschke-Kessler, 'The Production of Documents in International Arbitration: A Commentary on Article 3 of the New IBA Rules of Evidence' (2002) 18 Arbitration International 411 (hereafter 'Raeschke-Kessler').

[7] For example, the English Arbitration Act, s 34(2)(a). This provision grants to arbitrators broad powers to order disclosure by the parties to an arbitration but imposes no specific restrictions on the manner by which the tribunal arrives at a decision on this issue, subject always to the tribunal's underlying duties of fairness, impartiality and efficiency under the English Arbitration Act, s 33. A decision of the Argentinian Court confirms that the tribunal has a wide discretion in relation to production of evidence: '[e]very Arbitral Tribunal has the power to ponder the evidence offered by the parties and only order the production of such evidence that it deems useful for the resolution of the conflict'. *Sociedad de Inversiones Inmobiliarias del Puerto SA v Constructora Iberoamericana SA*, Chamber D of the National Court of Appeals on Commercial Matters.

[8] See, for example: SCC Rules Article 31(3); HKIAC Rules Article 22.3; UNCITRAL Rules Article 27.3; ICC Rules Article 25(5); Belgium Judicial Code Article 1700 s 4; Netherlands Code of Civil Procedure Article 1039 (4); English Arbitration Act 1996 s 34(2)(d).

6.11 Accordingly, although the power of a tribunal to order document production will nearly always exist, the exercise of that power will generally be a matter for the discretion of the tribunal. For a variety of reasons this may be unsatisfactory both to the parties and to the tribunal. As noted, depending on the backgrounds of individual tribunal members, a common law party may fear that it will not be able to obtain all of the documents that it considers it should have from the other party. A civil law party may fear that its common law opponent will obtain access to documents that the civil law party does not accept that its opponent should have. A tribunal may look for external guidance and a tried and tested route to navigate party disagreements. The regime for document production set out in the IBA Rules accommodates those concerns.

3. Development of the IBA Regime for Production of Documents

6.12 The IBA Rules make no provision for a general obligation of discovery of documents, under which a party has an automatic obligation to disclose to its opponent all documents that are germane to the dispute.

6.13 Accordingly, save for specific documents that may have been requested by a tribunal pursuant to Article 3.10,[9] documents on the record in the arbitration will derive only from those that each party has volunteered in support of its case, or that have been disclosed following a request for production made by one party to another. As mentioned, the latter process is regulated by Articles 3.2–3.8. The core provision is Article 3.3, which sets out the requirements that must be met in relation to the substance and content of a Request to Produce. Article 3.2 grants a party the right to deliver a Request to Produce and Articles 3.4–3.8 deal with the voluntary production of the requested documents by the party in possession, as well as with the raising and resolution of objections to production by that party. Article 9.2 sets out the grounds upon which objection to a request for production may be made.

6.14 Within the committee charged with drafting the 1999 IBA Rules, the issue of non-voluntary document production was the subject of heated debate between participants from different legal traditions. As noted in the commentary to the IBA Rules:

> The issue of whether and under what conditions one party should be able to request production of documents from another party occupied much of the Working Party's discussions in 1999. The vigour with which this issue was debated demonstrated that the question of document production was the key area in which practitioners from common law countries and civil law countries differ.[10]

6.15 The requirements of Article 3 of the IBA Rules were drafted in accordance with a number of principles articulated in the commentary to the 1999 IBA Rules and

[9] See 6.323-6.340.
[10] Commentary on the IBA Rules (n 5) 7.

expanded upon in the Commentary to the current (2010) IBA Rules. Those principles include the following:[11]

- Expansive American-style or English-style discovery is generally inappropriate in international arbitration;
- There is a general consensus, even among practitioners from civil law countries, that some level of document production is appropriate in international arbitration; and
- The scope of the permissible document production request is to be limited by certain objections set out in Article 9.2.

In broad terms, the regime arrived at in the IBA Rules has at its heart the requirement in Article 3.3 that, if a request for production of documents by another party is to be advanced, the document requested must be 'relevant to the case and material to its outcome'. The grounds for objection set out at Article 9.2 add further protections designed to contain the scope of document production under the rules to that representing a reasonable compromise between legal traditions, and in which the rights of the requesting and producing parties are properly balanced. **6.16**

The 1999 IBA Rules introduced the concept of 'relevant and material to outcome'. Provisions in the 1999 Rules expanded the limited document production contained in the 1983 Rules[12] and, for the first time, permitted a party to address a request to the tribunal for an order requiring production of internal documents from the other party's files. However, this right was made subject to a requirement that the request identify the documents with precision and include an explanation as to how those documents were 'relevant and material to the outcome of the case'.[13] The other party was permitted to raise an objection to the request on one of a number of grounds expressly provided for in the rules.[14] Those grounds for excluding evidence and denying requests for production (now set out in Article 9)—relevance and materiality, privilege, unreasonable burden, loss or destruction, commercial or technical confidentiality, political or institutional sensitivity, and considerations of fairness or equality—provided a series of checks and balances. These two mechanisms were the foundation for the provisions in the current IBA Rules. **6.17**

The 1999 IBA Rules attracted stinging criticism at a number of levels, including assertions that those rules facilitated unnecessary document production beyond what was necessary to protect a party's position, encouraged delay and costs, had the potential to increase antagonism between the parties, and could lead to a lack of party confidence in the tribunal when it was forced to make (arguably) premature **6.18**

[11] ibid 8.
[12] See Chapter 1 para 1.12.
[13] IBA Rules on the Taking of Evidence in International Commercial Arbitration 1999, Article 3.3 (hereafter '1999 IBA Rules').
[14] ibid Article 9.2.

decisions on document production without a proper appreciation of the issues in the case.[15]

6.19 Despite such criticisms, and with the benefit of the passage of time, the document production provisions contained in Article 3 have undoubtedly gained wide acceptance by arbitration practitioners from around the world. As noted in the Commentary to the IBA Rules, Article 3 represents a 'balanced approach' that is 'widely accepted by both common law and civil law practitioners'.[16] This is confirmed by statistical data that indicates there is no significant preference for use of IBA Rules in either common law countries or in civil law ones:

> In terms of the frequency with which the Rules on Evidence are referenced in common and civil law jurisdictions, the survey results interestingly do not indicate any significant difference between the two. By way of example, a relatively high number of English arbitrations referred to the [IBA Rules] (72%), while a lower number of U.S. arbitrations (56%) did so. The frequency of such references in France, however, appears to lie somewhere between the two (62 %).[17]

As one commentator puts it:

> A civil lawyer may find the Rules helpful when seeking to limit an extensive request for document production by a common law party; and a common law party may be able to use the Rules to obtain at least some internal documents from a civil law party which this party would otherwise not provide.[18]

6.20 However, there are still calls for amendment to Article 3, most often on the basis that the rules lean too far towards the common law approach to document production. An IBA Survey on the issue notes that:

> Respondents who call for a revision of Article 3 believe that the IBA Committee should further limit the scope of disclosure to strike a proper balance between the civil law tradition and the US legal culture. These respondents, based in both civil and common law jurisdictions, and from all regions but Africa, complained about the number and scope of document requests, as well as the cost and burden associated with addressing such requests. In their view, disclosure under Article 3 still resembles too closely discovery as it is practiced in common law litigation, or at least in the US.[19]

[15] Peter Hafter, 'The Provisions on the Discovery of Internal Documents in the IBA Rules of 1999' in Gerald Aksen (ed), *Global Reflections on International Law, Commerce and Dispute Resolution: Liber Amicorum in Honour of Robert Briner* (International Chamber of Commerce 2005) 347.

[16] Commentary on the IBA Rules (n 5) 7.

[17] 2016 IBA Report (n 3) para 39.

[18] Tobias Zuberbühler and others, *IBA Rules of Evidence: Commentary on the IBA Rules on the Taking of Evidence in International Arbitration* (Sellier European Law Publishers 2012) 40 (hereafter 'Zuberbühler')

[19] 2016 IBA Report (n 3) para 87. The development of the Prague Rules on the Efficient Conduct of Proceedings in International Arbitration issued in December 2018 are another manifestation of this disquiet. The Note from the Working Group, in the draft of 1 September 2018, explained the rationale of the Prague Rules: 'The drafters of the IBA Rules on the Taking of Evidence in International Arbitration (IBA Rules) bridged a gap between the common law and civil law traditions of taking evidence. The IBA Rules were very successful in developing a nearly standardized procedure in international arbitration, at least for proceedings involving Parties from different legal

Other mooted possibilities for change include a provision for automatic production of documents manifestly relevant to the dispute. This would be a radical amendment since, unlike the position under court rules in many common law jurisdictions,[20] there is no practice of automatic discovery of documents (helpful and adverse) in international commercial arbitration. It has been suggested that the introduction of such a requirement into the IBA Rules could be based on the obligation of parties to arbitration to act in good faith. There is force in this argument but, as has been recognized, pursuit of such a revision is probably best left for another day.[21] Despite these various suggestions for revision to the Article 3 regime, the prevailing view appears to be that the IBA Rules should not be amended for the time being.[22] In our view, if applied properly, the IBA regime for document production requests represents a reasonable compromise between legal traditions and is flexible enough to accommodate the majority of circumstances, and the diverse (or sometimes uniform) cultural mix existing in individual arbitrations. 6.21

O'Malley and other commentators suggest that the presumption in arbitration is that a party will establish its case based largely (if not entirely) on the documents within its own possession.[23] Applying that perspective, a wide-ranging discovery process that allows a party to substantiate a case by 'discovering' the primary evidence to support its arguments is not compatible with the threshold concept set out in Article 3.1, ie that a party to arbitration will produce the documents on which it relies. On the other hand, Article 3.3 avoids the restricted view of disclosure held in certain civil law jurisdictions. In particular, it expressly contemplates the production of categories of documents (rather than just specific identified documents), and (as a result of amendments first made in the 1999 IBA Rules) it does not exclude production of 'internal' documents held by another party. Overall, it represents a genuine compromise between the civil law approach of (predominantly) voluntary disclosure and the common law 'discovery' process described at 6.2. 6.22

traditions and those with significant amounts at stake. However, from a civil law perspective, the IBA Rules are still closer to common law traditions, as they follow a more adversarial approach regarding document production, fact witnesses and party-appointed experts. In addition the parties' entitlement to cross-examine witnesses is almost being taken for granted. [. . .]. In light of all of this, the drafters of the Prague Rules believe that developing the rules on taking evidence, which are based on the inquisitorial model of procedure and would enhance more active role of the Arbitral Tribunals, would contribute to increasing efficiency in international arbitration'.

---

[20] For example, this is the case in England. See CPR 31.6.

[21] See remarks in VV Veeder, 'Are the IBA Rules "Perfectible"?' in Teresa Giovannini and Alexis Mourre (eds), *Written Evidence and Discovery in International Arbitration: New Issues and Tendencies* (Kluwer Law International 2009) 321. An express obligation of good faith is contained in the IBA Rules on the Taking of Evidence in International Arbitration 2010, Preamble 3 (hereafter 'IBA Rules'). See Chapter 2. Veeder suggests that, in principle, the introduction of a requirement of production of all documents manifestly relevant to the substantive issues between the parties into the IBA Rules could be based on the obligation to act in good faith.

[22] 2016 IBA Report (n 3) para 79.

[23] Nathan O'Malley, 'Document production under Art.3 of the 2010 IBA Rules of Evidence' (2010) International Arbitration Law Review 186 (hereafter 'O'Malley Document Production'). See also Mark McNeil and Margaret Clare Ryan, 'Meeting the Requirements of Article 3(3) of the IBA Rules: Recommendations for Successful Requests for Document Production' in Julio César Betancourt (ed), *Defining Issues in International Arbitration: Celebrating 100 Years of the Chartered Institute of Arbitrators* (OUP 2016) para 17.06 (hereafter 'McNeil and Ryan').

6.23 However, it should be borne in mind that, although it is important not to lose sight of differing cultural perspectives, when it comes to operation of the Article 3 procedures in an individual arbitration those procedures should be applied as a standalone autonomous regime.

4. Changes Introduced by the 2010 IBA Rules

6.24 The current IBA Rules introduced some adjustments reflecting the ever-increasing volume of document production resulting from electronic communications. The definition of 'Documents' was revisited during drafting to ensure that it was adequate, and changes were made. The possible use of search teams to capture electronic documents was also introduced.[24] However, there was no fundamental rethinking of how document production of electronic documents should be managed. The draftsmen took a largely 'hands-off' approach towards such issues as data preservation measures, or possible limitations on the types of sources of electronic information that might be requested.[25] For the most part, electronic documents are treated in the same manner as paper documents.

6.25 A further related change influenced by the volume of e-documents introduced into arbitration, and the desire to cater for greater economy in the document production process, was the introduction of 'considerations of procedural economy' as a ground for excluding documents from production or oral testimony from evidence under Article 9.2.[26]

B. Documents Relied on by the Parties

3.1. Within the time ordered by the Arbitral Tribunal, each Party shall submit to the Arbitral Tribunal and to the other Parties all Documents available to it on which it relies, including public Documents and those in the public domain, except for any Documents that have already been submitted by another Party.

1. Obligation to Disclose Documents Relied upon

6.26 Article 3.1 imposes an obligation on each party to produce the documents upon which it relies in a timely fashion. This is consistent with the principle in Preamble 3 that each

[24] IBA Rules (n 21) Article 3.3(a)(ii). See also 6.69-6.75.

[25] See Richard Kreindler, 'The 2010 Revision to the IBA Rules on the Taking of Evidence in International Commercial Arbitration: A Study in Both Consistency and Progress' (2010) International Arbitration Law Review 157, 158 (hereafter 'Kreindler').

[26] See further Christopher Newmark, '"Efficient, Economical and Fair": The Mantra of the New IBA Rules' (2010) 13 International Arbitration Law Review 165.

party shall be entitled to know reasonably in advance of the evidentiary hearing the evidence on which the other parties rely. It helps avoid a situation in which a party is served with a large volume of documents shortly before the hearing.

2. What Is to Be Disclosed?

The requirement for disclosure of documents on which a party wishes to rely is uncontroversial. Leaving aside the question of timing, it is in that party's interests to produce these documents. The requirement has been present in the IBA Rules since they were first published.[27] Article 3.1 requires production of *all* documents available to a party upon which it relies. The only exception is that a party need not produce a document that has already been submitted by another party. It is not enough that the producing party believes that the other party already has a copy of the document. If it has not already been introduced into the arbitration then it must be produced under Article 3.1. There is no exception for documents that are in the public domain. Article 3.1 states expressly that these must be produced. **6.27**

3. Timing of Production

Under Article 3.1, production of documents relied on must take place 'within the time ordered by the Arbitral Tribunal'. The relevant deadlines will normally be set out in the procedural timetable. **6.28**

The parties may be required to produce the supporting documents that they rely on with their written submissions. They may be given an additional longstop date by which any other documents upon which they rely must be produced. That date may be the one contemplated by Article 3.11 (ie following document production, witness statements, and expert evidence) or an earlier one.[28] **6.29**

For the purposes of Article 3.1, we suggest that a date prior to delivery of witness/expert evidence is desirable since the witnesses/experts may not otherwise have an opportunity to address something important arising out of the documents. The further deadline referred to in Article 3.11 will provide a final opportunity to produce additional documents that have become relevant as a result of what is said in witness statements, expert evidence, or other documents produced (see 6.341-6.349 for more detail). **6.30**

[27] IBA Supplementary Rules Governing the Presentation and Reception of Evidence in International Commercial Arbitration 1983, Articles 4.1, 4.3.

[28] See 6.341-6.349.

6.31 The purpose behind these various deadlines is to ensure that other parties have sight of the documents at the earliest possible opportunity. This limits the possibility of any party gaining a tactical advantage by submitting documents late or so close to the hearing that the other party is not able to deal with them properly and, as a result, may suffer prejudice in presentation of its case. Of course, it is always open to the tribunal to adjust the timetable to give the receiving party more time, but this can then lead to procedural inefficiency.[29]

6.32 In practice, it is not uncommon to see a request from one or more parties to introduce new documentary evidence after the relevant deadline has passed. How the tribunal responds will depend on the facts of the case and the attitude of the individual tribunal members.

6.33 For example, a tribunal will generally admit new documents into the record where all parties agree to this.[30] Absent such agreement, some tribunals may expect the producing party to provide a compelling reason why the tribunal should admit the documents late. The tribunal may be willing to admit them if the producing party can demonstrate to the tribunal's satisfaction that it did not have, and could not have obtained, the documents any sooner.

6.34 In circumstances where the evidence suggests that the producing party *could* have submitted the documents earlier but *chose* not to in order to gain a tactical advantage, a robust tribunal may refuse to admit them after the deadline has passed. Other tribunals may take a pragmatic approach and admit documents even where there is no satisfactory explanation for the delay and the other party does not agree to their admission. If the tribunal has seen the documents it may conclude that they are not material to the tribunal's determination and so can be safely admitted, and discounted in the award, without prejudice to either party. Some tribunals may admit the documents without any such analysis simply because they are concerned that if they do not, the award will be vulnerable to challenge on the basis that the producing party was denied the opportunity to put its case.[31]

6.35 Decisions by tribunals not to admit documents filed after a procedural deadline has passed have been upheld by courts.[32] In one ICC case where the tribunal took a robust approach, the tribunal made the following comments:

> The arbitrators have a duty to take into account the fundamental right of each party to present its case properly, but they also have a duty to ensure that the

[29] Nathan D O'Malley, *Rules of Evidence in International Arbitration: An Annotated Guide* (Informa Law/ Routledge 2012) para 3.06 (hereafter 'O'Malley Rules of Evidence').

[30] For discussion see ibid para 3.08.

[31] Of course, if the documents are material, and the other party is prejudiced by their late admission, the award could be subject to a challenge from the other side.

[32] For discussion and examples of cases in the Netherlands, the US, and Switzerland, see O'Malley Rules of Evidence (n 29) para 3.06 and (n 9).

> arbitration progresses at a reasonable pace and to avoid unwarranted or deliberate delays. If a party which has had ample opportunity to prepare its case or to submit requests to the arbitral tribunal at an earlier stage of the proceedings, applies to the tribunal, belatedly and without giving legitimate reasons for tardiness, with requests which are liable to cause substantial delays, it may well be the duty of the arbitrators to continue the arbitration without accepting the request of the tardy party.[33]

Where it is clear that a party could have produced documents earlier and chose not to do so as a part of its tactical strategy then, even if the documents are admitted, a tribunal may consider it appropriate to sanction the producing party in costs pursuant to Article 9.7 of the IBA Rules. **6.36**

C. Request to Produce Documents

3.2. Within the time ordered by the Arbitral Tribunal, any Party may submit to the Arbitral Tribunal and to the other Parties a Request to Produce.

3.3. A Request to Produce shall contain:

(a) (i) a description of each requested Document sufficient to identify it; or

(ii) a description in sufficient detail (including subject matter) of a narrow and specific requested category of Documents that are reasonably believed to exist; in the case of Documents maintained in electronic form, the requesting Party may, or the Arbitral Tribunal may order that it shall be required to, identify specific files, search terms, individuals or other means of searching for such Documents in an efficient and economical manner;

(b) a statement as to how the Documents requested are relevant to the case and material to its outcome; and

(c) (i) a statement that the Documents requested are not in the possession, custody or control of the requesting Party or a statement of the reasons why it would be unreasonably burdensome for the requesting Party to produce such Documents, and

(ii) a statement of the reasons why the requesting Party assumes the Documents requested are in the possession, custody or control of another Party.

[33] Letter from the President of the Arbitral Tribunal in ICC Case No 6465 in Dominique Hascher (ed) *Collection of Procedural Decisions in ICC Arbitration 1993–1996* (Kluwer Law International 1997) 82

6.37 Articles 3.2 and 3.3 of the IBA Rules deal with the delivery and content of a request for production of documents made by one party to another.

1. Party Right to Deliver a Request to Produce

6.38 Article 3.2 states expressly that any party may deliver a request for documents to any other party to the arbitration.

6.39 It is, of course, open to parties to an international arbitration to agree to limit the scope of document production, or to exclude it altogether. The ICC Commission Report on Controlling Time and Costs in Arbitration identifies an agreement to limit the number of permitted document production requests as a technique for managing document production efficiently.[34] We are aware of cases in which parties have agreed that they will each make no more than five document production requests. The ICC Guide for Effective Management of Arbitration[35] highlights that the ICC Rules contain no specific provisions governing document production and that the parties may agree on the procedures to be applied. Suggested options mentioned in the Guide include no document production at all.

6.40 In practice, parties rarely consider document production procedures when drafting their arbitration agreement. In one survey on document production in international arbitration, 73 per cent of respondents said that they rarely or never included a procedure for document production in their arbitration clauses; 15 per cent said that they sometimes included such provisions; and only 6 per cent said that they frequently did so.[36] Even when parties consider the issue, they may be reluctant to agree to limit or exclude the right to request documents from an opponent party.[37] Until a dispute arises it is difficult to anticipate what categories of document will be relevant and therefore which party will hold them. Once a dispute has arisen, the potential for agreement is much diminished.

6.41 We suggest that the possibility of limiting document production requests should be on the agenda for discussion during the consultation process required under Article 2 of

[34] *ICC Arbitration Commission Report on Controlling Time and Costs in Arbitration* (International Chamber of Commerce 2018) paras 49–57 (hereafter 'ICC Report on Controlling Time and Costs').

[35] *Effective Management of Arbitration: A Guide for In-House Counsel and Other Party Representatives* (International Chamber of Commerce 2014) 33. Topic Sheet 6 goes on to describe some of the factors parties should take into account in deciding what approach to document production is sensible in an individual case, and advocates the use of a cost/benefit analysis.

[36] Berwin Leighton Paisner, '2013 International Arbitration Survey on Document Production in International Arbitration'.

[37] See further Marghitola (n 1) 160, who concludes that the practice of limiting or excluding document production is unlikely to gain broad acceptance in practice. See also Jarred Pinkston, 'The Case for a Continental European Arbitral Institution to Limit Document Production' in Nikolaus Pitkowitz and others, *Austrian Yearbook on International Arbitration 2011* (Manz'sche Verlags- und Universitätsbuchhandlung 2011) 87, which considers the potential for arbitral institutions to set limits to document production.

the IBA Rules. The parties' willingness to place limits on the number or scope of document production requests may aid efficiency in time and costs.

2. Timing of a Request to Produce

As to timing of the Request to Produce, Article 3.2 simply says that the Request to Produce should be delivered within the time ordered by the tribunal. A deadline for delivery of requests to produce is often contained in the first procedural order following discussion with the parties on the procedural timetable. In cases where such consultation takes place pursuant to Article 2 of the IBA Rules, one of the suggested agenda items for discussion set out in that provision is 'the requirements, procedure and format applicable to production of documents'. Discussion around this is likely to include debate on appropriate dates for delivery of requests to produce and how this step fits into the overall procedural timetable. What those dates are will depend on the individual circumstances of the case. **6.42**

In general, the procedural framework into which a Request to Produce will fit is relatively straightforward. Each party will volunteer in advance of the document production phase all of the documents on which it intends to rely (as prescribed by Article 3.1 of the IBA Rules), sometimes with its written submissions. Under Article 3.2 of the IBA Rules, the parties will then deliver—by a date fixed by the tribunal—their document production requests containing the information set out in Article 3.3, including a statement explaining the relevance and materiality of the requested documents. The parties will then usually be given a reasonable time in which to either produce the requested documents or to provide details of any applicable grounds of objection under Article 3.3 and/or Article 9.2. There may be an opportunity for the requesting party to respond to the objections. In the event that the objection to production cannot be resolved between the parties, the requesting party may ask the tribunal to make an order for production under Article 3.7. **6.43**

As discussed elsewhere, the Article 3.1 provision for voluntary production of documents relied on, the requirements of the IBA Rules as to the content of a Request to Produce, as well as other factors of more general application may all have some influence on the precise date for delivery of document production requests.[38] It has been suggested that best practice is for document production to take place between the first and second round of written submissions.[39] **6.44**

We agree that this is likely to be the approach adopted in many arbitrations, although it may require some adaptation according to the circumstances of the case, particularly **6.45**

[38] See 6.113-6.119.
[39] Zuberbühler (n 18) 46.

where English-style pleadings are utilized and the range of issues that can be identified from first round pleadings are limited.

3. The Content of a Request to Produce

a. Introduction and overview

6.46 Article 3.3 lays down requirements relating to the substantive content of a Request to Produce Documents.

6.47 These requirements are an important part of the checks and balances that exist within the IBA Rules, and which are designed to maintain an appropriate balance between 'too much' and 'too little' document production, as viewed from the perspectives of parties from different legal traditions, and in the interests of efficiency of process.[40]

6.48 In summary, under Article 3.3 of the IBA Rules, the Request to Produce must contain:

(a) a narrow and specific description of the document(s) requested;[41]
(b) a statement as to why the requested documents are relevant to the case and material to its outcome;[42]
(c) a statement that the requested documents are not in the possession, custody, or control of the requesting party, or a statement that it would be unreasonably burdensome for that party to have to produce them;[43] and
(d) the reasons why the requesting party assumes that the documents requested are in the possession, custody, or control of the party to whom the request is addressed.[44]

6.49 In general terms, even when contested, a Request to Produce documents should succeed under the IBA Rules where:

(a) the requirements of Article 3.3 have been met;
(b) the tribunal considers that the issues that the requesting party wishes to prove by means of the documents are relevant to the case and material to its outcome;[45] and

[40] See Commentary on the IBA Rules (n 5). Despite the wide acceptance of the IBA regime, the mechanisms for controlling documents production contained in the IBA Rules remain the subject of ongoing debate. For example, Jaffe, Dulani, and Stute say that 'the scope of production continues to divide scholars and practitioners alike'. Lotfi notes that 'Given the diverging domestic standards regarding document production, international arbitration is a prime battleground for conflicting approaches'. See Michael Jaffe, Jeetander Dulani, and David Stute, 'Burden of Proof as a Prerequisite to Document Production Under the 2010 IBA Rules: An Obituary' (2017) 1 Transnational Dispute Management <www.transnational-dispute-management.com/article.asp?key=2440> accessed 29 November 2018 (hereafter 'Jaffe, Dulani, and Stute'); Courtney Lotfi, 'Documentary Evidence and Document Production in International Arbitration' (2014) 4 Transnational Dispute Management <www.transnational-dispute-management.com/article.asp?key=2136> accessed 29 November 2018 (hereafter 'Lotfi').
[41] IBA Rules (n 21) Article 3.3(a).
[42] ibid Article 3.3(b).
[43] ibid Article 3.3(c)(i).
[44] ibid Article 3.3(c)(ii).
[45] ibid Article 3.7. See also 6.239-6.252.

(c) none of the grounds for objection raised under Article 9.2 of the IBA Rules is found to apply.[46]

Some commentators have expressed the view that a number of the requirements to be applied under Article 3.3 remain uncertain and subject to conflicting views, with the result that the document production phase of an arbitration remains highly contentious, and often costly and time-consuming.[47] We do not disagree that document production is often hotly disputed and extremely expensive. Whether that outcome can be laid at the door of the IBA Rules, rather than the parties themselves, is a different question. **6.50**

b. Description of the document

> **3.3 (a) (i) a description of each requested Document sufficient to identify it, or**
> **(ii) a description in sufficient detail (including subject matter) of a narrow and specific requested category of Documents that are reasonably believed to exist; in the case of Documents maintained in electronic form, the requesting Party may, or the Arbitral Tribunal may order that it shall be required to, identify specific files, search terms, individuals or other means of searching for such Documents in an efficient and economical manner;**

i. Introduction

Article 3.3(a) requires the requesting party to provide a description of the document it wants. **6.51**

A party may request either an individual document, or a narrow and specific category of documents.[48] Whatever document is sought, the description should be such that the producing party can easily understand whether a document it holds falls within the terms of the request. **6.52**

ii. Individual documents

Where an individual document is sought, the description provided in the Request to Produce must be 'sufficient to identify it'.[49] **6.53**

In many ways it is more straightforward to seek production of an individual document than a category of documents. When a party seeks production of an individual document, that party will generally have a very clear idea of what it is. In **6.54**

[46] See Chapter 12, paras 12.57–12.316.
[47] McNeil and Ryan (n 23) para 17.02.
[48] The Commentary on the IBA Rules (n 5) notes that the facility to make a request by reference to an individual document *or* by 'describing "in sufficient detail (including subject matter) . . . a narrow and specific requested category of Documents that are reasonably believed to exist" was a compromise between the common law and civil law systems'.
[49] IBA Rules (n 21) Article 3.3(a)(i).

some instances, the requesting party may have found a reference to or description of the document in another piece of evidence or in a public register. For example, a document already on the record in the arbitration may refer to a specific email or letter from the other party to a third party, or it may be clear from the first document that it addresses matters that have been raised in another document. In such circumstances, it is often relatively easy for the requesting party to identify the letter by date and sender/recipient, or by a description, perhaps cross-referenced to the document in which it is mentioned. In other cases, the requesting party may not know a precise date or author but is nonetheless able to describe the document in a way that will still permit the producing party to identify it. For example, in relation to payment of a certain amount made to company X in August of a given year, it may be possible to request production of the payment order by means of a description referencing those matters. The requirements of Article 3.3(a)(i) will be met because the description is sufficient for the respondent to search for and identify the document.

iii. Categories of document

6.55 Article 3.3(a) also allows parties to request a category of documents as long as the category of documents requested is 'narrow and specific' and the category of documents is 'reasonably believed to exist'.[50]

6.56 In many cases, a requesting party may not know the details of specific documents and will have to frame its request by reference to a category of documents. The requirements mentioned are designed to ensure that the right to request a category of documents is not used as a basis for a 'fishing expedition', while at the same time not shutting out reasonable requests for documents that are germane to issues in the case. The Commentary to the IBA Rules mentions the example of an arbitration involving the termination by one party of a joint venture agreement. The requesting party may know that a notice of the termination was given on a certain date, that the Board of the other party must have made the decision to terminate at a meeting shortly before that notice, that certain documents must have been prepared for the Board's consideration of that decision, and that minutes must have been taken concerning the decision. The requesting party cannot identify the dates or the authors of such documents, but nevertheless can identify with some particularity the nature of the documents sought and the general time frame in which they would have been prepared. Such a request may qualify as a 'narrow and specific category of Documents', as permitted under Article 3.3(a)(ii).[51]

50 ibid Article 3.3(a)(ii).

51 Commentary on the IBA Rules (n 5) describes the discussions on this topic that took place between those responsible for drafting the IBA provisions.

Narrow and specific Although the term 'narrow and specific' may sometimes be construed differently by arbitrators with civil or common law backgrounds (or even by arbitrators with the same legal background), it seems to be common ground that a request for a category of documents should not be couched in nebulous terms. For example, a request for 'any and all documents', references to lengthy time frames, and/or 'relating' to a broad description of subject matter are, in most cases, judged by tribunals to be too broad and failing to meet the 'narrow and specific' standard.[52] **6.57**

Where the inadequacy of a request is less obvious a more considered approach to assessing its legitimacy may be required and the approach taken by different tribunals may vary. **6.58**

It is suggested that the 'narrow and specific' standard has generally been understood to apply to both the time frame for a Request to Produce, as well as its subject matter.[53] Some tribunals have indicated other requirements. In one ICC case, in which the need for a high degree of specificity was acknowledged, it was suggested that a request for a category of documents should, for example, describe the kind of document, the identity of the authors and their addressees, cover a narrow time period, describe the contents and the other characteristics of the documents sought, and in general allow the other party to divine precisely what documents were responsive to the request.[54] **6.59**

In our view, the correct approach is to consider whether the description provided in the request is adequate to enable the party on whom the request is served to judge without too much difficulty whether a particular document it has in its possession falls within the category of documents requested or outside of it. **6.60**

Where a request for a category of documents is overbroad, and is contested, many tribunals will deny the request and there is therefore an element of risk in drafting requests too widely. However, some tribunals may invite the requesting party to refine the request. A certain amount of negotiation on the scope of a particular request may also take place between the parties. For more detail on this point see 6.258-6.261. **6.61**

Examples Box 6.1 provides some examples of ICC cases cited by Hamilton[55] where a tribunal regarded a request for a category of documents as being insufficiently specific and *refused* to make an order for production in the terms of the request. **6.62**

[52] O'Malley Rules of Evidence (n 29) para 3.35 (internal references are omitted).
[53] ibid para 3.34.
[54] Virginia Hamilton, 'Document Production in ICC Arbitration' in *Special Supplement 2006: Document Production in International Arbitration* (International Chamber of Commerce 2006) 63, 71 (hereafter 'Hamilton').
[55] ibid.

Box 6.1 Examples of ICC Cases Cited by Hamilton

Example 1
Correspondence, reports, meeting minutes, notes, internal memoranda, and emails relating to twelve specified topics and a period exceeding six years.

Example 2
Copies of any correspondence or other written communications to or from potential buyers or their representatives regarding or referring to their receipt of the internal audit reports and/or the internal audit reports themselves.

Example 3
Copies of documents setting out [Company X]'s policies with respect to (a) the [Y] business, and/or (b) the receipt of cash deposits in [country Z].

Example 4
All Field Site Instruction for Areas [A], [B], [C], and [D] . . .

Example 5
The requesting party was seeking production of 'documents assessing or relating to the assessment of [Company X]'s equity, created between [date A] and [date B], excluding [Company X]'s and [Respondent]'s financial statements and documents (such as documents produced by . . .) generated for the purpose of preparing [Company X]'s and [Respondent]'s financial statements in the normal course of business.'

In example 5, the tribunal made the following observation:

> The description 'assessing or relating to the assessment of [Company] X's equity' does not elicit the type of automatic understanding of the nature of the responsive document, or category of documents, sought, which a sufficiently detailed document request—indicating narrow parameters such as the authors, recipients, specific contents, and specific characteristics of the documents—would. Virtually any [Company X] document could be interpreted as 'relating' in some way to the assessment of its equity and, therefore, be covered by this document request.

6.63 National courts have in appropriate cases endorsed the decision of a tribunal to dismiss a request for documents not framed in sufficiently precise terms, and have found that such dismissal did not result in unfair treatment of the requesting party. For example, in one case drawn to our attention, proceedings were initiated before the Paris Court of Appeal to set aside an arbitral award for, inter alia, lack of due process.[56] The court

[56] CA Paris 19 January 1999 No. 133395. Case details provided by French respondent to the BCLP Survey on the use of the IBA Rules.

held that a tribunal rightly dismissed a request for production of another party's entire correspondence on grounds that the Request to Produce was not sufficiently specific.

Volume of documents An interesting question arises in relation to the volume of documents potentially caught by a document production request. If such volume is extremely large, does this suggest that the request is insufficiently narrow? We do not think that volume can be relevant to the adequacy of the description of the category of document requested, although it may give rise to other grounds of objection to production.[57] A request may describe a category of documents very precisely and it simply be the case that a large number of documents meeting that description exists.[58] **6.64**

Reasonably believed to exist In addition to the requirement that the category of documents requested be a narrow and specific category, Article 3.3(a) requires that the documents requested are 'reasonably believed to exist'. If the request is contested by the other party and the requesting party has to seek an order for production from the tribunal, the tribunal will have to be satisfied that there is a reasonable basis for belief in the existence of the documents. Accordingly, we suggest that it is an implied requirement, and that it would be prudent that the requesting party mention the grounds for belief in the request, particularly where this is not obvious from the nature of the documents requested. **6.65**

For example, in a construction dispute between an employer and main contractor relating to particular aspects of the project for which the contractor seeks an extension of time, the employer may be arguing that the delay was caused by problems with the contractor's design. The employer may wish to see correspondence between the main contractor and subcontractors relating to any problems with a particular component over the period when the alleged delay occurred. Where it is clear from the contract documents or other correspondence that the main contractor has used subcontractors on the relevant part of the project, the employer will have reasonable grounds for believing that correspondence between the main contractors and the subcontractor will exist and may wish to explain this in the document request. **6.66**

Individual documents can be sought without such qualification,[59] probably because when requesting a specific document, the description of the document will contain details such as a date and sender/recipient, which will tend to confirm its existence. When it comes to a category, the request is necessarily broader and to prevent a fishing exercise the requesting party must be able to point to circumstances that suggest the existence of the documents. **6.67**

4. Documents Maintained in Electronic Form

Article 3.3(a)(ii) also specifically deals with a situation where a party requests production of documents held in electronic form. The provision highlights ways in which the **6.68**

[57] For example, that it would be unreasonably burdensome to have to produce the documents; see IBA Rules (n 21) Article 9.2(c).

[58] See further O'Malley Rules of Evidence (n 29) para 3.38 (internal references are omitted).

[59] Article 3.3(a)(i) makes no mention of a reasonable belief that the individual document exists.

search for such documents may be made more efficient and economical by the provision of additional information.

a. General approach to electronic documents

6.69 A number of modest revisions introduced into the IBA Rules in 2010 are directed at the growing use of e-discovery.[60] Aside from these changes there was no fundamental re-thinking of how document production of electronic documents should be managed.[61] In substance, under the IBA Rules electronic documents are treated in the same way as paper documents. There is no additional express provision dealing with particular issues generated by the nature and volume of electronic documents—for example, data preservation measures, or a limitation on the types of sources of electronic information that may be requested—or a separate regime for production of electronic documents.

6.70 The absence of the latter has been seen by some as a positive feature of the 2010 IBA Rules. For example, it has been said that:

> Issuing an entire set of new rules for production of electronic documents as part of the 2010 Rules would have been likely to lead to unwanted and unfortunate results. In particular, new detailed rules may well have led to an increase of the production of electronic documents and hence document production in general. [...] it is thought that the 1999 Rules contributed to an overall increase of document production in international arbitration practice, and the same might have happened if the 2010 Rules had been amended by detailed rules on e-disclosure. Accordingly, a well-intended 'cure' may have eventually become a part of the 'disease' itself. Moreover, a new set of rules as to production of electronic documents might, in effect, jeopardise the flexibility of the parties and the arbitrators to address such issues in view of the particular circumstances of the case.[62]

6.71 In our view, and despite the absence of detailed provisions on electronic document production, it clearly lies within the discretionary powers of a tribunal operating under the IBA Rules to take an active role in relation to the management of e-documents or related issues should it wish to do so.[63]

b. Search parameters

6.72 Article 3.3(a)(ii) states expressly that:

> ... in the case of Documents maintained in electronic form, the requesting Party may, or the Arbitral Tribunal may order that it shall be required to, identify specific files,

[60] These included changes to the definition of 'Document', and the introduction into Article 3.3(a)(ii) of the provision described at 6.72. As mentioned earlier in the text, another change influenced by the volume of e-documents introduced into arbitration, and the desire to cater for greater economy in the document production process, was the introduction of 'considerations of procedural economy' as a ground for excluding documents or oral testimony from production or evidence; see 6.25.

[61] The Commentary on the IBA Rules (n 5) notes that the rules are 'neutral regarding whether electronic documents should be produced in any given arbitration; they simply provide a framework for doing so where the parties agree or the tribunal orders production of such documents'.

[62] Zuberbühler (n 18) 38.

[63] For example, pursuant to IBA Rules (n 21) Preamble 3 and Article 2. See further Kreindler (n 25) 157.

search terms, individuals or other means of searching for such Documents in an efficient and economical manner.

The proposed use of search terms and other search parameters is intended to assist in making the search for electronic documents that are the subject of a Request to Produce as efficient as possible, bearing in mind that the volume of electronic documents that a party may possess may often run into tens of thousands of documents, if not more. The availability of this mechanism applies to a request for production of a category of documents.[64]

Given the volume of documents held electronically by most commercial parties, it is simply not feasible or cost-efficient for a manual search/review of all of those documents to take place in all cases. Even where a party has the necessary resources, the costs associated with such a search may well be disproportionate. Out of necessity the parties must therefore employ search parameters as a filter to catch documents that may fall within the category of documents requested. A manual review of that set of captured documents (sometimes referred to as the review set) will then generally be done to identify those documents from the review set that do fall within the request, and those documents within that group that may be privileged or sensitive. The skill in this exercise is to formulate initial search parameters that are not too narrow so that the risk of missing important documents is high, and not so wide so that the set to be manually reviewed is too large. Although the advent of predictive coding[65] has the potential to improve upon and possibly supersede this approach to finding electronic documents, for the moment at least, the use of appropriate search criteria remains an important element in trying to manage and contain the burden of electronic document production while at the same time ensuring so far as possible that relevant and material documents are made accessible to the requesting party. **6.73**

This express reference to the power of a tribunal to require formulation of appropriate search terms is consistent with guidelines on production of electronic documents found elsewhere.[66] **6.74**

In our view a request for documents in electronic form should volunteer suggested search criteria formulated by reference to as many as possible of the following parameters: **6.75**

Date range: In most cases it should be relatively straightforward to identify a date range. It should be as narrow as possible and linked to the likely time period within which

[64] Formulation of appropriate search parameters to find an individual document required by IBA Rules (n 21) Article 3.3(a)(i) should be relatively straightforward.

[65] Predictive coding is machine-learning technology driven by human tuition. A senior lawyer reviews a small 'seed set' of documents, which is then analysed by the software programme and used to generate a further sample of documents for review. Through a process of iterative refinement, an algorithm in the software used to harvest relevant documents can reach a level of review accuracy that can be applied across the entire data set, identifying relevant documents in a manner that is far more efficient and scalable than a traditional document review. A series of sample reviews, privilege sweeps, and other human interventions can then be used to verify the results and finalize the documents prior to production. See further Chapter 5, paras 5.84–5.85.

[66] For example, see *ICDR Guidelines for Arbitrators Concerning Exchanges of Information* (International Centre for Dispute Resolution 2008) Article 4 (hereafter 'ICDR Guidelines').

documents in the particular category of documents described are likely to have been created, with perhaps a small degree of leeway either side of those dates. For example, a request for correspondence relating to what was agreed at a meeting between named individuals on a particular date is likely to have been generated in a relatively short period after the date of the meeting.

Custodians (identified by name or email address): Identification of individuals who are likely to be the sender, recipient, or author of documents requested, or likely to hold such documents by reason of their role or function is extremely useful. Searches can be made by reference to these details. Depending on how conscientious the requesting party is, there are various refinements that may be made to limit custodian related searches. For example, a request for emails passing between Mr A and Mr B will produce two copies of each email (the one sent and the one received). In contrast, if the request limits the search to email folders of Mr A and asks for emails to or from Mr B, only one copy should be produced. In practice, the wider search may not impose a significant additional burden because of the availability of software that can deduplicate a data set to remove identical copies. However, all such methods of limiting searches for documents in electronic form should be carefully considered.

Search terms. Date and custodian criteria can impose useful limits on a search for electronic documents. However, depending on the nature of the business being conducted by the party in possession of the documents, application of these filters alone may still produce a large volume of irrelevant documents. It is therefore useful to identify particular words or phrases that are likely to occur in the particular documents being sought, either on their own or in combination with other words or phrases. Clearly, to be useful, these must be specific to the particular subject matter of the documents. For example, in a dispute between an hotel owner and a large management company with responsibility for a number of hotels, where the owner claims the management company is in breach of contract for letting customer service standards slip at the owner's hotel, a search for 'complaint' in the management company's records has the potential to pull up a large number of documents unrelated to the owner's hotel. If that search were run in combination with the name of the owner's hotel, a more targeted set of documents might be produced.

File types: to avoid misunderstanding it is prudent to indicate the standard file types that the requesting party expects to receive (for example, .pst files (emails), Microsoft Word files, pdf files, .msg, .xls/xlsx, .ppt/.pptx, and jpg files, although some parties will wish to make clear that this is a non-exhaustive list.

5. Statement of Relevance and Materiality

3.3(b). a statement as to how the Documents requested are relevant to the case and material to its outcome.

a. Introduction

Article 3.3(b) expresses a requirement that a Request to Produce contain a statement as to why the documents requested of the other party are 'relevant to the case and material to its outcome'. The requirement of relevance and materiality, as well as the specificity requirement set out in Article 3.3(a),[67] are critical elements of a document production request made under the IBA Rules.[68] 6.76

The benchmark of relevance and materiality underpins each of the tests for introduction of evidence contained in the IBA Rules. In addition to the requirement at Article 3.3(b), there is express provision for application of this benchmark at Article 2.3(a); Article 3.7; Article 3.10;[69] Article 3.11; Article 4.9; Article 4.10; Article 8.2; Article 8.5; Article 9.1; and Article 9.2(a). Those provisions are addressed in detail elsewhere in this text. Although the benchmark is the same in each case, the stage of the proceedings at which it is applied, the facts of the case, and the other requirements of the particular provision being applied are all factors that will all influence the outcome of its operation in each case. 6.77

The benchmark of relevance and materiality is one of the tools given to a tribunal to help it ensure that document production assists, rather than frustrates, an efficient determination of the dispute. Importantly, the benchmark also sets parameters for document production that—for the most part—are acceptable to parties and practitioners from different legal traditions. As mentioned, if applied robustly it can prevent 'fishing expeditions', but will also facilitate introduction into evidence of documents that are germane to the dispute. 6.78

At a practical level, confining document production within reasonable parameters assists in reducing the number of documents introduced to the record in an arbitration. The large and growing volume of documentary evidence used in international arbitration brings a number of challenges. It often involves delay, as documents are searched for, reviewed, delivered, and digested. It can also involve significant additional costs that, as well as being generally undesirable, can exacerbate inequalities of resources between parties. In addition, while the parties may very often have teams of lawyers and experts available to pore over these documents, the same is not true of arbitrators, who are very often expected to wade through a vast amount of material that later turns out to be of little significance.[70] A review of the transcripts of evidentiary hearings, and of 6.79

[67] See 6.51-6.67.

[68] Although these two requirements are contained in two separate provisions, the point has been made that where a category of documents (rather than an individual document) is being requested under IBA Rules (n 21) Article 3.3(a)(ii), the requirement that the request contain 'a description in sufficient detail (including subject matter) . . . ' creates a direct link to the relevance requirement under Article 3.3(b); Marghitola (n 1) 37–39.

[69] Although this provision does not contain an express reference to relevance and materiality, a party to whom the arbitral tribunal has addressed a request for documents under this provision is entitled to object to such production on any of the grounds set out in IBA Rules (n 21) Article 9.2 (ie including on grounds that the documents lack 'sufficient relevance to the case or materiality to its outcome').

[70] Depending on the tribunal's appetite for reviewing files of documents and/or the time available to them to do so, the need to deal with a large volume of documents may have adverse consequences for the arbitration process. See Michael E Schneider, 'Chapter 9. The Paper Tsunami in International Arbitration: Problems, Risks for the Arbitrators' Decision Making and Possible Solutions' in Teresa Giovannini and Alexis Mourre (eds), *Written*

the final award(s) in many arbitrations, will show that the number of key documents referred to by the parties, and relied on by the tribunal, is usually few in number.

b. 'Relevant and material' as best practice in international arbitration

6.80 Whether the benchmark of relevance and materiality introduced under the 1999 IBA Rules[71] led the way, or followed an emerging approach, it is clear that the current IBA formulation represents accepted best practice for document production in international arbitration. In some cases, the benchmark may be stated expressly in the applicable arbitration rules (see, for example, SIAC Rules Article 27(b); SCC Rules Article 31(3); and HKIAC Rules Article 22.3). In other cases, it is not mentioned, but the test of relevance and materiality is nonetheless applied by the tribunal.

6.81 The LCIA Rules omit any reference to materiality;[72] however, in the leading commentary on the LCIA Rules, it is noted that the benchmark of relevance and materiality set out in the IBA Rules is frequently adopted by LCIA tribunals. When commenting on application of Article 22.1(v) the authors say:

> International arbitrators will have different approaches to the scope of disclosure each party must make. Arbitrators from civil law jurisdictions are often said to be less keen to order disclosure than their colleagues from common law jurisdictions. However, in recent years growing reliance has been placed by many international arbitrators, including in LCIA arbitration proceedings, on the provisions of the IBA Rules on the Taking of Evidence in International Arbitration. In particular, Articles 3 and 9.2 of the IBA Rules are regularly cited as containing the relevant principles governing documentary disclosure in international arbitration.

Thus, the requesting party will have to satisfy the Arbitral Tribunal that . . . the document is '. . . *relevant to the case, and material to the outcome* . . .'.[73]

6.82 The ICC Rules contain no provision dealing specifically with the production of documentary evidence.[74] However, the ICC Commission Report on Techniques for Controlling Time and Costs in Arbitration recommends that the parties and the

Evidence and Discovery in International Arbitration: New Issues and Tendencies (Kluwer Law International 2009) 366.

---

71 The formulation under the 1999 IBA Rules (n 13) was slightly different. Article 3.3(b) of those earlier rules required a statement as to how the documents requested are 'relevant and material to the outcome of the case'. The significance of the difference between the two formulations is discussed at 6.91.

72 LCIA Rules, Article 22.1(v).

73 Shai Wade, Philip Clifford, and James Clanchy, *Commentary on the LCIA Arbitration Rules 2014* (Sweet & Maxwell 2015) paras 22-013–22-014 (emphasis added).

74 ICC Rules Article 25(1): 'The arbitral tribunal shall proceed within as short a time as possible to establish the facts of the case by all appropriate means'. The manner in which this is to be achieved is left very much to the tribunal's discretion. Those rules also allow the tribunal to summon the parties to provide additional evidence at any point in the proceedings; ICC Rules Article 25(5). It should be noted that the provisions of the ICC Rules also contemplate that reference may be had to the rules of procedure of the applicable national procedural law. ICC Rules Article 19 states that the 'proceedings before the arbitral tribunal shall be governed by the Rules and, where the Rules are silent, by any rules which the parties or, failing them, the arbitral tribunal may settle on, whether or not reference is thereby made to the rules of procedure of a national law to be applied to the arbitration'. This is confirmed in Hamilton (n 54) 63.

tribunal should consider referring to Article 3 of the IBA Rules for guidance and limiting requests to the production of documents that are relevant and material to the outcome of the case.[75] The list of case management techniques available to tribunals for controlling time and costs suggested at Appendix IV of the ICC Rules suggests the same approach.[76]

One review of ICC procedural orders indicates that, in just over half of the ICC orders examined, the tribunal referred to the relevance and materiality of the documents when deciding whether or not to order their production. The review also noted a number of references made by tribunals to the IBA Rules as an embodiment of accepted good practice.[77] **6.83**

The ICC Task Force on E-Discovery adopted a broadly similar formulation to the relevance and materiality benchmark in the IBA Rules, providing also for considerations of proportionality in addition to picking up the requirements of specificity stated in Article 3.3(a)(ii).[78] There are many other examples.[79] **6.84**

There are exceptions to this approach. A small number of arbitration rules contain express reference to a different benchmark. For example, Article 50(b) of the WIPO Rules refers to the power of the tribunal to order production of documents that the tribunal considers 'necessary or appropriate'.[80] The ICSID Rules state that production of documents may be ordered by a tribunal where it 'deems it necessary'.[81] **6.85**

It might be argued that the standard for document production contained in these alternative formulations imposes a more onerous burden on the requesting party than the relevance and materiality test laid down in the IBA Rules. However, there is some evidence to suggest that, in practice, tribunals may see little difference between these benchmarks.[82] For example, a procedural order issued by one ICSID tribunal contained the following statement: **6.86**

[75] ICC Report on Controlling Time and Costs (n 34) paras 51, 52.
[76] ICC Rules 2012 Appendix IV: Case Management Techniques, para(d)(iii).
[77] Hamilton (n 54).
[78] *ICC Arbitration Commission Report on Managing E-Document Production* (International Chamber of Commerce 2012) para 3.12 (hereafter 'ICC Report on Managing E-Document Production'; emphasis added). See further Gary B Born, *International Commercial Arbitration* (2nd edn, Kluwer Law International 2014) 2359 (hereafter 'Born').
[79] See *CPR Protocol on Disclosure of Documents and Presentation of Witnesses in Commercial Arbitration* (International Institute for Conflict Prevention & Resolution 2009) Section 1(a) (hereafter 'CPR Protocol'); see also ICDR Guidelines (n 66) Article 2, Article 3(a).
[80] WIPO Arbitration Rules Article 50(b): 'At any time during the arbitration, the Tribunal may, at the request of a party or on its own motion, order a party to produce such documents or other evidence as it considers necessary or appropriate . . . '.
[81] ICSID Rules of Procedure for Arbitration Proceedings. Article 34 states: The Tribunal may, *if it deems it necessary* at any stage of the proceeding, (a) call upon the parties to produce documents . . . ' (emphasis added).
[82] See further O'Malley Rules of Evidence (n 29) para 3.77, where O'Malley suggests that the IBA Rules capture the 'pre-eminent test' and that questions of whether a requested document is 'necessary', required or otherwise important to a case, will be established by demonstrating the likely relevance and materiality of the evidence. Other commentators confirm the view that procedures and standards have emerged from practice that are codified (in particular) in the IBA Rules (n 21). Gabrielle Kaufmann-Kohler and Philippe Bartsch, 'Discovery in International Arbitration: How Much is Too Much?' (2004) 1 SchiedsVZ 13 (hereafter 'Kaufmann-Kohler and Bartsch') in relation to the 1999 IBA Rules (n 13). See also Born (n 78) 2320.

> The Tribunal further considers that in deciding whether or not it is necessary to order production of a document, it should be guided by the tests of relevance and materiality in the IBA Rules. The Tribunal finds no underlying conflict between these concepts.[83]

6.87 In another ICSID case, the tribunal gave guidance suggesting that necessity and relevance are synonyms in the context of document disclosure. It stated that the required analysis:

> [R]elates to a substantive inquiry into whether the documents requested are relevant to, and in that sense necessary for, the purposes of the proceedings where the documents are to be used.[84]

6.88 The review of ICC procedural orders mentioned supports this view. While noting that arbitrators have considerable freedom when deciding how to exercise the power to order document production, the review shows that tribunals tend to be guided by a number of recurrent standards and principles reflecting the position under the IBA Rules.[85]

6.89 Thus, while the manner in which tribunals exercise their discretion over document production will vary from one arbitration to another, a representative 'international' approach has begun to evolve in recent decades, consistent with the benchmark contained in the IBA Rules.[86]

c. Relevance and materiality under the IBA Rules: what do they mean?

i. Relevance versus materiality

6.90 The concepts of 'relevance' and materiality' find their origins in different legal traditions. Relevance to the case is a requirement for document disclosure that is typically used in common law jurisdictions where there is a broad understanding of what this description means. In these jurisdictions, provided a document is 'relevant', there is generally no inquiry as to whether the document is ultimately necessary in order to enable the court to decide the case. In contrast, civil law concepts strongly influence the IBA requirement that a document must be material to the outcome of the case. In civil law jurisdictions, the judge will examine and inquire what allegations are disputed and may order production of any document necessary to establish those allegations.[87]

6.91 Under the 1999 IBA Rules the benchmark adopted was 'relevant and material to the outcome of the case'. This is in contrast to the formulation used in the current IBA Rules: 'relevant *to the case* and material to its outcome'.[88] The formulation in the 1999 IBA Rules was often interpreted to mean that 'relevance' and 'materiality' were part of a

[83] *Tidewater Inc., Tidewater Investment SRL, Tidewater Caribe, C.A., et al. v The Bolivarian Republic of Venezuela* (Procedural Order No. 1, 29 March 2011) ICSID Case No. ARB/10/5 [14].
[84] *ADF Group Inc v United States* ICSID Case No ARB (AF)/001/1 Award of 9 January 2003, para 29.
[85] Hamilton (n 54).
[86] See further Born (n 78) 2320.
[87] See further Marghitola (n 1) 47.
[88] IBA Rules (n 21) Article 3.3(b) (emphasis added).

single requirement that carried a degree of redundancy between the two concepts.[89] It is widely accepted that the revised formula in the current IBA Rules contains two limbs ('relevant to the case' and 'material to its outcome') and that both limbs must be satisfied.[90] The IBA Rules do not contain a definition of either term.

In addition to the mentioned distinction between legal traditions, there is some suggestion that the two limbs reflect two differing perspectives—that of the parties, and that of the tribunal. This makes sense. 'Relevant to the case' may be seen as meaning that a document or content of a document will reasonably assist *a party* in establishing its case while 'material to its outcome' is to be seen as relating to the *tribunal's* right to evaluate a requested document in light of whether it will have a bearing upon the final award.[91] **6.92**

Some commentators suggest that the requirement of 'relevancy' continues to be wrapped up in the second limb of materiality—ie a document that is material to outcome is always relevant to the case.[92] While in some cases this may be true, it is a simplistic analysis that ignores the dual perspective highlighted earlier. **6.93**

A more general point to bear in mind in relation to both relevance and materiality is that the IBA Rules are not intended to limit a substantive right to documents that may exist independently of the document production process.[93] The benchmarks of relevance and materiality cannot be used by a party to resist operation of a substantive right—for example, a contractual or statutory obligation.[94] Both the form and substance of production requests based on a substantive right have to be examined by reference to rights and obligations existing under the applicable substantive laws, and not against the benchmark of relevance and materiality.[95] **6.94**

ii. Relevant to the case

The IBA Rules contain no definition of '*relevant to the case*'. **6.95**

Various descriptions of what must be demonstrated by a statement of relevance delivered under Article 3.3(b) have been put forward. We suggest that an appropriate **6.96**

[89] See further O'Malley Rules of Evidence (n 29) para 3.68

[90] See further O'Malley Document Production (n 23) 4. See also Born (n 78) 2360.

[91] See further Kreindler (n 25) 55. Marghitola (n 1) 49 also notes this dual perspective. When describing the relevancy requirement she suggests that the 'amendment to the wording involved a change of perspective. Contrary to the term "relevant to the outcome of the case" [the benchmark contained in the 1999 IBA Rules], the term "relevant to the case" considers the relevance from the parties' perspectives. "Relevant to the case" does not imply an analysis by the arbitral tribunal regarding whether the requested documents will be needed to resolve the case. Rather, the issue is whether the requesting party can use the requested document to present its case.'

[92] Born (n 78) 2360.

[93] See further Matthias Scherer, 'The Limits of the IBA Rules on the Taking of Evidence in International Arbitration: Document Production Based on Contractual or Statutory Rights' (2010) 13 International Arbitration Law Review 195 (hereafter 'Scherer'); Reto Marghitola, 'Document Production: New Findings on an Old Issue' (2016) 34 ASA Bulletin 78.

[94] A term providing for a right to provision of documents held or generated by the other party is not uncommon in certain types of contracts such as distributorship agreements or joint venture agreements, or in respect of audit rights in a production sharing agreement. As to statutory rights, one example cited elsewhere is the obligation of an agent to return, at the request of his/her principal, everything that he has received as a result of his/her agency activities.

[95] Scherer (n 93).

base test for relevance is whether the document will assist the requesting party, either to establish the truth of the allegations of fact relied on to support its legal case, or because it is inconsistent with the facts relied on by its opponent(s). Documents meeting this formulation will not be limited to documents relevant to witness evidence, and may include documents that establish or discredit facts on which expert evidence is based.

6.97 This approach is supported by other commentators. For example, it is said that to demonstrate relevance the requested document must be useful for a line of evidence followed by the requesting party in order to establish the truth of factual allegations on which legal conclusions are based.[96] In similar terms, a document is said to be relevant if it is likely to prove a fact from which legal conclusions are drawn.[97] Another view notes that the requested document may serve to support the requesting party's allegations in the case or, on the contrary, may be necessary to repudiate allegations made by the other party.[98]

6.98 Documents that contradict a written witness statement are relevant to the case. A party can typically use such documents to present them to an opponent's witness during cross-examination. A more interesting question concerns documents that are unrelated to the case, but which touch on the credibility of the witness. On one view, such documents are irrelevant to the issues in the case and therefore fall outside of the parameters laid down by Article 3.3(b).[99] However, if the documents are of a nature that are likely to substantially undermine the credibility of a key witness for the producing party, it is difficult to see why they would not be material to the outcome of the case and therefore also relevant to it within the context mentioned.

6.99 In order to demonstrate relevance in the terms described here, it is good practice for parties to explain in their document production requests the relationship between a document requested and the issue in the written submissions to which it is said to relate. One experienced arbitrator has put it in these terms:

> [T]he requesting party should be invited to make clear with reasonable particularity what facts or allegations(s) each document or category of documents sought is intended to establish.[100]

6.100 A ruling in an unpublished ICC award makes the point that:

> The request for production must establish the relevance of each document or each specific category of documents sought in such a way that the other party and the

96 Raeschke-Kessler (n 6) 427.
97 Kaufmann-Kohler and Bartsch (n 82).
98 Raeschke-Kessler (n 6) para 3.2.3.
99 See further Marghitola (n 1) 50.
100 Bernard Hanotiau, 'Document Production in International Arbitration: A Tentative Definition of "Best Practices"' in *Special Supplement 2006: Document Production in International Arbitration* (International Chamber of Commerce 2006) 113, para 14 (hereafter 'Hanotiau').

arbitral tribunal are able to refer to factual allegations in the submissions filed by the parties to date.[101]

Where production requests are to be made in the form of a Redfern Schedule, the explanation should be included within the schedule.[102] An example and template Redfern Schedule can be found at Appendix 4 and Appendix 5. 6.101

iii. Material to outcome of the case

As noted, under the current version of the IBA Rules the requirement of materiality to outcome of the case is a separate and more onerous requirement than that of 'relevant to the case'. It is a requirement formulated from the perspective of the tribunal. The key question to determine whether the requirement is met is if the requested document will have a material effect on the tribunal's award. The document(s) must add something to the evidence on a factual issue that is on the critical path to a determination of the dispute. If it is clear that the document will have no bearing on the matters to be decided then the requirement is not met. The more difficult ground is where a document is likely to fall within the scope of the evidence to be considered by a tribunal in relation to an important issue between the parties, but the significance of the document is not readily apparent. Whether an IBA tribunal will be satisfied that the requirement of materiality is met is likely to turn, in practice, on the individual predilections of tribunal members, the quality of the analysis put forward by the party in support of the request and (if the request is opposed), the quality of the argument made by the other party. That said, if a very large number of requests are made it is only the most diligent of tribunals that may give such opposing arguments the consideration they merit. 6.102

It is nonetheless useful to consider some of the different ways in which the 'material to outcome' test has been paraphrased. These include: '[the documents are] material to the tribunal's decision';[103] '[the document] is needed to allow complete consideration of the factual issues from which legal considerations are drawn';[104] '[a document which] would have a tendency to influence the tribunal's determination of issues in dispute'[105] or that will have a bearing upon the 'likely merit of the point the requesting party seeks to support'.[106] 6.103

Examples of documents likely to be material to outcome include: the test results of an allegedly defective product; sales statistics in relation to a claim for royalties; the 6.104

[101] McNeil and Ryan (n 23) 174, para 17.19.

[102] See 6.199–6.207 for a description and explanation of the use of Redfern Schedules.

[103] McNeil and Ryan (n 23) para 17.24.

[104] Marghitola (n 1) 79. A similar formulation is provided by Professor Raeschke-Kessler (n 6) para 11.1, who opines that 'the arbitral tribunal must deem it necessary that the document is needed as an element to allow complete consideration whether a factual allegation is true or not'. Although similar to the description offered by those commentators in relation to the requirement of relevance, the phrase 'complete consideration' is a distinguishing feature.

[105] Byung Chol Yoon and Joel Richardson, 'Discovery in Investment Arbitration Involving Republic of Korea' (2008) 4 Asian International Arbitration Journal 137, 139.

[106] O'Malley Rules of Evidence (n 29) para 3.73 citing *Aguas del Tunari, S.A. v Republic of Bolivia* (Procedural Order No. 1) ICSID Case No ARB/02/3.

metadata of a document where the issue is the timing or authenticity of the document; internal schedule analysis where there are claims of construction delay; or distributor sales figures in a claim for unpaid commission.

6.105 Examples of circumstances where a document may be found *not* to be material include: where an issue has already been conceded by one side and the document is not therefore material to the tribunal's determination; where the matter to which the document relates is connected with the events underlying the dispute but is not on the critical path to a determination by the tribunal; or where the tribunal already has sufficient evidence on the particular issue.

iv. Relevant but not material

6.106 'Relevant' and 'material' are two separate requirements and it therefore follows that a document may be found by a tribunal to be relevant to the case, but not material to outcome.[107] In such circumstances, a request for production may be denied.

6.107 There are a number of circumstances where a tribunal may feel that, despite its relevant content, a document or category of documents will not be material to outcome. An obvious example is where the tribunal does not believe that the argument to which a document is relevant will affect its final award. The decision of the English Court in *ABB v Hochtief Airport GmbH* is a good illustration of this point.[108] In that case, the complaining party argued before the court that it had been unfairly discriminated against when a number of its document requests were denied by the tribunal during the arbitration. It argued that it had clearly shown that the documents in question were relevant to one of its arguments. In reviewing the conduct of the tribunal in light of the standards found in the IBA Rules (which by order of the tribunal were to apply), the court noted that, even though there did appear to be a connection between the document requests and the complaining party's arguments in the case, the tribunal had not acted unfairly in denying document production. It was plain that the tribunal did not consider that the requested documents would assist with its determination. The argument to which the requested documents related was immaterial to outcome.[109] In practice, a tribunal will have to be very careful not to prejudge the issue, or to be perceived as doing so.

6.108 Likewise, where the issue to which a document is relevant is no longer in dispute between the parties, there is little purpose to be served by admitting evidence on it.[110]

[107] As Redfern and Hunter observe, 'the requirement of showing "materiality to the outcome of the case" . . . enables arbitral tribunals to deny document requests where, although the requested documents would clearly be relevant, they consider that the production of them will not affect the outcome of the proceedings'. Nigel Blackaby and others, *Redfern and Hunter on International Arbitration* (6th edn, OUP 2016) para 6.98.

[108] *ABB AG v Hochtief Airport GmbH* [2006] EWHC 388 (Comm).

[109] See further O'Malley Document Production (n 23) 5. See also *ABB AG* (n 108) [84]–[85]. The Court also noted that 'whether the arbitrators were wise to reject . . . [the] request for disclosure was not something it had to decide', suggesting that the court may have considered that admitting the documents would perhaps have avoided a possible basis of complaint by the requesting party.

[110] See, for example, O'Malley Rules of Evidence (n 29) para 9.12, where reference is made to a procedural order in ICC Case No. 6465.

As mentioned, another situation where 'relevant' evidence can have no bearing on outcome is where the evidence already before the tribunal is sufficient to decide the particular issue to which the requested document relates. One reported ICC decision refers to a requesting party seeking the production of notes of witness interviews referred to in a report in order that the requesting party could check the accuracy and veracity of the statements made in the report. The tribunal pointed out that the requesting party would have the opportunity to question the witnesses at the hearing and that there was other material already on the record that could be used to prove the truth or otherwise of the statements made in the report. The request for production was denied.[111]

v. Documents sought in aid of unformulated claims

In practice, depending upon the attitude of the tribunal, it may not always be essential for the issue to which the document production request relates to have been formally joined in the parties' submissions for a tribunal to allow a request for production. **6.109**

It is stated elsewhere that document production under the IBA Rules cannot be used as a means of 'fishing' to identify possible new allegations or claims[112] and that document production is aimed at obtaining evidence that is relevant and material to existing claims and issues in dispute between the parties. We agree with that position. However, the requirement of a current claim should not be applied too harshly. For example, a party may be about to amend its case to include new claims in circumstances where it would be inefficient to defer document requests relating to those new claims to a separate round of document production. The important point is that the requesting party should be in a position to explain and formulate the allegations being made in sufficiently precise terms for the benefit of the tribunal and its opponent. Provided such explanation can be provided, it will not always matter that the formal pleading containing the allegation follows shortly after the request. This will be something to be considered on a case-by-case basis. **6.110**

vi. Approach to drafting document requests

In order to address the requirements of Article 3.3(b), when drafting document production requests, parties should be careful in relation to each document or category of document they want to see to: **6.111**

[111] Hamilton (n 54). Although this article involves a review of ICC Decisions over a period prior to the current 2010 IBA Rules, the example cited concerned the issue of materiality. Another example quoted elsewhere is the decision of an ICSID tribunal to reject document production requests filed after a jurisdictional hearing on grounds that the evidence before the tribunal was '*sufficient to decide the jurisdictional issues raised by the respondent*'. *El Paso Energy International Company v The Argentine Republic* (Procedural Order No. 1, 28 July 2005) ICSID Case No. ARB/03/15, quoted in the Decision on Jurisdiction (*El Paso Energy International Company v The Argentine Republic* (Decision on Jurisdiction, 27 April 2006) ICSID Case No. ARB/03/15 [9]). See further McNeil and Ryan (n 23) para 17.24.

[112] McNeil and Ryan (n 23) para 17.19. See also Hamilton (n 54) 72.

(a) provide an explanation of the relevance of the requested document(s) that is supported by reference to the appropriate paragraphs of pleadings or submissions already before the tribunal; and
(b) provide an explanation as to why the issue to which the document is said to be relevant is on the critical path to a determination by the tribunal, thereby making the document material to outcome.

There are, of course, other requirements that the Request to Produce will also have to meet—for example, narrowness and specificity of requests relating to categories of documents. These are dealt with elsewhere in this text,[113] and are also described in the checklist at Appendix 7.

6.112 We are aware of a case in which the numerous strands of inter-related arguments pleaded by a respondent in an LCIA arbitration were systematically 'unpicked' by the claimant and an analysis carried out to determine which of those arguments were actually on the critical path to a determination of the dispute. The analysis was provided to the tribunal, which was conscientious in its review of the points made. A significant number of document requests made by the respondent were denied by the tribunal on the basis of a finding that the requested documents were not material to outcome.

vii. Importance of the timing of the request to produce to establishing relevance and materiality

6.113 A requesting party must explain in the Request to Produce why a document is relevant and material. Before ordering production of requested documents a tribunal must be satisfied that the benchmark of relevance and materiality has been met.[114] As noted earlier, these requirements dictate to some extent the point at which a party is in a proper position to draft a Request to Produce.

6.114 In many cases the Request for Arbitration and the Response to it will contain very rudimentary information about the dispute. It is only when the parties have exchanged fully developed factual and legal submissions in a first round of submissions that it will be possible for (a) the requesting party to make out a case as to why the documents sought are relevant to the case and material to its outcome and (b) the arbitral tribunal to determine under Article 3.7 whether the issues to be proved by the documents are relevant and material.[115]

6.115 It is implicit in the terms of Article 3.1 (providing for each party to produce all documents on which it intends to rely—generally done with the first round of pleadings/submissions)[116] that the tribunal will not entertain a request for document production

[113] See 6.51-6.67.
[114] See the requirements of IBA Rules (n 21) Article 3.7.
[115] Under IBA Rules (n 21) Article 3.7, the arbitral tribunal must determine that '*the issues that the requesting Party wishes to prove* are relevant to the case and material to its outcome' (emphasis added).
[116] Many institutional arbitration rules contain a similar provision. For example: LCIA Rules, Article 1.1(ii): The Request for Arbitration must be accompanied by a copy of the contract or other document containing the arbitration agreement and to which the claim relates. Further: LCIA Rules Articles 15.2, 15.3, 15.4, and 15.5: Written Statements

prior to the submission of the primary substantive pleadings. In order to avoid duplication, tribunals will generally expect voluntary production of documents to take place first. In addition, until the first round of submissions is completed, the main issues in the case may not be clearly understood and it may not be possible to formulate a request meeting the requirements of specificity, relevance, and materiality.[117] This view on the timing of requests for production under Article 3 is supported by the Commentary to the IBA Rules, which states:

> The specificity required in the request to produce makes it likely that a request will be made only after the issues have become sufficiently clear in the case. The precise timing of such a request will be determined by the arbitral tribunal. It will naturally depend upon the specificity of the initial pleadings and any terms of reference or other documents identifying the issues.[118]

Similar views have been expressed by Professor Kaufmann-Kohler[119] and by Yves Derains, the latter when writing more generally about achieving efficiency in international arbitration. Derains argues that document production should not take place until after the first round of submissions so that the tribunal can determine what documents are relevant and material, and to prevent fishing by the parties. He says that: 6.116

> It is generally held that the parties should submit the documents on which they rely at the same time as they file their memorials, and that requests for document production should not be allowed until the parties have exchanged their first memorials fully presenting their respective cases. Only then will the arbitrators be able to determine whether the requested documents are relevant and material to the issue in dispute. This is practically impossible beforehand, as the arbitrators will not have received sufficient information on the dispute. Moreover it discourages so-called 'fishing expeditions', by means of which a party endeavouring to construct its case on the basis of the documents that it hopes to find in the other party's files, without previously setting down its claims on the sole basis of the factual elements in its possession.[120]

The point has also been made that making a document production request after delivery of submissions has the practical advantage that it will focus the parties' respective document requests on the specific issues raised in submissions, and the tribunal will be better educated about what those issues are.[121] There seems to be a consensus that 6.117

are required to include 'all essential documents'; SIAC Rules, HKIAC Rules Article 16.3: 'The Claimant shall annex to its Statement of Claim all documents on which it relies'. HKIAC Rules Article 17.4: 'The Respondent shall annex to its Statement of Defence all documents on which it relies'. See also UNCITRAL Rules Articles 20.4 and 21.2.

117 O'Malley Document Production (n 23) 1.
118 Commentary on the IBA Rules (n 5) 10.
119 Kaufmann-Kohler and Bartsch (n 82).
120 Yves Derains, 'Towards Greater Efficiency in Document Production before Arbitral Tribunals-A Continental Viewpoint' in *Special Supplement 2006: Document Production in International Arbitration* (International Chamber of Commerce 2006) 83 (hereafter 'Derains').
121 Robert H Smit, 'Towards Greater Efficiency in Document Production before Arbitral Tribunals: A North American Viewpoint' in *Special Supplement 2006: Document Production in International Arbitration* (International Chamber of Commerce 2006) 93.

having document production requests after first round submissions represents best practice.[122]

6.118 By way of illustration, in one ICC case the tribunal rejected a request for production of accounting documents and sales information made by the claimant with its Statement of Claim because the respondent had not yet had an opportunity to submit its answer to the Statement of Claim with supporting documents.[123] In *Merrill & Ring Forestry LP v Canada*, a claim conducted under the UNCITRAL arbitration rules, the claimant made a request to have document production in the early stages of the arbitration, prior to the filing of the statement of claim, and the defence. The tribunal declined the claimant's request and ordered that the disclosure phase take place after the filing of primary evidence by both sides with their respective statements. In its comments to the parties, the tribunal noted that the document disclosure should be restricted to relevant evidence 'still missing' from the record, which may be deemed necessary'.[124]

6.119 US law firm respondents to a survey on use of the IBA Rules reported that they have seen tribunals resist very early requests for document production because the tribunal did not yet feel that it had enough context to understand whether a document or category was relevant. In one case, with the aim of resolving allegations that one party was engaged in a 'fishing expedition', the tribunal decided that documents would not be deemed relevant unless the responsive category of documents was 'undoubtedly perceived relevant at the time of the request'. In another case, the tribunal allowed a party to present a mini-summary of its case to establish to the tribunal's satisfaction that the documents it requested early on in the proceedings were relevant.[125]

viii. Metadata

6.120 A question that may arise for consideration under the IBA Rules is whether, where the production of metadata is requested by one of the parties or by the tribunal, a separate analysis of the relevance and materiality of the required metadata should be carried out. In our view, it should.

6.121 Document production in international arbitration often involves a significant volume of soft copy documents. The IBA Rules define documents to include electronic documents and the rules have a single set of provisions governing production of both hard and soft copy documents, with some limited additional provisions relating to electronic documents.[126]

[122] See further Lotfi (n 40) 7; Marghitola (n 1) 53, 97; Hanotiau (n 100) para 14.
[123] Hamilton (n 54) 66–67.
[124] See further O'Malley Rules of Evidence (n 29) para 3.29 fn 49.
[125] BCLP Survey on use of the IBA Rules.
[126] The 2010 IBA Rules (n 21) introduced new specific provisions to address issues raised by the production of electronic documents. The definition of document was expanded to include 'program or data . . . maintained . . . by electronic . . . means' as well as adding language to Articles 3(3)(a)(ii) and 3(12)(b).

In some cases issues may arise around whether documents should be produced in native format with all associated metadata.[127] The default position under the IBA Rules is that electronic documents shall be produced by a party 'in the form most convenient or economical to it that is reasonably usable by the recipients' unless the parties agree something else or the tribunal decides otherwise.[128] 6.122

The Commentary to the IBA Rules notes that the format of a document that is 'most convenient and economical' will generally not be the native format with full metadata because 'submission in this format can be unduly expensive and inconvenient'.[129] We suggest that a departure from the 'norm' can only be justified by reference to the relevance and materiality of the metadata to the issues in the case. 6.123

Support for this approach may be found in an ICC Report,[130] which notes that hidden metadata will usually be irrelevant to the dispute and it will therefore be unnecessary to produce it; even where metadata is potentially relevant, the burden of production may outweigh its potential evidentiary value. The report suggests that a separate test of relevance and materiality should be applied to the metadata in terms broadly consistent with the combined effect of Article 3.3(b) and Article 9.2(a) and (c).[131] The ICC Report states: 6.124

> Tribunals should consider applying a presumption against requiring the production of hidden metadata associated with a document that is to be produced, unless the requesting party establishes a degree of relevance and materiality that outweighs the burden and costs involved.[132]

For example, if there is a dispute as to the authenticity or date of a document, the metadata may well be relevant and material.

ix. Prima facie relevance and materiality

There appears to be widespread acceptance that a tribunal's assessment of a requested document as being prima facie relevant and material is sufficient to satisfy the requirements of Article 3.3(b) and to justify an order for production. 6.125

[127] See ICC Report on Managing E-Document Production (n 78), which contains a very helpful analysis of the nature and subcategories of metadata found embedded in documents generated by the computer system of which the document was created/stored. In that report 'metadata' at its most general level is described as 'data about (electronically stored) data. Documents or files created on a computer will typically contain embedded information that is not readily apparent on the screen view of a file or in a printed version of the document or file. This secondary "metadata" is information about the electronic document or file that describes its characteristics, origins, or usage'.

[128] IBA Rules (n 21) Article 3.12(b).

[129] Commentary on the IBA Rules (n 5) 12.

[130] ICC Report on Managing E-Document Production (n 78).

[131] The ICC Report also notes that in cases involving a suspicion of fraud, forgery, or deliberate tampering with evidence, hidden metadata may be valuable evidence. Even absent allegations of improper conduct it may be useful in some cases to know the author of a document, or when it was created or edited. ICC Report on Managing E-Document Production (n 78) para 4.10(b).

[132] ibid para 5.11.

6.126 It is said that if a party is able to put forward a credible argument as to the prima facie relevance of a document this will generally satisfy a tribunal.[133] This position is supported by practical examples. The review of ICC procedural orders already mentioned notes that:

> Inevitably, a tribunal's assessment of the relevance of a document is made on the basis of the knowledge it has of the case and the parties' claims at the time the document production order is made. This means it will rule on what one arbitral tribunal referred to as the 'prima facie relevance' of the requested documents.[134]

Among the procedural orders reviewed, several tribunals considered the relevance requirement met 'when there was a likelihood of relevance'.[135] A number of eminent arbitrators confirm this to be the position.[136]

6.127 The position is the same in relation to the test of 'material to [. . .] outcome'. One commentator suggests that 'the prevailing view of scholars' is that prima facie materiality to the outcome of the dispute is the applicable standard under the IBA Rules.[137]

6.128 While the same commentator goes on to indicate that prima facie means there is a degree of probability of over 50 per cent (more likely than not),[138] we think that is setting the bar too high. On the case as articulated to it at the time, the tribunal should consider it likely that the document in question is relevant and material to the decisions it has to make in the case.

6.129 However, a tribunal should be careful to distinguish between 'potential relevance' and 'prima facie' relevance and/or materiality, with only the latter meeting the test under the IBA Rules. In practice, many tribunals may regard the difference as academic.[139]

x. Burden of proof

6.130 It is widely accepted that the party seeking to obtain document production will generally have the burden of demonstrating the relevance and materiality of the requested evidence. We believe this to be correct.

6.131 A separate question, and one that has been the subject of much debate, is whether the requesting party must in all cases carry the burden of proof in relation to the issue to

[133] See further O'Malley Document Production (n 23) fn 24. O'Malley cites a definition of prima facie case used in an Iran–US Claim Tribunal as being ' . . . a case sufficient to call for an answer'.

[134] Hamilton (n 54).

[135] ibid. ICC Case 15583 is an example of where the requirement of relevancy was assessed by a tribunal on a prima facie basis and in which the final award makes reference to orders for disclosure by the tribunal. The tribunal in that case noted that materiality and relevance are assessed on a prima facie basis and found that it was: 'satisfied that the requested documents/information are prima facie relevant and material to the outcome of the dispute'. The final award is dated November 2010. It appears that the 1999 IBA Rules were applied; hence, the reference to the 1999 formulation of the relevance and materiality requirement rather than the clearly two-limbed test under the current 2010 Rules. The tribunal ruled in favour of the requesting party on that basis.

[136] See Hanotiau (n 100); Born (n 78) 2360.

[137] Marghitola (n 1) 54.

[138] ibid.

[139] ibid. See also (n 133).

which the document is said to relate. For example, it has been suggested that if a document production request is made on grounds that the other party has not provided those documents necessary to support its case, the request should generally be denied because the request relates not to the requesting party's burden of proof, but to its opponent's. In other words, the objecting party bears the risk of not proving its case.[140]

It is useful to consider the provenance of this approach and the extent to which it represents current practice. Being aware of the associated issues may assist parties when dealing with tribunal members who indicate that they intend to adopt it. **6.132**

The approach was advocated by eminent arbitrator Yves Derains in 2006 when he called for greater efficiency in document production under the previous 1999 IBA Rules. Derains argued that it was necessary in order to avoid an 'avalanche of needless documents' being introduced into arbitration proceedings. Although Derains acknowledged that the 1999 IBA Rules did not contain any express provision that the requesting party must carry the burden of proof on the relevant issue, he nonetheless reached the view that the requirement of relevance and materiality coupled with the goal of efficiency laid down in paragraph 1 of the Preamble to the IBA Rules should lead arbitrators to adopt this solution.[141] Other commentators agree with this approach.[142] We do not agree, not least because in broad terms a party should be entitled to production of documents that make its opponent's burden of proof more difficult to discharge. **6.133**

Furthermore, there exists a considerable body of opinion that rejects the notion that a burden of proof requirement has any place in application of the IBA Rules.[143] There **6.134**

[140] O'Malley cites by way of example the comments of an Iran–US Claims Tribunal where it was noted that the Tribunal did not intend to order disclosure of documents which the claimant would likely have to file to meet its own burden of proof. It was said by the tribunal that 'the Party who carries the burden of proof determines at its discretion what evidence it wishes to submit in support of its claim. It is not normally up to the Tribunal to give directions to any of the parties regarding the evidence to be submitted by them.' O'Malley Rules of Evidence (n 29) para 3.72. *The Offshore Oil Co v National Iranian Oil Co*, Case 133, Chamber Two, Order of 26 June 1986.

[141] Derains (n 120) 83, who said '[t]o be efficient, document production must serve the purpose of bringing to the arbitral tribunal's knowledge not just any documents relevant and material to the outcome of the dispute, but documentary evidence without which a party would not be able to discharge the burden of proof lying upon it [. . .] On the other hand, when a document production request is disputed, the arbitrators have the responsibility of determining whether the requesting party actually needs the documents to discharge its burden of proof. If not, the request should be denied [. . .] When assessing requests, arbitrators must carefully check that the burden of proof actually lies on the requesting party . . . '. At the date of publication, the 1999 IBA Rules were the then current version of the IBA Rules.

[142] O'Malley says that a 'party seeking to obtain document disclosure must demonstrate that the requested documents will reasonably assist it in discharging its burden of proof' and that the 'tribunal should consider whether the request clearly states why a document is needed to discharge the party's burden of proof'. O'Malley Document Production (n 23) 189. See also Ashford, who states that 'a party seeking to obtain document disclosure must demonstrate to the satisfaction of the arbitral tribunal that the requested documents are, in effect, necessary for it to discharge the burden of proof that it has'. Peter Ashford, *The IBA Rules on the Taking of Evidence in International Arbitration* (CUP 2013) 71 (hereafter 'Ashford'). See also Hanotiau (n 100) para 14.

[143] Jaffe, Dulani, and Stute (n 40). See also Born (n 78) 2319–2423. See also Marghitola (n 1) 54. The Derains approach has been roundly rejected by Born (n 78) 2364, who comments that there is 'no basis for this approach in . . . the IBA Rules . . . or sound arbitral procedures. The fact that a party bears the burden of proof on an issue does not make a document it has requested any less relevant or material, nor any less important to the tribunal's fact-finding mandate. Moreover, the fact that a party bears the burden of proof on an issue does not suggest that it will, absent the requested document(s), be able to discharge that burden: it is both illogical and unfair to deny a party disclosure of documents otherwise subject to disclosure, merely because it does not bear the burden of proof with respect to the underlying issue to which the document is relevant'.

is no reference to such a requirement in the current IBA Rules (or indeed in the 1999 IBA Rules). We take the view that a tribunal should consider the facts of an individual case very carefully before coming to such a view. A party may have legitimate reasons for wishing to 'flush out' the available evidence on a particular point. An early assessment of that evidence (or its non-production/existence) may affect the nature of further steps taken in the arbitration, with consequential impact upon costs and efficiency. Dealing with the matter in this way may also prevent the tactical late production of evidence that takes the requesting party by surprise. In addition, where the party with the burden of proof has produced documents on the relevant issue that assist it in relation to discharging that burden, there may nonetheless be other documents on the same issue that may help its opponent to raise the evidential burden that the party with the burden of proof has to surmount.

6.135 The only potential source of support for the contrary position that the authors can find in the IBA Rules is the requirement at Article 3.7 that, before making an order for production, the Arbitral Tribunal must determine that:

> *[T]he issues that the requesting Party wishes to prove* are relevant to the case and material to its outcome.[144]

6.136 However, in our view, the reference to 'the issues that the requesting party wishes to prove [by the documents requested]' are not restricted to issues on which the requesting party has the burden of proof. The same wording appeared in the 1999 IBA Rules, which Derains himself accepted did not contain an express statement of the blanket rule on burden of proof that he advocated. Furthermore, whenever a requesting party's opponent carries the burden of proof on a particular claim, application of such a rule would prevent a requesting party from being able to test the factual assertions of its opponent. As a result, allocation of the burden of proof would become a ground on which to reject a document production request and the relevance and materiality benchmark of the IBA Rules would be compromised. A document may meet the test of 'material to outcome'—the more onerous limb of the Article 3.3(b) benchmark—even where it provides no assistance to the requesting party in discharging its burden of proof in relation to facts relied on. It is also material if it prevents the producing party from proving a fact. We suggest that 'prove' at Article 3.7 should be read as including 'disprove'.

6.137 The Commentary to the IBA Rules highlights the position taken under many institutional rules that 'arbitral tribunals are to establish the facts of the case by all appropriate means' and that this includes 'the competence of the arbitral tribunal to order one party to introduce certain documents, including internal documents, into the arbitral proceedings upon request of the other party'.[145] This suggests that those responsible for

[144] Emphasis added.
[145] Commentary on the IBA Rules (n 5) 7.

drafting the IBA Rules saw tribunals as having broad arbitral authority to order the production of documents unfettered by the Derains approach.[146]

Whatever the rights and wrongs of this debate, practical experience suggests that the blanket rule on burden of proof suggested by Derains may be 'in play' in some arbitrations and parties should be alive to its implications. In the review of ICC procedural orders mentioned, it was noted that: **6.138**

> [the criteria of relevance and materiality] are frequently cited together to stress that the document sought must not only relate to the fact in question but, in the words of one arbitral tribunal, be '*necessary in the sense that the applicant would otherwise be unable to discharge the burden of proof in relation to such fact*'.[147]

For example, a 2010 procedural order made by one ICC tribunal suggests that the requesting party must carry the burden of proof because if it does not, the failure of the other party to volunteer the document may be addressed by other means. In that case it was said that: **6.139**

> The Tribunal notes that relevance and materiality must be considered from the perspective, inter alia, of *whether the requesting party actually requires the documents sought in order to discharge its burden of proof*. If the Respondents are of the view that the Claimant's Statement of Claim Memorial and accompanying witness statements and expert evidence are deficient because, for example, the Claimant has failed to provide supporting documents, they may so aver in their Statement of Defence Memorial. It will then fall to the Claimant to address this argument in its Statement of Reply Memorial. The Respondents will have other opportunities in their Statement of Rejoinder Memorial and the oral hearing to argue the Claimant has not discharged its burden of proof . . .[148]

A published extract from a 2013 ICC procedural order notes that: **6.140**

> [T]he document production procedure does not aim at enabling the parties to obtain documents relevant to the outcome of the dispute simpliciter, but rather *documents without which they would not be able to prove their respective allegations*;
>
> Therefore, a document requested in order to dispute the opposite party's allegations does not meet the criteria set forth in Procedural Order No. 1 and/or the IBA Rules.[149]

[146] See further Jaffe, Dulani, and Stute (n 40) 4–5.
[147] Hamilton (n 54) 69 (emphasis added).
[148] ICC Procedural Order from May 2013, 'Extracts from ICC Case Materials on the Taking of Evidence with References to the IBA Rules' (2016) 1 ICC Dispute Resolution Bulletin 127 (emphasis added).
[149] ibid (emphasis added).

xi. Good faith

6.141 Preamble 3 to the IBA Rules requires the parties to act in good faith in relation to all aspects of the taking of evidence.[150] There is debate as to the scope of that obligation. However, a deliberate attempt by a party to formulate intentionally burdensome requests without a legitimate basis on grounds of relevance and materiality would, in our view, breach the obligation and may provide a basis for objection or complaint outside of the grounds set out in Article 9.2. However, because such requests are very unlikely to meet the requirements of Article 3.3(b) there will generally be no need to base the dismissal of document production on the principle of good faith.[151]

xii. Cultural and practical perspectives on 'relevant and material'

6.142 Law firm respondents to a survey on use of the IBA Rules[152] confirm that, as described, the requirements of relevance and materiality are widely used across jurisdictions albeit with differing emphasis. Respondents reported that, in their experience, arbitral tribunals had excluded production of documents by reference to a lack of relevance,[153] and/or a requirement of relevance and materiality.

6.143 Australian Respondents observed that practice on the application of relevance and materiality requirements varies from tribunal to tribunal but the requirement of 'material to outcome' is becoming increasingly important. Swedish respondents reported that a lack of either 'relevance' or 'materiality' is a common basis on which on which to refuse document production. Respondents in Portugal and China reported that documents were only required to be relevant. Nigerian respondents reported that they had experience of cases where the tribunal had denied document production requests because the documents sought were not relevant and material to outcome. Argentinian respondents reported that 'the documents requested must be relevant to solve the case'. Interestingly, Spanish respondents reported that, in their experience tribunals are often flexible in their application of the criteria and, in cases of doubt, they prefer to order production/admit the documents and decide their relevance and materiality when assessing the totality of the evidence produced.

150 See Chapter 2, paras 2.43–2.99. The obligation to act in good faith is also stated elsewhere in 'soft law' guidance. For example, the IBA Guidelines on Party Representation in International Arbitration as adopted by the IBA Council on 25 May 2013 state in Article 13 that that a Party representative should not make any Request to Produce (or any objection to a Request to Produce), for an improper purpose such as to harass or cause unnecessary delay. These Guidelines also make clear that 'a Party Representative' should advise the party they represent to take reasonable steps to ensure that a reasonable search is made for documents that a party has either 'undertaken, or been ordered to produce', and to assist such party in taking such steps. We suggest that, where production is carried out under the IBA Rules (n 21), if a party does not object to a particular document request under one or more of the grounds set out in IBA Rules Article 9, it should be treated as having 'undertaken' to search for the relevant document(s). This view is supported by the wording of IBA Rules Article 3.4, which provides that: 'Within the time ordered by the Arbitral Tribunal, the Party to whom the Request to Produce is addressed shall produce to the other Parties . . . all the Documents requested in its possession, custody or control as to which it makes no objection'.

151 Marghitola (n 1) 111–12.

152 BCLP Survey on use of the IBA Rules.

153 ibid. Respondents reporting this position included those from France, China, and Portugal.

A decision of the Swedish Supreme Court[154] drawn to our attention dealt with a request by the claimant to arbitration proceedings for an order that a third party produce documents sought by the claimant in those arbitration proceedings. The court noted that the tribunal's consent for the application (as required under section 26 of the Swedish Arbitration Act) had been forthcoming on the basis that the documents sought might contain evidence important to the case. It was accepted that such assessment was for the tribunal to make and should not generally be revisited by the court.[155] However, the court noted that guidance for how to go about that exercise was contained both in domestic guidance, and in Article 3 of the IBA Rules.[156] **6.144**

US respondents reported that although the rules applied to disclosure in domestic litigation are different, the US courts will typically support use of the IBA Rules in arbitrations seated in the United States. For example, one decision of the New York Federal Court found that an arbitrator had not erred by first adopting the IBA Rules and then proceeding to deny document production requests on the basis that the requests made did not comply with the IBA requirements as to scope and description.[157] **6.145**

French respondents reported that tribunals in arbitrations seated in France will draw guidance from or will apply the IBA Rules and, in consequence, the criteria of relevance and materiality will apply. Portuguese respondents reported that, in arbitrations subject to Portuguese curial law, there is nothing to prevent the parties adopting an intermediary position between civil law and common law practice as set out in the IBA Rules, provided the parties had the opportunity to exercise a right of reply to requests made. **6.146**

6. Statement that Documents Are Not in Possession, Custody, or Control of the Requesting Party

3.3(c) (i) a statement that the Documents requested are not in the possession, custody or control of the requesting Party or a statement of the reasons why it would be unreasonably burdensome for the requesting Party to produce such Documents.

a. Introduction

Article 3.3(c)(i) provides that the Request to Produce must contain (a) a statement that the requested documents are not in the 'possession, custody or control' of the requesting party, or (b) a statement of the reasons why it would be unreasonably burdensome for the requesting party to produce them. **6.147**

[154] *Euroflon Tekniska Produkter AB v Flexiboys i Motala AB* Case No 0 1590-11 (Swedish Supreme Court, 10 May 2012).
[155] ibid 7–12.
[156] ibid 6.
[157] *Landmark Ventures Inc. v Insightec ltd* 63 F Supp 3d 343 (US District Court, SDNY, 25 November 2014).

6.148 In other words, if the requesting party already has the documents it should not ask another party to produce them unless there are good reasons why it would be unduly onerous for the requesting party to have to retrieve the documents itself. The Commentary to the IBA Rules explains the importance of this requirement in these terms:

> By requiring the requesting party to state that the documents sought are not in its own possession, the IBA Rules of Evidence seek to prevent unnecessary harassment of the opposing party by the requesting party.

6.149 Article 3.3(c)(ii) (see 6.160-6.198) goes on to say that the Request to Produce must also contain a statement of reasons why the requesting party believes that the documents it has requested are in the 'possession, custody or control' of another party.

b. Not in the possession, custody, or control of the requesting party

i. 'Possession, custody or control'

6.150 Article 3.3(c)(i) and Article 3.3(c)(ii) each use the same phrase—'possession, custody or control'. In the majority of cases a party will not request production of documents that it already has. As a result, it is generally not necessary to consider detailed application of that phrase to the requesting party. Much more often, arbitrators are asked to conclude, pursuant to Article 3.3(c)(ii), that the requested documents *are* in the possession, custody, or control of the party who has been asked to produce the documents. For that reason, the terms 'possession', 'custody', and 'control' are analysed at 6.160-6.198 in the context of Article 3.3(c)(ii). Where it is necessary to consider whether the requesting party has 'possession, custody or control' of documents that it requests then the same considerations will apply equally to that situation.

ii. Statement of non-possession by the requesting party

6.151 It may be self-evident that certain categories of document that the requesting party wants to see will never have been in its possession, custody or control. For example, correspondence between two individuals employed by another party. In such circumstances, the requesting party may feel very comfortable making a statement that those documents are not in its possession, custody or control. In other cases, the requesting party may not be entirely sure if it has some or all of the documents. In these cases, in order that it may make a statement in good faith that the documents are not in its possession, custody or control, the requesting party may wish to make enquiries of its officers, employees, contractors, and/or consultant, etc, to check that the documents are not already accessible to it.[158]

[158] In one unreported ICC case noted by Hamilton (n 54) 75, a party requesting production of documents was criticized by the tribunal for failing to first make adequate searches for the documents it wanted.

iii Publicly available documents

A question that sometimes arises is whether a party can request production of documents that are in the public domain. Although at the time of the request these documents may, strictly speaking, not be in the '*possession, custody or control*' of the requesting party, it may be perfectly possible for the requesting party to obtain them. As a general principle, documents in the public domain should be treated as documents to which the requesting party has available access and those documents should not therefore be the subject of a document production request. However, there may be legitimate exceptions to this approach. For example, a technical manual may be referred to in documents on the record and a copy held by one of the parties. The manual may be publicly available but only at significant cost. In those circumstances it may be reasonable for the party without a copy of the manual to ask for copies of the relevant parts of it so that it may understand the references made to it in the documents on the record. **6.152**

The position was fairly summarized by the tribunal in *ADF Group Inc. v United States of America*: **6.153**

> Where . . . the documents requested are in the public domain and equally and effectively available to both parties, we believe that there would be no necessity for requiring the other party physically to produce and deliver the documents to the former for inspection and copying. Where, however, the requesting party shows it would sustain undue burden or expense in accessing the publicly available material, the other party should be required to produce the documents for inspection.[159]

iv. Annotated documents

Parties sometimes wish to find out whether an opponent has made any annotations to the opponent's copy of a document that both parties have in their possession, and it may request production of the document on that basis. **6.154**

If there are annotated copies of the relevant document and those annotations are relevant to the case and material to its outcome, it may be possible to treat the requested document as a new document not in the possession, custody, or control of the requesting party. Such an approach can be found in the English Civil Procedure Rules, which provide that a copy of a document which contains 'a modification, obliteration or other marking or feature on which a party intends to rely or which adversely affects his own case or another party's case or support another party's case' is to be treated as a separate document.[160] However, those procedural rules concern a party's obligation to make automatic voluntary disclosure of documents. The position is more difficult under the IBA Rules, and in international arbitration generally, where a document need **6.155**

[159] *ADF Group Inc. v United States of America* (Procedural Order No.3, 4 October 2001) ICSID Case No. ARB (AF)/00/1 [4].

[160] CPR 31.9(2), <www.justice.gov.uk/courts/procedure-rules/civil/rules/part31#31.9> accessed 2 April 2019.

only be produced upon a legitimate request being made. It has been suggested that, in general, where the requesting party holds a 'clean' copy of the document, a request for any annotated copies of the documents should be dismissed unless there are reasonable grounds for belief that such annotations exist.[161]

c. Unduly burdensome for the requesting party to produce the documents

6.156 As mentioned, Article 3.3(c)(ii) provides one exception to the general rule that a party in possession of particular documents cannot ask another party to produce them. The exception is where it would be 'unreasonably burdensome' for the requesting party to produce the documents.

6.157 The grounds on which a party may argue that it would be onerous to produce documents in its possession will vary according to the circumstances of the case. However, possible examples include where the documents have been archived and can only be retrieved at significant expense, or perhaps where a party has only retained hard copy documents and in order to find the items wanted by its opponent it would have to undertake a manual review of a significant volume of documents. In addition, back-up tapes may not be easily recoverable or it is not possible to interrogate them by reference to search terms.[162] It has been suggested that the alleged burden on the requesting party should be assessed against the evidential value of the documents and the comparative ease with which the other party can produce them—essentially a matter of proportionality or 'balance of convenience'.[163]

6.158 We suggest that where a tribunal is satisfied that the document requested is relevant and material for the case, that the time or cost to the requesting party associated with production is very high and the non-requesting party has easy access to the document, the tribunal should be prepared to make an order for production. The Commentary to the IBA Rules suggests that this balancing of cost/convenience is the correct approach. It says:

> Article 3.3(c)(i) of the revised IBA Rules recognises one exception to [the principle that a party should not request documents in its possession]. In the age of electronic documents, it will become increasingly less likely that a particular document has been entirely deleted from a party's records, as it may continue to exist electronically, such as on back-up tapes or in electronic archives. Where a document is no longer easily accessible, for example because it is not in a server's active data, it may be less burdensome and costly for another party to produce it.[164]

[161] Jeffrey Waincymer, *Procedure and Evidence in International Arbitration* (Kluwer Law International 2012) 865 (hereafter 'Waincymer').

[162] Irene Warshauser, 'Electronic Discovery and Arbitration: A Shortcut Through E-Discovery' in Arthur Rovine (ed), *Contemporary Issues in International Arbitration and Mediation. Fordham Papers 2008* (Martinus Nijhoff Publishers 2009) 255; Ashford (n 142) 73.

[163] O'Malley Rules of Evidence (n 29) para 3.46.

[164] Commentary on the IBA Rules (n 5).

Tribunals will sometimes allow requests for production of documents which are said to be burdensome for the requesting party to produce, but at the expense of the requesting rather than the producing party.[165] 6.159

7. Statement of Reasons Why the Requesting Party Assumes that the Documents Are in the Possession, Custody, or Control of Another Party

3.3(c)(ii) a statement of the reasons why the requesting Party assumes the Documents requested are in the possession, custody or control of another Party.

a. Introduction

Article 3.3(c)(ii) provides that the Request to Produce should contain a statement setting out the reasons why the requesting party believes that the documents it wants are in the 'possession, custody or control' of another party. 6.160

Although we go on to discuss each of these terms, a party requesting production will generally simply use the phrase 'possession, custody or control' with supporting explanation as to why the opponent party either has the document or can obtain access to it. If the request is resisted and the tribunal is asked to make an order for production, the tribunal may also look at the requirement in the round without too much analysis as to which of the three terms are satisfied. 6.161

Article 3.3(c)(ii) does not require the requesting party to provide proof that the documents are held by another party. However, in practice, if the request is objected to by the opponent party, the requesting party will need to be able to persuade the tribunal that its assumption that the objecting party has the documents is a reasonable one. The circumstances giving rise to a belief that another party holds particular documents will be case-specific. 6.162

For example, in relation to the Article 3.3(a) requirement, we gave the example of a construction dispute between an employer and main contractor relating to particular aspects of the project for which the contractor is seeking an extension of time due to alleged default on the employer side, and where the employer is arguing that the delay was caused by problems with the contractor's design. The employer wants to see correspondence between the main contractor and subcontractors relating to any problems with the project over the period when the alleged delay occurred. If it is clear from the contract documents or other correspondence that the main contractor has used subcontractors on the relevant part of the project, the employer will have reasonable grounds for believing that correspondence between the main contractors and the subcontractor relating to the project will exist. By extension, it is reasonable to assume for 6.163

[165] Ashford (n 142) 64.

the purposes of Article 3.3(c)(ii) that copies of that correspondence will be in the possession of the main contractor.

6.164 A similar situation may arise where the party to whom a Request to Produce is addressed is required by legislation or regulation to keep such documents. We are aware of this point being addressed before the Chinese Court in *Long Tiwei v Chongqing Haoyouduo Department Store Co. Ltd*, where it was found that, if a party is under an obligation to keep a particular document in its records, it can be assumed that the documents are in the possession of that a party.[166]

b. Meaning of 'possession, custody and control'

i. Introduction

6.165 As mentioned, the phrase 'possession, custody or control' is used in both Article 3.3 (c)(i) and Article 3.3 (c)(ii). It is also used in Article 3.4, which makes clear that the obligation to produce a document (whether on a voluntary basis or pursuant to an order for production made by the tribunal) is limited to documents that a party has in its 'possession, custody or control'. Consideration of this phrase is most likely to be engaged where a requesting party has stated in a Request to Produce its belief that particular documents are held by the party to whom the request is addressed, and the party alleged to have the documents contends that they are not in that party's 'possession custody or control' and it cannot therefore produce them. Although the intention behind practical application of the phrase is reasonably clear—in essence, that by some legal means the party to whom the Request to Produce is addressed has a right of access to the documents in question—in a contentious environment such as international arbitration, there may be considerable debate between the parties, and with the tribunal, as to what constitutes 'possession, custody or control'.

6.166 The Commentary to the IBA Rules does not mention the origin of the phrase 'possession, custody or control',[167] but it is suggested by Marghitola that is derived from common law rules—in particular, the United States Federal Rules of Civil Procedure, which contain the very same formula of 'possession, custody and control'.[168] Although adoption of English-/US-style discovery was regarded by the drafting committee as being inappropriate in international arbitration, it may be that adoption of the concept of 'possession, custody or control' was considered useful as part of the package of measures by which a compromise between common law and civil law approaches could be found.

[166] *Long Tiwei v Chongqing Haoyouduo Department Store Co. Ltd* heard before the Chongqing No. 1 Intermediate People's Court. This was reported to us in BCLP Survey on use of the IBA Rules.

[167] IBA Working Party, 'Commentary on the New IBA Rules of Evidence in International Commercial Arbitration' (2000) 2 Business Law International 16 (hereafter 'Commentary on the 1999 IBA Rules') refers only to documents being in the 'possession' of another party, although those rules contain the same description 'possession, custody or power' as appears in the 2010 IBA Rules.

[168] United States Federal Rules of Civil Procedure, rr 26(a)(1)(A)(ii), 34(a)(1), and 45(a)(1)(iii). See further Marghitola (n 1) 64.

The terms 'possession', 'custody', and 'control' are not defined terms within the IBA Rules. It is suggested that this poses a problem because lawyers from different jurisdictions may understand these terms to mean different things. By way of example, in some civil law countries 'possession' includes 'indirect possession' or actual control over a document; while in many common law countries the term possession does not extend to documents that can be obtained on demand, that situation instead falling within the description of 'control'.[169] Given the lack of a definition in the IBA Rules, there exists the potential for disagreement on what each of the terms 'possession', 'custody', and 'control' means. However, that is not to say that the inclusion of a definition of those terms in the rules would remove argument on whether a particular situation falls within one or more of those definitions or outside all of them. The inclusion of a definition might also hinder the flexibility available to a tribunal when interpreting these terms in an individual case. **6.167**

As things stand, it is left to an individual tribunal to decide how the terms are to be interpreted on the facts of an individual case. In our view, the precise meaning of individual terms may not matter very much in practice. The idea behind the formula adopted in the IBA Rules was to capture all situations where the party to whom the Request to Produce is addressed can, in practice, obtain a requested document. Even if a different interpretation is applied to individual terms, the outcome may be the same. For example, a civil law arbitrator may take the view that a document is in the 'possession' of the party while an arbitrator with a common law background may treat the same document as being in that party's 'control'. It does not really matter because in both instances the tribunal is entitled to order production. The adoption of three alternative criteria for production suggests that a relatively liberal approach to establishing an ability to produce requested documents on the part of the non-requesting party was intended by those drafting the IBA Rules. **6.168**

However, given that the IBA Rules adopt three categories of access to a document (possession, custody and control), as a matter of analysis the reader must assume that each has a distinct meaning. The phrase is written in the disjunctive and therefore only one of the descriptions needs to be met. We therefore address below the difference in meaning often attributed to the each of the three terms. **6.169**

ii. Possession

The meaning of 'possession' differs according to jurisdiction. However, it is generally not limited to physical possession of the document. As mentioned, in some civil law systems possession includes 'indirect possession' by means of control over a document.[170] The provisions of the current English civil procedural rules treat 'possession' **6.170**

[169] See for more detail Marghitola (n 1) 64–65, who suggests that a uniform interpretation of the phrase 'possession, custody, and control' is desirable.

[170] In Germany, German Civil Code BGB, s 854(1).

as a sub-set of 'control'.[171] However, for the purposes of the IBA Rules, and to distinguish it from 'custody' or 'control', we suggest that a document may be said to be in the possession of the party if it has a legal right to hold the document, and is in physical possession of it—in either electronic or paper form. A statement of those circumstances should be included in the Request to Produce. A request for production that relies on some other circumstance enabling the opponent party to access the document may be better made by additional reference to one of the other terms in Article 3.3(c).

iii. Custody

6.171 In broad terms, 'custody' is generally understood to mean the mere physical holding of a document without rights over the document. For example, for the purposes of document disclosure, English procedure rules traditionally distinguished between an agent being in 'possession' of documents entrusted to him by the owner of the documents, and a servant merely carrying the documents and thereby having 'custody' of them.[172]

6.172 Where a party requests production of documents on the basis that they are in the custody of another party, they should explain the basis of that belief in accordance with the requirements of Article 3.3(c)(ii). For example, if there is evidence that a bank acted as a depositary for certain documents and there is no evidence of the termination of that depositary relationship, the requesting party may reasonably make a statement that it assumes that the documents are still in the custody of the bank.

iv. Control

6.173 Although a fairly straightforward concept, the issue of what constitutes 'control' is a frequent source of argument in relation to document production.

6.174 In broad terms, if a document is not in the possession or custody of a party, but that party has the ability to obtain the document without any assistance from the tribunal or any other third party, it may generally be assumed that the document is in the 'control' of the party. The party requested to produce the document may control a right of access to the document, or control the party holding the document. One United States authority defines control as 'the legal right, authority or ability to obtain upon demand documents in the possession of another'.[173]

6.175 In England, a previous version of the Civil Procedure Rules covering discovery and inspection of documents stated that: '. . . each party must . . . make and serve on that other party a list of the documents which are or have been in his possession, custody or power . . .'. 'Power' in this context was similar in concept to 'control' and, as in the case of the IBA Rules, that term was distinguished from 'possession' and 'custody'. The

[171] CPR 31.8. Under the previous version of the English Civil Procedure Rules, a party to litigation had an obligation to disclose 'documents which are or have been in its possession, custody or power' with the word 'power' then understood to be similar in concept to 'control'. RSC Ord 24, r2.

[172] RSC Ord 24, r 20.

[173] *American Rock Salt & Co. v Norfolk Southern Corp.* 228 FRD 426, 460 (US District Court, WDNY, 19 August 2004).

note to that rule comments on the meaning of '[d]ocuments that are or have been in his power' as including 'all documents which though they are not in his possession or custody, he has a right to obtain from the person who has them—e.g. where he is the owner and has not parted with the right to possession.'[174]

In *Lonrho Limited v The Shell Petroleum Company Limited & The British Petroleum Company Limited*, the English Court set out a test for what constituted 'power', with Lord Diplock stating that it meant 'a presently enforceable legal right to obtain from whoever actually holds the document inspection of it without the need to obtain the consent of anyone else.'[175] As discussed, the current version of the English Civil Procedure Rules adopts a different approach of limiting the obligation of disclosure to documents within a party's control, and defining control widely to include documents that are in a party's physical possession, or where the party has the right to possession of them or a right to inspect and take copies,[176] but the *Lonrho* test remains relevant.[177] **6.176**

The Irish Supreme Court has adopted a similar definition to that used by the English Court. In *Johnson v Church of Scientology*, it held that a document is in the power of a party where that party has an enforceable legal right to obtain the document from whoever actually holds the document without the need to obtain the consent of any other party.[178] **6.177**

Consistent with the national court approaches described above, Professor Waincymer describes 'control' as used in the IBA Rules by reference to the power of the respondent to obtain the document: **6.178**

> The concept of control should be interpreted in a practical and realistic fashion. Is the relationship between the party against whom the order is sought and the person in possession of the document such that the former could reasonably be expected to gain access from the latter? That should include situations where the party against whom the application is made could have power over a third party, either through a corporate group or some contractual or other right to gain access to the document . . . [179]

In similar fashion, the reference to 'control' in the IBA Rules may also be interpreted as covering documents that are in the possession of a third party but that can be obtained **6.179**

[174] RSC Ord 24, r 1(1). As mentioned, the current version of the English Civil Procedure Rules adopts a different approach of limiting the obligation of disclosure to documents within a party's control and defining control widely to include documents that are in a party's physical possession, or where the party has the right to possession of them or a right to inspect and take copies. CPR 31.8. However, it has been noted that, in substance, there may be little difference between the two formulations, although the CPR concept may be broader. See CPR 31.16.3.

[175] *Lonrho Ltd. and Another v Shell Petroleum Co. Ltd. and Another* [1980] 1 WLR 627, 635.

[176] CPR 31.8. As discussed, 'control' as used in the English Civil Procedure Rules describes a range of situations, including those where, under the previous version of the rules (RSC Ord 24, r 2), documents would have been found to be within the 'power' of a party and therefore required to be disclosed.

[177] For example, see discussions in *North Shore Ventures Limited v Anstead Holdings Inc.* [2012] EWCA Civ 11 (hereafter '*North Shore*').

[178] *Johnson v Church of Scientology* [2001] 1 IR 682.

[179] Waincymer (n 161) 864.

by the party to whom the Request to Produce is delivered without difficulty and without third-party consent.

6.180 A common-sense approach to such issues is desirable. As Gary Born indicates, the term 'control' should not be applied in an overly technical way:

> The essential point is that control is not a technical concept, but rather a practical one which should be liberally interpreted and applied.[180]

6.181 In similar vein, O'Malley notes that:

> In terms of evidentiary procedure, 'control' is not a strict concept that is defined by legal personage. In other words, if a document is held outside the files of a party, it does not necessarily mean it does not have 'control' over it. *Parties to arbitration are expected to attempt to obtain requested documents from related corporate entities or parties with whom they have a relationship.*[181]

6.182 There are many examples of control which are, to a large extent, uncontroversial.

6.183 One is a contractual right to request a document. If a party has entered into a contract with a third party under which it has provided certain documents to that third party (for example, for research or design purposes) but the contract provides that the party may call for their return at any time, then the document remains within the control of the contracting party.[182]

6.184 Another example is a power of a party to obtain documents from state authorities. In Russia, an abstract from a land registry showing the current owner or holder of the property can normally be obtained by any person. However, only the current owner (or holder of another proprietary title such as leaseholder) can request information relating to underlying documents of entitlement.[183] In such a case, if the applicant is seeking production of the abstract showing succession in title over the land and the respondent is currently a registered owner of the land, it is arguably within the respondent's control to apply to the land registry and to obtain the abstract sought.

6.185 There may, however, be less-straightforward situations. For example, it is less clear whether documents that a party has a right to inspect, but over which he has no other rights, can properly be said to be within that party's control. In domestic litigation in Australia, it was held by the Supreme Court of Victoria that a patient's medical records were not within the patient's power, despite the patient having a right of access to review the records.[184] Whether the same conclusion would be arrived at by application of the IBA Rules is uncertain. Leaving aside arguments around whether an objection to

180 Born (n 78) 2365.
181 O'Malley Rules of Evidence (n 29) para 3.49 (emphasis added).
182 Waincymer (n 161) 863–65.
183 Russian Federal Law on State Registration of Title to Real Estate, Article 62(14).
184 *Psalidis & Anor v Norwich Union Life Australia Limited* [2009] VSC 417.

production would succeed on grounds of doctor/patient privilege,[185] medical records might be said to be in the control of a (patient) party if that party not only has a right to review documents but also the right to take a photocopy, and can therefore produce it if so ordered by the tribunal.

The most hotly debated issue on control is the question of whether documents are in the control of a party if they are held by its affiliates or subsidiaries. Another issue concerns the question of whether a sovereign respondent has 'possession, custody or control' of documents if they are in the possession of its municipal authorities or other government agency. **6.186**

v. Documents held by affiliates and subsidiaries

A party requesting production of documents from a corporate entity will very often extend the scope of the request to include documents held by an affiliate of the corporate entity. Such requests are frequently resisted on the basis that the affiliate is an independent legal entity and that the party to whom the Request to Produce is addressed has no right to access or produce copies of documents held by the affiliate. Gary Born confirms the recurrence of this issue before tribunals and the fact that orders for production will very often be made: **6.187**

> A recurrent issue is whether a party may be ordered to produce documents in the possession of its corporate affiliates (e.g., subsidiaries, parents, sister subsidiaries). Tribunals have not infrequently ordered parties to produce documents held by other members of a corporate group, on the theory that these are generally in the control of a member of that group . . . [186].

In truth, the issue of whether a party to arbitration has sufficient 'control' to produce documents held by an affiliate company will involve—certainly by the party wishing to formulate an objection to production and ideally by the tribunal as well—an analysis of the nature of the relationship between the two entities,[187] as well as the ease with which the party to the arbitration may be able to obtain a copy. In relation to the latter, the Commentary to the IBA Rules notes that, even where a certain document is known to exist and considered to be within the 'possession, custody or control' of another party, where it would be unreasonably difficult for that party to obtain the documents, it may be possible for it to rely on an objection to production under Article 9.2 (c) of the IBA Rules (unreasonable burden to produce). **6.188**

A bare objection that a document is in the possession of an affiliated company (and therefore not available for production) should not be accepted as sufficient to resist production without further scrutiny. However, a situation in which the arbitrating party is **6.189**

[185] See, for more detail Richard M Mosk and Tom Ginsburg, 'Evidentiary Privileges in International Arbitration' (2001) 50 ICLQ 345, 353–55.
[186] Born (n 78) 2365 (internal references are omitted).
[187] See, for more detail, O'Malley Rules of Evidence (n 29) para 3.50.

the parent of the company in possession of the documents may be very different from one in which the arbitrating party is the subsidiary of that company. Overall, much may depend on the structure of the particular group of companies and where real control lies. In particular, whether the party to the arbitration has a right to obtain the document without its affiliate's agreement or, often more likely, where the relationship between the two entities is such that if the party to the arbitration asks for the documents to be made available that request will be met.[188]

6.190 The need to consider the precise relationship between the arbitrating party and the company holding the documents is reflected in decisions by national courts. For example, the Irish courts have taken the view that, within a corporate structure, documents will usually be understood to be within the control of the party if held by a wholly/majority owned subsidiary, but that is not the case in respect of documents held by a parent or sister company.[189] The approach taken by the Australian courts appears to be similar. They have held that an Australian subsidiary of a foreign holding company did not have possession of documents of the holding company and could not be compelled to produce them.[190]

6.191 The English Courts have also given helpful guidance on the need to look beyond the legal architecture of the corporate relationship. In *Schlumberger Holdings Limited v Electromagnetic Geoservices* the claimant was a holding company. The defendant applied for a disclosure order that would require the claimant to search the records of companies within the claimant group who were not parties to the action. The context of the application was that the claimant had already carried out searches of files held within the group. The judge made the order for the disclosure on the basis of evidence that, as a matter of fact, the claimant was provided with access to group company documents.[191] Mr Justice Floyd explained his reasoning as follows:

> I accept that the mere fact that a party to litigation may be able to obtain documents by seeking the consent of a third party will not of its own be sufficient to make that party's documents disclosable by the party to the litigation. They are not within his present or past control precisely because it is conceivable that the third party may refuse to give consent. But what happens where the evidence reveals that the party has already enjoyed, and continues to enjoy, the co-operation and consent of the third party to inspect his documents and take copies and has already produced a list of documents based on the consent that has been given and where there is no reason to suppose that that position may change? Because that is the factual situation with which I am confronted here. In my judgment, the evidence in this case sufficiently establishes that relevant documents are and have been within the control of the claimant.[192]

[188] ibid.
[189] See, eg *Thema International Fund plc v HSBC Institutional Trust Services (Ireland) Limited* [2013] IESC 5.
[190] *Gambro Pty Ltd v Fresenius Medical Care Australia Pty Ltd* [2002] FCA 1359.
[191] *Schlumberger Holdings Ltd v Electromagnetic Geoservices AS* [2008] EWHC 56 (PAT) (hereafter '*Schlumberger*'). This case was referred to in *North Shore* (n 177) in which the judge summarized the facts of *Schlumberger* in this way.
[192] ibid 21.

In *North Shore*,[193] the English court again focused on the substance of the relationship between the two parties involved. In that case, which concerned a situation in which the litigant parties who had been asked to provide the documents had set up a number of trusts under which those parties were discretionary beneficiaries, it was said that the court would have regard to 'the true nature of the relationship between the third party and the litigant' and interestingly, that even if the arrangements made between the two parties precluded the party in physical possession from handing the documents over to the true owner, it would nonetheless be open to the court to find that the documents remained within the control of the latter party.[194] **6.192**

In broad terms, the examples presented here are concerned with what Marghitola describes as the criteria of 'effective control'.[195] However, it has to be recognized that much will also depend upon the predilections of individual tribunals and the individual facts of the case. There is a school of thought that tribunals should be more liberal in their application of the requirements of 'control' than might be appropriate in national courts.[196] It is not uncommon for arbitral tribunals to order a party to search the records of affiliated entities, as well as its advisers or agents in order to find responsive documents.[197] **6.193**

Of course, if the party required to produce documents cannot comply with the order for production because the party in possession (either in truth or ostensibly) refuses to make the documents available, then the documents will not be produced. That might be said to be an end of the matter and no harm done to the party ordered to produce. However, it should be remembered that it is open to a tribunal to draw adverse inferences in circumstances where a party has failed to disclose a document ordered to be produced.[198] This raises related issues as to the burden of proof on the issue of 'possession, custody or control'. We suggest that a tribunal will need to be very confident that documents are in a party's control before drawing adverse inferences as a result of the non-production of documents. **6.194**

A middle ground adopted by some tribunals where the legal right or ability to obtain documents held by an affiliate is not clearly established is to direct that the arbitrating party take active steps to request a copy of the documents from the related company—sometimes couched in terms of that party using its 'best efforts' to obtain the documents. Tribunals are for the most part composed of individuals with broad commercial experience. They will know that, although a subsidiary may not have a legal right to obtain documents from its parent company, in many cases if the subsidiary makes a genuine effort to obtain the parent company's co-operation to facilitate **6.195**

193 *North Shore* (n 177).
194 ibid 40.
195 Marghitola (n 1) para 5.08.
196 ibid.
197 See, for more detail O'Malley Rules of Evidence (n 29) para 3.50.
198 See Chapter 12 paras 12.54–12.56 and 12.355–12.384.

the production of a document then this can be achieved.[199] An example of this approach is a decision of the tribunal in PCA case *Clayton v Canada*, where it was said by the tribunal that:

> [T]he Tribunal accepts that such documents may not be in the possession, custody or control of the Respondent. However, the Tribunal wishes to clarify that, for a party to claim that documents are not in its control, it must have made 'best efforts' to obtain documents that are in the possession of persons or entities with whom or which the party has a relevant relationship. This is consistent with the approach adopted by the Tribunal in *Vito G. Gallo v Government of Canada* in its Procedural Order No. 2 dated February 10, 2009.[200]

The tribunal held that Canada should use its 'best efforts' to obtain documents that are in the possession of persons or entities with whom or which the party has a relevant relationship.[201]

6.196 Another example is an ICC case where the order for production was couched in terms of using 'best efforts' to obtain documents. As pointed out by Marghitola, the requirement for production in that case was limited to documents of which the requesting party had actual knowledge.[202]

vi. Documents held by municipal authorities or other governmental bodies of a sovereign respondent

6.197 As mentioned, another issue that gives rise to debate is the extent to which one arm of a state may obtain documents from another state agency. This is touched upon in the Canadian cases mentioned earlier. The logic applicable to this situation is similar to that discussed in relation to a corporate structure. If a government has a legal right to request documents from its constituent parts (such as municipalities), a tribunal may find that the documents are in the control of the government party.

6.198 The tribunal in PCA arbitration *Vito G. Gallo v Government of Canada* refused to decide whether municipalities were within the control of Canada, but took note of Canada's offer to use its best endeavours and to write to certain municipalities to request that they voluntarily produce documents for the arbitration. The parties were also given liberty to apply to the tribunal should those efforts render no result.[203]

[199] In a litigation context, where the 'true' relationship means that the documents are effectively within the control of the party requested to make production, the English court has been prepared to make a disclosure order. See *North Shore* (n 177) 40.

[200] *William Ralph Clayton and others v Government of Canada* (Procedural Order No. 8, 25 November 2009) PCA Case No. 2009-04 [1(h)].

[201] Ibid. The award gives no general guidance as to what that 'relevant' relationship should be. However, in *Clayton and others*, the relevant agency was said (by the claimant) to have been a governmental entity established under the Canadian Environmental Assessment Act and an 'integral part of the government apparats of Canada'.

[202] Hamilton (n 54) 74.

[203] *Vito G. Gallo v The Government of Canada* (Procedural Order No. 2, 10 February 2009) PCA Case No. 55798 [7]–[9].

8. The Use of Redfern Schedules for Requests to Produce

It is common practice in international arbitration for a Request to Produce to be delivered in the form of a Redfern Schedule. This is a table containing a number of columns in which the party requesting production will set out the categories of document that it wishes to see, usually supported in a second column by the information required by Article 3.3(a), (b), and (c). The party to whom the request is addressed will then complete the next empty column in the table, indicating whether it intends to produce the requested documents on a voluntary basis pursuant to Article 3.4, or if it objects to production on one of the grounds for objection set out in Article 9.2. If it objects, it will also provide details of the grounds of objection relied upon in relation to each category of document to which objection is taken. Where the objection cannot be resolved, the tribunal will decide on the matter under Article 3.7 (see 6.232–6.262) and will often enter its ruling on the objection in a final column of the table. There will generally be a separate Redfern Schedule for each party's requests to produce. **6.199**

The Redfern Schedule is named after Alan Redfern,[204] who is credited for its introduction as standard practice in international arbitration. Redfern describes the provenance of the Redfern Schedule in these terms: **6.200**

> The Redfern Schedule was devised in order to crystallise the precise issues of document production which were in dispute between the parties. The arbitral tribunal would then know what position the parties had reached in the course of their exchanges, which may well have been going on for several months. The Redfern Schedule makes it possible for both the parties' lawyers and the arbitral tribunal to know where the parties finally stand in relation to detailed requests for document production and the reasons for objection to them. The tribunal can then go through the requests, one by one, and decide how each is to be dealt with.[205]

[204] At the time, Alan Redfern was a partner in an international law firm in the City of London, and is now a member of the English bar and a well-known arbitrator.

[205] Alan Redfern, 'Documentary Disclosure in International Arbitration: The IBA Rules and the Redfern Schedule' in Andrea Carlevaris and others (eds), *International Arbitration Under Review: Essays in Honour of John Beechey* (International Chamber of Commerce 2015) 343, 351. With the permission of Alan Redfern, we are able to share some further insight into the provenance of the Redfern Schedule. In around 2000, Mr Redfern was sitting on a tribunal with a retired English House of Lords judge as presiding arbitrator. The case concerned three companies—one claimant and two respondents. Over a period of several months there had been a series of exchanges between lawyers in relation to document production requests. When the tribunal came to deliberate on disputed requests the chairman found himself with a large pile of lawyers' letters in front of him and asked how on earth the issues could be distilled from correspondence? Mr Redfern replied: 'Well, the parties' lawyers know better than we do where they have got to. So why don't we get them to write down a sort of definitive list of what after all this exchange of correspondence represents their position today in terms of what they want and what they are prepared to give the other parties. We could have a schedule, couldn't we? We could have four columns: first column the request for production of the document. Second column: why do you want it, why is it material to the outcome of the case? Third column: what is the response—you can't find it or it's too wide or its legal professional privilege or we'll give you some but not everything. The fourth column: decision of the Tribunal.' The chairman liked the idea and said 'We will call it the Redfern Schedule.' Thus, the Redfern Schedule was born.

6.201 The Redfern Schedule was later picked up by other arbitrators and in 2012 the ICC published a report on Techniques for Controlling Time and Costs in Arbitration in which it recommended use of Redfern Schedules.[206] From that time onwards the Redfern Schedule has become the prevalent form of written vehicle for document production requests.

6.202 The original form of Redfern Schedule had only four columns (requested documents, reason for request, reply, and tribunal's decision). In current practice, counsel will often now make modifications to this format. For example, there may be a first column that identifies requests by number. Where there are a significant number of requests this provides an easy reference point. Another more substantive modification is an additional column in which the requesting party is given an opportunity to respond to objections raised by its opponent, either by taking issue with the grounds of objection or perhaps taking them into account and proposing a modification to the original request. This addition appears to be particularly prevalent among counsel from common law jurisdictions where an applicant is used to having the last word. If used, this last round of comments will need to be built into the procedural timetable. There are no rules about the format of a Redfern Schedule and its precise form will vary according to the preferences of the person drafting it. For example, there may not always be a discrete column or line reference in which the requesting party confirms (as required by Article 3.3(c)(i)) that it does not have the requested documents. Since this is a requirement applicable to all requests it is sometimes addressed by way of a general statement to this effect in the introductory part of the Redfern Schedule. However, any exceptions to that position (for example, where the requesting party has a particular document or category of documents in its possession, but claims (pursuant to Article 3.3(c)(i)) that it would be unreasonably burdensome to have to produce them itself), are generally best dealt with against the individual item requested as the explanation given will have to be tailored to those documents.

6.203 It is prudent *not* to make such a general statement in relation to the requirement at Article 3.3(c)(ii) that the requesting party provide a statement of the reasons why that party assumes that the requested documents are in the possession, custody, or control of the responding party. Those reasons will generally be specific to the particular document or category of documents being requested. It is more appropriate to include these reasons in the appropriate column against the relevant category of document. Appropriate cross-referencing can limit the need to repeat the same ground more than once.

6.204 A regrettable development in relation to use of the Redfern Schedule is the practice of some counsel to use it as a vehicle for making submissions on the merits of the case—in particular, unnecessarily stating again and again what their case is and referencing

[206] ICC Report on Controlling Time and Costs (n 34) para 52.

arguments relied upon that have no relevance to the critical path by which a requested document may be said to be relevant to the case and material to its outcome. In addition, as Shore describes it, 'the determination of counsel that what they say they need should control' the process, has resulted in Redfern Schedules that are complex and overlong; he continues:

> [W]e all now have the Redfern Schedule which, in its origins, reflected the developments of the newer editions of the IBA Rules of Evidence. What the Redfern Schedule meant to do was organize and discipline the parties in order to make sure that narrow, material, specific and relevant documents were the only ones—even though internal—that would be produced. But, as we all know, the Redfern Schedule has become a trial within a trial.[207]

Nonetheless the utility of the Redfern Schedule as a vehicle for distilling requests, objections, and outstanding issues should not be underestimated.

By way of illustration, the below is an extract from a Redfern Schedule published elsewhere concerning an objection to a request for production made on grounds that the requested documents were not relevant to the case or material to its outcome.[208] **6.205**

No.	Document Description	Relevance and Materiality/ Possession of Documents	Claimant's /Respondent's Response
3	An extract of the due diligence report in connection with X's acquisition of Y in 2012 and contained in the transaction files for the acquisition referred to in para. 20 of Mr Jones' witness statement, including all sections of that report which relate to the Contract.	The report will show what X and its advisers understood the Contract to mean in 2012 before the context of this arbitration. The interpretation of the Contract is at the core of the case and this document will be material to outcome in that it will show how the Contract might be interpreted absent pressure of this arbitration.	The documents are neither relevant to the case nor material to its outcome. The understanding of the contracting parties (Y and Z at the time they negotiated and concluded the contract) are relevant, not X's understanding when it acquired Y.

A more detailed fictional example of a Redfern Schedule and a template Redfern Schedule prepared by the authors can be found at Appendix 4 and Appendix 5. **6.206**

A variation on the traditional form of Redfern Schedule is to present the information that would normally appear in the various columns of one horizontal line in the form of an individual table for each request. **6.207**

[207] Laurence Shore, 'Chapter 3: Document Production, Witness Statements, and Cross-Examination: The Enduring Tensions in International Arbitration' in Stavros Brekoulakis and others (eds), *The Evolution and Future of International Arbitration* (Kluwer Law International 2016).

[208] Lotfi (n 40) 11.

D. Voluntary Production

3.4. Within the time ordered by the Arbitral Tribunal, the Party to whom the Request to Produce is addressed shall produce to the other Parties and, if the Arbitral Tribunal so orders, to it, all the Documents requested in its possession, custody or control as to which it makes no objection.

6.208 Article 3.4 is uncontroversial. It simply provides that, if a party has no objection to a document production request made on it, it should produce the requested document(s) by the date ordered by the tribunal. That date is likely to have been laid down in a previous procedural order. The timing of document production requests, to which the date for voluntary production will be linked, is discussed at 6.113-6.119.

6.209 The obligation to produce extends only to documents in that party's 'possession, custody or control'. The meaning of these terms is discussed at 6.165-6.198.

6.210 Under Article 3.4, the production of documents shall be made to all parties to the arbitration irrespective of which party actually made the request to which the documents are responsive. This is to ensure a level playing field between the parties to the arbitration and is consistent with the requirement of a fair process set out in the Preamble, as well as in many national law and institutional rules that may be applicable to the arbitration.

6.211 It is rarely the case that a party will take an extreme position in relation to document production requests made on it—most parties are unlikely to produce without objection everything that has been requested, or conversely to raise objections to each and every request. Parties will generally agree to produce some of the requested documents but take issue with others. Article 3.4 ensures that a respondent should not delay the production of the documents to which it makes no objection pending determination of objections to other requests.

6.212 There is no obligation under Article 3.4 to send produced documents to the tribunal unless there is a specific direction to do so. This is in contrast to the position under the 1999 IBA Rules where the default position was that the documents were to be produced both to the tribunal and the other parties. The Commentary explains that the rationale for the change was that it was often not efficient for a tribunal to review all of the documents at the stage of their production.[209]

6.213 The inefficiency to which the Commentary refers is an obvious one. It is rarely an efficient use of resources for arbitrators to review all of the documents provided by way of document production. Although the IBA Rules contribute to ensuring that such documents are relevant and material to the case,[210] in practice a large number of successful

[209] Commentary on the IBA Rules (n 5).

[210] IBA Rules (n 21) Article 3.3(b) requires the Request to Produce to contain a statement as to how the documents requested are relevant to the case and material to its outcome. If the request is contested, the Tribunal should

requests to produce will catch both highly relevant and less relevant or even irrelevant documents. It is the job of counsel for each party to review the universe of the produced documents and to select those that support the position of the party that counsel represents. It is these documents that are then introduced into the record in the arbitration for the tribunal to consider.[211]

Documents that a party obtains by means of the document production process will not generally, absent a specific order to this effect, be regarded as being 'on the record' or as having been 'filed' or 'submitted' unless and until they are produced with a submission or pleading, or as an exhibit to evidence filed.[212] Alternatively, the document should be submitted under Article 3.1 or Article 3.11. **6.214**

E. Objections to Production

Article 3.5 and 3.6

5. **If the Party to whom the Request to Produce is addressed has an objection to some or all of the Documents requested, it shall state the objection in writing to the Arbitral Tribunal and the other Parties within the time ordered by the Arbitral Tribunal. The reasons for such objection shall be any of those set forth in Article 9.2 or a failure to satisfy any of the requirements of Article 3.3.**
6. **Upon receipt of any such objection, the Arbitral Tribunal may invite the relevant Parties to consult with each other with a view to resolving the objection.**

1. Objections

Article 3.5 and 3.6 are best considered together. They are two elements of the same process by which a party may pursue an objection to a document production request made by another party. **6.215**

a. Introduction

Under the IBA Rules, when a request for production is made, the party to whom it is addressed must produce the requested document or make an objection. If that party **6.216**

only make an order for production if satisfied that the explanation given is adequate. In practice, the position is more complicated. See 6.76-6.146 .

211 This will be done pursuant to IBA Rules (n 21) Articles 3.1 and 3.11.

212 This is standard practice, but for an express direction in these terms see *Mesa Power Group LLC v Government of Canada* (Procedural Order No. 4, 12 July 2013) PCA Case No. 2012-17 [67.ii.d].

does not have a valid objection, it cannot withhold production. The documents must be produced pursuant to Article 3.4.

6.217 If the party receiving the request has an objection, it must state that objection in accordance with the requirements of Article 3.5. Under Article 3.6 the tribunal may then invite the parties to discuss the objection to see if it can be resolved.

b. Stating objections to production under Article 3.5

6.218 Article 3.5 provides that any objection must be stated in writing. If the parties are using Redfern Schedules the objections may be incorporated in to the appropriate column (see 6.199-6.207).

6.219 As with other requirements in Article 3, the objections must be delivered within the time ordered by the tribunal. Once again, that deadline is likely to have been laid down in a previous procedural order.

6.220 Under Article 3.5 the objections that may be raised fall into two categories. The first category of permitted objection concerns a failure of the requesting party to meet the requirements of Article 3.3 relating to the content of the Request to Produce. The second category comprises the various grounds for excluding evidence set out in Article 9.2.

i. Formal objections citing non-compliance with Article 3.3

6.221 As mentioned, Article 3.3 requires a description of an individual document, or a description 'in sufficient detail' of a narrow and specific category of documents sought; a statement that the documents are not in the possession, custody, or control of the requesting party (or that it would be unreasonably burdensome for that party to produce them); a statement as to why the requested documents are assumed to be in the possession, custody, or control of the opponent party; and a statement as to how the documents are relevant to the case and material to its outcome.

6.222 Provided the Request to Produce has been drafted with care by reference to the provisions of Article 3.3, it is unusual to see an objection based on a failure to include the information required by that provision.

6.223 More often, the objection founded on Article 3.3 is based on an alleged inadequacy or error in the information that has been provided. For example, the objection may be that the description of the document requested is too vague and therefore non-compliant with the requirement for specificity in description, or that, on proper analysis, the documents requested are not relevant to the case or material to its outcome. The latter objection is separately included in Article 9.2(a), but where this ground is available parties will often refer both to Article 9.2 and the failure to satisfy the requirements of Article 3.3.

ii. Objections under Article 9.2

Article 9.2 of the IBA Rules sets out a number of grounds on which the documents requested may be excluded from production. It should be noted that, under Article 9.2, these grounds are available to be raised by a party in relation to any evidence at issue in the arbitration and not just documents that it has been asked to produce. **6.224**

The available grounds set out in Article 9.2 are reproduced in full below. **6.225**

(a) lack of sufficient relevance to the case or materiality to its outcome;
(b) legal impediment or privilege under the legal or ethical rules determined by the Arbitral Tribunal to be applicable;
(c) unreasonable burden to produce the requested evidence;
(d) loss or destruction of the Document that has been shown with reasonable likelihood to have occurred;
(e) grounds of commercial or technical confidentiality that the Arbitral Tribunal determines to be compelling;
(f) grounds of special political or institutional sensitivity (including evidence that has been classified as secret by a government or a public international institution) that the Arbitral Tribunal determines to be compelling; or
(g) considerations of procedural economy, proportionality, fairness, or equality of the Parties that the Arbitral Tribunal determines to be compelling.

The interpretation and application of these grounds are discussed in Chapter 12.

Under Article 3.5 a party may rely on any of the grounds set out in Article 9.2. It may rely on more than one ground in relation to an individual request to produce and it is common practice to do so where more than one ground is applicable. A party may also rely on an Article 9.2 ground in combination with an objection that an Article 3.3 requirement has not been met. For example, if the request is broad and unfocused such that it will catch a large volume of irrelevant documents it may be objected to the basis that (a) under both Article 3.3 and Article 9.2(a) the documents lack sufficient relevance to the case and materiality to its outcome; (b) under Article 9.2(c) the request places an unreasonable burden on the party requested to produce the documents; and (c) under Article 9.2(g) runs against considerations of procedural economy and proportionality. **6.226**

In order to simplify dealing with objections by reference to the various paragraph numbers in Article 9.2 (often necessitating counsel and the tribunal to repeatedly refer to the IBA Rules in order to check the particular basis of objection) eminent arbitrator VV Veeder QC designed what has become known as the 'Veeder Code' or 'Veeder Protocol' by which each of the grounds of objection is given a code that is easier to associate with the particular ground of objection in question than the Article 9 paragraph reference. For example, 'M' stands for materiality. If an objection is based on the contention that the document is not relevant and material 'M' can be used in the Redfern Schedule in **6.227** combination with the Article 9.2 reference. The Veeder Code can also be used in arbitrations not subject to application of the IBA Rules. A copy of the Veeder Code can be found in Appendix 6.

2. Obligation to Meet and Confer under Article 3.6

6.228 Article 3.6 empowers the tribunal to invite the parties to consult with each other with a view to resolving an objection to production. This is a new provision that did not exist in the 1999 IBA Rules.

6.229 As one commentator explains:

> Requiring parties to meet and confer regarding disputes over evidence is obvious because it places a certain 'onus' on them to act in a reasonable manner. When a tribunal requests cooperation between the parties, it is only the most recalcitrant of participants who flatly refuses to seek a reasonable way of addressing its concerns. Often such a conference is all that is required to resolve disputes over document production, and thus the addition of Article 3.6 to the IBA Rules was a welcome innovation.[213]

6.230 The word 'may' indicates that it is a right, but not an obligation, of the tribunal to invite the parties to consult. In the majority of cases it is useful to invite discussion and to build into the procedural timetable a period within which such consultation may take place. Where parties are genuinely constructive in their approach to consultation it may be possible to resolve a large part of the disagreement, sometimes by withdrawal or acceptance of a request, but more often by the parties negotiating a compromise position that involves a narrowing of the date range or description of the documents sought. Even where parties are not really interested in cooperation they may nonetheless, for tactical reasons, seek to narrow the areas of dispute. Counsel on both sides will understand that the tribunal is unlikely to be impressed with unmeritorious technical arguments that simply seek to obstruct the document production process.

6.231 Unfortunately, there will be some matters where there is no scope for agreement between the parties. While it would perhaps be wrong to shut out the possibility of negotiation altogether, the tribunal may decide under Article 3.6 to keep the period within which consultation is to take place relatively short. In exceptional circumstances—for example, if the history of the proceedings shows that good faith cooperation between the parties is not possible—the tribunal might decide that there is no purpose to be served by inviting the parties to consult.

[213] O'Malley Rules of Evidence (n 29) para 3.66.

F. Order for Production

3.7. Either Party may, within the time ordered by the Arbitral Tribunal, request the Arbitral Tribunal to rule on the objection. The Arbitral Tribunal shall then, in consultation with the Parties and in timely fashion, consider the Request to Produce and the objection. The Arbitral Tribunal may order the Party to whom such Request is addressed to produce any requested Document in its possession, custody or control as to which the Arbitral Tribunal determines that (i) the issues that the requesting Party wishes to prove are relevant to the case and material to its outcome; (ii) none of the reasons for objection set forth in Article 9.2 applies; and (iii) the requirements of Article 3.3 have been satisfied. Any such Document shall be produced to the other Parties and, if the Arbitral Tribunal so orders, to it.

1. Introduction

Article 3.7 lays down the procedure for the final step in the document production process by which a party can ask the tribunal to rule on the validity of an objection to production. **6.232**

As mentioned, under Article 3.2 each party to the arbitration is entitled to make a request for documents. The party to whom the request is addressed can either voluntarily produce the document (Article 3.4) or make an objection (Article 3.5). In some instances, the requesting party may be given an opportunity to reply to the objections. Following completion of these formal steps the tribunal may invite the parties to consult on the outstanding objections, or the parties may themselves decide that some negotiation would be sensible. However, once it becomes apparent which requests are not capable of being resolved, the party making the request must decide whether to abandon it or to ask the tribunal to rule on the validity of the objection. The request must be made within the time ordered by the tribunal as laid down in the procedural timetable. Where the tribunal rules in favour of the requesting party it may make an order for production. **6.233**

2. The Process for Determination by the Tribunal

When a request for a ruling under Article 3.7 is made by one of the parties, the tribunal must 'in consultation with the parties' and 'in timely fashion' consider the Request to Produce and the objections. **6.234**

The requirement that the tribunal deal with the matter 'in timely fashion' emphasizes the desirability of the tribunal making a ruling as soon as possible. A late ruling may affect the procedural timetable and the parties' preparations. For example, the documents **6.235** requested may be relevant to the witness evidence that a party is collecting or be something that one of its experts needs to see in order to address a particular point in expert evidence. As mentioned, the procedural timetable will generally contain a date by which requests for a ruling are to be filed. During discussions on the procedural timetable, it is good practice to ask the tribunal to set a date by which a ruling on production requests is to be given. Although some tribunals are occasionally reluctant to commit themselves to a date, if pressed they may still be prepared to agree a provisional date or date range.

6.236 As to the requirement that the tribunal consider the Request to Produce and objection 'in consultation with the parties', tribunals will sometimes agree to hold an oral hearing if requested by one of the parties. More often, they may convene a conference call during which they may ask questions and give each party an opportunity to explain its position more fully. In most cases, the matter is dealt with on paper only, the tribunal having discharged its obligation to consult through the Redfern Schedule process.

3. The Making of an Order for Production

6.237 Under Article 3.7, the tribunal may (but is not obliged to) order production of the requested documents where it is satisfied that:

(a) the issues that the requesting party wishes to prove are relevant to the case and material to its outcome;[214]
(b) none of the reasons for objection set forth in Article 9.2 applies;[215] and
(c) the requirements of Article 3.3 have been met.[216]

These requirements are dealt with in more detail at 6.239–6.256.

6.238 In practice, a tribunal may also take into account a number of factors relevant to the individual arbitration. It will generally, to the extent possible, wish to leave the parties feeling that they have been treated fairly and that the amount of document production obtained or given is relatively balanced. Of course, in some cases (for example, in a breach of warranty dispute following the sale of a company) the documents may be all or mostly on one side and such obvious even-handedness may not be possible. However, in every case, the tribunal will wish to pay close attention to the circumstances of the individual dispute. Although writing in respect of the 1999 IBA Rules, rather than the current version of the rules, Professor Hanotiau refers to the then-current best practice developed in the several years following introduction of the 1999 IBA Rules, and summarizes that practice in relation to these more nebulous factors:

214 IBA Rules (n 21) Article 3.7 (i).
215 ibid Article 3.7 (ii).
216 ibid Article 3.7 (iii). This third requirement was added in the 2010 revisions to the IBA Rules. See Commentary on the IBA Rules (n 5).

As rightly pointed out by Mr Veeder, the best procedures for document production will differ from case to case depending upon the dispute, the parties and their legal representatives. In a similar vein, Mr Hwang and Mr Chin emphasized that in dealing with applications for document production arbitral tribunals should take into consideration the expectations of the parties and their lawyers, the amount in dispute, the nature of the issues in dispute, and various other factors such as whether or not there are other means of obtaining the requisite information without resorting to discovery. It is paramount that in each case the arbitral tribunal strike a balance between a number of fundamental requirements: the integrity of the arbitral process, its efficiency in terms of time and costs, fairness to the parties and, to the best extent possible, satisfaction of their legitimate expectations and, above all, compliance with due process.[217]

a. Relevance and materiality

Before making an order for production the tribunal must be satisfied that the benchmarks of relevance and materiality have been met. Those benchmarks are discussed in detail at 6.74-6.146. **6.239**

The description of the standard described in Article 3.7 to which the tribunal must be satisfied is in slightly different terms to that appearing in Article 3.3(b) (which states that the Request to Produce shall contain 'a statement as to how *the documents are relevant to the case and material to its outcome*'). Article 3.7 provides that the tribunal may order production where (among other things) 'the Arbitral Tribunal determines that . . . *the issues that the requesting Party wishes to prove* are relevant to the case and material to its outcome . . . '.[218] There is some divergence of opinion on this issue but, in our view, nothing turns on the difference in formulation.[219] Article 3.3 concerns a requirement as to the content of the Request to Produce imposed on the parties. Article 3.7 is concerned with the tribunal's assessment of the Request to Produce. Although it is sometimes relied upon to support an argument that the burden of proof in relation to the issue to which the document is said to relate must lie with the requesting party, we disagree with that view. This issue is discussed in more detail at 6.131-6.140. **6.240**

217 Hanotiau (n 100) para 8. Other commentators make the same point. See, for example Pierre Tercier and Tetiana Bersheda, 'Chapter 7 Document Production in Arbitration: A Civil Law Viewpoint' in Markus Wirth, Christina Rouvinez, and Joachim Knoll (eds), *The Search for 'Truth' in Arbitration: Is Finding the Truth What Dispute Resolution Is About?* (JurisNet 2011) 90–92 (hereafter 'Tercier and Bersheda'); Kaufmann-Kohler and Bartsch (n 82). Hamilton (n 54) 73 refers to the desirability of the burden imposed on the producing party being proportionate to the evidentiary value of the documents.

218 Emphasis added. The other requirements of IBA Rules (n 21) Article 3.7 are that the document(s) should be in the possession, custody, or control of the producing party; none of the reasons for objection set out in Article 9.2 apply; and that the various requirements of Article 3.3 (including the provision by the requesting party of a statement explaining the relevance and materiality of the requested documents) have been met.

219 At least one commentator—Marghitola (n 1) 53—suggests that the requirement is to be interpreted as simply requiring the tribunal to be convinced of the relevance and materiality of the requested document. Others suggest that the tribunal must consider it from the perspective of the allegations relied on by the requesting party. For example, Tercier and Bersheda (n 217) 82 suggest that, when a tribunal has to determine whether the benchmark of relevance and materiality has been met, it should consider the following questions: if the requesting party has pleaded the factual circumstances in sufficient detail; if the opposing party has contradicted the factual allegation in sufficient detail; are the factual allegations are relevant and material?

6.241 Determination of whether a document or category of documents is relevant or material to outcome rests solely with the tribunal.[220] The tribunal will have to make that decision by reference to the matters referred to at 6.237 and the particular circumstances of the case. Associated factors that may arise in individual cases include those described next.

i. Tribunal reluctance to make a final decision on relevance and materiality

6.242 A tribunal will very often be asked to order document production after written submissions but prior to witness or expert evidence.[221] This is still a relatively early stage in the proceedings and a tribunal may have concerns that to indicate a position on relevance and materiality—particularly a decision to exclude documents from production on that basis—may compromise later developments, and even the award itself. This problem is one of the justifications given for application of a test of prima facie relevance and materiality in relation to document production requests.[222]

6.243 An arbitral tribunal is not bound by the prima facie finding of its procedural decisions when it issues the final award. However, a tribunal may wish to make an express statement of this position.[223]

6.244 If a tribunal is unsure, but not positive, about whether the requested production will be material, it may postpone a decision about whether to order production until it has a better understanding of the issues in the case.[224] This is unlikely to find favour with the parties but is an alternative way of dealing with cases where the tribunal is uncomfortable making a ruling, even on a prima facie basis. Of course, the tribunal may also be tempted simply to grant the request, rather than risk shutting out valuable evidence. However, if used too often, and depending on the volume of documents at play in the arbitration, the latter approach may simply store up problems for a later date, as well as creating unnecessary costs.

ii. Tribunal review of documents to determine relevance and materiality

6.245 Where a tribunal is in doubt about whether the requested documents meet the test of relevance and materiality the tribunal may feel that it would be useful to see the requested documents in order to determine this question.

220 IBA Rules (n 21) Article 3.7 makes express reference to a determination by the Arbitral Tribunal on relevance and materiality as a condition of the exercise of its discretion to order document production. Further, IBA Rules Article 9.1 states that the Tribunal shall determine the 'relevance [and] materiality' of evidence. Although documents requested to be produced are not yet evidence on the record it seems very clear that the power to make a determination on this issue rests solely with the tribunal.

221 As mentioned, the need for particular categories of document may not become apparent until issues between the parties can be identified from the submissions. Many counsel will wish to have completed document production prior to serving witness statements or experts' reports. Of course, if the memorial style approach of submissions is adopted production may be ordered to take place between first and second round submissions.

222 See 6.125-6.129 . See further Marghitola (n 1) 54.

223 For examples, see ibid and Philipp Habegger, 'Document Production: An Overview of Swiss Court and Arbitration Practice' in *Special Supplement 2006: Document Production in International Arbitration* (International Chamber of Commerce 2006) 21, para 41. For another similar example of an order in these terms, see paras 34 and 42 of 'Procedural Order No. 3 in Terms of Reference and Procedural Orders from ICC Case 18033 (Extracts)' (2016) 1 ICC Dispute Resolution Bulletin 165.

224 O'Malley Rules of Evidence (n 29) para 3.76.

It has been argued in some quarters that such an approach is not consistent with the Article 3 process, by which the tribunal should rule on an objection to production. It is pointed out that if a party has to produce a document to the tribunal before the tribunal has decided on the relevance or materiality of the requested documents, a requirement of prima facie relevance and materiality is de facto waived. In addition, production of documents to the tribunal prior to an order for production being made may raise issues of due process around fair treatment and the right to be heard on the evidence.[225] **6.246**

In addition, as mentioned elsewhere, the Commentary to the IBA Rules states that '[i]t is generally preferable that the arbitral tribunal not review any . . . documents itself . . . '.[226] The Commentary explains that '(i) if after reviewing the document the arbitral tribunal upholds the objection, it could not eliminate its knowledge of the document once it has been reviewed, or (ii) there may be confidentiality concerns'.[227] In extreme cases, the tribunal may consider it appropriate to utilize the procedure set out in Article 3.8. Similar issues arise where a party unilaterally produces documents to the tribunal (but not to the other party).[228] As O'Malley describes it: **6.247**

> [P]arties have attempted in the past to produce evidence only to the tribunal, without copying the opponent, with the purported aim of asking the tribunal to review the evidence in order to determine the validity of its objection. This procedure should be avoided, unless the parties have agreed beforehand that it is permissible or the tribunal has ordered that. To submit evidence to the tribunal without copying an opponent raises the possibility of a serious procedural irregularity.

iii. *Good faith and weight to be attached to counsel's submissions on relevance and materiality*

When considering objections to a request for production, a tribunal will sometimes have to consider arguments from opposing counsel as to why the requested documents are not relevant or material.[229] In many cases, these will be presented on paper, but in some cases, they may be the subject of oral argument. **6.248**

Absent evidence to the contrary a tribunal will generally assume that counsel are acting in good faith. In addition to considering arguments from counsel for the requesting party on why documents *are* relevant and material, a tribunal must also give weight to arguments made by opposing counsel as to why they are *not*. The tribunal may accept **6.249**

[225] Marghitola (n 1) 49–50.
[226] Commentary on the IBA Rules (n 5) 10–11.
[227] The judgment of the Singapore High Court in *Dongwoo Mann+Hummel Co Ltd v Mann+Hummel* [2008] 3 SLR(R) 871; [2008] SGHC 67 [74]–[75] provides some interesting observations on the position where a tribunal has had sight of documents provided by one party to the tribunal, but that were not provided to the other party, and what it will be necessary to show in order to make out an argument that the party not provided with the documents has been prejudiced.
[228] See further O'Malley Rules of Evidence (n 29) para 3.60 (internal references are omitted).
[229] McNeil and Ryan (n 23) para 17.20.

factual representations made by opposing counsel in aid of those arguments without the need for supporting evidence. The following statement made by an experienced arbitrator in an unreported ICC arbitration is cited as representing the appropriate approach:

> The affirmation of counsel, for the objecting party, whose good faith is assumed, that the documents in question are neither directly relevant nor material, while not determinative, has to be accorded weight.[230]

6.250 This manner of looking at things is one shared by others. For example, an ICC procedural order in a different arbitration notes that:

> [At the document production stage] . . . the Tribunal has to be guided, to a large extent, by the affirmation of counsel that documents requested are neither directly relevant nor material.[231]

6.251 Our view is that tribunals should listen to the arguments put forward by counsel for all parties. They may have a better grasp of the detail than the tribunal and be better able to assess why a particular document/category of document is (or is not) relevant and material to outcome. However, determination of whether the document is relevant and material is a matter for the tribunal alone.[232] Submissions to the effect that documents are not relevant and material should not be accepted at face value. It is the tribunal, and not counsel, that is the final arbiter on this issue. The tribunal's ability to assess issues of relevance and materiality on a prima facie basis[233] should assist it to discharge this responsibility regardless of what stage of the arbitration the document production process takes place. Of course, the ease with which a tribunal is able to do this may depend to a large extent upon how much 'reading in' to the dispute members of the tribunal have undertaken so as to be adequately prepared for making the relevant determinations.

6.252 This matter also raises issues relating to the duty of good faith enshrined in Preamble 3 to the IBA Rules and, more generally, to standards of conduct expected of counsel in relation to document production.[234] As a general matter, the obligation to provide good faith answers and objections in international arbitration has been affirmed by a number of tribunals.[235] Further discussion on the obligation of good faith may be found in Chapter 2.[236]

[230] O'Malley Document Production (n 23) 4. The author does go on to make clear that 'the mere cursory review of records by opposing counsel does not support a good faith objection that no relevant records exist. A reasonable investigation is required on behalf of the party claiming that there are no "relevant" documents available'.
[231] ICC Procedural Order from July 2010, 'Extracts from ICC Case Materials on the Taking of Evidence with References to the IBA Rules' (2016) 1 ICC Dispute Resolution Bulletin 127.
[232] IBA Rules (n 21) Article 9.1, Article 9.2(a).
[233] See 6.125-6.129.
[234] See also Chapter 2 paras 2.81–2.86.
[235] See further O'Malley Rules of Evidence (n 29).
[236] Paras 2.43–2.86.

b. None of the reasons for objection set forth in Article 9.2 applies

Objections may be made to a request to produce documents. The available grounds are set out at 6.225 and are addressed in detail in Chapter 12. In summary, they comprise a lack of relevance and materiality; a legal impediment or privilege; loss or destruction; commercial or technical confidentiality; special political or institutional sensitivity; considerations of procedural economy, proportionality, fairness, or equality of the parties; or it being an unreasonable burden to produce the material. 6.253

In substance, the majority of the Article 9.2 grounds concern the nature and/or content of the particular documents that have been requested. In addition to weighing any procedural concerns that arise (whether under Article 9.2(g) or otherwise), in relation to each ground of objection the tribunal will therefore have to consider whether that objection has valid application to the document(s) requested. This can be a challenging task. As described in Chapter 12, difficult and complex issues may arise in relation to each of those grounds. 6.254

c. The requirements of Article 3.3 have been satisfied

As mentioned, the need for the tribunal to be satisfied that the requirements of Article 3.3 are met is a new provision that did not exist in the 1999 IBA Rules. The nature of those requirements are addressed at 6.46-6.198. 6.255

O'Malley argues that a failure to meet the requirements of Article 3.3 is fatal to a request for production under the IBA Rules: 6.256

> Failure to meet the requirements of Article 3.3 means that a request may be simply denied on its face as not compliant with the standard found in the IBA Rules.[237]

O'Malley's view is supported by the text of Article 3.7, which reads:

> The Arbitral Tribunal may order the Party to whom such Request is addressed to produce any requested Document in its possession, custody or control as to which the Arbitral Tribunal determines that (i) the issues that the requesting Party wishes to prove are relevant to the case and material to its outcome; (ii) none of the reasons for objection set forth in Article 9.2 applies; *and* (iii) the requirements of Article 3.3 have been satisfied.[238]

It is certainly true that the fact of the requirement at 3.7(iii) being specially added in 2010 suggests that the draftsmen intended the provision to have some force. Given the use of the preposition 'and' in the last part of the Article 3.7, it seems clear that, in fact, all *three* elements of the provision must be satisfied. The question of whether they have been satisfied will be a matter for determination by the individual tribunal. In practice, some tribunals may be prepared to overlook technical non-compliance—for example, 6.257

[237] O'Malley Rules of Evidence (n 29) para 3.79.
[238] Emphasis added.

where a party omits to confirm that the requested documents are not in its possession, custody or control, but is able to confirm this to the tribunal if asked to do so.

d. Reformulation of the Request for Production

6.258 An interesting issue arises in relation to the power of a tribunal to reformulate a document production request either because it is not sufficiently narrow to meet the requirements of Article 3.3(a)(ii) or (for example) because, as drafted, it is not sufficiently targeted at issues material to outcome in the case.

6.259 It has been said that, in circumstances where the IBA Rules have been formally adopted, rather than just being used as guidelines, a requesting party should not be assisted in this way where it fails to describe the requested document sufficiently narrowly to meet the requirements of Article 3.3(a)(ii). The IBA Rules contain no provision that contemplates the power of the arbitral tribunal to reformulate requests and a party should not be given a 'second chance' to obtain documents when it has failed to meet the requirements of Article 3. The IBA Rules place the burden on the requesting party to identify the document or documents they want in sufficient detail, so that the tribunal may make a determination on whether the requirements of Article 3 are met. If this analysis is correct, it might in principle also apply to any reformulation by the tribunal by reference to the relevance and/or materiality supporting a particular document request. A decision by a tribunal to unilaterally reformulate a party's document request could raise concerns of procedural unfairness, particularly where the other party is not given a further opportunity to raise objections.[239]

6.260 While this analysis has merit, as a matter of practice a more pragmatic approach is often adopted. In the early stages of the document production process there is often a significant amount of dialogue between participants around the formulation of requests and supporting reasons with revisions and refinements appearing in a Redfern Schedule or correspondence passing between the parties.[240] If a hearing before the tribunal takes place in relation to the outstanding disputed items, that dialogue may continue with participation from the tribunal. In some cases, the scope of the documents requested and the accepted basis of relevance and materiality of documents may not exactly mirror that expressed in the original document production request. However, provided that due process has been observed by ensuring that both parties have had the opportunity to make submissions on those matters, the tribunal should not be subject to criticism for active engagement in that process. Giving a party an opportunity to revise a request for production aids, rather than frustrates, procedural efficiency. It also ensures that the tribunal is presented with the evidence that it may require to determine the case before it.

[239] McNeil and Ryan (n 23) para 17.16.

[240] The Commentary on the IBA Rules (n 5) notes that '[p]arty-to-party consultation may in some circumstances be the more effective means of resolving objections, including those based on insufficient descriptions and other deficiencies in the form of request to produce'.

Clearly a tribunal should not overstep the mark—for example, by itself fundamentally redrafting the request. However, in our view (and subject to the particular circumstances) it would not be desirable for a tribunal to strike out a document request that is too widely drawn when it is clear that within it lies a set of documents capable of being identified, and where that more limited category of documents is prima facie relevant to the case and material to its outcome. While wholesale redrafting is not appropriate, saving part of the request may be. It may be possible to do this by cutting down the sub-categories of document listed, imposing a temporal limitation or restricting the number of individuals whose files are to be searched. Dialogue between the tribunal and the parties on such matters is not unusual and should be not discouraged. This more pragmatic approach may be particularly important when a party is represented by counsel unfamiliar with the IBA Rules and/or the Redfern Schedule process. **6.261**

4. Production of Documents Ordered to Be Produced

Unsurprisingly, Article 3.7 states expressly that any documents ordered by the tribunal to be produced are to be provided to the other parties to the arbitration. As is the case in relation to voluntary production under Article 3.4, the IBA Rules incorporate a revision to the 1999 Rules as a result of which the producing party is no longer required to provide a copy of the documents to the tribunal. For the reasons given at 6.212-6.13 , this is generally regarded as an improvement to the rules. **6.262**

G. Review of Documents

Article 3.8

8. In exceptional circumstances, if the propriety of an objection can be determined only by review of the Document, the Arbitral Tribunal may determine that it should not review the Document. In that event, the Arbitral Tribunal may, after consultation with the Parties, appoint an independent and impartial expert, bound to confidentiality, to review any such Document and to report on the objection. To the extent that the objection is upheld by the Arbitral Tribunal, the expert shall not disclose to the Arbitral Tribunal and to the other Parties the contents of the Document reviewed.

1. Introduction

Article 3.8 makes express provision for the power of the tribunal, in consultation with the parties, to appoint an 'independent and impartial expert' to review documents that **6.263** are the subject of a document production request to which the party in possession of the document has made an objection. The tribunal may do so where it determines (a) that a decision on the validity of the objection can only be made following a review and (b) it would not be appropriate for the tribunal to carry out that review. The Commentary to the IBA Rules suggests that the appointment *may* be made under Article 6 of the IBA Rules (Tribunal-Appointed Experts) but this is not a requirement.[241] A number of similar considerations arise in relation to the appointment of an expert under Article 3.8 as arise under Article 6. Article 6 is discussed in Chapter 9.

6.264 Article 3.8 refers expressly to the requirement of prior consultation with the parties before the tribunal appoints an expert. As discussed later, decisions around the appointment of a third-party expert can raise difficult issues. These include the risk of the tribunal improperly delegating part of its decision-making function or, if the tribunal decides to review the documents itself (rather than appointing an expert) and upholds the objection to production, the possibility that its view of the case may nonetheless be influenced by what it has seen. Consultation with the parties in which they may express their views on the best course of action is therefore important.

6.265 The first sentence of Article 3.8 contains an ambiguity. It is not clear whether the reference to exceptional circumstances attaches to the need for the documents in question to be reviewed prior to a ruling on the objection, or a situation in which it would not be appropriate for the tribunal itself to carry out the review. In practice, both situations are likely to be the exception to the general position that the tribunal can make a decision on an objection without sight of the documents in issue. Only in exceptional circumstances will it be the case that an objection can be ruled on only after a review of the documents. What those circumstances are will be case specific.

2. The Need to Review the Documents

6.266 Grounds of objection most likely to give rise to a need to review the document in order to rule on it are objections raised under Article 9.2(b) (legal impediment or privilege), Article 9.2(e) (commercial or technical confidentiality), or Article 9.2(f) (special political or institutional sensitivity).[242] Consideration of arguments put forward by counsel in relation to objections to production on these grounds will, in some cases, benefit from an opportunity to review the content of the document to see if the objection stands up.

[241] ibid 11.

[242] It is possible that issues may also arise in relation to IBA Rules (n 21) Article 9.2(a) (lack of sufficient relevance and materiality). However, this is less likely given the nature of the objection being advanced by the non-requesting party. The tribunal should be able to determine this objection on the basis of its knowledge of the case and submissions from counsel.

It will generally not be appropriate for the requesting party to see the documents in question in advance of a ruling on the objection. However, to permit a tribunal to review those documents in order to determine whether the objection is legitimate may also be inappropriate where the documents contain information that, once seen by the tribunal cannot be unseen, and which may taint its view of the case.[243] 6.267

It would be potentially unfair to both the requesting and producing parties if the tribunal were to be influenced by the content of a document without both parties having an opportunity to make submissions on that content. That will not be possible where, having looked at the document, the tribunal rules against its production. In this situation the appointment of a third party to review and report to the tribunal on whether the grounds for objection have any substance may be the preferred solution. 6.268

3. Review of Documents by an 'Independent and Impartial Expert'

Article 3.8 provides that the review of documents may be undertaken by an 'independent and impartial expert' instead of by the tribunal. 6.269

As mentioned, the perceived desirability of any review being undertaken by someone other than the tribunal may be more acute where production of a document has been objected to on the basis of a claim to legal privilege under Article 9.2(b) of the IBA Rules. However, since determination of that claim will involve application of a legal principle, it would appear inappropriate for any part of the process leading to a ruling to be delegated to a third party. In such circumstances, a tribunal may prefer to rely instead on assurances from counsel as to the existence of privilege and the completion by the parties of a privilege log.[244] 6.270

The tribunal and/or the party holding the document may prefer confidential documents to be examined by someone other than the tribunal, although in this situation those concerns are, in substance, more likely to be directed at the opponent party seeing confidential business information than worries about the tribunal having sight of the documents. However, this does not address the risk that, if the documents are not subsequently made available to the other party, that party may argue that it has been denied the opportunity to make submissions on evidence that the tribunal has seen and cannot 'unsee'. 6.271

The Commentary to the IBA Rules suggests that a review of documents that are said to be confidential in nature may be better undertaken by a third party from a 6.272

243 Commentary on the IBA Rules (n 5) 11, which explains that '(i) if after reviewing the document the arbitral tribunal upholds the objection, it could not eliminate its knowledge of the document once it has been reviewed, or (ii) there may be confidentiality concerns'.

244 A privilege log is a document produced to the tribunal, and often to the other parties, in which basic details about the nature and content of a document withheld from production on grounds of legal privilege are provided by the withholding party. See further Chapter 12 paras 12.238–12.240.

confidentiality perspective as the third-party expert appointed under Article 3.8 will be expressly bound to confidentiality.[245] In relation to the latter, Article 3.8 refers expressly to the third-party expert appointed under that provision being 'bound to confidentiality' and that 'the expert shall not disclose to the Arbitral Tribunal and to the other Parties the content of the Documents reviewed'. Article 3.8 is silent as to the method by which these obligations are to be imposed on the third-party expert. If the expert is appointed pursuant to Article 6 (Tribunal-Appointed Experts) then the imposition of confidentiality obligations can be addressed as part of the terms of reference and retainer arrangements discussed in relation to that article (see Chapter 9). If the appointment of the expert is not made under Article 6, the tribunal should address the issue of confidentiality as part of its terms of instruction to the expert.

6.273 If a third party has specialist knowledge of the industry sector, the third party may be better equipped than the tribunal to decide whether the confidentiality concern is a legitimate one.[246]

6.274 Where a third party is appointed to review documents the tribunal will make a decision based on the third party's report. If the objection to production is upheld, the third party will not disclose the content of the document to either the tribunal or to the parties. However, although a potentially useful procedure on paper, this mechanism adds an extra layer of complexity and requires careful handling by the tribunal. A third-party appointment may result in a significant decision-making power being placed with the third party, whose status, if appointed under Article 3.8, may mean that the party protections expressly set out in Article 6 may not apply.[247]

6.275 The Commentary to the IBA Rules cautions that 'the expert . . . would provide a report on the objection, but *the arbitral tribunal* is to make the final ruling as to its validity'.[248] However, in practice, the line between a reporting and decision-making function may be a difficult one to draw.[249] If the expert reports in detail on the content of the documents the tribunal may as well have looked at them. If the expert merely makes a recommendation or states the expert's opinion on whether the objection has merit, and such recommendation or opinion is then acted upon, this is delegation of the decision in all but name. The proposed terms of the confidentiality expert's appointment, and how it feeds in to the decision-making process, should be carefully considered and the parties given an opportunity to comment on it as part of the consultation discussed earlier.

245 Commentary on the IBA Rules (n 5) 10–11; IBA Rules (n 21).

246 For an example of where a tribunal used a third party to review evidence see 6.276. Although not a situation concerning an objection to document production, the case illustrates where a review by a third party may be useful.

247 Domitille Baizeau and Juliette Richard, 'Chapter 4: Addressing the Issue of Confidentiality in Arbitration Proceedings: How Is This Done in Practice?' in Elliott Geisinger (ed), *Confidential and Restricted Access Information in International Arbitration* (JurisNet 2016) 53, 66–67 (hereafter 'Baizeau and Richard'). The Commentary to the IBA Rules (n 5) 11 notes that the appointment of the expert may be made under Article 6.

248 Emphasis added. See further O'Malley Rules of Evidence (n 29) para 3.85.

249 Baizeau and Richard (n 247) 67.

Although not related to a document production request, an interesting example of a tribunal appointing a third party to review documents is *Bechtel v Islamic Republic of Iran*. In *Bechtel*, the tribunal appointed an accounting firm to inspect corporate books and records alleged to establish that individual United States citizens owned shares in the relevant companies, thus bringing the dispute within the jurisdiction of the tribunal. The accounting firm reported to the tribunal its opinion that the necessary shareholding was indeed owned by the relevant individuals. Based on this report and the other evidence in the record, the tribunal concluded that the jurisdiction requirements had been satisfied. **6.276**

Was this an inappropriate delegation of the tribunal's decision-making responsibility? The issue in question was a question of fact, which it was the tribunal's obligation to determine. The role of a third-party expert is merely to provide a reasoned opinion that the tribunal will take into account when reaching its decision.[250] The approach adopted by the tribunal was a pragmatic one. The question of whether the tribunal relied too heavily on the opinion of the expert to the extent that it constituted improper delegation may depend on the nature of information and reasoning that the expert provided to the tribunal in support of its conclusion that the requisite relevant shareholding had been established. **6.277**

It may be possible to avoid this issue if the parties are prepared to agree to grant the third-party expert power to make a final determination on the relevant issue in substitution for a determination by the tribunal. Just as parties to a contract may carve out certain types of dispute for expert determination, rather than arbitration, there is nothing in principle to prevent them from carving out an issue for expert determination during the arbitration.[251] Any such arrangement will require careful formulation and drafting. **6.278**

Article 3.8 states expressly that the expert to be appointed should be 'independent and impartial'. In our view, if read literally, this description makes it inappropriate for a tribunal secretary to be asked to carry out a review under Article 3.8, although this is a practice sometimes adopted in international arbitration.[252] In some cases the parties may regard it as a pragmatic approach they are prepared to agree to or accept without challenge. **6.279**

Respondents to a recent survey on use of the IBA Rules[253] reported very few examples of tribunals appointing a third party to review documents objected to on grounds of commercial confidentiality or political sensitivity. German respondents had experience of one case in which a third party was instructed by the tribunal to **6.280**

[250] Waincymer (n 161) 947–48.
[251] See further O'Malley Rules of Evidence (n 29) para 3.85.
[252] For example, see *Dr Horst Reineccius and others v Bank for International Settlements* (Procedural Order No. 6, 11 June 2002) PCA Case No 2000-04 1. In that case the parties appear to have agreed that the review be undertaken by the tribunal secretary.
[253] BCLP Survey on use of the IBA Rules.

review certain documents and to submit answers to a question previously agreed between the parties. Interestingly, this was a case where the objection raised was one of legal privilege. Respondents in Sweden were aware of another case in which such an approach had been proposed, but where the proposal was rejected by the parties.

H. Documents Held by Third Parties

Article 3.9

9. If a Party wishes to obtain the production of Documents from a person or organisation who is not a Party to the arbitration and from whom the Party cannot obtain the Documents on its own, the Party may, within the time ordered by the Arbitral Tribunal, ask it to take whatever steps are legally available to obtain the requested Documents, or seek leave from the Arbitral Tribunal to take such steps itself. The Party shall submit such request to the Arbitral Tribunal and to the other Parties in writing, and the request shall contain the particulars set forth in Article 3.3, as applicable. The Arbitral Tribunal shall decide on this request and shall take, authorize the requesting Party to take, or order any other Party to take, such steps as the Arbitral Tribunal considers appropriate if, in its discretion, it determines that (i) the Documents would be relevant to the case and material to its outcome, (ii) the requirements of Article 3.3, as applicable, have been satisfied and (iii) none of the reasons for objection set forth in Article 9.2 applies.

1. Introduction

6.281 Article 3.9 sets out a procedure by which a party may obtain assistance or permission from the tribunal in relation to efforts to obtain documents from persons and organization that are not parties to the arbitration.

6.282 Each party is responsible for presenting the evidence it relies on to support its case. However, in some disputes documents of evidential value may be held by another party to the arbitration. The provisions of Articles 3.2–3.7 provide a procedure by which the party wanting access to documents held by another party can obtain them. This procedure works because the tribunal has jurisdiction over the other parties to the arbitration. Where germane documents are held by a non-party to the arbitration the tribunal cannot compel production by that party. Article 3.9 provides a practical mechanism involving similar considerations by which other available routes to obtain documents of evidential value may be considered and, if appropriate, pursued.

2. Requirements for an Application and Order under Article 3.9

In order for a party to make an application to the tribunal under Article 3.9, and for the tribunal to grant relief in the terms provided for in Article 3.9, the following requirements must be met: 6.283

(a) The documents to which the application relates (i) must be documents held by a person or organization who is not a party to the arbitration and (ii) must be documents that the requesting party 'cannot obtain on its own';
(b) The documents to which the application relates are documents that the tribunal determines to be 'relevant to the case and material to its outcome';
(c) The requirements of Article 3.3 'as applicable' have been satisfied; and
(d) None of the reasons for objection set out in Article 9.2 applies.

a. Held by a non-party to the arbitration and not possible to obtain

The requirement mentioned at (a) in 6.283 may be regarded as a threshold requirement. 6.284

If the documents are in the possession of another party to the arbitration the procedures set out in Articles 3.2–3.7 are engaged and should be utilized. Likewise, if the party wanting the documents has the power to obtain them without intervention of the tribunal, then it should do so. 6.285

A question arises around the proper interpretation of the requirement that the applicant party 'cannot obtain the Documents on its own'. It might be said that this requirement is met if the applicant party can demonstrate to the tribunal that the applicant has no legal entitlement to the documents. However, it appears likely that where there are possible active steps still open to the applicant party by which it may be able to obtain the documents, those steps should be pursued prior to an application being made under Article 3.9. If this position is accepted, a further question arises as to how far the applicant party must go to meet the requirement. One interpretation—claimed by some to be the safer interpretation—is that the steps required are limited to those directed at obtaining voluntary production of the evidence from the third party,[254] eg by formal request or completion of an available administrative procedure by which the document may be obtained. Another possible interpretation is that the applicant party is also expected to pursue any legal process available by which it may obtain the document. However, on the basis that the pursuit of court process without the consent of the tribunal is both controversial and undesirable (see 6.316-6.322)[255] this appears unlikely to be the intended meaning of this provision. 6.286

[254] O'Malley Rules of Evidence (n 29) para 3.92. There is at least one authority for that proposition: NAFTA Arbitration, *Methanex Corp v United States of America* (Letter from Tribunal, 16 March 2004). In *Methanex*, the tribunal appears to have regarded the exhaustion by the party wanting production of available steps to itself obtain voluntary production of the evidence as a requirement of an application by that party under the 1999 IBA Rules (n 13) Article 3.8 (now IBA Rules (n 21) Article 3.9).

[255] See also Chapter 7 paras 7.204–7.206 in relation to the application of the similar provision at Article 4.9.

6.287 Where an application is made under Article 3.9 the applicant party should provide an appropriate statement of the reasons why it is unable to obtain the documents, including, where apt, an explanation of why, as a matter of applicable law, the claimant has no legal right of access to the relevant documents. If the applicant has made unsuccessful efforts to obtain the documents (for example, by writing to the party in possession to request a copy of the documents) it should describe those steps. If there is a connection between another party to the arbitration and the party in possession of the documents that might explain obstacles placed in the way of the applicant party in trying to obtain the documents, or which might make it easy for that other party to obtain the documents, it would be sensible to also set these out in the application.

6.288 A related question is the potential for overlap between the provisions of Article 3.9 and the provisions of Article 3.7 pursuant to which a tribunal may order the production of documents from a party to the arbitration if satisfied that those documents are in the 'possession, custody or control' of that party. Situations may exist where a party to the arbitration effectively 'controls' documents held by a non-party, eg a subsidiary company in common ownership. We think it unlikely that the party requesting the documents was intended to have a right of election between the provisions of Articles 3.2–3.7 and Article 3.9. If it can be demonstrated that the documents are, in fact, under the control of another party to the arbitration the requesting party should in the first instance make its application under Articles 3.2–3.7.

b. Relevant to the case and material to its outcome

6.289 The factors relevant to a party's submission and tribunal determination that documents are relevant to the case and material to its outcome are addressed in detail at 6.76-6.146.

6.290 The requirement that the tribunal should be satisfied that the documents are relevant and material helps to avoid time and costs being wasted in efforts to secure production of documents having little evidential value. As the express reference in Article 3.9 to the tribunal's discretion makes clear, the tribunal is to be the final arbiter of whether this benchmark test is met. If the tribunal determines that the documents are *not* relevant to the case, or would *not* be material to its outcome, the tribunal should refuse the application.

c. The requirements of Article 3.3 have been satisfied

6.291 Article 3.3 sets out requirements as to the content of a request for production made by one party to the arbitration on another. Those same requirements are expressly adopted into Article 3.9. In summary, under Article 3.3, the party seeking the documents must provide a description of the document/narrow and specific category of documents; a statement of why the documents are relevant and material; a statement confirming that the documents are not in the possession, custody, or control of the requesting party (or that it would be unreasonably burdensome for that party to produce them); and a statement of the reason why the requesting party believes the documents to be in the possession, custody, or control of another party to the proceedings. Under Article 3.9 these requirements apply 'as applicable'. In our view, this means no more than that they should be adjusted, as appropriate, to meet the different set of circumstances with which Article 3.9 is concerned. So, for example, instead of a statement of why the requesting party believes the documents to be in the possession of 'another Party', the applicant party should explain why it believes the documents wanted are held by the third party mentioned in the application.

d. None of the reasons for objection in Article 9.2 apply

Article 3.9 does not state as much, but it seems logical to assume that the right to raise an objection under Article 9.2 in relation to an Article 3.9 application rests with any other party to the arbitration. **6.292**

An interesting question arises as to whether the party raising the objection must have a personal interest in the ground of objection raised. For example, could a claim of legal privilege be raised when that privilege attaches to the third party, and not to the 'other' party to the arbitration? In cases when the third party and its affairs are not known to the other parties to the arbitration, they are unlikely to have the necessary information on which to ground such an objection. However, it may be that where a connection exists between a party to the arbitration and the third party from whom the documents are sought, the party to the arbitration may try to shield the third party from the proposed action to obtain production. Of course, certain bases of objection may clearly be of interest and/or relevance to all participants in the arbitration, eg the question of whether the documents are relevant to the case and material to its outcome (9.2(a)), or considerations of procedural efficiency (9.2(g)) where it is suggested that steps in the arbitration should be delayed until after the proposed external action to obtain the documents has been completed. **6.293**

3. The Exercise of the Tribunal's Discretion: Decision on Steps to Be Taken

A tribunal has a discretion, but no obligation, to grant an application under Article 3.9. The tribunal must be satisfied that the documents of which production is sought are relevant and material, that all other requirements of the provision are met, and that there are available steps for obtaining the documents that it considers it is appropriate to take. The nature of any steps to be taken is a matter for the tribunal's discretion, and will vary according to the circumstances of the case. **6.294**

The words 'shall take, authorize the requesting Party to take or order any other Party to take' in the final part of Article 3.9 make clear that the tribunal may consider, take, authorize, or order (as appropriate) action by (a) the tribunal itself; (b) the requesting party; and/or (c) a non-requesting party. Possible steps in each category are discussed at 6.297-6.322. **6.295**

6.296 The tribunal should authorize only 'such steps as the Arbitral Tribunal considers appropriate'. The tribunal will wish to understand the likely timeline and costs involved in each available step, and whether the taking of those steps will have an impact on the procedural timetable. If, in exceptional circumstances, the tribunal is prepared to take action itself, it will also wish to be satisfied that it holds sufficient party funds to cover the costs of doing so.

4. Possible Steps to Obtain Production of Documents

a. Introduction

6.297 Article 3.9 covers two possible forms of application by a party seeking production of third-party documents. The first is where a party wishes the tribunal to take active steps to obtain production of documents from a non-party. The second is where the party wishes to obtain the permission of the tribunal to take steps itself—perhaps because this is a requirement of the national court from whom it intends to seek assistance, or for other reasons. The issue of whether, by operation of the IBA Rules, a party is always obliged to obtain permission from the tribunal prior to taking action itself, is discussed at 6.316-6.322.

6.298 Importantly, when responding to such an application, a tribunal is not restricted to granting the precise relief sought by the applicant party. In broad terms it may authorize the applicant party to take steps that the tribunal considers appropriate, require a non-applicant party to take such steps, or take appropriate steps itself.

6.299 The steps that follow a successful application to the tribunal may involve the issue of proceedings in a state court, generally either the courts of the seat of arbitration or the courts of the place where the documents are held. National arbitration laws will differ as to what assistance is available to compel the production of documents for use in arbitration proceedings—in particular, whether a request for assistance can be made by one of the parties to the arbitration or by the tribunal and, in the former situation, whether the consent of the tribunal is required.

6.300 The menu of steps available to be taken in each case will differ according to the circumstances of the dispute.

b. Steps available to the tribunal

6.301 In relation to the first situation (steps to be taken by the tribunal) Article 3.9 makes clear that the tribunal may only be asked 'to take whatever steps are legally available to obtain the requested Documents . . . '. This is a recognition that the tribunal has no jurisdiction over a person or organization who is not a party to the arbitration, and that the nature and scope of any assistance that the tribunal can obtain from state courts will be determined by the particular provisions of the relevant arbitration laws and/or the court's inherent jurisdiction.

Some national arbitration laws contain express provision permitting an arbitral tribunal to seek assistance from the state court in relation to the production of documents. It will often be appropriate to look first to the courts at the seat. If parties have chosen an 'arbitration-friendly' jurisdiction as the seat of arbitration, the relevant arbitration laws may provide some measure of support and assistance for the arbitral process. For example, in states that have adopted the UNCITRAL Model Law,[256] a party may seek to rely on Article 27 of that Law. That provision states: **6.302**

> The *arbitral tribunal* or a party with the approval of the arbitral tribunal *may request from a competent court of this State* assistance in taking evidence. The court may execute the request within its competence and according to its rules on taking evidence.[257]

The language of Article 27 permits argument as to whether its scope includes applications for disclosure of documents.[258] However, it has certainly been used in some jurisdictions to compel a third party to attend before the tribunal for the purpose of producing particular identified documents.[259] Article 1(2) of the Model Law provides that its provisions will apply only where the place of arbitration is in the territory of the State. **6.303**

However, the documents that are sought may be held in a jurisdiction other than the seat. In these circumstances, the courts of the seat may have difficulty in compelling production of documents from a party based overseas. In theory, a tribunal may therefore have to look to another national court to provide assistance. In the United States, Section 1782 28 U.S.C. gives the court power to order discovery from specified persons 'for use in a proceedings in a foreign or international tribunal'.[260] This provision has been used for the purpose of seeking documents. Assistance is available at the request of either a 'foreign or international tribunal' or 'any interested person' to proceedings before the relevant tribunal.[261] **6.304**

Despite the express power granted to a tribunal to seek assistance from a state court, in our view, a tribunal will be reluctant to take such steps itself and will prefer that any application to a state court is made by one of the parties. **6.305**

A tribunal may be more willing to make a formal request to the third party asking it to produce a document. For example, in ICSID case *Aguas del Tunari v Bolivia*[262] the tribunal wrote to the Ministry of Foreign Affairs of the Netherlands seeking disclosure of information concerning the interpretation of the relevant treaty under which the claim **6.306**

[256] UNCITRAL Model Law on International Commercial Arbitration (as adopted by UNCITRAL on 21 June 1985 and as amended by UNCITRAL on 7 July 2006) (hereafter 'UNCITRAL Model Law').

[257] ibid Article 27 (emphasis added).

[258] Born (n 78) 2325–26 and 2397–98.

[259] ibid; see also *Vibroflotation AG v Express Builders Co. Ltd* [1995] 1 HKLR 239 (Hong Kong Court of First Instance), and *Jardine Lloyd Thompson Canada Inc. v SJO Catlin* [2006] ABCA 18 (Alberta Ct. App.).

[260] 28 U.S.C. s 1782.

[261] The scope and application of Section 1782 is the subject of ongoing debate. For further discussion see Jonathan Blackman and Peter Fox, 'Discovery in Aid of Arbitration under 28 USC 1782' The Arbitration Review of the Americas 2017 [online] (16 August 2016) <http://globalarbitrationreview.com/insight/the-arbitration-review-of-the-americas-2017/1067594/discovery-in-aid-of-arbitration-under-28-usc-1782> accessed 3 December 2018.

[262] ICSID Case No. ARB/02/3.

was made.[263] Of course, the tribunal will have to be careful not to violate any confidentiality obligations in the arbitration.

c. Steps to be taken by the applicant party

6.307 Just as a tribunal may seek the assistance of national courts, so may a party to the arbitration. There may be situations where a party wishes, or has no option other than, to take steps itself to obtain the production of documents from non-parties by seeking direct assistance from state courts. Again, depending on where the party who has the documents is based, this may be the courts at the seat of arbitration or, if different, the courts of the jurisdiction in which the documents are held.[264] Very often, the parties are as well placed as the tribunal to seek assistance from national courts and there is no real need for the tribunal to take direct action.

6.308 The availability of state court assistance varies from jurisdiction to jurisdiction and can also vary according to whether the third party is within the jurisdiction. A number of national arbitration laws provide for local court assistance to a party to an arbitration having its seat in that jurisdiction. Under some national laws, the consent of the tribunal is a pre-condition of an application by a party to the state court.[265] Article 3.9 makes express provision for a party to be able to seek such permission. The 1999 IBA Rules did not contain this mechanism. Those earlier rules only provided for a party to request that the tribunal itself take appropriate steps.[266]

6.309 Section 26 of the Swedish Arbitration Act provides that parties to an arbitration seated in Sweden have the right, with the approval of the arbitrators, to seek the assistance of local courts in the production of documents '*as evidence*'. In France, parties can, subject to authorization of the tribunal, submit a request to the President of the First Instance Court (Tribunal de Grande Instance) seeking the production of documents.[267] In

[263] See, for more detail O'Malley Rules of Evidence (n 29) para 3.97 and fn 133.

[264] For example, the US courts have the power to order production of documents by specified persons 'for use in a proceeding in a foreign or international tribunal'. USA: 28 U.S.C. s 1782. Laurence Shore, 'Chapter 3. State Courts and Document Production' in Teresa Giovannini and Alexis Mourre (eds), *Written Evidence and Discovery in International Arbitration: New Issues and Tendencies* (Kluwer Law International 2009) 57 (hereafter 'Shore').

[265] England: English Arbitration Act 1996, s 43(2): Application may only be made with the permission of the tribunal or the agreement of the other parties. English Arbitration Act 1996, s 44(4): the court shall act only on the application of a party or proposed party to the arbitral proceedings (upon notice to the other parties and the tribunal made with the permission of the tribunal or the agreement in writing of the other parties; Hong Kong: *Vibroflotation AG v Express Builders Co. Ltd* [1995] 1 HKLR 239 (H.K. Ct. First Inst.) The Court held that the arbitral tribunal's approval (under UNCITRAL Model Law (n 256) Article 27) might be inferred, but added that the better course was to obtain the express approval of the arbitrator. Switzerland: Article 184 (n 32) parallels the UNCITRAL Model Law, providing the possibility for parties to an arbitration seated in Switzerland, 'with the consent of the Arbitral Tribunal,' to seek judicial assistance in the 'taking of evidence'; Sweden: Swedish Arbitration Act, s 26 (n 224) provides that parties to an arbitration seated in Sweden have the right, with the approval of the arbitrators, to seek the assistance of local courts in taking sworn witness testimony or the production of documents. For an interesting discussion on the ability of a party to an arbitration to obtain assistance from the US courts see John Fellas, 'Expert Analysis: Using Section 1782 to Obtain Evidence for International Arbitration Proceedings' New York Law Journal [online] (29 March 2017) <www.law.com/newyorklawjournal/almID/1202782394403/using-section-1782-to-obtain-evidence-for-international-arbitration-proceedings/> accessed 10 December 2018 (hereafter 'Fellas').

[266] 1999 IBA Rules (n 13) Article 3.8.

[267] French Code of Civil Procedure Article 1469.

Australia, under Section 23 of the International Arbitration Act 1974, subpoenas are available.

There are two potential procedures available under the English Arbitration Act 1996. Some limited assistance may be available under Section 43 of the English Arbitration Act. That section provides that a party may use the same court procedures as are available in relation to legal proceedings to secure the attendance before the tribunal of a witness in order to produce documents or other evidence. Section 43 may be used to obtain delivery of documents from a non-party, provided the documents are specifically identified.[268] However, Section 43 cannot be used as a back door to obtain wider third-party disclosure. In *BNP Paribas v Deloitte & Touche*,[269] the tribunal gave permission to the parties to request production of documents from Deloitte & Touche that were 'relevant to the issues in dispute' and, if necessary, by application pursuant to Section 43 of the Arbitration Act for a witness summons. The court rejected the application on the basis that the twenty or so categories of documents listed in the application were too generally described so that the application was in fact an application for third-party disclosure under the guise of a witness summons requesting that the documents be brought to the tribunal under a subpoena.[270] 6.310

Another possible route, where appropriate, is to use Sections 44(1) and 44(2) of the English Arbitration Act 1996. These sections provide that, unless otherwise agreed by the parties, the court has the power to make orders in relation to various matters including: (a) the taking of the evidence of witnesses [44(2)(a)]; and (b) the preservation of evidence [44(2)(b)]. In *Assimina Maritime Ltd v Pakistan Shipping Corp*[271] the court held that an order could be made under section 44(2)(b) of the Arbitration Act for the production of a report and working documents held by a British marine engineering firm for use in an arbitration in London, provided that the documents could be identified specifically or by class.[272] In that case, the court held that the preservation of the content of the documents for the purposes of resolving the issues in the arbitration was a consideration of sufficient weight to justify the court exercising its discretion under Section 44 of the Arbitration Act. There has been conflicting authority as to whether and in what circumstances the court's powers under Section 44 may extend to third parties outside the jurisdiction.[273] 6.311

[268] The procedural mechanism for this is the issue of a witness summons requiring a party in possession of the documents to attend at court with the requested documents.

[269] [2003] EWHC 2874.

[270] *Tajik Aluminium Plant v Hydro Aluminium AS* [2005] EWCA Civ 1218.

[271] [2005] 1 Lloyd's Rep 525.

[272] In that case Coleman J held that English Arbitration Act 1996 s 44 does 'not include an order for disclosure by a non-party of documents relevant to an issue in the arbitration. [. . .] Accordingly, it is only where it can be shown that a question arises in relation to a particular document or documents of a non-party which need to be inspected or photocopied that an order under this section can be made'.

[273] See *DTEK Trading SA v Sergey Morozov* [2017] EWHC 94 (Comm), which contains a useful analysis of the authorities. See also Robert Merkin and Louis Flannery, *Arbitration Act 1996* (5th edn, Informa Law/Routledge 2014) 175–76.

6.312 The scope of the assistance available from the United States courts under Section 1782 28 U.S.C. is potentially broader. This has given rise to some debate over the utility and desirability of such measures. For example, Shore argues that mechanisms such as Section 1782 28 U.S.C. raise the possibility of material imbalance in the scope of evidence available to parties to an arbitration because evidence located in jurisdictions that have such mechanisms is more obtainable than similar evidence located in other countries.[274]

d. Steps a tribunal may order 'any other' party to take

6.313 As mentioned, in response to an application under Article 3.9, the tribunal may require *any* party to the arbitration to take such steps as the tribunal considers appropriate in order to obtain the relevant documents.

6.314 In our view, the cases in which a tribunal will order a party to the arbitration who is not also a party to the application under Article 3.9 to issue legal proceedings in order to obtain documents from a third party will be relatively rare. In the event it were to do so, the same considerations in relation to available mechanisms would apply as in the case of an applicant party.[275]

6.315 However, legal process is not the only possibility. Where a party to the arbitration other than the applicant has the ability to obtain the documents, it may be ordered by the tribunal to do so under Article 3.7 (see 6.173-6.198). For example, documents of title may be relevant and material to the issues between the parties and the other party may have the legal right to obtain a copy from the local register of title. However, where the party with possession, or a right of access to the documents, is merely an associated company of a non-applicant corporate party to the arbitration (but the legal relationship between the two companies is not such as to place the documents within the 'possession, custody or control' of the non-applicant party for the purposes of Article 3.3(c)(ii)),[276] the applicant party may ask and/or the tribunal may consider it appropriate to order that the non-applicant party take reasonable steps or use 'best efforts' to obtain those documents from its connected company.

5. Does Article 3.9 Restrict a Party's Ability to Seek Assistance from National Courts?

6.316 An important question concerning application of Article 3.9 is whether a party intending to seek national court assistance must first obtain the permission of the tribunal, ie is the permission of the tribunal a pre-condition to the intended action?

274 Shore (n 264).
275 See 6.307-311..
276 See 6.173-6.198 .

For example, as a matter of US federal law, it is not necessary to obtain the permission of a foreign tribunal before making an application seeking judicial assistance under Section 1782 U.S.C.[277] However, some commentators argue that, even if national law allows a party to apply to a state court without the tribunal's permission, where Article 3.9 applies it will prevent that party from obtaining evidence by that means without first obtaining permission from the tribunal.[278] 6.317

This position also finds support in the Commentary on the IBA Rules, which says that Article 3.9 permits parties to seek leave from the tribunal to take action itself under national arbitration laws '*as long as the arbitral tribunal determines* that [the] documents would be "relevant to the case and material" to its outcome, the requirements of Article 3.3 have been satisfied and none of the reasons for objection set forth in Article 9.2 applies'.[279] 6.318

How the provision at Article 3.9 is found to interact with provisions of individual national laws when an application to the courts of that jurisdiction is made will be a matter for those courts. Questions of whether the IBA Rules have been expressly adopted between the parties, have been imposed by the tribunal, or are simply being used as guidelines may be relevant. However, this is an issue that must be taken seriously by parties considering an application to a national court since, at the very least, it may involve them in wasted time and costs. In the United States District Court for the District of Columbia, in a Section 1782 application for production of documents made in connection with an ICSID arbitration in which the 1999 IBA Rules were being used as guidelines, the court held that the applicant had 'side-stepped' the IBA Rules, and thus undermined 'the tribunal's control over the discovery process.' The application was dismissed.[280] The fact that the application was made under the 1999 IBA Rules is significant in that the equivalent article under those rules made no provision for a party to seek tribunal consent to the taking of court action by a party. However, the argument that any unilateral action by a party is improper without oversight by the tribunal could apply equally—and perhaps with more force—to applications under Article 3.9 of the 2010 IBA Rules, which makes express provision for such permission to be sought. 6.319

However, the opposite view has also been expressed. One commentator puts it this way: 6.320

> Given the general rather than detailed language of the Rules, it seems fair to assume that the drafters had no intention to limit the parties' option, but rather wanted to provide for a further option.[281]

[277] *In re Malev*, 964 F2d 97, 101 (2nd Cir. 1992). For more detail see Fellas (n 265).

[278] O'Malley Rules of Evidence (n 29) paras 3.90, 3.109.

[279] Commentary on the IBA Rules (n 5) 11 (emphasis added).

[280] *Caratube International Oil Company LLP and Devincci Salah Hourani v Republic of Kazakhstan* ICSID Case No. ARB/13/13. For more detail, see Ashford (n 142) 78. The application in this case was made under 1999 IBA Rules (n 13) Article 3.8 (the equivalent of IBA Rules (n 21) Article 3.9).

[281] Zuberbühler (n 18) 73.

6.321 Although our view is that Article 3.9 is designed to make sure that supervisory jurisdiction over the initiation of the steps contemplated in Article 3.9 (and Article 3.10) should remain with the tribunal,[282] there may be justified exceptions to this general rule in certain circumstances where it may be impossible or impractical to seek the tribunal's permission.

6.322 The most obvious exception is where a tribunal has not yet been formed or cannot, for some reason, act effectively. Another is where the documents are held by a third party connected in some way to one of the parties to the arbitration. If the third party is made aware of an application being made to the tribunal, this may prompt that party to destroy the documentary evidence. In such a case, the only viable option for the applicant would be to apply to the tribunal without informing the other parties. However, a substantial obstacle to this route is that tribunals are for good reason reluctant to hear *ex parte* applications in which the other parties will not have an opportunity to respond.[283] Many institutional rules have express provisions guarding against this.[284] A possible solution may be for the applicant party to seek a retrospective permission from the tribunal once an *ex parte* application to the national court has been made and granted. The applicant may provide an undertaking to the relevant national court that it will do so. The court can therefore be satisfied that it will be acting to assist the tribunal, and not acting in a way which interferes with the exercise of the tribunal's jurisdiction.

I. Documents Sought by the Tribunal

Article 3.10

10. At any time before the arbitration is concluded, the Arbitral Tribunal may (i) request any Party to produce Documents, (ii) request any Party to use its best efforts to take or (iii) itself take, any step that it considers appropriate to obtain Documents from any person or organisation. A Party to whom such a request for Documents is addressed may object to the request for any of the reasons set forth in Article 9.2. In such cases, Article 3.4 to Article 3.8 shall apply correspondingly.

1. Introduction

6.323 Article 3.10 permits a tribunal to ask a party to produce, facilitate production of documents, or to take steps itself to obtain documents on its own initiative and without any application to do so being made by the parties.

[282] The commentary states this expressly in relation to IBA Rules (n 21) Article 3.10. It says that 'Ultimate oversight and control over this process should remain with the arbitral tribunal'.
[283] Maxi Scherer, Lisa Richman, and Rémy Gerbay, *Arbitrating under the 2014 LCIA Rules: A User's Guide*, (Kluwer Law International 2015) 264.
[284] See, for example, LCIA Rules Article 13.4.

2. The Rationale for Permitting a Tribunal Request

The right of the tribunal to request production of documentary evidence is widely accepted. Although more frequent in the civil tradition of inquisitorial procedures than in common law practice, it is now relatively commonplace in international arbitration. An express power on the part of the tribunal to actively call for evidence may be found in a number of national laws. These are not confined to civil law jurisdictions. For example, the English Arbitration Act 1996 makes express reference to the right of a tribunal to decide 'all procedural and evidential matters', and goes on to say that: 6.324

> [P]rocedural and evidential matters include '(g) whether and to what extent the tribunal should itself take the initiative in ascertaining the facts and the law'.

A tribunal's power to take the initiative in gathering evidence is also found in a number of institutional rules. For example, Article 25(5) of the ICC Rules provides that: 6.325

> At any time during the proceedings, the arbitral tribunal may summon any party to provide additional evidence.

The ICC's Commentary to the 2012 ICC Rules notes that this provision is most commonly used to order the production of additional documents.[285]

It is also acknowledged that the right to request production will continue through the life of an arbitration. As O'Malley says: 6.326

> A tribunal may request the production of evidence at any moment prior to termination of the proceedings, or until it is otherwise *functus officio*.[286]

This raises the question of why and when it may be appropriate for a tribunal to do so. If a claimant fails to produce evidence to support its claim, should a tribunal decide that the claimant's case has failed because it has not discharged its burden of proof or should a tribunal instead request documents that may fill the gaps on its own initiative? Much will depend on the individual facts of the case, but many tribunals will be reluctant to request production of documents other than in response to an application from one of the parties. 6.327

As mentioned, the right of a tribunal under Article 3.10 to actively request production of documents is more in the civil law tradition. As a result, arbitrators from different legal backgrounds may each have a different perspective on the matter. For example, if a claimant fails to produce a key piece of evidence, an arbitrator from a common law jurisdiction may be more willing to dismiss the claim on the basis that the claimant has not discharged its burden of proof. A civil law arbitrator may have a cultural preference 6.328

[285] Jason Fry, Simon Greenberg, and Francesca Mazza, *The Secretariat's Guide to ICC Arbitration* (International Chamber of Commerce 2012) paras 3–977. Other similar provisions in institutional rules include: SIAC Rules Rule 27(f); HKAC Rules Article 22.3; and LCIA Rules Article 22.1(v).

[286] O'Malley Rules of Evidence (n 29) para 3.115 and fn 159.

towards a more inquisitorial approach and may feel more comfortable making a request for production of the documents. However, there are no hard rules around this. An experienced common law arbitrator may be just willing as a civil law arbitrator to call for documents s/he believes to be important to the case.

6.329 The Commentary on the IBA Rules indicates that the rationale for including express provision for the tribunal's right to request production of documents is that the tribunal may be required (under certain institutional rules) to establish the facts of the case by all appropriate means. Therefore, it should be entitled to order a party to produce documents it considers to be relevant and material to the extent those documents have not already been introduced as evidence into the proceedings.[287]

6.330 This justification for the provision is a good one. In addition, because the party ordered to produce/take steps to obtain the documents may object on any of the grounds set out in Article 9.2, the controls on this form of document production remain consistent with other provisions of the IBA Rules.

3. The Available Routes

6.331 The options available to a tribunal under Article 3.10 are:

(a) to request a party to the arbitration to produce a document;
(b) to request such party to use its best efforts to take appropriate steps to obtain a document from a 'person or organisation'; and
(c) for the tribunal itself to take any steps it considers appropriate to obtain a document from a 'person or organisation'.

6.332 Option (a) covers a simple request made to a party to the arbitration for a document that the tribunal believes to be in the possession of that party. Options (b) and (c) concern documents held by a non-party to the arbitration. Option (b) appears to be intended for use where the tribunal believes that one of the parties to the arbitration has some special status in relation to the document or party in possession of it that makes a request addressed to that party appropriate. Option (c) appears most likely to be engaged where none of the parties to the arbitration has any particular attribute that makes it more likely that they can obtain the documents, or for other reasons in the case the tribunal believes it is more appropriate or desirable for the tribunal to take steps itself.

6.333 In exercising its jurisdiction to make an order in any of the terms mentioned, the tribunal should proceed cautiously. It will wish to ensure so far as possible that the selection of the particular document(s) requested carries with it no indication of a predisposition as to its evidential value. It is sensible for the tribunal to indicate the reason

[287] Commentary on the IBA Rules (n 5) 11. Examples of institutional rules requiring the tribunal to establish the facts of the case cited in the Commentary are ICC Rules Article 25(1) and LCIA Rules Article 22.1.

why it believes the documents it seeks are relevant and material with an express invitation to the parties to raise an objection if they disagree.

4. The Right to Object

Article 3.10 makes express provision for a right of objection to a tribunal's request on any of the grounds set out in Article 9.2. Those grounds of objection are described at 6.225, and in more detail in Chapter 12. There is no requirement in Article 3.10 that the tribunal deliver a request for documents in terms that comply with the requirements of Article 3.3 relating to a Request to Produce delivered by a party to the arbitration, and therefore no reference to a right of objection based on the tribunal's non-compliance with those requirements. Where the documents requested lack sufficient relevance to the case or materiality to its outcome, this will be caught by the ground of objection set out at Article 9.2(a). However, despite the absence of a reference to the requirements of Article 3.3, it is desirable that the tribunal nonetheless set out in the request the reasons why it believes the documents are relevant and material.[288] **6.334**

On a strict reading, the right of objection referred to in Article 3.9 would appear to apply only in relation to the tribunal's exercise of option (a) i.e. where the tribunal delivers a simple request to produce to a particular party, that party (and that party only) may raise an objection—and possibly option (b) at 6.331. The Commentary to the IBA Rules suggests that the right to object is also engaged in relation to option (b). If the right of objection does apply to option (b), it would make no sense for it to not also apply to action by the tribunal itself under option (c), although in that case the reference to 'a party to whom such a request for Documents is addressed' in Article 3.9 would have to be read as applying to all parties to the arbitration. **6.335**

If an objection is raised, the provisions of Articles 3.4–3.8, by which party objections to a request for production made by another party are resolved, are to apply 'correspondingly'. It appears uncontentious that those procedures should be followed.[289] However, as a matter of practice (and supported by the use of the word 'correspondingly' in Article 3.10) the provisions will have to be read with appropriate adjustments to take account of the fact that it is the tribunal, rather than another party, that is pursuing the request. For example, it cannot be necessary for a party to actively request the tribunal to rule on an objection as provided for in Article 3.7 or, if documents are in the possession of a third party 'person or organisation' as contemplated by Article 3.10, there can **6.336**

[288] IBA Rules (n 21) Article 3.3(b) includes a requirement that the request to produce include a statement as to how the documents requested are relevant to the case and material to its outcome.

[289] For example, O'Malley (n 29) para 3.116 notes that the tribunal is bound to follow the procedure set forth in IBA Rules (n 21) Articles 3.4–3.8 before ordering the production: 'Because the parties are to be treated equally, and must be afforded the same opportunities to provide comments on the disclosure requests, irrespective of whether they come from a tribunal on its own motion or from another party, a tribunal must give the party ordered to submit the evidence an opportunity to object to any proposed disclosure. For this reason, a tribunal should follow the procedure in articles 3.4 to 3.8 before ordering the production of documentary evidence'.

be no question of the tribunal reviewing those documents as provided for in Article 3.8 prior to making a ruling. In substance, the tribunal should request the documents and give the party (or parties, in the case of option (c)) time to raise objections (if any) or produce/take steps to produce the documents. If objections are raised, the tribunal will have to give them proper consideration before deciding whether to pursue its request by available means.

5. The Taking of Appropriate Steps

6.337 The decision as to what steps are 'appropriate' for a party to take when requested by a tribunal to obtain documents from a third party under option (b) at 6.331 is a matter for the tribunal, as is a decision as to the steps that a tribunal might itself take under option (c). However, in each case, and even when formal objections are not raised under Article 9.2, it is desirable that the tribunal invites comments from the party (or parties) as to the steps the tribunal has in mind. What steps are appropriate to consider will be specific to the facts of the case.

6.338 The procedures that may be available to a party, or to the tribunal, in relation to the obtaining of documents from 'any person or organisation' will be similar to those described in relation to Article 3.9. The only material difference is that those steps will be triggered by a tribunal's request for production, rather than by a party request.

6.339 In relation to option (b) at 6.331, although the wording used in Article 3.10 appears sufficiently wide to permit a tribunal to require a party to take steps by way of available legal proceedings to compel a third party to make documents available, our view is that such a course of action is likely to be rare, and that most tribunals will be reluctant to consider compelling a party to take legal action. This course would also be fraught with problems at a practical level. For example, who would pay the cost of such proceedings, and would decision making in relation to the conduct of the litigation have to be overseen by the tribunal?

6.340 Much more likely is that a party will be asked to take such steps as are available to it, short of legal action, to obtain the documents sought. The phrase requiring the party to 'use its best efforts' also appears more consistent with such an approach. The same phrase is used in Article 4.10 in relation to a request by the tribunal that a party to the arbitration provide for the appearance of a witness to give oral testimony.[290] In relation to that provision we suggest that it might include such action as contacting the witness in positive terms to request their participation, or arranging travel and accommodation to enable the witness to attend the evidentiary hearing. In relation to documents, it is likely to comprise the taking of similar practical steps. For example, in a construction

[290] See Chapter 7 paras 7.219-7.230.

dispute between employer and main contractor, where that contractor has a right under its contract with a subcontractor to obtain certain documents relevant to the dispute, the contractor may be asked to write to the subcontractor in appropriate terms exercising its rights under the subcontract.

J. Additional Production by the Parties

Article 3.11

11. Within the time ordered by the Arbitral Tribunal, the Parties may submit to the Arbitral Tribunal and to the other Parties any additional Documents on which they intend to rely or which they believe have become relevant to the case and material to its outcome as a consequence of the issues raised in Documents, Witness Statements or Expert Reports submitted or produced, or in other submissions of the Parties.

1. Introduction

Article 3.11 of the IBA Rules should be read in conjunction with Article 3.1. The latter requires each party to submit within the time ordered by the tribunal all documents upon which it relies.[291] Article 3.11 of the IBA Rules gives the parties a right to submit further documents where the requirements laid down in Article 3.11 are met, and where this is done within the time ordered by the tribunal.[292] **6.341**

In an ideal world, each party would submit the entirety of its case and all supporting evidence at the outset of the arbitration. In the real world, claims give rise to defences and cross-claims and, as matters are investigated further by the parties, additional categories of document may become important. Sometimes this is at a relatively late stage in the arbitration where there is no longer the opportunity to exhibit those documents to witness statements or expert reports. Article 3.11 provides a mechanism by which such additional documents may be introduced. **6.342**

2. Requirements for Introduction of Documents under Article 3.11

Subject to meeting the deadline for delivery imposed by the tribunal, Article 3.11 permits parties to introduce further documents on which they intend to rely. In addition, parties may submit documents that 'they believe' have become relevant to the case and **6.343**

[291] See 6.26–6.36.

[292] Article 4.5(b) of the IBA Rules may provide an additional opportunity to introduce documents. See Chapter 7 para 7.110.

material to its outcome as a result of issues raised in documents, witness or expert evidence, or submissions of the parties.

6.344 In relation to the first category of documents mentioned, it is not unusual for a tribunal to set a long stop date by which any documents on which a party intends to rely must be introduced on to the record. Key documents on which a party relies are likely to have already been introduced with submissions or witness/expert evidence. However, new helpful documents may come to light during the case or may have been obtained from the other parties during document production. The key point is that by a certain date the presenting party must indicate to the other parties what those documents are. This is consistent with Preamble 3 and the principle underlying the IBA Rules that 'each party shall be entitled to know reasonably in advance of any Evidentiary Hearing or any fact or merits determination, the evidence on which the other Parties rely'.[293] It is also consistent with the right of each party to have a proper opportunity to present its case. This includes the right to produce documents relied on in support of that case, provided the timing of this is not such as to breach the principle just mentioned. The documents introduced may include (and, on one view, ought to comprise) documents that are relevant to the case and material to its outcome.

6.345 The second category of documents permitted to be introduced are documents that have not previously been put onto the record at an earlier stage (eg as exhibits to submissions or witness evidence) but that, as a result of issues later raised in submissions and evidence, have become relevant and material. It may be that these documents are relevant and material to another party's case and so are not technically documents relied on by the introducing party under the first category mentioned earlier.

6.346 This raises the interesting question of whether under Article 3.11 a party is obliged to produce documents that appear to it to be relevant and material, even if those documents are adverse to its position? The IBA Rules do not expressly impose such a requirement on the parties. However, it is a matter of debate as to whether it might be said that the requirement of good faith set out in Preamble 3 to the IBA Rules imposes an obligation to produce such documents even when they do not fall within a document production request made by another party under Article 3.2.[294]

6.347 The benchmark for consideration of whether the new documents are relevant to the case and material to its outcome will engage the same factors as considered in relation to Article 3.3(b).[295] Whether the proposed production meets the other requirements of Article 3.11 is another relevant consideration, although in the majority of cases this may not be tested unless an objection to introduction of the documents on that basis is raised by one of the other parties in accordance with Article 9.2(a).

[293] See IBA Rules (n 21) Preamble 3.
[294] See discussion in Chapter 2 para 2.79.
[295] See 6.76-6.146.

3. Timing of the Production of Documents under Article 3.11

Where a party wishes to rely on the provisions of Article 3.11 the documents must be introduced '[w]ithin the time ordered by the Arbitral Tribunal'. This is a standard form of wording used throughout the IBA Rules. As is the norm in any arbitration, the tribunal will set deadlines for the various procedural steps to be undertaken in the arbitration guided by the principle contained in Preamble 1, and in arbitration rules and practice, to ensure an efficient, economical, and fair process, and after consultation with the parties under Article 2 of the IBA Rules.[296] If the tribunal has already set a deadline for submitting additional documents under Article 3.11 (in a first procedural order or elsewhere), a party may simply submit the additional documents within that deadline. If that step has not been provided for, then the party wishing to introduce the new documents should, strictly speaking, seek permission from the tribunal to do so by a particular date. Many tribunals will insert into their procedural orders a requirement that the 'late' introduction of documents will only be allowed following a special application to the tribunal and with its permission. **6.348**

Where a party seeks to introduce documents *after* a date ordered by the tribunal for that step to take place, different considerations to those mentioned in Article 3.11 will apply. It then becomes a matter for balancing the right of a party to present its case by reference to the evidence it wishes to rely on and the prejudice to the other parties of having to deal with new evidence tendered at the last moment. Chapter 7 discusses similar considerations that arise as occur in relation to the late introduction of witness evidence. **6.349**

K. General Issues Regarding Documents

Article 3.12

12. With respect to the form of submission or production of Documents:
- **(a) copies of Documents shall conform to the originals and, at the request of the Arbitral Tribunal, any original shall be presented for inspection;**
- **(b) Documents that a Party maintains in electronic form shall be submitted or produced in the form most convenient or economical to it that is reasonably usable by the recipients, unless the Parties agree otherwise or, in the absence of such agreement, the Arbitral Tribunal decides otherwise;**
- **(c) a Party is not obligated to produce multiple copies of Documents which are essentially identical unless the Arbitral Tribunal decides otherwise; and**
- **(d) translations of Documents shall be submitted together with the originals and marked as translations with the original language identified.**

[296] See Chapter 5.

6.350 Article 3.12 addresses a number of general issues relating to documents. These provisions aid efficiency of the arbitration process and ensure a uniformity of approach by each of the parties to the dispute in relation to the matters covered

1. Conformity of Copy with the Original and Obligation to Present Original for Inspection

3.12 (a) copies of Documents shall conform to the originals and, at the request of the Arbitral Tribunal, any original shall be presented for inspection.

6.351 Article 3.12(a) is concerned with the use of copy documents.

a. Use of copy documents is permitted

6.352 Article 3.12(a) permits the production and submission into evidence of copies of documents, rather than originals.[297]

6.353 Historically, many arbitral tribunals required the production into evidence of original documents, or duly certified copies. Although this is still the case in certain jurisdictions (for example, in some countries of the former Soviet Union), it is general practice in international arbitration for tribunals to accept copies of documents unless the authenticity of the document or conformity of the copy with its original is disputed by a party or witness.

6.354 Although they permit the use of copy documents, the IBA Rules require that the copy should conform to the original.[298] Under the previous 1999 IBA Rules it was a requirement that a copy should 'fully conform' to the original. In the current IBA Rules, the word 'fully' has been omitted. Noting the change, O'Malley suggests that a distinction is to be drawn between minor or irrelevant discrepancies and those that are material in nature. As he puts it:

> Such a rule would appear to be consistent with the approach that . . . evidence produced in an arbitration should have material conformity to an original, but minor and/or irrelevant discrepancies (such as irrelevant notes in the margins which do not feature on the original) should not bar a copy from being introduced into evidence.[299]

6.355 However, the Commentary on the 2010 IBA Rules (like the commentary to the 1999 Rules) still states expressly that the copy document 'must *fully* conform' to the original.[300] This is either an oversight in the Commentary or an indication that there is no real change in the substance of the requirement that a document conform to the

[297] Commentary on the IBA Rules (n 5) 12.
[298] IBA Rules (n 21) Article 3.12(a).
[299] O'Malley Rules of Evidence (n 29) para 3.131.
[300] Commentary on the IBA Rules (n 5) 12 (emphasis added).

original. However, it is difficult to understand how the deletion of an additional qualifying word in the rules themselves could not have been intended to change the meaning of the requirement in some way.

In our view, O'Malley's point concerning the difference between minor/irrelevant differences and those that are more significant could be made in relation to the earlier ('fully conform') description, even if it was intended that this should mean something different and more onerous. The real question is whether the copy document conforms in substance with the original of which the document is said to be a copy. For example, in relation to the 1999 IBA Rules, Professor Raeschke-Kessler went so far as to argue that irrelevant material that would not mislead or distort the evidence could be removed from the copy document. He says that: 6.356

> The copy of the original must only conform to the document as it was initially established by the author. The recipient of the letter, for example, may later add handwritten notes on the letter. These notes do not belong to the original document of the sender. If the recipient wants to introduce the latter into the arbitral proceedings as a document written by the sender, the recipient may remove from the copy his or her own handwritten notes on the original because they do not belong to the original document.
>
> This is of course different if the recipient has written his or her own manifestations of legal importance on the document. If, for example the person received an offer to conclude a contract from the sender and signed the document, a contract between sender and recipient will have been concluded by that signature. When introducing this document into the arbitral proceedings, the signature of the document must remain visible on the copy.[301]

Thus, a party to the arbitration may have taken a telephone call and, during that call, jotted down on an original piece of correspondence the telephone number of the person calling. The call and the person calling had no connection to the dispute. This is clearly a different situation from one in which that same party writes 'correct' at the bottom of a draft minutes of a meeting relating to the dispute. 6.357

Article 3.12(c)—which relieves a party from an obligation to produce multiple copies of a document that is 'essentially identical'—may also be relevant in this context in providing guidance on what might be regarded as a non-conformity for the purposes of Article 3.12 (a). See further at 6.374–6.377. 6.358

b. Production of the original document

Although the use of copy documents is permitted, Article 3.12(a) provides that 'at the request of the Arbitral Tribunal, any original shall be presented for inspection'. 6.359

301 Raeschke-Kessler (n 6) 413.

6.360 Article 3.12(a) does not give any guidance on the circumstances that may prompt the tribunal to ask the party whose document it is to produce the original document. Those circumstances will be case specific. In general terms, a request for inspection of the original is most likely to be prompted by an issue raised by one of the other parties to the arbitration. It may be sensible for a tribunal to set a deadline for the parties to indicate if the authenticity of a document is disputed. Such disputes raise difficult issues and may call for further factual or expert evidence (including of a forensic nature). This cannot be left until late in the proceedings.[302] Circumstances that may justify a request by the tribunal for sight of the original documents include where another party has made allegations that the copy produced is materially different from the original, or that the document is a forgery.[303]

c. Available options if a copy does not conform to the original or gives rise to doubts about the authenticity of the document

6.361 If a copy does not conform with the original when inspected, or if doubts exist about the authenticity of the original document, the tribunal may be faced with the question of what to do about it, either on its own initiative or following an application by one of the parties. Much may depend on the facts of the case but available options include:

(a) excluding the document from evidence;
(b) admitting it into evidence but attaching no/less weight to the document if its authenticity is in question. In particular, a tribunal may decide that it attaches no weight to the document unless it is corroborated by other reliable evidence.

6.362 In nearly all cases it is desirable for the tribunal to give the parties an opportunity to make submissions on the implications of the lack of conformity and the consequences that should flow from that position.

6.363 In relation to allegations of forgery, it must be borne in mind that most tribunals will be very slow to make a finding to that effect without compelling evidence of the forgery. As one commentator puts it:

> When confronted with challenges to evidence based on the allegation of forgery, customarily arbitrators begin with the presumption that the evidence is authentic, and require a high or enhanced standard of proof be met by the party alleging the forgery before disqualifying the evidence from the record.[304]

6.364 In practice, in many cases, the tribunal may not need to make a finding that a document has been forged, but may simply address the problem as a question of weight of

[302] 'Procedural Order of 19 May 2004 in ICC Case 13046 (Extract)' in *Special Supplement 2010: Decisions on ICC Arbitration Procedure: A Selection of Procedural Orders Issued by Arbitral Tribunals Acting under the ICC Rules of Arbitration (2003–2004)* (International Chamber of Commerce 2010).

[303] For further discussion on the issues raised in relation to circumstances justifying a Request to Produce an original, and doubts as to the authenticity of a document, see Simon Gabriel, 'Dealing with "Challenged Documents"' (2011) 4 ASA Bulletin 823.

[304] O'Malley Rules of Evidence (n 29) para 3.135.

evidence, eg in *Reza Said Malek v the Islamic Republic of Iran*,[305] where the tribunal was faced with inconsistent evidence in relation to the authenticity of a document. In that case, the tribunal decided that the document should be afforded no evidential weight and, on that basis, the tribunal held it was unnecessary to decide whether the document was a forgery.

If, of course, the forgery is proven to the satisfaction of the tribunal then, in addition to any other consequences that may flow from this finding, the act of forgery (and therefore the document) may, depending on the issues in the case, be very important evidence, just not of the fact for which it was originally offered as support. **6.365**

2. Format for Submission of e-Documents

3.12(b) Documents that a Party maintains in electronic form shall be submitted or produced in the form most convenient or economical to it that is reasonably usable by the recipients, unless the Parties agree otherwise or, in the absence of such agreement, the Arbitral Tribunal decides otherwise . . .

Article 3.12(b) addresses the form in which documents held in electronic form should be submitted or produced in an arbitration. The limited special provision in the IBA Rules concerning electronic documents is addressed at paragraphs 6.69-6.75. **6.366**

The IBA Rules define 'Documents' to include electronic documents and, in practice, document production in international arbitration will nearly always involve a significant volume of soft copy documents. Despite this, there is a single set of rules governing both hard and soft copy document production with some relatively minor additions relating to electronic documents.[306] Article 3.12(b) contains a useful addition to the provisions addressing soft copy documents by removing uncertainty around the default position in relation to the format in which electronic documents should be produced. **6.367**

The approach adopted in the IBA Rules is straightforward. Electronic documents are to be produced by a party in 'the form most convenient or economical to it'. However, there are a number of caveats to this. The first is that, whatever form the document is delivered in, it must be 'reasonably usable by the recipients'. The second is that the parties may agree otherwise or (in the absence of any such agreement) the tribunal may order otherwise. **6.368**

305 *Reza Said Malek v the Islamic Republic of Iran* (Final Award No. 534-193-3, 11 August 1992) 9 Iran–US Cl Trib.

306 For example, IBA Rules (n 21) contain a reworking of the definition of 'Document' contained in 1999 IBA Rules (n 13), and IBA Rules (n 21) Article 3.3(a) contains express reference to the power of the tribunal to order a party to identify specific files, search terms, and other means of searching for electronic documents that are the subject of a document production request.

6.369 Electronic files will be held in a number of different formats.[307] The format in which a document is originally created is often referred to as its 'native format'. However, it is nearly always possible to convert the document into a different format. Sometimes this will be done in the ordinary course of business, but in relation to document production a party may have the ability to produce a soft document in one of a number of different formats. The format in which a document is produced may affect the amount of information about the document that is transferred to the recipient as attached metadata. For example, the same email can be produced electronically in its native format (normally .pst or .msg format), or in a pdf file. The latter can still be read and understood but the available metadata will generally only contain details of the date of the document format conversion or pdf scan. This will not allow the recipient to check the electronic history of the original email. The format in which a document is produced may also affect the ease with which the document may be loaded on to a document database and/or interrogated with the use of forensic software.[308] It may also affect such minor (but often practically important) matters as whether the content of the document can be cut and pasted into submissions or other documents created in connection with preparation of a party's case.

6.370 As mentioned, the IBA Rules provide that the parties may produce e-documents in the form most convenient to them. The Commentary contains the following observations—most notably, a recognition that this approach may result in something less than the native format document with all available metadata

> The cost of the taking of evidence in electronic form can vary widely depending on the form in which documents are to be submitted. Thus, absent agreement by the parties or determination by the arbitral tribunal to another form, the revised text of the IBA Rules . . . provides that the default form of production for electronic documents shall be the form most convenient or economical to the producing party that is reasonably usable by the recipient. This format will generally not be the native format with full metadata, as submission in this format can be unduly expensive and inconvenient.

6.371 Issues around electronic document production are also something that parties may wish to raise with the tribunal at an early stage as part of the consultation process provided for by Article 2 of the IBA Rules.[309] The Commentary to the IBA Rules confirms that this approach is desirable, and says:

> Where electronic disclosure is likely to play a role in an arbitration, the question of the form of production should be addressed early in Article 2.1 consultation . . . .[310]

[307] For example, .pst, .msg, .xls/xlsx, .ppt/.pptx, .jpg, etc.
[308] As mentioned, the amount of metadata provided will vary according to format. The less metadata the fewer available fields by which the data may be interrogated. For example, an email produced in .pst format will allow searching by reference to sender, recipient, subject, etc. A .pdf copy may not.
[309] See Chapter 5.
[310] Commentary on the IBA Rules (n 5) 12.

If a party is keen to obtain document production from other parties in native format with some or all available metadata, then it is prudent to raise this at an early stage in the arbitration. It may be seen as mutually beneficial by parties at that stage and be possible for them to agree a protocol for e-production. There are a number of protocols available to parties who wish to address such issues early on, eg the CIArb Protocol for E-Disclosure in International Arbitration and the TECSA & Disclosure Protocol.[311] 6.372

The circumstances in which a tribunal may make an order requiring a party to produce electronic documents in a format different from that in which they been have produced (or it is intended they be produced) will vary from case to case. In many cases, it ought to be possible for the parties to reach a solution without troubling the tribunal. 6.373

3. Multiple Identical Copies

3.12(c) a Party is not obligated to produce multiple copies of Documents which are essentially identical unless the Arbitral Tribunal decides otherwise.

Article 3.2(c) contains the very sensible provision that, during the document production process, a party is not required to produce more than one copy of the same document where the documents are 'essentially identical'. As mentioned elsewhere, the volume of documents—particularly electronic documents—introduced in international arbitration is often very significant. The more that can be done to restrict the introduction of documents that have no additional evidential value and merely serve to increase costs, the better for all concerned. Article 3.12(c) is therefore consistent with the objective set out in Preamble 1 of an 'efficient' and 'economical' process. 6.374

The practical implications of the provision are self-explanatory. If during the document production process a party locates more than one copy of the same document it need produce only a single copy, provided the two copies are 'essentially identical'. 6.375

The meaning of 'essentially identical' requires careful consideration. If a search for documents has found two copies of the same document, but one of them contains manuscript annotations or has an additional stamp of some significance to the dispute, Article 3.12(c) is not triggered because these documents are not essentially identical. They are to be treated as separate documents for the purposes of Article 3.12(c). In such a case, and provided they fall within the scope of a legitimate request for production, the party in possession should produce both documents. 6.376

[311] See also CPR Protocol (n 79), and ICC Report on Managing E-Document Production (n 78).

6.377 A practical difficulty can sometimes arise in relation to electronic documents. Historically, documents (principally hard copy) were reviewed manually and counsel would make a decision as to whether the copies in front of him or her were essentially the same. More recently, with the bulk of document production involving e-documents, the volume of documents to be searched has grown exponentially. It is not unheard of to have document production involving hundreds of thousands of documents. In addition, the very nature of electronic documents lends itself to multiple copies. For example, one email sent to two recipients will be found in the email boxes of the sender and two recipients. If a search is made of all three custodians, three copies will be found. Where, as is very often the case, an email has been copied to numerous recipients the volume of copies may be significant. Fortunately, forensic document management software is often able to carry out a process of 'de-duplication' by which it can identify multiple copies of the same document by reference to certain parameters that may be applied. For example, all emails having the same sender, recipients and subject and sent/received at the same time are to be identified as duplicates.

6.378 The search for documents to produce may also be approached using 'threading' by which the software will retrieve only those parts of the communication 'tree' that contain unique material. For example, a reply to an email that includes the email to which it responds will be retrieved but not the original email. Such software is also capable of identifying copies that have minor variations—for example, if one of the recipients forwarded the email to someone else with only 'FYI' added on top of the email. It is for counsel to determine the parameters to be applied to identify duplicates, and whether any category of duplicate needs to be manually reviewed to determine whether it is 'essentially identical' or should be produced. For instance, in the example given of the forwarded email simply marked 'FYI', if the knowledge (or lack of knowledge) of the subject matter of the email by the person to whom it was forwarded is an issue in the arbitration, then the email may be material.

4. Translations

3.12(d) translations of Documents shall be submitted together with the originals and marked as translations with the original language identified.

6.379 Article 3.12(d) concerns the submission of translations of documents. The provision of translations is a common practice in international arbitration where very often documents submitted or produced will include documents in a language other than the language of the arbitration.

6.380 Article 3.12(d) simply says that where translations are submitted, they shall be (a) submitted together with the originals and (b) marked as translations with the original language identified. Requirement (a) might be read as indicating that the translation should be submitted at the same time as the original language document is submitted or produced into the arbitration. However, the Commentary to the IBA Rules expressly states that the IBA Rules do not govern 'the timing of submission of translations'. The requirement must therefore be read as meaning that when a translation is submitted it should be accompanied by a copy of the original language document. This will ensure that a translation is not mistaken for an original document.

The Commentary to the IBA Rules also state that those rules do not govern: **6.381**

> [W]hether translations are required in particular arbitral proceedings, whether particular documents may be translated in part only, [or] the resolution of disputes regarding translations.[312]

A number of institutional rules grant the tribunal an express power to decide whether translations are required. For example, see Article 17.5 of the LCIA Rules and Rule 22 of the SIAC Rules. **6.382**

As already mentioned, it is advisable for parties to discuss these and other issues relating to the translation of documents as part of the consultation process under Article 2 of the IBA Rules, not least so that the most cost-effective way of managing translation costs can be determined. Some of those issues are discussed in Chapter 5. **6.383**

Article 3.12(d) does not mention the form that the translation must take. For example, is an informal translation prepared by one of the parties acceptable, or must it have been prepared by a qualified translator and contain an appropriate certificate as to the accuracy of the translation? This is another issue about which it is prudent for the parties to agree or consult the tribunal at an early stage in the arbitration.[313] **6.384**

In very rare cases, 'competing' translations may be submitted by different parties. In such cases the tribunal may direct that the parties consult to agree a translation or, failing that, if interpreters are to be present at the evidentiary hearing the tribunal might also defer consideration of the issue until the hearing if there is a possibility of discussing the meaning of the document direct with its author. **6.385**

L. Confidentiality

> **3.13 Any Document submitted or produced by a Party or non-Party in the arbitration and not otherwise in the public domain shall be kept confidential by the Arbitral Tribunal and the other Parties, and shall be used only in connection with the arbitration. This requirement shall apply except and to the extent that disclosure may be required of a Party to fulfil a legal duty, protect or pursue a legal right, or enforce or challenge an award in bona fide legal proceedings before a state court**

[312] Commentary on the IBA Rules (n 5) 12.
[313] See Chapter 5.

or other judicial authority. The Arbitral Tribunal may issue orders to set forth the terms of this confidentiality. This requirement shall be without prejudice to all other obligations of confidentiality in the arbitration.

6.386 Article 3.13 sets out an express obligation of confidentiality in relation to documents introduced into the arbitration. Parties to the arbitration, and the tribunal, can use documents submitted or produced by another party or non-party in the arbitration only for the purposes of the arbitration. All such documents must be kept confidential.[314]

6.387 As stated elsewhere, there is no general rule of confidentiality in international arbitration, and obligations of confidentiality must therefore be looked for in the parties' agreement to arbitrate, in applicable arbitration rules, and in the national laws of the seat of arbitration.[315] Article 3.13 provides a measure of protection in respect of documents used in the arbitration. It goes some way to addressing potential concerns that dissemination of documents produced in an arbitration is uncontrolled, leading to parties being reluctant to present or produce evidence in the case.

6.388 Article 3.13 is applicable to all documents introduced into the proceedings, regardless of why or how they were introduced—including documents volunteered by a party in support of its own case, documents produced in response to a Request to Produce and/or order of the tribunal, as well as to documents submitted by a third party.[316] The equivalent provision in the 1999 IBA Rules was said to apply only to documents submitted by a party against its will pursuant to a Request to Produce or other procedural order.[317] The provision does not affect the right of a party to publish its own documents.[318]

6.389 The confidentiality requirement does not apply to documents that are already in the public domain or are made public by the parties prior to production in the arbitration. Parties remain free to make their own documents public at any time.[319]

6.390 The requirement of confidentiality applies except and to the extent that disclosure may be required of a party to fulfil a legal duty, protect or pursue a legal right, or enforce or challenge an award. An express 'carve out' of these circumstances was introduced by the current IBA Rules.[320] Similar exceptions to obligations of confidentiality are seen routinely in commercial documents. These provisions generally acknowledge that, as a matter of general law, a duty of confidentiality may be over-ridden in circumstances

[314] See further Tercier and Bersheda (n 217) 77, 97.

[315] See further O'Malley Rules of Evidence (n 29) para 3.142. See also Michael Hwang and Nicholas Thio, 'A Proposed Model Procedural Order on Confidentiality in International Arbitration: A Comprehensive and Self-Governing Code' (2012) 29 Journal of International Arbitration 137.

[316] Commentary on the IBA Rules (n 5) 13.

[317] Commentary on the 1999 IBA Rules (n 167) 24. See also Born (n 78) 2319–2423; and (n 312); and Raeschke-Kessler (n 6) 414.

[318] Article 3.13 obliges the tribunal and the 'other parties' to keep documents confidential: 'Any Document submitted or produced by a Party or non-Party in the arbitration and not otherwise in the public domain shall be kept confidential by the Arbitral Tribunal and the other Parties' (emphasis added).

[319] Commentary on the IBA Rules (n 5) 13. See Procedural Order No. 7 in *Gramercy Funds Management LLC and another v. The Republic of Peru* dated 10 May 2019 for a decision upholding the principle embodied in Article 3.13.

[320] See further Tercier and Bersheda (n 217).

where a party may be compelled by reason of law to disclose a document, or where the law recognizes that circumstances exist that justify the disclosure—for example, the pursuit of a legal right.[321] The usual procedure followed where an event falling within an exception arises is for the party relying on the exception to provide notice of impending disclosure to the tribunal and to the party who produced the document.[322]

Article 3.13 applies to documents only. The IBA Rules take no position in relation to the confidentiality of non-documentary evidence, eg oral testimony (although a written transcript recording oral testimony would be subject to confidentiality protection as a document submitted or produced by a non-party).[323] That is not to say that other confidentiality obligations may not apply. Potential sources of such obligations include the parties' arbitration agreement, the legal regime at the seat of arbitration, any applicable institutional rules or, in the case of investment arbitration, any relevant BIT, as well as any confidentiality regime agreed or directed in the first procedural order or under Article 9.4 of the IBA Rules.[324] For this reason, Article 3.13 states that this 'requirement shall be without prejudice to all other obligations of confidentiality in the arbitration'. **6.391**

Article 3.13 also goes on to provide that the 'Arbitral Tribunal may issue orders to set forth the terms of this confidentiality'. Some tribunals may wish to address the issue of confidentiality of documents in the first procedural order. If the applicable institutional rules do not contain satisfactory confidentiality provisions and/or the IBA Rules are being used as guidelines only, an express statement of confidentiality may be an important first step in establishing an appropriate level of confidentiality. It is suggested that, even where the applicable national law may independently impose confidentiality obligations on the parties with regard to materials produced in the arbitration, it is prudent to remove any doubt by use of express confidentiality orders.[325] **6.392**

The Commentary to the IBA Rules suggests that, to prevent inadvertent disclosure of documents, 'tribunals and parties are well-advised to discuss procedures for consideration of confidentiality in any consultation under Article 2.1 [of the IBA Rules] (eg proper retention or deletion of evidence following conclusion of the proceedings and any challenge of enforcement proceedings)'.[326] Tribunals may sometimes also set out a **6.393**

[321] In a similar way, the 'carve out' at Article 3.13 recognizes that most systems of law admit of exceptions to the duty of confidentiality if necessary to protect the parties' legitimate interests or to protect the more general public interest. For example, English law recognizes limited exceptions to the duty of confidentiality where disclosure is reasonably necessary for the protection of parties' legitimate interests against a third party (see *Hassneh Insurance Co of Israel v Mew* [1993] 2 Lloyd's Rep 243). In addition, there may be circumstances where an agreement regarding confidentiality will be unenforceable on public policy or mandatory law grounds, for example, in circumstances involving mandatory reporting obligations by publicly held companies. See also O'Malley Rules of Evidence (n 29) para 3.156.

[322] See further ibid para 3.157.

[323] Commentary on the IBA Rules (n 5) 13.

[324] See Chapter 12 paras 12.317–12.356.

[325] See Born (n 78) 2387.

[326] Commentary on the IBA Rules (n 5) 13.

protocol by which any materials of a potentially confidential nature are to be identified or processed during the arbitration.[327]

6.394 The nature of such an agreement or order will vary according to the facts of the case. The nature of specific provisions that may be adopted are dealt with in more detail in the context of Article 2 consultation, and Article 9.4, which makes express provision for the tribunal to make necessary arrangements to permit identified types of evidence to be presented or considered subject to suitable confidentiality protections.[328]

M. Separate Issues or Phases

> **3.14. If the arbitration is organised into separate issues or phases (such as jurisdiction, preliminary determinations, liability or damages), the Arbitral Tribunal may, after consultation with the Parties, schedule the submission of Documents and Requests to Produce separately for each issue or phase.**

6.395 Article 3.14 allows a tribunal to order production of documents in stages by reference to issues or phases where the arbitration is being organized in that way. It is a new provision that introduces a consistent approach in relation to all types of evidence. As the Commentary explains:

> This procedure was already contemplated by the previous text of the [1999] IBA Rules with reference to witness testimony (Article 4.4), and has now been expanded to encompass documentary evidence as well.[329]

6.396 A simple arbitration will be conducted in a relatively straightforward manner—the parties will exchange pleadings or submissions and evidence, and there will then be an evidentiary hearing, after which the tribunal will make an award. In some instances, the tribunal may even decide the case on paper without a hearing.

6.397 However, in more complex cases there may be threshold issues (eg limitation or jurisdiction issues) that are potentially dispositive of the entire arbitration, or discrete issues that usefully could be addressed early in order to narrow or simplify other issues in dispute (eg a decision on the applicable law or a decision on the meaning of a particular contractual provision). This may affect the organisation of the arbitration. For example, a tribunal may decide to bifurcate the proceedings into two phases: Stage 1 submissions

[327] See Hanotiau (n 100) para 22. The following text was proposed for insertion into a first procedural order: 'If any documentary evidence which the Arbitral Tribunal orders a party to produce or file contains privileged and proprietary information or trade secrets, that party shall so indicate to the Arbitral Tribunal and to the other party. In that case, after consultation with the parties, the Arbitral Tribunal shall determine what measures should be taken to respect the proprietary nature of the information while allowing as much evidence as possible to be produced for the purpose of the arbitration proceeding'.

[328] See Chapter 5 and Chapter 12.

[329] Commentary on the IBA Rules (n 5) 14.

and hearing will deal only with jurisdiction or liability; Stage 2 (if any) will be used to determine the merits or quantum of the claim.

If the proceedings are bifurcated in such a way, it may be sensible to also separate document production into different stages. For example, if Phase 1 deals with liability only, the first round of document production could be limited to issues relevant to liability. If the claimant were to lose on liability this approach could result in considerable savings in costs. **6.398**

Article 3.14 says that if the arbitration is organized into phases the tribunal 'may' organize document production in the same way. However, it is not obliged to do so. The tribunal retains discretion over whether it is appropriate in a given case to limit document production in this way. There are arguments for and against such an approach. Just as having document production limited to liability issues may result in savings if the claimant fails to establish liability, so costs may be increased if liability is established. The document production process will have to be conducted a second time and it is very likely that this will involve some duplication of associated costs. In addition, in relation to bifurcation of liability and quantum it may be reasonably easy to isolate one set of documents from another. In relation to one discrete issue among many that it has been decided should be hived off, it may be more difficult to do so. These sorts of issues should be considered in the consultation process required under Article 2 and as part of more general discussions regarding the desirability of bifurcation or separation of issues for preliminary determination. **6.399**

7

Article 4: Witnesses of Fact

Article 4 Witnesses of Fact

1. **Within the time ordered by the Arbitral Tribunal, each Party shall identify the witnesses on whose testimony it intends to rely and the subject matter of that testimony.**
2. **Any person may present evidence as a witness, including a Party or a Party's officer, employee or other representative.**
3. **It shall not be improper for a Party, its officers, employees, legal advisors or other representatives to interview its witnesses or potential witnesses and to discuss their prospective testimony with them.**
4. **The Arbitral Tribunal may order each Party to submit within a specified time to the Arbitral Tribunal and to the other Parties Witness Statements by each witness on whose testimony it intends to rely, except for those witnesses whose testimony is sought pursuant to Articles 4.9 or 4.10. If Evidentiary Hearings are organised into separate issues or phases (such as jurisdiction, preliminary determinations,**

liability or damages), the Arbitral Tribunal or the Parties by agreement may schedule the submission of Witness Statements separately for each issue or phase.

5. Each Witness Statement shall contain:
   (a) the full name and address of the witness, a statement regarding his or her present and past relationship (if any) with any of the Parties, and a description of his or her background, qualifications, training and experience, if such a description may be relevant to the dispute or to the contents of the statement;
   (b) a full and detailed description of the facts, and the source of the witness's information as to those facts, sufficient to serve as that witness's evidence in the matter in dispute. Documents on which the witness relies that have not already been submitted shall be provided;
   (c) a statement as to the language in which the Witness Statement was originally prepared and the language in which the witness anticipates giving testimony at the Evidentiary Hearing;
   (d) an affirmation of the truth of the Witness Statement; and
   (e) the signature of the witness and its date and place.
6. If Witness Statements are submitted, any Party may, within the time ordered by the Arbitral Tribunal, submit to the Arbitral Tribunal and to the other Parties revised or additional Witness Statements, including statements from persons not previously named as witnesses, so long as any such revisions or additions respond only to matters contained in another Party's Witness Statements, Expert Reports or other submissions that have not been previously presented in the arbitration.
7. If a witness whose appearance has been requested pursuant to Article 8.1 fails without a valid reason to appear for testimony at an Evidentiary Hearing, the Arbitral Tribunal shall disregard any Witness Statement related to that Evidentiary Hearing by that witness unless, in exceptional circumstances, the Arbitral Tribunal decides otherwise.
8. If the appearance of a witness has not been requested pursuant to Article 8.1, none of the other Parties shall be deemed to have agreed to the correctness of the content of the Witness Statement.
9. If a Party wishes to present evidence from a person who will not appear voluntarily at its request, the Party may, within the time ordered by the Arbitral Tribunal, ask it to take whatever steps are legally available to obtain the testimony of that person, or seek leave from the Arbitral Tribunal to take such steps itself. In the case of a request to the Arbitral Tribunal, the Party shall identify the intended witness, shall describe the subjects on which the witness's testimony is sought and shall state why such subjects are relevant to the case and material to its outcome. The Arbitral Tribunal shall decide on this request and shall take, authorize the requesting Party to take or order any other Party to take, such steps as the Arbitral Tribunal considers appropriate if, in its discretion, it determines that the testimony of that witness would be relevant to the case and material to its outcome.
10. At any time before the arbitration is concluded, the Arbitral Tribunal may order any Party to provide for, or to use its best efforts to provide for, the appearance for

testimony at an Evidentiary Hearing of any person, including one whose testimony has not yet been offered. A Party to whom such a request is addressed may object for any of the reasons set forth in Article 9.2.

A. Introduction

7.1 Article 4 of the IBA Rules, supplemented by Article 8 dealing with procedural aspects of oral testimony at the evidentiary hearing, provides a comprehensive framework for use and management of witness evidence.

7.2 This chapter deals primarily with Article 4. Related provisions found in Article 8 are referenced where appropriate, but will be dealt with in more detail in Chapter 11, which considers the text of Article 8. Other provisions relevant to the use of witness evidence include the duty to consult set out in Article 2,[1] the obligation of good faith contained in the Preamble 3,[2] and the tribunal's power to determine the admissibility, relevance, materiality, and weight of evidence found in Article 9.[3]

7.3 The importance that a party's legal team attaches to presentation of witness evidence may be influenced by the legal tradition of the jurisdiction with which those representatives are most familiar. It is dangerous to generalize, since practice varies considerably even among jurisdictions within each of the common law and civil law traditions. However, the differences that exist may colour the perspective that a party, its legal advisers, and each member of the tribunal may bring to an arbitration.

7.4 In the common law tradition, significant emphasis is placed on the use of witness evidence. Common law court proceedings will typically include oral witness testimony with cross-examination by counsel for the opposing party. In many civil law procedures, greater weight will be given to documentary evidence. There may be no or little oral evidence and, if there is, questioning of the witness may be undertaken by the court, rather than by counsel.[4] In international arbitration, civilian lawyers often prefer to deliver witness statements with written submissions[5] as part of a complete presentation of the case (the 'memorial' style approach), whereas common law

[1] IBA Rules on the Taking of Evidence in International Arbitration 2010, Articles 2.2(a), 2.2(b) (hereafter 'IBA Rules'). See Chapter 5.

[2] See Chapter 2 paras 2.43–2.99.

[3] IBA Rules (n 1) Article 9.1 says 'The Arbitral Tribunal shall determine the admissibility, relevance, materiality and weight of evidence'. See also Chapter 12.

[4] An examination of the use of witness testimony in different legal traditions appears in Peter Spuijbroek, *Witness Evidence in International Commercial Arbitration* (University of Amsterdam 2013) (hereafter 'Spuijbroek'). See also Roland Ziade and Charles-Henri De Taffin, 'Fact Witnesses in International Arbitration' (2010) International Business Law Journal 115.

[5] Written submissions in international arbitration proceedings (whether served with or without witness evidence) will generally contain a much fuller exposition of a party's case than would be the case with pleadings before a court in a number of (principally) common law jurisdictions such as England, Singapore, Australia, Ghana, Malaysia, Nigeria, and the United States. In international arbitration, issues of fact and law will generally be addressed in a more narrative style of drafting.

lawyers may wish to have delivery of pleadings/written submissions first in order to carry out a forensic examination of those documents before submitting witness evidence.[6] An appreciation of those differences will be useful to the parties, their legal counsel, and the tribunal when consulting about the procedure to be adopted for the taking of evidence.

The use of witness evidence may require direction and management by the tribunal in a number of areas. These include decisions about the identity and number of witnesses, the scope and content of the statements, a timetable for delivery of evidence, requests for oral examination and directions for attendance, and the management of questions put during oral evidence. The IBA Rules provide a useful set of provisions that can be adopted, or can guide, the parties' discussions as they search for common ground on the procedure to be adopted both on matters of detail and questions of principle.[7] **7.5**

Although many institutional rules make provision for the use of witness statements, and some include express reference to matters such as the manner of questioning of witnesses during oral testimony[8] or party contact with witnesses,[9] there is generally very little provision on matters of detail such as the required content of a witness statement or delivery of reply evidence.[10] Absent a reference to the IBA Rules, the parties to arbitration proceedings will generally not have agreed anything about these matters in their arbitration agreement. **7.6**

In practice, and in keeping with the principle of party autonomy, the procedure and timetable for presentation of witness evidence will very often be negotiated between the parties early in the arbitration process, with guidance and/or intervention from the tribunal as necessary, consistent with the consultation process provided for in Article 2 of the IBA Rules.[11] **7.7**

B. Witness Identification

4.1. Within the time ordered by the Arbitral Tribunal, each Party shall identify the witnesses on whose testimony it intends to rely and the subject matter of that testimony.

[6] See further Chapter 5 paras 5.74–5.76.

[7] Article 4 is a development and refinement of provisions first found in the IBA Supplementary Rules Governing the Presentation and Reception of Evidence in International Commercial Arbitration 1983 (hereafter '1983 IBA Rules'). The framework for management of witness evidence introduced by those rules was intended to be a bridge between the different practices found in common law and civil law systems.

[8] For example, see DIAC 2007, Article 29.3.

[9] For example, see SIAC Rules, Rule 25.5. This topic is also sometimes addressed by a tribunal in the first procedural order.

[10] See, for example, the brief provision contained in ICC Rules, Article 25(3) and the lack of any clear provision in ADCCAC Rules and CIETAC Rules.

[11] See Chapter 5.

7.8 Article 4.1 stipulates the first step in the procedure for presentation of witness evidence. It requires each party to the arbitration to identify:

(a) the witnesses on whose testimony it relies;[12] and
(b) the subject matter of that testimony.

7.9 In practice, consultation on the procedure by which the admission and presentation of witness evidence is to be managed may already have taken place. Article 2 (Consultation on Evidentiary Issues) includes reference to 'the preparation and submission of Witness Statements . . . ' and 'the taking of oral testimony at any Evidentiary Hearing' as being appropriate topics on which the tribunal may consult the parties at an early stage in the proceedings with the objective of agreeing an efficient, economical, and fair process.[13]

7.10 Article 4.1 implements the second principle set out in Preamble 3 to the IBA Rules—ensuring that no party is taken by surprise by its opponent's introduction of evidence on a particular topic. It reduces the scope for tactical games designed to keep details of witnesses hidden until the last possible moment. Article 4.1 also enables each party to collect evidence on the same subject matter as its opponent well in advance of the evidentiary hearing. These safeguards will contribute to the efficiency of the arbitration and assist the parties in preparing their case.

7.11 Article 4.1 may also facilitate direct examination or interrogation by a tribunal in cases where the tribunal has not made an order for the delivery of witness statements. These cases are likely to be rare, but they may occur—for example, where the parties wish to keep down costs or where the tribunal was appointed under terms of special expedition.[14] It may also happen that a witness not connected to either party is prepared to give oral testimony but has neither the time nor the inclination to produce a statement. The information provided under Article 4.1 will at least provide an outline of the likely evidence against which preparation for the evidentiary hearing may be undertaken by the non-presenting party, and by the tribunal.

7.12 Provisions similar to Article 4.1 encouraging advance notification of the identity of witnesses appear in a number of institutional rules.[15] Even where such provisions are absent, it is reasonable to expect a tribunal to issue a similar direction as part of its general case management of the arbitration.[16]

[12] Each party to an arbitration must prove the facts upon which it relies. It will do this by means of documentary evidence, factual witness testimony, and expert witness opinion. IBA Rules (n 1) Article 2 provides for early consultation on how this evidence is to be presented.

[13] IBA Rules (n 1) Articles 2.1, 2.2(a), and 2.2(b).

[14] For example, under the SCC Rules for Expedited Arbitration.

[15] For example, see SCC 2017, Article 33(1): 'In advance of any hearing, the Arbitral Tribunal may order the parties to identify each witness or expert they intend to call and specify the circumstances intended to be proved by each testimony'; and SIAC Rules, Rule 25.1: 'Before any hearing, the Tribunal may require the parties to give notice of the identity of witnesses, including expert witnesses, whom the parties intend to produce, the subject matter of their testimony and its relevance to the issues'.

[16] Michael Bühler and Carroll Dorgan, 'Witness Testimony Pursuant to the 1999 IBA Rules of Evidence in International Commercial Arbitration: Novel or Tested Standards?' (2000) Journal of International Arbitration 3 (hereafter 'Bühler and Dorgan').

The parties must provide the information described in Article 4.1 'within the time ordered by the Arbitral Tribunal'.[17] That deadline is likely to be decided upon during or after consultation with the parties and will very often be recorded in the first procedural order. The tribunal may stipulate that the information specified in Article 4.1 be provided with pleadings/written submissions or at some other time prior to the date for delivery of witness statements. The appropriate procedural timing will vary from case to case. **7.13**

There may be legitimate reasons for having a deferred date for notification of witness information. Until submissions have closed, it may not be possible to establish the scope of the matters in issue between the parties so as to identify what witness testimony is necessary. In other cases, the issues of fact between the parties may be clear early on from the face of the Request for Arbitration and the answer or response to that request. If Party A's claim is for the price of goods sold and delivered to Party B, and Party B's defence is that the price has already been paid, it ought to be possible to identify relatively quickly which witnesses are able to offer evidence regarding payment having been received/not received. In other, more complex, cases the subject matter and factual issues in dispute between the parties may not emerge or crystallize until a much later stage. For example, in a complex construction dispute, all of the potential causes of a delay in completion for which witness evidence will be required may not be capable of being identified until a detailed examination of relevant documents has taken place. **7.14**

Selection of individual witnesses may also take place at different stages. In many cases, counsel for the parties will have had some contact with potential witnesses as part of their initial investigation of the dispute or in order to gather information for written submissions. Where a memorial approach is adopted, witness statements may already have been taken. However, there will be other cases where fact-finding is ongoing during the early stages of the procedure, or situations in which the parties and their legal counsel have not yet identified the best or only witness on a particular subject. **7.15**

If the parties are able to agree a date for notification of the required information this is likely to be adopted by the tribunal. **7.16**

Having considered the parties' written submissions, it is possible that a tribunal will indicate to the parties issues of fact that the tribunal has identified, and it may request details of the witnesses who will address those facts. As with any communication prior to the award by which the tribunal provides insight into its thinking on the issues between the parties, the tribunal will need to be careful not to give an impression of bias—for example, by formulating an issue in a way that carries an underlying assumption in favour of one of the parties. A common way of avoiding this problem is for the tribunal to ask the parties to agree a list of the issues to be addressed by the fact witnesses. **7.17**

[17] IBA Rules (n 1) Article 4.1.

C. Witness Relationship with a Party to the Arbitration

4.2. Any person may present evidence as a witness, including a Party or a Party's officer, employee or other representative.

1. Introduction

7.18 Article 4.2 addresses the important question of whether an individual with a connection to one of the parties to the arbitration may offer evidence as a witness or must tender information in a different capacity. This provision provides that 'any person' may present evidence as a witness. As a result, a party-related witness is treated in the same way as any other witness. For example, under Article 8.4 of the IBA Rules, the tribunal may order a party-related witness to affirm 'in a manner determined by the Arbitral Tribunal to be appropriate'[18] that s/he commits to tell the truth, just as it would with a witness having no connection to a party.

7.19 The Commentary on the IBA Rules[19] points out that differences exist between legal systems on the question of whether an executive employee, agent, or other person affiliated with one of the parties to a dispute can be heard as a witness. In common law systems, any person (including the parties themselves), their employees, or their representatives may generally present evidence as a witness. In contrast, many civil law systems do not permit a party to be a witness in its own case. For example, many Swiss Cantonal civil procedure rules traditionally had a relatively narrow definition of a witness: a witness can only be a person who is independent of the parties and has no interest in the outcome of the proceedings. German law distinguishes between the examination of witnesses and the examination of a party—technically, a party and certain directors and officers of a party cannot serve as witnesses.[20]

7.20 That is not to say that a related party cannot be heard. Very often, applicable restrictions simply mean that the connected individual will not be categorized as a witness and that certain consequences may follow from that position.[21] For example, as mentioned in the Commentary, the information they give will not be provided under oath or a similar commitment to tell the truth.[22] For these and other reasons, in some jurisdictions the evidence of a connected party may be treated as having less weight. In one case, the French Court of Appeal considered an ICC award in which the Egyptian Government was found to be a party to an arbitration agreement with Southern Pacific Properties

[18] IBA Rules (n 1) Article 8.4.

[19] 1999 IBA Working Party and 2010 IBA Rules of Evidence Review Subcommittee, 'Commentary on the Revised Text of the 2010 IBA Rules on the Taking of Evidence in International Arbitration' (*International Bar Association*, 2010) 15 <www.ibanet.org/Document/Default.aspx?DocumentUid=DD240932-0E08-40D4-9866-309A635487C0> accessed 27 November 2018 (hereafter 'Commentary on the IBA Rules').

[20] See Christian Oetiker, 'Witnesses Before the International Arbitral Tribunal' (2007) ASA Bulletin 253.

[21] Nigel Blackaby and others, *Redfern and Hunter on International Arbitration* (6th edn, OUP 2015) para 6.125.

[22] Commentary on the IBA Rules (n 19).

(SPP). The tribunal had relied on the testimony of SPP's chairman, in which he explained that he had refused to sign the agreement unless the Egyptian Government was added. The French Court was dismissive of the testimony of the SPP chairman, who it regarded as an interested party. The award was set aside.[23]

2. Party Witnesses in International Arbitration: The IBA Rules

Despite some civil law scepticism, in international arbitration it is now accepted that a party may be heard as a witness, and tribunals will generally listen to that evidence with an open mind. There are many good reasons for this, not least that such witnesses may have the best knowledge of the facts underlying the dispute. In some cases, there may be no other witnesses who can speak to the relevant events. To deny a party the right to rely on evidence from its directors and employees might also be viewed by practitioners from the common law tradition as frustrating that party's right to present its case in the way it wishes. Acceptance of this position is reflected in the terms of Article 4.2 of the IBA Rules, which expressly state that 'a Party or a Party's officer, employee or other representative' may present evidence 'as a witness'. **7.21**

Notwithstanding the terms of Article 4.2, parties may find it helpful to be alive to cultural differences and perceptions during discussions around arrangements for witness testimony. This may aid understanding of a position taken by an opponent or, where there is a choice of possible witnesses, inform a decision about which of them is likely to have most credibility with the tribunal. **7.22**

Similar express provisions permitting party witnesses can be found in some institutional rules.[24] Other rules are silent on the issue.[25] In our view, the latter position should not be taken to exclude the right to admit party witnesses. In most cases, the general discretion afforded to a tribunal to conduct proceedings as it thinks fit will enable admission of related-party evidence. International practice also supports the view that, even where the position on party witnesses is unclear under the applicable arbitration rules, a tribunal is entitled to permit a party representative to appear as a witness.[26] **7.23**

[23] See *République Arabe d'Egypte v Southern Pacific Properties Limited* 23 ILM 1048 (1984) (Paris Court of Appeal, 12 July 1984); See Alan Redfern, 'International Commercial Arbitration. Jurisdiction Denied: The Pyramid Collapses' (1986) Journal of Business Law 15, 20–21. In Siegfried H Elsing and John M Townsend, 'Bridging the Common Law–Civil Law Divide in Arbitration' (2002) Arbitration International 59, the authors make the point that '[t]he civil law believes that the best evidence comes from documents. While witness testimony can be crucial to a civil law case, the civil law generally gives far less weight to live testimony than the common law, and treats the testimony of witnesses affiliated with or employed by a party with considerable scepticism'.

[24] For example, see the LCIA Rules, Article 20.6: 'Subject to any order by the Arbitral Tribunal otherwise . . . '; International Arbitration Rules of Zurich Chamber of Commerce, Article 37; and SCAI Rules, Article 25.2.

[25] Institutional rules not containing an express provision on this point include the SCC Rules (n 15) and SIAC Rules (n 9).

[26] This view is supported by a number of commentaries, eg Emmanuel Gaillard and John Savage (eds), *Fouchard Gaillard Goldman on International Commercial Arbitration* (Kluwer Law International 1999) para 1280, which states: 'In an international arbitration, in the absence of an agreement between the parties to the contrary, the arbitral tribunal can allow the parties to appear as witnesses. It is up to the arbitral tribunal to decide whether it is

7.24 If the IBA Rules are being used as guidance only (and the applicable institutional rules do not deal with this issue in terms acceptable to the parties), the parties may wish to make an agreement in the terms of Article 4.2, or the tribunal may wish to incorporate such a provision in the first procedural order.

3. Assessment of the Evidence

7.25 Acceptance of a party representative as a witness under Article 4.2 of the IBA Rules does not mean that the weight given to that evidence by the tribunal will necessarily be unaffected by the relationship between the witness and a party to the dispute. Article 9.1 of the IBA Rules, reflecting modern practice in international arbitration, provides that the tribunal 'shall determine the admissibility, relevance, materiality and weight of evidence' presented to it'. In consequence, the tribunal is still free to consider the identity of a witness, and his or her connection or affiliation to a party, as one of the factors to be taken into account in assessing the weight to be attributed to the evidence offered by that witness.[27]

7.26 This position is confirmed in the Commentary on the IBA Rules[28] and is unsurprising. For example, just as a tribunal may consider it appropriate to give less weight to the evidence of a hostile witness whose employment has been terminated by one of the parties to the arbitration, the tribunal may take into account a sympathetic relationship between the witness and a party. As is always the case, this will be subject to the tribunal's overall assessment of the quality and truth of the evidence presented by an individual witness during oral testimony.

4. Enforcement

7.27 A further factor to note is the potential for challenge to the award if the place of enforcement takes a hard line in relation to reliance on party-witness testimony. For example, not only are many Arab countries influenced by civil law scepticism associated with party witnesses, but Islamic Sharia law does not accept the testimony of a witness

appropriate to hear them in the circumstances, and to assess the evidentiary weight of their testimony . . . Others draw a distinction between the parties' officers, who can only be heard as parties, and their employees, who can be heard as witnesses. In fact, these distinctions are of little significance, as the witnesses themselves generally do not testify under oath and the arbitrators always have the power to assess the weight to be given to their testimony'. In relation to arbitration in Sweden, see Stefan Brocker and Kristoffer Löf, 'Chapter 8: The Proceedings' in Ulf Franke and others (eds), *International Arbitration in Sweden: A Practitioner's Guide* (Kluwer Law International 2013) 153, 193, where it is said that: 'There are no restrictions [in the Swedish Arbitration Act] as to who may testify in arbitral proceedings. Consequently, party representatives may appear to give testimony in the same way as witnesses not formally affiliated with a party'.

[27] See Chapter 12 paras 12.31–12.42.

[28] Commentary on the IBA Rules (n 19) 15.

with a vested interest in the evidence that they give, because it is regarded as untrustworthy. Such distrust extends to evidence given by an employee of that party. It has been argued that Article 4.2 of the IBA Rules is in direct conflict with this principle of Islamic jurisprudence. This situation poses potential problems with respect to the enforceability of arbitration awards in certain jurisdictions. For example, in Saudi Arabia, where the principles of Sharia law are recognized and where the relevant arbitration legislation states in terms that the rules of procedure adopted in an arbitration must not conflict with Sharia law.[29] The potential for tension is recognized in some institutional rules where express provision is made for mandatory provisions of national law to be accommodated. For example, the issue is acknowledged in the Cairo Rules, which provide that:

> Witnesses, including expert witnesses, who are presented by the parties to testify to the arbitral tribunal on any issue of fact or expertise may be any individual, notwithstanding that the individual is a party to the arbitration or in any way related to a party, *to the extent permitted under the law governing the relevant issues . . .*[30]

D. Contact with Witnesses

> **4.3. It shall not be improper for a Party, its officers, employees, legal advisors or other representatives to interview its witnesses or potential witnesses and to discuss their prospective testimony with them.**

Article 4.3 deals with interaction between a party/party representative and a witness/ potential witness for that party. It makes clear that it is not improper for a party (or its representative) to meet with and discuss the evidence that an individual witness is able to give. **7.28**

1. Background

As mentioned, witness testimony, both written and oral, is now an accepted part of international arbitration. However, as pointed out in the Commentary on the IBA Rules, there are important differences between legal systems concerning the permitted nature and extent of the contact parties may have with witnesses whose testimony they offer **7.29**

[29] See further William Kirtley, 'Do the IBA Rules on the Taking of Evidence in International Arbitration Conflict with Islamic Sharia?' (*International Arbitration Information*, 30 November 2018) <https://international-arbitration-attorney.com/international-arbitration-conflict/> accessed 28 November 2018 in which reference is made to Royal Decree No. M/34 Dated 24/5/1433H (16 April 2012) approving the Saudi Arabia Arbitration Law 2012 which, at Article 25, states: '1. The two parties to arbitration may agree on procedures to be followed by the arbitration tribunal in conducting the proceedings, including their right to subject such proceedings to effective rules of any organization, agency or arbitration center within the Kingdom or abroad, provided said rules are not in conflict with the provisions of Sharia; 2. In the absence of such an agreement, the arbitration tribunal may, subject to the provisions of Sharia and this Law, decide the arbitration proceedings it deems fit'.

[30] Cairo Regional Centre for International Commercial Arbitration Rules 2011, Article 27.2 (emphasis added).

in support of their case.[31] Even where the formal restrictions that apply are not significantly different, cultural variances in approach may exist. In particular, there is a range of opinion on the nature of the support that it is appropriate to offer a witness in preparation for giving oral evidence at an evidentiary hearing. In light of these matters, and in the absence of an express agreement or other applicable provision, parties may find themselves operating on an uneven playing field. Thus, although Article 4.3 confirms that witness contact is acceptable in arbitration proceedings conducted under the IBA Rules, in implementing or considering that provision, it is necessary to bear in mind the differences in practice that exist at an international level.

a. Professional codes of conduct and cultural variances

7.30 The rules and practice prevailing in a particular counsel's home jurisdiction may influence how s/he interacts with witnesses in the arbitration. Different national codes of conduct applying to counsel on each side of a case may require different standards of conduct in connection with witness contact.

7.31 Professional rules in some civil law countries prohibit or restrict contact between counsel and potential witnesses in litigation. Such limitations may arise in relation to both litigation and arbitration, although in recent years, in a number of jurisdictions, there has been a softening of approach in connection with the conduct of international arbitration. For example, both the Dutch-speaking and French-speaking Brussels Bar have adopted exemptions to their professional rules allowing counsel to have prior contact with witnesses in the conduct of international arbitration.[32]

7.32 In England, in line with common law practice, solicitors are permitted to interview witnesses. However, they cannot do anything during the interview that may result in the court being misled.[33] Indicative behaviours demonstrating that this rule has been

[31] Commentary on the IBA Rules (n 19) 15.

[32] On 12 October 2010, the Council of the French Speaking Bar of Brussels introduced a new section 462-2 in its Rules of Conduct. The rule explicitly permits attorneys to have preparatory contact with witnesses, both for the purpose of written statements and oral hearings within the framework of arbitration and other alternative dispute resolution methods (such as mediation or conciliation). The rule explicitly applies to both international and domestic proceedings. The rule nonetheless emphasizes that in contact with witnesses, an attorney's general obligations of loyalty, consideration, and dignity remain unaffected. In particular, the attorney must, at all times, observe the perception of truth of the witness and may not influence, or even appear to have influenced, the witness. Following that decision, the Council of the Dutch Speaking Bar of Brussels extended on 11 January 2011 its existing exemption to domestic arbitration as well. See Pascal Hollander and Maarten Draye, 'Belgium: Brussels Bar Lifts the Traditional Prohibition on Preparatory Contacts Between Attorneys and Witnesses in Arbitration' (2011) ASA Bulletin 496. The Council of the Paris Bar adopted a similar rule on 26 February 2008, although applicable only to international arbitration. The rule provides that, within the scope of international arbitration proceedings before tribunals situated in France or in other countries, a lawyer shall evaluate the appropriateness and trustworthiness of the testimony given in order to support his client's action by observing all applicable rules of procedure. In the same context, the manner in which a lawyer prepares a witness for a hearing shall not be contrary to the code of conduct of the legal profession and shall be in line with established and accepted practice in proceedings in which a lawyer acts in this capacity as a defence counsel. The Swiss Bar Association has for many years had in place professional rules providing that arbitral proceedings are excluded from the general prohibition of contact between lawyers and witnesses. See Swiss Bar Association Rules of Professional Conduct for Barristers, Article 7(2).

[33] Solicitors Regulation Authority's Code of Conduct 2011, Chapter 5 (Version 21, Solicitors Regulation Authority, 6 December 2018).

breached include attempting to influence the witness with regard to the content of their witness statement and seeking to persuade a witness to change their evidence.[34] The English Bar Standards Board's Code of Conduct prohibits the drafting of a witness statement that contains any statement of fact other than the evidence it is reasonably believed the witness would give if giving evidence orally.[35] It also prohibits counsel from encouraging a witness to give misleading or untruthful evidence.[36] The code of conduct states expressly that counsel must not 'rehearse, practice with or coach a witness in respect of their evidence'.[37]

Compliance with applicable professional rules is a matter for individual legal counsel.[38] In theory, if counsel on the same case are operating to different rules or codes of practice, the 'disadvantaged' party and its legal team may consider enlisting the assistance of co-counsel not bound by the same restrictions. However, this may not always be a convenient or practical solution. Depending on the precise terms of the applicable professional rules, the risk remains that counsel is culpable in respect of conduct by co-counsel working as part of the same legal team. **7.33**

Questions have been raised as to whether, if necessary, an arbitral tribunal should determine and apply an applicable law on witness preparation and, if so, what the law should be. While the idea that determining a single applicable set of professional conduct rules to remove potential inequality between the parties appears superficially attractive, in practice, attaining such an objective is illusory. For example, in applying a 'closest connection' test, the applicable law might be found to be that of the law of the seat. Such a finding necessarily assumes that local rules intended for local counsel are appropriate to apply in an international arbitration with a seat in the jurisdiction. Even if this assumption were correct, application of the law of the seat would not automatically exempt individual counsel from more onerous requirements of other professional conduct rules that are also applicable to them. An alternative finding that the applicable law was the law of the jurisdiction of admission to practise as counsel would simply reinforce any potential inequality that might otherwise exist.[39] **7.34**

[34] ibid para IB(5.10).

[35] 'Code of Conduct', *The Bar Standards Board Handbook* (3rd edn, Bar Standards Board 2018) rC9.2.d (hereafter 'BSB Code of Conduct').

[36] ibid rC9.3.

[37] ibid rC9.4. See also The Ethics Committee of the Bar Council, 'Witness Preparation' (*The General Council of the Bar*, August 2017) <http://www.barcouncil.org.uk/media/438420/witness_preparation.pdf> accessed 28 November 2018.

[38] Born has written on the possible professional conduct rules applicable to a lawyer's actions in an international arbitration. They include the national rules of the bar to which the lawyer is admitted, professional conduct rules at the seat of arbitration, and standards of professional conduct for counsel in International Arbitration (eg *IBA Guidelines on Party Representation in International Arbitration* (International Bar Association 2013; hereafter 'IBA Guidelines on Party Representation'). See Gary B Born, *International Commercial Arbitration* (2nd edn, Kluwer Law Arbitration 2014) 2872–75 (hereafter 'Born').

[39] See further Fabian von Schlabrendorff, 'Interviewing and Preparing Witnesses for Testimony in International Arbitration Proceedings: The Quest for Developing Transnational Standards of Lawyers' Conduct' in Miguel Angel Fernandez-Ballester and David Arias (eds), *Liber Amicorum Bernardo Cremades* (La Ley 2010) (hereafter 'von Schlabrendorff').

7.35 As mentioned, in addition to differences in the codes of conduct applicable to individual counsel, international arbitration practitioners will have different cultural approaches to preparation of witness evidence. This may also inform the nature of their interaction with witnesses. For example, in contrast to much civil law practice, common law counsel view it as an essential part of case preparation to be able to conduct interviews with potential witnesses and, if testimony is to be used, to support that witness in the drafting of a witness statement and preparation for the evidentiary hearing. Even within that tradition practice may differ. For example, English lawyers often view with suspicion the intensive witness preparation in the form of 'mock' cross-examinations undertaken by some US counsel. Those US counsel may feel that they are doing no more than assisting their client's witnesses to recall key events as part of proper and professional preparation of the case for hearing. US counsel may, in turn, take a sceptical view of the direct testimony in written witness statements that has been carefully crafted by English lawyers.

7.36 The nature of desirable limits around witness preparation for an evidentiary hearing is a topic that generates considerable debate. At one end of the spectrum is a meeting with the witness to explain the procedure that will be followed at the evidentiary hearing. At the other extreme is a full-scale rehearsal or mock cross-examination on the facts of the case. In the latter situation some counsel may suggest or indicate to the witness how they should respond to particular questions—so-called 'coaching'.

7.37 There are a number of recognized advantages of witness contact in preparation for an evidentiary hearing. It clearly makes sense that a lawyer should be permitted to explain the order of events and conventions to be adopted at the hearing so that the witness knows what to expect. A witness who feels relatively comfortable with his surroundings and what is expected of him is much more likely to present credible and useful evidence.[40] In nearly all cases it will be useful for witnesses to review the relevant documents in order to refresh their memory of events and to collect their thoughts on a particular point. This may reduce the time taken for reading documents during cross-examination and may avoid the witness either contradicting themselves as events come back to them, or being unable to produce any helpful evidence because they are taken by surprise on a topic they have not considered for many months or years.[41]

[40] Even in the English case of *R v Momodou* [2005] EWCA Crim 177 [62] and [64] (hereafter '*Momodou*'), in which the court was critical of some forms of witness preparation, it was accepted that some form of witness familiarization was perfectly proper. In paragraph 62, the judge said that '[The principle stated] does not preclude pre-trial arrangements to familiarise witness with the layout of the court, the likely sequence of events when the witness is giving evidence, and a balanced appraisal of the different responsibilities of the various participants'. In *Momodou* the court went on to indicate the procedure that should be followed if witness familiarization takes place: the process should normally be supervised or conducted by a qualified lawyer suitably accredited by the appropriate bar rules; none of those involved should have any personal knowledge of the matters in issue; records should be maintained of all those present and the identity of those responsible for the familiarization process; the programme should be retained, together with all the written material (or appropriate copies) used during the familiarization sessions; none of the material should bear any similarity whatever to the issues in the proceedings to be attended by the witnesses; and nothing in it should play on or trigger the witness's recollection of events.

[41] See further Bühler and Dorgan (n 16) 20–21.

7.38 On the other hand, over-preparation can undermine the credibility of a witness. The most important thing for a party tendering a witness is that the tribunal believes the witness to be honest. If this is the case, the tribunal will not expect the witness to remember accurately every detail of events that may have occurred some time ago, and minor inconsistencies with other evidence may be forgiven. However, if the tribunal believes that the evidence given by a witness has been coached or rehearsed, it may be less inclined to accept that evidence as genuine and may give it less (or no) weight. It is also possible that the view the tribunal takes of that witness may contaminate its assessment of other witnesses tendered by the same party. Many experienced arbitrators express confidence that they can tell when a witness has been coached and will adjust their assessment of that evidence accordingly.

7.39 The following extract from the judgment of Mr Justice Fraser in a commercial dispute in the English Technology and Construction Court,[42] although addressing evidence given in Court rather than arbitration, illustrates the sorts of dangers inherent in over-preparation:

> Mr Colwill adopted a style of giving evidence that became increasingly common throughout the trial for the majority of the witnesses for Energy Solutions. [. . .] it appears that witness training was provided . . . Whether that training was responsible for the style of giving evidence, I do not know. [. . .] This was, at times, to avoid the question and embark upon something of a corporate presentation. The linguistic device adopted for this approach was, usually, to state that it was necessary to put a question 'in context' and then embark upon an exposition that was essentially sketching out the Claimant's case, and avoiding giving a clear answer to sensible questions.[43]

7.40 It appears that some form of mock questioning between counsel and witness is relatively common practice in international arbitration. In a Queen Mary survey of international practitioners conducted in 2012,[44] 55 per cent of respondents said that mock cross-examination had taken place in their arbitrations at some stage. In addition, 62 per cent of all respondents, and 81 per cent of North American respondents, considered mock cross-examination of witnesses appropriate. Only a small minority (24 per cent) considered it inappropriate.

7.41 The real issue may lie in the extent to which counsel seek to influence what the witness will say in response to questions from opposing counsel or the tribunal. There is a divergence of opinion on this issue. Some practitioners take the view that there is nothing wrong in suggesting an answer that witnesses may use, as long as it is not a false answer.[45] For example, one US bar opinion states in the following terms the view that it

[42] *EnergySolutions EU Limited v Nuclear Decommissioning Authority* [2016] EWHC 1988 (TCC) [81]–[82].
[43] ibid 81.
[44] Queen Mary University of London, '2012 International Arbitration Survey: Current and Preferred Practices in the Arbitral Process' (*White & Case*, 2012) <www.arbitration.qmul.ac.uk/media/arbitration/docs/2012_International_Arbitration_Survey.pdf> accessed 28 November 2018.
[45] Shai Wade and others, *A Commentary on the LCIA Arbitration Rules 2014* (Sweet & Maxwell 2015) para 20-016 (hereafter 'Wade'), confirms this to be the position.

is wholly irrelevant that a lawyer has suggested the response a witness give in evidence if the evidence itself is true:

> [T]he governing consideration for ethical purposes is whether the substance of the testimony is something the witness can truthfully and properly testify to. If he or she is willing and (as respects his or her state of knowledge) able honestly so to testify, the fact that the inclusion of a particular point of substance was initially suggested by the lawyer rather than the witness seems to us wholly without significance . . . The mere fact of a lawyer having prepared the witness for presentation of testimony is simply irrelevant, indeed a lawyer who did not prepare his or her witness for testimony, having had an opportunity to do so, would not be doing his or her professional job properly.[46]

7.42 The subject of witness 'coaching' has received attention before the courts of a number of jurisdictions. The English court has given some guidance as to where the line is to be drawn between what is acceptable and what is not. Those guidelines adopt a more restrictive approach than the North American example given, and suggest that *any* discussion on the evidence to be given may influence its delivery and is to be discouraged. In *R v Momodou* Lord Justice Judge commented that:

> [T]he witness should give his or her own evidence, so far as practicable uninfluenced by what anyone else has said, whether in formal discussions or informal conversations. The rule reduces, indeed hopefully avoids any possibility, that one witness may tailor his evidence in the light of what anyone else said, and equally, avoids any unfounded perception that he may have done so. These risks are inherent in witness training. Even if the training takes place one-to-one with someone completely remote from the facts of the case itself, the witness may come, even unconsciously, to appreciate which aspects of his evidence are perhaps not quite consistent with what others are saying, or indeed not quite what is required of him. An honest witness may alter the emphasis of his evidence to accommodate what he thinks may be a different, more accurate, or simply better remembered perception of events. A dishonest witness will very rapidly calculate how his testimony may be 'improved'.[47]

7.43 In a case before the Singapore High Court,[48] the Judge took the decision to give 'negligible weight' to the evidence of one of the witnesses of fact in the case. During the course of the trial it became apparent that the witness had participated in group training

[46] 'D.C. Bar Opinion 79: Limitations on a Lawyer's Participation in the Preparation of a Witness's Testimony' in, *D.C. Bar, Code of Professional Responsibility and Opinions of the D.C. Bar Legal Ethics Committee* (D.C. Bar 1991) 138–39. See also Born (n 38) 2859. For an interesting exposition of the US perspective, see von Schlabrendorff (n 39).

[47] *Momodou* (n 40) 61. The guidelines in *Momodou* were applied by the English Court of Appeal in *R v Salisbury* [2005] EWCA Crim 3107 [60] (hereafter '*Salisbury*') where a description of the relevant boundary in the following succinct terms by Mr Justice Pitchford in the lower Court was approved by the Court of Appeal: '27. There is, in my view, a difference of substance between the process of familiarisation with the task of giving evidence coherently and the orchestration of evidence to be given. The second is objectionable and the first is not'. *Momodou* and *Salisbury* were also cited with apparent approval in a civil context in *Ultraframe (UK) Limited v Fielding and others* [2005] EWHC 1638 (Ch) [22]–[26].

[48] *Compania de Navegacion Palomar, S.A. v Ernest Ferdinand Perez De La Sala* [2017] SGHC 14 [257]–[290].

sessions where, in effect, the witnesses had 'practised' their evidence. In addition, the witness had been provided with a document containing a series of questions that he might be asked in cross-examination and including a set of answers in the nature of a script—a document that was described by the Judge as going 'to the very veracity of [the party's] witnesses and the evidential value of [the party's] evidence'. The Judge concluded that 'the credibility and accuracy of the important and relevant parts of . . . the evidence on the issues before me has been severely compromised'.[49]

Responses to a survey on the IBA Rules containing questions on the issue of preparation and 'coaching' of a witness for an evidentiary hearing were varied. Respondents from Argentina and Italy said that this was not permitted, while respondents from China, Canada, and the United States said that it was. The experience of many practitioners appeared to be that there is a boundary beyond which it is improper and imprudent to go. There was consistency around the idea that counsel could assist and support witnesses to express their testimony fully and effectively, but that they must not do anything to distort the witness's version of events. For example, the position in Australia was described as being that it is possible to direct the witness's attention to points in his/her evidence that may arise in cross-examination. It is also possible to direct a witness to points in his/her evidence that appear contradictory. However, coaching a witness so that the witness's live recollection of events is supplanted by another version suggested by the interviewer is not possible. In Ireland, directing a witness to answer a question in a particular way would be impermissible. The position in Nigeria was reported to be that interviewing a witness is permissible, but that the counsel interviewing must avoid any suggestion calculated to result in the witness supressing evidence or deviating from the truth.[50] **7.44**

b. Development of common standards in international arbitration

As described, there exists a wide spectrum of practice around witness contact in international arbitration. However, as has occurred in relation to other aspects of the arbitration process, international guidelines are emerging that seek to articulate a common understanding of what constitutes accepted best practice. **7.45**

For example, as noted in the Commentary on the IBA Rules, 'in transnational arbitration, it is now generally well established "that a party and its counsel are, as a general rule, permitted to contact a potential witness on its behalf and question him or her about the facts in dispute"'.[51] However, the IBA Guidelines on Party Representation in International Arbitration,[52] drafted by an IBA Task Force on Counsel Conduct, **7.46**

[49] In the course of the judgment reference was also made to a decision of the Hong Kong Court of Appeal, *HKSAR v Tse Tat Fung* [2010] HKCA 156, approving the principles set out in the *Momodou* (n 40) case; see ibid 280.

[50] BCLP Survey on use of the IBA Rules.

[51] Commentary on the IBA Rules (n 19) quoting M Schneider, 'Witnesses in International Arbitration' (1993) ASA Bulletin 302, 306.

[52] IBA Guidelines on Party Representation (n 38).

emphasize the need to protect and preserve the authenticity of the evidence to be given by a witness.

7.47 Guidelines 18–25 concern the interaction between party representatives and witnesses. Guideline 24 provides that a party representative may meet or interact with witnesses and experts in order to discuss and prepare their prospective testimony. Guidelines 20 and 21 provide that counsel may 'assist Witnesses in the preparation of Witness Statements' while always 'seek[ing] to ensure that a Witness Statement reflects the Witness's own account of relevant facts, events and circumstances'.[53] These provisions are mirrored in the Comments to the Guidelines 18–25 which emphasize the need to preserve the authenticity of the evidence.[54] We suggest that the Guidelines represent best practice in international arbitration.

2. Maintaining a Level Playing Field and Application of Article 4.3

7.48 In practice, witness contact takes two main forms: interviewing a witness to take a witness statement, and preparation for an evidentiary hearing. Practical issues around both forms of witness contact may arise in any arbitration. The IBA Rules contain useful provisions for the parties, and for the tribunal, in relation to each aspect.

a. Witness interviews

7.49 Article 4.3 of the IBA Rules makes clear that it is not improper for 'a Party, its officers, employees, legal advisors or other representatives *to interview* its witnesses or potential witnesses'.[55] This reflects current practice in international arbitration. It is not uncommon to find express provision for such contact in the first procedural order, even when the situation is already covered by application of the IBA Rules or other similar institutional rule.[56]

7.50 A number of institutional rules contain provisions reflecting the acceptance of such contact between witness and a party's lawyer,[57] although the LCIA Rules make the position subject to the mandatory provisions of any applicable law.[58]

[53] IBA Guidelines on Party Representation (n 38) 13.
[54] ibid 15 (emphasis added).
[55] IBA Rules (n 1) Article 4.3 (emphasis added). The 1983 IBA Rules (n 7) were silent on the issue of contact between a party and a witness, although the rules clearly contemplated that witness statements would be prepared. See 1983 IBA Rules (n 7) Article 5. The IBA Rules on the Taking of Evidence in International Commercial Arbitration 1999 (hereafter '1999 IBA Rules') clarified the position and introduced the current provision.
[56] One example of an order known to the authors simply states that 'Counsel may discuss with the witnesses . . . , in accordance with normal international practice, the content of their statements . . . prior to their submissions'. The order stopped short of reference to witness contact after submissions of witness statement and pre-evidentiary hearing, perhaps because of the difficulty in formulating a non-contentious form of wording.
[57] See, for example, the SIAC Rules, Rule 25.5, and the Swiss Rules, Article 25.2.
[58] LCIA Rules, Article 20.5. Application of IBA Rules (n 1) Article 1.1 may provide a similar outcome. At the time of writing the authors could not find any other major institutional rule with the same provisions.

The majority of respondents to a survey on this point confirmed that it was considered permissible in their jurisdiction for a party/counsel to interview a witness and to prepare a witness statement for use in international arbitration.[59] 7.51

b. Preparation for the evidentiary hearing

Article 4.3 of the IBA Rules also makes clear that, in addition to interviewing witnesses or potential witnesses, it is not improper for 'a Party, its officers, employees, legal advisors or other representatives . . . to discuss their prospective testimony with them'.[60] This wording did not appear in the 1999 IBA Rules and the Commentary on the current rules suggest that the additional wording is intended to clarify that an interview with a witness need not remain general, but may relate to the subject matter of the testimony that the witness will give. In our view, this area of practice will continue to generate debate. When asked about possible areas for improvement to the IBA Rules, respondents to an IBA Survey 'called for greater clarity on the boundaries between fact witness interviews and preparation'.[61] 7.52

In practice, there is unlikely to be a fundamental conflict between the IBA Rules and applicable institutional rules.[62] Most institutional rules provide little guidance on preparation for the evidentiary hearing. They either refer only to interviewing a witness or are silent on the matter.[63] Thus, to the extent that a tribunal takes the view that the IBA Rules reflect current best practice in international arbitration, a similar approach may be followed even when the IBA Rules have not been formally adopted in the arbitration. 7.53

Policing the proper observance of boundaries set by Article 4.3 of the IBA Rules may be problematic. It is difficult for another party or the tribunal to know what goes on behind the scenes in relation to witness preparation. While counsel subject to local bar restrictions on witness contact may advocate transparency, the same may not be true of counsel who intend to push the boundaries of what is deemed acceptable. Complaints about witness preparation made to the tribunal by the other party's counsel may not always result in sanctions, or removal of the witness testimony from the 7.54

59 This was the reported position across a range of common law and civil law systems that included France, Germany, Spain, Portugal, Sweden, Australia, USA, China, Nigeria, and Canada in the responses to the BCLP Survey on use of the IBA Rules.

60 IBA Rules (n 1) Article 4.3 (emphasis added).

61 The IBA Arbitration Guidelines and Rules Subcommittee, 'Report on the Reception of the IBA Arbitration Soft Law Products' (*International Bar Association*, 2016) para 96 <www.ibanet.org/Document/Default.aspx?DocumentUid=105d29a3-6261-4437-84e2-1c8637844beb> accessed 27 November 2018 (hereafter '2016 IBA Report'). The respondents who responded in these terms were from Argentina and Singapore.

62 Under IBA Rules (n 1) Article 1.3, in the event of conflict between those rules and the institutional rules, the Arbitral Tribunal is to apply the provision so as to accomplish the purposes of both sets of rules and, by reference to Commentary on the IBA Rules (n 19) 5, to 'try to harmonise the two sets of rules to the greatest extent possible'. The objectives underlying the IBA Rules are set out in the Preamble. In relation to witness contact, the most relevant objectives are likely to be ensuring a fair process, as well as upholding the obligation to act in good faith. See the IBA Rules (n 1) Preambles 1 and 3.

63 The LCIA Rules refer only to interviewing the witness, as do the Swiss Rules. LCIA Rules, Article 20.5: 'it shall not be improper for any party or its legal representatives to interview any potential witness for the purpose of presenting his or her testimony in written form to the Arbitral Tribunal or producing such person as an oral witness at any hearing'. See also the Swiss Rules, Article 25.2. Both the SIAC Rules and ACICA Rules say nothing on the matter.

record.[64] Opposing parties may have to place their trust in the ability of the tribunal to identify a witness who has been coached beyond acceptable boundaries and to take this into account when weighing the evidence of that witness. Many experienced arbitrators will be adept at doing this.

7.55 As a result of the differing approaches to witness contact it may be desirable for the parties to an arbitration to agree—or the tribunal to lay down—some ground rules to ensure, as far as possible, that the parties are operating on a level playing field, whether by reference to particular rules or guidelines or to a discrete agreement. Ideally, there should be openness and transparency around what each party may be expected to do and what the tribunal will find acceptable.

7.56 The UNCITRAL Notes on Organizing Arbitral Proceedings[65] suggest that a tribunal may wish to address such matters at the outset of arbitral proceedings; paragraph 90 states:

> The arbitral tribunal may consider clarifying at the outset of the arbitral proceedings the nature of the contact a party or its representative is permitted to have with its witnesses, when inquiring about the facts of the case, when preparing written witness statements and when a witness is preparing to give oral testimony.[66]

7.57 It is not wholly clear whether this approach is intended to foster transparency about restrictions contained in professional conduct rules applicable to individual counsel, or to encourage the tribunal to indicate the nature of contact with witnesses that the tribunal would find appropriate, subject always to any applicable conduct or local rules.[67] Both objectives have merit.

E. Witness Statements

> **4.4. The Arbitral Tribunal may order each Party to submit within a specified time to the Arbitral Tribunal and to the other Parties Witness Statements by each witness on whose testimony it intends to rely, except for those witnesses whose testimony is**

[64] See Born (n 38) 2863, where the point is also made that improper conduct is also unlikely to be a proper basis for annulment or non-recognition of the award, on that basis alone.

[65] UNCITRAL Notes on Organizing Arbitral Proceedings (United Nations Commission on International Trade Law 2016).

[66] ibid 20.

[67] See UNCITRAL Working Group II, 'Report of Working Group II (Arbitration and Conciliation) on the Work of its Sixty-First Session' (A/CN.9/826) para 148 <http://daccess-ods.un.org/access.nsf/Get?OpenAgent&DS=A/CN.9/826&Lang=E> accessed 28 November 2018 and UNCITRAL Working Group II, 'Settlement of Commercial Disputes: Revision of the UNCITRAL Notes on Organizing Arbitral Proceedings' (A/CN.9/WG.II/WP.183) para 107 <http://www.uncitral.org/uncitral/en/commission/working_groups/2Arbitration.html> accessed 28 November 2018. The first document noted that it had been said that the 'language set out at paragraph 107 of document A/CN.9/WG.II/WP.183 provided a good basis for making clear that all parties should have the same information in relation to the possibility of contact between a party and a witness while a witness was giving evidence, but that it should be clear . . . that the arbitral tribunal should clarify at the outset of proceedings whether any contact would be appropriate prior to testimony being given . . . '.

sought pursuant to Articles 4.9 or 4.10. If Evidentiary Hearings are organised into separate issues or phases (such as jurisdiction, preliminary determinations, liability or damages), the Arbitral Tribunal or the Parties by agreement may schedule the submission of Witness Statements separately for each issue or phase.

1. Introduction

Article 4.4 of the IBA Rules gives the tribunal express power to order the submission of witness statements from witnesses upon whose testimony a party intends to rely, and to determine the time period for doing so. **7.58**

In the majority of cases, the tribunal will already have power under the applicable institutional rules to direct the use of witness statements. In such cases, the IBA Rules contain helpful provisions providing detail of how the presentation of that evidence should be managed, with a focus on transparency. **7.59**

Article 8.4 of the IBA Rules provides that a witness attending an evidentiary hearing who has submitted a witness statement shall confirm that statement and the Parties may agree, or the tribunal may order, that the witness statement shall serve as that witness's direct testimony. In practice, the submission of witness statements, and their standing as direct testimony, is what happens in most international arbitrations.[68] This was not always the case. The use of witness statements in which the witness sets out, in written form, the substance of his or her evidence, is a relatively new practice. Even in the English Court, where the presentation and testing of witness evidence is considered to be a critical part of the litigation process, the use of witness statements in substitution for oral direct testimony did not become commonplace until the 1990s. **7.60**

Article 4.5 (see 7.82– 7.126) sets out details of the required content of a witness statement served under the IBA Rules. **7.61**

2. Advantages and Disadvantages of Witness Statements

As mentioned, Article 4.4 does not *require* the tribunal to order the submission of witness statements; rather, the article states that the tribunal '*may* order' (emphasis added). There may still be occasions in international arbitration where the parties and the tribunal are content that witness statements should not be served, perhaps for reasons of economy. However, in the majority of cases, witness statements will be used. **7.62**

[68] All respondents to the BCLP survey on use of the IBA Rules on this issue confirmed the widespread use of witness statements in arbitration, although a Swedish respondent reported that counsel will sometimes argue that witness statements should not be produced unless all parties agree. Portuguese respondents indicated that practice in domestic arbitrations has seen a recent trend towards the use of witness statements. The conventional practice in those arbitrations had traditionally been the presentation of direct evidence orally at the evidentiary hearing.

7.63 The Commentary on the IBA Rules suggests that the use of witness statements is desirable in the interests of procedural efficiency. As the Commentary points out, if witness statements are used, the evidence that a witness plans to give orally at the hearing is known in advance. The other party can better prepare its examination of the witness and select the witnesses that it will present on the same issues of fact. The tribunal is also better placed to understand the evidence and formulate its own questions to the witness. Because in most cases the witness statement will stand as the direct evidence of the witness, the examination can move straight to cross-examination by the other party.[69]

7.64 The use of witness statements contributes to a fair process by ensuring that parties are not taken by surprise, thereby meeting the objective referred to in the Preamble to the IBA Rules that each party should be given reasonable advance notice of the evidence relied on by its opponent.[70] The following remarks capture the problems inherent in not using witness statements:

> Fairness is the overriding objective in arbitration. The party offering the witness has ample time to put together the direct testimony. Without witness statements the opposing party would be confronted with direct testimony for the first time during the hearing. Preparation time would be reduced to zero. The opposing counsel would have to prepare the cross examination while listening to the direct testimony. Accordingly, the playing field would not be level.[71]

7.65 There are other possible advantages. The use of witness statements may assist the parties in identifying areas of agreement and narrowing the scope of disputed facts. The 'cards on the table' approach to witness evidence may also assist in facilitating settlement of the dispute.

7.66 Of course, if witness statements are not used, the attendant difficulties of anticipating and cross-examining witnesses, as well as the inability to narrow factual issues, would apply to all parties. However, this might still work to the 'net disadvantage' of one party if, for example, the bulk of the available witness evidence on disputed facts came from one side only.

7.67 On the other hand, there are a number of criticisms of witness statements. Some critics say that such statements are little more than a vehicle by which counsel make further submissions[72] and that they have little evidential value. In addition, the practice of having the witness statement stand as direct testimony means that the direct testimony

[69] See Chapter 11 paras 11.56–11.67.

[70] IBA Rules (n 1) Preambles 1 and 3.

[71] Ragnar Harbst, *A Counsel's Guide to Examining and Preparing Witnesses in International Arbitration* (Kluwer Law International 2015) 68 (hereafter 'Harbst').

[72] Michael Hwang and Andrew Chin, 'The Role of Witness Statements in International Arbitration' in Albert Jan van den Berg (ed), *International Arbitration 2006: Back to Basics?* (Kluwer Law International 2007) 650–51. See also Andrea Menaker and Noor Davies, 'The Direct Examination of Witnesses and Experts Not Called for Cross-Examination: Balancing Efficiency and Fairness' (2015) BCDR International Arbitration Review 135 (hereafter 'Menaker and Davies').

given orally at an evidentiary hearing is, at best, often limited to answering a few questions directed at correction or clarification of a written statement before the witness is plunged into a challenging cross-examination.[73] The tribunal does not have the benefit of seeing and listening to the witness give his recollection of events. This may be seen by some as unfair, as well as not always getting the best out of the witness. There is also debate around whether the use of witness statements necessarily results in savings in time and costs, as is often claimed.[74]

3. Timing

In the absence of agreement between the parties, it is for the tribunal to decide when the witness evidence is to be submitted. The IBA Rules merely provide that the tribunal may order the submission of witness statements to the tribunal and to the other parties 'within a specified time'. The date for delivery of statements is likely to be one that has been discussed and agreed during consultation on the procedural timetable for the arbitration.[75] **7.68**

In addition to determining a date for delivery, the tribunal will need to consider whether the parties should deliver witness statements simultaneously or consecutively. There are advantages and disadvantages to both approaches. The Commentary on the IBA Rules suggests that simultaneous exchange causes less delay, leads to more disclosure and equality between the parties, and results in less tailoring of statements to neutralize witness evidence received from the other party.[76] Conversely, consecutive statements may allow parties to focus on the relevant points that arise out of the statements received from the other party, thus potentially making the process more efficient.[77] The Commentary goes on to suggest that a combination of the advantages of both simultaneous and consecutive delivery may be achieved if the tribunal directs two rounds of simultaneous exchange, with the second round being limited to matters raised in the other party's first-round statements.[78] **7.69**

To an extent, the choice of one approach over the other may depend upon whether a memorial style[79] of submissions is being used in the arbitration. If it is, the parties' **7.70**

[73] In some cases, a tribunal may agree to a short period of direct examination, but this is generally very limited. For example, in a case known to the authors the relevant procedural order provided that: 'Each witness giving oral evidence shall first be briefly examined in direct examination (up to 15 minutes of direct examination per witness), followed by the examination by the other side ("cross-examination") . . . The scope of direct examination shall be limited to matters covered in the Parties' written submissions and new matters that have arisen since the witness submitted his/her last witness statement . . . or had an opportunity to do so.'

[74] See further discussions at 7.100– 7.101.

[75] See Chapter 5 paras 5.71–5.76.

[76] IBA Working Party, 'Commentary on the New IBA Rules of Evidence in International Commercial Arbitration' (2000) 2 Business Law International 16, 28 (hereafter 'Commentary on the 1999 IBA Rules').

[77] ibid.

[78] ibid.

[79] This is where witness statements (and sometimes expert reports) are served together with written submissions/pleadings. For more detail, see Chapter 5 paras 5.74–5.76.

written submissions will generally be accompanied by supporting witness statements and documents, and sometimes expert evidence as well. Some counsel (often common law lawyers) prefer that witness statements follow as a separate step after the process of pleading has been completed. By way of example, witness statements in LCIA arbitrations are said to be generally exchanged after the parties' written statements of case.[80]

7.71 If witness evidence is delivered after the pleadings have been delivered, the witness statements can be more focused, with emphasis on the issues that have crystallized on the earlier pleadings or written submissions.

7.72 On the other hand, where a pleading or memorial is accompanied by witness statements, the submissions and evidence are generally more closely aligned, ie the evidence supports the factual matters relied on in the pleadings. This approach may avoid the embarrassment of a party arguing a point in submissions and only later finding out that it cannot be made good in witness evidence.

7.73 The practice of serving witness evidence with a memorial/pleading may also avoid additional procedural steps. In practice, witness statements served after an exchange of pleadings sometimes go far beyond a party's case as stated in its prior written submissions. In addition, Article 4.5(b) of the IBA Rules permits a witness statement to be accompanied by additional documents not already submitted. As a result, a witness statement delivered after pleadings have closed may serve as a trigger for a further round of submissions,[81] at the risk of further responsive steps and consequential delay.

7.74 Issues also sometimes arise about whether the witness statements (or at the very least, second-round statements), should be served after document production. In cases where the bulk of the relevant documents are in one party's possession (for example, in a construction dispute where only the contractor holds a complete set of documents relating to project performance, or in a dispute following the sale of a company where the relevant documents have all remained within the company, which has been sold) the other party may want to have access to relevant categories of documents when preparing its evidence. The first party may say this is unnecessary as the witnesses should speak only to matters within their own knowledge. In truth, when taking witness statements, most counsel will want the comfort of access to all contemporaneous documents in order to raise with the witness any factual issues arising out of those documents. It is sensible and appropriate to raise these matters with the tribunal during the consultation process contemplated by Article 2 of the IBA Rules.

7.75 In a survey on this issue,[82] a number of respondents from civil law jurisdictions reported that, in their experience, witness statements are generally served with written submissions. These respondents included law firms in France, Germany, Spain, Portugal and

[80] Wade (n 45) 20-008.

[81] These points are made in Markus Wirth, 'Fact Witnesses' (2010) International Arbitration Law Review 207, 208 (hereafter 'Wirth').

[82] BCLP Survey on the use of the IBA Rules.

Sweden. The experience of respondent practitioners in China, Nigeria, Ireland, Italy, Australia and Canada was more mixed, with delivery of witness statements reported as sometimes taking place at the same time as written submissions, and sometimes subsequently. In the latter case, there was a mix of simultaneous and consecutive exchange.[83]

4. Organizing Witness Statements by Reference to Issue or Phase

Consultation on the preparation and submission of witness statements is expressly referred to as a topic on which early consultation may be desirable under Article 2 of the IBA Rules.[84] During discussions between the parties, and in consultation with the tribunal, it will be appropriate to consider and discuss all of the various factors relating to process and timing that may be relevant in the particular circumstances of the case. One of those factors will be the desirability of organizing witness evidence appropriately according to the agreed phases of the arbitration. **7.76**

Article 4.4 of the IBA Rules provides that the tribunal may order, or the parties may agree, that the timetable for delivery of witness evidence should reflect the fact that evidentiary hearings have been organized by reference to separate issues or phases and thus permit witness evidence on different issues at different times. It states: **7.77**

> If Evidentiary Hearings are organised into separate issues or phases (such as jurisdiction, preliminary determinations, liability or damages), the Arbitral Tribunal or the Parties by agreement may schedule the submissions of Witness Statements separately for each issue or phase.[85]

This provision should encourage parties and the tribunal to think about what 'tailoring' of the witness evidence is possible in the interests of efficiency. For example, where it has been decided that a challenge to the jurisdiction of the tribunal will be dealt with as a preliminary step, there may be a direction for witness evidence to be limited to matters relevant to that challenge. If there is a possibility that the proceedings will fall away as a result of a successful challenge, there is little point in the parties incurring time and costs in preparation of evidence of a wider scope. Similar considerations may apply where it has been decided that there should be a bifurcation of the arbitration to deal with liability and quantum, or another determinative preliminary issue. **7.78**

Although the particular situations mentioned here are expressly highlighted in Article 4.4, in our view the flexibility inherent in the opening line of Article 4.4 means that it is possible to tailor the timing of witness evidence to other circumstances. For **7.79**

[83] Reported general practice was as follows: China—delivery with written submissions or separately by simultaneous exchange; Nigeria—with written submissions in sequential exchange; Ireland, Italy and Australia—separate sequential or simultaneous exchange; Canada—separate sequential exchange other than in arbitrations subject to the IBA Rules where delivery with written submission or simultaneous delivery is also used. BCLP Survey on use of the IBA Rules.

[84] IBA Rules (n 1) Article 2.2(a). See Chapter 5 paras 5.56–5.64 and 5.71–5.76.

[85] IBA Rules (n 1) Article 4.4 (emphasis added).

example, if a party's expert witnesses are not all available to work on expert evidence during the same time period, or the preparation of evidence by one expert is dependent on the conclusions of another expert, it may make sense to expedite or defer a particular strand of expert evidence and the witness evidence on which it depends. Of course, the parties will need to be wary of proposals that, although superficially attractive, may in practice introduce an unwarranted degree of procedural complexity or simply increase costs.

5. Other Considerations

7.80 A tribunal may not wish to receive a copy of the witness statements when served by the parties but may prefer to wait until it receives bundles containing a complete set of witness evidence in preparation for the evidentiary hearing. It is sensible to clarify this point with the tribunal during discussions on the procedural timetable. A tribunal-expressed wish to defer delivery may indicate that a tribunal does not intend to look at the evidence before the hearing. This is an approach that many parties may dislike but which is relatively common in arbitration and elsewhere.[86]

7.81 The fact that a party has provided a witness statement does not always mean that the witness will be required to attend an oral hearing. Article 8.1 of the IBA Rules provides that witnesses need attend only if their presence is requested by any party to the proceedings, or by the tribunal. It is possible that the parties may reach a position where the written evidence of a particular witness is not contested or, as issues and evidence develop, the witness evidence is not considered material to the outcome of the case.[87] Where attendance at the evidentiary hearing is requested by the other party, in the absence of good cause, the witness must attend the hearing or the tribunal may disregard the witness statement.[88]

F. Content of Witness Statements

4.5. Each Witness Statement shall contain:

(a) the full name and address of the witness, a statement regarding his or her present and past relationship (if any) with any of the Parties, and a description of his or her background, qualifications, training and experience, if such a description may be relevant to the dispute or to the contents of the statement;

[86] For example, this is the approach adopted in English litigation where the Judge will not look at witness evidence until shortly before the evidentiary hearing. There is always the possibility that the parties may settle their dispute and court/tribunal time/legal fees will be wasted if the evidence is reviewed earlier than necessary.

[87] See Bühler and Dorgan (n 16) 16–17.

[88] See discussion on Article 4.7 at 7.137– 7.167.

(b) a full and detailed description of the facts, and the source of the witness's information as to those facts, sufficient to serve as that witness's evidence in the matter in dispute. Documents on which the witness relies that have not already been submitted shall be provided;

(c) a statement as to the language in which the Witness Statement was originally prepared and the language in which the witness anticipates giving testimony at the Evidentiary Hearing;

(d) an affirmation of the truth of the Witness Statement; and

(e) the signature of the witness and its date and place.

1. Introduction

Article 4.5 of the IBA Rules lays down a number of requirements concerning the content of a witness statement submitted under the IBA Rules. **7.82**

The opening line of Article 4.5 includes the words 'shall contain'. As a result, where the IBA Rules have been formally adopted, in the absence of agreement between the parties or an order of the tribunal to the contrary, these requirements must be met in relation to any witness statements submitted. In light of this, it seems to us that the tribunal is entitled to order that any formal defect in a delivered statement should be corrected, either at the request of another party or on its own initiative. **7.83**

In any event, Article 4.5 is useful in providing a form of checklist for the content of a witness statement. In broad terms, the requirements described in Article 4.5 reflect good practice as to the form and content of written witness testimony. **7.84**

2. Formal Details

(a) the full name and address; present and past relationship (if any) with any of the Parties; description of background, qualifications, training and experience

A witness is required to state his or her full name and address. **7.85**

In practice, the address provided will very often be a business or professional address, but it need not be. As long as some form of contact address is provided this is unlikely to present a problem. If a witness has no business address and, for some reason, the witness does not wish to give a personal residential address, it may be possible for the witness's personal address to be provided confidentially to the tribunal only, without objection being taken by other parties. **7.86**

Any relationship between the witness and any of the parties must be disclosed. The existence of such a relationship, and its nature, may be relevant to the tribunal's assessment of the weight it should attribute to the evidence presented by the witness. **7.87**

In practice, the tribunal's assessment of the quality of evidence given by a witness will be heavily influenced by the tribunal's judgment on the credibility of that witness after hearing him or her give oral evidence. However, in circumstances where a tribunal relies on written witness testimony only, the existence of a relationship between that witness and one or more of the parties may assume greater significance. It may be one of a number of factors the tribunal will take into account in weighing the evidence.

7.88 Article 4.5(a) requires the disclosure of present and past relationships. A witness should think very carefully about the existence of any prior relationships. Clearly, the fact that a witness is or has been an employee of one of the parties, or has provided business or professional services to them, or has some other professional or personal connection must be disclosed. Even where the relationship is from a considerable time ago, or appears insignificant, the prudent course is to mention it in the opening paragraphs of the statement. This will protect the witness (and the party tendering that witness) from criticism or tactical challenge by the other party. There may also be situations where a witness is known to a member of the tribunal and disclosure of that relationship may assist the tribunal. In all of these cases transparency will enhance the credibility of the witness.

7.89 The witness statement must include a description of the witness's background, qualifications, training, and experience *if* such description 'may be relevant to the dispute or to the contents of the statement'.

7.90 In many cases, such a description will be relevant. A witness tendered by a party will very often be an employee whose role in the organization is the reason the witness has relevant evidence to offer. Similar considerations will apply to outside contractors and agents retained by that party. For example, a head of finance may have noticed that funds are being diverted away from the company's accounts, or an IT consultant may have been given project management for an outsourced software development project and can speak to the failures in performance by the party to whom the work was outsourced. In such cases, the status and role of the witness within or in relation to the organization, as well as their professional qualifications and experience in the relevant professional or industry discipline, add context and possibly weight to the evidence they offer.

7.91 Some tribunals may ask that witness statements include photographs of the witnesses so that there is no doubt about the identity of the person submitting the statement. It may also help the tribunal to recollect 'who testified to what' when it revisits the evidence after the evidentiary hearing.[89]

[89] See Harbst (n 71) 68.

3. Evidence

(b) a full and detailed description of the facts, and the source of the witness's information as to those facts, sufficient to serve as that witness's evidence in the matter in dispute.

The witness statement must contain a complete statement of the facts intended to be relied upon. It must also indicate the source of the witness' information about those facts. **7.92**

a. Witness testimony

Article 4.5(b) of the current IBA Rules provides that the witness statement must contain a 'full and detailed description of the facts . . . sufficient to serve as that witness's evidence . . .'. This requirement makes sense when viewed in the context of the current general practice in international arbitration (provision for which is made at Article 8.4 of the IBA Rules)[90] that witness statements stand as direct testimony. The requirement of a 'full' and detailed description of the facts also reduces the risk that, as the dispute develops, the scope of the available direct testimony is found to be too narrow. **7.93**

The statement should explain the facts from the perspective of the witness. Although not expressly referred to in the IBA Rules, adoption of the words actually used by the witness is generally the best practice. **7.94**

The word-for-word repetition by lawyers of precisely the same description of a meeting in the statements of two separate witnesses is unlikely to enhance their credibility. Allowing the witness to tell the story in his or her own words will not only maintain the integrity of the evidence but, under cross-examination, the witness is more likely to tell the same narrative and, as a result, contribute to his or her credibility before the tribunal. Finessing evidence to express it in terms that fit neatly with a legal argument or concept is likely to be quickly identified by the tribunal as lawyers' drafting, with a possible adverse effect on the weight that the tribunal will attach to it. **7.95**

In the witness evidence it produces, a party should focus on the evidence necessary to prove the facts underpinning its case. We agree with the suggestion that it is helpful (at least internally) for counsel to mark up a copy of the written submissions with details of those witness who can prove the facts relied upon in order to ensure that there are no gaps.[91] **7.96**

There is no guidance given as to the form that the required description of the facts must take. This matter is left to the witness and assisting counsel. As a matter of convention, **7.97**

[90] IBA Rules (n 1) Article 8.4 provides that a witness attending an evidentiary hearing who has submitted a witness statement shall confirm that statement and the parties may agree, or the tribunal may order, that the witness statement shall serve as that witness's direct testimony.

[91] Peter Ashford, *The IBA Rules on the Taking of Evidence in International Arbitration: A Guide* (CUP 2013) 101 (hereafter 'Ashford').

and in order to provide a coherent account that the tribunal can follow, the narrative provided in a witness statement is generally chronological or issue-based, and is set out in numbered paragraphs that facilitate ease of review and cross-referencing in any later supplemental or reply witness statements, or during cross-examination and in the award itself.

7.98 Preferences as to the general content and structure of a witness statement may be influenced by cultural background and individual experiences. However, in general, it is sensible to confine the statement to events of which the witness has direct knowledge. To expand the statement beyond these events may result in cross-examination of the witness on matters about which s/he has no knowledge and, depending on how the witness copes with questioning on those points, may adversely affect the credibility of that witness. Restricting the content to matters on which the witness has direct knowledge will also minimize the use of hearsay (see further at 7.104– 7.106).

7.99 A further common (but unhelpful) practice is to have a witness comment on or explain each and every document in the case. This is wasteful of both time and costs. Other categories of content that will offer little assistance to the tribunal, and which may detract from the substance of the evidence of value that the witness can offer, include statements of opinion and speculation.

7.100 Given the extensive use of witness statements in the English Courts, some useful observations may be gleaned from published reports considering (and criticizing) the significant cost and length of witness statements filed in that forum. Those reports note that court time has not been saved by the introduction of witness statements—rather than listening to the examination-in-chief, the Judge simply spends time reading a very lengthy witness statement, and loses the opportunity to observe the witness's demeanour during direct examination as well as cross-examination.[92] Many of the adverse factors identified in those reports are equally applicable in international arbitration. Those factors include counsel's perception that witness statements have to be drafted as precisely as pleadings, leading to many rounds of drafts before the finished (often lengthy) statement is produced and, in some cases, attempts to 'bury' certain key facts among many pages of minor detail.

7.101 However, the reports on court practice mentioned[93] also note a number of mechanisms that may reduce the length and cost of witness statements. In appropriate cases, and bearing in mind that considerations of due process, efficiency, and economy are an express objective under the IBA Rules,[94] these approaches may be considered for use in

[92] Rupert Jackson, *Review of Civil Litigation Costs: Preliminary Report Volume 2* (The Stationary Office 2009) Ch 42 para 1.3, which says that in substantial cases the use of written witness statements, instead of saving costs and promoting fairness, had the opposite effect. See also James Hope, 'Witness Statements: The Cost of Gilding the Lily' (*Commercial Dispute Resolution*, 17 June 2014) <www.cdr-news.com/categories/arbitration-and-adr/5071-witness-statements> accessed 28 November 2018, where the author draws attention to these matters and their relevance to the use of witness statements in international arbitration. There also appears to be some dissatisfaction with the use of witness statements among some arbitration practitioners.

[93] See (n 92).

[94] IBA Rules (n 1) Preamble 1.

international arbitration. Suggested possibilities include a requirement for a one-page summary of the witness evidence, stipulating a maximum length for the statements, as well as (in appropriate cases) early identification (by argument if necessary) as to the facts that need to be proved by witness evidence, and the imposition of costs sanctions where directions as to the scope or form of witness statements have been flouted.

The lack of express provision in the IBA Rules on the format in which the evidence is to be drafted provides scope for innovation or tailoring of the statement to suit the needs of the case, should the parties agree, or the tribunal guide them towards, a variation on the conventional. For example, 'bullet points' or 'telegraphic style'[95] or a statement in question-and-answer format could be used.[96] Another helpful approach requested by some tribunals is a requirement that the witness statement identify the factual issue to which each part of the witness statement is relevant.[97] **7.102**

If parties are concerned that their opponent may take a very different approach from them in preparing witness evidence (for example, in relation to the level of detail), the best way to tackle this concern is to clarify the matter early in the process, either by discussion with the other party or as part of the consultation with the tribunal provided for in Article 2 of the IBA Rules. **7.103**

b. Source of the information

The source of the witness's information as to those facts

Article 4.5(b) states that the witness statement shall contain details of the source of the information for the facts described in the witness statement. As a result, in addition to expressly indicating the matters that are based on the witness' own knowledge, the witness should identify any parts of the statement based on what is referred to in the common law tradition as hearsay—namely, something that the witness has learned 'second-hand', generally through something said by someone other than the person testifying, or as reported in a document issued or prepared by someone else. Under many institutional rules, and under the arbitration laws of most arbitration-friendly seats, it is up to the tribunal to decide on the admissibility of evidence, and thus there is no rule against the admission of hearsay evidence.[98] However, the requirement to state **7.104**

[95] See, Bühler and Dorgan (n 16) 13. Telegraphic style is a technique of eliminating a word or words necessary for complete grammatical construction, but understood in context.

[96] Laurence Shore, 'Chapter 3: Document Production, Witness Statements, and Cross-Examination: The Enduring Tensions in International Arbitration' in Stavros Brekoulakis and others (eds), *The Evolution and Future of International Arbitration* (Kluwer Law International 2016) para 3.14 and fn 16 (hereafter 'Shore').

[97] 'Procedural Order of 19 May 2004 in ICC Case 13046 (extract)' in *Special Supplement 2010: Decisions on ICC Arbitration Procedure: A Selection of Procedural Orders issued by Arbitral Tribunals acting under the ICC Rules of Arbitration (2003-2004)* (International Chamber of Commerce 2010) para 5.4(c) is an example of such an order where the tribunal directed that each witness statement should contain 'appropriate captions or internal references indicating with reasonable specificity the factual and legal issues to which it is relevant'.

[98] The majority of institutional rules make clear that the admissibility, relevance, and materiality of evidence, and the weight to be attributed to it, are all matters to be determined by the arbitral tribunal. See, for example, SCC Rules, Article 31; Swiss Rules, Article 24.2; SIAC Rules, Rule 19.2; HKIAC Rules, Article 22.2; and UNCITRAL Rules, Article 27.4. The ICC Rules do not contain a specific provision to this effect. ICC Rules, Article 25(1) simply

the source of knowledge will assist the tribunal in assessing the weight to be accorded to that evidence.[99] Witness statements sometimes contain an introductory paragraph confirming that the facts stated are based on the personal knowledge of the witness unless otherwise stated. In that case, the witness need refer specifically to a source of knowledge *only* if a particular piece of evidence is based on hearsay or other 'second-hand' knowledge.

7.105 In principle, the other party might raise an objection to hearsay evidence under mechanisms available in the IBA Rules. For example, Article 9.2 of the IBA Rules states that the tribunal shall, 'at the request of a Party, or on its own motion' exclude from evidence any statement on grounds that it lacks 'sufficient relevance to the case or materiality as to its outcome' or for considerations of ' . . . fairness or equality of the Parties that the Arbitral Tribunal considers to be compelling'.[100] It is possible to see how such provisions might be used to argue that all or a portion of a witness statement based on the knowledge or statements of a third party, to whom one of the parties does not have access, is unfair, or that hearsay testimony gleaned from a third party not offering oral testimony can have such little weight that it has no evidential value and cannot therefore be considered material to outcome.

7.106 If the party asserting the facts supported by the hearsay statements has better evidence to support its position, there is little point in including the hearsay statements, which may serve only to detract from the more valuable evidence. However, if hearsay evidence is included it is likely to be admitted. Even in the face of objection from one of the parties, unless the statement made is clearly irrelevant (in which case one wonders why it has been included at all), or the subject of the statement is addressed adequately elsewhere in the evidence, a tribunal is likely to permit its admission and address any shortcomings by means of the weight it attributes to the hearsay evidence. There are reported cases where a tribunal has made an express finding that the IBA Rules do not, per se, require the exclusion of evidence by reason of its hearsay nature.[101] While we agree with that view, it seems to us that the strict application of the specific provisions of the IBA Rules mentioned may nonetheless, in some cases, provide a mechanism for the exclusion of hearsay evidence, should that be considered appropriate.

provides that the 'arbitral tribunal shall proceed within as short a time as possible to establish the facts of the case by all appropriate means'. A similar position may be found under the arbitration laws of many seats of arbitration. See, for example English Arbitration Act 1996, s 34(1); German Code of Civil Procedure (Zivilprozessordnung 'ZPO'), s 1042(4); Belgian Judicial Code, Article 1700(3); and Dutch Code of Civil Procedure, Article 1039-5.

---

[99] For a discussion of the tribunal's power to assess the weight of evidence, see Chapter 12 paras 12.31–12.42 relating to IBA Rules (n 1) Article 9.1. See also SI Strong and James Dries, 'Witness Statements under the IBA Rules of Evidence: What to Do about Hearsay?' (2005) Arbitration International 301 (hereafter 'Strong and Dries').

[100] IBA Rules (n 1) Articles 9.2(a) and 9.2(g). The nature and application of these grounds are dealt with in more detail in Chapter 12. Application of the grounds mentioned are dealt with in Strong and Dries (n 99) 309–12. In theory, an objecting Party might also make use of IBA Rules (n 1) Article 4.10 to ask the Arbitral Tribunal to order the other Party to require the author of the hearsay to appear at the Evidentiary Hearing to give first-hand evidence, a course of action that may not be straightforward.

[101] ICC Partial Award dated November 2012 cited in 'Extracts from ICC Case Materials on the Taking of Evidence with References to the IBA Rules' (2016) 1 ICC Dispute Resolution Bulletin 127 7 (hereafter 'ICC Partial Award dated November 2012').

Issues of a similar nature arose on interesting facts in an arbitration conducted under the NAFTA/UNCITRAL Arbitration Rules. In that case, one of the parties had obtained witness testimony by means of an application to the US court under Section 1782 28 U.S.C. Exhibits to written submissions filed by the claimant in the arbitration contained reference to the testimony obtained. The respondent objected to the introduction of this evidence on grounds that the claimant was relying on witness testimony without submitting witness statements and the respondent (and subsequently the tribunal) would be unable to examine the witnesses and assess their credibility. The respondent contended that this would be contrary to the IBA Rules. In response, among other arguments, the claimant submitted that the exhibits objected to were documents and there was no reason why this documentary evidence—which the claimant submitted was clearly and directly relevant to the dispute—should be inadmissible. The tribunal found that the witness evidence should be treated like any other document and that there was no prohibition on it being presented. However, the tribunal went on to say that it would 'assess the weight of that evidence taking into account other elements on the record as well as the fact that the persons making the statements had not appeared as witnesses and thus had neither been cross-examined nor questioned by the tribunal. In addition, the tribunal could always request that these persons be produced as witnesses'.[102] **7.107**

Assessment of the weight of evidence by a tribunal is discussed in more detail in Chapter 12 in relation to Article 9.1.[103] **7.108**

c. Documents

Documents on which the witness relies that have not already been submitted shall be provided

The rules of most arbitral institutions require parties to file with the Request for Arbitration a copy of the arbitration agreement and any underlying contract. After the Response/Answer to the Request for Arbitration has been served, there will then follow one or more rounds of formal submissions in which each party's case will be set out in more detail. Those submissions are likely to be accompanied by an additional set of documents upon which that party relies in support of its case and many institutional rules (and some arbitrators) will require this.[104] In addition, the parties will generally engage in one or more rounds of document production requests that will generate yet further documents on which the parties may wish to rely. Depending on whether the memorial or common law pleading approach is adopted, this may be before or after first-round witness statements. Delivery of documents on which a party wishes to rely **7.109**

[102] *Mesa Power Group LLC v Government of Canada* (Procedural Order No. 6) PCA Case No. 2012-17 [2]–[8].

[103] Chapter 12, paras 12.31–12.42.

[104] For example, see the LCIA Rules, Articles 15.2–15.5: written Statements are required to include 'all essential documents'; SIAC Rules, Rule 20.7: 'All submissions referred to in this Rule shall be accompanied by copies of all supporting documents which have not previously been submitted by any party.' Also see the 2018 HKIAC Rules, Articles 16.3 and 17.4; SCC Rules, Article 29; and UNCITRAL Rules, Articles 20.4 and 21.2.

are addressed in Article 3.1 and Article 3.11 of the IBA Rules, and are discussed in Chapter 6.[105]

7.110 Article 4.5(b) contains express provision that a witness statement must be accompanied by any documents on which the witness relies that are not already on the record. For this purpose, new documents obtained by means of document production will not generally, absent a specific order to this effect, be regarded as being 'on the record' or as having been 'filed' or 'submitted' unless and until they are produced with a submission or pleading, or with witness evidence.[106] Thus, if a witness wishes to rely on it the document should be provided with the witness statement. Although the parties will have access to a document obtained by means of document production (as either the producing or receiving party), the tribunal will not.[107]

7.111 It follows from the closing text of Article 4.5(b) that if the document on which the witness relies has already been filed—for example, with an earlier submission—then it does not need to accompany the witness statement. The witness may simply refer to the document by the exhibit number that document was allocated when it was previously introduced.

7.112 If more than one document is being served (for example, as is likely to be the case when a memorial-style submission is delivered), the documents will generally be delivered as a single set of uniquely numbered exhibits to which reference can be made both in the submissions and/or in any accompanying witness and expert evidence. If reference is made to exhibits already in the record, then the original exhibit number should be used. There is no need to deliver a further copy of the document. To have duplicate exhibits with different exhibit numbers will only lead to complications when it comes to preparing the hearing bundles.

d. Language of testimony

> **(c) a statement as to the language in which the Witness Statement was originally prepared and the language in which the witness anticipates giving testimony at the Evidentiary Hearing.**

7.113 At some point either before or early in the life of an arbitration a decision will be made as to the language or languages in which the arbitration proceedings will be conducted ('the language of the arbitration'). A well-drafted arbitration agreement will make express provision for this.

[105] See Chapter 6, paras 6.26–6.36 and 6.341–6.349.

[106] This is standard practice, but for an express direction in these terms, see *Mesa Power Group LLC v Government of Canada* (Procedural Order No. 4) PCA Case No. 2012-17 [67.ii.d], a case conducted under the NAFTA, the 1976 UNCITRAL Rules, and the IBA Rules, where the direction stated that: 'The documents produced shall not be considered part of the record unless and until one of the Parties submits them as exhibits with their forthcoming submissions'. See also IBA Rules (n 1) Article 3.1 and Article 3.11.

[107] See also the terms of IBA Rules (n 1) Article 3.11, and the discussion of that article at Chapter 6 paras 6.341–6.349.

Absent such provision, the applicable institutional rules will generally provide a mechanism and/or criteria by which the language of the arbitration is to be determined.[108] The chosen language of the arbitration will be the language in which submissions, witness statements, and expert evidence are filed, and the language in which any oral hearings will be conducted.[109] Any documentary exhibits filed in the arbitration, or at least the relevant parts, will generally have to be translated into the language of the arbitration if the original document is in a different language.[110] 7.114

Where a witness is not fluent in the language of the arbitration, s/he may elect to prepare a witness statement in their native language. This will then need to be translated into the language of the arbitration for filing in the proceedings. Article 4.5(c) of the IBA Rules requires that, in such circumstances, the witness evidence contain a declaration indicating the language in which the witness evidence was originally prepared. In many cases, both the originally prepared witness statement and the translation into the language of the arbitration will be submitted. It is good practice to do so as the opposing party will not otherwise have a proper opportunity to verify or test the accuracy of the translation. It will assist to have both documents in the record in case of a later dispute as to the correctness of the translation. The IBA Rules do not require a translation to be certified by the translator, although some parties may wish to arrange for this to be done. 7.115

Article 4.5(c) of the IBA Rules also requires that, where a witness has made a statement in a language other than the language of the arbitration, the statement should indicate the language in which the witness anticipates giving evidence at the evidentiary hearing.[111] It is sensible for this to be made known in advance so that appropriate arrangements can be made for the attendance at the evidentiary hearing of an independent interpreter. This can sometimes take time to organize as the parties may wish to conduct a joint interview so that both sides are happy about the expertise of the interpreter. It may also have an impact on the anticipated length of the evidentiary hearing. Several witnesses giving evidence through an interpreter can significantly slow down progress in the taking of evidence, although this can be ameliorated by the use of simultaneous translation where appropriate.[112] 7.116

108 For example, Article 20 of the ICC Rules: 'In the absence of an agreement by the parties, the arbitral tribunal shall determine the language or languages of the arbitration, due regard being given to all relevant circumstances, including the language of the contract'. Also, LCIA Rules, Article 17.4: 'Following the formation of the arbitral tribunal, unless the parties have agreed upon the language or languages of the arbitration, the arbitral tribunal shall decide upon the language(s) of the arbitration after giving the parties a reasonable opportunity to make written comments and taking into account the initial language(s) of the arbitration and any other matter it may consider appropriate in the circumstances'.

109 Although it is possible to have more than one language of the arbitration, the use of multiple languages can bring problems (eg translation and interpretation costs, as well as difficulty in finding suitable arbitrators sufficiently fluent in all of the relevant languages) and is relatively rare.

110 See discussion of IBA Rules (n 1) Article 3.12(d) at Chapter 6 paras 6.379–6.385.

111 Where no witness statement is prepared for a witness, but where the witness intends to testify in a language other than the language of the arbitration, this should be notified to the tribunal and to other participants in the arbitration. See Commentary on the IBA Rules (n 19).

112 See, for more detail, Chapter 11 paras 11.108–11.110.

7.117 Although the tactic is frowned upon by tribunals, a witness will sometimes be advised by counsel to give oral testimony through an interpreter; it is thought that the intervening interpretation period will give them additional time to consider their response to the question being asked. This can raise issues around fair allocation of time at the evidentiary hearing, particularly if the tribunal is operating a 'chess clock' arrangement, although some tribunals may allocate any extended translation time against the party who produced the witness.[113] These and other matters related to the language in which evidence is presented are dealt in more detail in Chapter 11 on Article 8 of the IBA Rules.[114]

e. Affirmation of truth

(d) an affirmation of the truth of the Witness Statement.

7.118 The IBA Rules do not require the witness statement to be made under oath. As the Commentary on the IBA Rules notes,[115] arbitration practice and domestic legal systems differ too much on this point for such a requirement to be appropriate.[116]

7.119 Where express provision on the point is included in institutional rules, such provision generally permits delivery of a statement that is merely signed (although not excluding other forms of confirmation) sometimes coupled with a requirement that the testimony contain a statement as to the truth of the matters stated.[117]

7.120 The IBA Rules adopt a requirement that the witness simply confirm that her or his witness statement is true.[118] One much-used approach is for the witness to state at the end of the witness statement immediately above their signature the phrase 'This statement is true to the best of my knowledge, information and belief'. We agree with the view that something short and simple like this is likely to be the most prudent course. An over-elaborate affirmation that later turns out to be inaccurate may lead to embarrassment under cross-examination.[119]

[113] Such an approach was adopted in an ICC case known to the authors. In that case the tribunal decided to use a chess clock at the evidentiary hearing. A prior procedural order stated that '. . . in the case where consecutive translation from Turkish to English is used for any particular witness, half the time used for cross-examination of that witness will be counted *against* the time available to the Party *producing* that witness'. It is assumed that simultaneous translation would not have incurred the same penalty (emphasis added).

[114] See Chapter 11 paras 11.101–11.107.

[115] Commentary on the IBA Rules (n 19) 28.

[116] For example, as noted in the Commentary on the IBA Rules, in many civil law systems, a sworn declaration can only be made before the state court authorities, or a 'notaire', making them too cumbersome. In English Court proceedings a simple statement of truth is generally sufficient.

[117] LCIA Rules, Article 20.2 states that 'Subject to any order otherwise by the Arbitral Tribunal, the testimony of a witness may be presented by a party in written form, *either as a signed statement or like document*' (emphasis added). The SIAC Rules, Rule 25.4 says that 'the Tribunal may direct the testimony of witnesses to be presented in written form, *either as signed statements or sworn affidavits* or any other form of recording' (emphasis added). SCC Rules, Article 33(2) provides that 'The testimony of witnesses or party-appointed experts *may be submitted in the form of signed statements*' (emphasis added).

[118] IBA Rules (n 1) Article 4.5(d), which mirrors the requirement in Article 8.4 in relation to oral testimony.

[119] See further Harbst (n 71) 71.

A number of commentators quote the suggestion by VV Veeder QC that counsel who assisted in preparation of the witness statement should append to it a declaration as to when and where the statement was prepared, and the amount of time that was spent on it by the witness and the lawyer, respectively. This suggestion contains an implied and wide-spread concern about the 'over-lawyering' of witness statements. As far as we are aware, the suggestion has not been implemented in practice. **7.121**

The witness will generally be asked to re-affirm the truth of the statement at the evidentiary hearing immediately prior to being examined by counsel.[120] If not already corrected in advance of the hearing, it is customary for the witness at that stage to identify for the tribunal any inaccuracies in the statement they have identified since the date of its preparation.[121] **7.122**

f. Signature and date

(e) the signature of the witness and its date and place.

Article 4.5(e) of the IBA Rules requires that the witness statement be signed. This is consistent with the giving of an affirmation of truth as required by Article 4.5(d). **7.123**

If a witness is unavailable to sign a statement by the date due for service, it is usually possible to agree with the opposing party that an approved unsigned statement may be served with a signed version following as soon as the signature can be obtained. **7.124**

In addition, under Article 4.5(e) the witness statement should set out the date and place of its signature. **7.125**

It is universal practice to include a date on any document to be filed in court or arbitration, although lay witnesses may forget to do so if not prompted by counsel. The addition of the place of signature is more unusual and does not appear in institutional arbitration rules. This requirement has appeared in all iterations of the rules since their introduction in 1983, but the provenance and basis for it is not clear. It may be that the requirement for a place of signature is simply something that was considered appropriate by reason of the combined legal backgrounds of the members of the committee responsible for drafting the original rules. One of the authors of the Commentary on the IBA Rules mentions elsewhere that practice varies between jurisdictions and the requirement of the place of signature may simply reflect this. **7.126**

[120] IBA Rules (n 1) Article 8.4 requires this. This is often done by simple oral confirmation of the statement, although certain witnesses may elect to take an oath. See Chapter 4 paras 4.36–4.37 where the possible implications of mandatory provisions of law in this respect are discussed.

[121] See Chapter 11 paras 11.56–11.64.

G. Additional Witness Statements

4.6. If Witness Statements are submitted, any Party may, within the time ordered by the Arbitral Tribunal, submit to the Arbitral Tribunal and to the other Parties revised or additional Witness Statements, including statements from persons not previously named as witnesses, so long as any such revisions or additions respond only to matters contained in another Party's Witness Statements, Expert Reports or other submissions that have not been previously presented in the arbitration.

1. Introduction

7.127 Article 4.6 deals with delivery of a second round of written witness evidence. This provision permits submission of 'revised or additional Witness Statements' responsive to matters contained in another party's witness statements, expert evidence, or submissions not yet filed when the witness statement was prepared (referred to in this text as 'responsive witness evidence').

7.128 It is not unusual in international arbitration for there to be two (or more) rounds of witness statements. This reflects the general principle that, in order to have a fair hearing, a party should have the opportunity to present its case.[122] This will include the opportunity to respond to allegations or evidence filed by the party's opponent in which new issues are raised.[123]

7.129 Article 4.6 provides for delivery of responsive witness evidence 'within the time ordered by the Arbitral Tribunal'. It may follow from this wording that, even where the IBA Rules have been formally adopted as binding in the arbitration, absent direction from the tribunal or agreement between the parties,[124] the terms of Article 4.6 will not confer a right to serve responsive witness statements.[125] If there is no pre-existing direction permitting further witness statements, a party wishing to serve such evidence must make application to the tribunal explaining why the introduction of that additional evidence is justified. An alternative view is that the use of the word 'may' in the

[122] The requirement of a fair hearing is a fundamental requirement in international arbitration. It is often expressly embedded in national arbitration laws (see, for example, the English Arbitration Act 1996, s 33) but, even without this, the non-observance of this requirement will give rise to grounds for challenge. See, for example, the New York Convention on the Recognition and Enforcement of Foreign Arbitral Awards 1958, Article V1(b), which sets out that recognition and enforcement of an award may be refused by the courts of the jurisdiction where recognition and enforcement of the award is sought if the 'party against whom the award is invoked . . . was . . . unable to present his case'.

[123] See, for example, *Fraport AG Frankfurt Airport Services Worldwide v The Republic of the Philippines* (Decision on the Application for Annulment of Fraport AG Frankfurt Airport Services Worldwide, 23 December 2010) ICSID Case No. ARB/03/25 [202]. See also Nathan O'Malley, *Rules of Evidence in International Arbitration: An Annotated Guide* (Informa Law 2012) 124–25.

[124] An agreement between the parties to the arbitration that responsive evidence should be filed will prevail over the terms of IBA Rules (n 1) Article 4.6. See further Harbst (n 71) 87.

[125] See Harbst (n 71) 86.

statement 'any Party *may*, within the time ordered by the Arbitral Tribunal, submit to the Arbitral Tribunal . . . revised or additional witness statements'[126] creates an implied duty on the tribunal to set a date.[127] However, this latter reading might be thought inconsistent with the tribunal's general discretion not to admit evidence at all.[128]

In practice, delivery of responsive witness evidence is a common practice in international arbitration and express provision for it is often included in the first procedural order.[129] However, if the tribunal takes the view that the other party's evidence to which a party wishes to serve responsive evidence does not have an impact on the case, responsive evidence may not always be permitted. This was the view taken in *Malaysian Historical Salvors SDN v The Government of Malaysia*,[130] in which the respondent objected to the late introduction of evidence by the claimant. The tribunal decided that it was not necessary to give the respondent an opportunity to submit responsive evidence because, even on the claimant's best case, its claim on the particular point was not made out. Such circumstances will not arise very often as a tribunal is unlikely to be in a position to assess, at the stage of responsive witness evidence, that further evidence is not required. The tribunal may also be wary of giving the impression of having prejudged any part of the case. **7.130**

2. Timing of Responsive Statements

If first-round witness statements have been served simultaneously, a further round of responsive statements will almost certainly be necessary. The parties may have focused on different topics in the first-round statements, and responsive statements are likely to be necessary in order to achieve clarity on what the factual issues are between the parties. **7.131**

3. Substance of Responsive Statements

As noted, the IBA Rules provide that, where there is a second round of evidence, it should be limited to matters raised in the other party's witness statements, expert report/s, or submissions that were not available when the first round of witness evidence was delivered. However, very often there will be 'evidence creep' in the content **7.132**

[126] IBA Rules (n 1) Article 4.6 (emphasis added).

[127] As already noted, there exists a reasonable argument that a right to deliver responsive evidence flows from the parties' right to be heard so that the parties are entitled to deliver responsive evidence even without authorization from the tribunal. See Tobias Zuberbühler and others, *IBA Rules of Evidence: Commentary on the IBA Rules on the Taking of Evidence in International Arbitration* (Schulthess 2012) 98.

[128] See, in particular, IBA Rules (n 1) Articles 9.1 and 9.2.

[129] For an example, see Sigvard Jarvin and Corinne Nguyen, *Compendium of International Commercial Arbitration Forms: Letters, Procedural Instructions, Briefs and Other Documents* (Kluwer Law International 2017) 161–70.

[130] *Malaysian Historical Salvors, SDN, BHD v The Government of Malaysia* (Award on Jurisdiction, 17 May 2007) ICSID Case No. ARB/05/10 [145].

of responsive witness statements. Parties may decide that they would like to introduce new material (both witness testimony and documents) not directly relevant to what is said by their opponent's witnesses. They may have taken an earlier tactical decision to hold back some evidence until responsive statements are delivered.

7.133 As mentioned, a responsive statement that attempts to introduce a new version of events may fall outside of what is permitted by Article 4.6 of the IBA Rules. Furthermore, it may raise questions about (a) the reliability of the earlier statement and (b) whether the opponent will have a fair opportunity to deal with the new evidence in the time available prior to the evidentiary hearing.[131]

7.134 Each situation has to be considered on the facts of the particular case, but where possible the tribunal should try to prevent abuse under Article 4.6.[132] There may be circumstances where even the very late delivery of new evidence may be considered justified in order to ensure that a party has a proper opportunity to present its case. However, there will also be situations where the late delivery of evidence under cover of a 'responsive' statement is simply a tactic by the introducing party—for example, it may follow a pattern of conduct by that party designed to delay and disrupt the proceedings. Where a party or counsel has demonstrated a track record of abusive or bullying tactics in the arbitration, a tribunal should consider adopting a robust approach,[133] although it will naturally be concerned not to provide the introducing party with a ground for challenge to the award by excluding material evidence. Even where part of the statement is properly responsive, a tribunal should consider declaring inadmissible those parts of the statement that are unresponsive to the other party's last round of evidence.[134]

4. New Witnesses

7.135 Article 4.6 makes clear that responsive witness evidence may come from a new witness who has not previously submitted a witness statement. It may be that the evidence of that witness had not previously been considered as relevant to the issues in dispute but, because of something said in the other party's evidence, it has become so. For example, the other party may make reference to an event not addressed in a party's first-round witness evidence, but in which the new witness had a key role. Or perhaps, in relation to a conversation not previously thought to be controversial, a party may deny that it took

[131] See further Philip Yang, 'Procedural Issues at the Interlocutory and Hearing Stages: Part 2' (2013) Asian Dispute Review 138.

[132] Ashford (n 91) 103.

[133] See Lucy Reed, 'Chapter 2, §2.04: Sanctions Available for Arbitrators to Curtail Guerrilla Tactics' in Günther Horvath and Stephan Wilske (eds), *Guerrilla Tactics in International Arbitration* (Kluwer Law International 2013) 99; the author makes the point that tribunals too rarely exclude 'a suddenly available rebuttal statement'.

[134] For an example of a case where witness evidence determined not to be responsive was declared inadmissible, see *William J. Levitt v The Islamic Republic of Iran* (Award No. 297-209-1 of 22 April 1987) (2013) 14 Iran–U.S. Cl. Trib. Rep. 191 [22]–[24].

place, and the other party may wish to put in a statement from a second witness who was also at the meeting.

5. 'Revised or Additional' Statements

The use of the phrase 'revised or additional' in Rule 4.6 is interesting. In practice, most 'second-round' evidence is delivered by means of new witness statements. However, where the witness providing the new evidence has already submitted a witness statement, there is no reason—in principle—why the new evidence should not be introduced by way of revisions (whether corrections or additions) to the existing statement. In many ways, this method of dealing with the matter has much to recommend it. The tribunal will have only one statement to read, rather than two. The changes can be made in a differently coloured font to maintain full transparency about the date at which the new evidence was introduced. It also makes it easier for the tribunal to identify changes in position. This may be why, in practice, this approach is rarely used by parties. **7.136**

H. Non-Attendance at an Evidentiary Hearing

> **4.7. If a witness whose appearance has been requested pursuant to Article 8.1 fails without a valid reason to appear for testimony at an Evidentiary Hearing, the Arbitral Tribunal shall disregard any Witness Statement related to that Evidentiary Hearing by that witness unless, in exceptional circumstances, the Arbitral Tribunal decides otherwise.**

1. Introduction

Article 4.7 sets out the consequences of a witness failing to comply, without a valid reason, with a request made under Article 8.1 to attend an evidentiary hearing. Save in exceptional circumstances, in the event of such failure the witness statements of that witness are to be disregarded. Article 4.7 thereby addresses a number of issues relating to a party's 'right' to conduct an oral examination of an opponent's witness. **7.137**

Article 8.1 of the IBA Rules provides that each party shall inform the tribunal, and other parties to the arbitration, of the fact (and expert)[135] witnesses whose appearance it requests at the evidentiary hearing. The notice required by the IBA Rules must be given 'within the time' ordered by the tribunal. This will generally be after all written **7.138**

[135] IBA Rules (n 1) Article 8.1 states expressly that the term 'witness' for the purposes of that article includes both witnesses of fact and any experts.

evidence has been delivered and the parties have had an opportunity to consider what evidence of the other parties they accept, and what they do not. It may be possible for the parties to agree that witnesses whose evidence is not contested do not have to attend the hearing.[136]

2. A Party's Right to Cross-Examine

7.139 In line with accepted practice in international arbitration, the effect of Article 8.1 of the IBA Rules is that where a party has tendered a witness statement in support of its case, that witness should be available for cross-examination at the evidentiary hearing. A number of institutional rules contain express provision adopting a similar position.[137]

7.140 In order to understand why Article 4.7 takes such a strict approach, it is necessary to consider the value that many practitioners and legal traditions place on the ability to question a witness. Cross-examination is regarded by some as an essential opportunity to challenge and test the evidence contained in a witness statement. Only by cross-examination can a proper assessment of the truth, or accuracy of recollection, of the evidence set out in the witness statement be carried out. Evidence that has not been tested by cross-examination may be given less, or no, weight by a tribunal.

7.141 A tribunal placed diminished weight on the evidence of a witness not available for cross-examination in *Bayindir Insaat Turizm Ticaret Ve Sanayi A.S. v Islamic Republic of Pakistan*, where the respondent relied on witness evidence from a witness who (for confidential reasons that the respondent was not prepared to disclose) was unable to attend the hearing to be cross-examined. In its award on the merits the tribunal stated that:

> [T]he tribunal has carefully reviewed all circumstances and concluded that, because the Claimant had no opportunity to cross-examine Mr Mirza, the latter's written evidence could only be considered if corroborated by other evidence in the record.[138]

7.142 Despite such acknowledgments as to the reduced value of witness evidence not tested by oral examination, there remains a wide spectrum of views as to the importance of cross-examination. Representative of one end of this spectrum is the view expressed

[136] Some institutional rules make express provision for this situation. The SCC Rules, Article 33(3) states 'any witness . . . on whose testimony a party seeks to rely shall attend a hearing for examination, unless otherwise agreed by the parties'.

[137] For example, see LCIA Rules, Article 20.4; ICDR Rules, Article 23.4; SCC Rules, Article 33(3); and SIAC Rules, Rule 25.4.

[138] *Bayindir Insaat Turizm Ticaret Ve Sanayi A.S. v Islamic Republic of Pakistan* (Award, 27 August 2009) ICSID Case No. ARB/03/29 [303] (hereafter '*Bayindir*'). See also *Generica Limited v Pharmaceutical Basics Inc* 125 F3d 1123 (7th Cir. 1997) (hereafter '*Generica*'), in which the tribunal would not permit cross-examination of a third-party witness because it did not regard the proposed subject matter of the examination as being germane to its award. Despite this, when the tribunal came to assess the evidence, it acknowledged the restrictions that had been placed upon the respondent's cross-examination of the witness. The award made in favour of the claimant expressly noted that, for that reason, the tribunal placed diminished reliance on the direct testimony of the witness.

by the United States Supreme Court that cross-examination is the 'greatest legal engine ever invented for the discovery of truth'.[139] At the other end of the scale is the view that documentary evidence is the most reliable form of evidence and that witness evidence, even when subject to cross-examination, is often unreliable[140] and/or self-serving, and so should be given little weight.[141]

One author refers to the emergence of a 'counter-movement' against the idea of cross-examination as a state-of-the-art feature of international commercial arbitration.[142] The process of cross-examination is criticized for being destructive and of low efficiency. It is said that the: **7.143**

> . . . approach seeks to destroy the credibility of the witness or simply get the witness to confirm the propositions of the cross-examiner, and it often achieves both. However, who cares about those achievements (apart from super-aggressive counsel), because they are of limited importance and often of little use to the arbitrator, who is the only objective player in the process. Accordingly, it is more productive if the process is geared to what the arbitrator needs.[143]

The truth as to the value of cross-examination is likely to lie somewhere in the middle. However, if one party has the opportunity to interview and take a statement from a witness for use in the arbitration, it is fair that the other party should also have the opportunity to question that witness on the evidence that has been submitted. Witness statements and cross-examination may be regarded as two sides of the same process of taking evidence. **7.144**

Although not required under the IBA Rules, some tribunals may direct that a witness statement should contain a statement confirming that the witness is willing and able to attend the evidentiary hearing, if required.[144] In certain circumstances, loss of the opportunity to cross-examine might be argued to be a denial of due process.[145] **7.145**

[139] Spuijbroek (n 4) para 9.

[140] There is research to suggest that individuals can inadvertently—sometimes influenced by how questions are framed—create false memories. This may undermine the value of oral evidence given under pressure in response to carefully constructed questions put by examining counsel. For example, see Daniel Kahneman, 'What You See Is All There Is (WYSIATI)' in *Thinking, Fast and Slow* (Reprint edn, Penguin 2012).

[141] We have also seen an interesting public exchange of views between arbitration practitioners on the additional point that it is sometimes difficult to assess the veracity of witnesses under cross-examination where—as has become more common—the examination takes place by means of video conference and that such difficulties may increase as other technological advances become adopted—for example, three-dimensional holographic projection. It is suggested that it may be possible to address such difficulties by harnessing other technological developments such as improved (non-invasive) lie-detection methods.

[142] Wirth (n 81) 210.

[143] Shore (n 96) para 3.15 and fn 18.

[144] In one example known to the authors the relevant procedural order stated in terms that 'All factual witness statements shall contain . . . confirmation that the witness is able and willing to attend the hearing in London, if so required'. It also went on to direct that 'The parties shall inform their potential witnesses of the hearing dates to ensure their availability to attend the hearing, and to enable the witness to obtain in good time the necessary visa to attend the hearing in London if required'.

[145] This view is shared by other commentators. See Spuijbroek (n 4) paras 43, 48, and 52–53, as well as para 55 and fn 182 for an example in *Generica* (n 138) of a challenge being brought where one party had not been allowed to complete its cross-examination of the other party's witness, and Spuijbroek (n 4) para 56 for another example in *Paklito Investment Ltd. v Klockner East Asia Ltd.* [1993] HKLR 39, where one party had had no opportunity to question a witness, even though cross-examination had been requested. In the first case, the challenge was

Article 4.7 addresses the issue by providing—in substance—that witness statements will not be taken into account by a tribunal unless there has been a corresponding opportunity for the other parties to cross-examine the witness.[146]

3. Requirements to Be Satisfied before a Witness Statement Is Disregarded

7.146 Where a witness has failed to attend an evidentiary hearing when requested to do so by notice under Article 8.1, certain conditions must be satisfied before the statement of that witness is disregarded by a tribunal under Article 4.7. Those conditions are that:

(a) the witness must have failed to provide a valid reason for not attending the hearing; and
(b) there are no exceptional circumstances that cause the tribunal to decide that the statement should not be disregarded.

a. Valid reason

7.147 If the witness can provide a valid reason as to why they are not able to attend the evidentiary hearing the witness statement need not be disregarded.

7.148 It is for the tribunal to decide whether the reason given is 'valid'. In practice, submissions on this issue are likely to be made by one party and responded to by the other parties in advance of the tribunal making a decision on the validity of the explanation. Reasons likely to be accepted as valid include physical incapacity by reason of serious illness or accident, or the need to undergo some form of medical procedure within a particular time frame,[147] subject to provision of certification by a doctor.[148] Other possibilities include an inability to travel to the hearing as a result of visa requirements, a compelling need to be somewhere else on the date of the hearing (for example, a court

dismissed because the tribunal had attached 'little or no weight' to the witness statement. In the second case, enforcement of the award was denied. In *Bayindir* (n 138), after reviewing all of the circumstances, the tribunal concluded that, because the Claimant had no opportunity to cross-examine a witness, the latter's written evidence could only be considered if corroborated by other evidence in the record.

---

[146] Where the IBA Rules do not apply, some tribunals may wish to make provision for such a power where express provision does not otherwise exist under the applicable institutional rules. Respondents to the BCLP Survey on use of the IBA Rules based in France and Sweden told us that they had experience of tribunals incorporating express reference to such a power when drawing up a first procedural order.

[147] In addition to incidents of serious illness or infirmity the authors are aware of one case where the witness sought to be excused because she was having a course of IVF treatment that required the procedure to be carried out on particular dates.

[148] By way of example, in an ICC case known to the authors the procedural order dealing with such a situation provided that: '*Subject to the submission of medical evidence before the beginning of the hearing*, the First Witness statement of [redacted] shall remain on the evidentiary record, on the basis that there is a valid reason for his non-attendance' (emphasis added). In that case, the tribunal also went on to note that the weight to be attached to the witness statement might nonetheless be affected by the other party's loss of opportunity to cross-examine: 'In weighing the value to attach to his evidence, the tribunal will take into account the fact that the [. . .] Respondents will not have had an opportunity to cross-examine Mr [redacted]'.

appearance under subpoena or where the witness is the accused in a criminal trial), and threats made to the witness that have been proven to the satisfaction of the tribunal.[149]

A further aspect to be considered when reasons for non-attendance at a hearing are proffered is whether some other means of facilitating the oral testimony of the witness can be arranged. For example, subject to considerations of procedural efficiency, if the unavailability of the witness is temporary, the hearing may be deferred. If a physical condition renders the witness immobile but capable of giving evidence, the witness could attend by video-conference. The tribunal may wish to explore all possible avenues for securing the attendance of the witness for cross-examination whether in person or remotely, even where (subject to procedural fairness and efficiency) this has to take place after the main evidentiary hearing.[150] If the witness, through counsel, rejects reasonable ways of dealing with the problem, this may be taken into account by the tribunal when considering whether the reason given for non-attendance is valid. **7.149**

b. Exceptional circumstances

Even where a witness is unable to provide an adequate reason to excuse his or her attendance, the tribunal may nonetheless determine that there are exceptional circumstances justifying the witness statement being taken into account. This approach is expressly permitted under Article 4.7. **7.150**

As with consideration of a 'valid reason', if the party with the non-attending witness wishes to rely on the existence of exceptional circumstances (or the tribunal raises the issue) it is very likely that the parties to the arbitration will make submissions on those matters in advance of the tribunal making a decision on this point. In practice, it is hard to see what exceptional circumstances would justify the acceptance into evidence of a witness statement where a valid reason for the non-attendance cannot be provided. **7.151**

c. Practical application

In our view, the tribunal should apply a high standard to the question of whether a 'valid reason' or 'exceptional circumstances' exist as this carve out from the consequences of Article 4.7 could otherwise be too easily abused by parties. Claims of a 'family emergency' or 'urgent business needs' without some further explanation should not be regarded as adequate. Of course, as a matter of practice, the approach taken by individual tribunals—and the stringency of the benchmark they apply—may vary considerably. A review of ICC decisions in arbitrations referencing the IBA Rules describes contrasting examples of the view taken by two ICC tribunals on the question of whether a 'valid reason' under Article 4.7 had been established.[151] In the first case, the tribunal decided to admit the witness statement of the witness. The tribunal took account of **7.152**

[149] See also Harbst (n 71) 91–93. An example of threats made to witnesses can be found in *Caratube International Oil Company LLP v The Republic of Kazakhstan* (Award, 5 June 2012) ICSID Case No. ARB/08/12 69-77.

[150] For example, as may be the case where the witness simply fails to turn up at that hearing.

[151] ICC Partial Award dated November 2012 (n 101) 6.

the fact that (a) the witness was based in the United States (ie not in the jurisdiction in which the hearing took place); (b) that although no evidence to this effect was provided, the witness had limited means and might struggle to meet the costs of attendance; and (c) the statement did not go much, if at all, beyond confirming the content of another statement. Accordingly, the tribunal found that there was a valid reason for the non-attendance (and that the matters identified also constituted extraordinary circumstances justifying a refusal to disregard the statement). The tribunal therefore admitted the statement, but made clear that the weight to be attributed to it remained a matter for submissions. In a second case, where a witness (within the jurisdiction) failed to attend the evidentiary hearing, the tribunal found that:

> [T]here was no valid reason for his non-attendance, for the purposes of Article 4.7 of the IBA Rules. Further there were no exceptional circumstances justifying the Tribunal nonetheless having regard to [the] statement. [The witness] was in the United Kingdom and could apparently have attended the hearing if he had so wished.

4. Disregarding the Witness Evidence

7.153 Subject to the two requirements just described (the absence of a valid reason, and/or no exceptional circumstances) being met, Article 4.7 of the IBA Rules provides that a tribunal 'shall disregard' a witness statement served by one of the parties if, after having been requested to make themselves available for questioning at an oral hearing, that witness fails to attend.

a. Application of the requirement to disregard witness evidence

7.154 The use of the word 'shall' in Article 4.7 indicates that, save in the excepted circumstances described, the tribunal must disregard the witness statement entirely if the witness fails to appear at the hearing. As mentioned, an important argument in support of this position is that, until tested by cross-examination, the witness statement has little or no value.[152] In addition, if without further explanation, a witness is not prepared to attend and affirm a witness statement already filed, this may suggest that they are resiling from all or part of that evidence.

7.155 There are different points of view as to whether the position adopted under Article 4.7 is too inflexible and whether it attributes too much significance to oral examination of a witness.[153]

[152] It should be noted that IBA Rules (n 1) Article 8.3(b) (describing the procedure to be adopted at the Evidentiary Hearing) does not use the phrase 'cross-examination' but, in essence, this is the process provided for in that rule: '. . . following direct testimony, any other Party may question such witness in an order to be determined by the Arbitral Tribunal. The Party who initially presented the witness shall subsequently have the opportunity to ask additional questions on the matters raised in the other Parties' questioning.'

[153] As described at 7.142– 7.143, not everyone agrees that cross-examination actually has the value often attributed to it.

The alternative approach of simply adjusting the weight to be attributed to the witness statement is regarded by some as a more flexible option. 7.156

Whatever the position taken, and depending on the facts of the case, there undoubtedly are risks attached to application of the requirement to disregard the evidence of a witness who fails to attend a hearing. For example, if the only evidence that a party has on a particular issue is the witness statement of a witness who is no longer under the control of that party (for example, because he has left their employment and now works for a competitor), is it fair to disregard that witness statement when the witness refuses to attend the evidentiary hearing? Could such a situation lead to a challenge to the award? 7.157

In practice, the tribunal's power not to disregard a statement when a valid reason has been tendered by the party affected provides a mechanism for balancing the legitimate interests of the parties. In the example just mentioned, it may be open to the party relying on the witness statement to explain to the tribunal that—despite all reasonable efforts on its part, including an offer of reasonable time costs and expenses—the witness is not prepared to attend the hearing and has made clear that his refusal is the result of pressure being exerted on him by the new employer. A tribunal may regard such circumstances as constituting a 'valid reason' for the purposes of the Article 4.7 exception. 7.158

Conversely, in circumstances where no reason is given and no exceptional circumstances are identified, the tribunal may risk a challenge to the award if it admits the statement of the non-attending witness. As mentioned, in some circumstances, loss of the opportunity to cross-examination may be argued to be a denial of due process.[154] Of course, if the IBA Rules are adopted as guidelines only, the tribunal may decide not to exclude the witness statement and instead adjust the weight attributed to it. If there is corroborative evidence, the tribunal may be prepared to take it into account. 7.159

b. Practice in international arbitration

Whatever reservations may exist about the strict application of Article 4.7, the requirement that a tribunal shall, in certain circumstances, disregard the statement of a witness who fails to attend an evidentiary hearing is not out of line with international arbitration practice. Provision for this step can be found in a number of published procedural orders. One example of this provides that: 7.160

> The Arbitral Tribunal may consider the witness statement of a witness who provides a valid reason for failing to appear when summoned to a hearing, having regard to all the surrounding circumstances. *The arbitral tribunal shall not consider the witness statement of a witness who fails to appear and does not provide a valid reason.*[155]

[154] See 7.139–7.145.

[155] See 'Procedural Order of 12 May 2004 in ICC Case 12990 (extract)' and 'Procedural Order of 12 May 2003 in ICC Case 12169 (extract)' in *Special Supplement 2010: Decisions on ICC Arbitration Procedure: A Selection of Procedural Orders issued by Arbitral Tribunals acting under the ICC Rules of Arbitration (2003-2004)* (International Chamber of Commerce 2010) 4.7; 10 (emphasis added).

7.161 Another states that:

> A witness duly summoned, who does not appear at the hearing of the Arbitral Tribunal scheduled to hear his testimony, shall, in principle, only be summoned a second time on timely presentation of a valid excuse.
>
> *Where a witness should ultimately not be able to attend for a valid reason, the Arbitral Tribunal shall in principle not be entitled to consider his written statement, except if extraordinary circumstances so warrant.* In such event the Arbitral Tribunal shall hear the parties and decide by taking, however, into account all relevant circumstances, including the parties' legitimate interests.[156]

7.162 The latter form of wording might be regarded as more draconian than the IBA Rules as the existence of a 'valid reason' does not of itself provide an exception to the witness statement being disregarded.

7.163 Some institutional rules take no position on the matter.[157] Others provide some guidance as to the range of approaches open to the tribunal. For example, the LCIA Rules, while also acknowledging that the existence of circumstances justifying non-attendance ('just cause', rather than the IBA's 'valid reason') provides an exception, state that:

> If the Arbitral Tribunal orders that other party to secure the attendance of that witness and the witness refuses or fails to attend the hearing without good cause, the Arbitral Tribunal may place such weight on the written testimony or exclude all or any part thereof altogether as it considers appropriate in the circumstances.[158]

7.164 The SIAC Rules adopt a similar approach, but the relevant provision does not contain an express proviso for a situation where good reasons for the non-attendance have been provided.[159] In the authors' experience, absent mandatory application of the IBA Rules,[160] it is relatively common for tribunals to include in the first procedural order express provision for the approach of adjusting the weight attributed to the statement.[161]

156 'Procedural Order of 20 September 2004 in ICC Case 13054 (extract)' in ibid 10 (emphasis added).

157 For example, the UNCITRAL Rules, Article 17.3; and the ICC Rules, Articles 25.2 and 25.3.

158 LCIA Rules, Article 20.4.

159 SIAC Rules, Rule 25.4: 'If the witness fails to attend for oral examination, the Tribunal may place such weight on the written testimony as it thinks fit, disregard such written testimony, or exclude such written testimony altogether'. The WIPO Arbitration Rules adopt a softer line than the IBA Rules in providing that the tribunal may make the admissibility of witness statements conditional upon the witness being made available for oral testimony; see the WIPO Arbitration Rules, Article 56(d).

160 Or where an agreed adjustment to the rules has been made.

161 Orders we have seen include: 'Should a witness who has submitted a written statement not appear at the witness hearing, *the Sole Arbitrator shall at its discretion assess his written statement*, taking into account all relevant circumstances'; 'If a witness does not appear at the hearing without a valid reason, the Tribunal *may use its discretion to limit the evidentiary weight to be given to the witness statement*'; 'If a witness is required to attend for cross-examination but fails to do so, the arbitral tribunal may in its discretion receive the statement, disregard the statement, *or accept it but attach less weight to it, to be determined in the Arbitral Tribunal's discretion*'; 'Should a witness who has submitted a written statement not appear at the witness hearing, *the Sole arbitrator shall at its discretion assess his written statement*, taking into account all relevant circumstances'; 'Where a witness should ultimately not be able to attend for a valid reason, the Arbitral Tribunal shall in principle not be entitled to consider his written statement, except if extraordinary circumstances so warrant. In such event the Arbitral Tribunal shall hear the parties and decide by taking, however, into account all relevant circumstances, including the parties' legitimate interests' (emphasis added).

c. Other mechanisms under the IBA Rules

Other mechanisms exist under the IBA Rules to assist a tribunal in dealing with absent witnesses. These should be considered together with Article 4.7. 7.165

For example, as mentioned, a witness statement may be admitted under Article 4.7 on the basis that a valid reason for non-attendance has been tendered. However, the tribunal will still have the power to assess the weight of that evidence in accordance with Article 9.1 of the IBA Rules.[162] The tribunal may take note of the fact that the witness was unwilling to attend to confirm the evidence and that the evidence of the witness was not challenged under cross-examination. 7.166

Under Article 9.6, where a party fails to make oral testimony available at an evidentiary hearing in circumstances where that testimony has been requested by another party, a tribunal may draw adverse inferences as to the nature of the evidence withheld. However, it should be borne in mind that, even in circumstances where the drawing of adverse inferences appears appropriate, it can problematic for a tribunal to identify the precise nature of the inference that it is appropriate to draw.[163] In the context of Article 4.7, in the BCLP Survey on the use of the IBA Rules, one respondent in the United States reported the example of a case where a party had withdrawn a witness statement on the day of the hearing in order to avoid being under an obligation (and failing) to produce the witness at the evidentiary hearing. The tribunal accepted that the witness statement should be disregarded. However, the tribunal declined to draw adverse inferences from the fact that the testimony had been withdrawn. 7.167

I. No Acceptance of Content of the Witness Statement

4.8. If the appearance of a witness has not been requested pursuant to Article 8.1, none of the other Parties shall be deemed to have agreed to the correctness of the content of the Witness Statement.

Rule 4.8 of the IBA Rules provides that, where a witness has not received an Article 8.1 request to attend the evidentiary hearing, this is not taken to mean that the content of the witness statement submitted by that witness is agreed by opponent parties. The Commentary on the IBA Rules suggests that this provision was included for the sake of efficiency to encourage agreement between parties that a witness whose evidence may not be material to outcome need not attend the evidentiary hearing.[164] 7.168

[162] Under IBA Rules (n 1) Article 9.1, the weighing of evidence is left entirely to the tribunal.

[163] Article 9.6 is covered in Chapter 12; see paras 12.357–12.386.

[164] Commentary on the 1999 IBA Rules (n 76) where the substance of the current provision was first introduced. In the section dealing with 1999 IBA Rules (n 55) Article 5, where 1999 IBA Rules (n 55) Article 5.6 is in similar terms to IBA Rules (n 1) Article 4.8, Commentary on the 1999 IBA Rules (n 76) 31 states: 'Article 5.6, like Article 4.9 [now 4.8] was added . . . mostly for the sake of efficiency and completeness. If the parties can agree that an expert witness or fact witness need not appear . . . the progress of the arbitration may be enhanced. To encourage such agreements where the content of the expert report or witness statement may not be material to the outcome,

7.169 Given the apparent intention behind the provision, it appears likely that the phrase 'other Parties' is intended to refer to all parties other than the party that presented the witness statement. It can also reasonably be assumed that the party submitting and relying on the witness statement will accept the truth of the statement, and that there is therefore no need for application of the provision to extend to that party. However, the provision could have been more tightly drafted and other interpretations are possible.[165]

1. Not Calling a Witness for Cross-Examination

7.170 There are many reasons why a party may decide not to require the attendance for cross-examination of another party's witness. Some of these may relate to efficiency. For example, with increasing use of a chess clock at evidentiary hearings, and as contemplated to some extent by the Commentary on the IBA Rules, where the evidence of a particular witness is only of marginal importance, counsel for the opposing party may prefer to use the hearing time on potentially more important and fertile cross-examination. Other reasons for not calling a witness may be more tactical. For example, the evidence of an individual witness may relate to a particular issue where the party's case is weak and not calling the opposing key witness may form part of an effort to downgrade the importance of the issue. Another reason may be that a party recognizes that a witness for the opposing party will make a good witness, that under cross-examination they may offer additional testimony helpful to the other side, and that they are very unlikely to make any concessions when cross-examined.

7.171 Article 4.8 provides a measure of protection for the party not calling a witness for cross-examination. The provision confirms that a decision not to cross-examine a witness shall not constitute agreement to the correctness of the evidence contained in their witness statement. This is an important clarification, particularly if counsel for the opposing parties are from different legal traditions.

7.172 In some legal systems there are restrictions on the reliance that counsel may place on unchallenged evidence. For example, in a number of common law jurisdictions, it is a well-established principle that a party must challenge in cross-examination the witness evidence of the opposing party on a particular issue if they intend later—perhaps in closing submissions—to argue that the evidence on that point should not be believed. This is sometimes called the rule in *Browne v Dunn*.[166]

Articles 4.9 [now 4.8] and 5.6 state that such an agreement does not reflect agreement on the content of the expert report or witness statement'.

---

[165] For example, in a dispute where there are two or more respondents (or claimants) and one calls a witness for cross-examination while the others do not, is it only the party that *does* call for cross-examination (the 'other' party) that it is intended should have the protection offered by IBA Rules (n 1) Article 4.8.

[166] This rule is so-called because the first reported judgment dealing with it appears in the English case of *Browne v Dunn* (1893) 6 R 67, HL (hereafter '*Browne*') 70–71. In that case, heard before the then-House of Lords, it was said by Lord Herschell that: '. . . I cannot help saying that it seems to me to be absolutely essential to the proper conduct of a case, where it is intended to suggest that a witness is not speaking the truth on a particular point, to

It is said that the rule has two aspects. The first is procedural fairness. The witness must be given the opportunity to deal with the case that will be relied upon in contradiction of his or her evidence (including any inferences that it is said can be drawn from other evidence), and the party presenting the witness testimony must have the opportunity to call further evidence either to corroborate what the witness says or to contradict any inference relied upon by the other party. These requirements are said to be rules of conduct 'which are essential to fair play at the trial'.[167] 7.173

The second aspect relates to weight and cogency of evidence. Although a failure to put points in cross-examination will not always be regarded as conceding the truth of the evidence presented,[168] the weighing of the available evidence by the court on the relevant point may be affected. In *Bulstrode*, the point was made in these terms: 'In this aspect the rule says no more than that if a witness is not cross-examined upon a particular matter, upon which he has given evidence, then that circumstance will often be very good reason for accepting the witness's evidence upon that matter. If I may say so, this is little more than common sense'.[169] 7.174

Despite these factors, the rule has been criticized for the uncertainty around its application, the risk that cautious counsel will lengthen hearings unnecessarily by exhaustive 7.175

direct his attention to the fact by some questions put in cross-examination showing that that imputation is intended to be made, and not to take his evidence and pass it by as a matter altogether unchallenged, and then, when it is impossible for him to explain, as perhaps he might have been able to do if such question had been put to him, the circumstances which it is suggested indicate that the story he tells ought not to be believed, to argue that he is a witness unworthy of credit. My Lords, I have always understood that if you intend to impeach a witness you are bound, whilst he is in the box, to give him the opportunity of making any explanation which is open to him; as it seems to me, that is not only a rule of professional practice in the conduct of a case, but it is essential to fair play and fair dealing with witnesses'. See also Colin Tapper, *Cross & Tapper on Evidence* (12th edn, OUP 2010) 314, fn 446 (hereafter '*Tapper*'). The rule appears to be recognized in a number of other jurisdictions, including South Africa, Canada, Ireland, and Australia, where it is said to be 'taken very seriously'; and *Markem Corp v Zipher Ltd* [2005] EWCA Civ 267 [57]). See also *Allied Pastoral Holdings Pty Ltd v Commissioner of Taxation* [1983] 1 NSWLR 1; *Bulstrode v Trimble* [1970] VR 840 (hereafter '*Bulstrode*'); and *Chen v NG (British Virgin Islands)* [2017] UKPC 27 (hereafter '*Chen*'). There is debate on the precise scope and application of the rule across jurisdictions but it appears to be widely accepted that (a) in practice, it may be unrealistic in light of restrictions on allocated court hearing time for cross-examination to extend to each and every statement made by the witness with which issue is taken, although the substance of any evidence that it is intended to challenge should be raised; and (b) where the witness (and the party presenting that witness) are already on clear notice (for example, by means of pleadings or written evidence) that the evidence is challenged, cross-examination may not be required under the rule. Note the comments of the Privy Council in the judgement delivered by Lord Neuberger and Lord Mance in *Chen*, 52 that: 'In a perfect world, any ground for doubting the evidence of a witness ought to be put to him, and a judge should only rely on a ground for disbelieving a witness which that witness has had the opportunity to explain. However, the world is not perfect, and, while both points remain ideals which should always be in the minds of cross-examiners and trial judges, they cannot be absolute requirements in every case. Even in a very full trial, it may often be disproportionate and unrealistic to expect a cross-examiner to put every possible reason for disbelieving a witness to that witness, especially in a complex case, and it may be particularly difficult to do so in a case such as this where the Judge sensibly rationed the time for cross examination . . . '. See also *Browne*, 70–72, and *White Industries (Qld) Pty Ltd v Flower & Hart* [1998] FCA 806. In *P v D, E and F* [2019] EWHC 1277 a failure to cross-examine a witness on a core issue led to the award being successfully challenged under Section 68 of the English Arbitration Act 1996. The judgment contains a useful review of the English authorities.

---

[167] See the Judgment of Lord Herschell in *Browne* (n 166). The substance of the rule may also be found in professional conduct rules. For example, see BSB Code of Conduct (n 35) r C7 states that: 'You must not make a serious allegation against a witness whom you have had an opportunity to cross-examine unless you have given that witness a chance to answer the allegation in cross-examination'.

[168] See Tapper (n 166) 314.

[169] *Bulstrode* (n 166) 840.

cross-examination, and because the rule hinders the ability of counsel to control cross-examination and to make tactical decisions about how far to push a witness on a particular point.[170]

7.176 However, although the rule does not appear to be of universal application across common law systems,[171] it may be that those tasked with drafting the IBA Rules—intended to be a set of rules on evidence that can be accepted by lawyers from both civil and common law traditions—had in mind that, in the interests of clarity, it might be prudent to include express provision in the terms of Article 4.8 (and its predecessor provisions). In relation to the first mentioned rationale for the rule—that a witness must be given the opportunity to address the case relied on in contradiction of the evidence given by that witness—a relevant factor may be that, in international arbitration, greater emphasis is placed on written submissions and that those submissions are generally more discursive and leave parties in little doubt about which parts of the factual case are challenged and on what basis.

7.177 An important point to note is that the wording of Article 8.4 makes no distinction between matters of minor or no importance to outcome, and evidence on which the outcome of the dispute might turn. It applies to all of the written evidence of a witness not called for cross-examination. An opponent party may still tender its own witness to give evidence contradicting that of the 'opposing' witness not called, or make submissions as to the unreliability or lack of weight to be attributed to the evidence of the absent witness, perhaps by reference to other witness or documentary evidence available to the tribunal. Some practitioners regard this as unfair. If an opponent party chooses not to cross-examine a witness, why should the written evidence of that witness not be deemed accepted? An IBA survey report on use of the IBA Rules notes this concern and a comment from one respondent that 'parties engage in the "unfair practice" of not calling a witness while making attempts to undermine his or her credibility through their written submissions'.[172]

7.178 In our view, and notwithstanding the terms of Article 4.8, there are considerable dangers in a party not calling for cross-examination a witness whose evidence touches on important issues of fact potentially relevant to outcome (or, having called such a witness, not challenging by cross-examination that part of the witness evidence). Under Article 4.8, the evidence of that witness may not be deemed accepted by the non-calling party, but the tribunal may still regard it as credible. When the tribunal comes to assess the weight of evidence on either side of the dispute, it may well take into account the fact that the written evidence of the witness was not challenged by cross-examination. While there can be no certainty around whether this factor will influence the tribunal to attach less or more weight to the evidence, the tribunal may wonder why the

[170] See Hugh Kennedy, 'Putting the Case Against the Rule in *Browne v Dunn*' (2006) The Bar Review: Journal of the Bar of Ireland 39.

[171] For example, it does not appear to extend to the US.

[172] 2016 IBA Report (n 61) para 98.

opportunity to conduct cross-examination was not utilized. In some cases, on balance, the tribunal may still feel that the weight of evidence is with the opponent party, but that party may have done itself no favours by not calling the witness for cross-examination.

Even allowing for pressure of time, the prudent course for counsel will be to identify the best witness to challenge on each issue and to take the opportunity to cross-examine them on the points that matter to success of the case. To avoid any misunderstanding between the parties, and to avoid post-hearing arguments on an alleged failure to challenge evidence on the critical path to a determination, it is sensible for counsel for the parties to discuss such issues at an early stage in order to establish clear ground rules. 7.179

2. A Party's Right to Call Its Own Witness

As mentioned, in circumstances where a party has elected not to call a witness for cross-examination, the statement at Article 4.8 that it should not, as a result, be deemed to accept the correctness of a witness statement, may in certain circumstances leave the other party feeling aggrieved. For example, it may feel that the witness would have stood up well to cross-examination, would have impressed the tribunal, and that the substance of the evidence contained in the statement would be accepted in its entirety. There may also have been matters raised by other witnesses upon which some short direct examination would be helpful. This raises the issue of whether a party should be entitled to call its own witness when the attendance of that witness has been waived by the other party/parties, possibly for tactical reasons 7.180

International arbitration tribunals do not appear to adopt a consistent approach on this issue. In a 2015 survey of publicly available decisions made by arbitral tribunals in investment treaty cases it was found that, in the cases surveyed, tribunals tended to adopt one of three approaches: 7.181

(a) only the tribunal or the party entitled to cross-examine the witness may request attendance;[173]
(b) a party submitting a witness statement may request the attendance of the witness at the hearing;[174] and
(c) the parties may request permission from the tribunal to call their own witnesses when not required for cross-examination by another party.[175]

Article 8.1 of the IBA Rules gives each party an express right to request a witness to attend an evidentiary hearing and does not limit the category of witness to whom that provision applies. Subject to the tribunal's overall control over who should appear,[176] 7.182

[173] The cases falling into this category appear to have been investment arbitrations conducted under the ICSID Convention Arbitration Rules or the UNCITRAL Rules.
[174] The cases falling into this category are said to have been conducted under various arbitration rules.
[175] Menaker and Davies (n 72) 139–47.
[176] IBA Rules (n 1) Article 8.2.

Article 8.1 says in terms that a witness shall appear at the hearing if the attendance of that witness 'has been requested by *any* party'.[177] Thus, in principle, Article 8.1 permits a party to give notice under Article 8.1 that it requires the attendance of its *own* witness, although it makes no special provision for how this is to be done. The Commentary on the IBA Rules supports this interpretation.[178] However, in practice, and unless there are questions that the tribunal wishes to put to the particular witness, it is open to a tribunal to exclude such witness on the basis that the evidence that they can offer is already contained in the witness statements.[179] These issues are discussed further at Chapter 11.[180]

J. The Unwilling Witness

4.9. If a Party wishes to present evidence from a person who will not appear voluntarily at its request, the Party may, within the time ordered by the Arbitral Tribunal, ask it to take whatever steps are legally available to obtain the testimony of that person, or seek leave from the Arbitral Tribunal to take such steps itself. In the case of a request to the Arbitral Tribunal, the Party shall identify the intended witness, shall describe the subjects on which the witness's testimony is sought and shall state why such subjects are relevant to the case and material to its outcome. The Arbitral Tribunal shall decide on this request and shall take, authorize the requesting Party to take or order any other Party to take, such steps as the Arbitral Tribunal considers appropriate if, in its discretion, it determines that the testimony of that witness would be relevant to the case and material to its outcome.

1. Introduction

7.183 A tribunal has jurisdiction only over the parties to the arbitration. Therefore, there may be limits to the steps that it can take to compel a witness to give evidence.[181] Article 4.9 of the IBA Rules provides a practical mechanism by which a party desiring to call a reluctant witness can seek active engagement from the tribunal in the taking of available

[177] ibid Article 8.1 (emphasis added).

[178] Commentary on the IBA Rules (n 19) 17 makes the point that Article 8.1 aligns the IBA Rules to current best practice 'according to which witnesses appear only if cross-examination has been requested *or the party presenting the testimony wishes to do so by means of live testimony rather than written statements alone*' (emphasis added). Even against this background, we suggest that if the live evidence of the witness concerns only peripheral matters not material to outcome of the case, then the opponent party may wish to make submissions on costs should the attendance of the witness add significantly to hearing time or other costs (eg interpreters).

[179] In principle, a witness should not be allowed to supplement its evidence during oral examination.

[180] Chapter 11 paras 11.26–11.42.

[181] See further Judith Levine, 'Can Arbitrators Choose Who to Call as Witnesses? (and What Can Be Done if They Don't Show Up?)' in Albert Jan Van den Berg (ed), *Legitimacy: Myths, Realities, Challenges* (Kluwer Law International 2015) 346 (hereafter 'Levine'). Levine includes reference to national law provisions that may mitigate this position. For example, she cites the example of US Federal Arbitration Act 9 USC, s 7 (hereafter 'US FAA'), which provides that arbitrators may 'summon in writing any person to attend before them as a witness'.

steps—including seeking the assistance of a national court—to make this possible. This is in contrast to most institutional rules, which contain little or no express provision for this situation.[182]

Each party is responsible for presenting at the hearing the witnesses upon whose evidence that party wishes to rely. This is a natural corollary of the obligation of a party to prove the facts underpinning its claim or defence. In practical terms, this means that the relevant party will organize the taking of a witness statement and underwrite any costs associated with the attendance of the witness at the evidentiary hearing.[183] **7.184**

However, occasionally a witness may refuse to cooperate with a party that would like to present the evidence of that witness to the tribunal. For example, the witness may be a former employee who feels that they have been badly treated, they may feel a loyalty to the other party, or they may simply not wish to become embroiled in a dispute. If the dispute was before a state court the litigant party would almost certainly be able to ask the court to issue an order or subpoena requiring the witness to attend to give evidence. The legal landscape is more complex when the dispute is being heard before an arbitral tribunal because the tribunal's jurisdiction extends only to the parties to the arbitration. **7.185**

Article 4.9 makes provision for two types of application to the tribunal. The first is where a party wishes the tribunal to take active steps to compel the testimony of a witness. The second is where a party wishes to obtain the permission of the tribunal to take active steps itself—perhaps because this is a requirement of a national court from whom it intends to seek assistance, or for other reason—perhaps as a matter of courtesy. **7.186**

2. Requirements for an Application and Order under Article 4.9

In order for a party to make an application to a tribunal under Article 4.9, and for the tribunal to grant relief in the terms provided for in that provision, the applicant must supply the tribunal with the following information: **7.187**

(a) the identity of the intended witness;
(b) a description of the subjects on which the witness's testimony is sought; and
(c) an explanation as to why such subjects are relevant to the case and material to its outcome.

A tribunal has a discretion, but no obligation, to grant an application under Article 4.9. The tribunal must be satisfied that the evidence of the potential witness is both relevant and material, and that there are steps available to facilitate the testimony of the **7.188**

[182] The terms of some institutional rules will nonetheless provide for discretionary or inherent powers sufficiently wide to cover such a situation should the tribunal wish to exercise them. See, for example, ICC Rules, Article 25.1: 'The arbitral tribunal shall proceed within as short a time as possible to establish the facts of the case by all appropriate means'. See also ICC Rules, Article 25.5; Swiss Rules, Article 24(3); HKIAC Rules, Article 22.3; UNCITRAL Rules, Article 27.3.

[183] Bühler and Dorgan (n 16) 18.

witness that the tribunal considers to be appropriate to be taken in the circumstances of the particular arbitration. Article 4.9 thus provides for a two-pronged approach to the making of a decision by the tribunal to grant the application.

a. Relevant and material

7.189 The applicant must demonstrate to the tribunal that there are good reasons why it is appropriate for efforts to be made to obtain the testimony of the unwilling witness. The applicant should do this by reference to the value of the witness evidence to the tribunal's determination of the issues in the case. As with other types of evidence, the key test will be whether the evidence the witness can offer is both relevant to the case *and* material to its outcome. As mentioned, this benchmark is used consistently within the IBA Rules and is also one of the yardsticks by which a tribunal may decide to exclude evidence (whether document, statement, oral testimony, or inspection) not considered appropriate for admission in the arbitration.[184]

7.190 If strictly interpreted, the requirement that evidence be both 'relevant to the case and material to outcome' is an onerous one. Parties should not assume that all evidence touching upon disputed events will meet the standard required. Parties should focus upon both elements of the requirement when preparing an application under Article 4.9. This may require careful analysis of the issues and evidence already on the record to assess whether the evidence is likely to impact the ultimate outcome of the case. Further guidance on the meaning of 'relevant to the case and material to outcome' can be found in Chapter 6.[185]

7.191 The requirement that the tribunal should be satisfied that the testimony of the witness would be relevant to the case *and* material to its outcome helps to avoid time and costs being wasted in efforts to bring an irrelevant witness before the tribunal.

7.192 Article 4.9 refers expressly to the tribunal's discretion to determine whether the benchmark of relevance *and* materiality is met. The tribunal is the final arbiter on this matter. If the tribunal determines that the evidence sought to be obtained is *not* relevant to the case, or would *not* be material to its outcome, the tribunal should refuse to grant the relief sought.

b. Consideration of available steps

7.193 If the benchmark of relevance and materiality *is* met, the tribunal will have to assess what steps (if any) are available to persuade or compel the witness to provide testimony, and to decide whether the taking of any of those steps is desirable. The tribunal should authorize only 'such steps as the tribunal considers appropriate'.

7.194 As mentioned, Article 4.9 covers two forms of application by a party seeking assistance in obtaining witness testimony—one in relation to action by the tribunal, and the other

[184] See IBA Rules (n 1) Article 9.2(a).
[185] See Chapter 6 paras 6.76–6.146.

relating to proposed action by the applicant party. Importantly, when responding to such an application, a tribunal is not restricted to granting the precise relief sought by the applicant party. It may:

(a) authorize the applicant party to take steps that the tribunal considers appropriate;
(b) require a non-applicant party to take such steps; or
(c) take appropriate steps itself.

The steps taken in each case will differ according to the circumstances of the dispute and may involve the issue of proceedings in state courts. National arbitration laws will differ as to what assistance is available to compel the attendance of a witness, and whether the consent of the tribunal is required before such action may be taken. **7.195**

The tribunal must consider the likely timeline involved in each available step and the impact that it may have on the procedural timetable. If, in exceptional circumstances, the tribunal is prepared to take action itself it will wish to be put in funds to cover the costs of doing so. **7.196**

i. Steps available to the applicant party

The applicant party may be able to enlist direct assistance from state courts. This will generally be the court at the seat of arbitration, or where the witness is resident. Various forms of assistance subject to differing requirements may be available. **7.197**

Many national arbitration laws provide for local court assistance to a party to an arbitration having its seat in that jurisdiction. Article 184 of the Swiss Private International Law Statute (PILS) provides that a party to an arbitration seated in Switzerland may seek the assistance of Swiss courts in taking evidence: **7.198**

> If the assistance of state judiciary authorities is necessary for the taking of evidence, the Arbitral Tribunal or *a party with the consent of the Arbitral Tribunal, may request the assistance of the state judge* at the seat of the Arbitral Tribunal; the judge shall apply his own law.[186]

Section 26 of the Swedish Arbitration Act provides that parties to an arbitration seated in Sweden have the right, with the approval of the arbitrators, to seek the assistance of local courts in taking sworn witness testimony or the production of documents 'as evidence'. **7.199**

Other courts may offer assistance where the hearing is to take place within the jurisdiction. In such circumstances, it is possible that a sympathetic tribunal may agree to hold a hearing in a particular place other than the seat in order to facilitate court-assisted compulsion of a witness. For example, Section 43 of the English Arbitration Act 1996 provides that: **7.200**

[186] Emphasis added.

> A party to arbitral proceedings may use the same court procedures as are available in relation to legal proceedings to secure the attendance before the tribunal of a witness in order to give oral testimony . . .

7.201 The power under Section 43 may be exercised only if the witness is in the United Kingdom and the arbitral proceedings are being conducted in England, Wales, or Northern Ireland.[187] This does not necessarily require the arbitration to be seated in those locations, just that the proceedings are conducted there.

7.202 *Stemcor (S.E.A.) Pte Limited v Mideast Integrated Steels Limited* was a case concerning an arbitration seated in Mumbai. In *Stemcor*, one of the parties wished to cross-examine a witness based in Singapore; that witness refused to come to India for the hearing due to concerns he might be prosecuted or have his passport confiscated. The requesting party obtained leave from the tribunal to seek assistance from the Bombay High Court under Section 27 of the Arbitration and Conciliation Act. The Bombay Court made an order appointing the arbitrator as a court commissioner and directed the team of lawyers, along with the commissioner, to travel to Singapore to record the evidence of the witness.[188]

7.203 Some national courts may offer assistance in the taking of evidence for use in arbitration proceedings taking place outside the jurisdiction. For example, in the United States, Section 1782 28 U.S.C. gives the court the power to order discovery from specified persons 'for use in a proceeding in a foreign or international tribunal'. This provision has mainly been used for the purpose of obtaining documents, but it does extend to orders requiring a person to give evidence. Assistance is available at the request of either a 'foreign or international tribunal' or 'any interested person' in proceedings before the relevant tribunal.[189]

7.204 Under many laws, the consent of the tribunal is a pre-condition of an application by a party to the state court.[190] Article 4.9 provides a mechanism by which a party may seek

[187] In contrast to the steps that will follow a successful application under the English Arbitration Act 1996, s 44 in relation to a witness overseas, the process under English Arbitration Act 1996, s 43 will be relatively straightforward because an order of the English Court should be relatively easy to enforce against a witness within the jurisdiction.

[188] *Stemcor (S.E.A.) Pte Limited v Mideast Integrated Steels Limited*, Arbitration Petition No. 332 of 2018 (Bombay High Court).

[189] The scope and application of 28 U.S.C., s 1782 is the subject of ongoing debate. For further discussion, see Jonathan Blackman and Peter Fox, 'Discovery in Aid of Arbitration under 28 USC 1782' (*The Arbitration Review of the Americas*, 16 August 2017) <https://globalarbitrationreview.com/insight/the-arbitration-review-of-the-americas-2017/1067594/discovery-in-aid-of-arbitration-under-28-usc-1782> accessed 29 November 2018.

[190] See, for example, England: English Arbitration Act, s 43(2), where application may only be made with the permission of the tribunal or the agreement of the other parties, and s 44(4), where the court shall act only on the application of a party or proposed party to the arbitral proceedings (upon notice to the other parties and the tribunal made with the permission of the tribunal or the agreement in writing of the other parties; Hong Kong, in *Vibroflotation AG v Express Builders Co. Ltd* [1995] 1 HKLR 239 (Hong Kong Court of First Instance), the Court held that the arbitral tribunal's approval (under UNCITRAL Model Law on International Commercial Arbitration (as adopted by UNCITRAL on 21 June 1985), Article 27) might be inferred, but added that the better course was to obtain the express approval of the arbitrator. In Switzerland, PILS, Article 184 parallels the UNCITRAL Model Law on International Commercial Arbitration (as adopted by UNCITRAL on 21 June 1985 and as amended by UNCITRAL on 7 July 2006)—(hereafter 'UNCITRAL Model Law'), providing the possibility for parties to an arbitration seated in Switzerland, 'with the consent of the Arbitral Tribunal,' to seek judicial assistance in the 'taking

such permission. The 1999 IBA Rules made provision only for a party to request that the tribunal take action itself.[191] We discuss at Chapter 6 whether the similar provision at Article 3.9 of the IBA Rules imposes an *obligation* on a party to obtain the permission of the tribunal before taking action itself, regardless of whether such prior permission is a requirement of the national law under which assistance is sought.[192] Similar issues arise in relation to Article 4.9. The Commentary on the IBA Rules indicates that the tribunal is the proper arbiter of whether an application to a state court should be pursued. It refers to the right of the tribunal to exercise its discretion to 'refuse the request if it does not consider the potential testimony to be relevant to the case or material to its outcome', thus suggesting that, under Article 4.9, the tribunal's permission is intended to be a pre-condition to the proposed action.[193]

ALC v ALF[194] heard before the Singapore Court is an interesting example of where the **7.205** relationship between the mechanisms provided for at Article 4.9 of the IBA Rules and the powers of a local court came under consideration. *ALC* concerned a domestic arbitration conducted under SIAC rules. By Procedural Order No. 1, the parties adopted the (2010) IBA Rules as guidance on procedural matters. The claimant to the arbitration was not satisfied with the adequacy of the document production given by the respondent and made an application to the arbitrator for an order directing that the respondent obtain sworn statements from two of its employees in relation to the disclosure that had been given. The arbitrator rejected this request because he did not consider it appropriate to require sworn testimony on that issue. Its request for witness statements having been denied, the claimant decided that the relevant employees should attend the evidentiary hearing. However, rather than making an application to the arbitrator for assistance[195] or permission to apply to the court under Article 4.10 of the 1999 IBA Rules (the equivalent of Article 4.9 of the current IBA Rules), the claimant applied for and obtained direct from the Singapore Court a subpoena requiring the employees to attend the hearing to give evidence on matters relating to the respondent's disclosure. The respondent applied to the Singapore Court for that subpoena to be set aside.

of evidence'; in Sweden, Swedish Arbitration Act, s 26 provides that parties to an arbitration seated in Sweden have the right, with the approval of the arbitrators, to seek the assistance of local courts in taking sworn witness testimony or the production of documents. For an interesting discussion on the ability of a party to an arbitration to obtain assistance from the US courts, see John Fellas, 'Using Section 1782 to Obtain Evidence for International arbitration Proceedings' (New York Law Journal, 30 March 2017) <www.law.com/newyorklawjournal/almID/1202782394403/Using-Section-1782-to-Obtain-Evidence-for-International-Arbitration-Proceedings/> accessed 29 November 2018.

[191] 1999 IBA Rules (n 55) Article 4.9.

[192] SeeChapter 6, 6.316–6.322.

[193] Commentary on the IBA Rules (n 19) 18. See discussion at 6.319-6.322 on possible exception to such a requirement.

[194] *ALC v ALF* [2010] SGHC 231 (hereafter '*ALC*').

[195] Procedural Order No. 1 in the arbitration also contained express provision that the arbitrator had power to order a party to use its best efforts to provide the appearance for testimony at a hearing of any person, including one whose testimony has not been offered.

7.206 In the course of its judgment setting aside the subpoena, the Singapore Court made two observations. First, that (among other matters) taking into account the terms of the IBA Rules, it was clear that the parties had contractually agreed on the procedure to be adopted in relation to the calling of witnesses (namely, that an application should first be made to the arbitrator) and the respondent should have followed that procedure.[196] Secondly, that although the right of a litigant to bring all evidence relevant to its case before the court is immutable, in relation to arbitration proceedings, questions relating to the relevance and/or materiality of the evidence sought to be obtained from the recalcitrant witness fall to be decided not by the court, but by the arbitrator as the 'trial judge' with power to determine both the procedure and the substance of the arbitration.[197] In an arbitration in which the IBA Rules have been adopted or applied, this will involve satisfying the tribunal as to the relevance and materiality to outcome of the witness testimony sought to be introduced.[198] This decision is therefore broadly supportive of the regime set out in the IBA Rules by which, to the extent practicable and subject to considerations of due process, evidence put before the tribunal is limited to that which is relevant to the case and material to its outcome, and the tribunal is the final arbiter of whether those criteria have been met and whether steps to pursue the witness are merited.[199]

ii. Steps available to a non-applicant party

7.207 As mentioned, in response to an application under Article 4.9, the tribunal may require any other party to the arbitration to take such steps as the tribunal considers appropriate.

7.208 We think it unlikely in the majority of cases that a tribunal would order a party to the arbitration who is not also a party to the application made under Article 4.9 to issue legal proceedings to compel the testimony of a recalcitrant third-party witness. In the event that it was to do so, the same considerations in relation to available mechanisms would apply as in the case of the applicant party.[200]

7.209 However, legal process may not be the only option. It is possible that there may be more steps open to the non-applicant party than are available to the applicant party. For example, the reluctant witness may be a former employee or independent consultant retained by the non-applicant party over whom the latter has a degree of control or influence. In such circumstances, the tribunal may order the non-applicant party to make a formal request for testimony to the proposed witness, or direct that the non-applicant party use best efforts to obtain the agreement of the witness to offer evidence. [201]

[196] *ALC* (n 194) [28], [34], [42]–[43], [52]–[53], and [56].
[197] ibid [22], [29], and [49]–[51].
[198] IBA Rules (n 1) Article 4.9.
[199] Commentary on the IBA Rules (n 19) 18.
[200] See 7.197– 7.206.
[201] See also Article 4.10 and the commentary on that article that follows.

iii. Steps available to the tribunal

The tribunal may decide that the most appropriate step is action by the tribunal itself. 7.210

Article 4.9 makes clear that the tribunal may only be asked 'to take whatever steps are legally available to obtain the testimony . . . '. In part, this provision acknowledges that the tribunal has no jurisdiction over an individual who is not a party to the arbitration. 7.211

The action that the tribunal proposes to take may include a direct application for assistance to a national court. The Commentary on the IBA Rules makes express reference to the taking of such action by a tribunal (although it notes that in some cases it may be more practical or efficient for the tribunal to instead authorize the applicant party to approach the court itself—for example, where 'the party requesting the evidence was located in that country, spoke the local language or already had local legal counsel'). If assistance is to be sought from national courts, the nature and scope of any assistance that the tribunal can obtain from those courts will be determined by the particular terms of the relevant arbitration laws and/or the relevant court's inherent jurisdiction. 7.212

Some national arbitration laws contain express provision permitting an arbitral tribunal to seek an order from the state court to compel a witness to appear before the tribunal, or for the court to examine the witness itself. In most cases, it will be appropriate to look first to the courts at the seat. If the parties have chosen an 'arbitration-friendly' jurisdiction as the seat of arbitration, the relevant arbitration laws should provide some measure of support and assistance for the arbitral process. For example, in states that have adopted the UNCITRAL Model Law, Article 27 provides that: 7.213

> The *arbitral tribunal* or a party with the approval of the arbitral tribunal *may request from a competent court of this State* assistance in taking evidence. The court may execute the request within its competence and according to its rules on taking evidence.[202]

Article 1(2) of the Model Law provides that its provisions will apply only where the place of arbitration is in the territory of the state. Other examples of where national courts will assist where the arbitration is seated within that jurisdiction include Switzerland (Article 184 of the Swiss PILS)[203] and the United States (Section 7 of the Federal Arbitration Act).[204] 7.214

However, as mentioned, potential witnesses in an international arbitration will frequently be domiciled in a different jurisdiction from that of the seat of arbitration. The courts of the seat may themselves have difficulty in compelling the witness to participate. In theory, a tribunal may therefore have to look to another national court to 7.215

[202] UNCITRAL Model Law (n 190) Article 27 (emphasis added).

[203] *A v B* [2015] ASA Bulletin 2015 919 (Court of First Instance of the Canton of Geneva, 9 February 2015) is an example of a recalcitrant witness being summoned by the state court at the seat of arbitration to attend an arbitration hearing.

[204] US FAA (n 181) s 7.

provide assistance. For example, as mentioned in 7.203, in the United States, Section 1782 28 U.S.C may provide some assistance.

7.216 Despite the express power granted to a tribunal to seek assistance from a state court, in our view a tribunal will be reluctant to make an application itself and will prefer that any application to the appropriate court is made by one of the parties. Support for this view may be found in commentary on the Swiss law provision (mentioned at 7.214) that says:

> The practical relevance of Art. 184(2) PILS, however, has been limited so far. Arbitral tribunals generally are hesitant to apply to state courts for judicial assistance in connection with the taking of evidence and only revert to this possibility as a last resort.[205]

7.217 However, the action open to the tribunal need not be limited to the pursuit of proceedings in a national court. Even if not fully addressed in the applicant-party's application, or any response delivered by the other party, the tribunal may wish to explore with the parties other possible steps available to secure the attendance of the witness on a voluntary basis, rather than by compulsion. Those steps will depend very much on the circumstances of the case and (if known) the reasons for the unwillingness of the witness to offer evidence. For example, in appropriate circumstances, the tribunal might consider simply writing to the potential witness to request their agreement to provide evidence. Although such power should be exercised cautiously, the tribunal has the ability to do so under Article 8.5 of the IBA Rules.[206] Some witnesses may be more willing to cooperate if invited to do so by the tribunal—a neutral in the dispute—rather than one of the parties. Having received an invitation from the tribunal, they may feel more confident resisting an attempt by one of the parties to discourage them from offering evidence, or they may understand better that their evidence is important to the proceedings. They may be reassured by confirmation that any associated expenses they incur will be reimbursed or, if necessary, that the tribunal can provide a letter to their employer explaining why they may need to take time off to attend a hearing.

7.218 Before making any direct contact with a potential witness, it would be prudent for the tribunal to share a draft of the communication with the parties. The tribunal should also ensure that the parties are willing to put in place all necessary practical and logistical arrangements for the witness's attendance, should that individual agree to give evidence.

205 Marc D Veit, 'Chapter 2, Part II: Commentary on Chapter 12 PILS, Article 184 [Procedure: taking of evidence]' in Manuel Arroyo (ed), *Arbitration in Switzerland: The Practitioner's Guide* (2nd edn, Kluwer Law International 2018) para 68.

206 IBA Rules (n 1) Article 8.5 states that '... the Arbitral Tribunal may request any person to give oral or written evidence on any issue that the Arbitral Tribunal considers to be relevant to the case and material to its outcome'. The circumstances and manner in which the tribunal may exercise its powers under IBA Rules (n 1) Article 8.5 are dealt with later in this commentary. See Chapter 11 paras 11.86–11.92.

K. Request for Witness Testimony by the Tribunal

4.10. At any time before the arbitration is concluded, the Arbitral Tribunal may order any Party to provide for, or to use its best efforts to provide for, the appearance for testimony at an Evidentiary Hearing of any person, including one whose testimony has not yet been offered. A Party to whom such a request is addressed may object for any of the reasons set forth in Article 9.2.

Article 4.10 relates to the power of the tribunal to call witnesses on its own initiative and without request by a party. **7.219**

1. Power of the Tribunal to Call Witnesses

Unless the parties have agreed otherwise, Article 4.10 enables a tribunal to order a party to take steps (or use its best efforts) to secure the attendance of a witness at the evidentiary hearing. **7.220**

Witnesses of fact are the responsibility of the parties. Based on an assessment of its own case and that of its opponent, as well as the evidential burden that it must discharge, each party will select its own witnesses and decide the issues on which those witnesses will give evidence. Tribunals will generally play no part in this process. However, occasions may arise when, following a reading of the submissions and/or written evidence, it appears to the tribunal that a witness who may have important evidence to offer has not provided a witness statement and/or is not being called to attend for examination at the evidentiary hearing. **7.221**

An order by the tribunal for the attendance of a witness is more in the civil law tradition of inquisitorial procedures than in the common law tradition of an adversarial process. However, whatever distinctions may exist in relation to national courts, this is not necessarily so in the practice of international arbitration and relevant tribunal powers may be found in the national arbitration laws of both legal traditions. **7.222**

For example, the German Arbitration Law states that the 'arbitral tribunal is empowered to determine the admissibility of taking evidence, *take evidence* and assess freely such evidence'.[207] The English Arbitration Act 1996 contains similar provision. It states at Section 34 that 'the tribunal [shall] decide all procedural and evidential matters, subject to the right of the parties to agree any matter' and that 'procedural and **7.223**

[207] German Arbitration Law, s 1042(4) (emphasis added). See also the Arbitration Law of the People's Republic of China, Article 43: 'The parties concerned shall provide evidence to support their respective claims. Where an arbitration tribunal deems it necessary to collect evidence, it may collect it on its own initiative.'; and the Brazilian Arbitration Act 1996 (as revised in 2015), Article 22: 'A tribunal has the power to compel the production of evidence (documentary or testimonial), which it deems necessary for resolving a dispute'.

evidential matters' include '(g) whether and to what extent the tribunal *should itself take the initiative in ascertaining the facts and the law*'.[208]

7.224 A tribunal's power to take the initiative is also reflected in a number of institutional rules. For example, Article 25(5) of the ICC Rules provides that '[a]t any time during the proceedings, the arbitral tribunal may summon any party to provide additional evidence'. The ICC Secretariat's Guide to the 2012 ICC Rules notes that:

> This provision is most commonly used to order the production of additional documents, *but could potentially be used for any type of additional evidence.* Article 25(5) can be applied at a party's request or on the tribunal's own initiative.[209]

7.225 The power available to the tribunal under Article 4.10 should be exercised cautiously. The tribunal must ensure that there is no perception of unfairness or bias in relation to the choice of witness. Prior consultation with the parties is a good idea, as it will reduce the risk of challenge to the award—for example, on grounds that the parties were deprived of the right to be heard in relation to the introduction of the evidence, or the opportunity to offer other evidence on the topic on which the tribunal wished to hear the witness.

7.226 In some limited circumstances, the tribunal may elect to contact the potential witness directly. As mentioned, Article 8.5 of the IBA Rules makes it clear that a tribunal has the power to do so.[210] However, as with a decision to call the witness, the tribunal should first consult with the parties. If the tribunal does decide to make direct contact, it will need to ensure that the confidentiality of the arbitration process is not compromised, and any communication with a potential new witness will have to be drafted in neutral and circumspect terms.

7.227 In most cases, the tribunal will direct one of the parties to take steps to secure attendance of the witness. Article 4.10 is likely to be of most value where one of the parties has a degree of control or influence over the witness concerned. An obvious example of this is where the witness is an employee or officer of a corporate party.[211] There also may be other situations, eg where the witness is a supplier or professional consultant to one of the parties. Provided the witness values that commercial relationship, it is likely to agree to a request for assistance.

7.228 Depending on the nature of the relationship (if any) between the relevant party and the proposed witness, the tribunal may prefer to direct a party to use 'best efforts' to secure

[208] English Arbitration Act 1996, s 34 (emphasis added).

[209] Jason Fry, Simon Greenberg, and Francesca Mazza, *The Secretariat's Guide to ICC Arbitration* (International Chamber of Commerce 2012) para 3-977 (emphasis added).

[210] Chapter 11 paras 11.86–11.92.

[211] Gary Born notes that the 'classic examples of such witnesses are corporate officers, directors or senior employees of a party to the arbitration'. See Gary B Born, *International Commercial Arbitration* (Kluwer Law International 2009) 1900–02. In the current (2014) edition of that text, Born puts it this way: '. . . where a party fails to offer evidence from an apparently important witness, particularly its own officer or director, tribunals will request or, occasionally, order attendance of the individual(s) at a hearing', see Born (n 38) 2284.

the attendance of the witness rather than ordering it to provide for the witness to attend the evidentiary hearing. For example, where the witness is an employee of a party, the tribunal may be prepared to make an order. Where the witness is an independent third party with whom the party has only an intermittent professional relationship, the tribunal may prefer to direct that party to use 'best efforts' to secure the witness. Such 'best efforts' are likely to comprise practical steps, eg contacting the individual in positive terms, making financial and logistical arrangements for their travel to the hearing, and liaising with the other parties about the timetable for the hearing to ensure that any dates on which the witness is unavailable are accommodated.

The nature of these circumstances in which a tribunal may make an order under Article 4.10 will be fact specific, but publicly cited examples of where a tribunal has found it appropriate to direct the attendance of a witness include: **7.229**

(a) the calling of consultants who, at the request of an expert witness, had created technical simulations forming part of and relied upon in the expert reports.

In this example, the parties were ordered to 'take the measures necessary' to ensure that two of the three consultants appear for cross-examination at the evidential hearing. (A third consultant had ceased providing services to an expert of one of the parties as a result of—it was alleged—pressure applied by one of the other parties to the arbitration. In relation to that individual, the tribunal decided to contact the dismissed consultant to request that he attend the hearing to answer questions the tribunal might consider relevant and that the expert might not be in a position to address).[212]

(b) the calling of individuals who had close involvement in events underlying the dispute, but who were not related to or within the control of the parties.[213]

In this case, after receiving the parties' witness lists, the tribunal informed the parties that, in light of its review of the written submissions, the tribunal would benefit from the testimony of two individuals whom the parties had not presented as fact witnesses. The tribunal considered that testimony from those individuals would help shed further light on the facts of the case and the parties' arguments. The tribunal stated the topics on which it would be interested in hearing the individuals' accounts. Invoking the provisions of an earlier procedural order,[214] the tribunal requested the parties 'to use their best efforts to provide for the appearance for testimony of these two persons at the hearing'.

[212] *Guaracachi America, Inc. and Rurelec PLC v The Plurinational State of Bolivia* (Procedural Order No. 16, 21 March 2013) PCA Case No. 2011-17.

[213] This example is cited in Levine (n 181) 327–28.

[214] The procedural order included the following provision: 'The Tribunal may, after consulting with the Parties at a reasonable time in advance of the hearing, request a Party to make available for testimony at the hearing a witness whose appearance has not been requested by the other Party. The Tribunal may also request the Parties to provide for, or to use their best efforts to provide for, the appearance for testimony of a person for whom no witness statement has been submitted'.

2. Party Objection

7.230 Where, in accordance with its powers under Article 4.10, a tribunal asks a party to secure the attendance of a witness at an evidentiary hearing, the party so requested has a right (also under Article 4.10) to object to that request on any of the grounds set out in Article 9.2 of the IBA Rules.[215] This provision ensures that the otherwise far-reaching power of the tribunal to direct the attendance of a witness is counter-balanced by the right of a party opposing that step to voice its disagreement by reference to the carefully crafted grounds of objection to the introduction of evidence set out in Article 9.2. Those grounds include a situation where the evidence is not sufficiently relevant to the case or material to its outcome, as well as circumstances of commercial or technical confidentiality, legal privilege or impediment, political or institutional sensitivity, and considerations of procedural economy, proportionality, and fairness. These matters are dealt with in Chapter 12.

[215] The same caveat appears in IBA Rules (n 1) Article 8.5.

8

Article 5: Party-Appointed Experts

Article 5 Party-Appointed Experts

1. A Party may rely on a Party-Appointed Expert as a means of evidence on specific issues. Within the time ordered by the Arbitral Tribunal, (i) each Party shall identify any Party-Appointed Expert on whose testimony it intends to rely and the subject-matter of such testimony; and (ii) the Party-Appointed Expert shall submit an Expert Report.

2. The Expert Report shall contain:

(a) the full name and address of the Party-Appointed Expert, a statement regarding his or her present and past relationship (if any) with any of the Parties, their legal advisors and the Arbitral Tribunal, and a description of his or her background, qualifications, training and experience;

(b) a description of the instructions pursuant to which he or she is providing his or her opinions and conclusions;

(c) a statement of his or her independence from the Parties, their legal advisors and the Arbitral Tribunal;

(d) a statement of the facts on which he or she is basing his or her expert opinions and conclusions;
(e) his or her expert opinions and conclusions, including a description of the methods, evidence and information used in arriving at the conclusions. Documents on which the Party-Appointed Expert relies that have not already been submitted shall be provided;
(f) if the Expert Report has been translated, a statement as to the language in which it was originally prepared, and the language in which the Party-Appointed Expert anticipates giving testimony at the Evidentiary Hearing;
(g) an affirmation of his or her genuine belief in the opinions expressed in the Expert Report;
(h) the signature of the Party-Appointed Expert and its date and place; and
(i) if the Expert Report has been signed by more than one person, an attribution of the entirety or specific parts of the Expert Report to each author.

3. If Expert Reports are submitted, any Party may, within the time ordered by the Arbitral Tribunal, submit to the Arbitral Tribunal and to the other Parties revised or additional Expert Reports, including reports or statements from persons not previously identified as Party-Appointed Experts, so long as any such revisions or additions respond only to matters contained in another Party's Witness Statements, Expert Reports or other submissions that have not been previously presented in the arbitration.
4. The Arbitral Tribunal in its discretion may order that any Party-Appointed Experts who will submit or who have submitted Expert Reports on the same or related issues meet and confer on such issues. At such meeting, the Party-Appointed Experts shall attempt to reach agreement on the issues within the scope of their Expert Reports, and they shall record in writing any such issues on which they reach agreement, any remaining areas of disagreement and the reasons therefore.
5. If a Party-Appointed Expert whose appearance has been requested pursuant to Article 8.1 fails without a valid reason to appear for testimony at an Evidentiary Hearing, the Arbitral Tribunal shall disregard any Expert Report by that Party-Appointed Expert related to that Evidentiary Hearing unless, in exceptional circumstances, the Arbitral Tribunal decides otherwise.
6. If the appearance of a Party-Appointed Expert has not been requested pursuant to Article 8.1, none of the other Parties shall be deemed to have agreed to the correctness of the content of the Expert Report.

A. Introduction

8.1 Article 5 of the IBA Rules, supplemented by Article 8 dealing with procedural aspects of oral testimony at the evidentiary hearing, provides a comprehensive framework for use and management of evidence from party-appointed experts.

The sections that follow deal primarily with Article 5. Related provisions found in Article 8 are referenced where appropriate, but will be dealt with in more detail in Chapter 11. Other provisions relevant to the use of evidence from party-appointed experts include the duty to consult set out in Article 2,[1] and the tribunal's power to determine the admissibility, relevance, materiality, and weight of evidence found in Article 9.1.[2] 8.2

Although Article 5 is self-contained, it is important to understand how it corresponds with Article 6 which deals with tribunal-appointed experts. 8.3

There are generally two distinct mechanisms for adducing expert evidence in an arbitration: 8.4

(a) Party-appointed experts, where each party is responsible for the selection and appointment of their own expert; and
(b) Tribunal-appointed experts, where an expert is appointed by the tribunal.

A third approach proposed by German arbitrator Dr Klaus Sachs, and sometimes referred to as 'The Sachs Protocol', avoids the use of either party-appointed or tribunal-appointed experts. Under the Sachs Proposal, the tribunal invites each party to draw up a short-list of candidates who could serve as an expert. After receiving comments from the parties, the tribunal then selects two experts, one from each list, and appoints these experts jointly as an expert team.[3] The proposal was first outlined at the 2010 ICCA Annual Conference in Rio de Janeiro and the extent to which the suggestion will be taken up in international arbitration remains to be seen. 8.5

1. Expertise and the Role of the Expert in International Arbitration

As international arbitration has grown in popularity, so has the size and complexity (both legal and technical) of the cases that are referred to arbitration. Experts may be needed to help the tribunal to understand and/or reach a determination on factual or legal issues presented in the arbitration. When it comes to the selection of individual arbitrators, the relevant experience each has in the particular industry or commercial sector in which the dispute has arisen may be an important factor, but in practice, even with such experience, the tribunal may lack the relevant technical expertise or other specialized knowledge required to decide a case without some assistance from experts. 8.6

The importance a party's legal team attaches to presentation of evidence by party-appointed experts may be affected by the legal tradition of the jurisdiction with which 8.7

[1] IBA Rules, Articles 2.2(a), (b). See Chapter 5.

[2] IBA Rules (n 1) Article 9.1: 'The Arbitral Tribunal shall determine the admissibility, relevance, materiality and weight of evidence.' See Chapter 12.

[3] Klaus Sachs and Nils Schmidt-Ahrendts, 'Protocol on Expert Teaming: A new Approach to Expert Evidence' in Albert Jan van den Gerg (ed), *Arbitration Advocacy in Changing Times* (Kluwer Law International 2011) 135–48.

those representatives are most familiar. It is dangerous to generalize since practice varies considerably even among jurisdictions within each of the common law and civil law traditions. However, the differences that exist may colour the perspective that a party, its legal advisers, and each member of the tribunal, bring to this issue.

8.8 In the common law tradition, parties normally find and appoint their own experts. The party retaining the expert is responsible for preparing instructions to the expert, outlining the issues that the expert should address, and providing the expert with relevant background documents, as well as paying the expert and dealing with related practical issues.[4] Although in some jurisdictions a party-appointed expert has an overriding duty to the court, such an expert is generally treated as a witness for that party. This is reflected in institutional arbitration rules that refer to the testimony of 'witnesses' as including witnesses of fact or expert witnesses.[5]

8.9 In the civil law tradition, the expert is a court appointee, although generally as a result of an application by a party, rather than initiated by the court on its own initiative. In France, for example, the expert is chosen by the judge from a list of experts maintained by the relevant court. Only experts who have been formally recognized as qualified to act in such capacity by the state may act as an expert in French proceedings.[6] The expert will provide specialist evidence for the court on the basis of instructions given by the judge. Although reports from party-appointed experts may be submitted to the court (or tribunal), such evidence will seldom be recognized as expert evidence. This reflects the civil law tradition of attributing little weight to opinions put forward by the parties. The existence of this distinction is reflected in institutional arbitration rules, which generally include separate provisions dealing with tribunal-appointed experts.[7]

8.10 In recent years, the line separating civil law and common law practice has become more blurred. For example, the English Civil Procedure Rules (CPR) include express provisions dealing with the instruction and use of joint experts by the parties and the powers of the court to order their use.[8] However, while the CPR encourage the use of joint experts, their use tends to be confined to less complex, lower-value claims where the use of joint experts is seen as a cost-saving device.[9]

[4] For an analysis of the implications of the contractual relationship of a party-appointed expert to the participants in an arbitration, see Friederike Schäfer, 'Practical Problems Arising from the Contractual Relationship between Expert and Participants in an Arbitration' in Nikolaus Pitkowitz and others (eds), *Austrian Yearbook on International Arbitration 2011* (Manz'sche Verlags- und Universitätsbuchhandlung 2011) 113–27.

[5] See for example the LCIA Rules, Article 20.3; and the SIAC Rules, Rule 25.1.

[6] David Brown, 'Chapter 5. Oral Evidence and Experts in Arbitration' in Laurent Lévy and VV Veeder (eds), *Arbitration and Oral Evidence* (International Chamber of Commerce 2004) 77.

[7] LCIA Rules, Article 21; SIAC Rules, Rule 26.

[8] CPR 35.7-8 and 35 PD 7.

[9] Harry Woolf, *Access to Justice: Final Report to the Lord Chancellor on the Civil Justice System in England and Wales* (Stationery Office Books 1996).Other considerations are also mentioned. Chapter 13 para 19 contained a recommendation that single joint experts should be used whenever the case (or the issue) is concerned with (1) a substantially established area of knowledge; and (2) where it is not necessary for the court to sample a range of opinions. The recommendation resulted in the introduction of CPR 35.7, 'Provisions for the Instruction of a Single Joint Expert in Appropriate Cases'.

The IBA Rules accommodate both legal traditions by incorporating provisions for the use of party-appointed experts (Article 5) and tribunal-appointed experts (Article 6), leaving it to the tribunal and the parties to utilize the provisions most suitable to the particular arbitration.[10] Although the IBA Rules do not favour one type of expert testimony over the other, in practice, parties to international arbitration proceedings will very often rely on party-appointed experts with tribunal-appointed experts being used less frequently.[11] 8.11

On some occasions there may be a need for both party-appointed and tribunal-appointed experts. For example, a tribunal may decide that it is appropriate for the tribunal to appoint an expert to provide evidence going to the merits of a particular technical issue in dispute between the parties. In such cases, party-appointed experts may be used to deal with other issues or, if the issue being dealt with by the tribunal-appointed expert is the only technical issue, the parties may still wish to instruct experts to help them and to comment on the report of the tribunal-appointed expert. 8.12

In practice, the timing and method for presenting expert evidence will be discussed by the parties and the tribunal at an early stage of the arbitration, usually at the first procedural hearing or during the consultation process required by Article 2. That discussion is likely to include consideration of the need for expert evidence, the issues on which expert evidence is required, and whether the evidence should be provided by party-appointed and/or tribunal-appointed experts. In keeping with the overriding objective of the IBA Rules, the tribunal will also wish to consider the impact that different possible approaches to presentation of expert evidence will have on the costs of the arbitration. In appropriate circumstances, and in order to reduce time and costs, the tribunal may wish to encourage the parties to retain a single joint expert.[12] 8.13

2. Development of Article 5

The 1983 IBA Rules provided that witness statements could be delivered by 'a witness of fact' as well as by 'an expert', without any further differentiation.[13] Article 7(g) of the 8.14

[10] In contrast, the Prague Rules on the Efficient Conduct of Proceedings in International Arbitration adopt a default position of a tribunal-appointed expert. Article 6.1 provides that 'At the request of a party or on its own initiative and having heard the parties, the arbitral tribunal may appoint one or more independent experts to present a report on disputed matters which require specialised knowledge'. Article 6.5 provides that the appointment of any expert by the arbitral tribunal does not preclude a party from submitting an expert report by any expert appointed by that party.

[11] See Rolf Trittmann and Boris Kasolowsky, 'Taking Evidence in Arbitration Proceedings between Common Law and Civil Law Traditions: The Development of a European Hybrid Standard for Arbitration Proceedings' (2008) UNSW Law Journal 330, 338.

[12] See *ICC Arbitration Commission Report on Issues for Arbitrators to Consider Regarding Experts* (International Chamber of Commerce 2010) Section D para(v) (hereafter 'ICC Report on Issues for Arbitrators Regarding Experts').

[13] See the IBA Supplementary Rules Governing the Presentation and Reception of Evidence in International Commercial Arbitration 1983, Articles 5.2 and 5.2(c); Article 'Definition of Witness Statement' (hereafter '1983 IBA Rules').

1983 IBA Rules allowed the tribunal to regulate the right of the parties to call expert witnesses and to make provision with regard to their activities and the presentation of their evidence.[14]

8.15 The 1999 IBA Rules introduced detailed provisions relating to both party-appointed experts and tribunal-appointed experts. The commentary to the 1999 IBA Rules notes that many modern arbitration rules refer to party-appointed experts and make express provision for a party to present its own expert witness to give evidence on points at issue. In view of this growing recognition of the notion of party-designated experts, the drafting subcommittee referred to the expansion of the IBA Rules in this regard as a 'welcome improvement'. However, as with other provisions in the IBA Rules, the drafting subcommittee also felt the need to recognize the alternative approach to expert evidence followed in the civil law tradition. As a result, the 1999 IBA Rules introduced two separate articles dealing with expert evidence: Article 5 (party-appointed experts) and Article 6 (tribunal-appointed experts). The commentary to the 1999 IBA Rules notes that, although the appointment of an independent expert witness by a tribunal is more generally followed in the civil law tradition, the practice was becoming more frequent in international arbitration generally. This dual provision is in keeping with the purpose behind the IBA Rules of providing a framework within which lawyers from all legal traditions feel comfortable.[15] However, it should be noted for completeness that the co-existence of provisions for both party-appointed and tribunal-appointed experts in the IBA Rules is sometimes criticized as being an inefficient practice.[16]

8.16 The current IBA Rules retained the structure of the 1999 IBA Rules, but introduced amendments to Article 5 intended to address concerns about the independence of party-appointed experts and to extend the duty of party-appointed experts to cooperate in preparation of their evidence—for example, by seeking to narrow the issues between them.[17]

8.17 In relation to the application of Article 5 and Article 6, it is important to bear in mind that the rival approaches of party-appointed experts and tribunal-appointed experts raise different issues in their operation. These differences are reflected in the different terms of those two articles, and in the areas in which revisions to those provisions have occurred. For example, the 1999 IBA Rules were criticized in respect of the potential for a lack of impartiality of party-appointed experts and the lack of coordination between experts selected by different parties.[18] Provisions addressing these issues of

[14] The tribunal's power to appoint an expert is mentioned in 1983 IBA Rules (n 13). Articles 7(f) and 7(e) also refer to the right of tribunal members to rely on his/her own expertise.

[15] See Chapter 1 for further discussion as to the provenance of these provisions.

[16] The IBA Arbitration Guidelines and Rules Subcommittee, 'Report on the Reception of the IBA Arbitration Soft Law Products' (International Bar Association 2016) para 70 <www.ibanet.org/Document/Default.aspx?DocumentUid=105d29a3-6261-4437-84e2-1c8637844beb> accessed 29 November 2018, with reference to Prof. Dr. Siegried H Elsing, 'Procedural Efficiency in International Arbitration: Choosing the Best of Both Legal Worlds' (2011) ShiedsVZ 114.

[17] Klaus Sachs and Nils Schmidt-Ahrendts, 'Expert Evidence under the 2010 IBA Rules' (2010) International Arbitration Law Review 216 (hereafter 'Sachs and Schmidt-Ahrendts, Expert Evidence').

[18] ibid.

independence and cooperation represent the biggest changes in Article 5 of the current IBA Rules and are addressed in more detail later in this chapter. Concern about the independence of a tribunal-appointed expert is much less likely to arise. The greater risk in the context of Article 6 is that the tribunal will be too reliant on the expert it has appointed. As a result, Article 6 provides a process whereby parties can challenge the tribunal-appointed expert and/or his or her findings. This process is discussed further in Chapter 9.

3. Other Guidelines on the Use of Party-Appointed Experts

An interesting comparator to Article 5 is the CIArb Protocol for Use of Party-Appointed Expert Witnesses in International Arbitration.[19] The Protocol was first issued in 2007. It was structured along similar lines to the IBA Rules and was aligned with those provisions dealing with party-appointed experts. However, in a number of significant respects, highlighted later in the chapter, the CIArb Protocol goes further than the IBA Rules. Unlike the IBA Rules, the CIArb Protocol follows English judicial practice and, perhaps for this reason, has not been widely adopted in international arbitration. **8.18**

B. Is Expert Evidence Required, and If So, on Which Issues?

1. A Party may rely on a Party-Appointed Expert as a means of evidence on specific issues. Within the time ordered by the Arbitral Tribunal, (i) each Party shall identify any Party-Appointed Expert on whose testimony it intends to rely and the subject-matter of such testimony; and (ii) the Party-Appointed Expert shall submit an Expert Report.

1. Assessing the Need for Expert Evidence

It is good practice for the parties and the tribunal to consider at an early stage in the proceedings whether there is any need for expert evidence. In some cases, it is not necessary because a determination of the particular dispute does not require technical or other specialized knowledge. **8.19**

An interesting approach in this respect is that advocated by the ICC Commission Report on Controlling Time and Costs: **8.20**

[19] Chartered Institute of Arbitrators, Protocol for Use of Party-Appointed Expert Witnesses in International Arbitration (hereafter 'CIArb Protocol').

> It is helpful to start with a presumption that expert evidence will not be required. Depart from this presumption only if expert evidence is needed in order to inform the arbitral tribunal on key issues in dispute.[20]

8.21 In some cases, expert evidence may not be necessary because the tribunal has the necessary technical or specialist expertise. The parties may deliberately have selected arbitrators who will be able to understand the relevant technical issues without the need for explanation from a party-appointed expert. However, even in these cases the parties may wish to appoint their own experts, either to help them (and counsel) to understand the technical evidence or in order to take the lead in investigating what can be agreed with the other party. Particular care should be taken in cases where only one or two arbitrators on the tribunal have the relevant technical expertise or specialized knowledge, since to rely on their assessment may be to shut out the remaining arbitrator/s from the decision-making process. As has been highlighted:

> If the dispute involves specialized knowledge . . . and only one member of a three-arbitrator tribunal possesses the required expert knowledge, the situation becomes more complex because of the need to avoid a de facto in camera expertise proceeding. In other words, unless the parties expressly agree, it is neither expected nor recommended that one arbitrator will perform an independent expert investigation or evaluation on which the other arbitrators would rely in making their decision. Many problems exist with this approach, not the least of which is that it reduces the parties' ability to comment on, ask questions about and, if appropriate, challenge what the expert has done.[21]

8.22 Similar considerations may arise in disputes involving issues of foreign law. Where a dispute involves an issue of French law, and the tribunal consists of French lawyers, the tribunal may not need to hear testimony from an expert on French law. In other cases, there may be an issue as to how evidence of applicable law should be adduced. The tribunal and individual parties may have different perspectives. In some legal systems, foreign applicable law must be proven as if it were a fact; in others it is considered to be a matter of law. The existence of contrasting positions on this issue has been usefully summarized as follows:

> Court approaches to ascertaining applicable law vary considerably, at least in theory. For present purposes, it may nevertheless be useful to divide them into three theoretical categories: (i) those in which the court has considerable powers to apply foreign law and to ascertain its contents on its own motion (this is typically the approach followed in civil law systems), (ii) those in which the court is required essentially to rely on the initiative of the parties to plead and prove foreign law as if it were a factual

[20] *ICC Arbitration Commission Report on Controlling Time and Costs in Arbitration* (International Chamber of Commerce 2018) para 62 (hereafter 'ICC Guide to Controlling Costs').

[21] ICC Report on Issues for Arbitrators Regarding Experts (n 12) 33.

matter (this is typically the approach of English-based common law systems), and (iii) those intermediate systems . . . where pleading foreign law primarily rests with the parties and where responsibility with regard to ascertaining its contents is divided between the court and the parties.[22]

These different perspectives may need to be given special consideration in an arbitration context.

For example, in the English courts, foreign applicable law will generally be proven by reference to expert evidence.[23] **8.23**

However, in an arbitration seated in London (or elsewhere) involving parties from different jurisdictions, different approaches may be taken. One party may wish to put its arguments in submissions without adducing expert evidence from foreign lawyers. Another may seek to prove foreign law with reference to expert evidence. The tribunal may or may not regard itself as suitably qualified to deal with the particular 'foreign' law issues involved on the basis of pleadings alone.[24] As a result, the approach to presentation of argument and evidence on foreign law is something best agreed between participants to the arbitration at as early a stage as possible.[25] **8.24**

There are a number of perceived advantages of party-appointed experts. For example, in relation to many technical or scientific issues that arise, there will invariably be differing academic viewpoints. As a result, and even though a professional expert would be expected to refer in his or evidence to the range of available opinion, appointment of a single expert who only represents one of the competing views may result in an imperfect presentation of relevant evidence. In addition, a party-appointed expert can play a useful role in assisting the appointing party prepare its case for the evidentiary hearing.[26] This may extend to providing input on questions to be put to the opponent party's expert (or a tribunal-appointed expert) in cross-examination with a view to stress-testing the expert evidence presented. **8.25**

The ability to use party-appointed experts is also consistent with a party's right to present its case as it wishes. This is a fundamental right, forming part of accepted due **8.26**

[22] 'International Law Association Committee on International Commercial Arbitration Ascertaining the Contents of the Applicable Law in International Commercial Arbitration Report for the Biennial Conference in Rio de Janeiro, August 2008' (2008) 20 Revista Brasileira de Arbitragem 163.

[23] Lord Collins of Mapesbury and others (eds), *Dicey, Morris and Collins on The Conflict of Laws* (15th edn, Sweet & Maxwell 2012) 318–34. But, if there is no expert evidence offered, the court is entitled to treat foreign law as being the same as English law.

[24] Some commentators refer to this as a widely-used approach. See, eg Alison Ross, 'Let Counsel Not Experts Set Out the Law, Donovan argues' (*Global Arbitration Review*, 5 January 2018) <https://globalarbitrationreview.com/article/1152192/let-counsel-not-experts-set-out-the-law-donovan-argues> accessed 10 December 2018. However, a number of authors suggest that a tribunal may come under annulment scrutiny in circumstances where it fails to require proof of the relevant law and acts on the assumption that it knows the law. See Frédéric G Sourgens, Kabir AN Duggal, and Ian A Laird, *Evidence in International Investment Arbitration* (OUP 2018) para 7.06.

[25] See further discussion at Chapter 5 paras 5.68–5.70.

[26] Julian Lew, Loukas Mistelis, and Stefan Michael Kröll, *Comparative International Commercial Arbitration* (Kluwer Law International 2003) para 22-89 (hereafter 'Lew, Mistelis, and Kröll').

process, breach of which might arguably give rise to a justifiable challenge to the resulting award.[27]

8.27 On the other hand, permitting the parties to present expert evidence without any restriction can also have drawbacks. The evidence may be unnecessary, and instructing two party-appointed experts may, in some cases, incur more costs than appointing a single tribunal-appointed expert (or no experts at all). Given that one of the objectives behind the IBA Rules is to provide an 'efficient' and 'economical' process, these are proper issues to consider. Of course, the IBA Rules also refer to the need for a 'fair' process and this will include the right of each party to present its case. These are competing considerations that must be borne in mind when the presentation of expert evidence is discussed between the parties and the tribunal.

8.28 If consensus is reached then preparation and presentation of the expert evidence should be relatively trouble-free. If a party insists on using a party-appointed expert where the tribunal takes the view that such evidence is unnecessary then it should be aware of the risk that the tribunal may exclude oral testimony from that expert, or that the tribunal may place little or no weight on the evidence presented. Likewise, if one party insists on using a party-appointed expert (and thus effectively forcing the opponent party also to use one) in circumstances where the opponent party and the tribunal feel that a single tribunal-appointed expert would make more sense, it is possible that the tribunal may impose some form of costs penalty.[28]

2. The Right of a Party to Present Party-Appointed Expert Evidence

8.29 An issue that arises in relation to the use of party-appointed experts is whether a party may, as of right, submit an expert report prepared by a party-appointed expert or whether leave to do so is required from the tribunal. We first will consider current practice in international arbitration and then the position under Article 5.1.

a. Current practice in international arbitration

8.30 Many national arbitration laws and rules give the parties the right to adduce independent expert evidence without the permission of the tribunal.[29] Even in the absence of express provision, it is widely accepted that a party's right to be given a fair opportunity to present its case includes a right to call independent experts to give evidence.[30]

[27] See further Doug Jones, 'Party-Appointed Expert Witnesses in International Arbitration: A Protocol at Last' (2008) Arbitration International 137, 149–50 (hereafter 'Jones').

[28] For example, by directing that, whatever the outcome of the case, the party that insisted on instructing party-appointed experts should bear all of its own costs in that respect. Such an order would have to be made under the tribunal's powers in relation to costs under the applicable institutional rules since (save in relation to bad faith conduct). The power does not exist under the IBA Rules.

[29] SCC Rules, Article 33; SCAI Rules, Article 25.2; see also *UNCITRAL Notes on Organizing Arbitral Proceedings* (United Nations 2016) para 94 (hereafter 'UNCITRAL Notes').

[30] CIArb Protocol (n 19).

It seems to us that this is the correct starting point, subject to the application of sensible caveats designed to ensure efficiency of process.

However, it is also worth remembering that some legal practitioners (counsel and judges/arbitrators) in a number of common law countries are now trying to encourage the use of single joint experts (historically the preserve of civil law practitioners), not least because parties, hoping to strengthen a weak case, have exhibited a tendency to call multiple experts where perhaps one would have sufficed, or to call an expert where none was needed. This can lead to unnecessary delay and cost that, especially where there is financial inequality between the parties, may also result in a process that is perceived to be unfair.[31] **8.31**

Where permission from the tribunal is required, it may be relatively easy to obtain. An ICC Commission Report notes that tribunals may be reluctant to refuse a party's request to offer expert testimony because of concern that this may be regarded as interference with that party's right to present its case, and that such refusal may expose the arbitral award to the risk of being set aside.[32] The perception of risk may be greater than its substance where the tribunal has exercised its powers reasonably and fairly. Refusal by a tribunal to allow a party to adduce expert evidence does not, in all cases, lead to the setting aside of the award, nor should it. For example, in *Egmatra AG v Marco Trading Corporation*[33] concerning a trade arbitration conducted under the rules of the London Metal Exchange, the losing party sought to vacate the award on the basis of an alleged serious irregularity in that the tribunal had rejected an invitation by that party to permit introduction of expert evidence to assist the tribunal. The tribunal had declined that invitation on the basis that it had the necessary expertise. Article 9.2 of the applicable LME Rules expressly permitted the tribunal to 'allow, refuse, or limit the appearance of witnesses, whether witnesses of fact or expert witnesses'. Counsel for the party seeking vacation of the award suggested that the arbitrators were not experienced in the particular matter at issue. The English Court found that it had heard nothing that supported that conclusion. It noted that the tribunal '[h]aving considered the matter carefully . . . politely said that they did not think they needed such help'. The Court found that there was no serious irregularity and the challenge to the award was rejected. **8.32**

A related factor is that some institutional rules allow the tribunal to limit or exclude expert evidence. For example, Article 20.3 of the LCIA Rules provides that a tribunal 'may allow, refuse or limit the written and oral testimony of witnesses (whether witnesses of fact or expert witnesses)'. The tribunal may consider the evidence to be irrelevant to the issues to be determined, or it may even prefer its own expertise on the point in dispute. Some commentators suggest that the tribunal may go one step further and disregard **8.33**

31 Jones (n 27) 138–39.
32 ICC Report on Issues for Arbitrators Regarding Experts (n 12) Section II.C.
33 [1999] 1 Lloyd's Rep 862.

such evidence—for example, where the tribunal chooses to rely on its own expertise. In those circumstances, the tribunal should exercise caution and take all necessary steps to ensure that the parties have been given a fair opportunity to address the matters on which the tribunal does intend to rely:

> Where expert evidence is adduced, it is quite proper for an arbitral tribunal to reject it and rely on its own skill and experience—it is quite proper for them to employ such knowledge in reaching the decision. However, the arbitral tribunal should not adopt a theory of its own without putting it to the parties for comment for while they are . . . entitled to use their knowledge and expertise to fill gaps in the evidence about matters which will be obvious to them but which might be obscure to a layman . . . they ought to draw to the attention of the witnesses the experience which seems to them to suggest that the evidence given is wrong, and ought not to prefer their own knowledge or experience without giving the witness an opportunity to deal with it.[34]

b. The right of a party to present party-appointed expert evidence under Article 5.1

8.34 Article 5.1 of the IBA Rules provides that a party 'may' rely on a party-appointed expert 'as a means of evidence on specific issues'. There is a significant body of opinion to support the view that Article 5.1 is an express statement of the right of a party to rely on party-appointed expert evidence.[35] Certainly, the Commentary on the IBA Rules suggests that the right of a party to present its own expert witness is a well-established concept. When referring to the fact that modern arbitration rules refer expressly to party-appointed experts, the Commentary notes that 'Most of these rules codify the well-established notion that a party can present its own expert witnesses to testify on the points at issue'.[36] That must be right. Whether it is for the tribunal alone to dictate the precise issues on which expert evidence is required is another question. The fact that Article 5.1 goes on to say that each party is to give notice of the intended subject matter of the expert testimony suggests that the parties have the right to specify those matters, subject to consultation and discussion with the tribunal and opponent party as required by Article 2 of the IBA Rules. The tribunal will decide the date by which the evidence is to be delivered.[37]

[34] Peter Ashford, *The IBA Rules on the Taking of Evidence in International Arbitration: A Guide* (CUP 2013) para 5-2 (hereafter 'Ashford'). With reference to *Dugdale v Kraft Foods* [1976] 1 WLR 1288, 1294–95.

[35] Gary B Born, *International Commercial Arbitration* (2nd edn, Kluwer Law International 2014) 2277; Sachs and Schmidt-Ahrendts, Expert Evidence (n 17) 216; Ashford (n 34) 5-1; Jeffrey Waincymer, *Procedure and Evidence in International Arbitration* (Kluwer Law International 2012) 935–36; Michael McIlwrath and John Savage, *International Arbitration and Mediation: A Practical Guide* (Kluwer Law International 2010) para. 5-209.

[36] 1999 IBA Working Party and 2010 IBA Rules of Evidence Review Subcommittee, 'Commentary on the Revised Text of the 2010 IBA Rules on the Taking of Evidence in International Arbitration' (*International Bar Association*, 2010), <www.ibanet.org/Document/Default.aspx?DocumentUid=DD240932-0E08-40D4-9866-309A635487C0> accessed 6 August 2018 (hereafter 'Commentary on the IBA Rules').

[37] IBA Rules (n 1) Article 5.1(ii).

If this is correct, subject to any mandatory provisions of the *lex arbitri*, Article 5.1 allows each party to adduce evidence from a party-appointed expert without first obtaining the tribunal's permission, but subject always to the tribunal's right to exclude or place restrictions on the presentation of expert evidence on the grounds set out in Article 8.2 and 9.2 of the IBA Rules. **8.35**

As mentioned, the right of a party to appoint an expert under Article 5.1 is broadly consistent with current practice in international arbitration and recognizes the value that party-appointed expert evidence may bring to the proceedings. Like some institutional rules, the IBA Rules also contain certain safeguards designed to permit the tribunal to control oral testimony from a party-appointed expert on whose written evidence a party relies. In particular, Article 8.2 of the IBA Rules provides that the Arbitral Tribunal may limit or exclude the appearance of a witness (which term includes an expert) at an evidentiary hearing if it considers 'such . . . appearance to be irrelevant, immaterial, unreasonably burdensome, duplicative or otherwise covered by a reason for objection set forth in Article 9.2'.[38] It is worth noting that, unless otherwise agreed by the parties, the operation of Article 8.2 means that the tribunal has the final say on whether oral testimony from a party-appointed expert tendering an expert report is ultimately heard. **8.36**

The decision not to hear from an expert (so-called 'gating') has obvious possible advantages. It can shorten the hearing and reduce costs by avoiding the use of duplicate or irrelevant evidence. However, the power to exclude expert evidence will be exercised very cautiously by a tribunal. As mentioned, a refusal to permit the presentation of evidence may constitute (or be elevated by a party to be) a denial of a party's right to fully present its case, leading to a challenge to the award. It may also be more difficult for a tribunal to assess the potential value of expert evidence than it can in relation to fact evidence. **8.37**

It is helpful that Article 8.2 states expressly the circumstances in which the tribunal may restrict or exclude evidence. Those circumstances are consistent with other provisions of the IBA Rules directed at excluding evidence that is unlikely to assist the tribunal in arriving at a determination or that, for other good reasons, it is not appropriate to admit on to the record. **8.38**

If the tribunal does not believe that evidence from a party-appointed expert is necessary but has no wish to exclude the evidence from the record, it may allow the expert report into evidence, but place little reliance upon it. The tribunal will generally retain discretion as to the weight it attaches to the expert evidence.[39] **8.39**

[38] See Chapter 11 paras 11.25–11.42.

[39] IBA Rules (n 1) Article 9.1. See also LCIA Rules (n 5) Article 22.1(vi); HKIAC Rules (n 6) Article 22.2; and SIAC Arbitration Rules (n 5) Rule 19.2.

3. Notification that a Party Intends to Rely on Party-Appointed Expert Evidence

8.40 Article 5.1 stipulates the first step in the procedure for presentation of evidence from a party-appointed expert. It requires a party intending to present such expert evidence in the arbitration to describe:

(a) the identity of the party-appointed expert on whose testimony it intends to rely; and
(b) the subject matter of such testimony.

8.41 In practice, consultation on the procedure by which the admission and presentation of expert evidence is to be managed is likely to have already taken place under Article 2 of the IBA Rules, which includes reference to 'the preparation and submission of Expert Reports . . . ' and 'the taking of oral testimony at any Evidentiary Hearing' as being appropriate topics on which the tribunal may consult the parties at an early stage in the proceedings with the objective of agreeing an efficient, economical and fair process.[40] As part of that consultation process, there may have been discussions on the nature and scope of expert evidence and/or agreement on the date by which the information referred to in Article 5.1 is to be provided.

8.42 The Preamble to the 1999 IBA Rules required a party intending to rely on expert testimony to notify the other party in advance. The Commentary on the 1999 IBA Rules made it clear that such notification should be provided as soon as possible. The current IBA Rules expand on this so that a party intending to rely on party-appointed expert evidence must now disclose the details described at 8.40.

8.43 The introduction of this requirement was dictated by considerations of fairness and in accordance with the principles laid down in the Preamble to the IBA Rules. Those principles include (a) the provision of an 'efficient, economical and fair' process and (b) that 'each party shall be entitled to know, reasonably in advance of any evidentiary hearing or any fact or merits determination, the evidence on which the other Parties rely'.

8.44 Article 5.1 supports achievement of these principles. Provision of the information referred to in Article 5.1 will ensure that no party is taken by surprise in relation to the nature and scope of the expert evidence served by its opponent. It reduces the scope for tactical games designed to keep details of experts hidden until the last possible moment. This is particularly important where, as under the IBA Rules, the parties are entitled to submit expert evidence without permission.

8.45 The notification described in Article 5.1 may also allow each party to make a more informed decision on the nature and scope of its own evidence. For example, the other party may notify an intention to rely on expert evidence in a discipline not considered

[40] IBA Rules (n 1) Articles 2.1 and 2.2(a), (b). See Chapter 5.

necessary by the first party (or vice versa). This may lead to further consultation between the parties. If the exchange of information under Article 5.1 causes any change in either party's list of experts or subject matter for expert evidence, it may be necessary for that party to deliver a revised notice under that provision.

A number of institutional rules contain provisions similar to Article 5.1 encouraging advance notification of the identity of witnesses (including expert witnesses).[41] Even where such provisions are absent, it is reasonable to expect a tribunal to issue a similar direction as part of its general case management of the arbitration and as a means of promoting time and cost efficiency.[42] **8.46**

4. Timing of Delivery of the Article 5.1 Notification

The parties must provide the information described in Article 5.1 '*within the time ordered by the Arbitral Tribunal*'.[43] That deadline is likely to be decided upon by the tribunal during or after consultation with the parties, whether that consultation is conducted pursuant to Article 2 of the IBA Rules or otherwise, and it will very often be recorded in the first procedural order. The tribunal may stipulate that the information specified in Article 5.1 be provided with pleadings/written submissions or on some other date prior to the date for delivery of expert reports. The appropriate procedural timing will vary from case to case. **8.47**

There may be legitimate reasons for having a deferred date for notification of expert information. For example, until submissions have closed it may not be possible to establish the scope of the technical matters in issue between the parties so as to identify what expert evidence is necessary, or the matters upon which expert comment is desirable may not emerge until after document production. **8.48**

5. Timing of Delivery of Expert Evidence

Article 5.1 also states that the party-appointed expert shall submit an expert report '*Within the time ordered by the Arbitral Tribunal*'. That date will be chosen after consultation between the tribunal and the parties as contemplated by Article 2 of the IBA Rules, as will the manner of delivery. As mentioned elsewhere,[44] there are several different approaches. A common approach is for expert evidence to be exchanged between **8.49**

[41] SCC Rules, Article 33(1): 'In advance of any hearing, the Arbitral Tribunal may order the parties to identify each witness or expert they intend to call and specify the circumstances intended to be proved by each testimony'; SIAC Arbitration Rules, 25.1: 'Before any hearing, the Tribunal may require the parties to give notice of the identity of witnesses, including expert witnesses, whom the parties intend to produce, the subject matter of their testimony and its relevance to the issues'.

[42] ICC Guide to Controlling Costs (n 20).

[43] IBA Rules (n 1) Article 5.1.

[44] See Chapter 5 paras 5.71–5.76.

the parties at the same time.[45] Simultaneous exchange tends to keep the evidence focused on the matters that the relevant party and its expert regard as being material to the case without reference to what is said by the opponent's expert. While there are no fixed rules, delivery is often sequential where memorials are used. The party going first has a blank slate, while the party going second has an opportunity to put its own case while simultaneously rebutting that advanced by its opponent.

8.50 Whether simultaneous or consecutive exchange of evidence is more appropriate will depend on the facts of the case. Unlike fact evidence, where witnesses of fact ought generally to know what they have to say on a particular issue of fact between the parties without benefit of the other side's witness statements, depending on the purpose for which the expert evidence is required, consecutive delivery may sometimes be most appropriate. For example, if expert forensic accountants are to be instructed to address the claimant's quantum claim then, depending upon the particularity with which the claim is articulated in the pleadings or submissions, the respondent's expert may need to see that claim, and the expert accounting evidence that supports it, before writing a report identifying flaws in the claim. The parties ought to be able to reach agreement on such matters, but if not, the tribunal will have to decide on the correct approach to be followed. The UNCITRAL Notes on Organizing Arbitral Proceedings make express reference to the need for the tribunal to consider whether expert reports should be filed consecutively or simultaneously, and whether such submission should be made along with a statement of claim or statement of defence.[46]

8.51 The tribunal will generally address issues of timing and sequence during its preliminary discussions with the parties on the procedural timetable whether pursuant to Article 2 or otherwise.

C. The Content of the Expert Report

5.2 The Expert Report shall contain:

(a) the full name and address of the Party-Appointed Expert, a statement regarding his or her present and past relationship (if any) with any of the Parties, their legal advisors and the Arbitral Tribunal, and a description of his or her background, qualifications, training and experience;

(b) a description of the instructions pursuant to which he or she is providing his or her opinions and conclusions;

(c) a statement of his or her independence from the Parties, their legal advisors and the Arbitral Tribunal;

[45] The CIArb Protocol (n 19) mentioned at 8.18recommends that expert reports and the reply expert reports should be exchanged simultaneously.

[46] UNCITRAL Notes (n 29) para 99.

(d) a statement of the facts on which he or she is basing his or her expert opinions and conclusions;

(e) his or her expert opinions and conclusions, including a description of the methods, evidence and information used in arriving at the conclusions. Documents on which the Party-Appointed Expert relies that have not already been submitted shall be provided;

(f) if the Expert Report has been translated, a statement as to the language in which it was originally prepared, and the language in which the Party-Appointed Expert anticipates giving testimony at the Evidentiary Hearing;

(g) an affirmation of his or her genuine belief in the opinions expressed in the Expert Report;

(h) the signature of the Party-Appointed Expert and its date and place; and

(i) if the Expert Report has been signed by more than one person, an attribution of the entirety or specific parts of the Expert Report to each author.

1. Introduction

Article 5.2 lays down a number of requirements concerning the content of a party-appointed expert report submitted under the IBA Rules. It substantially expands on the requirements set out in the 1999 IBA Rules. **8.52**

The requirements of Article 5.2 are driven by various objectives. Some of the requirements concern necessary formal requirements (such as name and address) and some of them are directed at safeguarding the independence of the expert. There are also a number of provisions aimed at making the expert report capable of verification—ie that all parties (and the tribunal) should be in a position to be able to test the correctness of the conclusions drawn by the expert by reference to the matters relied on. For example, there is a requirement that the expert describe the methodology used[47] and the facts on which the expert's conclusions are based.[48] Even if counsel for the other party or the tribunal do not have sufficient knowledge or expertise to test the conclusions themselves, the opinion should contain all the necessary information so that an expert instructed by another -party can review the report and confirm or question the findings made. **8.53**

The opening line of Article 5.2 includes the words '*shall contain*'. As a result, where the IBA Rules have been formally adopted, in the absence of agreement between the parties or an order of the tribunal to the contrary, these requirements must be met in relation to any expert report submitted. **8.54**

[47] IBA Rules (n 1) Article 5.2(e).
[48] ibid Article 5.2(d).

8.55 The IBA Rules do not provide any sanction for non-compliance with the requirements in Article 5.2. In practice, tribunals will approach this issue on a case-by-case basis and according to the severity of the breach.[49]

8.56 If the non-compliance is material, the tribunal may rule—most likely on an application from the opposing party—that the expert evidence the party is seeking to introduce is not admissible, or that it must be corrected. This approach may be justified where the defects in the expert report raise questions as to its completeness or value. For example, if the expert has failed to describe the methodology used to arrive at his or her conclusions, or to identify the facts/documents relied upon in reaching the stated conclusions. An alternative approach would be for the tribunal to admit a non-compliant expert report into evidence with the caveat that the omissions may affect the weight attached to it by the tribunal.

8.57 As mentioned, Article 5.2 says that the expert report 'shall' contain the stated information. The drafters of the IBA Rules intended Article 5.2 to be mandatory and must have regarded all of the listed content as being sufficiently important to include in Article 5.2. Furthermore, compliance with the IBA Rules is squarely within the parties' control. If upon receipt of a draft expert report a party finds that it does not conform to the provisions of the IBA Rules, the party can ask its expert to amend the report to include the missing details. It is obviously good practice to let the expert know the requirements of the IBA Rules at the time of instructing the expert, so that the requirements of Article 5.2 are kept well in mind while drafting.

2. Matters to Be Included in the Expert Report

8.58 Article 5.2 is useful in providing a form of checklist for the content of an expert report. In broad terms, the requirements described in Article 5.2 reflect good practice as to the form and substance of an expert report.

a. Details of the expert, expertise, and any relationship with the parties/tribunal

> **5.2 (a) the full name and address of the Party-Appointed Expert, a statement regarding his or her present and past relationship (if any) with any of the Parties, their legal advisors and the Arbitral Tribunal, and a description of his or her background, qualifications, training and experience.**

8.59 Article 5.2(a) incorporates three distinct requirements on content. The expert report must contain:

(a) the name and address of the party-appointed expert;
(b) details of his or her relationship/s with any of the parties, their legal advisors, and the tribunal; and

[49] See, eg ICC Report on Issues for Arbitrators Regarding Experts (n 12) Section II.G.1.

(c) a description of the background, qualifications, training, and experience of the expert.

The first requirement is straightforward. It simply requires the expert to give his or her full name and address. The name and address will help the parties and the tribunal to identify the expert and to see whether they have had any previous dealings with the expert. It is very common, especially among professional experts, for the address to be a business, rather than home, address. 8.60

If the tribunal has not ordered earlier disclosure of the identity of each party's experts as contemplated under Article 5.1, delivery of expert reports by the appropriate deadline may be the first time that each party finds out who the experts for the other party will be. This is in contrast to the position under the 1983 IBA Rules, which made provision for the identity of witnesses (including experts) to be disclosed in 'Introductory Submissions'[50] (defined widely to include any form of pleading or submissions). 8.61

The second requirement concerns any (past or present) relationship the expert may have with one of the parties, their counsel, or with any member of the tribunal. Article 5.2(a) of the 1999 IBA Rules only required the expert to disclose a relationship with any of the parties. The expanded provision contained in the revised Article 5.2(a) was intended to foster transparency and confidence in the independence of the expert. 8.62

In formulating these new provisions, the drafting subcommittee adopted a similar approach to that applied in the IBA Guidelines on Conflicts of Interest[51] designed for use by arbitrators—namely, to employ a mechanism of enhanced disclosure of connections in order to aid transparency and strengthen the perceived (and, we assume, encourage the real) independence of experts from the parties, their legal advisors, and the tribunal.[52] However, unlike the IBA Guidelines on Conflicts of Interest, which set out general standards and list specific situations with an indication as to whether they warrant disclosure or disqualification of an arbitrator, the IBA Rules do not define the nature of the relationships that should be disclosed or provide any guidance as to the extent of the disclosure required. 8.63

For example, under the Guidelines on Conflicts of Interest, relationships not listed in the 'Red List' or 'Orange List'[53], or falling outside the time limits used in some of the 8.64

[50] 1983 IBA Rules (n 13) Article 3 and the definition of 'Introductory Submission'. 1983 IBA Rules (n 13) Article 6 (Scope of proceedings) also provided that whenever terms of reference are drawn up they shall contain a list of the witnesses who will be called upon to give evidence at the hearing, and the issues upon which each witness will testify.

[51] *IBA Guidelines on Conflicts of Interest in International Arbitration* (International Bar Association 2014) (hereafter 'IBA Guidelines on Conflicts of Interest').

[52] Christopher Harris, 'Expert Evidence: The 2010 Revisions to the IBA Rules on the Taking of Evidence in International Arbitration' (2010) International Arbitration Law Review 212, 213 (hereafter 'Harris').

[53] The IBA Guidelines on Conflicts of Interest (n 51) uses a traffic light system categorizing circumstances into red, orange and green lists.

situations cited are generally not subject to disclosure. In contrast, Article 5.2(a) requires an expert to disclose *any* present or past relationship to the parties, legal advisors, or the tribunal. The fact that the expert may have worked with a member of the tribunal more than 30 years ago makes no difference to the obligation to disclose under Article 5(2)(a).

8.65 Where there is a relationship, that relationship should be disclosed. The question of whether the expert has any pre-existing personal or professional relationships with any of the parties, counsel, or individual members of the tribunal is one that the party instructing the expert is likely to have canvassed with the expert when first considering them for appointment. That party generally will hope that there are no such relationships. However, even if there are, if the party is satisfied that the relationship is too old or remote for it to be of any consequence, it may nonetheless instruct the expert. However, this is not without some risk. The other party may attempt to undermine the credibility of the expert by reference to the disclosure. Depending on the nature of the relationship and whether the expert has had any involvement in the events leading up to the dispute, these circumstances may affect the weight that the tribunal attributes to the evidence.

8.66 There may be situations where it is necessary, for various reasons, for the expert to be someone with close ties to the instructing party. For example, where the dispute has occurred between parties working in a very specialist niche industry, a party employee or consultant known to the party may be the best qualified person to speak to the technical issues in dispute. Another situation known to us is where a forensic accountant employed by counsel to one of the parties had supported that party through early quantification of the opponent party's quantum claim, and the associated document production process, and for reasons of economy, was appointed to provide the expert evidence for that party. If the expert has a connection to the appointing parties, a convincing statement of the expert's knowledge and expertise may help to enhance their credibility in circumstances where, because of that connection, the tribunal might otherwise be cautious about relying on the opinion of that expert.

8.67 A judgement about disclosure may have to be made where a relationship exists (or existed) between the expert and a company or person connected to a party. Strictly speaking, Article 5.2(a) is confined to relationships with a defined circle of participants. 'Party' is defined narrowly in the IBA Rules as '*as a party to arbitration*'. As a result, it is arguable that any past or present relationship with a subsidiary or affiliate of a party need not be disclosed. Of course, an existing relationship with an affiliate or subsidiary of a party is just as capable of influencing an expert's conduct as is a relationship with a party. However, it may be that the drafting subcommittee felt that there were difficulties around establishing exactly where the line should be drawn—ie how far removed the relationship must be on paper before it need not be disclosed. In addition, confidentiality issues may arise if an expert is expected to disclose work undertaken for related third parties.

However, even where the relationship with the third party is an old one, or appears insignificant, the prudent course is often to mention it in the opening paragraphs of the report. This will protect the expert (and the party tendering that expert) from criticism or tactical challenge by the other party. **8.68**

If the relationship is with a member of the tribunal (even if it is historic or remote), the transparency encouraged by Article 5.2(a) will avoid the risk of the tribunal later being compromised with potential adverse consequences in time and cost. **8.69**

Lastly, the expert report must also include a description of the expert's background, qualifications, training and experience. This is very important, as the role of the expert is to opine on specialist matters beyond the expertise of the tribunal in order to assist it to form an opinion on those matters.[54] **8.70**

The tribunal has no say in the choice of a party-appointed expert. S/he is chosen by one of the parties. However, if the evidence is to be of value to the tribunal, the tribunal needs to be provided with the information necessary for it to assess whether the expert evidence comes from somebody with expertise/specialist knowledge in the relevant field. It is the responsibility of each party (and that party's counsel) to make sure that the expert is properly qualified. The qualifications and experience of the expert will be an important factor for the tribunal in considering what weight to attribute to the expert's testimony. If the expert is inadequately qualified in the field about which s/he is opining, this is a point that counsel for the other party is likely to take up on cross-examination of that expert. **8.71**

b. A description of the instructions provided to the expert

> **5.2(b) a description of the instructions pursuant to which he or she is providing his or her opinions and conclusions.**

Article 5.2(b) requires the expert to describe in the report the instructions given to him or her by the appointing party. This is another new provision introduced by the current IBA Rules in order to foster transparency and independence. Requiring the expert to describe the instructions given reduces the risk of a party seeking to influence the opinion of the expert. **8.72**

The importance of this provision cannot be overstated. The opinion of an expert can be influenced significantly by the instructions given—for example, by the assumptions that the expert is asked to make, or by the documents and other information provided. **8.73**

[54] Lew, Mistelis, and Kröll (n 26) paras 22–80.

A statement of the instructions is essential to enable the other party and its counsel to evaluate and test the expert's conclusions.

8.74 The expert is only required to describe the instructions given. There is no obligation for a copy of the instructions to the expert to be provided or annexed to the report as is required, eg under the English Civil Procedure Rules. It has been suggested that this is one of the areas in which compromise was required in order to gain the widest possible acceptance of the revisions made in the current IBA Rules.[55]

8.75 The approach adopted in the IBA Rules avoids to some extent the complex issue of discoverability of communications between counsel- and party-appointed experts in international arbitration in circumstances where formal international guidelines are rare and national rules vary.[56] By encouraging transparency around the nature of the instructions given, the cases in which disclosure of counsel/expert communications is necessary are likely to be rare. The CIArb Protocol suggests that disclosure of such communications should not be ordered without good cause:

> All instructions to, and any terms of appointment of, an expert shall not be privileged against disclosure in the Arbitration, but the Arbitral Tribunal shall not, in relation to the instructions or terms of appointment:
>
> (a) order disclosure of the instructions or appointment or any document relating thereto; or
>
> (b) permit any questioning of the expert about such instructions or appointment unless it is satisfied that there is good cause.[57]
>
> In the meantime, the drafts of expert opinion and working papers should be privileged.[58]

8.76 The CIArb Protocol goes further than Article 5.2(b) in requiring disclosure of the 'basis of remuneration of the expert'. Some commentators see this as information that is plainly relevant to the independence of the expert, particularly if the remuneration of an expert is based on the outcome of the case.[59] Such factors may be relevant to the statement of independence required from an expert under Article 5.2(c). Although the Commentary on the IBA Rules makes it clear that receiving payment for services as an expert (eg an hourly rate for time spent) does not preclude 'independence', it appears likely that a financial stake (eg a 'success fee') in the outcome of the case might do so.

[55] Harris (n 52).

[56] Paul D Friedland and Kate Brown de Vejar, 'Discoverability of Communications Between Counsel and Party-Appointed Experts in International Arbitration' in Albert Jan van den Berg (ed), *Arbitration Advocacy in Changing Times* (Kluwer Law International 2011) 160–78.

[57] CIArb Protocol (n 19) Article 5(1).

[58] ibid Article 5(2).

[59] Harris (n 52) 213.

c. Statement of independence

5.2 (c) a statement of his or her independence from the Parties, their legal advisors and the Arbitral Tribunal.

i. Introduction

Article 5.2(c) requires a statement of the expert's independence from the parties, their legal advisors, and the tribunal. This complements Article 5.2(a), which requires disclosure of any and all relationships an expert may have with the parties, their legal advisors, and the tribunal. In order to satisfy this requirement, an expert is required to evaluate any such relationships and confirm that—whether or not those relationships exist—s/he is able to provide an independent opinion. As explained in the Commentary: **8.77**

> While the former requirement requires disclosure, satisfaction of the latter requirement requires the expert to evaluate any such relationships and attest that he or she is 'independent', for example in the sense that he or she has no financial interest in the outcome or otherwise has relationships that would prevent the expert from providing his or her honest and frank opinion. Receiving payment for services as an expert does not preclude 'independence'. Article 5.2(c) is intended to emphasise the duty of each party-appointed expert to evaluate the case in an independent and neutral fashion rather than to exclude experts with some connection to the participants or the subject-matter of the case.[60]

Article 5.2(c) is a new provision. As highlighted, one of the main concerns expressed with regard to party-appointed experts prior to 2010 was that their evidence may be compromised by a lack of independence and impartiality.[61] The IBA Rules drafting subcommittee sought to address these concerns by requiring a statement of independence and highlighting the need for the party-appointed expert to be independent not only from the parties, but also from the parties' legal advisors and the tribunal. **8.78**

ii. Independence versus impartiality

Article 5.2(c) of the IBA Rules refers only to 'independence'. It makes no mention of other terms that appear in some institutional rules, such as 'impartiality' and 'objectivity'.[62] It has been suggested that the provision in the IBA Rules conflates such terms.[63] In our view, although Article 5.2(c) refers only to independence, the expert should also be impartial. **8.79**

In substance, independence is an objective factor emphasizing a lack of ties (professional, social or other) between the expert and those appointing him/her. Impartiality is **8.80**

[60] Commentary on the IBA Rules (n 36) 19.

[61] Sachs and Schmidt-Ahrendts, Expert Evidence (n 17) 216.

[62] LCIA Rules, Article 21.2; UNCITRAL Rules, Article 29 specifically require the expert to be both impartial and independent. The CIArb Protocol (n 19) Article 4(1) requires impartiality, independence, and objectivity.

[63] See further Mark Kantor, 'A Code of Conduct for Party-Appointed Experts in International Arbitration: Can One be Found?' (2010) Arbitration International 323.

a state of mind as to whether the expert can approach the evidence in a neutral fashion with no bias or favouritism shown towards those instructing him/her. Arguably, it is possible to be dependent, but impartial. Equally it is possible to be independent, but partial. However, at the end of the day, it is impartiality, ie mental objectivity, that matters.

8.81 It is for this reason that some national laws and arbitration rules impose only a requirement of impartiality on arbitrators, eg Section 24 of the English Arbitration Act, which provides that an arbitrator may be removed where circumstances exist that give rise to that are justifiable doubts as to his/her 'impartiality'. Independence is not mentioned.

8.82 However, impartiality, as a state of mind, is very difficult to detect, whereas independence can at least be judged by reference to tangible parameters. As a result, a number of institutional rules and arbitration laws often include a requirement for experts to be both independent and impartial.[64]

8.83 Only in limited instances is independence mentioned on its own, either in relation to experts or arbitrators.[65] However, there are some arbitration rules that do not contain any express requirement that the expert be either impartial or independent.[66]

8.84 The Article 5.2(c) focus on independence alone has attracted some criticism:

> In opting to focus more strongly on the independence of the expert than his or her impartiality, the IBA subcommittee has preferred the (possible) outward manifestation of partiality over tests which focus on the arguably more relevant but less tangible state of mind of the expert. Whilst that is legitimate per se, and is indeed the route taken by some notable institutional rules and arbitration laws, the disclosure of connections in this way is a rather blunt instrument, as it is the quality of those connections which is really of importance. Indeed, there is an inherent tension between the concept of independence and a relationship of retainer, such as the relationship between a party and the expert it appoints and pays.[67]

8.85 Furthermore, it is also recognized that there are significant differences in what is meant by 'impartiality' when talking about an expert, and when talking about an arbitrator.[68]

---

[64] LCIA Rules, Article 21.2 and UNCITRAL Rules, Article 29 specifically require the expert to be both impartial and independent.

[65] Swiss Private International Law Statute, Article 180(1); ICSID Arbitration Rules, Article 25. This was also the only requirement in ICC Rules 1998, Article 7(1), but the current ICC Rules, Article 11(1) refers to both independence and impartiality.

[66] Eg CIETAC Rules, Article 44; HKIAC Rules, Articles 22 and 25.

[67] Harris (n 52) 213.

[68] This is a topic discussed in ICSID decision *Bridgestone Licensing Services Inc. and Bridgestone Americas Inc. v The Republic of Panama* (ICSID Case No. ARB/16/34, Ruling on Claimant's application to remove the Respondent's expert witness as to Panamanian law, para 14). In that case, the tribunal accepted that a party-appointed expert for the respondent had inadvertently, in breach of Article 5.2(a) of the IBA Rules, failed to disclose in his report that he had engaged in earlier limited communications with the claimant's counsel in respect of the same matter. In reliance (inter alia) on Article 9.2(b) of the IBA Rules, the claimant sought to have the expert removed on the basis that, during the communications between the expert and the claimant's counsel, the expert had received confidential information that precluded him from acting for the respondent. Following analysis of the communications the tribunal found that it did not. The ruling discusses issues of independence and impartiality as they relate to party-appointed experts.

In particular, that an expert is not expected to remain distant from the party appointing him or her, and that a strong opinion on an issue does not mean that an expert is not qualified to perform the role assigned to him as it might in relation to an arbitrator who might be perceived as having prejudged a matter without having heard from the parties. As has been pointed out by Sir Bernard Rix, a retired English Lord Justice of Appeal:

> A party-appointed expert is not forbidden to speak to his appointing party save in the presence of the other party. A party-appointed expert may be chosen for the very reason that he adheres to a particular scientific, academic or professional point of view. As long as he is sincere in that point of view, and that point of view is a respectable one, there can be no complaint about that. So I suppose that in this context talk of impartiality is emphasising a number of slightly different things. It emphasises above all, I think, a lack of partisanship. Impartiality here means above all an eschewal of partisanship or if you like an adherence to neutrality. The tribunal is entitled to feel confident that, given the same set of facts, the expert would express the same opinion by whichever side he is appointed.[69]

iii. Independence from legal advisers

It seems likely that the objective behind requiring a statement of independence of an expert from the instructing party's 'legal advisors' in Article 5.2(c) was to discourage parties from selecting experts who have a long-standing business relationship with counsel in the proceedings, or who otherwise have a high financial dependency on the relationship with counsel. For example, if a law firm regularly instructs one particular expert for evidence on quantum work, there may be a concern that the expert will be keen to get the right result on the case because this will help to maintain a profitable workflow from the law firm. **8.86**

The inclusion of a reference to 'legal advisors' at Article 5.2(c) has attracted some criticism.[70] However, the drafting subcommittee must have considered that the relationship between counsel and the expert to be sufficiently important to include it in the IBA Rules. **8.87**

iv. The expert's duty to the tribunal

It is generally accepted that, although a party-appointed expert is retained by the parties, s/he has a duty to assist the tribunal. However, there is no explicit reference to such a duty in the IBA Rules. Provision for operation of such a duty is referred to elsewhere and may be adopted by the parties. For example, the CIArb Protocol includes a specific statement to that effect in the following terms that is required to be provided in the expert's report: **8.88**

[69] Sir Bernard Rix, 'The Ethical Duties of Experts to the Tribunal' (2014) Arbitration 290, 291–92.

[70] Ashford (n 34) 5–7; Harris (n 52) 213.

> I understand that my duty in giving evidence in this arbitration is to assist the arbitral tribunal decide the issues in respect of which expert evidence is adduced. I have complied with, and will continue to comply with, that duty.[71]

8.89 We suggest that it is sensible practice for an expert to include such as statement in his/her report, even if not required to do so under any applicable set of arbitration rules.

8.90 The CIArb provision is focused on an expert's obligation to provide an opinion that will assist the tribunal in its determination on the relevant technical issues, the subtext being that in his/her opinion the expert should be neutral and should not be seeking to advance the position of the appointing party. A further useful benchmark question is contained in the UK Civil Justice Council civil claims guidance.[72] When acknowledging the nature of an independent opinion, the Protocol states that 'a useful test of "independence" is that the expert would express the same opinion if given the same instructions by another party'.[73]

v. Additional obligations with which the expert may need to comply

8.91 In addition to requirements contained in the IBA Rules or other applicable rules or protocols, an expert witness may be bound by professional codes of conduct. Many experts—eg accountants, surveyors, and engineers—will be members of professional bodies with codes of practice that impose ethical duties covering all aspects of their professional activities, including giving evidence as a party-appointed expert.

8.92 There are also associations for professional expert witnesses, which have promulgated their own codes of practice. For example, the Academy of Experts has a Code of Practice for Experts that is to be followed by all members of the Academy. The Code of Practice sets a number of 'minimum standards of practice' that should be maintained by all its members

d. Statement of facts on which the expert opinion is based

> **5.2(d) a statement of the facts on which he or she is basing his or her expert opinions and conclusions.**

8.93 Article 5.2(d) requires the expert to set out in his or her report the facts that s/he has relied upon in reaching the opinion and conclusions set out in the report. As mentioned, this requirement is included so that the other experts of like discipline may verify the validity of the opinion expressed by reference to those facts and so that opposing counsel and the tribunal can test the evidence relied on. In addition, if the expert has been provided with an incomplete set of facts by the appointing party, this may affect the

[71] CIArb Protocol (n 19) Article 8(1)(a).

[72] UK Civil Justice Council, 'Guidance for the Instruction of Experts in Civil Claims' (1 December 2014) <www.judiciary.uk/related-offices-and-bodies/advisory-bodies/cjc/cjc-publications/guidance-for-the-instruction-of-experts-in-civil-claims/> accessed 10 December 2018.

[73] ibid para 11.

value of the opinion expressed. For example, if an expert is asked to provide an opinion on whether the quality of raw material supplied was in compliance with the contract standard on moisture content, but is supplied with the wrong contract standard, the opinion on whether the product complied with the contract may be wrong.

Article 5.2(d) is very focused in scope in that it requires an expert to provide only a statement of the facts on which s/he is basing opinions and conclusions. It does not require the expert to state the facts, matters, and documents the expert has considered, but on which his or her opinion is not based. There are advantages and disadvantages to this formulation. On the one hand, it keeps the statement of facts fixed on the matters that have influenced the opinion and which the other party may wish to verify. On the other hand, it may restrict the ability of the other party to carry out a more meaningful evaluation of the report by highlighting any matters that were considered by the expert but (perhaps, in error) not relied upon for one reason or another. Some provisions found elsewhere go further than this. For example, the CIArb Protocol requires an expert to indicate both categories of material. It says that an expert opinion must: **8.94**

> (e) state which facts, matters and documents, including any assumed facts or other assumptions, *have been considered* in reaching the opinion;
>
> (f) state which facts, matters and documents, including any assumed facts or other assumptions, *the opinion is based on*'.[74]

In practice, many experts will provide in their expert report a list of all of the materials that they have considered. An interesting issue arises in relation to documents provided by the instructing party to the expert, but not relied upon, that have not been produced to the other party. The generally held view is that it would be improper to provide materials to an expert that the expert of like discipline has not had the opportunity of seeing, even when the first expert regards them as irrelevant to the issues being considered by the experts. The opponent expert might take a different view on the relevance of those materials. In our experience, it is prudent for counsel to obtain confirmation from an opponent in correspondence that everything provided to the other party's expert has also been made available to all of the other parties. If a party were to refuse to produce such documents to the other side, (whether the arbitration was being conducted under the IBA Rules[75] or otherwise) in our view it would then be open to the other party requesting production to apply to the tribunal for an order directing that they be provided. **8.95**

Individual tribunals may approach the issue in different ways. On one view, in order to ensure fairness between the parties, it is only right that both experts should have the **8.96**

[74] CIArb Protocol (n 19) Articles 4(4)(e) and (f) (emphasis added).

[75] In our view, the IBA Rules would be engaged since they are expressed to govern 'the taking of evidence'—see IBA Rules (n 1), Article 1.1—which we believe would cover the situation mentioned. The IBA Rules Preamble contains the principle that operation of the rules should provide a fair process for the taking of evidence.

opportunity to see the same material, even if the second expert subsequently agrees that it is irrelevant to the issues. If the material is truly irrelevant then, subject to issues of confidentiality and/or cost, it is hard to see why the party with the documents should object to providing them. On the other hand, the test for production under the IBA Rules is that documents should be 'relevant to the case and material to its outcome'. If the first expert to whom the documents have been provided considers them to be irrelevant to issues on which expert evidence is offered, then the tribunal may be minded to hear argument from the parties on whether the documents/categories of document that have been provided are potentially relevant and material or not. Article 6.3 of the IBA Rules suggests that this is an appropriate test to apply in relation to the provision of documents to an expert in the arbitration.[76] In our view it would not be right for the tribunal to decide the issue simply on the basis of the first expert's opinion that the documents have no relevance.

e. The expert opinion/conclusions together with details of methodology and evidence relied upon

5.2(e) his or her expert opinions and conclusions, including a description of the methods, evidence and information used in arriving at the conclusions. Documents on which the Party-Appointed Expert relies that have not already been submitted shall be provided.

8.97 Article 5.2(e) is a key provision and deals with the core elements of the expert report.

8.98 First, it provides that the report should contain the expert's 'opinions and conclusions'. In so doing, it stops short of more expansive formulations found elsewhere. For example, the provisions of the CIArb Protocol require the expert to also:

(h) state which matters the expert has been unable to reach an opinion on;
(i) state which matters (if any) are outside the expert's area of expertise.[77]

8.99 The IBA Rules do not expressly require these matters to appear in the report. The requirements of Article 5(2)(e) are met as long as it is clear from the report what the expert's conclusions are and how s/he has arrived at them. However, in practice, experts tend to identify any matters on which they have been unable to reach an opinion in order to avoid any suggestion that they have overlooked or failed to address a particular point. Similar considerations will apply to any matters that the expert concludes are outside their area of expertise. Identifying such matters, with reasons why the expert

[76] IBA Rules (n 1) Article 6.3 addresses the provision of document to a tribunal-appointed expert. It provides that such expert may request access to documents held by a party to the arbitration to the extent that those documents are 'relevant to the case and material to its outcome', with any disagreement between the expert and the party holding the document/s on this point is to be decided by the tribunal. However, it is also worth noting that under IBA Rules (n 1) Article 6.5, both parties are entitled to have access to any documents that the tribunal-appointed expert has examined.

[77] CIArb Protocol (n 19) Articles 4(4)(h) and (i).

cannot address them (for example, that they require specialist knowledge in a different discipline), is sound protective practice.

Another good practice is for the expert to set out and describe contrary views/opinions. This helps to demonstrate that the expert is independent and impartial and has considered a broad range of expert opinion or approaches relevant to the issue under consideration. One commentator suggests that: **8.100**

> It is often advisable as a matter of tactics for an expert to identify and rebut matters which undermine or contradict his or her views. This formal requirement, however, serves to reinforce in the expert's mind the importance of their independence and impartiality, as well as giving the arbitral tribunal increased confidence that it is being presented with the whole picture. It might be added that this approach is also in accordance with one of the fundamental tenets of the IBA Rules —the requirement to act in good faith in relation to the taking of evidence.[78]

The second requirement of Article 5.2(e) is that, in addition to a statement of the expert opinion and conclusions, the report must contain a description of 'the methods, evidence and information used in arriving at the conclusions'. This information is required in order to put the other party and the tribunal in a position where they can meaningfully evaluate the expert evidence presented (see8.53 for more detail). **8.101**

Lastly, Article 5.2(e) contains express provision that an expert report must be accompanied by any documents upon which the expert relies that are not already on the record. This requirement appeared in the 1999 IBA Rules and is repeated in 2010 Rules. **8.102**

This rule assumes that new documents may be filed with the report that are not already on the record, eg documents that originate with the expert, or that have been produced by another party during document production, but which are not yet on the record. New documents obtained by means of document production will not generally, absent a specific order to this effect, be regarded as being 'on the record' or as having been 'filed' or 'submitted' unless and until they are produced with a submission or pleading, or with fact/expert evidence.[79] If an expert wishes to rely on a document not on the record, Article 5.2(e) requires that it be produced with the expert report. **8.103**

If a memorial-style submission is being served with accompanying evidence then it will generally be accompanied by one set of numbered exhibits to which reference can be made, both in the submissions and in the accompanying expert evidence. In this situation there is no need for further copies of documents to be provided with the **8.104**

[78] Harris (n 52) 214.

[79] This is standard practice, but for an express direction in these terms, see *Mesa Power Group, LLC v Government of Canada* (Procedural Order No. 4, 12 July 2013) PCA Case No. 2012-17 [67(ii)(d)], a case brought under the North American Free Trade Agreement (NAFTA) and conducted under the 1976 UNCITRAL Rules and IBA Rules (n 1), which states in relation to documents produced as part of the document production process: 'The documents produced shall not be considered part of the record unless and until one of the Parties submits them as exhibits with their forthcoming submissions'.

expert report/s; to do so will only lead to complications when it comes to preparing the hearing bundles.

8.105 Although the provision is clear, there have been some instances where a party has refused to provide such documents. In the NAFTA arbitration *Methanex Corporation v United States of America*, an issue arose as to whether the party-appointed experts were under an obligation to produce to the other side copies of all materials, documents, data, or other information on which Methanex's scientific experts relied for the opinions and conclusions they expressed in their expert reports. The Tribunal issued an order requiring the provision of such documents. In issuing that decision, reference was made to Article 3.1 of the IBA Rules by which a party is required to produce all documents available to it upon which it relies by a date ordered by the tribunal. This provision is addressed elsewhere, but its terms add weight to the requirement contained in Article 5.2(e). A date given under Article 3.1 is likely to be a final date for production of such documents. It makes sense to have a separate provision relating to delivery of documents relied on in expert evidence, since the other party's expert may need sight of such documents in order to be in a position to evaluate and comment on the other's expert's report. In *Methanex*, among other things, the tribunal said:

> (2) As also previously ordered by the Tribunal and in accordance with the time-table already established by the Tribunal, each Disputing Party is required by Article 3(1) of the IBA Rules to submit to the Tribunal and the other parties, all documents available to that party on which that party relies, including public documents and those in the public domain (except for any documents that have already been submitted by another party);
>
> (3) Whilst the Tribunal accepts the reluctance of Methanex at this stage of the proceedings not to burden the Tribunal unnecessarily 'with voluminous and often highly technical scientific papers and reports on which [Methanex's] expert reports rely . . . ' (Methanex's Summary of Evidence, ¶2), that consideration does not apply to the USA currently studying Methanex's Expert Reports;
>
> (4) Accordingly, as regards the USA, Methanex's Expert Reports must comply fully with the requirements of the IBA Rules and the Tribunal's orders; exactly the same position shall apply to the Expert Reports served by the USA, as regards Methanex; and the Tribunal asks both Disputing Parties to note that in the event of any failure to comply with those requirements, the Tribunal may exercise its power to exclude or limit expert evidence sought to be adduced by the Disputing Party in default.[80]

8.106 Therefore, no matter how voluminous the materials are, the experts are under an obligation to provide to the other side those documents upon which they rely and that have

[80] *Methanex Corporation v United States of America* (Letter from Tribunal (on documents relied upon by Methanex Experts), 10 October 2003) NAFTA.

not previously been submitted. Production of these documents is essential for a fair hearing.

f. Statement of the language in which the report was prepared, and in which the expert intends to give oral testimony

> **5.2(f) if the Expert Report has been translated, a statement as to the language in which it was originally prepared, and the language in which the Party-Appointed Expert anticipates giving testimony at the Evidentiary Hearing.**

Article 5.2(f) addresses circumstances in which the expert report has been prepared in a language other than the language of the arbitration,[81] and then translated. The provision requires disclosure of this fact and the language in which the report was originally prepared. It also requires the expert report to confirm the language in which the expert anticipates giving oral testimony. These are new requirements not present in the 1999 IBA Rules. The requirement is only triggered if the expert report served in the arbitration is a translation. **8.107**

Given the often-technical nature of expert evidence, it is clearly desirable that any expert instructed be fluent in the language of arbitration. However, this may not always be possible. For example, the expert evidence required may relate to the quality of coal mined in a particular remote location for which the pool of suitably qualified experts is small and none are fluent in the language of the arbitration. **8.108**

Where an expert is not fluent in the language of the arbitration, s/he may elect to prepare an expert report in their native language. This will then need to be translated into the language of the arbitration for filing in the arbitration. Article 5.2(f) of the IBA Rules ensures that there is full transparency around these circumstances. **8.109**

In many cases, both the originally prepared report and the translation will be submitted. It is good practice to do so as the opposing party will not otherwise have a proper opportunity to verify or test the accuracy of the translation. It will assist to have both documents on the record in case of a later dispute as to the correctness of the translation. Even where the translation is of a good standard, certain aspects of the evidence or important nuances thereof may be lost in translation. Given the technical nature of some expert evidence, ensuring accuracy of translation may be more challenging than is the case in relation to fact evidence. **8.110**

[81] At some point either before or early in the life of an arbitration a decision will be made as to the language or languages ('the language of the arbitration') in which the arbitration proceedings will be conducted. A well-drafted arbitration agreement will make express provision for this. Absent such provision the applicable institutional rules will generally provide a mechanism and/or criteria by which the language of the arbitration is to be determined. For example, see the ICC Rules, Article 20 and LCIA Rules, Article 17.4. The chosen language of the arbitration will be the language in which submissions, witness statements, and expert evidence are filed, and the language in which any oral hearings will be conducted. Any documentary exhibits filed in the arbitration, or at least the relevant parts, will generally have to be translated into the language of the arbitration if the original document is in a different language.

8.111 Additionally, without the original report, it may be difficult, if not impossible, to cross-examine the expert. Without the original, the expert is often able to say that the translation is incorrect and that is not exactly what s/he meant. Although even in these circumstances a skilled cross-examiner may be able to demonstrate inconsistencies in the report, it is much easier for the tribunal and the parties if the expert can be taken to the original text so that the expert's comments about the translation can be verified at the hearing.

8.112 As mentioned, Article 5.2(f) of the IBA Rules also requires that the expert indicate the language in which s/he will give evidence at the evidentiary hearing. It is important for this to be made known in advance so that, if necessary, appropriate arrangements can be made for the attendance at the hearing of an independent interpreter.[82]

g. Affirmation of genuine belief

> **5.2(g) an affirmation of his or her genuine belief in the opinions expressed in the Expert Report.**

8.113 Article 5.2(g) requires the expert to include in the report 'an affirmation of his or her genuine belief in the opinions expressed in the Expert Report'. This provision is a modification of Article 5.2(d) of the 1999 IBA Rules. Those earlier rules required the expert to include 'an affirmation of the truth of the Expert Report'. The modification reflects the fact that a party-appointed expert is not testifying to matters of fact, but is rather providing an expert opinion.

8.114 Article 8.4 of the IBA Rules requires that the expert re-affirm at the evidentiary hearing his or her genuine belief in the opinions expressed in the report immediately prior to being examined by counsel.[83] If not already corrected in advance of the hearing, it is customary for the expert at that stage to identify for the tribunal any inaccuracies in the report that they have identified since the date of its preparation.

h. Signature

> **5.2(h) the signature of the Party-Appointed Expert and its date and place.**

8.115 Article 5.2(h) of the IBA Rules requires that the expert report be signed. This is consistent with the giving of an affirmation of genuine belief in the content of the report as required by Article 5.2(g). If there is more than one author, each of the contributors should sign and the requirements of Article 5.2(i) should be addressed.

[82] See Chapter 7 paras 7.116–7.117 and Chapter 11 paras 11.108–11.110 in relation to interpretation of oral witness testimony.

[83] IBA Rules (n 1) Article 8.4 requires this, and that the expert 'confirm' the expert report. This is often done by simple oral confirmation of the statement, although, in exceptional cases, experts may elect to take an oath. See Chapter 11 paras 11.78–11.85. See also Chapter 4 paras 4.36–4.37.

In addition, under Article 5.2(h) the expert report should set out the date and place of its signature. **8.116**

It is universal practice to include a date on any document to be filed in court or arbitration. The addition of the place of signature is more unusual and does not appear in institutional arbitration rules. This requirement has appeared in all iterations of the rules since they were introduced in 1983, but the provenance and basis for it is not clear.[84] **8.117**

When a report is prepared in a language other than the language of the arbitration (and then translated), a practical issue can arise as to whether it is necessary to sign the translation, or the original, or both. There is no one-size-fits-all answer. Generally, an expert will feel more comfortable signing the opinion in their native language, in which case the presenting party can furnish the unsigned translation. Alternatively, the expert can sign the translation only since Article 5.5(f) suggests that it is the translation that is formally 'served'. Another approach is for the expert to sign the original language report, and for the translator to certify the accuracy of the unsigned translation. Finally, in some instances the expert may sign both the original and the translation. **8.118**

i. Attribution

> **5.2(i) if the Expert Report has been signed by more than one person, an attribution of the entirety or specific parts of the Expert Report to each author.**

Article 5.2(i) requires that where the report is signed by more than one person, the report should indicate which parts of the report have been prepared by which author/s. This is a new provision not present in the 1999 IBA Rules. **8.119**

The practical significance of this rule is that counsel and the tribunal should understand to whom they should address specific questions about the report. The requirement is also intended to help parties determine which experts they wish to attend the evidentiary hearing, and what preparation they need to do for questioning one or more of the co-authors.[85] **8.120**

The fact that the rule is not engaged unless the report is signed by more than one person suggests that each of the signatories is to be regarded as a party-appointed expert in the case and that they will be available for cross-examination if required. In practice, agreement may be reached between the parties that only one signatory should be cross-examined. **8.121**

Article 5.2(i) may be engaged where a joint report has been prepared by two experts. These may be experts in different areas of expertise or in the same field. For example, a **8.122**

[84] See Chapter 7 paras 7.125–7.126.
[85] Commentary on the IBA Rules (n 36) 19–20.

valuation of a business may require input from a valuation expert as well as an expert in that particular industry (for instance, in choosing relevant comparators for the valuation expert to apply). In such a case, different parts of the reports should be explicitly attributed to their authors or (if it is the case) they should indicate that the entire report has been prepared together. Another approach is for the experts to prepare separate (signed) reports, but for one to be attached as an appendix to the other. This may be appropriate where the expert preparing the covering report relies on certain conclusions stated in the appended report. There may also be situations where two people from the same organization, and with the same professional qualifications, work together on a report.

8.123 A related issue concerns reports prepared by an expert with the help of others. It is very common for an expert witness to have help from his or her team in preparing the report. In such circumstances, it is usually only the nominated expert who will sign off on the report. Provided the expert has considered all of the material on which the report is based and the conclusions stated in the report are those of the expert, this should not pose a problem. If the expert has not done this preparatory work, then s/he may be vulnerable to challenge on cross-examination.

D. Reply Expert Reports

5.3. If Expert Reports are submitted, any Party may, within the time ordered by the Arbitral Tribunal, submit to the Arbitral Tribunal and to the other Parties revised or additional Expert Reports, including reports or statements from persons not previously identified as Party-Appointed Experts, so long as any such revisions or additions respond only to matters contained in another Party's Witness Statements, Expert Reports or other submissions that have not been previously presented in the arbitration.

1. Introduction

8.124 Article 5.3 deals with delivery of a second round of expert evidence. It permits submission of 'revised or additional Expert Reports' responsive to matters contained in another party's witness statements, expert evidence, or submissions not yet filed when the expert report was prepared (referred to here as 'responsive expert evidence').

8.125 The provision gives the parties the opportunity to respond to such matters by submitting revised or additional expert reports. The reports may be provided by experts who have not previously delivered expert evidence in the arbitration.

8.126 Article 5.3 is a new provision that did not exist in the 1999 IBA Rules.

2. Timing of Responsive Statements

Article 5.3 provides for delivery of responsive expert evidence 'within the time ordered by the Arbitral Tribunal'. It appears to follow from this wording that, even where the IBA Rules have been formally adopted in the arbitration, absent direction from the tribunal or agreement between the parties, the terms of Article 5.3 will not confer a right to serve responsive expert evidence. If there is no pre-existing direction permitting further expert reports, a party wishing to serve such evidence must make application to the tribunal explaining why the introduction of that additional evidence is justified. An alternative view is that the use of the word 'may' in the statement 'any Party *may*, within the time ordered by the Arbitral Tribunal, submit to the Arbitral Tribunal . . . revised or additional Expert Reports'[86] creates an implied duty on the tribunal to set a date.[87] However, this latter reading may be inconsistent with the tribunal's general discretion not to admit evidence at all.[88] **8.127**

Delivery of responsive evidence is a common practice in international arbitration and express provision for it is often included in the first procedural order. In theory, if the tribunal takes the view that the expert evidence to which a party wishes to respond does *not* have an impact on the case, responsive evidence may not always be permitted. However, such circumstances may not arise very often as a tribunal is unlikely to be in a position to assess, at the stage of responsive expert evidence, that further evidence is not required. As with fact evidence, the tribunal may also be wary of giving the impression of having prejudged any part of the case. **8.128**

If first-round expert reports have been served simultaneously, a further round of responsive reports will almost certainly be necessary. The parties may have focused on different points in the first-round reports and responsive evidence may be necessary in order to achieve clarity on the issues between the parties. It is for this reason that some counsel and arbitrators prefer consecutive first- round reports so that the respondent's reports cover at least the same issues as the claimant albeit that new areas of evidence may also be raised. As mentioned elsewhere (see 8.50), depending on the nature of the expert evidence, consecutive evidence may sometimes be essential. Actual delivery of responsive expert reports is often most efficiently done by simultaneous, rather than consecutive, delivery, but both approaches are relatively common. In either case, the purpose is to give each party an opportunity to respond to points raised in the other party's first-round reports that may not have been addressed. **8.129**

[86] Emphasis added.

[87] As already noted, there exists a reasonable argument that a right to deliver responsive evidence flows from the parties' right to be heard, so that the parties are entitled to deliver responsive evidence even without authorization from the tribunal. Tobias Zuberbühler and others, *IBA Rules of Evidence: Commentary on the IBA Rules on the Taking of Evidence in International Arbitration* (Schulthess 2012) 98 para 50. Similar considerations arise in relation to fact evidence. See Chapter 7.

[88] See in particular IBA Rules (n 1) Article 9.1.

3. Substance of Responsive Statements

8.130 The IBA Rules provide that a second round of evidence should be limited to matters raised in the other party's first round witness statements, expert report/s, or submissions that were not available when the first round of expert evidence was delivered. However, there may sometimes be 'evidence creep' in the content of responsive expert reports. Parties may decide that they would like to introduce new material (both expert testimony and documents) not directly relevant to what is said by their opponent's experts.

8.131 As mentioned, a responsive report that attempts to introduce new evidence may fall outside of what is permitted by Article 5.3. Furthermore, it may raise questions about (a) the reliability of the earlier report and (b) whether the opponent will have a fair opportunity to deal with the new evidence in the time available prior to the evidentiary hearing.[89]

8.132 The intention of the rule seems to be to exclude evidence that the party serving the second-round reports could have included in first round reports. As a matter of principle, it seems unlikely that it would extend to new (non-responsive) material for the same side.[90] However, in practice, this form of analysis rarely takes place and all of the additional evidence may be 'dressed up' as arising from the other party's new evidence. If the other party were to raise a legitimate objection on this basis to part of the 'responsive' evidence submitted, it might be necessary to obtain permission from the tribunal for the introduction of that evidence.

8.133 Each situation has to be considered on the facts of the particular case, but where possible the tribunal should try to prevent abuse under Article 5.3.

4. New Experts

8.134 As mentioned, Article 5.3 makes clear that responsive expert evidence may come from a new expert who has not previously delivered evidence in the arbitration. It may be that the evidence of that expert had not previously been considered to be relevant to the issues in dispute, but because of something said in the other party's evidence, it has become so. For example, the opposing party may make reference to a technical issue not thought to be relevant in a party's first-round expert evidence delivered first.

[89] See further Philip Yang, 'Procedural Issues at the Interlocutory and Hearing Stages: Part 2' (2013) Asian Dispute Review 138.

[90] The Commentary on the IBA Rules (n 36) appears to confirm this. It refers to the responsive statement being limited to matters 'contained in another party's witness statements, expert reports or other submissions that have not been previously presented . . . '.

5. 'Revised or Additional' Statements

The use of the phrase 'revised' in Article 5.3 is an interesting one. In practice, most 'second-round' evidence is delivered by means of an additional report. However, there is no reason in practice why the new evidence should not be introduced by way of 'tracked' revisions (whether corrections or additions) to an existing report. **8.135**

E. Consultation between Opposing Experts

> **5.4. The Arbitral Tribunal in its discretion may order that any Party-Appointed Experts who will submit or who have submitted Expert Reports on the same or related issues meet and confer on such issues. At such meeting, the Party-Appointed Experts shall attempt to reach agreement on the issues within the scope of their Expert Reports, and they shall record in writing any such issues on which they reach agreement, any remaining areas of disagreement and the reasons therefore.**

Article 5.4 gives the tribunal discretion to make an order requiring experts of like (or related) disciplines to meet and seek to agree the issues on which they agree and the issues that remain in dispute (between the experts).[91] **8.136**

This rule is driven by the desire to make the process more efficient. If the experts are able to agree on certain issues before submitting the rebuttal expert reports, those reports and any later cross-examination can normally be limited to the areas of disagreement. This leads to greater efficiency and costs savings. **8.137**

In practice, the meeting of experts will generally take place on a 'without prejudice' basis. Only when a note of the meeting has been agreed between the experts will that note have an 'open' status so that it may be introduced into the arbitration. **8.138**

The tribunal and counsel will very often encourage the experts to identify the key issues between them in the case so that these can be used as an agenda for the meeting of experts. Some tribunals may even go so far as to give procedural directions identifying the issues that the experts should discuss and how the expert meeting should be conducted. For example, in one ICSID case, the tribunal issued a procedural order specifically requiring the parties' experts to meet, confer, and produce jointly a report addressing three specific issues.[92] Where pursuant to Article 2.3, the tribunal has identified one or more technical issues as being material to the outcome of the case, then encouraging the experts to focus on that issue may in some cases be desirable. **8.139**

[91] A similar approach can be found, inter alia, in ICC Guide to Controlling Costs (n 20) para 67; see also UNCITRAL Notes (n 29) para 97.

[92] *Gold Reserve Inc. v Bolivarian Republic of Venezuela* (Procedural Order No. 2) ICSID Case No. ARB(AF)/09/1

8.140 After the meeting of experts has taken place, the experts will generally prepare a joint report/statement listing the points of agreement and disagreement. In relation to points of disagreement, it is often helpful for the experts to explain the basis on which they disagree. In some instances, and depending on the number of issues, it can be helpful to produce a joint statement in a table format with separate columns for the issue, agreed part, disagreed part, and the position of each expert in relation to those matters upon which they disagree. Below is an example of such a statement produced in an arbitration between parties to a minority shareholder dispute. A template joint statement is included at Appendix 10.

	Dr Smith	**Mr Doe**	**Similarities and areas of agreement**	**Differences and areas of disagreement**
Valuation methodology				
Consideration of benchmarks derived from transactions in Company X's shares	Dr Smith expressed his opinion on the transaction by which the Claimant acquired shares from Company A in August 2015 in his first report, ¶¶ 8.4–8.9.	Mr Doe does not consider that the transaction by which the Claimant acquired shares from Company A in August 2015 provides a useful valuation benchmark for his four dates in 2016 and 2017. This is because the target company appears to have significantly underperformed against the business plan targets communicated in 2015.	We both agree that the valuation benchmarks derived from transactions in Company X's shares should be treated with caution, though our reasons differ.	Dr Smith reservations stated in his first report, ¶¶ 8.8 and 8.9. In Mr Doe's opinion the target company's worsening financial position means that transactions involving the target's shares that occurred in 2015 may not provide useful guides to the value of the target's shares in 2016 and 2017.
EV/Revenue multiple	Dr Smith used the EV/Revenue multiple in the valuation based on the Guideline Public Company method.	Mr Doe used the EV/Revenue multiple in the valuation based on the Guideline Public Companies and Guideline Transaction methods.	We agree that the EV/Revenue multiple is the most appropriate multiple to be used in Company X's share valuation under the market approach.	We disagree on the Guideline Public Companies to be used to value Company X and also on the availability of suitable Guideline Transactions.

8.141 Article 5.4 is mandatory in the sense that, if the tribunal exercises its discretion and orders the experts to meet, the experts have an obligation to do so.

8.142 However, what the IBA Rules do not do is explicitly state that the expert should *not* accept instructions from his/her appointing party or counsel not to agree, a requirement that is advocated by some practitioners:

> Another element of the court reforms that could render the provisions of the IBA Rules on Evidence more effective is the prohibition on accepting instructions not to agree, which . . . has the potential to undermine the joint conference and waste further time and money.[93]

A further practical issue around joint meetings that can sometimes hinder efficiency is that the experts may reach a measure of consensus, even producing a draft note recording that agreement, but are put under pressure by counsel after the meeting to change/amend what they have agreed. As a result, the drafting of the note of agreement/disagreement can sometimes become a matter of further debate and negotiation as counsel try to 'nuance' the experts' conclusions to better fit their respective client's position prior to the note being finalized. **8.143**

In light of this, some practitioners may have liked to see an express provision in the IBA Rules that a party-appointed expert should not discuss the drafting of the note of meeting with counsel prior to it being agreed. Where counsel and expert are conducting themselves in a professional manner, and where (as required by the IBA Rules) the parties are acting in good faith,[94] such a provision should not be necessary. However, poor practice does occur from time to time, occasionally leading to a suspicion that the expert has accepted instructions from the appointing party *not* to reach agreement with the opposing expert on a particular point at issue, or to step back from an agreement reached during the meeting. That said, we anticipate that any proposal to incorporate an express provision would be met with significant resistance from counsel. Many practitioners will have experienced the situation where, during the meeting of experts, a weak expert is taken advantage of by an aggressive opponent and may end up appearing to concede matters that s/he does not actually agree. In any event, it is always open to the tribunal to issue express directions around such matters. **8.144**

F. Failure to Attend the Evidentiary Hearing

5.5. If a Party-Appointed Expert whose appearance has been requested pursuant to Article 8.1 fails without a valid reason to appear for testimony at an Evidentiary Hearing, the Arbitral Tribunal shall disregard any Expert Report by that Party-Appointed Expert related to that Evidentiary Hearing unless, in exceptional circumstances, the Arbitral Tribunal decides otherwise.

93 Jones (n 27) 145.
94 IBA Rules (n 1) Preamble 3.

1. Introduction

8.145 Article 5.5 concerns the expert's obligation to attend the evidentiary hearing and the consequences of non-appearance.

8.146 The 1999 IBA Rules required party-appointed experts to appear at an evidentiary hearing unless the parties agreed otherwise. The position under the IBA Rules is somewhat different.

8.147 The IBA Rules no longer have a default position whereby an expert is required to attend the hearing. The expert is only required to attend if his or her appearance is requested to attend pursuant to Article 8.1 of the IBA Rules.

8.148 Article 8.1 provides that each party shall inform the tribunal, and other parties to the arbitration, of the expert[95] witnesses whose appearance it requests at the evidentiary hearing.

8.149 The notice required by Article 8.1 must be given 'within the time' ordered by the tribunal. This will generally be after all written evidence has been delivered and the parties have had an opportunity to consider what evidence of the other parties they do and do not wish to challenge in cross-examination. It may be possible for the parties to agree that experts whose evidence is not contested do not have to attend the hearing.[96] In practice, this is relatively rare.

8.150 Article 5.5 sets out the consequences of a party-appointed expert failing to comply with a request to attend an evidentiary hearing made under Article 8.1 without a valid reason. Save in exceptional circumstances, in the event of such failure the expert reports of that expert related to the evidentiary hearing are to be disregarded.

2. A Party's Right to Cross-Examine

8.151 In line with accepted practice in international arbitration, the effect of Article 8.1 of the IBA Rules is that, where a party has tendered an expert report in support of its case, the expert should be available for cross-examination at the evidentiary hearing. A number of institutional rules contain similar provision.[97]

8.152 In order to understand why Article 5.5 takes such a strict approach, it is necessary to consider the value that many practitioners and legal traditions place on the ability to question a party-appointed expert. Cross-examination is regarded by some as an

[95] IBA Rules (n 1) Article 8.1 states expressly that the term 'witness' for the purposes of Article 8.1 shall include both witnesses of fact and any experts.

[96] Some institutional rules make express provision for this situation. The SCC Rules, Article 33(3) states 'any witness . . . on whose testimony a party seeks to rely shall attend a hearing for examination, unless otherwise agreed by the parties'.

[97] For example, see LCIA Rules, Article 20.4; SCC Rules, Rule 33(3); and SIAC Rules, Rule 25.4.

essential opportunity to challenge and test the evidence contained in an expert report. Only by cross-examination can a proper assessment of the opinions and expert views set out in the report be made. This matter is discussed further in Chapter 7 in relation to fact evidence.[98]

3. Requirements to Be Satisfied before an Expert Report Is Disregarded

Article 5.5 provides that, where an expert has been asked to attend for cross-examination by notice under Article 8.1 but has failed to do so, the evidence of a non-appearing expert will have to be disregarded unless: **8.153**

(a) the expert provides a valid reason for not attending the hearing; or
(b) there are exceptional circumstances that cause the tribunal to decide otherwise.

Unlike witnesses of fact, party-appointed experts are retained by the parties to whom they owe a contractual obligation. The expert retainer will usually include an obligation to appear at the evidentiary hearing if so required. For that reason, a tribunal is likely to apply a very high standard to the question of whether a valid reason or exceptional circumstance exists that justifies the non-attendance of an expert at an evidentiary hearing.[99] **8.154**

Reasons that may be accepted as valid are likely to be limited to matters that could not have been anticipated or planned for when the expert was first retained. Examples include physical incapacity by reason of serious illness or accident, or the need to undergo some form of urgent medical procedure within a particular time frame, subject to provision of certification by a doctor. Other possibilities may include an inability to travel to the hearing as a result of newly imposed travel bans. **8.155**

As with fact witnesses, a further aspect to be considered when reasons for non-attendance at a hearing are proffered is whether some other means of facilitating the oral testimony of the expert can be arranged. For example, subject to considerations of procedural efficiency, if the unavailability of the expert is temporary, perhaps the hearing can be deferred. Similarly, if a physical condition renders the expert immobile but capable of giving evidence, the expert could attend by video conference. If the expert report was prepared with assistance from a wider team, it is perhaps possible for someone else on the team to attend the evidentiary hearing in place of the original expert. **8.156**

[98] See specifically 7.139–7.145.

[99] For example, in *Compañiá de Aguas del Aconquija S.A. and Vivendi Universal S.A. v Argentine Republic* (Award, 20 August 2007) ICSID Case No. ARB/97/3, the respondent applied to the tribunal for an order permitting one of its experts to testify by video conference instead of attending in person at the oral hearing. The respondent was unable to provide a good reason why the expert was unable to attend and the claimants applied to have the evidence struck from the record. The tribunal denied the respondent's application and granted the claimants' application to have the evidence removed from the record.

4. Disregarding the Expert Report

8.157 Subject to the two requirements in Article 5.5 just mentioned, ie the absence of a valid reason and/or no exceptional circumstances, Article 5.5 of the IBA Rules provides that a tribunal 'shall disregard' any expert report by that party-appointed expert relating to that evidentiary hearing.

8.158 The use of the word 'shall' in Article 5.5 indicates that the tribunal must disregard the expert report entirely if the expert fails to appear at the hearing. There are various arguments in support of this provision, including the fact that, when first retaining the expert, the appointing party ought to have obtained the necessary commitment/made appropriate arrangements to ensure the expert's attendance at the hearing. Another available argument in support of this position is that, until tested by cross-examination or witness conferencing, the expert evidence has little or no value.[100] In addition, if without further explanation, an expert is not prepared to attend and affirm to the opinions expressed in the expert report already filed, this may suggest that they are resiling from all or part of that evidence.

8.159 Furthermore, in circumstances where no good reason is given and no exceptional circumstances are identified, the tribunal may risk a challenge to the award if it admits the report of the non-attending expert. As already mentioned, loss of the opportunity to cross-examine may amount to a denial of due process.[101]

8.160 The counter-argument is that Article 5.5 lacks flexibility. However, in practice, the tribunal's power not to disregard an expert report when a valid reason has been given or where exceptional circumstances exist provides a satisfactory mechanism for dealing with this situation. The tribunal will be the final arbiter of whether these exceptions apply in the particular circumstances of the case. If the report is admitted, it still will be subject to the tribunal's power to assess the weight of evidence in accordance with its powers under Article 9.1 of the IBA Rules.[102] The tribunal may take into account (according to the circumstances) the fact that the expert was not tested in cross-examination.

8.161 A further factor when it comes to the weighing of evidence is that the tribunal will have the assistance of the other party's expert evidence, including any additional oral testimony that expert gives at the evidentiary hearing. This can make non-attendance of the opponent expert a perilous situation for the party who appointed that expert.

8.162 Where, without proper justification, an expert fails to attend an evidentiary hearing following a request to do so, it is also open to the tribunal, under Article 9.6, to infer that

[100] It should be noted that IBA Rules (n 1) Article 8.3(c) (describing the procedure to be adopted at the Evidentiary Hearing) does not use the phrase 'cross-examination' but, in essence, this is the process provided for in that rule.

[101] See discussion at Chapter 7 paras 7.139–7.145.

[102] Under IBA Rules (n 1) Article 9.1, the weighing of evidence is left entirely to the tribunal.

the testimony that would have been presented would be adverse to the presenting party. Article 9.6 is discussed in more detail in Chapter 12. However, as a matter of practice, the drawing of adverse inferences can be problematic for a tribunal, even in relation to fact evidence.[103] In relation to expert evidence, the position will be even more difficult because expert opinions are rarely binary, and it will be extremely difficult to pinpoint a particular inference that it is reasonable to draw from the non-attendance.

G. Content of Expert Report Not Accepted Where Expert Not Called to Evidentiary Hearing

5.6. If the appearance of a Party-Appointed Expert has not been requested pursuant to Article 8.1, none of the other Parties shall be deemed to have agreed to the correctness of the content of the Expert Report.

1. Introduction

Rule 5.6 of the IBA Rules provides that, in circumstances where a party-appointed expert has not received an Article 8.1 request to attend the evidentiary hearing, this does not mean that the other parties will be treated as having agreed the content of the expert report submitted by that expert. The phrase '*other Parties*' is used because it can reasonably be assumed that the party submitting and relying on the expert report will accept the correctness of its content. **8.163**

2. Not Calling an Expert for Cross-Examination

It is possible (although relatively rare in our experience) that a party may decide not to call the opposing party's expert for cross-examination. For example, there may be circumstances where an expert has provided an uncontroversial report and there is little to be gained from the expert giving oral testimony.[104] **8.164**

Article 5.6 provides a measure of protection for the party not calling an expert for cross-examination. It confirms that a decision not to cross-examine an expert shall not constitute agreement to the correctness of the content of the expert report. This is an important clarification, particularly if counsel for the opposing parties are from different legal traditions. In many common law systems, there are restrictions on the right to dispute evidence that has not been challenged on cross-examination. See Chapter 7 paras 7.170–7.179 for further discussion on this topic. **8.165**

[103] See Chapter 12.
[104] Christopher Newmark , 'Efficient, Economical and Fair: The Mantra of the New IBA Rules' (2010) International Arbitration Law Review 168.

8.166 Article 5.6 applies to all of the written evidence of an expert not called for cross-examination. Thus, for example, an opponent party may still tender its own expert to give evidence contradicting that of the 'opposing' expert not called, or make submissions as to the unreliability or lack of weight to be attributed to the evidence of the absent expert, perhaps by reference to its own expert evidence, or documentary evidence available to the tribunal. When the tribunal comes to assess the weight of evidence on either side of the dispute, it is a matter for the tribunal to decide how much reliance to place on the evidence of the expert not called for cross-examination. However, if the evidence relates to an important issue in the case it may also wonder why the expert was not called to be cross-examined. As a result, it might place more weight on the evidence of a non-attending expert. Given all of the attendant risks, it is very unlikely that a party will not call an opposing expert to the evidentiary hearing unless the parties have agreed between themselves that the relevant discipline of expert for all parties should not attend.

3. A Party's Right to Call Its Own Expert

8.167 Article 8.1 of the IBA Rules gives each party an express right to request an expert to attend an evidentiary hearing and does not limit the category of expert to whom that provision applies. Subject to the tribunal's overall control over who should appear,[105] Article 8.1 says in terms that a witness (a term that includes any experts) shall appear at the hearing if the attendance of that witness 'has been requested by *any* party'.[106] Thus, in principle, a party is permitted to give notice under Article 8.1 that it requires the attendance of its *own* expert, although it makes no special provision for how this is to be done. In our view, for the reasons given in 8.166, this situation is unlikely to arise very often in practice. While exceptional cases may occur, in the vast majority of instances, either all of the experts in a particular discipline will appear, or none of them will.

[105] IBA Rules (n 1) Article 8.2.
[106] Emphasis added.

9

Article 6: Tribunal-Appointed Experts

Article 6 Tribunal-Appointed Experts

1. **The Arbitral Tribunal, after consulting with the Parties, may appoint one or more independent Tribunal-Appointed Experts to report to it on specific issues designated by the Arbitral Tribunal. The Arbitral Tribunal shall establish the terms of reference for any Tribunal-Appointed Expert Report after consulting with the Parties. A copy of the final terms of reference shall be sent by the Arbitral Tribunal to the Parties.**
2. **The Tribunal-Appointed Expert shall, before accepting appointment, submit to the Arbitral Tribunal and to the Parties a description of his or her qualifications and a statement of his or her independence from the Parties, their legal advisors and the Arbitral Tribunal. Within the time ordered by the Arbitral Tribunal, the Parties shall inform the Arbitral Tribunal whether they have any objections as to**

the Tribunal-Appointed Expert's qualifications and independence. The Arbitral Tribunal shall decide promptly whether to accept any such objection. After the appointment of a Tribunal-Appointed Expert, a Party may object to the expert's qualifications or independence only if the objection is for reasons of which the Party becomes aware after the appointment has been made. The Arbitral Tribunal shall decide promptly what, if any, action to take.

3. Subject to the provisions of Article 9.2, the Tribunal-Appointed Expert may request a Party to provide any information or to provide access to any Documents, goods, samples, property, machinery, systems, processes or site for inspection, to the extent relevant to the case and material to its outcome. The authority of a Tribunal-Appointed Expert to request such information or access shall be the same as the authority of the Arbitral Tribunal. The Parties and their representatives shall have the right to receive any such information and to attend any such inspection. Any disagreement between a Tribunal-Appointed Expert and a Party as to the relevance, materiality or appropriateness of such a request shall be decided by the Arbitral Tribunal, in the manner provided in Articles 3.5 through 3.8. The Tribunal-Appointed Expert shall record in the Expert Report any non-compliance by a Party with an appropriate request or decision by the Arbitral Tribunal and shall describe its effects on the determination of the specific issue.
4. The Tribunal-Appointed Expert shall report in writing to the Arbitral Tribunal in an Expert Report. The Expert Report shall contain:
   (a) the full name and address of the Tribunal-Appointed Expert, and a description of his or her background, qualifications, training and experience;
   (b) a statement of the facts on which he or she is basing his or her expert opinions and conclusions;
   (c) his or her expert opinions and conclusions, including a description of the methods, evidence and information used in arriving at the conclusions. Documents on which the Tribunal-Appointed Expert relies that have not already been submitted shall be provided;
   (d) if the Expert Report has been translated, a statement as to the language in which it was originally prepared, and the language in which the Tribunal-Appointed Expert anticipates giving testimony at the Evidentiary Hearing;
   (e) an affirmation of his or her genuine belief in the opinions expressed in the Expert Report;
   (f) the signature of the Tribunal-Appointed Expert and its date and place; and
   (g) if the Expert Report has been signed by more than one person, an attribution of the entirety or specific parts of the Expert Report to each author.
5. The Arbitral Tribunal shall send a copy of such Expert Report to the Parties. The Parties may examine any information, Documents, goods, samples, property, machinery, systems, processes or site for inspection that the Tribunal-Appointed Expert has examined and any correspondence between the Arbitral Tribunal

and the Tribunal-Appointed Expert. Within the time ordered by the Arbitral Tribunal, any Party shall have the opportunity to respond to the Expert Report in a submission by the Party or through a Witness Statement or an Expert Report by a Party-Appointed Expert. The Arbitral Tribunal shall send the submission, Witness Statement or Expert Report to the Tribunal-Appointed Expert and to the other Parties.

6. **At the request of a Party or of the Arbitral Tribunal, the Tribunal-Appointed Expert shall be present at an Evidentiary Hearing. The Arbitral Tribunal may question the Tribunal-Appointed Expert, and he or she may be questioned by the Parties or by any Party-Appointed Expert on issues raised in his or her Expert Report, the Parties' submissions or Witness Statement or the Expert Reports made by the Party-Appointed Experts pursuant to Article 6.5.**
7. **Any Expert Report made by a Tribunal-Appointed Expert and its conclusions shall be assessed by the Arbitral Tribunal with due regard to all circumstances of the case.**
8. **The fees and expenses of a Tribunal-Appointed Expert, to be funded in a manner determined by the Arbitral Tribunal, shall form part of the costs of the arbitration.**

A. Introduction

Article 6 of the IBA Rules addresses the use of tribunal-appointed experts. Read together with Article 8, which deals with procedural aspects of oral testimony at the evidentiary hearing, it provides a comprehensive framework for the use and management of evidence from such experts. **9.1**

The matters covered in Article 6 include the appointment and terms of reference of a tribunal-appointed expert, a party's right to object to the appointment, the content of the expert's report, the parties' right of response to the expert evidence, and the right to examine the expert at the evidentiary hearing. **9.2**

As already mentioned in relation to Article 5, although Article 6 is a relatively self-contained code on tribunal-appointed experts, it is important to understand the relationship and differences between the provisions of Article 6 and those contained in Article 5 dealing with party-appointed experts. Those drafting the IBA Rules faced the same challenges in reconciling the competing historical and cultural preferences of different legal traditions in relation to expert evidence as they did in connection with other aspects of procedure affecting the taking of evidence. However, rather than adopting a single or merged approach from one or other legal tradition, the drafting committee adopted a dual approach representing prevailing practice in both common law and civil law systems.[1] Article 5 makes provision for party-appointed **9.3**

[1] See Chapter 8 paras 8.7–8.11 for more detail of the background to and evolution of Articles 5 and 6.

experts (the traditional common law preference) while Article 6 addresses tribunal-appointed experts (most commonly used in civil law systems[2] and in the UNCITRAL Model law).[3] These two articles reflect the available mechanisms under the IBA Rules (and in the practice of international arbitration generally) by which expert evidence is introduced.

9.4 The terms of Articles 5 and 6 reflect the different concerns and issues that arise in relation to the use of each of party-appointed and tribunal-appointed experts. As mentioned, a key objective of Article 5 is to make sure that there is transparency and a degree of assurance around a party-appointed expert's independence. Article 6 contains checks and balances designed to ensure that the tribunal does not delegate its decision-making function to a tribunal-appointed expert, that the parties have a proper opportunity to make representations on the choice of expert, and to examine and comment on the evidence presented by that expert.

9.5 Issues that routinely arise in relation to the appointment of a tribunal-appointed expert include the following:

(i) whether or not the case is suited to the use of a tribunal-appointed expert;
(ii) selection of the expert and the expert's terms of reference;
(iii) what material is to be provided to the expert;
(iv) whether the expert is to be able to seek further material or information from the parties and, if so, what the procedure is for such requests;
(v) the procedure for enabling the parties to comment on the expert's report;
(vi) the procedure to be adopted at the hearing in relation to presentation of the expert's evidence; and
(vii) whether and in what circumstances the parties are to be entitled to rely on party-appointed expert evidence.

9.6 A number of published materials contain useful guidelines on issues that the parties and/or a tribunal may wish to consider in connection with the use of tribunal-appointed experts.[4]

9.7 An IBA report indicates that Article 6 is relied upon in about 8 per cent of cases in which reference is made to the IBA Rules.[5]

[2] Christopher Harris, 'Expert Evidence: The 2010 Revisions to the IBA Rules on the Taking of Evidence in International Arbitration' (2010) International Arbitration Law Review 212 (hereafter 'Harris').

[3] UNCITRAL Model Law on International Commercial Arbitration (as adopted by UNCITRAL on 21 June 1985 and as amended by UNCITRAL on 7 July 2006), Article 26 (hereafter 'UNCITRAL Model Law'). For more detail, see Julian DM Lew, Loukas A Mistelis, and Stefan Michael Kroll, *Comparative International Commercial Arbitration* (Kluwer Law International 2003) paras 22–87.

[4] For example, see Chartered Institute of Arbitrators, International Arbitration Practice Guidelines: Party-appointed and Tribunal-appointed Experts; *UNCITRAL Notes on Organizing Arbitral Proceedings* (United Nations 2016); and *ICC Arbitration Commission Report on Issues for Arbitrators to Consider Regarding Experts* (International Chamber of Commerce 2010) (hereafter 'ICC Report on Issues for Arbitrators Regarding Experts').

[5] The IBA Arbitration Guidelines and Rules Subcommittee, 'Report on the Reception of the IBA Arbitration Soft Law Products' (*International Bar Association*, 2016) para 45 <www.ibanet.org/Document/Default.aspx?DocumentUid=105d29a3-6261-4437-84e2-1c8637844beb> accessed 27 November 2018.

B. Party Involvement in the Tribunal's Expert Appointment

6.1 The Arbitral Tribunal, after consulting with the Parties, may appoint one or more independent Tribunal-Appointed Experts to report to it on specific issues designated by the Arbitral Tribunal. The Arbitral Tribunal shall establish the terms of reference for any Tribunal-Appointed Expert Report after consulting with the Parties. A copy of the final terms of reference shall be sent by the Arbitral Tribunal to the Parties.

Article 6.1 deals with the process for appointment of a tribunal-appointed expert. **9.8** Importantly, it provides for consultation with the parties. This is desirable both to engage the confidence of the parties in the appointment, and to ensure that the issues to be put to the expert meet the needs of the case.

1. Can a Tribunal Appoint an Expert without the Consent of the Parties?

Article 6.1 expresses the right of a tribunal to appoint an expert to report on specific **9.9** issues selected by the tribunal. It may do so 'after consulting with the parties'. Subject to observing the requirement of consultation, Article 6.1 appears to give a tribunal the right to appoint an expert even where party consent is not obtained. While the Commentary to the IBA Rules makes clear that an important principle underlying Article 6 is the substantial involvement of the parties at all stages of the process, it does not suggest that the tribunal may not make an appointment unless it has the consent of the parties.

A number of institutional arbitration rules contain similar provision giving the tribunal **9.10** broad authority to retain experts directly, after consultation with the parties.[6]

Many national arbitration laws also make provision for the appointment of tribunal- **9.11** appointed experts where the parties have not agreed otherwise - for example, Article 26 of the UNCITRAL Model Law[7] and Section 37 of the English Arbitration Act.[8] Section 25 of the Swedish Arbitration Act provides that the tribunal may appoint an expert unless both parties are opposed to such a course. Although the formulation adopted by the Swedish legislation differs from that in the UNCITRAL Model Law and the English legislation, from a practical perspective the outcome is the same. In other countries—for example, Switzerland, France, Belgium, and

[6] See, for example, ICC Rules, Article 25.4; LCIA Rules, Article 21.1; HKIAC Rules, Article 25.1; and SIAC Rules, Rule 26.

[7] UNCITRAL Model Law (n 3) Article 26 provides that 'Unless otherwise agreed by the parties, the arbitral tribunal . . . (a) may appoint one or more experts to report to it on specific issues to be determined by the arbitral tribunal'.

[8] The English Arbitration Act 1996, s37 states that: '(1) Unless otherwise agreed by the parties . . . (a) the tribunal may . . . (i) appoint experts or legal advisers to report to it and the parties . . . '.

the United States—the parties' right, and the tribunal's power, to determine the arbitral procedure has generally been interpreted as permitting the appointment of tribunal-appointed experts.[9] However, regardless of any formal requirements imposed in relation to the appointment of such an expert, there are very good reasons why a tribunal should consult and/or seek approval from the parties before making the appointment—not least because of the need to fund payment of the expert's fees, which is impossible without the cooperation of at least one party. In all cases, building a consensus around the use of a tribunal-appointed expert, as well as the choice of expert, will aid the smooth running of the arbitration and minimize the risk that one of the parties will feel dissatisfied and/or later claim that the appointment adversely affected presentation of its case.

9.12 Where both parties are actively opposed to the use of a tribunal-appointed expert, a question arises in relation to party autonomy, ie is the tribunal entitled to proceed with the proposed appointment in the face of party agreement that it should not. Party autonomy is of fundamental importance to the arbitration process. However, a tribunal has obligations in connection with the arbitration that it may regard as inconsistent with an agreed position presented by the parties. For example, if the tribunal believes that the appointment of a tribunal-appointed expert will be the most efficient and useful way in which to obtain expert evidence, it may take the view that abandonment of that proposed approach breaches its general duty to conduct the proceedings in a fair, efficient, and economic manner.[10] Such a position can create a dilemma for the tribunal, to which there is no easy answer. However, in practice, it is unlikely that the tribunal will proceed to make the appointment.[11]

9.13 Although relatively rare, in some cases, the parties' arbitration agreement may exclude the right of a tribunal to appoint an expert. This may mitigate the tribunal dilemma of balancing party autonomy and tribunal duties, but it is not without risk. Situations do sometimes arise in which the tribunal feels that expert evidence presented by party-appointed experts is inadequate in some way, or that it would benefit from the assistance of a third 'independent' expert in relation to certain aspects of the case. For example, in a situation where, despite opportunities given to the parties to supplement that evidence, the tribunal feels that the available party-appointed expert evidence is not convincing or is inconclusive. If the tribunal cannot appoint its own expert, it may simply decide that the relevant party has not discharged its burden of proof. By depriving the tribunal of the opportunity to appoint an expert, the parties may jeopardize the outcome they seek.

[9] Chartered Institute of Arbitrators, Practice Guideline 10: Guidelines on the use of Tribunal-Appointed Experts, Legal Advisers and Assessors, para 2.3.

[10] See Preamble to the IBA Rules on the Taking of Evidence in International Arbitration 2010 (hereafter 'IBA Rules'). Such duty may also be a mandatory requirement of the law of the seat. For example, see English Arbitration Act 1996, s 33; and Swedish Arbitration Act 1999, s 21.

[11] See further discussion on this issue at Chapter 5 paras 5.30–5.38.

In summary, under the IBA Rules, unless the parties have agreed otherwise, a tribunal may appoint a tribunal-appointed expert after consulting with the parties. If both parties are against such an appointment, the tribunal would be ill-advised to proceed with it. However, where one party is for and another is against a tribunal appointment, the tribunal has the power to proceed with the appointment and should do so where considerations of efficiency, economy, and fairness support that decision. **9.14**

2. Consultation with the Parties

Article 6.1 requires that the tribunal first consult with the parties before appointing an expert. The Commentary to the IBA Rules emphasizes how important it is that the parties are involved at each stage of the process. This is desirable in itself and may also reduce the risk of potential future challenges to the expert, the expert's report, and/or to the award. **9.15**

Consultation between the tribunal and the parties will generally involve consideration of a number of different topics relevant to the appointment. **9.16**

a. Is it necessary/appropriate to appoint a tribunal-appointed expert

The first question is whether it is necessary or appropriate to retain a tribunal-appointed expert. There are a variety of reasons why a tribunal may wish to do so. **9.17**

For example, in a small number of cases, the tribunal may require assistance on technical issues that it finds difficult to understand without assistance, but which are not necessarily disputed. The tribunal may also wish to appoint an independent expert to review confidential or sensitive documents in relation to a disputed document production request and form the view that this is most appropriately done pursuant to the provisions of Article 6.[12] **9.18**

More generally, the reasons for the appointment will be similar to decisions underpinning appointment of a party-appointed expert—most commonly, that there are disputed facts that the tribunal will find difficult to resolve without hearing expert evidence on the issue. In these circumstances, the key question will be whether it is better to use a single tribunal-appointed expert, or party-appointed experts (or possibly both). Pursuit of the overall objective of an 'efficient, economical and fair process **9.19**

[12] IBA Rules (n 10) Article 3.8 makes express provision for the power of the tribunal, in consultation with the parties, to appoint an independent third party to review documents that are the subject of a document production request to which the party in possession of the document has made an objection. The tribunal may do so where it determines (a) that a decision on the validity of the objection can only be made following a review and (b) it would not be appropriate for the tribunal to carry out that review. The 1999 IBA Working Party and 2010 IBA Rules of Evidence Review Subcommittee, 'Commentary on the Revised Text of the 2010 IBA Rules on the Taking of Evidence in International Arbitration' (International Bar Association) 11 <www.ibanet.org/Document/Default.aspx?DocumentUid=DD240932-0E08-40D4-9866-309A635487C0> accessed 27 November 2018 (hereafter 'Commentary on the IBA Rules') suggests that the appointment may be made under IBA Rules (n 10) Article 6 (Tribunal-Appointed Experts) but need not be. See Chapter 6 paras 6.263–6.265.

for the taking of evidence' provided for in the Preamble to the IBA Rules may require careful consideration in relation to this matter.

9.20 The particular considerations relevant to this debate, and its timing, will be specific to an individual case. Where a tribunal requires general assistance to understand technical matters not in dispute, a single tribunal-appointed expert may be an obvious choice. Where expert evidence on disputed issues is required, then, depending on the preferences of counsel and the parties, positions may differ. Some tribunals may see a tribunal-appointed expert as being more efficient in terms of time and costs, as well as more independent. However, it should not be assumed that the appointment of a single tribunal-appointed expert will necessarily be faster or less expensive than the use of party-appointed experts. For example, the right of parties to be involved in the selection of an individual expert to be appointed by the tribunal, and the parties' right to respond to the expert evidence presented by such an expert by means of evidence from a party-appointed expert can make this approach as time consuming and expensive as the appointment of experts by the parties.

9.21 In addition, it is possible that the parties may, in any event, exercise their right under Article 5 to present expert evidence on the same issue. The entitlement of a party to rely on party-appointed expert evidence is addressed in Chapter 8.[13] Moreover, even without the formal appointment of a party-appointed expert, parties will sometimes appoint 'shadow experts' to assist them in formulating questions to the tribunal-appointed experts or a challenge to the expert's conclusions. Counsel for the parties—particularly if they are from a common law jurisdiction—may oppose the appointment of a tribunal-appointed expert and argue that the requirement of a 'fair' process[14] dictates that they should have the opportunity to present expert evidence from a party-appointed expert. Finally, it should be borne in mind that, in many cases, experienced party-appointed experts prepared to work cooperatively may be able to narrow the technical issues between the parties, thereby reducing the amount of evidence to be prepared and presented to the tribunal.

9.22 The English court has identified a number of factors to be considered when the court has to decide whether to order parties to an individual piece of litigation to appoint a single 'joint' expert, rather than individual party-appointed experts. Some of these factors are equally relevant to the decision to appoint a tribunal-appointed expert. They include:[15]

- the value of the dispute;
- the complexity of the issue;
- whether a party has already instructed an expert on the issue in question;

[13] See Chapter 8 paras 8.29–8.39.
[14] IBA Rules (n 10) Preamble.
[15] 35 PD 7.

- whether the instruction of a single joint expert is likely to assist the parties and the court to resolve the issue more speedily and in a more cost-effective way than separately instructed experts; and
- whether the expert evidence falls within a substantially established area of knowledge that is unlikely to be in dispute or there is unlikely to be a range of expert opinion.

If the tribunal and the parties can discuss and agree on either a tribunal-appointed expert or party-appointed experts, then this is clearly desirable. Where parties insist on introducing party-appointed expert evidence, the tribunal may abandon the idea of a tribunal-appointed expert where it will simply duplicate costs and effort. However, as mentioned, if having considered party-appointed expert evidence a tribunal forms the view that such evidence is inadequate in some way, or that the tribunal would nonetheless benefit from the assistance of a third expert in relation to the technical matters in issue, then it may propose or revisit the idea of a tribunal-appointed expert. For example, both party-appointed experts may be credible, but they may be adopting materially different positions in their evidence such that the tribunal feels it necessary to appoint a third expert in order to assist the tribunal navigate through the competing views contained in the available evidence, even though this may result in additional delay and/or expense.[16] **9.23**

b. The choice of expert

Article 6 does not lay down any guidance as to the selection process of the tribunal-appointed expert. This is unsurprising. Much will depend on the facts of the case, the nature of the issues on which expert evidence is required, the knowledge and experience of counsel and the tribunal in relation to that discipline of expert, and the personalities involved. In practice, there are generally three options for a tribunal wishing to appoint an expert: **9.24**

(i) The tribunal may invite the parties to suggest a suitable expert, with a suggested default appointment mechanism in the event that the parties are unable to agree;
(ii) The tribunal may approach a specialist institution for assistance in identifying a suitable expert[17]; and/or
(iii) The tribunal may identify an expert using their own contacts.[18]

[16] See also Chartered Institute of Arbitrators, Practice Guideline 10: Guidelines on the use of Tribunal-Appointed Experts, Legal Advisers and Assessors, para 3.2.3.

[17] The tribunal may want to approach relevant specialist institutions, such as the Expert Witness Institute, the Society of Expert Witnesses, and the Academy of Experts. Similarly, for a fee, the ICC can assist with finding a suitable expert in a particular field. See 'Proposal of Experts and 'Neutrals' (*International Chamber of Commerce*, 2014) <https://iccwbo.org/dispute-resolution-services/experts/proposal-experts-neutrals/> accessed 10 December 2018. This is governed, inter alia, by the ICC Rules for the Proposal of Experts and Neutrals (in force as of 1 February 2015).

[18] A similar approach can be found in ICC Report on Issues for Arbitrators Regarding Experts (n 4) Section III (A)(2)–(3).

Depending on the facts of the case, there may be advantages and disadvantages to each of these three options. However, where the tribunal identifies an expert without prior consultation with the parties it would be prudent for it to seek prompt input from the parties on whether they believe the proposed expert to be suitable.

9.25 The search for an expert can be time-consuming and a tribunal may not always have access to the same level of resources as large law firms in carrying out that search. Its approach to the search may also be different. When counsel for one of the parties is looking for an expert, consciously or subconsciously they will be looking for an expert who will support their client's case. To that end, lawyers often conduct a background check on the expert's published works, in addition to his or her professional background and experience. A tribunal is likely to approach a search in a more objective way, ie it will merely wish to satisfy itself that the expert has the necessary qualifications and experience. The tribunal will also need to be alive to potential conflicts. In some areas of expertise there may be a very small pool of experts, some of whom may have an existing relationship with one of the parties or a member of the tribunal.

c. The scope of the mandate to be given to the tribunal-appointed expert

9.26 Article 6.1 provides that the tribunal may appoint an expert 'to report to it on specific issues designated by the Arbitral Tribunal'. Those issues should be directly relevant to the dispute.

9.27 Depending on the stage reached in the proceedings, the tribunal may have a relatively clear view on the nature of the issues on which it requires assistance from an expert. However, it is important that the tribunal consult the parties. Not only is this an express requirement of the IBA Rules, but the parties may have a deeper understanding of the issues in dispute and the matters that they will need to demonstrate by reference to expert evidence in order to make their case. In order to avoid any suggestion that a party's ability to present its case has been hindered in any way, it is essential that the parties be involved in formulating the issues to be addressed by the expert.

9.28 Efficiency and costs should also be borne in mind. The scope of the expert's mandate will have a direct impact on the expert fees incurred. In general terms, limiting the scope of the evidence to that required to assist the tribunal to determine the dispute, or necessary to provide important background context for material issues, should be the underlying agenda.

d. Consultation on the terms of reference

9.29 Article 6.1 requires the tribunal to establish formal terms of reference for the Tribunal-Appointed Expert Report 'after consulting with the Parties'.

9.30 The terms of reference to be provided by the tribunal to the tribunal-appointed expert is the equivalent of the instructions given by a party to a party-appointed expert. If done properly, instructions to a party expert will be couched in relatively objective terms. However, the instructing party will still have full control over what it wishes to say in the instructions and the directions it gives to the expert. The drawing up of terms of reference under Article 6 is a more tightly controlled process. During consultation on that document each party will wish to do what it can to ensure that (a) the matters it considers important are put to the expert and (b) the instructions given to the expert are not expressed in terms that favour one party over another. In our experience, it is common practice for draft terms of reference to be circulated to the parties for comment before being finalized. Another approach is for the tribunal to invite the parties to try to agree terms of reference. The terms of whatever they can agree is then produced and any points of disagreement are resolved by a decision of the tribunal.

The IBA Rules require the tribunal to send a copy of the final terms of reference to the parties. **9.31**

Similar provision requiring consultation on terms of reference by which a tribunal expert is to be appointed can be found in Article 25 (4) of the ICC Rules:[19] **9.32**

> The arbitral tribunal, after having consulted the parties, may appoint one or more experts, define their terms of reference and receive their reports. At the request of a party, the parties shall be given the opportunity to question at a hearing any such expert.

The UNCITRAL Arbitration Rules approach the issue slightly differently. They require the Tribunal to communicate the terms of reference to the parties but contain no explicit requirement for the tribunal to consult with the parties on that document. In particular, Article 29(2) of the UNCITRAL Arbitration Rules provides: **9.33**

> A copy of the expert's terms of reference, *established by the arbitral tribunal*, shall be communicated to the parties.[20]

In our view, the express requirement to consult on the terms of reference found in in the IBA Rules is the better approach. **9.34**

Article 6 does not contain any guidance as to what should be included in the terms of reference. The possible content of terms of reference is addressed in the next section, but, as a minimum, that document must set out clearly the scope and substance of the questions to be answered by the expert.[21] The tribunal and the parties may also wish to include instructions on what is to happen should the expert identify an issue that has not been specifically addressed in the terms of reference.[22] The tribunal and the parties will generally wish to indicate the documents and information to be considered by **9.35**

[19] The desirability of consultation is also noted elsewhere. See, for example, the Chartered Institute of Arbitrators, International Arbitration Practice Guidelines: Party-Appointed and Tribunal-Appointed Experts.

[20] Emphasis added.

[21] See also ICC Report on Issues for Arbitrators Regarding Experts (n 4) 9.

[22] See Herman Verbist, Erik Schäfer, and Christophe Imhoos, *ICC Arbitration in Practice* (2nd edn, Kluwer Law International 2015) 486 (hereafter 'Verbist, Schäfer, and Imhoos'), where it is said that: 'If the expert, while carrying out the mission, becomes aware that any issue to be addressed in the expert report is not appropriately phrased, or if the expert becomes aware of a relevant issue not mentioned in these terms of reference, then the expert shall advise the arbitral tribunal thereof immediately. The arbitral tribunal shall have the right to modify and/or amend these terms of reference as it deems fit after having heard the parties'.

the expert, and any tests or investigations that should be conducted. A communication protocol between the expert, the tribunal, and the parties may also be considered for inclusion, along with appropriate procedural directions, and a timetable for production of the expert report.

3. Content of the Terms of Reference

9.36 The terms of reference provided to a tribunal-appointed expert will be tailored to the circumstances of the individual dispute and in practice are likely to be heavily influenced by the consultation with the parties on content that has taken pace. However, the following housekeeping points and general topics are frequently identified as matters to consider:[23]

- Identification of the arbitration proceedings (parties to the proceedings and any institution number, etc.);
- Name and address of the expert. Where a professional partnership or other body is retained the individual assuming the role of expert should be identified;
- Any other aspects of the desired organization, preparation, and presentation of the evidence. For example, the format in which the expert report should be presented;
- A provisional timetable for preparation and delivery of the expert evidence;
- Definition of the expert's tasks and the questions/issues that the expert must address in the expert report;
- An express statement of the power of the tribunal to adjust the expert's terms of reference if so required by the expert's findings (normally exercised after consulting the parties);
- Identification of information (documents, specimens, etc.) that are to be provided to the expert on which the expert should base his or her report;[24]
- A procedure by which the expert may collect further information that the expert may require in order to prepare the report. For example, the rules under which the expert can contact the parties to request information or hold interviews with them;
- Rules for communications between the expert, the parties, and the tribunal designed to ensure transparency around the process by which the evidence is prepared;
- An express statement of the parties' right to comment on the expert's report and to question the expert at an oral hearing upon request, as well as confirmation of the expert's agreement to attend the hearing;[25]

[23] See Verbist, Schäfer, and Imhoos (n 22) 490 and Claus von Wobeser, 'The Arbitral Tribunal-Appointed Expert', in Albert Jan van den Berg (ed), *International Arbitration 2006: Back to Basics?* (Kluwer Law International 2007) 801–12 (hereafter 'Wobeser'). Various examples of tribunal orders and terms of reference may be found in published materials. For example, see Michael E Schneider, 'Technical Experts in International Arbitration' (1993) ASA Bulletin 446.

[24] See also IBA Rules (n 10) Articles 6.3 and 6.5.

[25] See also IBA Rules (n 10) Article 6.5.

- A statement of the expert's related obligations. For example, the duty to maintain confidentiality, the obligation to be truthful and impartial, the duty to disclose the expert's contacts with the parties, and potential conflicts of interests prior to and during the arbitration proceedings;
- Scope of the expert's liability, and grounds for termination of the retainer;
- A statement of the expert's rights in relation to the role for which the expert has been retained, and what the expert expects from the tribunal/parties;
- A statement of agreed arrangements in relation to remuneration and reimbursement of expenses (including fees for the expert's employees and charges for travel and accommodation, if appropriate)—note that any advance payment should be recorded; and[26]
- Basic rules for monitoring costs and readjusting the advance on expert's fees.

A checklist of points to consider in relation to appointment of a tribunal-appointed may be found at Appendix 11.

It has been suggested that it is desirable for each member of the tribunal, the parties, **9.37**
and the expert to sign the terms of reference.[27] However, this is not a requirement of the IBA Rules and may not always be practical.

C. Party Objection to a Proposed Choice of Tribunal-Appointed Expert

6.2 The Tribunal-Appointed Expert shall, before accepting appointment, submit to the Arbitral Tribunal and to the Parties a description of his or her qualifications and a statement of his or her independence from the Parties, their legal advisors and the Arbitral Tribunal. Within the time ordered by the Arbitral Tribunal, the Parties shall inform the Arbitral Tribunal whether they have any objections as to the Tribunal-Appointed Expert's qualifications and independence. The Arbitral Tribunal shall decide promptly whether to accept any such objection. After the appointment of a Tribunal-Appointed Expert, a Party may object to the expert's qualifications or independence only if the objection is for reasons of which the Party becomes aware after the appointment has been made. The Arbitral Tribunal shall decide promptly what, if any, action to take.

[26] In tandem with the drawing up of terms of reference, there may need to be a formal letter of retainer recording who is contracting with the expert. One approach is for the tribunal to contract with expert in the name of and on behalf of all the parties, with a suitable indemnity for fees or payment on account being provided by the parties. See also IBA Rules (n 10) Article 6.8.

[27] Wobeser (n 23) 810.

1. Introduction

9.38 When a potential expert has been identified, the tribunal will normally approach the expert and ask whether they are able and willing to accept the appointment. The initial contact with a potential expert will focus on whether the expert has the required skills and expertise, is willing and available to assist without delaying the schedule for the arbitration, is independent and neutral, and does not have any conflicts of interest. It is advisable that all communications between the tribunal and a potential expert are conducted in writing and copied to all parties to avoid giving any grounds for future challenge to the expert, the report, and/or the award for lack of due process. It is good practice for the tribunal to send to the tribunal-appointed expert a copy of the IBA Rules.

9.39 Article 6.2 requires the nominated expert to provide the tribunal, and the parties, with details of the expert's qualifications and a statement of independence so that the parties have an opportunity to raise any concerns they may have in relation to either of these matters. The provision goes on to set out a procedure by which any concerns are to be articulated and determined.

9.40 Article 6.2 does not require the expert to provide a statement of availability. However, during initial contact with a potential expert it is sensible for the tribunal to establish that the expert has sufficient time to devote to the proceedings and is available to attend any hearing dates that have been fixed.

2. Grounds on which Party Objection May Be Made

a. Introduction

9.41 Article 6.2 provides that the parties may object to the appointment of the tribunal-appointed expert on only two grounds: (a) the expert's qualifications; and/or (b) the expert's lack of independence.

9.42 In practice, there are other grounds on which the parties might reasonably take objection to an individual expert. These may include the inexperience of the proposed expert in giving expert evidence, the level of fees associated with the appointment, a reasoned preference for party-appointed experts, or that the proposed appointment will reduce the efficiency of the proceedings and/or increase time and costs to an extent that will outweigh any benefits to be derived from the appointment.[28] However, the arena for raising these issues is the consultation process prescribed by Article 6.1. After such consultation, and at a point where the tribunal has identified an expert that it wishes

[28] See further eg ICC Report on Issues for Arbitrators Regarding Experts (n 4) 41.

to appoint, the parties' right of participation in the appointment process is limited to its right to raise a formal objection on one of the two discrete grounds mentioned. Although narrowly defined, these grounds provide important safeguards in relation to the expert evidence to be presented. The evidence of the expert will be of no value, and may even mislead the tribunal, if the expert is not suitably qualified to speak to the matters in issue. Likewise, if the expert is not independent, the evidence the expert gives may be partisan and therefore misleading or, if obviously one-sided, not something to which the tribunal can properly attach any weight.

b. Statement of qualifications

Unlike a party-appointed expert, who is only obliged to describe his or her qualifications and independence in the expert report that is produced, a tribunal-appointed expert is required under Article 6.2 to submit this background information *before* being appointed. Clearly, in practice, the parties can only raise an objection to appointment on the grounds of lack of qualification if they have information on those qualifications. If the parties know the identity of the proposed expert, they can try to conduct independent research, but it is much more satisfactory for the expert to provide full details of his or her expertise so that each of the parties has access to the same information. **9.43**

Against this background it is unclear why Article 6.4(a) requires the expert's report to include a description of the expert's background, qualifications, training, and experience while only a description of his or her qualifications is required at the stage of appointment pursuant to Article 6.1, in relation to which an objection may be raised. In practice, it is sensible for all of this information to be provided at the earliest stage. **9.44**

As mentioned, the early timing of provision of information under Article 6.2 is in contrast to the position in respect of party-appointed experts where such details are only provided to all participants at the report stage. However, in that case, each party will have its own expert who it will have vetted carefully to check that the expert has the requisite knowledge and will make a good witness. The opportunity to challenge the credentials of the opposing expert will come during cross-examination or in closing submissions, where arguments are made as to the weight to be attributed to a particular piece of evidence. **9.45**

c. Statement of independence

As with the statement of qualifications, the provision of a statement of independence by the proposed expert prior to appointment is in contrast to the position in respect of party-appointed experts, where that statement need only be included in the expert's report. The underlying rationale is also broadly the same. In the case of party-appointed experts, each party will have taken appropriate steps to investigate whether the expert has any connection with the opposing party. The appointing party is unlikely to select an expert with whom the appointing party has a significant existing relationship **9.46** because this will ultimately have to be disclosed and, when it is, the tribunal may take this into account when weighing the evidence of that expert. Even if the appointing party is prepared to take this risk, the other party will have the opportunity to challenge the expert about the relationship during cross-examination. To some extent, these matters operate as checks on the risks and consequences of a non-independent expert being appointed by a party to the arbitration. These mechanisms do not have the same degree of force in relation to a tribunal-appointed expert.

9.47 In many cases, the evidence to be presented by the tribunal-appointed expert will be the only evidence that the tribunal has before it on a particular issue. In the majority of those cases the tribunal will therefore rely on that evidence in reaching its determination. The parties need to be in a position to trust the expert's objectivity and impartiality. Early provision of a statement of independence and an opportunity to raise objections on the basis of a lack of independence *prior* to the expert being appointed are extremely important parts of the process for appointment of a tribunal-appointed expert.

9.48 Article 6 requires the proposed tribunal-appointed expert to provide a single statement of that expert's independence from the parties, their legal advisers, and the tribunal—the statement of independence. This requirement is in contrast to the position under Article 5, which requires a party-appointed expert to provide a statement of his or her present or past relationship with any of the parties, their legal advisors, and the tribunal[29] *in addition* to a 'statement of independence from the Parties, their legal advisers and the Arbitral tribunal'.[30] The reason for the difference in approach is unclear.[31] There is nothing in the Commentary on the IBA Rules to explain the reason for the additional requirement contained in Article 5, although it may be directed at achieving as much transparency as possible around the nature of any pre-existing relationship between a party and its appointed expert. In our view, an express requirement of transparency about the nature of any relevant pre-existing relationship is equally desirable in relation to a tribunal-appointed expert.

9.49 Article 6.2 requires a statement of independence, but make no reference to impartiality, even though in some cases applicable institutional rules or local arbitration law may impose this requirement. This position has attracted some criticism and debate, as has the requirement (introduced for the first time in the 2010 IBA Rules) that the expert declare themselves independent of the parties' legal advisers. These matters are addressed in more detail in Chapter 8.[32]

[29] IBA Rules (n 10) Article 5.2(a).
[30] ibid Article 5.2(c).
[31] The same concern is expressed in Harris (n 2) 215.
[32] See Chapter 8 paras 8.77–8.89.

3. The Procedure for Raising an Objection

Article 6.2 sets out the procedure that is to be followed when, following delivery of the expert's description of qualifications and statement of independence, a party wishes to raise an objection to the proposed appointment. 9.50

Under Article 6.2, the tribunal is to set a deadline by which any objections are to be raised and, if an objection is raised, the tribunal should decide 'promptly' whether to accept the objection. 9.51

In practice, there may be some dialogue between the tribunal, parties, and the proposed expert in the event an objection is received. The tribunal may wish to ask questions of the expert in relation to the basis of objection, or to invite submissions from the non-objecting party. Provided there is full transparency around such communications, there is nothing wrong in these (or other appropriate) steps being taken. However, the tribunal is likely to want these matters addressed and resolved as soon as possible so that there is no delay to progress in the arbitration. If the objection is upheld, the tribunal will need to find another suitable expert. The requirement in the IBA Rules that the tribunal rule on an objection promptly is consistent with the desirability for speed in relation to these matters. 9.52

It is important that a party act promptly in the event that it has concerns about the expert's qualifications or independence. It must make known its objection by the deadline laid down by the tribunal. It will not be able to rely on those matters as a basis for objection after that deadline has passed. Only circumstances not known to the objecting party at the date of the deadline may be relied upon as a basis for objection at a later date. This is made clear by the following new provision in Article 6.2 not present in the 1999 IBA Rules: 9.53

> After the appointment of a Tribunal-Appointed Expert, a Party may object to the expert's qualifications or independence only if the objection is for reasons of which the Party becomes aware *after the appointment* has been made.[33]

The rationale for this addition was to prevent belated and/or tactical challenges to the appointment of an expert intended to derail or delay the process. The parties are required to either raise their objections before the appointment or to be deemed to accept the position unless new circumstances come to light on which a later objection may be based. 9.54

[33] Emphasis added.

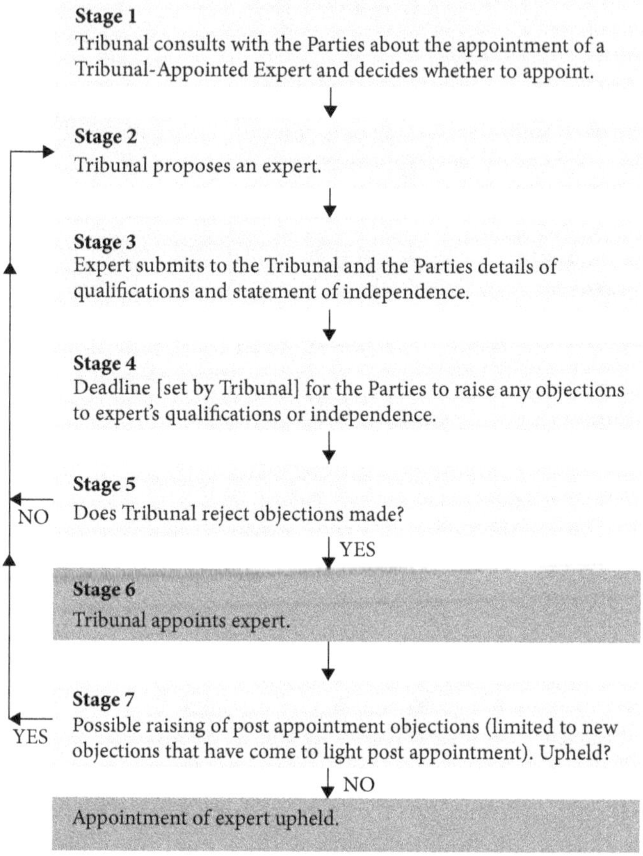

Figure 9.1 Flowchart for Appointment of a Tribunal-Appointed Expert

D. Provision of Information, Documents, and Other Materials to the Expert

6.3 Subject to the provisions of Article 9.2, the Tribunal-Appointed Expert may request a Party to provide any information or to provide access to any Documents, goods, samples, property, machinery, systems, processes or site for inspection, to the extent relevant to the case and material to its outcome. The authority of a Tribunal-Appointed Expert to request such information or access shall be the same as the authority of the Arbitral Tribunal. The Parties and their representatives shall have the right to receive any such information and to attend any such inspection. Any disagreement between a Tribunal-Appointed Expert and a Party as to the relevance, materiality or appropriateness of such a request shall be decided by the Arbitral Tribunal, in the manner provided in Articles 3.5 through 3.8. The Tribunal-Appointed Expert shall record in the Expert Report any non-compliance by a Party with an appropriate request or decision by the Arbitral Tribunal and shall describe its effects on the determination of the specific issue.

1. Introduction

Article 6.3 sets out the procedure by which a tribunal-appointed expert may obtain information from the parties that the expert needs to prepare the expert evidence that he or she has been asked to provide. 9.55

Whatever volume of information is provided to the expert with the terms of reference it is almost inevitable that the expert will have questions and/or will require further information when s/he comes to consider the issues upon which s/he must opine. In the event that a party objects to provision of the requested information, Article 6.3 confirms the mechanism by which that objection is to be resolved and the steps to be taken where a party refuses to make the information available. 9.56

The formal procedure for obtaining information set out in Article 6.3 is necessary for a number of reasons. A tribunal-appointed expert does not enjoy the same proximity of relationship to the parties as a party-appointed expert. Where the latter is used, the parties will take all appropriate steps to ensure that 'their' expert is provided with all necessary documents, goods, and samples. The same facility is not available to a tribunal-appointed expert who is, and must remain, wholly independent of any party to the dispute. In addition, if the tribunal-appointed expert is to retain the confidence of the parties, it is desirable to maintain transparency around the making of requests for information by the expert, and the nature of information provided by a party in response to such request. 9.57

The provisions of Article 6.3 may be supplemented by measures agreed by the parties in the terms of reference provided under Article 6.1. As mentioned, it is desirable that the tribunal and the parties agree a communication protocol to ensure transparency of process. Ideally, the expert should not communicate with a party without the other party being copied on that communication, and all requests for information and access should be made in writing and copied to all parties. 9.58

2. Requests for Information Made by the Tribunal-Appointed Expert

Article 6.3 gives the tribunal-appointed expert the same authority as the tribunal to request information/access 'to the extent relevant to the case and material to its outcome'. As mentioned elsewhere, the benchmark of relevance and materiality constitutes the gold standard for introduction of evidence under the IBA Rules. However, Article 6.3 also refers expressly to the application of Article 9.2 of the IBA Rules pursuant to which a party may object to, or the tribunal may exclude, material from the arbitration on a number of grounds. Those grounds include a lack of relevance and materiality.[34] In our 9.59

[34] Under IBA Rules (n 10) Article 9.2, either on application by a party or on its own motion, a tribunal may exclude evidence from the arbitration on a number of grounds. These include a lack of relevance and materiality, a legal impediment or privilege, loss or destruction, commercial or technical sensitivity, special political or institutional sensitivity, considerations of procedural economy, or it being an unreasonable burden to produce the material. See Chapter 12.

view, the inclusion of the additional express reference to the benchmark of relevance and materiality in connection with a request made by a tribunal-appointed expert highlights that the expert should consider carefully whether what is being requested meets that benchmark. It is sensible to flag this matter in the terms of reference so that the expert is aware that he or she may have to provide a justification for the request by reference to this standard. Chapter 6 provides more in-depth discussion on the terms 'relevant to the case' and 'material to its outcome'.[35]

9.60 Under Article 6.3, the tribunal-appointed expert may ask a party to the arbitration to provide:

(a) information;
(b) access to any documents, goods, samples, property, machinery, systems, and/or processes; or
(c) access to site for inspection.[36]

9.61 The tribunal-appointed expert may make the request directly to a party to the arbitration without prior reference to the tribunal. However, as mentioned, it is desirable that the request be copied to the tribunal and to the other parties. The application of Article 9.2 of the IBA Rules (anticipated by Article 3.3) depends upon the parties being aware of the requests made.

9.62 Practice varies in relation to the ability of a tribunal-appointed expert to address a request for information direct to a party and different arbitration rules approach the issue in different ways. For example, under some rules, any request for additional information must be made by the tribunal rather than by the expert themselves. Article 21.3 of the LCIA Rules provides that:

> *The Arbitral Tribunal may require* any party at any time to give to such expert any relevant information or to provide access to any relevant documents, goods, samples, property, site or thing for inspection under that party's control on such terms as the Arbitral Tribunal thinks appropriate in the circumstances.[37]

9.63 Other rules impose an obligation on the parties to produce documents and information requested but are silent as to who can request those materials. An example of this approach is Article 29(3) of the UNCITRAL Rules which provides that:

> The parties shall give the expert any relevant information or produce for his or her inspection any relevant documents or goods that he or she may require of them. Any dispute between a party and such expert as to the relevance of the required information or production shall be referred to the arbitral tribunal for decision.[38]

[35] See Chapter 6 paras 6.76–6.146.

[36] In relation to site inspections, Article 6.3 should be read together with IBA Rules (n 10) Article 7 (Inspection), which makes express reference to site inspection by a tribunal-appointed expert. Site inspections are not addressed in this chapter. See Chapter 10 on Article 7 for more detail.

[37] LCIA Rules, Article 21.3 (emphasis added). In similar fashion, UNCITRAL Model Law (n 3) Article 26.1(b) grants the right to request documents or inspection to the tribunal but not to the expert.

[38] UNCITRAL Rules, Article 29(3). Similar provision is laid down in ICDR Rules, Article 25.2.

Although 'as he or she may require of them' might be read as meaning a request from the expert, the position is by no means clear.

A third approach, adopted in Article 6.3 of the IBA Rules, is to make express provision for a direct request to be made by the expert to a party.[39] Article 6.3 goes as far as to say that the authority of a tribunal-appointed expert to request such information or access 'shall be the same as the authority of the Tribunal'. **9.64**

3. Party Objection to a Request for Information/Access by the Tribunal-Appointed Expert

A party has the right to object to a request for information/access made by a tribunal-appointed expert. The objection may be made on grounds that the information requested is not relevant to the case or material to its outcome, or on any of the other grounds set out in Article 9.2.[40] **9.65**

It appears from the wording of Article 6.3 that, if the expert accepts the objection, that is the end of the matter. However, where the objecting party and the expert disagree as to the 'relevance and materiality or appropriateness' of the request the disagreement will be decided by the tribunal 'in the manner' provided in Articles 3.5 to 3.8 of the IBA Rules. It is assumed that the reference to 'appropriateness' is a shorthand for the grounds of objection available under Article 9.2.[41] **9.66**

Articles 3.5 to 3.8 of the IBA Rules set out a procedure by which a party objection to a request for production of documents by another party may be resolved or determined by the tribunal, including provision for the material subject to the objection to be reviewed by another independent third party where this is necessary to establish the validity of the objection and the tribunal does not consider it appropriate to review the material itself. The provisions of Articles 3.5 to 3.8 are dealt with in Chapter 6 at 6.215–6.280. It is not clear whether, in the context of Article 6.3, those provisions are to be read simply as substituting the tribunal-appointed expert for the 'Party [submitting] a Request to Produce' or more literally. We suggest that the substance of any objection to a request made by a tribunal-appointed-expert is properly to be resolved between the parties to the dispute, or absent that, to be determined by the tribunal. Accordingly, any objection to an expert's request should be delivered to the tribunal, and be copied to all other parties and to the expert. The parties should consult and endeavour to reach an agreed position on whether the information/access requested is or is not relevant and material, or whether another **9.67**

[39] Another example of this approach may be found at HKIAC Rules, Article 25.2, which provides: 'The parties shall give the expert any relevant information or produce for his or her inspection any relevant documents or goods that he or she may require of them . . .'.

[40] See (n 34).

[41] There would otherwise be a disconnect between the available grounds of objection under Article 9.2 and the disagreement between the opposing party and the expert on the 'appropriateness' of the request that the tribunal has to determine.

ground for objection is made out. If the parties cannot reach agreement, then the matter will be determined by the tribunal. This is consistent with the tribunal being the final arbiter of what material may be introduced into the arbitration.

4. Right to Receive the Information Provided to the Tribunal-Appointed Expert

9.68 Article 6.3 establishes the right of the parties and their representatives to receive the same information that the tribunal-appointed expert receives from another party, and to attend any inspection that the expert conducts. This right is repeated in Article 6.5, and is uncontroversial.[42] For the process to be fair, each party must be given the same opportunity as the expert to have the information and access in order that it may draw its own conclusions. For example, the other party may consider the information/access to be incomplete and therefore misleading.

9.69 Where the information requested involves trade secrets or other confidential commercial information, the party in possession may need to consider seeking confidentiality protections from the tribunal. Article 9.4 provides a mechanism for such an application.[43]

5. Party Non-Compliance with a Request

9.70 If the request for information/access is made to a party and that request is not withdrawn or overruled by the tribunal, the party asked to provide the information or access is obliged to comply with the request. However, in practice, where the party refuses to do so there is little that the tribunal-appointed expert, or the tribunal, can do to compel provision of what has been requested.

9.71 One possible sanction is for the tribunal to draw an adverse inference against the non-providing party. Article 9.6 of the IBA Rules grants the tribunal express power to do so where a party has not objected to a request for evidence made by the other party or the tribunal has ordered that it should be produced:

> If a Party fails without satisfactory explanation to make available any other relevant evidence, including testimony, sought by one Party to which the Party to whom the request was addressed has not objected in due time or fails to make available any evidence, including testimony, ordered by the Arbitral Tribunal to be produced, the Arbitral Tribunal may infer that such evidence would be adverse to the interests of that Party.

[42] Commentary on the IBA Rules (n 12) 21.
[43] See Chapter 12 paras 12.317–12.356.

Although such provision makes no reference to a request for information/access made by a tribunal-appointed expert it may be read as applying to circumstances where a tribunal has overruled a party objection and made an order that information be provided to the expert. Other provisions of Article 6.3 support this reading. In order to assess whether an adverse inference may be drawn, and what that inference might be, the tribunal will need to understand the nature of the information withheld and what impact that information might have had on the evidence of the tribunal-appointed expert. Article 6.3 requires the expert to include in the expert report a description of the effect of the non-compliance on the determination of the specific issue to which it relates. 9.72

In our view, it would in any event be open to the tribunal to draw an adverse inference in appropriate circumstances pursuant to its general powers under Articles 9.1, 9.5, and 9.6. The use of adverse inferences is dealt with in more detail at Chapter 12 at 12.357–12.386. 9.73

E. Content of the Report Prepared by the Tribunal-Appointed Expert

6.4. The Tribunal-Appointed Expert shall report in writing to the Arbitral Tribunal in an Expert Report. The Expert Report shall contain:

(a) the full name and address of the Tribunal-Appointed Expert, and a description of his or her background, qualifications, training and experience;

(b) a statement of the facts on which he or she is basing his or her expert opinions and conclusions;

(c) his or her expert opinions and conclusions, including a description of the methods, evidence and information used in arriving at the conclusions. Documents on which the Tribunal-Appointed Expert relies that have not already been submitted shall be provided;

(d) if the Expert Report has been translated, a statement as to the language in which it was originally prepared, and the language in which the Tribunal-Appointed Expert anticipates giving testimony at the Evidentiary Hearing;

(e) an affirmation of his or her genuine belief in the opinions expressed in the Expert Report;

(f) the signature of the Tribunal-Appointed Expert and its date and place; and

(g) if the Expert Report has been signed by more than one person, an attribution of the entirety or specific parts of the Expert Report to each author.

1. Introduction

Article 6.4 sets out requirements for the content of the report prepared by the tribunal-appointed expert. In some instances, these mirror the requirements that apply to the 9.74

report of a party-appointed expert dealt with in detail in Chapter 8. However, as mentioned, Articles 5 and 6 have slightly different issues to tackle. This is why the requirements as to the content of the expert's report in each case are tailored to the role of either tribunal-appointed or party-appointed expert. Where a provision is the same as that under Article 5 in relation to the report of a party-appointed expert, we make no further comment on the position under Article 6. Where the wording differs, the difference is addressed.

9.75 As a further preliminary point, it is worth noting those requirements for the content of a party-appointed expert that are missing from Article 6.4, specifically:

(a) Article 6.4 does not contain a requirement that the expert report include a statement of the expert's independence from the parties, the parties' legal advisors and the tribunal as is required by Article 5.2(c). This requirement is redundant in Article 6 because a statement of independence should have been provided prior to appointment in accordance with Article 6.2.

(b) Another difference is that a tribunal-appointed expert is not required to include 'a description of the instructions pursuant to which he or she is providing his or her opinions and conclusions' as is required in relation to a party-appointed expert by Article 5.2(b) introduced in the current 2010 version of the IBA Rules.[44] The parties will already be aware of the instructions provided to the tribunal-appointed expert by means of the terms of reference copied to the parties pursuant to Article 6.1.

9.76 Finally, the additional requirement found in Article 6.3 that the expert should record in the report any non-compliance by a party with a request for information, and the effect of that non-compliance on the expert's determination, should also be borne in mind when considering a report prepared by a tribunal-appointed expert.

9.77 Article 6.4 is drafted as mandatory requirement—'The Expert Report *shall* contain . . . '. If the application of the IBA Rules has been agreed or ordered, reports submitted by a tribunal-appointed expert must comply with the requirements set out in Article 6.4. Ideally, the terms of reference given to the expert under Article 6.1 will have highlighted those provisions for the expert's attention.

9.78 The IBA Rules do not provide any sanction for non-compliance with the requirements in Article 6.4. In practice, tribunals are likely to approach this on a case-by-case basis.[45] If the non-compliance is material, the tribunal is likely to direct the expert to remedy the omission. The expert has been appointed by the tribunal and should accede to directions given by the tribunal after consultation with the parties.

[44] The IBA Rules on the Taking of Evidence in International Commercial Arbitration 1999 did not require inclusion of a description of the instructions in either Article 5 or Article 6 at all. However, in 2010, the requirement was added as IBA Rules (n 10) Article 5.2(b) for the Party-Appointed Expert, but no similar provision was added for the Tribunal-Appointed Experts.

[45] See, eg ICC Report on Issues for Arbitrators Regarding Experts (n 4) Section II(G)(1).

For example, the tribunal may have noticed a deficiency in the evidence itself or it may have been alerted to it by one or more of the parties. In circumstances where, on a particular issue, the tribunal has only the evidence of the tribunal-appointed expert, it is extremely important that such evidence be complete, that the expert set out the facts relied on in giving the opinion expressed in the report, and that the methodology and technical materials that the expert used in reaching his or her conclusions are provided in order that the tribunal may understand it, and so that each party may challenge during presentation of its case any part of the report with which it takes issue. Any deficiency in relation to these aspects of content will need to be remedied. **9.79**

In theory, an available alternative approach is for the tribunal to admit the non-compliant expert report into evidence with the caveat that the omissions may affect the weight attached to it by the tribunal. However, while this approach may work in relation to party-appointed expert evidence where there may be other party-expert evidence on the same issue available to fill the gaps, it is unlikely to be satisfactory where there is a single tribunal-appointed expert and the parties have not instructed their own experts. **9.80**

2. Matters to Be Included in the Expert Report

Article 6.4 is useful in providing a form of checklist for the content of the expert report to be produced by the tribunal-appointed expert. The requirements in Article 6.4 reflect good practice in relation to the form and content of an expert report. **9.81**

a. Name, address, qualifications, training, and experience

> **6.4(a) the full name and address of the Tribunal-Appointed Expert, and a description of his or her background, qualifications, training and experience.**

Article 6.4(a) requires the report to include the expert's name and address and a description of his or her background, qualifications, training, and experience. This requirement is similar to that in Article 5.2 of the IBA Rules with the omission of a statement of independence.[46] Although the expert should have already provided a description of his or her qualifications pursuant to Article 6.1, the requirement at Article 6.4 to include in the report the much broader description of 'background, qualifications, training and experience' should pick up the full spectrum of attributes that qualify that individual to provide an expert opinion. **9.82**

b. Statement of facts on which the expert opinion is based

> **6.4(b) a statement of the facts on which he or she is basing his or her expert opinions and conclusions.**

[46] See Chapter 8 paras 8.59–8.71.

9.83 Article 6.4(b) provides that the expert report set out the facts upon which the expert is basing his or her opinion. This requirement is the same as that appearing in Article 5.2(d) in relation to party-appointed experts. The same considerations will apply.[47]

c. The expert opinion and the methodology/evidence used

6.4(c) his or her expert opinions and conclusions, including a description of the methods, evidence and information used in arriving at the conclusions. Documents on which the Tribunal-Appointed Expert relies that have not already been submitted shall be provided.

9.84 Article 6.4(c) is an important provision stating the core requirement that the expert set out in the report the expert's opinions and conclusions on the matters s/he has been asked to address. It is these opinions/conclusions upon which (subject to challenge from the parties) the tribunal is likely to rely in reaching a determination.

9.85 A second requirement of Article 6.4(c) is that the report must contain a description of 'the methods, evidence and information used in arriving at the conclusions'. This information is necessary to put the other party and the tribunal in a position where they can meaningfully evaluate and/or question the expert evidence presented.

9.86 Lastly, Article 6.4(c) contains express provision that the expert report must be accompanied by any documents on which the expert relies that are not already on the record.

9.87 These requirements are the same as those appearing in Article 5.2(e) in relation to party-appointed experts. Similar considerations will apply.[48]

d. Statement of the language of the report and oral testimony

6.4(d) if the Expert Report has been translated, a statement as to the language in which it was originally prepared, and the language in which the Tribunal-Appointed Expert anticipates giving testimony at the Evidentiary Hearing.

9.88 Where the version of the expert report delivered to the tribunal is a translation, Article 6.4(d) requires the expert to disclose in the report the original language of the report and the language in which the expert anticipates giving oral testimony. These requirements are the same as those appearing in Article 5.2(f) in relation to party-appointed experts and the similar considerations will apply in relation to practical application of what is needed in order to comply with them.[49] However, in relation to tribunal-appointed experts, this information should (in most cases)

[47] See Chapter 8 paras 8.93–8.96.
[48] See Chapter 8 paras 8.97–8.106.
[49] See Chapter 8 paras 8.107–8.112.

come as no surprise to any of the parties. The question of whether the expert is able to present evidence in the language of the arbitration is something that is likely to have been explored during the appointment process. The size of the pool of suitably qualified experts may influence whether the tribunal selects an expert able to give evidence in the language of the arbitration over one that is not. An interesting question arises as to whether the language skills (or lack of them) of a tribunal-appointed expert forms part of the 'qualifications' to be disclosed to the tribunal and the parties under Article 6.2, and in relation to which a party may raise an objection under that provision.

e. Affirmation of genuine belief, signature, and attribution

> **6.4 (e) an affirmation of his or her genuine belief in the opinions expressed in the Expert Report;**
> **(f) the signature of the Tribunal-Appointed Expert and its date and place; and**
> **(g) if the Expert Report has been signed by more than one person, an attribution of the entirety or specific parts of the Expert Report to each author.**

Articles 6.4(e), (f), and (g) require the report to contain an affirmation of belief in the opinions expressed, the signature of the tribunal-appointed expert (with date and time of signature), and, where there is more than one signature, a statement explaining which parts of the report may be attributed to each signatory. These provisions are in identical terms to those appearing in Article 5.2(g), (h), and (i) in relation to the report of a party-appointed expert.[50] **9.89**

F. The Parties' Right to Respond to Evidence Produced by the Tribunal-Appointed Expert

> **6.5 The Arbitral Tribunal shall send a copy of such Expert Report to the Parties. The Parties may examine any information, Documents, goods, samples, property, machinery, systems, processes or site for inspection that the Tribunal-Appointed Expert has examined and any correspondence between the Arbitral Tribunal and the Tribunal-Appointed Expert. Within the time ordered by the Arbitral Tribunal, any Party shall have the opportunity to respond to the Expert Report in a submission by the Party or through a Witness Statement or an Expert Report by a Party-Appointed Expert. The Arbitral Tribunal shall send the submission, Witness Statement or Expert Report to the Tribunal-Appointed Expert and to the other Parties.**

[50] See Chapter 8 paras 8.113–8.123.

1. Introduction

9.90 Article 6.5 makes express provision for the parties to receive a copy of the expert report and to have a right of response to that report prepared by the tribunal-appointed expert.

9.91 Article 6.5 is concerned with natural justice, particularly the right of a party to have reasonable notice of evidence that may be relied on in the arbitration, and to be able to prepare and present its own case.[51] It comprises two main elements. The first is a right of access to the report and materials on which the expert prepared his or her evidence. The second is the right to respond to that evidence.

9.92 In summary, each party to the arbitration must be provided with:

(i) a copy of the report produced by the tribunal-appointed expert;
(ii) all of the materials that the expert has examined in the course of preparing the report; and
(iii) any correspondence that has passed between the tribunal and the expert.

9.93 Each party is entitled to respond to the expert report by means of submissions, a witness statement, or an expert report prepared by an expert instructed by the party.

2. Provision of the Expert Report and Related Materials

9.94 Article 6.5 suggests that the tribunal is to act as a conduit for provision of the expert report to the parties, and for provision of the parties' responses (if any) to the expert. In practice, if the parties have agreed a communication protocol as part of the terms of reference for the expert under Article 6.1, this may provide for delivery of correspondence and materials to all participants simultaneously. However, it is still up to the tribunal to take the lead in guiding the participants through the various steps described in Article 6.5, even if some or all of these have been anticipated and laid out in the terms of reference.

9.95 Article 6.5 is silent as to the point at which the expert's report is to be provided by the tribunal to the parties, but we suggest that it should be delivered to them as soon as possible after receipt by the tribunal. As mentioned, a copy may have been sent by the expert direct to the parties at the same time as it was sent to the tribunal. The tribunal may nonetheless wish to write to the parties to note this and to remind them of any dates agreed by which party responses to the report must be provided. If there are no dates ordered or agreed in the existing procedural timetable then the tribunal will need to indicate a date by which responses should be delivered.

[51] These are widely accepted principles embodied in arbitration laws and institutional rules. They are also captured in the principles set out in the Preamble to the IBA Rules.

9.96 In addition to seeing the report it is important that the parties have full transparency around the facts and materials relied upon by the expert in reaching his or her conclusions. Without this information the parties cannot properly evaluate the quality of the evidence and decide whether they wish to take issue with anything contained in the report. Like Article 6.3, Article 6.5 makes provision for the parties to have the right to see the categories of material described in Article 6.5 that the expert has 'examined' in reaching his or her conclusions.

9.97 The categories of material referred to in Article 6.5 are broad. They comprise 'any information, Documents, goods, samples, property, machinery, systems, processes or site for inspection'. 'Documents' is itself a defined term in the IBA Rules and, taking this into account, it is very unlikely that any material the expert has seen would fall outside of the description in Article 6.5.

3. *Ex Parte* Communications

9.98 Article 6.5 also states that the parties are entitled to examine 'any correspondence between the Tribunal and the Tribunal-Appointed Expert'. This provision suggests that *ex parte* correspondence may have taken place between the tribunal and the expert. On this basis, it appears that *ex parte* correspondence is permissible, subject to the safeguard contained in Article 6.5 giving the parties the right to examine that correspondence. We suggest that it may be prudent for parties to make an express request for sight of such correspondence where this is not provided for by means of an agreed communication protocol.

9.99 The possibility of *ex parte* communications between a tribunal and an expert is not yet ruled out in the practice of international arbitration. For example, until very recently the HKIAC Rules included express provision at Article 25.1 that 'The arbitral tribunal may meet privately with any tribunal-appointed expert'.[52]

9.100 On the other hand, as mentioned, much may depend on what might have been agreed between the parties and the tribunal during initial consultation on appointment of the expert, and the individual preferences of the particular tribunal. For example, in a survey on this issue, respondents from Spain indicated that they had experience of a tribunal making an express direction that there should be no *ex parte* communications between tribunal and expert (as well as that the expert should not attend the tribunal's deliberations).[53]

[52] This provision does not appear in Article 25.1 of the HKIAC Rules, which came into force on 1 November 2018.
[53] BCLP Survey on the use of the IBA Rules.

4. Party Right to Respond

9.101 Article 6.5 makes express provision for the parties to have an opportunity to respond to the report produced by the tribunal-appointed expert. This is unsurprising and reflects accepted practice in international arbitration.[54] In the interests of fairness and natural justice the parties must have an opportunity to present their views on the evidence so that they may, where necessary, point out any errors or omissions and/or have the opportunity to present reasons why the tribunal ought not to accept the conclusions of the expert. This is particularly important where the tribunal is relying on the evidence of a single tribunal-appointed expert, rather than weighing the evidence from 'competing' party-appointed experts.

9.102 Consistent with the above position, the commentary to the rules states that:

> The Working Party and the Subcommittee believed strongly that parties should know what the arbitral tribunal is being told by a Tribunal-Appointed Expert and should have an opportunity to rebut his or her conclusions.[55]

9.103 Other guidelines on the use of tribunal-appointed experts also stress the need for a party to have a right of response. For example, Practice Guideline 10 of the Chartered Institute of Arbitrators (Guidelines on the Use of Tribunal-Appointed Experts, Legal Advisers and Assessors) recommends that:

> [I]f the tribunal does decide to appoint an expert legal adviser or assessor the procedure to be followed must be closely defined in an order made by the tribunal at or about the stage of the appointment. Section 37 leaves the details of that procedure to the discretion of the tribunal save in one respect, that is, that any information, opinion or advice offered by any person appointed by the tribunal must be communicated to the parties and the parties must be given a reasonable opportunity to comment on it.[56]

9.104 Under Article 6.5, a party must exercise its right to respond by a date to be determined by the tribunal. Article 6.5 describes the form such a response may take. Each party may choose to respond:

- in a submission;
- through a witness statement; or
- by means of an expert report from a party-appointed expert.[57]

[54] Chartered Institute of Arbitrators, International Arbitration Practice Guidelines: Party-Appointed and Tribunal-Appointed Experts, Commentary on Article 5.1.

[55] Commentary on the IBA Rules (n 12) 21.

[56] Chartered Institute of Arbitrators, Practice Guideline 10: Guidelines on the Use of Tribunal-Appointed Experts, Legal Advisers and Assessors, para 1.6.

[57] Institutional arbitration rules, while very often stipulating a party's right to respond to the expert evidence of a tribunal-appointed expert in writing, do not generally contain a provision similar to that of the IBA Rules in which the form of the permitted response is set out. For example, see SCC Rules, Article 34(2) and HKIAC Rules, Article 25.3. One exception is LCIA Rules, Article 21.4, which gives the parties a right 'to present witnesses in order to testify on relevant issues arising from the report'. In practice, see the terms of the Final Award in ICC Case 17272 (extract, ICC Digital Library, 2013).

In our view, it is not intended that the parties have to make an election between these forms of response. In some instances, it may be necessary or appropriate for a party to use a combination of them.

Subject to any tribunal direction or agreement to the contrary, the wording of Article 6.5 suggests that the response should be sent to the tribunal, who will then pass it on to the expert. Although not provided for in Article 6.5, the tribunal may consider it appropriate in some cases for there to be a further round of expert evidence. **9.105**

An alternative approach to inviting responses to a completed expert report is for the tribunal to instruct the expert to submit a report in draft and for the tribunal to then invite the parties to comment on the expert's provisional findings. This allows the expert to take the parties' comments into account when finalizing the report. The advantage of this is that it may allow errors or omissions to be picked up and corrected before the report is issued in final form. A significant drawback is that it may result in protracted communications between all participants and a potential dilution of the evidence. In one reported case the tribunal departed from the guidelines laid down in Article 6.5 and adopted a procedure providing for the expert to submit a draft report so that the parties could request additional explanation or justification for the findings made. Although the tribunal saw this step as enhancing the efficiency of the process by avoiding unnecessarily long and complicated expert reports, it unfortunately led to a challenge to the expert and to the admissibility of the report.[58] **9.106**

G. The Attendance of the Tribunal-Appointed Expert at the Evidentiary Hearing

> **6.6 At the request of a Party or of the Arbitral Tribunal, the Tribunal-Appointed Expert shall be present at an Evidentiary Hearing. The Arbitral Tribunal may question the Tribunal-Appointed Expert, and he or she may be questioned by the Parties or by any Party-Appointed Expert on issues raised in his or her Expert Report, the Parties' submissions or Witness Statement or the Expert Reports made by the Party-Appointed Experts pursuant to Article 6.5.**

Article 6.5 addresses the attendance of a tribunal-appointed expert at an evidentiary hearing. **9.107**

[58] ibid.

1. Introduction

9.108 In line with other provisions of the IBA Rules, a tribunal-appointed expert who submits an expert report is only required to appear at the evidentiary hearing if a party or the tribunal requests that attendance. If no such request is made, there is no requirement that the expert attend.

2. Examination of the Tribunal-Appointed Expert

9.109 Article 6.6 states expressly that, where an expert does attend an evidentiary hearing, the expert may be questioned by the tribunal, or by the parties or their appointed experts.

9.110 This is an important provision. It is essential that each party be given an opportunity to question the expert in order to test his or her evidence. Although the parties will have had an opportunity under Article 6.5 to respond to the expert evidence, the expert may not have accepted the points made and counsel for the parties will wish to pursue those matters in cross-examination. It is also useful for the tribunal to see the evidence tested. In most cases, the tribunal will only form a final view as to the weight to be attached to expert evidence after it has had the opportunity to hear the expert under questioning from the parties.

9.111 The scope of the permitted questioning is limited to issues arising out of the expert's report or a party's response to that report delivered pursuant to Article 6.5. The Commentary on the IBA Rules explains that this provision is intended to ensure that the tribunal-appointed expert knows in advance the subjects on which s/he might be questioned, in order to prepare his or her responses and avoid the possibility of an adjournment being required as a result of new issues being put to the tribunal-appointed expert for the first time at the hearing.[59]

9.112 The express provision for a party-appointed expert to question the expert is interesting. While there may be advantages to an expert being questioned by another expert in the same discipline, the general practice in international arbitration is for cross-examination of an expert to be undertaken by counsel. An expert qualified in a discipline other than law may have a different skill set to that of an experienced advocate.

9.113 That said, where witness conferencing[60] is being employed by the tribunal, a discussion between a tribunal-appointed expert and any party-appointed experts qualified in the same discipline may be a useful way of assessing the evidence. There appears to be

[59] Commentary on the IBA Rules (n 12).

[60] Witness-conferencing, or 'hot-tubbing', is where witnesses or experts are subject to questioning at the same time, either by the tribunal or by counsel for the parties. Tribunals sometimes like to put the same question to each expert in turn and/or to encourage dialogue between the experts on a particular point with a view to encouraging consensus or highlighting the real differences between the witnesses/experts and judging who is more credible on the point. See for more detail Chapter 11 paras 11.72–11.74.

general acceptance that witness conferencing involving a tribunal-appointed expert is permitted under the provisions of Article 8 of the IBA Rules.[61] We agree with that view. Of course, witness conferencing is only possible where there is more than one expert on the same issue.

3. Consequences of Non-Attendance at the Evidentiary Hearing

Article 6 does not provide any consequences if a tribunal-appointed expert fails to attend the hearing if so requested. This is in stark contrast with the position of a party-appointed expert whose failure to appear will, under Article 5.5 of the IBA Rules, result in the expert report being disregarded by the tribunal unless it considers that there are exceptional circumstances that warrant its inclusion. It is not clear why the approach is different with respect to different types of experts. One possible explanation is that application of the Article 5 provision to the tribunal-appointed expert may leave the tribunal with no expert evidence at all, while in case of party-appointed experts, at least the tribunal can rely on the evidence of the other party's expert who *has* appeared. **9.114**

If the parties do not have an opportunity to cross-examine the tribunal-appointed expert, reliance by the tribunal on that evidence alone could be a failure of due process (or at least give one or other of the parties an opportunity to argue that it is). When weighing the evidence of a non-attending expert, the tribunal will have to take into account the responses to the report of the tribunal-appointed expert filed by the parties under Article 6.5, any reply to those responses made by the expert, and the fact that the expert was not available at the evidentiary hearing to answer further questions on the disputed issues. **9.115**

In practice, the non-attendance of a tribunal-appointed expert is likely to be rare. In addition to failing to meet the requirements of Article 6.6, it is also likely to constitute a breach of the expert's retainer with the tribunal and may have financial consequences for the expert. Where there are bona fide reasons for the expert not being able to attend, the tribunal may also decide that it should adjourn the hearing, or at least that portion concerned with the issues addressed by the expert, until a later date. **9.116**

4. Additional Role at the Evidentiary Hearing

The IBA Rules are silent as to what further role (if any) the expert may play at the hearing, eg if members of the tribunal should be permitted to have the expert sit with them as an adviser during questioning of any experts of the same discipline appointed **9.117**

[61] IBA Rules (n 10) Article 8 (Evidentiary Hearing). See, for example Nils Schmidt-Ahrendts and Klaus Sachs, 'Expert Evidence under the 2010 IBA Rules' (2010) International Arbitration Law Review 216, 218, where it is said that: '. . . the broad formulation of art. 8(3) of the 2010 IBA Rules allows the conclusion that not only party-appointed experts but also tribunal-appointed experts may be examined via witness-conferencing'.

by the parties, or when counsel for the parties are making submissions on the evidence of the tribunal expert. We are aware of cases where the tribunal has invited a tribunal-appointed expert to sit with the tribunal throughout the evidentiary hearing. We suggest that it is prudent for a tribunal considering such a step to first canvass it with the parties or, at the very least, to make known the intended scope of the expert's intended involvement so as to address as far as possible any concerns that the parties may have about the expert assuming a decision-making role (which is clearly prohibited).

5. Attendance during Tribunal Deliberations and *Ex Parte* Meetings with the Tribunal

9.118 Article 6 does not contain any reference to the attendance of a tribunal-appointed expert at tribunal deliberations or other meeting with the tribunal at which the parties are not present. However, nor does it contain an express prohibition on such attendance.

9.119 The presence of a tribunal-appointed expert in private meetings or at tribunal deliberations has advantages and disadvantages. On the one hand, the tribunal may benefit from expert assistance. The presence of the expert may help avoid any errors when the tribunal comes to consider the expert evidence and the parties' submissions on the evidence. Meeting with the expert and the parties may be less useful. The tribunal may be hesitant about discussing particular issues with the expert in an open way for fear of giving an appearance of bias. In addition, the parties may wish to intervene unnecessarily so as to make such meetings time-consuming and/or counter-productive.

9.120 On the other hand, the Article 6 mechanism must achieve the right balance between the tribunal's need for assistance on expert issues and the rights of the parties. The tribunal must not become so dependent on the expert that the case is effectively decided by the expert rather than the tribunal. For this reason, the parties may have justified concerns if the tribunal-appointed expert attends deliberations and expresses his or her views in the absence of the parties.

9.121 We suggest that there are serious risks associated with allowing the expert to be present in meetings with the tribunal without the parties also being present. Article 6 allows a tribunal to seek assistance from an expert, but does not allow the tribunal to delegate its decision-making function.[62] If a tribunal were to listen to additional input from the expert during a meeting or deliberations without giving the parties the opportunity to comment on that input before taking it into account, this would undoubtedly breach rules of natural justice. While the tribunal may want the expert present to walk them through the available evidence, it would be very easy for the line between explanation and comment to be crossed.

[62] See the ICC Report on Issues for Arbitrators Regarding Experts (n 4) Section III(A).

Unsurprisingly, there have been instances where national courts have found that *ex parte* meetings between a tribunal and a tribunal-appointed expert amount to an irregularity. In *Hussmann (Europe) Ltd v Al Ameen Development & Trade Co & Ors.*,[63] the applicant (HCN) challenged the award on the basis of alleged serious procedural irregularities including the fact that—without the parties being present—the tribunal had met with a tribunal-appointed expert on Saudi law to discuss the expert's report. Although what had occurred was not sufficient to sustain a proper challenge to the award, Mr Justice Thomas found that the meeting breached a provision of English arbitration law that required a tribunal to give the parties a reasonable opportunity to comment on 'information, opinion or advice' offered by a tribunal-appointed expert. In his judgment, Thomas J said that: 9.122

> Given that the pleadings raised no issues of Saudi law and that it was for the parties to allege that foreign law differed from English law, the tribunal should have followed the course of asking the parties whether there were any points where the law of Saudi Arabia differed from the law of England and Wales or to have itself raised with the parties specific points on which it might need assistance. However there was no irregularity in the tribunal instructing its own expert since the parties had left the way in which the expert was to be instructed to the tribunal.[64] The private meeting with the expert to discuss his draft report was contrary to s. 37(1) (b) of the 1996 Act and failure to inform the parties of it was an irregularity.
>
> [...]
>
> The point was taken that in the meeting with Dr Al-Qasem, the tribunal was not taking evidence and so the provisions of s. 37(1) (b) did not apply; I do not agree. They were plainly discussing with him the law of Saudi Arabia and the content of his report; in my judgment the provisions of the section were applicable to this meeting at which his evidence was discussed.[65]

Thomas J went on to make some further general observations in relation to discussions between a tribunal and tribunal-appointed expert at which the parties were not present. He said that: 9.123

> A tribunal should generally not hear evidence in the absence of the parties.
>
> I agree with the observation of Professor Merkin in his work on arbitration at para. 13.46(e): '. . . consultation with the experts should not take place after the close of the hearing or otherwise in the absence of the parties as this deprives the parties of their right to comment'.[66]

While the IBA Rules do not expressly rule out *ex parte* meetings with a tribunal-appointed expert, a tribunal must be vigilant about protecting each party's right to 9.124

63 *Hussmann (Europe) Ltd v Al Ameen Dev & Trade Co* [2000] 2 Lloyd's Rep. 83; [2000] 4 WLUK 617.
64 ibid [3].
65 ibid [4], [45].
66 ibid [45].

present its case and to know the evidence against it. The tribunal should not rely on views and conclusions of the expert about which the parties have had no opportunity to comment.

H. Assessment of the Evidence by the Tribunal

6.7. Any Expert Report made by a Tribunal-Appointed Expert and its conclusions shall be assessed by the Arbitral Tribunal with due regard to all circumstances of the case.

9.125 As mentioned, a primary area of concern relating to the use of a tribunal-appointed expert is that the tribunal may delegate its decision-making function to the expert. Article 6.7 addresses this problem and appears to be a reminder to the tribunal that it should not place undue reliance on the expert report produced by a tribunal-appointed expert without reference to the other available evidence and the circumstances of the case.

9.126 Furthermore, it highlights that the weight to be attached to the expert evidence on the facts of the case is to be assessed by the tribunal. The tribunal must not delegate its mandate to determine the dispute and the tribunal is not bound by the expert's findings. It is the role of the tribunal to assess the evidence. In exceptional circumstances, the tribunal may decide to place little or no reliance on the evidence of the tribunal-appointed expert, or it may prefer the evidence of a party-appointed expert over that of its own expert. For example, it might decide to disregard the evidence where:

- there are rebuttal reports from two or more party-appointed experts in which those experts reach the same conclusion, being a conclusion that is different to that of the tribunal-appointed expert; and/or
- the conclusions of the tribunal-appointed expert are based on assumptions/conditions that are not borne out by the facts; and/or
- the expert report produced by the tribunal-appointed expert contradicts the majority of the evidence on the record and common sense.

I. Fees and Expenses of the Expert

6.8. The fees and expenses of a Tribunal-Appointed Expert, to be funded in a manner determined by the Arbitral Tribunal, shall form part of the costs of the arbitration.

9.127 Article 6.8 confirms that the fees and expenses of the party-appointed expert are to be treated as a cost incurred in the arbitration in the same way as would be the case with the fees of a party-appointed expert. 'Costs of the arbitration' are generally understood to include the tribunal's fees and expenses, the legal or other costs of the parties, and the fees and expenses of any arbitral institution involved in the case.[67] The IBA Rules are silent on this point, but where the expert is appointed directly by the tribunal it seems appropriate that the fees would fall under the category of 'expenses of the tribunal'.[68]

The real question is how the expert's fees are to be funded in the interim period until they are allocated for payment by one or other of the parties as part of the general allocation of costs at the end of the arbitration. **9.128**

Article 6.8 simply says that the manner of funding is to be determined by the tribunal. The approach taken will depend on the facts of the case. This makes perfect sense. A provision that was in any way prescriptive might hinder, rather than facilitate, the appointment of the expert. **9.129**

Article 5 of the IBA Rules does not contain any provision about the fees of party-appointed experts. This is no doubt because in the ordinary course of events these are generally borne by the appointing party who, in turn, will (if appropriate) claim the fees as part of its costs in the arbitration when arguments on costs are heard by the tribunal. **9.130**

In the case of a tribunal-appointed expert, the situation is different. If called upon to pay the fees of a tribunal-appointed expert, one or both parties may be unwilling or slow to do so. Of course, there may be exceptional cases—for example, where one party insists in the face of opposition that expert evidence is required and is willing to provide up-front funding for the appointment of a single expert.[69] However, in general, the tribunal will need to ensure that arrangements are in place to ensure that the fees and expenses of the expert will be paid by the parties as and when they are incurred. The tribunal may try to agree a fixed fee with the expert. At the very least, it will wish to obtain an estimate of the fees likely to be incurred. Ideally, the tribunal will then obtain the parties agreement that they should advance an appropriate sum to be held on account of the expert's fees—very often in an account held by the supervising arbitral institution, where there is one. In an ad hoc arbitration, the tribunal may choose to use another third-party fund holder. **9.131**

It is common practice for the tribunal to ask the parties to advance the expert's fees in equal shares. Where one party refuses to do so, the other parties may have to make up the balance. If they are not prepared to do this, the tribunal (and possibly the expert) may be reluctant to proceed with the appointment. Any applicable institutional arbitration rules will also need to be taken into account and in some cases may provide assistance in relation to the mechanism by which the fees are to be advanced or paid. For **9.132**

[67] See, for example, English Arbitration Act 1996, s 59, which contains an express definition of the term 'costs of the arbitration', as used in that legislation, in the terms mentioned.

[68] The English Arbitration Act 1996 contains express provision to this effect. English Arbitration Act 1996, s 37(2) states that: 'The fees and expenses of an expert, legal adviser or assessor appointed by the tribunal for which the arbitrators are liable are expenses of the arbitrators for the purposes of this Part'.

[69] In theory, under the IBA Rules the tribunal should only sanction expert evidence on an issue that is relevant to the case and material to its outcome in relation to which one would expect there to be a general recognition by the parties and the tribunal that such is the case. In practice, the position may not be so clear.

example, the Rules of the International Commercial Arbitration Court at the Russian Federation Chamber of Commerce and Industry require the claimant to pay all of the fees and then seek to recover those fees through costs submissions.[70] Article 21.5 of the LCIA Rules provides that the fees and expenses of any expert appointed by the tribunal may be paid out of the deposits payable by the parties under Article 24 of those rules. If a party fails to pay its share of the deposit, the other party may be asked to pay the shortfall, but will have the right to ask the tribunal to make an award in its favour against the defaulting party for the relevant sum. A failure to pay a deposit by a claimant or cross-claimant may also result in the claim or cross-claim being struck out.[71]

[70] See, eg Section 14(2) of the Rules of the International Commercial Arbitration Court at the Russian Federation Chamber of Commerce and Industry (ICAC). However, the Arbitral Tribunal is still entitled to order that the Respondent pays part or all of the Tribunal-Appointed Expert Fees pursuant to Section 7 of the Costs Schedule annexed to the ICAC Rules.

[71] LCIA Rules, Articles 24.4, 24.5, and 24.6.

10
Article 7: Inspection

Article 7 Inspection

Subject to the provisions of Article 9.2, the Arbitral Tribunal may, at the request of a Party or on its own motion, inspect or require the inspection by a Tribunal-Appointed Expert or a Party-Appointed Expert of any site, property, machinery or any other goods, samples, systems, processes or Documents, as it deems appropriate. The Arbitral Tribunal shall, in consultation with the Parties, determine the timing and arrangement for the inspection. The Parties and their representatives shall have the right to attend any such inspection.

A. Introduction

The Commentary to the IBA Rules describes Article 7 as a: **10.1**

> simple provision, making possible inspections of relevant site, property, machinery or any other goods, samples, systems, processes or documents that may help the decision-making process, wherever they may be located.[1]

Article 7 enables the tribunal to direct that the tribunal, a tribunal-appointed expert, or a party-appointed expert, should make an inspection of a relevant site or thing. The inspection should be one that 'may help the decision-making process'. This objective is underpinned by the fact that the tribunal's power to order an inspection is made subject to the provisions of Article 9.2. **10.2**

[1] 1999 IBA Working Party and 2010 IBA Rules of Evidence Review Subcommittee, 'Commentary on the Revised Text of the 2010 IBA Rules on the Taking of Evidence in International Arbitration' (*International Bar Association*, 2014) 22 <www.ibanet.org/Document/Default.aspx?DocumentUid=DD240932-0E08-40D4-9866-309A635487C0> accessed 27 November 2018.

10.3 The Commentary on the IBA Rules notes that inspections most frequently occur in construction arbitrations in which the tribunal may wish to visit the construction site under dispute.[2] However, the making of an inspection may have value in a number of different situations. For members of the tribunal, as well as for counsel, a physical inspection of the piece of equipment, manufacturing process, layout of a half-built holiday complex, or scene of an incident can offer clarity to submissions and evidence that appear impenetrable on paper. For an expert witness, an inspection may be critical. In some circumstances, the object or site under dispute may be subject to further change or removal and an early inspection may be the only opportunity the experts have to gather evidence and inform themselves about its physical condition at the relevant time. Relevant physical evidence or data may have to be selected or identified so that steps can be taken to preserve it for future reference in the proceedings. Inspection of proprietary material related to the matter in dispute may provide additional insight.

10.4 In addition, the evidential value of the information obtained may be compromised if the inspection does not take place under supervision and in documented conditions in accordance with guidelines laid down by the tribunal or agreed between the parties.

10.5 The point is often made that, in modern practice, the need for an inspection by the tribunal can often be answered by use of visual aids such as models, photographs, drawings, and film, eg chartering a helicopter to make a video showing the terrain in which a road was to be constructed.[3] However, such solutions may not be an adequate substitute for inspection in all cases. In addition, such solutions are less likely to answer the needs of experts instructed to collect and present evidence.

B. What May Be Inspected?

10.6 The broad spectrum of circumstances in which an inspection may be appropriate is acknowledged in the revisions made to the predecessor provision of Article 7. The title was changed from 'On-site inspection' to 'Inspection' as an inspection will not always be connected with a geographical location.

10.7 Under Article 7, an order for inspection may be made in relation to:

> [A]ny site, property, machinery or any other goods, samples, systems, processes or Documents.

[2] ibid 22.

[3] Nigel Blackaby and others, *Redfern and Hunter on International Arbitration* (6th edn, OUP 2016) para 6.148 (hereafter 'Redfern and Hunter'). In the example cited, the matter was settled before the proposal could be acted upon.

The description extends the definition appearing in the 1999 IBA Rules by the inclusion of 'samples' and 'systems'.[4] This expanded description is broad enough to encompass most places and items that a tribunal may determine to be appropriate for inspection in the course of a dispute.

Some terms mentioned in Article 7 require no explanation—'site', 'property', 'machinery', or 'other goods' generally have meanings that are understood and unlikely to give rise to much serious dispute. 'Samples' may have different meanings, depending upon the context—for example, it could mean inspection of particular retained samples held by one of the parties, or a representative sample the tribunal wishes to see of something collected under agreed conditions. The descriptions 'systems' and 'processes' are also capable of wide interpretation, being terms that could apply equally to IT systems, manufacturing processes, accounting/audit procedures, etc. 'Documents' is a defined term in the IBA Rules, meaning: 'a writing of any kind, whether recorded on paper, electronic means, audio or visual recordings or any other mechanical or electronic means of storing or recording information'. The right to request/order the inspection of a 'Document' extends to documents of which a copy has been produced under Article 9 of the IBA Rules. **10.8**

On-site inspections are most likely to be proposed in disputes relating to the operation of an industrial plant or in construction, engineering, and mining disputes, or possibly in complex financial matters where an inspection of additional documents or processes is deemed necessary.[5] In theory, the possibilities are endless and may range from inspection of a commodity not meeting contractual specification to the inspection of computer hardware to determine whether soft copy documents said to have been deleted or lost can be retrieved. **10.9**

C. The Arbitral Tribunal's Power to Order an Inspection

There is no deadline specified in the IBA Rules by which an application or direction for inspection is to be made or given. As a result, and absent any party agreement or applicable provision to the contrary, it is open to a party or to the tribunal to propose an inspection at any stage. In practice, an inspection is likely to take place in advance of any evidentiary hearing, but, in principle, the suggested need for an inspection may arise out of events as late as the parties' closing written submissions. **10.10**

[4] IBA Rules on the Taking of Evidence in International Commercial Arbitration 1999, Article 7: '. . . the Arbitral Tribunal may . . . inspect or require the inspection . . . of any site, property, machinery or any other goods or process, or documents . . .'.

[5] Tobias Zuberbühler and others, *IBA Rules of Evidence: Commentary on the IBA Rules on the Taking of Evidence in International Arbitration* (Schulthess 2012) 146 (hereafter 'Zuberbühler').

10.11 Under Article 7, an order for inspection may arise in one of two ways. The tribunal may decide itself that an inspection is appropriate, or one of the parties to the arbitration may request it.

10.12 The tribunal is empowered to make an order for an inspection to be carried out by:

(a) the tribunal;
(b) a tribunal-appointed expert;[6] or
(c) a party-appointed expert.

10.13 Subject to any agreement by the parties to the contrary, the right of a tribunal to carry out or order an inspection is likely to exist in any event under the tribunal's general case-management authority. All of the major institutional rules confer a wide discretion on the tribunal in relation to the conduct of the proceedings and it is very likely that this would include the power to order an inspection if the tribunal considers it necessary in its proper conduct of the proceedings.[7]

10.14 When considering whether to exercise its power to order an inspection, the tribunal must bear in mind any provisions relating to inspection laid down in any applicable arbitration rules (eg Article 22.1(iv) of the LCIA Rules[8] and SIAC Rule 27(d)).[9] In addition, where the tribunal has already made provision for a possible inspection in a first procedural order, the terms of that order will need to be considered.

10.15 Save for compliance with the safeguards put in place by Article 9.2,[10] and subject to party agreement to the contrary, it is for the tribunal alone to decide whether an inspection should take place. The tribunal may make a direction for inspection 'as it deems appropriate'. This makes sense. Whether an inspection will add value to the proceedings will depend very heavily upon the particular facts of the case.

10.16 When a tribunal is considering an inspection under Article 7, it should bear in mind the cost and disruption to the parties of an inspection relative to the potential benefit to be gained.[11]

[6] For example, an expert appointed by the tribunal under the provisions of the IBA Rules on the Taking of Evidence in International Commercial Arbitration 2010, Article 6 (hereafter 'IBA Rules').

[7] See, for example, SCC Rules, Article 23(1): 'The Arbitral Tribunal may conduct the arbitration in such manner as it considers appropriate, subject to these Rules and any agreement between the parties'; HKIAC Rules, Article 13.1: 'Subject to these Rules, the arbitral tribunal shall adopt suitable procedures for the conduct of the arbitration in order to avoid unnecessary delay or expense, having regard to the complexity of the issues, the amount in dispute and the effective use of technology, and provided that such procedures ensure equal treatment of the parties and afford the parties a reasonable opportunity to present their case.'; SIAC Rules, Rule 19.1: 'The Tribunal shall conduct the arbitration in such manner as it considers appropriate, after consulting with the parties, to ensure the fair, expeditious, economical and final resolution of the dispute'; LCIA Rules, Article 14.5: 'The Arbitral Tribunal shall have the widest discretion to discharge these general duties [regarding the conduct of the arbitration] subject to such mandatory law(s) or rules of law as the Arbitral Tribunal may decide to be applicable.'

[8] 'The arbitral tribunal may decide to order any party to make any documents, goods, samples, property, site or thing under its control available for inspection by the arbitral tribunal, any other party, any expert to such party and any expert to the tribunal.'

[9] 'Unless otherwise agreed by the parties, the Tribunal has the power to order the parties to make any property or item in their possession or control available for inspection.'

[10] See Chapter 12 paras 12.57–12.316.

[11] See further Zuberbühler (n 5) 146.

If the site or object to be inspected lies within the control of one of the parties and that party fails to comply with the order for inspection of what may constitute 'relevant evidence', the tribunal is permitted to draw adverse inferences against the non-cooperating party in accordance with the provisions of Article 9.6 of the IBA Rules.[12] In the context of Article 7, 'relevant evidence' may include, for example, a piece of allegedly defective equipment the subject of the claim, or a database of customers in a dispute under a distributorship agreement. 10.17

D. Restrictions Imposed by Article 9.2

The power of the tribunal to carry out or order an inspection is made expressly subject to the provisions of Article 9.2 of the IBA Rules. These provisions state the grounds upon which the tribunal may exclude an inspection from evidence or production.[13] Such exclusion may manifest itself as a refusal to inspect or permit an expert to inspect, or by a decision to exclude evidence of an inspection—for example, by not admitting on to the record documentary or audio-visual material generated during an inspection, and not permitting oral testimony in relation to it. The tribunal may exclude such matters either on its own motion or as a result of an objection raised by one of the parties. 10.18

Although this is not stated expressly at Article 7, the decision as to whether grounds exist for excluding a proposed inspection, or evidence of an inspection that has taken place, rests solely with the tribunal.[14] Where the tribunal concludes that one of the grounds set out in Article 9.2(a)–(g) applies, it can exclude an inspection. In the context of Article 7, this will, in broad terms, include circumstances where: 10.19

- the information to be gleaned from the proposed inspection is not sufficiently relevant or material to outcome [9.2 (a)], eg a requested inspection of part of a construction site where the experts for the parties have already agreed that the item of work proposed to be inspected is not on the critical path of the delay claim being advanced by the claimant;
- that some legal impediment or privilege applies to the carrying out of an inspection [9.2 (b)], eg one party wishes to 'inspect' an audio recording held by another party, the content of which attracts legal privilege;
- that the carrying out of the inspection would be burdensome or disproportionate [9.2 (c) and (g)], eg where one of the party-appointed experts wishes to inspect a component part in a process engineering plant, but where the inspection would

[12] 'If a Party fails without satisfactory explanation . . . to make available any evidence, including testimony, ordered by the Arbitral Tribunal to be produced, the Arbitral Tribunal may infer that such evidence would be adverse to the interests of that Party'. IBA Rules (n 6) Article 9.6.

[13] The opening lines of IBA Rules (n 6) Article 9.2 expressly state that: 'The Arbitral Tribunal shall, at the request of a Party or on its own motion, exclude from evidence or production any Documents, statements, oral testimony *or inspection* for any of the following reasons' (emphasis added).

[14] See further Zuberbühler (n 5) 147.

cause material disruption to the respondent's business and the value of the particular claim to which the component is relevant is a very small part of the claimant's money claim;
- that the subject matter of the proposed inspection has been lost or destroyed [9.2 (d)], eg one of the parties wishes to inspect records relating to operation of a logistics business, but those records are demonstrated to have been destroyed during a fire at the relevant party's office premises;
- that there are compelling grounds of commercial or technical confidentiality, or special political or institutional sensitivity, that make an inspection inappropriate [9.2 (e) and (f)], eg where one party wishes to inspect unredacted files held by another party that contain politically sensitive communications between that party and its national government;
- or that considerations of procedural economy, proportionality, fairness, or equality of the parties militate against an inspection and the tribunal finds those considerations to be compelling [9.2 (g)], eg a party wishes the tribunal to inspect a top-secret military facility but, within the available procedural timeline, security clearance can only be obtained for the tribunal and one party's expert.

The grounds for exclusion under Article 9.2 are dealt with in more detail in Chapter 12.

E. Arrangements for the Inspection

10.20 Site inspections normally require considerable preparation. Born succinctly summarizes the typical routines and concerns:

> The logistics and procedures for a site inspection can be complex. Visits must be scheduled, following consultations and planning with the parties, with appropriate security, explanation and other assistance. All parties have the right to attend such inspections and the parties will typically be concerned to ensure that arrangements for any inspection not enable their counter-parties to present their case or 'spin' the presentation through employees responsible for accompanying the tribunal. Video recordings, photographs and other records of the inspection of a site, goods, or other property can sometimes be made, although the arrangements for this can again be cumbersome.[15]

10.21 The IBA Rules do not provide any detail about the arrangements for an inspection under Article 7. These will have to be determined on a case-by-case basis. However, the power given to a tribunal under Article 7 to determine the timing and arrangement of the inspection is very sensibly made subject to the requirement that the tribunal shall do so 'in consultation with the parties'. This is an important requirement and should not be regarded simply as a box to tick. As a matter of practice, an inspection is much

[15] Gary B Born, *International Commercial Arbitration* (2nd edn, Kluwer Law International 2014) 2353–54 (footnotes omitted).

more likely to run smoothly if there is agreement between the parties—with intervention where necessary from the tribunal—as to the appropriate arrangements for the inspection. In addition, a process of consultation gives each party an opportunity to voice its concerns and make proposals to address aspects of the inspection that might not otherwise have occurred to the tribunal.

Fair treatment of all parties is an important consideration. When a tribunal orders an inspection, it must ensure that the procedures and arrangements laid down for that inspection ensure due process and are fair to all parties. As mentioned, this principle is reflected in the grounds of exclusion set out at Article 9.2(g). As a result, a number of safeguards may need to be put in place in order to ensure that one party does not gain an unfair advantage over any other party as a result of or in connection with the inspection. **10.22**

The practical arrangements for an inspection may be relatively simple and flexible, or very detailed and prescriptive. What the tribunal determines to be appropriate will depend very much on the facts of the case, the attitudes of the parties, and the purpose of the inspection. **10.23**

When appropriate arrangements have been determined, it is good practice for the tribunal to issue a procedural order or protocol setting out the inspection arrangements in order to remove any doubt about what has been agreed or ordered.[16] As a minimum, this should include the following: **10.24**

- The date/s of the inspection;
- What is to be inspected;
- The nature and purpose of the inspection;
- Who is permitted to attend;
- The rights and role of each of the individuals attending the inspection and the content of any accompanying explanatory commentary; and
- Whether any record of the inspection is to be produced and what use is to be made of any information collected.

1. Timing and Date

As noted, there is no deadline by which an inspection must be undertaken. In consequence, an inspection may be proposed or take place at any stage of the proceedings. Where it is known early in the proceedings that an inspection is likely to be required—whether because the tribunal has signalled that it wants to make an inspection or the parties themselves are in agreement that one should take place or where one party has laid down a marker that its expert will require access to a site or object material to the **10.25**

[16] See further Redfern and Hunter (n 3) para 6.151.

dispute—it may be possible to build in to the procedural timetable some provision for an inspection. Where access to evidence is required urgently or where the need for an inspection arises on short notice or close to the evidentiary hearing, arrangements for the inspection may have to be made very quickly.

10.26 Agreement on the precise date and timing for an inspection may raise a number of factors for consideration. In many cases, the inspection will be of a site or facility controlled by one of the parties. When determining the date and time for an inspection the tribunal will need to be sensitive to the need not to disrupt more than is necessary any development or business being carried on there. There may also be debate around the best timing for an inspection in order to maximize the value of any evidence to be collected. For example, one of the parties may argue that an inspection should take place as soon as possible in order to avoid evidence being lost or destroyed, or there may be discussions around whether an inspection should take place in certain weather conditions or when a certain business process or activity is in full operation. Each party will wish to consider very carefully what will suit its case best before making proposals or submissions about date and timing. The tribunal will need to balance these submissions and make the final decision if disagreement between the parties cannot be resolved.

2. The Nature and Purpose of the Inspection

10.27 Whether the order for inspection has been precipitated by a party application or a tribunal request, once a decision to inspect has been made it is sensible to seek a consensus about what the inspection is intended to achieve. This will inform the nature and scope of the arrangements being discussed. In addition, even the simplest inspection involves time and cost and, in many cases, it will not be possible to repeat the inspection. To the extent possible, arrangements made should ensure that those participating are able to obtain what they need with minimum disruption. For example, in an IT dispute, inspection arrangements may include a clear definition of what is being searched for and on what systems; a means of inspection that interrupts the systems as little as possible (such as imaging, ie copying, of computers or servers, which can then be reviewed in isolation from the live systems); and a process by which the data retrieved is to be filtered (usually by the parties' respective experts under an agreed set of guidelines) before being released.

3. Attendance at the Inspection

10.28 Article 7 provides for inspection by the tribunal or by an expert. Depending on the purpose of the inspection some or all of these parties may attend. For example, if the purpose of the inspection is the collection of samples by party-appointed experts, the tribunal may take the view that there is no need for members of the tribunal to attend. If the purpose of the inspection is for the tribunal to be shown a particular piece of manufacturing plant relevant to the dispute, then the tribunal and experts in the relevant discipline may all attend.

Regardless of for whose benefit the inspection is taking place (ie tribunal or expert/s), Article 7 contains an express statement that the parties and their representatives have the right to attend any inspection. This is important, as transparency around what is said and done during an inspection is fundamental to ensuring fairness to both sides. If the purpose of the inspection is to collect evidence, transparency is particularly important. If a party does not know what the tribunal or another party's expert was shown, or what explanation of a process or problem may have been proffered to the tribunal, it may be disadvantaged. The presence of both parties will ensure 'fair play' and make more likely the observance of any protocol that may have been agreed for the inspection. **10.29**

The terms of Article 7 would appear to preclude a situation in which only one of the parties is barred from attending the inspection. The need for caution in relation to such matters is highlighted in the UNCITRAL Notes on Organizing Arbitral Proceedings: **10.30**

> If an on-site inspection of property or goods will take place, the arbitral tribunal may consider matters such as timing, meeting places, other arrangements to provide the opportunity for all parties to be present, and the need to avoid communications between arbitrators and a party about points at issue without the presence of the other party or parties.[17]

It has been pointed out that to make an inspection in the presence of one party alone may have potentially damaging consequences for the successful party when it comes to enforce the award.[18] **10.31**

As a general rule, the tribunal should therefore order that any inspection by the tribunal, or by a party-appointed or tribunal-appointed expert, should be carried out in the presence of the parties and/or their representatives.[19] Parties have the right to waive that right, but this would be unusual unless both parties agree to do so. Accordingly, given the clear wording of Article 7 on this point, such exclusion could only be justified by reference to other principles contained in the IBA Rules—for example, in order to protect confidential information pursuant to Article 9.4. All other options would have to be considered in consultation with the parties before the decision to exclude party representatives is made. **10.32**

In exceptional circumstances a tribunal may consider that it is appropriate to exclude party representation at the inspection. In all cases, the tribunal will have to observe the requirements of due process and fair and equal treatment, and limit any potential disadvantage as much as possible. For example, it may be possible to make a video and/or **10.33**

[17] UNCITRAL Notes on Organizing Arbitral Proceedings (United Nations 2016) paras 57 and 58.
[18] See further Redfern and Hunter (n 3) para 6.150.
[19] ibid.

audio recording of the inspection, which then may be provided to the non-attending parties.

10.34 Situations do arise where the party controlling the site does not allow access to it by the representatives of other parties. For example, where the site forms part of a classified area because of its military significance and has different access regimes for citizens and non-citizens, the controlling party may rely on local legislation preventing it from providing access. Where one party's expert is not permitted to attend, the tribunal may have to consider appointing an independent expert to inspect and report in preference to permitting the other party's expert to attend without his/her counterpart being present.

10.35 Where one party's representatives are denied access to a site only at the point of inspection, those conducting the inspection will have to make a choice as to whether to cancel the inspection or to continue with it in the absence of the party being denied access. For the reasons given mentioned, a tribunal is unlikely to want to continue without exploring further with the parties who should continue with the inspection and whether expanded access can be granted at a later date (assuming this is practicable).

10.36 Where a tribunal-appointed expert is refused access, that expert may seek guidance from the tribunal leading to the same considerations. That expert may then prepare a report and record in it what difference to his or her conclusions the site visit could have made.[20] The tribunal may draw negative inferences if it believes that the controlling party did not have a valid reason to refuse access to the site.[21]

10.37 Legal counsel are very often present at inspections. There are advantages to this. If the inspection is to be carried out by a tribunal or experts who may wish to ask questions of party representatives, counsel may assist in ensuring 'fair play'. In the event of an unanticipated issue or problem arising, it may be possible for counsel to agree a solution that can save the inspection from being abandoned. However, there are also possible disadvantages. For example, the presence of counsel may inhibit constructive discussion between experts on each side that may assist in narrowing the issues.

4. The Rights of Those Attending the Inspection

10.38 In all cases, it is prudent to have clear, simple guidelines on where those attending the inspection may go during the inspection, and what they are permitted to do or say. Additionally, it will be sensible to anticipate and/or to record any necessary security or confidentiality measures.

[20] As required by IBA Rules (n 6) Article 6.3.
[21] See ibid Article 9.6.

The arrangements that are made will necessarily be fact specific. What is observed during an inspection may be easily understood by all attendees with little or no accompanying explanation. In other cases—for example, if the tribunal is visiting a factory to inspect a manufacturing process or a piece of equipment alleged to be defective—it may be desirable for the parties to agree a neutral explanatory commentary to be given during the inspection so that everyone knows what it is they are looking at, and how it fits into the manufacturing process or commercial operation. **10.39**

It may also be sensible to discuss who should accompany the tribunal and who should answer any questions that the tribunal may have. The parties may wish to have an express agreement that none of the party representatives will attempt to advocate a position or argument, or that the tribunal will not talk to a party representative unless legal counsel for the other party is present. **10.40**

In other cases, and provided legal counsel are present, the tribunal may be keen to ask questions of the experts on each side in order to gain a better understanding of the process, and any technical issues between the parties. It has been suggested that, during the inspection, if a member of the tribunal observes something they regard as material to the dispute, this should be drawn to the attention of the parties in order that both parties may have an opportunity to comment.[22] **10.41**

If the purpose of the inspection is to gather evidence—perhaps a visit by the expert witness of the party not in possession of the property or object being inspected—other considerations may also come into play. For example, if the expert wishes to take samples, under what conditions can this be done and are the experts for the other parties entitled to supervise or take away part of the same sample? If non-destructive testing, eg the taking of physical measurements, is to be undertaken is it necessary that the parties agree a protocol for how this should be carried out? **10.42**

It is also helpful to have agreement or direction on whether those attending the inspection are permitted to make any form of visual or audio recording of the inspection. **10.43**

5. Record of Inspection and Use of Evidence

A tribunal may wish to issue directions about whether and how the inspection itself and any evidence or information arising out of it are to be recorded and/or circulated. **10.44**

Parties may agree to some form of joint visual or audio recording of the inspection being made. Counsel may sometimes wish to agree a joint note of what was inspected, by whom, and any significant matters arising during the inspection. The tribunal and the parties should think carefully about whether they would like a contemporaneous transcript made of the inspection as well as any questions and answers passing between **10.45**

[22] Zuberbühler (n 5) 149.

those who attend. While it can be useful to have a complete record of events, the formality of a transcript may, in some circumstances, inhibit useful dialogue with the experts.[23]

10.46 Direction may also be needed on how and to whom any material observations, evidence gathered, or the results of any associated sampling/testing are to be recorded and distributed. There should be a clear understanding of what material is, and is not, to be introduced on to the record as evidence. For example, it may be agreed or directed that the test results of a sample taken during the inspection will be introduced into the record, whereas the informal remarks made by an employee operating machinery during an inspection will not.

6. Practical Example of an Inspection

10.47 The following is an example of an inspection protocol agreed in relation to a tribunal inspection of a power generation plant, the performance of which was the subject of the dispute. The tribunal wished to gain a better understanding of a number of technical points made about plant components in expert evidence. Provision was also made for the parties' representatives to take photographs of the plant in operation.

Purpose

1. The purpose of the Site Visit is to (a) provide the Tribunal with an opportunity to familiarize itself with the power plant (the 'Plant') so as to be better able to understand the evidence of the parties relating to technical performance of the Plant and (b) to permit the parties to take photographs of certain parts of the Plant when in operation, under the same conditions and at the same time.

Site Visit Participants

2. The Tribunal will be accompanied on the Site Visit by one (1) technical representative nominated by each party (the 'Party Representatives') (excluding the parties' external legal counsel), who will jointly lead the Site Visit. The Tribunal has indicated that it would be preferable if the Party Representatives leading the Site Visit are not the same as those who will be testifying at the hearing.
3. The Tribunal will also be accompanied on the Site Visit by no more than two (2) members from each party's legal counsel ('Legal Counsel').
4. The Party Representatives and Legal Counsel shall be the same people for the duration of the Site Visit.

[23] See further Redfern and Hunter (n 3) para 6.151, which suggests that if a transcript is made the usefulness of the inspection may be lost as a result of the delay and formality that accompanies the presence of a reporter.

5. The parties shall notify the Tribunal and each other of the names and positions of the respective Party Representatives and Legal Counsel by [DATE].

Logistics

6. The Site Visit will take place on [DATE].
7. The Site Visit, including entry to the Plant site (where necessary), shall be co-ordinated by the Party Representative of the Respondents.
8. All participants attending the Site Visit agree to comply with the applicable safety rules and regulations and the directions of the Respondent's Party Representative who are co-ordinating entry to the site. All Site Visit participants will attend a mandatory safety briefing before commencing the visit.
9. Casual clothing will be appropriate for the Site Visit, including sturdy footwear. Any safety or protective clothing that may be necessary will be provided by the Respondents.

Conduct and Itinerary of the Site Visit

10. The Chairman of the Tribunal shall oversee the Site Visit and shall be responsible for ensuring its proper conduct in accordance with this Protocol.
11. The Site Visit shall be conducted in English.
12. All participants shall remain in a group at all times for the duration of the Site Visit.
13. The Party Representatives will lead the Tribunal through the Plant. Subject to further discussion and final agreement between the parties (to be reached by [DATE]), it is expected that the itinerary will comprise:
    (a) the fuel unloading station;
    (b) the sampling station;
    (c) the boiler, including:
        i. the firing system (burners, fuel and air supply); and
        ii. the flue gas ducts (including primary air injection and gas recirculation dampers).
14. Prior to the Site Visit, the parties shall send the Tribunal a plan of the Plant along with the agreed itinerary, such that the identification of what phenomena will be observed (and where) are clearly marked at the various stages of the plan. The parties shall attach images of each 'stage' for identification purposes. The parties may also wish to highlight some exhibits in the record for the Tribunal to be familiar with prior to the Site Visit, but any such submissions must be joint.
15. At each location, at the invitation of the Tribunal, the Party Representatives will briefly describe the equipment being observed and its function and the process or phenomena being observed in relation to that piece of equipment.
16. The Parties Representatives will be professional and neutral, and their descriptions and responses to questions of the Tribunal will be factual, neutral and objective and aimed solely at educating the Tribunal, not advocating any position or argument of the parties in the arbitration. There shall be no discussion amongst the

participants of the allegations by the parties or the merits of the case during the Site Visit. For the avoidance of doubt, the parties shall not make submissions to the Tribunal during the site visit.

17. The Tribunal shall not engage in discussions with the Party Representatives in the absence of the presence of the Legal Counsel for both parties.
18. Legal Counsel may object if he or she believes:
    (a) a Party Representative's description is breaching or may breach the above rules; or
    (b) the Tribunal has asked a question that Legal Counsel believes may elicit a response from a Party Representative that will advocate a position or argument of a party in the arbitration.
19. The parties shall not submit any documents to the Tribunal during the Site Visit, except as otherwise agreed by both parties on a document-by-document basis. In the event that both parties agree that a document is to be provided to the Tribunal, such document shall form part of the evidentiary record.
20. The Parties' Representatives may take photographs of any part of the Plant subject to inspection as described at paragraph 13 above save that before doing so each Party Representative will inform the other Party Representative of such intention so that both Party Representatives may have the opportunity to take a photograph at the same time, of the same piece of equipment during its operation. Such photographs may be introduced into evidence.
21. Nothing that is said on the Site Visit shall form part of the evidentiary record in the arbitration.

11

Article 8: Evidentiary Hearing

Article 8 Evidentiary Hearing

1. **Within the time ordered by the Arbitral Tribunal, each Party shall inform the Arbitral Tribunal and the other Parties of the witnesses whose appearance it requests. Each witness (which term includes, for the purposes of this Article, witnesses of fact and any experts) shall, subject to Article 8.2, appear for testimony at the Evidentiary Hearing if such person's appearance has been requested by any Party or by the Arbitral Tribunal. Each witness shall appear in person unless the Arbitral Tribunal allows the use of videoconference or similar technology with respect to a particular witness.**
2. **The Arbitral Tribunal shall at all times have complete control over the Evidentiary Hearing. The Arbitral Tribunal may limit or exclude any question to, answer by or appearance of a witness, if it considers such question, answer or appearance to be irrelevant, immaterial, unreasonably burdensome, duplicative or otherwise covered by a reason for objection set forth in Article 9.2. Questions to a witness during direct and re-direct testimony may not be unreasonably leading.**
3. **With respect to oral testimony at an Evidentiary Hearing:**
   (a) **the Claimant shall ordinarily first present the testimony of its witnesses, followed by the Respondent presenting the testimony of its witnesses;**

(b) following direct testimony, any other Party may question such witness, in an order to be determined by the Arbitral Tribunal. The Party who initially presented the witness shall subsequently have the opportunity to ask additional questions on the matters raised in the other Parties' questioning;

(c) thereafter, the Claimant shall ordinarily first present the testimony of its Party-Appointed Experts, followed by the Respondent presenting the testimony of its Party-Appointed Experts. The Party who initially presented the Party-Appointed Expert shall subsequently have the opportunity to ask additional questions on the matters raised in the other Parties' questioning;

(d) the Arbitral Tribunal may question a Tribunal-Appointed Expert, and he or she may be questioned by the Parties or by any Party-Appointed Expert, on issues raised in the Tribunal-Appointed Expert Report, in the Parties' submissions or in the Expert Reports made by the Party-Appointed Experts;

(e) if the arbitration is organised into separate issues or phases (such as jurisdiction, preliminary determinations, liability and damages), the Parties may agree or the Arbitral Tribunal may order the scheduling of testimony separately for each issue or phase;

(f) the Arbitral Tribunal, upon request of a Party or on its own motion, may vary this order of proceeding, including the arrangement of testimony by particular issues or in such a manner that witnesses be questioned at the same time and in confrontation with each other (witness conferencing);

(g) the Arbitral Tribunal may ask questions to a witness at any time.

4. A witness of fact providing testimony shall first affirm, in a manner determined appropriate by the Arbitral Tribunal, that he or she commits to tell the truth or, in the case of an expert witness, his or her genuine belief in the opinions to be expressed at the Evidentiary Hearing. If the witness has submitted a Witness Statement or an Expert Report, the witness shall confirm it. The Parties may agree or the Arbitral Tribunal may order that the Witness Statement or Expert Report shall serve as that witness's direct testimony.

5. Subject to the provisions of Article 9.2, the Arbitral Tribunal may request any person to give oral or written evidence on any issue that the Arbitral Tribunal considers to be relevant to the case and material to its outcome. Any witness called and questioned by the Arbitral Tribunal may also be questioned by the Parties.

A. Introduction

11.1 Article 8 is concerned with arrangements for the taking of oral and other evidence at an evidentiary hearing. 'Evidentiary Hearing' is broadly defined in the IBA Rules to mean:

> [A]ny hearing, whether or not held on consecutive days, at which the Arbitral Tribunal, whether in person, by teleconference, videoconference, or other method receives oral or other evidence.

Thus, regardless of the length of hearing, and whether the participants are all physically present in the same place or communicating by telephone or video link,[1] the provisions of Article 8 will apply to a hearing where evidence is to be received. **11.2**

Parties are free to agree that the tribunal should make a determination without a hearing. However, in the majority of international arbitrations, an evidentiary hearing does take place. One or all of the parties to the dispute may feel that an oral hearing is necessary for proper presentation of its case, particularly where direct challenge to the witness and expert evidence of the other party/parties is a key part of that presentation. The question of whether an evidentiary hearing is necessary and/or desirable will depend on the circumstances of the individual dispute, but if one is held, Article 8 will apply. **11.3**

There is an absence of guidance in institutional rules on how to structure a hearing. Although Article 8 does not provide a complete code, it sets out a series of important controls and practical steps for the management of a hearing. **11.4**

The terms of Article 8 are very general in nature. At its heart is Article 8.2 which gives the tribunal complete control over the evidentiary hearing at all times, including the right to limit or exclude questions to, or the appearance of, a witness. Other important provisions include the requirement that fact and expert witnesses for one party shall attend the hearing to be cross-examined if requested to do so by another party, the right of a tribunal to request a party to give evidence, and the right to ask questions of witnesses at the hearing. Other parts of Article 8 are concerned with the structure and order of events at the hearing and practical matters associated with the giving of oral evidence. **11.5**

As noted in the Commentary to the IBA Rules, in most cases an evidentiary hearing will have been preceded by a considerable amount of work by all parties, including a number of procedural steps in keeping with the principle set out in Preamble 3 that each party is entitled to know reasonably in advance of a hearing the evidence upon which its opponent intends to rely.[2] For example, there are likely to have been written submissions, document production, and in the majority of cases, the delivery of fact and expert evidence. The evidentiary hearing is the culmination of those efforts, although in a large number of cases post-hearing submissions 'wrapping-up' and addressing the available evidence on the matters heard will follow the hearing. **11.6**

[1] See definition of 'evidentiary hearing' at Chapter 3.
[2] See Chapter 2 paras 2.100–2.107.

B. Attendance of Witnesses for Cross-Examination

8.1 Within the time ordered by the Arbitral Tribunal, each Party shall inform the Arbitral Tribunal and the other Parties of the witnesses whose appearance it requests. Each witness (which term includes, for the purposes of this Article, witnesses of fact and any experts) shall, subject to Article 8.2, appear for testimony at the Evidentiary Hearing if such person's appearance has been requested by any Party or by the Arbitral Tribunal.

11.7 Article 8.1 is a new provision introduced into the IBA Rules in 2010. It provides that each party shall inform the tribunal and the other parties of the identity of the fact and expert witnesses of another party that it requests attend the evidentiary hearing. The notification is to be given by a date ordered by the tribunal. In practice, that date is often contained in the first procedural order or other direction setting out the procedural timetable. As is noted in the Commentary on the IBA Rules, Article 8.1 aligns the IBA Rules with current best practice according to which witnesses appear at the hearing only if cross-examination has been requested or the party presenting the testimony wishes to do by means of live testimony.[3] Where a party does wish to cross-examine the fact witness or expert whose evidence has been tendered by its opponent, then that witness or expert should attend the evidentiary hearing so that the opportunity is provided.

11.8 Article 4.7 (Witnesses of Fact) and Article 5.7 (Party-Appointed Experts) provide that if a witness/expert who has been asked to attend the hearing under Article 8.1 fails without valid reason to do so, the tribunal must disregard the written evidence of that witness unless, in exceptional circumstances, the tribunal decides otherwise. The importance that is often attached to the right of a party to cross-examine the witnesses of another party is discussed in Chapter 7,[4] where we also discuss the right of a party to call its own witness to attend the hearing where its opponent has not done so.

11.9 It is important to note that Article 4.8 (Fact Witnesses) and Article 5.6 (Party-Appointed Experts) provide that where the attendance of a witness or party-appointed expert has not been requested pursuant to Article 8.1, none of the other parties are deemed to have agreed to the correctness of the written evidence of the witness/expert not called. We discuss in Chapter 7 paras 7.168–7.179 and Chapter 8 paras 8.163–8.167 the meaning and application of these provisions.

[3] There are various reasons why a party may adopt the latter position. See Chapter 7 paras 7.170–7.182.

[4] See Chapter 7 paras 7.139–7.145 and 7.180-7.182. See also Chapter 8 paras 8.145–8.152 in relation to party-appointed experts. Those chapters also discuss the application and operation of Articles 4.7 and 5.7 of the IBA Rules.

C. Attendance in Person

Each witness shall appear in person unless the Arbitral Tribunal allows the use of videoconference or similar technology with respect to a particular witness.

Article 8.1 makes clear that, where a witness is requested to attend, the witness should attend in person unless the tribunal has agreed that the witness may give evidence by video conference or similar technology.[5] **11.10**

Video conferencing is now a widely recognized communication method that comes in many shapes and forms—it can be provided at a formal video conferencing facility or live interface via Skype, Viber, WhatsApp, or another application or programme that transmits a video signal. All of these different types of video communications can broadly be described as video conference. Article 8.1 also mentions 'similar technology'. It has been suggested that, in the future, parties to arbitration may be able to use telepresence technologies or 3D holograms.[6] If and when such technologies become available, they may be treated as 'similar technology' under Article 8.1 of the IBA Rules. **11.11**

Because Article 8.1 refers only to 'video conference' or 'similar technology', it is reasonable to infer that it was not the intention of those drafting the rules to permit cross-examination by telephone conference. This is unsurprising. Body language and facial expression form an important part of the evidence given orally by a witness and may assist the listener in forming a view on whether the witness is telling the truth. **11.12**

Where a party is aware that its witnesses may wish to give evidence by video conference, this should be raised during the consultation process provided for by Article 2, or as soon as the need for the use of video conferencing becomes apparent. In all cases, the consent of the tribunal should be sought. The party whose witness it is should provide reasons why it is necessary to present evidence in this way and the other parties should have an opportunity to respond. **11.13**

The giving of evidence by video conference can result in significant savings in time and costs. It may also enable evidence to be given in circumstances where this would not otherwise be possible, eg where the witness is prevented from travelling by illness or other commitments. **11.14**

However, there are a number of drawbacks to receiving evidence by video conference. Firstly, and despite significant improvements in technology, the medium can still be unreliable. Most arbitration practitioners will have experience of a conference facility where a connection cannot be established, where there is distortion in received sound, **11.15**

[5] See also Chapter 7 para 7.149 and Chapter 8 para 8.156.

[6] Robert H Smit, 'Chapter 24: The Future of Science and Technology in International Arbitration: The Next Thirty Years' in Stavros L Brekoulakis, Julian D M Lew, and Loukas A Mistelis (eds), *The Evolution and Future of International Arbitration* (Kluwer Law International 2016) paras 24.10–24.16.

and/or a time lag between question and answer. There have also been unsatisfactory instances where the connection has been lost halfway through the taking of evidence and, as a result, the witness has been given an unexpected opportunity to reconsider some of the answers s/he has given. Secondly, in terms of the tribunal's perception of the witness, video conference is seldom as good as having the witness physically present in the same room. As mentioned, the witness's body language may be very important for assessing whether the witness is telling the truth—observing a witness via video conference is never the same as observing them while in the same room, particularly where the quality of the image is less than perfect. Finally, there have been instances where a witness has received outside assistance during the testimony—for example, by someone writing and showing the witness suggested answers from behind the camera, or by the witness consulting email or messages on a mobile device.

11.16 If the decision is taken to allow a witness or expert to testify by way of video conference, there are a number of practical issues that will need to be considered and agreed in advance of the evidence being given.

11.17 A rehearsal of the technology between the two venues is a good idea, as is a contingency plan in the event of problems occurring on the appointed date and time. Perhaps a 'fall-back' window the following day, or the use of a different form of technology.

11.18 Another obvious consideration is the time difference between the place where the witness is located and the venue for the evidentiary hearing. This will need to be taken into account when a provisional timetable for witness evidence is agreed. Some contingency should be built into the video conference arrangements to meet the risk of another witness overrunning, although parties are often willing to agree that the timetable be interrupted if there is a genuine need to hear a witness operating in a significantly different time zone.

11.19 There may also need to be discussion and agreement on the materials that the witness will have in front of him or her during the examination. A witness giving evidence remotely should not have any advantage (or disadvantage) in terms of the materials available. Ideally, the witness should have available to them a printed set of the trial bundles in the same way as any other witness, or at least those parts of the bundles that the parties agree may be relevant to the evidence of that witness. However, it can sometimes be difficult to limit the volume of documents in any meaningful way, as parties are naturally reluctant to signpost particular documents to which they may wish to refer during cross-examination.

11.20 Precautions should be taken to ensure that a witness or expert will not be guided by someone present in the room in relation to answers given by the witness. In addition, the witness should not have any personal notes or other documents in front of them and only should have access to the trial bundles when referred to them by counsel during direct and cross-examination in the same way as a witness present in person. The party whose witness it is will generally make the arrangements for use of a video conference facility, but the opponent parties may insist on having someone present with the witness during the examination to ensure due process—for example, to ensure that the witness is not being passed notes. They may appoint a local agent to attend since such supervision does not require a detailed knowledge of the case and this will assist in managing costs. The tribunal may also give directions regarding how the identity of the witness or expert on the other end of the line can be verified by the agent or a representative.

It is prudent for the parties to agree a protocol covering the matters mentioned, as well as any other arrangements specific to the case. The Commentary on the IBA Rules states expressly that application for permission for a witness to appear by video conference should propose a protocol and 'that the tribunal's decision should depend, among other things, on the ability of the proposed protocol to maintain equality and fairness between the parties.[7] **11.21**

Against this background, it is clear that in many cases an 'in-person' appearance will offer greater reliability of communication, and is likely to result in the tribunal gaining a more accurate impression of the evidence that is presented. When considering whether to permit evidence to be given by video conference, a tribunal will often have to weigh these factors against considerations of economy and efficiency. The decision that the tribunal makes will be dependent on the facts, but it may be that the evidence of the particular witness is so critical to the dispute that the desirability for that evidence to be delivered in person outweighs all other considerations. In other cases, where the relevant party has demonstrated that there are good reasons why the witness is unable to attend, the tribunal may simply accept the position and rely on the parties to ensure that the best available arrangements are put in place. **11.22**

If the tribunal makes an order that a witness appear in person at the evidentiary hearing and the witness fails to attend, but offers themselves for cross-examination by video conference on the required date and time, the question arises as to whether the written evidence of that witness should be disregarded pursuant to Article 4.7 of the IBA Rules. On a strict reading of that rule it appears that it should be disregarded. Article 4.7 has application in the event of a witness failing to attend in response to a request made 'pursuant to Article 8.1'. Article 8.1 states that the attendance shall be in person unless otherwise ordered by the tribunal. However, there may be some tension between application of this provision and the right of a party to present its witnesses. As discussed in Chapter 7, Article 8.1 gives each party the right to call its own witness to attend the evidentiary hearing. While the tribunal has the right under Article 8.2 to exclude evidence at the hearing, this right arises only where the tribunal considers such evidence to **11.23**

[7] 1999 IBA Working Party and 2010 IBA Rules of Evidence Review Subcommittee, 'Commentary on the Revised Text of the 2010 IBA Rules on the Taking of Evidence in International Arbitration' (*International Bar Association*, 2014) 26 <www.ibanet.org/Document/Default.aspx?DocumentUid=DD240932-0E08-40D4-9866-309A635487C0> accessed 27 November 2018 (hereafter 'Commentary on the IBA Rules').

'irrelevant', 'immaterial', 'unreasonably burdensome', 'duplicative', or one of the grounds of objection to evidence set out in Article 9.2 applies. Some tribunals may be reluctant to shut out the evidence of such a witness tendered in this way.

D. Tribunal Control of Examination of Witnesses

8.2 The Arbitral Tribunal shall at all times have complete control over the Evidentiary Hearing.

The Arbitral Tribunal may limit or exclude any question to, answer by or appearance of a witness, if it considers such question, answer or appearance to be irrelevant, immaterial, unreasonably burdensome, duplicative or otherwise covered by a reason for objection set forth in Article 9.2.

Questions to a witness during direct and re-direct testimony may not be unreasonably leading.

11.24 Article 8.2 is primarily concerned with the tribunal's management of the evidentiary hearing.

1. Control Rests with the Tribunal

11.25 Article 8.2 makes clear that the tribunal, not the parties, control what happens at the hearing. The first sentence of this provision states expressly the principle that the tribunal 'shall at all times' have 'complete control' over the hearing. The Commentary to the IBA rules confirms this position and notes that the idea of the tribunal having supremacy of control comes from the civil law tradition. It also notes that the position has been widely adopted in the practice of international arbitration as reflected in similar provisions contained in institutional rules[8] and in some national arbitration laws.[9]

2. Grounds for Limitation or Exclusion of Evidence

11.26 The next part of the provision goes on to emphasize the degree to which the tribunal may exercise control over the oral evidence that is being presented. Article 9.1 of the IBA Rules refers to the power of the tribunal to determine the 'admissibility, relevance and materiality' of evidence. Article 9.2 provides that the tribunal may exclude oral testimony. Article 8.2 contains a clarification or extension of those powers by expressly providing that the tribunal may (i) limit or (ii) exclude a question put to a witness, or an answer given by a witness, or the appearance of the witness, on four specified

[8] See for example ICC Rules, Article 26(3).
[9] See, for example, the English Arbitration Act 1996, s 34.

grounds. It also restates the position under Article 9.2 pursuant to which the tribunal may limit or exclude the oral testimony of a witness on any of the grounds set out in that provision.

In high-value or important cases, the parties want to present as many witnesses as are available to support key elements of their case. However, the tribunal may wish to consider the potential probative value of the corroborative evidence against any increase in costs or hearing time necessary to facilitate the hearing of potentially duplicative evidence.[10] 11.27

The tribunal may take steps to exclude evidence on its own initiative where it considers the question, answer or appearance to be irrelevant, immaterial, unreasonably burdensome, duplicative, or otherwise covered by a reason for objection set out in Article 9.2. 11.28

The objective behind these provisions is efficiency of process and protection of the legitimate expectations of the parties. It makes no sense for valuable hearing time to be taken up with matters that contribute nothing of value to the evidence upon which the tribunal's determination will be based. The decision not to hear from a witness (so-called 'gating') has obvious advantages. It can shorten the hearing and reduce costs by avoiding the use of duplicative or irrelevant witnesses.[11] 11.29

The next sections discuss the various circumstances in which the power available to the tribunal under Article 8.2 may be exercised. 11.30

a. Irrelevant or immaterial

'Irrelevant' and 'immaterial' in Article 8.2 are shorthand for evidence that fails to meet the benchmarks of 'relevant to the case' and 'material to its outcome' that underpin the IBA Rules. The meaning of those benchmarks is discussed in detail in Chapter 6 paras 6.76–6.146. By the time that the evidentiary hearing takes place, the tribunal, and certainly the parties, will have an informed view on what oral evidence is likely to be relevant and material. Counsel are generally allowed a fair amount of latitude as to how they spend their allocated time for examination of witness. However, if it seems to the tribunal (either on its own initiative or at the suggestion of counsel for one of the other parties) that too much time is being spent on matters that have only peripheral relevance, then there may by an intervention by the tribunal. 11.31

b. Unreasonably burdensome

The 1999 IBA Rules used the term 'burdensome' without qualification. The word 'unreasonably' was introduced in the IBA Rules in 2010. 11.32

[10] See Chapter 7 para 7.182.

[11] The tribunal may feel that there is sufficient evidence on the record to address an issue without wasting further costs in presentation of more evidence. Judith Levine discusses trends and cultural perspectives among arbitrators in exercising their powers in this way in Judith Levine, 'Can Arbitrators Choose Who to Call as Witnesses? (And What Can Be Done If They Don't Show Up?)' in Albert Jan Van den Berg (ed), *Legitimacy: Myths, Realities, Challenges* (Kluwer Law International 2015) 333–41.

11.33 'Unreasonably burdensome' is a ground of objection to document production (as well as a basis for exclusion of evidence) under Article 9.2(c) of the IBA Rules. As explained in Chapter 12,[12] in considering this ground as a basis for exclusion of witness evidence at the evidentiary hearing, the tribunal may weigh the potential evidential value of the evidence in question against the burden (whether in time, costs, or other circumstances) associated with presentation of the evidence. If the tribunal believes that the burden is disproportionate to the potential probative value of the evidence, the evidence may be excluded.

11.34 In practice, 'unreasonably burdensome' is more likely to be applied as a ground of objection to document production[13] than as a basis for exclusion of evidence, whether at the evidentiary hearing or at any other time. As mentioned elsewhere, if the evidence is already available, the burden of maintaining that evidence in the record is likely to be negligible or non-existent.[14] However, there may be some circumstances where the operation of this provision is useful, eg if an expert is asked at the hearing to opine on a new issue that has not been addressed in his expert report. Although the expert may be perfectly capable of providing such an opinion, if it requires additional tests and research to be done in order to be able to reach an informed decision during the hearing, it may be regarded as unreasonably burdensome to do so.

c. Duplicative

11.35 The exclusion of evidence that is duplicative, and therefore adds nothing to the body of evidence available to the tribunal, is discussed at Chapter 6 paras 6.374–6.378 in relation to documentary evidence, and at Chapter 7 para 7.182 in relation to witness evidence. There will clearly be circumstances where oral testimony, although duplicative, may have some evidential value and should be admitted. For example, if there is a difference in evidence between two witnesses as to what was said at a meeting that is material to the dispute, the evidence of a third witness who was present at the meeting and may be able to corroborate one version of the facts may have value.

d. Otherwise covered by a reason for objection set out in Article 9.2

11.36 Article 9.2 is a key provision of the IBA Rules that applies to all forms of evidence. In broad terms, Article 9.2 operates as a limitation on the introduction/production of evidence where this would be improper on legal grounds or where, balancing the competing interests of the parties, it would be inappropriate to permit its introduction. The seven grounds for excluding evidence under Article 9.2 are discussed in detail in Chapter 12 paras 12.57–12.316.

[12] See Chapter 12 paras 12.242–12.257. In particular, paras 12.247–12.253.

[13] As mentioned elsewhere, the examples for application of IBA Rules (n 4) Article 9.2(c) described in the Commentary on the IBA Rules (n 7) refer only to situations involving document production. See Chapter 12 para 12.245.

[14] Chapter 12 para 12.249.

11.37 One situation in which the grounds set out in Article 9.2 may become relevant during an evidentiary hearing is where the subject matter of the questions put by counsel during cross-examination touches on matters that may be privileged[15] or politically sensitive,[16] and the evidence given by a witness in response inadvertently strays into evidence that is subject to those protections. For example, the company director of a party to the arbitration, who is also a witness in the case, may mention during cross-examination the content of legal advice that he has received as the company's representative. Under certain circumstances, this reference may be treated as a waiver of legal advice privilege.[17] However, counsel for the relevant party, or the tribunal itself, may intervene to clarify whether the witness intended/is entitled to waive the privilege. If the intention to waive the privilege is not clear, the tribunal may decide to exclude from the record the answer that was given by the witness.

11.38 Another example may be the late introduction of oral testimony that will cause prejudice to one of the parties and, thereby, arguably, engage Article 9.2(g) (fairness or equality of the parties). If a witness who has not provided a witness statement is tendered as a witness at the evidentiary hearing, the tribunal must balance a party's right to be heard against the other party's right not to be ambushed with evidence. If the parties have agreed the requirement of prior witness statements, the tribunal should not overrule that requirement. While Article 8.5 of the IBA Rules gives the tribunal a wide discretion to admit oral testimony at the evidentiary hearing, that provision is intended for witnesses that have been called at the request of the tribunal. The tribunal may be seen as 'bending the rules' if it applies this provision to an unexpected witness tendered by one of the parties.[18] However, much will depend on the individual circumstances of the case and there may be good reasons why the presenting party was not able to provide a statement from the witness (for example, because the witness was not permitted by an employer to provide a statement, or because the presenting party had to obtain a court order to compel the attendance of the witness). The potential value of the evidence will need to be weighed against any unfairness that may be caused by its late introduction.

3. Exercise of the Tribunal's Power to Limit or Exclude Evidence

11.39 Where, for reasons of efficiency, a tribunal wishes to tailor the evidence to that which will assist the tribunal in reaching its determination, it will generally wish to discuss this with the parties in advance of the hearing with the objective of achieving a consensus on how best to manage matters.[19]

[15] See IBA Rules (n 4) Article 9.2(b); Chapter 12 paras 12.77–12.241.

[16] See IBA Rules (n 4) Article 9.2(f); Chapter 12 paras 12.293–12.307.

[17] See: IBA Rules (n 4) Article 9.3(d). Chapter 12 para 12.223.

[18] Ragnar Harbst, *A Counsel's Guide to Examining and Preparing Witnesses in International Arbitration* (Kluwer Law International 2015) 92–93.

[19] This approach is recommended in the *ICC Arbitration Commission Report on Controlling Time and Costs in Arbitration* (International Chamber of Commerce 2018) para 37.

11.40 In some cases, such active intervention by the tribunal may meet resistance from counsel for the parties who are likely to have their own ideas about how they wish to present their client's case. In addition, depending on the facts of the case, counsel may occasionally fear that such intervention indicates that the tribunal has prejudged some of the issues in the case. Despite these factors, the tribunal may nonetheless, at a suitable time, wish to make appropriate directions pursuant to its powers under Article 8.2—for example, indicating the matters upon which it wishes to hear evidence and/or indicating those witnesses whose evidence may no longer be material given developments in the case.

11.41 A tribunal may also feel it appropriate to restrict witness evidence during oral testimony. It may decide to limit further questions or answers where it has heard several questions and answers put on a particular topic and decides for one of the reasons identified that there is no need, or that it is undesirable, to hear more. For example, this may occur where there is a long, drawn-out cross-examination on matters that have peripheral or no relevance to the issues on the critical path to a determination. In practice, the need for such measures may be mitigated by the 'chess-clock' system of limiting parties' use of hearing time. Where time is limited, counsel will generally be keen to use the time to best effect on evidence that will affect outcome. In many cases, an objection to evidence based on one of the grounds set out in Article 9.2 is most likely to be raised first by the one of the parties.

11.42 Where a tribunal does exclude evidence, it is possible that the party affected may seek to challenge the award. Much will depend on the particular facts of the case, the stated basis for the exclusion, the extent to which the tribunal has heard submissions on the proposed exclusion, and whether the tribunal has properly discharged its obligation to give each party a fair hearing. However, subject to those considerations, the view has been expressed that a tribunal that refuses to hear the testimony of a particular witness is unlikely to have its award set aside solely on that ground.[20]

4. The Use of Leading Questions

11.43 Article 8.2 also contains a statement that questions put to a witness during direct and re-direct testimony may not be unreasonably leading. A leading question is one that is asked in such a way as to suggest the desired answer.[21]

[20] Peter R Griffin, 'Recent Trends in the Conduct of International Arbitration: Discovery Procedures and Witness Hearings' (2000) 17(2) Journal of International Arbitration 19. Two cases are cited in support of this statement. The first a decision of the English Court of Appeal (*Dalmia Dairy Industries v National Bank of Pakistan* [1978] 2 Lloyd's Rep 223, 270) and the second a decision of the French Court of Appeal (*Soubaigne v Limmareds Skogar* 1985 Rev Arb 285). In the latter case, the Court found that arbitrators, like all judges, were only required to proceed to further investigation if they did not have sufficient material on which to base their decision, and were entitled to limit this to the measures they considered useful, and the most simple and the least onerous methods. Having before them relevant documents on the point at issue they could sufficiently decide on them without the oral testimony.

[21] *Halsbury's Laws* (2015) vol 12A para 840, which cited *Nicholls v Dowding & Kemp* (1815) 1 Stark 81.

A leading question is often framed to call for a 'Yes' or 'No' answer that allows counsel to guide the witness to the answer that is wanted.[22] This contrasts with an open question—usually involving the interrogatives who? what? when? where? how? or why?—that permit a witness to explain his or her side of the story, but to which the response may be much more uncertain.[23] Examples of open-ended questions are: 11.44

- Where was the meeting held?
- Can you please tell the tribunal who was at the meeting?

These examples can be compared with leading questions on the same topic:

- The meeting was held in Geneva, correct?
- Mr Smith was present at that meeting, was he not?

The general rule against leading questions in direct examination developed in the common law tradition where oral examination by counsel was a common practice.[24] Historically, counsel was not permitted to ask 'his' witness leading questions but was free to frame questions to his opponent's witness in any manner he pleased. The prohibition of leading questions in direct examination appears to derive from a concern that such questions might corrupt the evidence given by the witness, thus making the evidential process less fair. In a 1943 Scottish case, the justification for the rules was articulated in this way: 11.45

> [T]he leading question has its place in dealing with introductory narrative, non-controversial matters and the like, but its habitual and persistent use when examining in chief witnesses on central issues of disputed fact will not only 'displace entirely the confidence we ought to put in the deposition of a witness' (per Lord Kinnear in *Bishop v Bryce* at p. 435), but may make the answer as it is given a 'worthless answer' (per Lord Dunedin ibid., p. 431).[25]

A later Australian case, *R v Thynne*, held that the prohibition of leading questions in examination-in-chief is intended to prevent the examination being unfairly conducted, and therefore to avoid the risk that a witness, when asked a 'leading question', may adopt the suggestion implied in the question, rather than answering it truthfully from his/her own knowledge.[26] 11.46

[22] Ben H Sheppard Jr, 'Taking Charge: Proven Tactics for Effective Witness Control' in Lawrence W Newman and Ben H Sheppard Jr (eds), *Take the Witness: Cross-Examination in International Arbitration* (JurisNet/LLC 2010) 7.

[23] ibid 4.

[24] *Halsbury's Laws* (2015) vol 12A para 840. The rule still exists in many common law countries. See, for example, US Federal Rules of Evidence, r 6.11; and Australian Evidence Act 1995, ss 37 and 42. In England, the earliest case acknowledged to recognize it was the 1684 trial of Thomas Rosewell for treason, in which certain leading questions were not permitted in examination in chief (*R v Rosewell* (1684) 10 State Trials 147 per Jeffreys CJ). The principle was built on in cases such as *Nicholls v Dowding & Kemp* (1815) 1 Stark 81, *Gregory v Marychurch* 50 ER 1113, and *Moor v Moor* [1954] 2 All ER 459.

[25] *McKenzie v McKenzie* 1943 SC 108 (IH), citing *Bishop v Bryce* 1910 SC 426 (IH).

[26] *R v Thynne* [1977] VR 98. In an earlier Australian case, *Mooney v James* [1949] VLR 22, it was held that the prohibition on leading questions in examination-in-chief serves to inhibit the natural bias that a witness has in favour of the party calling him/her.

11.47 The prohibition against leading questions does not extend to cross-examination of a witness by opposing counsel. Leading questions are permitted in cross-examination as an aid to test the credibility of the witness, and to facilitate the examination of evidence given in written statements and direct examination by allowing the cross-examiner to direct questions to the elements of the evidence that they wish to tease out. In civil law jurisdictions where the distinction between examination-in-chief and cross-examination is understandably not as well-developed, the rules often simply require the questions to be asked clearly and affirmatively.[27]

11.48 Some civil law practitioners advocate against use of the common law practice of cross-examination in international arbitration.[28] However, despite the existence of scepticism in certain quarters, it is fair to say that some form of cross-examination is now widely accepted as part of the practice of international arbitration.[29] The inclusion in Article 8.1 of the prohibition against leading questions during direct and redirect testimony reflects this.

11.49 It should be noted that Article 8.2 qualifies the restriction on leading questions. It states that questions to a witness during direct and redirect testimony may not be 'unreasonably' leading. Whether the substance of a question strays into territory that is 'unreasonably' leading will be for the tribunal to determine, although opposing counsel may intervene to explain why it does. In practice, a tribunal will very often permit counsel a greater degree of latitude than would be permitted before a court. Some arbitration practitioners may have little or limited experience of oral examination of witnesses, perhaps because they come from a civil law jurisdiction where the scope for counsel examination of witnesses is limited, or because they are a relatively junior member of the team who has yet to perfect his or her examination techniques. Many arbitrators are also skilful advocates. They will be aware when a witness is being led, whether deliberately or unconsciously. They can make an appropriate adjustment to the weight they attribute to the evidence, or perhaps put some follow-up questions to the witness in order to clarify what their evidence actually is on a particular point.

E. Order and Organization of Questions to a Witness

8.3 With respect to oral testimony at an Evidentiary Hearing:

(a) the Claimant shall ordinarily first present the testimony of its witnesses, followed by the Respondent presenting the testimony of its witnesses;

[27] Bernardo M Cremades and David J A Cairns, 'Cross-Examination in International Arbitration: is it Worthwhile?' in Lawrence W Newman and Ben H Sheppard Jr (eds), *Take the Witness: Cross-Examination in International Arbitration* (JurisNet, LLC 2010) 232–35.

[28] ibid 223–42.

[29] See for example: Robert H Smit, 'Cross-Examining Witnesses Before Civil Law Arbitrators' in Lawrence W Newman and Ben H Sheppard Jr (eds), *Take the Witness: Cross-Examination in International Arbitration* (JurisNet/LLC 2010) 243–44 and Sophie Nappert and Christopher Harris, 'The English Approach to Cross-Examination in International Arbitration' in Lawrence W Newman and Ben H Sheppard Jr (eds), *Take the Witness: Cross-Examination in International Arbitration* (JurisNet/LLC 2010) 254 (hereafter 'Nappert and Harris').

(b) following direct testimony, any other Party may question such witness, in an order to be determined by the Arbitral Tribunal. The Party who initially presented the witness shall subsequently have the opportunity to ask additional questions on the matters raised in the other Parties' questioning;

(c) thereafter, the Claimant shall ordinarily first present the testimony of its Party-Appointed Experts, followed by the Respondent presenting the testimony of its Party-Appointed Experts. The Party who initially presented the Party-Appointed Expert shall subsequently have the opportunity to ask additional questions on the matters raised in the other Parties' questioning;

(d) the Arbitral Tribunal may question a Tribunal-Appointed Expert, and he or she may be questioned by the Parties or by any Party-Appointed Expert, on issues raised in the Tribunal-Appointed Expert Report, in the Parties' submissions or in the Expert Reports made by the Party-Appointed Experts;

(e) if the arbitration is organised into separate issues or phases (such as jurisdiction, preliminary determinations, liability and damages), the Parties may agree or the Arbitral Tribunal may order the scheduling of testimony separately for each issue or phase;

(f) the Arbitral Tribunal, upon request of a Party or on its own motion, may vary this order of proceeding, including the arrangement of testimony by particular issues or in such a manner that witnesses be questioned at the same time and in confrontation with each other (witness conferencing);

(g) the Arbitral Tribunal may ask questions to a witness at any time.

1. Introduction

Article 8.3 sets out an order for presentation of fact and expert witnesses, and the order in which counsel for each party are to put questions to the witness. The 1999 IBA Rules did not include reference to presentation of evidence by party-appointed and tribunal-appointed experts. This omission was remedied by the inclusion of paragraphs (c) and (d) of Article 8.3 into the 2010 IBA Rules. Article 8.3 also makes clear that the tribunal may vary the order of business to suit the circumstances of the case, and that the tribunal may ask questions of a witness at any time. **11.50**

2. The Order of Witnesses and Questions by Counsel

Article 8.3 establishes a default order for the taking of evidence at the evidentiary hearing. **11.51**

11.52 It is widely accepted (both in common and civil law jurisdictions) that the claimant should set out its case first. This is based on two considerations:

(a) the principles of natural justice, which require a person whose interests may or will be affected by the decision-making body to be informed of and given the opportunity to see the evidence against them and have the opportunity to respond to it. Thus, natural justice dictates that the respondent should be able hear the evidence relied on by the claimant before responding;[30] and
(b) allocation of the burden of proof—the claimant has the burden of proving its case. It generally follows that the evidence should start by the claimant setting out its case.[31]

11.53 Article 8.3 adopts as a default position the same practice of requiring the claimant to go first before going on to lay down an order of business similar in pattern to that followed in many national courts and comprising:

Claimant's Fact Witnesses
- Direct examination (also known as examination-in-chief) of the claimant's witnesses by the claimant's counsel;
- Cross-examination of the claimant's witnesses by the respondent's counsel;
- Re-examination (also known as 're-direct') of the claimant's witnesses by the claimant's counsel;

Respondent's Fact Witnesses
- Direct examination of the respondent's witnesses by the respondent's counsel;
- Cross-examination of the respondent's witnesses by the claimant's counsel;
- Re-examination of the respondent's witnesses by the respondent's counsel.

(If there are party-appointed experts)
- Direct examination of the claimant's experts by the claimant's counsel;
- Cross-examination of the claimant's experts by the respondent's counsel;
- Re-examination of the claimant's experts by the claimant's counsel;
- Direct examination of the respondent's experts by the respondent's counsel;
- Cross-examination of the respondent's experts;
- Re-examination of the respondent's experts;

[30] The principles of natural justice are applicable to arbitration. See *Re Brook, Delcomyn and Badart* (1864) 16 CBNS 403, 143 ER 1184.

[31] The general test for the burden of proof in civil litigation was set down in *Jane Wakelin (Pauper) v The London and South Western Railway Company* (1886) 12 App Cas 41, 45. Lord Halsbury held that 'it is true that the onus of proof may shift from time to time as a matter of evidence, but still the question must ultimately arise whether the person who is bound to prove the affirmative of the issue, which is in this case the negligent act, has or has not satisfied that burden'.

(If there is a tribunal-appointed expert present)

- Questioning of the tribunal-appointed expert (if any) by the tribunal;
- Questioning of the tribunal-appointed expert by the parties; and/or
- Questioning of the tribunal-appointed expert by party-appointed experts.

As mentioned, the tribunal may put questions to a fact witness or expert at any time.

Although the above is the default position under Article 8.3, the tribunal and/or the parties (by agreement) may deviate from it. Article 8.3(f) states expressly that the tribunal, either upon request by the parties, or on its own initiative, may vary the default order. What is considered appropriate in an individual case will depend very much on the facts of the case, the legal backgrounds of counsel and the tribunal, the nature of the evidence, and the time available. For example, if the parties and the tribunal are all from civil law backgrounds they may prefer to adopt a procedure more akin to that used in that tradition.[32] Another possible circumstance is where the tribunal and/or the parties may feel that certain disciplines of expert (perhaps relating to liability) are more conveniently heard immediately after fact witnesses for the same party, or that experts of like discipline may be more conveniently heard back to back. **11.54**

From a practical perspective, it is sensible for the tribunal and the parties to agree in advance of the hearing the order in which the taking of evidence is to take place. Normally it is for the calling side to decide in which order they will call witnesses, but the opposing counsel should be given advance notice so that they may know the order in which they have to prepare for cross-examination of the witnesses. Other considerations that may need to be taken into account when deciding on the order of witnesses are the possibility of witness non-availability on particular dates and, where witnesses are to be sequestered, the desirability of hearing early in the timetable the evidence of any party representatives also responsible for instructing counsel.[33] **11.55**

3. Direct Oral Testimony

In international arbitration, as in many other fora, the evidence of a witness of fact is generally presented in advance of the evidentiary hearing in the form of a witness statement, and that of an expert witness in the form of an expert report. Article 4.4 and Article 5.1 makes express provision for the delivery of witness statements and expert reports respectively. **11.56**

Article 8.4 provides that the parties may agree, or the tribunal may order, that the written witness statement or expert report should stand as that witness's direct testimony. **11.57**

[32] Commentary on the IBA Rules (n 7) 24 notes that: 'Nothing in the IBA Rules of Evidence, however, prevents an arbitral tribunal from hearing witnesses in another manner, such as the traditional method in certain civil law countries where witnesses are initially questioned by the arbitral tribunal, followed by questioning by the parties'.

[33] See also 11.99.

In practice, this is the approach adopted in the majority of international arbitrations as it has the advantage of saving valuable hearing time. A disadvantage is that it can encourage the preparation of long and detailed witness statements.[34]

11.58 If written evidence stands as direct testimony, direct examination of a witness by counsel will generally comprise the introduction of the witness and a question asking the witness to confirm the accuracy of the matters contained in their witness statement or expert report (and as expressly required by Article 8.4 of the IBA Rules). Where there are matters in that written evidence that need to be corrected, the opportunity will be taken at this point to place those corrections on the record before the witness is handed over for cross-examination to opposing counsel.

11.59 Of course, although witness statements are used in the majority of arbitrations, their use is not compulsory. As mentioned, Article 4.4 of the IBA Rules states that the tribunal 'may' order each party to submit witness statements. The Commentary to the IBA Rules states that:

> The arbitral tribunal, in consultation with the parties, should determine whether or not to require such witness statements, depending on the circumstances of each case.

If witness statements are not used, the witness will need to provide direct oral testimony.

11.60 Even where witness statements are used, a question may arise as to whether a witness is nonetheless entitled to give comprehensive direct evidence at the evidentiary hearing. For example, under Article 8.1 a party may request one of its witnesses to attend the evidentiary hearing even where the opponent party has not requested that attendance for cross-examination.[35] The Commentary to the IBA Rules indicates that this may be because the party wishes the witness to give direct oral testimony. It makes the point that Article 8.1 aligns the IBA Rules to current best practice:

> [A]ccording to which witnesses appear only if cross-examination has been requested *or the party presenting the testimony wishes to do so by means of live testimony rather than written statements alone.*[36]

11.61 Even where a witness is to be cross-examined, the same issue may arise. There is a school of thought that favours direct oral testimony over reliance on witness statements.[37] A party may believe that if its witness is permitted to present direct evidence

[34] See Chapter 7 para 7.67.

[35] IBA Rules (n 4) Article 8.1 gives each party an express right to request a witness to attend an evidentiary hearing and does not limit the category of witness to whom that provision applies. Subject to the tribunal's overall control over who should appear (IBA Rules (n 4) Article 8.2), Article 8.1 says in terms that a witness shall appear at the hearing if the attendance of that witness 'has been requested by *any* party' (emphasis added). See further Chapter 7 paras 7.180–7.182.

[36] Emphasis added.

[37] See, for discussion: Anne Véronique Schlaepfer and Vanessa Alarcón Duvanel, 'Direct and Re-Direct Examination' in Stephen Jagusch and Philippe Pinsolle (eds), *The Guide to Advocacy* (Global Arbitration Review 2016) 63–65.

in his or her own way prior to being cross-examined, this may be advantageous to its case. The tribunal may also find it helpful to hear direct oral testimony, rather than rely on a witness statement that is likely to have been drafted by, or with the assistance of, counsel.

A potential disadvantage of direct examination is that the witness may say something new that is not covered in a witness statement. Although, in principle, the witness should not introduce new evidence, if it does happen this may result in unfairness to the opponent party if counsel for that party in unable to address that new matter in cross-examination without additional preparation. Another disadvantage of direct examination is that it will take up time and perhaps eat into the allocated time available to the party whose witness it is. In *Abaclat*,[38] the tribunal refused a request by the respondent that it be permitted to conduct direct examination of its witnesses. The tribunal said that the very purpose of requesting witness statements is to gain time and increase efficiency, and to avoid having to start at zero with direct examination at the hearing. However, the tribunal went on to indicate that direct examination might be warranted in special circumstances, eg where new documents or allegations are submitted with the last round of written submissions and the other party has no opportunity to respond to such allegations other than through direct examination of its witness. **11.62**

If the parties can reach agreement on whether or not direct examination should take place, such agreement will usually be accepted by the tribunal. If there is no agreement then the decision will have to be made by the tribunal. Article 8.4 of the IBA Rules makes express provision authorizing the tribunal to decide the point. The tribunal might also consider limiting the appearance of a witness to cross-examination and re-direct examination pursuant to Article 8.2 on the grounds that the evidence is duplicative of the evidence contained in a witness statement. **11.63**

Another way to approach the matter is for the tribunal is to apply the chess-clock approach to both direct and cross-examination. Given that each party will have an equal amount of time at the hearing, it will be left to counsel for each party to decide whether s/he wants to use up a portion of the time allocated to them for direct examination of that party's witnesses and/or experts.[39] **11.64**

[38] *Abaclat and Others v Argentine Republic* (Procedural Order No. 27, 30 May 2014) ICSID Case No. ARB/07/5.

[39] Such an approach was suggested in Gary B Born, *International Commercial Arbitration* (2nd edn, Kluwer Law International 2014) 2286 (hereafter 'Born'), as quoted in Andrea Menaker and Noor L Davies, 'The Direct Examination of Witnesses and Experts Not Called for Cross-Examination: Balancing Efficiency and Fairness' (2015) BCDR International Arbitration Review 135; Richard Kreindler, 'Cross-Examination Against the Clock' in Lawrence W Newman and Ben H Sheppard Jr (eds), *Take the Witness: Cross-Examination in International Arbitration* (JurisNet/LLC 2010) 119 (hereafter 'Kreindler').

4. Cross-Examination and the Scope of Questions to the Witness

11.65 Cross-examination is the questioning of a witness by counsel for the opposing side.[40] In multi-party arbitrations, if a witness is called by the claimant, the witness can be cross-examined by counsel for each co-respondent. As mentioned at 11.43-11.49, there is no prohibition on the use of leading questions in cross-examination. However, Article 8.3 makes no reference to the scope of permitted cross-examination, in particular, whether it is possible for the cross-examining counsel to stray outside of the matters covered in the relevant witness statement or expert report.

11.66 There are various practices in relation to this issue. For example, the 'English' rule on the permitted scope of cross-examination is that it is not limited to the matters addressed in the witness statement but (absent an application to the tribunal during cross-examination) it is generally limited to 'matters in issue'.[41] The 'American' rule (sometimes honoured in the breach) is that cross-examination is limited to the scope of direct examination, ie if the written witness statement serves as direct evidence, cross-examination is limited to matters covered in the statement.[42] It is prudent for the parties and the tribunal to agree before the hearing the approach that is to be taken.[43]

5. Re-Examination

11.67 When cross-examination is concluded, counsel for the party presenting a witness or party-appointed expert is permitted to re-examine the witness. The re-examination is normally limited to matters raised with the witness during cross-examination,[44] although the tribunal may sometimes be prepared to allow some limited latitude on this unless objected to by the other party.[45] As mentioned, under Article 8.2 counsel for the party presenting the witness should not ask unreasonably leading questions during re-examination.

[40] It should be noted that IBA Rules (n 4) Article 8.3(c) (describing the procedure to be adopted at the evidentiary hearing) does not use the phrase 'cross-examination' but, in essence, this is the process provided for in that rule.

[41] There is English authority to the effect that seemingly irrelevant points may be shown by counsel to be relevant through subsequent evidence. See *Haigh v Belcher* (1836) 7 Carrington and Payne 389, 173 ER 173.

[42] See, for more detail: Laurence Shore, 'Cross-Examination without Discovery: Not Blind, but with Blinders' in Lawrence W Newman and Ben H Sheppard Jr (eds), *Take the Witness: Cross-Examination in International Arbitration* (JurisNet/LLC 2010) 59. However, it is suggested that some states, eg Mississippi, Alabama, Ohio, Massachusetts, North Carolina, and Texas follow a more English style of cross-examination where a witness may be cross-examined on any matter in issue. See Harbst (n 18) 107–09.

[43] See also paragraphs 7.172–7.179.

[44] See IBA Rules (n 4) Articles 8.3(b) (Fact Witness) and 8.3(c) (Party-Appointed Experts).

[45] If during re-examination the tribunal permits counsel to go outside matters raised in cross-examination, the tribunal should also offer opposing counsel an opportunity to cross-examine the witness again on any new matters.

6. Tribunal-Appointed Experts

In the case of a tribunal-appointed expert, Article 8.3(d) expressly provides that the tribunal and the parties may question that expert on issues raised in the expert's report, parties' submissions, or reports made by party-appointed experts. **11.68**

7. Tailoring of the Proceedings to Meet the Circumstances of the Case

Although Article 8.3(a)–(d) sets out a basic order for the questioning of witnesses, Article 8.3(e) and (f) make very clear that timing and organization of oral testimony may be tailored to suit the circumstances of an individual dispute. **11.69**

Article 8.3(e) makes express provision for a situation in which the arbitration is organized into separate issues or phases. In such circumstances, the tribunal may order the scheduling of testimony separately for each issue or phase. The provision is consistent with other provisions in the IBA Rules that may clear that the taking and presentation of all types of evidence may be organized in this way.[46] **11.70**

Article 8.3(f) empowers the tribunal to vary the order of witnesses as it considers appropriate. This may include (but is not limited to) the organization of testimony to be presented at a hearing by reference to particular issues. For example, it may be desirable for the tribunal to hear all of the expert evidence on a particular issue before moving on to the next group of experts. This arrangement also facilitates the use of witness conferencing (see 11.72–11.74) and avoids experts having to be present at the hearing for longer than is necessary. In some cases, similar considerations will apply in relation to the organization of fact evidence. **11.71**

Article 8.3(f) contains express reference to the organization of testimony 'in such manner that witnesses be questioned at the same time and in confrontation with each other (witness conferencing)'. Witness conferencing (also known as 'hot-tubbing') is widely used in international arbitration. There is no single method of witness conferencing, but it generally involves witnesses (more commonly expert witnesses, but sometimes witnesses of fact) sitting together and being asked questions on the same subject matter at the same time.[47] **11.72**

[46] See Articles 2.3, 3.14, 4.4, and 8.3(e).

[47] See, for example, John M Townsend, 'Crossing the Hot Tub: Examining Adverse Expert Witnesses in International Arbitration' in Lawrence W Newman and Ben H Sheppard Jr (eds), *Take the Witness: Cross-Examination in International Arbitration* (JurisNet/LLC 2010) 165. In April 2019 the Chartered Institute of Arbitrators issued 'Guidelines for Witness Conferencing in International Arbitration prepared by a sub-committee of the Singapore branch of the Chartered Institute chaired by Michael Lee. The Guidelines are comprehensive and comprise a checklist of matters to consider when considering use of witness conferencing, standard directions that provide a general framework for its use, and specific directions providing alternative directions depending on whether the conferencing is to be led by the tribunal, the witnesses, or the parties' counsel.

11.73 Although much depends on the individual circumstances of the case, witness conferencing can be effective. It enables the tribunal to hear evidence from competing quarters simultaneously and so be better able to judge the comparative strengths of that evidence. Witness conferencing is also thought to encourage a narrowing of the issues and, in the case of fact witnesses, to sometimes embarrass the witness into a more accurate version of the truth.[48] As noted in the Commentary to the IBA Rules:

> Such techniques may enable arbitral tribunals to better understand the contradictions in testimony and to be better able to determine the weight and credibility to be given to the testimony.

11.74 However, witness conferencing needs to be carefully orchestrated and a tribunal will need to control proceedings very closely. The tribunal will sometimes start the process by putting a series of questions to which they will expect an answer from each of the witnesses in turn. In some cases, this may lead to some form of quasi-discussion between the witnesses on the topic and the raising of follow-up questions by the tribunal. Counsel with little or no experience of witness conferencing may feel unnerved by it, particularly counsel from common law jurisdictions who are used to carefully structured cross-examination. Counsel often wish to preserve the right to conduct cross-examination or re-examination when the witness conferencing part of the evidence is concluded.[49] For this reason, witness conferencing may not always save time because it ends up being an addition to cross-examination, rather than replacing it.[50]

8. Tribunal Questions

11.75 Article 8.3(g) contains the simple statement that the tribunal may ask questions to a witness at any time.

11.76 In most national courts—whether in common law or civil law jurisdictions—the judge may wish to direct a question to the witness. However, in the civil law tradition, the judge or an arbitrator plays a much more proactive role at the hearing and is normally tasked with establishing the truth even if the parties do not present or volunteer it.[51] This approach is dubbed 'inquisitorial' in contrast to the adversarial approach adopted in common law countries where the judges may be more passive and to a very large extent will leave it to the parties to present the evidence as they wish. The inclusion in the IBA Rules of an express power permitting the tribunal to put questions to a witness may

[48] See further Wolfgang Peter, 'Witness "Conferencing"' (2002) 18 Arbitration International 47, and Carol Mulcahy, 'Opportunity or Threat (the benefits and pitfalls of witness conferencing in international arbitration)' Legal Business Arbitration Report 2006.

[49] Kreindler (n 39) 124.

[50] Born (n 39) 2293.

[51] See, for example, David Haigh, 'When to be Friendly and When to Impeach' in Lawrence W Newman and Ben H Sheppard Jr (eds), *Take the Witness: Cross-Examination in International Arbitration* (JurisNet/LLC 2010) 18 (hereafter 'Haigh').

be a recognition of civil law practice or simply reinforcement of the tribunal's general power to control the evidentiary hearing.[52]

As noted in the Commentary on the IBA Rules, in practice many tribunals will reserve their questions until towards the end of a witness' testimony other than in the case of questions designed to move the process along, or to make a witness feel comfortable. Counsel will have prepared and structured their questions carefully and frequent interruptions from the tribunal can sometimes disrupt the flow of examination to the disadvantage of counsel. However, in some cases, the tribunal may wish to take a more interactive approach and will ask a number of questions as the evidence unfolds. This sometimes happens in relation to expert technical evidence where the tribunal wishes to be sure that it has understood all of the evidence. Leaving questions until the end may hinder its understanding of earlier parts of the evidence. The tribunal may also wish to ask questions relating to the witness' direct evidence, particularly where this has not been given orally.[53] **11.77**

F. Affirmation and Confirmation by the Witness

> **8.4 A witness of fact providing testimony shall first affirm, in a manner determined appropriate by the Arbitral Tribunal, that he or she commits to tell the truth or, in the case of an expert witness, his or her genuine belief in the opinions to be expressed at the Evidentiary Hearing. If the witness has submitted a Witness Statement or an Expert Report, the witness shall confirm it.**
>
> **The Parties may agree or the Arbitral Tribunal may order that the Witness Statement or Expert Report shall serve as that witness's direct testimony.**

Article 8.4 provides that, prior to giving oral testimony, a witness of fact shall affirm that s/he commits to tell the truth during that testimony. **11.78**

Article 8.4 stipulates a different requirement for expert witnesses. Prior to giving oral testimony, an expert (whether party-appointed or tribunal-appointed) is to affirm his or her genuine belief in the opinions to be expressed during that testimony. **11.79**

The reason for the distinction is self-evident. A witness speaks to matters of fact. An expert can only give his expert opinion on the issues that have been put to him based on his knowledge and experience. In most instances there is no absolute truth in relation to those matters. **11.80**

52 IBA Rules (n 4) Article 8.2 states that the tribunal shall have complete control over the evidentiary hearing at all times.

53 For example, where it has been agreed or directed that the written statement of a witness should serve as direct testimony. See IBA Rules (n 4) Article 8.4.

11.81 The IBA Rules make no reference to the possibility of a witness or expert giving evidence on oath, but neither do they exclude the possibility.

11.82 In some cases, parties may prefer that their witnesses offer evidence on oath. This may be because it believes the tribunal will give it greater weight or because the other party is proffering its witnesses on that basis and it feels it will be at a disadvantage if it does not do the same. It is certainly true that in a number of jurisdictions the giving of evidence on oath may cloak the evidence with some additional weight. This may be because there are sanctions attached to the giving of false evidence. For example, in arbitral proceedings in England and Wales, if the evidence of a witness given under oath proves to be a lie, the witness may be held criminally liable under the Perjury Act 1911, for which offence the maximum sentence is seven years' imprisonment.[54]

11.83 Although the majority of institutional rules are silent on the administration of oaths, express provision for the tribunal to administer an oath can be found in some institutional rules and national arbitration laws.[55]

11.84 If a party wishes its witnesses to give evidence under oath it is usual to raise this with the other party and the tribunal in advance of the hearing. Some tribunals will ask for the appropriate form of oath and holy book to be made available at the hearing so that the oath may be administered by the tribunal.

11.85 There may be occasions where a specific mandatory provision of the law of the seat requires evidence to be given on oath. If it does, this will override the less prescriptive requirements of Article 8.4, which do not require the giving of evidence on oath. The practical implications of this may be important. A failure of the witnesses to give testimony under oath in the manner prescribed may put the award at risk of being set aside by the local courts.[56]

G. Tribunal Request for Evidence

8.5 Subject to the provisions of Article 9.2, the Arbitral Tribunal may request any person to give oral or written evidence on any issue that the Arbitral Tribunal

[54] For more detail, see Audley Sheppard, 'Oaths and Perjury' in Julio César Betancourt (ed) *Defining Issues in International Arbitration: Celebrating 100 Years of the Chartered Institute of Arbitrators* (OUP 2016) 197–206; in particular, see paras 20–24. Interestingly, we understand from respondents to the BCLP Survey on the use of the IBA Rules that, in the United States, a witness can in some circumstances be liable to perjury before an arbitral tribunal regardless of whether s/he actually took an oath.

[55] For example, see LCIA Rules, Article 20.1 and English Arbitration Act, s 38(5). A very different approach is taken in Sweden. Under Articles 25 and 26 of the Swedish Arbitration Act, the arbitrators may not administer oaths or even affirmations of truth. Where a party wishes a witness or an expert to testify under oath, or a party to be examined under an affirmation of truth, the party must submit an application for permission to the District Court, after first obtaining the consent of the tribunal. Swedish Arbitration Act 1999, s 25(3); Finn Madsen, *Commercial Arbitration in Sweden: A Commentary on the Arbitration Act (1999:116) and the Rules of the Arbitration Institute of the Stockholm Chamber of Commerce* (2nd edn, OUP 2006) 178.

[56] See Chapter 4 paras 4.36–4.37, which discuss the requirements of UAE law in this respect.

considers to be relevant to the case and material to its outcome. Any witness called and questioned by the Arbitral Tribunal may also be questioned by the Parties.

Subject to the protections afforded by Article 9.2, Article 8.5 gives the tribunal an express power to request written or oral evidence on any issue that the tribunal considers to be relevant to the case and material to its outcome. **11.86**

There is no restriction on the timing of such a request under Article 8.5, although it is clearly desirable that the tribunal give the parties as much notice as possible of the request, particularly if the tribunal wishes to hear oral testimony. The intention behind Article 8.5 is explained in the Commentary to the IBA Rules: **11.87**

> Inquisitorial powers of the arbitral tribunal follow from the *lex arbitri* of the seat of the arbitration.[57] Inquisitorial powers may also follow from the arbitration rules agreed by the parties. The IBA Rules of Evidence do not provide for similarly sweeping inquisitorial powers of the arbitral tribunal, but Article 8.5 covers the main case where inquisitorial powers may be exercised: the hearing of a key witness who typically had an earlier association with both parties but whom the parties for some reason failed to persuade to appear, perhaps because they no longer have close ties with the witness. Such a tribunal witness will often be questioned in the inquisitorial fashion described above. To proceed in this fashion is not mandated, but is contemplated by the second sentence of Article 8.5.[58]

Thus, it is contemplated that the exercise of the tribunal's powers under Article 8.5 will be directed at obtaining 'key' evidence. This is reflected in the requirement at Article 8.5 that the evidence sought by the tribunal be 'relevant to the case and material to its outcome'. **11.88**

As mentioned, the benchmarks of 'relevant to the case' and 'material to its outcome' are a cornerstone of the IBA Rules designed to ensure that evidence put before the tribunal is limited to that which has an evidential value for a determination of the dispute. The meaning of the two phrases is discussed in detail at Chapter 6 paras 6.76-6.146. **11.89**

The tribunal has the power, exercisable at any time up to the end of the arbitration, to request production of documents (Article 3.10), and to request that a party make arrangements for the attendance of a person to give oral testimony at an evidentiary hearing (Article 4.10). It may be that Article 8.5 is principally directed at requests for evidence during the evidentiary hearing but there is clearly potential for overlap between these provisions and the terms of Article 8.5. **11.90**

For example, Article 8.5 may be utilized where, during cross-examination, a witness or expert has referred to a document not in the record. If the document is in the **11.91**

[57] Examples given in the commentary are the English Arbitration Act, s 34(2) and the Swiss Private International Law Statute, Article 184.

[58] Commentary on the IBA Rules (n 7) 24.

possession of one of the parties, and the tribunal is of the view that the document may be important, it can ask the relevant party to produce it. The time given for production may be short—normally before the end of the hearing, or even before the end of cross-examination in order that the document can be put to a witness. If any of the objections to production available under Article 9.2 are raised, the tribunal will generally consider them there and then.

11.92 Cases where the tribunal requests additional oral evidence at the hearing will be relatively rare. However, one example known to the authors concerned an LCIA arbitration in which important witness testimony centred around a particular meeting attended by the beneficial owner of the claimant, its CEO, and the beneficial owner of the respondent. The claimant produced evidence from the CEO, but had not proffered the claimant's beneficial owner as a witness because of the direct evidence about what was said at the meeting being already available from the CEO. Notwithstanding this, at the beginning of the hearing the tribunal expressed the view that the beneficial owner of the claimant should also produce a witness statement. The statement was produced during the course of the hearing and special arrangements were made for that witness to be cross-examined at the conclusion of the hearing.

H. Issues Not Addressed in Article 8

11.93 There are a number of matters relating to the organization and management of an oral hearing that are not addressed in Article 8. In many cases, it will be desirable to supplement the provisions of Article 8 by agreement between the parties (or absent such agreement by direction from the tribunal) on a number of practical matters.

11.94 Some of these matters (for example, a provisional date for the hearing, the hearing venue, and perhaps the date by which parties will give notification of which of an opponent's witnesses they wish to cross-examine) are likely to have been agreed relatively early in the proceedings, perhaps as part of an Article 2 consultation. However, there will be other matters that in practice are frequently only agreed upon much closer to the hearing. These include such matters as the content and organization of hearing bundles, allocation of time at the hearing, the use of interpreters, transcripts, the timetabling of witnesses participating by video conference, etc.

1. Sequestration of Witnesses

11.95 Sequestration of witnesses is a practice that requires a witness not to be present at a hearing before that witness has given testimony. The basis for sequestration is that attending a hearing before giving evidence will 'permit a witness to tailor his or her subsequent testimony'[59] to the evidence that the witness has heard during earlier testimony by other witnesses. The practice of sequestration is one that has existed in many national courts for a considerable time and is considered common practice in a number of fora. In one case decided by the English Court of Appeal, it was held that the exclusion of a prospective witness for part of a hearing (while another witness gave evidence on substantially the same facts) did not give rise to unfairness, and that it was within the power of the court to order the exclusion.[60] However, sequestration of witnesses is not used in all cases and witnesses (including expert witnesses) are frequently allowed into the hearing room before giving evidence.

The approach in international arbitration varies. Some authors suggest that the tribunal will generally permit witnesses to be present at the hearing at a time when they are not giving evidence, unless there are particularly contentious factual questions in issue.[61] Others suggest that it makes sense and that it is common practice to exclude witnesses who have yet to give evidence. Born suggests that: **11.96**

> Although there is no invariable rule, in most cases, tribunals exclude a fact witness from attending other witnesses' examinations prior to his or her own testimony, on the (correct) basis that this may permit a witness to tailor his or her subsequent testimony. This is a common-sense and time-tested means for attempting to safeguard the integrity of the arbitral procedure and to achieve the tribunal's mandate of ascertaining the facts. After a witness has testified, he or she will usually be permitted to attend subsequent parts of the hearing (on the basis that there is no longer any material risk that the witness will be recalled to testify).[62]

The IBA Rules are silent on the issue of sequestration. The Commentary on the IBA Rules explains that this is left for the arbitral tribunal to decide 'because it depends on the circumstances of the case, the nature of the dispute and the persons involved'.[63] Since under Article 8.2 the tribunal remains in control of the hearing at all times, it **11.97**

[59] Born (n 39) 2288.

[60] *Da Costa v Sargaco* [2016] EWCA Civ 764.

[61] Nigel Rawding, Gregory Fullelove, and Penny Martin, 'Chapter 18: International Arbitration in England: A Procedural Overview' in Julian D M Lew and others (eds), *Arbitration in England, with Chapters on Scotland and Ireland* (Kluwer Law International 2013) para 18-97. The manner in which this matter is dealt with in arbitration rules varies. For example, the UNCITRAL Arbitration Rules, Article 28(3) provides that the tribunal may require the retirement of any witness, including the expert witnesses, during the testimony of other such witnesses, except that a witness, including an expert witness, who is a party to the arbitration shall not, in principle, be asked to retire. In contrast, the Swiss Rules, Article 25(6) provides that the tribunal may order witnesses or expert witnesses to retire during the testimony of other witnesses or expert witnesses.

[62] Born (n 39) 2288–89 (footnotes omitted). See also: International Council for Commercial Arbitration, *ICCA Drafting Sourcebook for Logistical Matters in Procedural Orders* (International Council for Commercial Arbitration 2015) para 25.1 (hereafter 'ICCA Drafting Sourcebook') notes that witnesses should be isolated once their testimony has begun particularly if their testimony extends over a number of days). This practice is uncontroversial. However, ICCA Drafting Sourcebook para 26.1 also provides that the parties should attempt to agree on the presence of witnesses and experts in general. ICCA Drafting Sourcebook paras 26.2–26.4 set out options by which no fact witnesses and/or experts can be present at all unless giving evidence or that fact witnesses or experts can only be present after giving evidence.

[63] Commentary on the IBA Rules (n 7).

lies within its power to exclude a witness from the hearing room if this is considered appropriate.

11.98 In practice, the issue of sequestration is often discussed between the parties and they are able to reach an agreement on whether or not it should be applied. Where the parties cannot agree, the tribunal may have to give a ruling on the matter.[64] Where sequestration is ordered or agreed, the witness should not be permitted to see the transcript of earlier evidence.[65]

11.99 One such basis on which parties sometimes seek to avoid sequestration is where a witness is also a party to the arbitration, or the principal representative of a party.[66] If they are excluded from the hearing room this may give rise to a number of issues—for example, is it fair to disallow a party to the arbitration to attend the hearing (even for a limited time), and who will give instructions to counsel in the event that instructions are needed during the period that the witness is excluded? These points justify serious consideration and the tribunal will sometimes need to find the right balance between protecting the integrity of the oral testimony and the protection of individual party rights.[67] As Born explains in relation to the right to have party representatives present at all times:

> Tribunals often recognize the force of this position, but nonetheless impose limits on the number of persons that may be designated as party representatives (to avoid circumvention of sequestration requirements). Tribunals also generally seek to schedule the witness testimony so that party representatives will be examined first, before other witnesses testify.[68]

11.100 The position in relation to expert witnesses is generally more relaxed. Tribunals will ordinarily permit expert witnesses to attend testimony of both fact and expert witnesses, prior to their own testimony. The broad rationale is that the expert is not giving evidence on matters of fact and that exposure to the oral testimony of witnesses (which on some issues may be relevant to the expert evidence that the expert has produced) is beneficial, rather than harmful.[69] This approach makes sense and, we believe, should be followed.

[64] ICCA Drafting Sourcebook (n 62) paras 26.1–26.6 set out a number of template provisions that vary according to the category of witness to be excluded.

[65] Appropriate confirmation on this point from counsel, and from the sequestered witness, may be considered desirable.

[66] IBA Rules (n 4) Article 4.2 states expressly that any person may present evidence as a witness, including a party or a party's officer, employee, or other representative.

[67] For example, in England the discretion of the judge to exclude witnesses from the courtroom was held in *Tomlinson v Tomlinson* [1980] 1 WLR 322 not to extend to the parties themselves, their solicitors, or experts.

[68] Born (n 39) 2289 (footnotes omitted).

[69] ibid.

2. Allocation of Time Allowed for Direct Examination, Cross-Examination, and Re-Examination

Another very important issue for the parties to agree and/or for the tribunal to resolve is allocation of time at the hearing. Arbitration hearings tend to be short and, as a result, parties often compete for time. A standard practice in arbitration is to allocate time equally between the parties. This is widely known as a 'chess-clock approach' for the obvious reason that it necessitates very precise time-keeping during the hearing. The principle of 'equal time' is generally accepted as reflecting the principle of equal treatment of the parties.[70] However, there are a number of practical considerations that arise. 11.101

a. Equal division and time allocation

In theory, an equal allocation of time appears straightforward. In practice, a number of issues may start to creep in as the allocation discussion begins. What if one party has a significantly greater number of witnesses than the other? Should the other party be given more time so that they have an adequate opportunity to cross-examine each of them? If there are two co-respondents to a claim made by a single claimant, should the claimant have 50 per cent of the time, and the co-respondents each have only 25 per cent? 11.102

The first example is recognized as a difficult area. Kreindler summarizes the problem in this way: 11.103

> The tribunal need not be concerned early on with tactical considerations of written advocacy and witnesses. At the same time, the tribunal does need to consider whether a chess clock method makes sense for a particular case. The method is a seemingly reliable way of imposing discipline and equilibrium on the case and fulfilling the duty to ensure equal treatment. However, it is not fail-safe. Thus, for example, where one party has two witnesses and the other 40, the imposition of a clock method may raise issues. Indeed, it may be seen as a windfall for the one side and an unacceptable constraint for the other.[71]

Some tribunals will employ a formula to give the party with fewer witnesses additional cross-examination time in proportion to the disparity in the number of witnesses. However, this approach is not universally accepted and will need to be tailored to the circumstances of the case. For example, if a claimant has six witnesses and a respondent has only four witnesses, it might be thought that the respondent should have 60 per cent of the time allocated to oral examination. However, what if the majority of those witnesses deal with minor issues that occupy very little time, or the respondent makes a last-minute tactical decision to call only two of the claimant's six witnesses—should there be a reallocation of time? 11.104

[70] Born (n 39) 2273.
[71] Kreindler (n 39) 115.

11.105 Normally, the amount of time spent with a particular witness within the agreed time budget for each party is a matter for counsel—s/he may decide to spend more time with one witness and much less time with another witness. However, other matters of detail that arise include whether time taken for objections by counsel should be counted against that party, and not against the party whose examination is interrupted,[72] and whether any of the time taken for interpretation of oral testimony given in a language other than the language of the arbitration should be counted against the party on whose behalf the witness testifies. In relation to the latter, a relevant factor may be whether the witness is able to speak the language of the arbitration and chooses to testify in a different language.[73]

b. Active tribunal and allocation of time

11.106 Another important issue is how the time taken up by tribunal questions is to be allocated. In a complex case, particularly one involving technical evidence, several hours of hearing time may be occupied by tribunal questions and the ensuing responses.

11.107 A tribunal comprised of arbitrators who actively engage with the evidence is generally a good thing. However, if this eats into the time available for cross-examination then it may become an issue for the parties. Of course, in some cases, the questions asked by the tribunal may bring out evidence that cross-examining counsel intended to cover and there may therefore be savings in time. In other cases, the tribunal will be sensitive to issues of time and may rein in the number of questions asked. However, if the parties and the tribunal have not made any prior provision for how time spent on tribunal questions is to be allocated, they may need to do so if that time becomes significant. For example, should the time be counted against the party calling or against the party cross-examining a witness, or should it be allocated on an equal basis? There are no hard rules around these matters. If counsel on all sides are cooperative it may be possible to tailor time allocation according to need.

3. Oral Testimony, Language, and the Use of Translators/Interpreters

11.108 Evidence may be presented in different languages. Articles 4.5(c), 5.2(f), and 6.4(d) include a requirement that the author of a witness statement or expert report should indicate in that document the language in which the witness/expert anticipates giving evidence at a hearing. If a witness or expert gives evidence in a language that is not the language of the arbitration, arrangements should be made for an interpreter to attend the hearing.[74] However, cross-examination through an interpreter can present a number of challenges for counsel. As Haigh explains:

[72] Born (n 39) 2274. The merits and time taken for the objection may be relevant considerations.
[73] ibid. See also Chapter 7 para 7.117.
[74] See further discussion in Chapter 7 paras 7.116–7.117.

> For a cross-examination to be effective, it is usually important to know what the answers will be. Such knowledge is thrown into doubt when one cannot be entirely sure of the facts due to uncertainty over the nuances of translation of records or the interpretation of the witness's answers. It is also difficult to control a combative witness. His answer in another language may go on and on, but you cannot cut him off until you hear the ultimate answer filtered through the interpreter. The shifting sands of translation and interpretation will therefore often make the bilingual cross-examination very challenging.[75]

In order to mitigate these potential problems it is important to find an interpreter who is experienced in providing translation during a court or arbitration hearing. As mentioned elsewhere, the parties may wish to interview the interpreter. If the evidence is concerned with technical matters that will involve use of a specialist vocabulary it is desirable to ensure that the interpreter has the requisite knowledge. Another important consideration is what interpretation mode—simultaneous or consecutive (also known as 'sequential')—is to be used. Simultaneous interpreters convert what is said in real-time; there are no pauses in conversation. In consecutive interpretation, the interpreter waits for the speaker to finish a sentence or an idea, and then renders the speaker's words into the target language. Not every interpreter is prepared to do simultaneous interpretation and special equipment (interpreter booth, headphones, microphones, etc.) is likely to be required. **11.109**

Some practitioners suggest that simultaneous interpretation is essential if the cross-examination is to have any chance of success because the interpretation should interrupt the flow of question and answer as little as possible.[76] It also has the advantage of saving time—sequential translation will take much longer. However, simultaneous translation also has disadvantages. During high-speed cross-examination, the risk that the interpreter misses words or phrases, or does not have time to find the most appropriate word in the target language, is much greater. As a rule, sequential translation is generally more accurate. The parties and/or the tribunal should decide what is more important for them—to keep the flow uninterrupted or to have a potentially more accurate interpretation of the witness evidence. **11.110**

4. Use of Transcripts and Electronic Bundles

Another consideration not addressed in Article 8 is the use of transcripts (verbatim stenographic records). A clear advantage of having a transcript is that it avoids future disputes as to what has been said at the hearing. If real-time transcription is used, it can also be a valuable tool during the hearing—for example, a witness may be taken by counsel back to earlier oral testimony. Given the relatively modest costs involved, and **11.111**

[75] Haigh (n 51) 26.
[76] Nappert and Harris (n 29) 267.

the availability of stenographers in all of the main arbitration centres, the use of transcripts is almost universal in high-value arbitrations. In addition to providing a record of what has been said, they provide a valuable tool for counsel and arbitrators to copy and paste extracts from oral evidence and submissions into an award or closing written submissions.

11.112 In some cases, parties will also agree to use electronic hearing bundles. These can be more portable and more convenient than paper files, and often bring other advantages—for example, the facility to simply 'click' through to another document in the hearing bundle referred to in the document being considered (for example, an exhibit referred to in a witness statement). Use of electronic bundles is a matter that should be discussed between the parties as early as practicable as it may affect the way in which counsel prepare for the hearing; if the discussion is left too late the use of electronic bundles may not be possible.

5. Provision for Closing Statements or Post-Hearing Briefs

11.113 Once the taking of evidence is over, both parties generally like to present a summary of their position to the tribunal that takes account of events during the hearing. For example, a key piece of evidence may have come out on cross-examination that one party wishes to emphasize, or the tribunal may have asked a lot of questions on a particular topic and counsel may wish to address specific points about which they believe the tribunal may be concerned.

11.114 By and large this can be done in two ways: (i) oral closing statements or (ii) written post-hearing briefs. Sometimes the tribunal combines these two methods—for example, by allowing the parties to have oral closing arguments after filing written post-hearing briefs, or vice versa.

11.115 There is no 'one-fits-all' solution, and each option has its advantages and disadvantages. Oral closings are cheaper and faster, but counsel sometimes require time to consider the transcripts and reflect on developments before making final submissions in the case. Written post-hearing briefs prolong the proceedings and entail additional costs, but in complex cases they may be the only practicable way of dealing with matters. Where written post-hearing briefs are to be permitted the tribunal may decide to impose a page limit.

12

Article 9: Admissibility and Assessment of Evidence

Article 9 Admissibility and Assessment of Evidence

1. **The Arbitral Tribunal shall determine the admissibility, relevance, materiality and weight of evidence.**

2. The Arbitral Tribunal shall, at the request of a Party or on its own motion, exclude from evidence or production any Document, statement, oral testimony or inspection for any of the following reasons:
   (a) lack of sufficient relevance to the case or materiality to its outcome;
   (b) legal impediment or privilege under the legal or ethical rules determined by the Arbitral Tribunal to be applicable;
   (c) unreasonable burden to produce the requested evidence;
   (d) loss or destruction of the Document that has been shown with reasonable likelihood to have occurred;
   (e) grounds of commercial or technical confidentiality that the Arbitral Tribunal determines to be compelling;
   (f) grounds of special political or institutional sensitivity (including evidence that has been classified as secret by a government or a public international institution) that the Arbitral Tribunal determines to be compelling; or
   (g) considerations of procedural economy, proportionality, fairness or equality of the Parties that the Arbitral Tribunal determines to be compelling.
3. In considering issues of legal impediment or privilege under Article 9.2(b), and insofar as permitted by any mandatory legal or ethical rules that are determined by it to be applicable, the Arbitral Tribunal may take into account:
   (a) any need to protect the confidentiality of a Document created or statement or oral communication made in connection with and for the purpose of providing or obtaining legal advice;
   (b) any need to protect the confidentiality of a Document created or statement or oral communication made in connection with and for the purpose of settlement negotiations;
   (c) the expectations of the Parties and their advisors at the time the legal impediment or privilege is said to have arisen;
   (d) any possible waiver of any applicable legal impediment or privilege by virtue of consent, earlier disclosure, affirmative use of the Document, statement, oral communication or advice contained therein, or otherwise; and
   (e) the need to maintain fairness and equality as between the Parties, particularly if they are subject to different legal or ethical rules.
4. The Arbitral Tribunal may, where appropriate, make necessary arrangements to permit evidence to be presented or considered subject to suitable confidentiality protection.
5. If a Party fails without satisfactory explanation to produce any Document requested in a Request to Produce to which it has not objected in due time or fails to produce any Document ordered to be produced by the Arbitral Tribunal, the Arbitral Tribunal may infer that such document would be adverse to the interests of that Party.
6. If a Party fails without satisfactory explanation to make available any other relevant evidence, including testimony, sought by one Party to which the Party to whom the request was addressed has not objected in due time or fails to make

available any evidence, including testimony, ordered by the Arbitral Tribunal to be produced, the Arbitral Tribunal may infer that such evidence would be adverse to the interests of that Party.

7. If the Arbitral Tribunal determines that a Party has failed to conduct itself in good faith in the taking of evidence, the Arbitral Tribunal may, in addition to any other measures available under these Rules, take such failure into account in its assignment of the costs of the arbitration, including costs arising out of or in connection with the taking of evidence.

A. Introduction

Article 9 is a key provision of the IBA Rules. It deals with assessment and admissibility of evidence, contains the benchmarks by reference to which evidence may be excluded, and provides certain mechanisms by which the tribunal may address bad-faith conduct by a party to the arbitration. **12.1**

The results of an IBA survey show that Article 9 is the second most referenced provision of the IBA Rules (approximately 13 per cent of all references), second only to Article 3.[1] **12.2**

The equivalent provision in the 1999 IBA Rules[2] was similar in scope to the present provision. However, material changes have been introduced into Article 9 of the current IBA Rules. Two key amendments are: **12.3**

(i) A new set of provisions with respect to privilege and legal impediment has been incorporated into what is now Article 9.3; and
(ii) The addition of Article 9.7—this allows tribunals to impose costs sanctions on a party that fails to conduct itself in good faith in the taking of evidence.

The provisions of Article 9—in particular, Article 9.2 which sets out the grounds upon which documents, statements, oral testimony, or inspection may be excluded from evidence or production—operate in tandem with a number of other provisions of the IBA Rules. Accordingly, Article 9 is expressly referenced elsewhere in the IBA Rules. For example, in Article 3 (Documents), Article 6 (Tribunal-Appointed Experts), Article 7 (Inspection), and Article 8 (Evidentiary Hearing).[3] The provisions contained in Article 9 play an important role in the successful operation of the IBA Rules. **12.4**

[1] See: The IBA Arbitration Guidelines and Rules Subcommittee, 'Report on the Reception of the IBA Arbitration Soft Law Products' (*International Bar Association*, 2016) paras 46–48 <www.ibanet.org/Document/Default.aspx?DocumentUid=105d29a3-6261-4437-84e2-1c8637844beb> accessed 27 November 2018 (hereafter '2016 IBA Report'). It should be noted that the distribution of references to different provisions of the IBA Rules varies according to jurisdiction.

[2] IBA Rules on the Taking of Evidence in International Commercial Arbitration 1999, Article 9.

[3] IBA Rules on the Taking of Evidence in International Arbitration 2010, Articles 3.5, 3.7, 3.9, 3.10, 6.3, 7, 8.2, and 8.5 (hereafter 'IBA Rules') contain references to Article 9.2.

B. Assessment of Evidence

9.1. The Arbitral Tribunal shall determine the admissibility, relevance, materiality and weight of evidence.

1. Introduction

12.5 Article 9.1 states the general principle that the tribunal shall determine the admissibility, relevance, materiality, and weight of evidence. The exercise of the tribunal's discretion in determining these matters is central to its role in arbitration proceedings.

12.6 The terms of Article 9.1 reflect accepted practice in international arbitration and provision in similar terms may be found in a number of institutional rules and national arbitration laws. For this reason, practical application of Article 9.1 operates in a similar manner to practice and procedure adopted in arbitrations not conducted under the IBA Rules, and it has relatively few distinguishing features.

12.7 An important consequence of the principle expressed in Article 9.1 is that (subject to any mandatory provisions of law applicable at the seat of arbitration)[4] the tribunal is not obliged to follow strict rules of evidence that might apply in a national court, either at the seat of arbitration or one of the home jurisdictions of the parties to the dispute. Nonetheless, a tribunal may, in practice, take account of or be sensitive to the law of the seat of arbitration, the national legal backgrounds (and expectations) of the parties and their advisers, any agreements made between the parties, and any applicable institutional rules or guidelines.

2. Article 9.1: An Accepted Principle in International Arbitration

12.8 As mentioned, the principle stated in Article 9.1 can be found in nearly all institutional and other arbitration rules.[5]

12.9 The same principle is also found in many national arbitration laws. For example, the German Code of Civil Procedure states that: 'The arbitral tribunal is empowered to determine the admissibility of taking evidence, take evidence and assess freely such

[4] See Chapter 4 paras 4.10–4.56.

[5] See SCC Rules, Article 31(1); DIAC Rules, Article 28.2; SIAC Rules, Rule 19.2; LCIA Rules, Article 22.1(vi); PCA Rules, Article 27.4; WIPO Arbitration Rules, Article 50(a); PRIME Finance Arbitration Rules, Article 27.4; ADR Institute of Canada (ADRIC) Arbitration Rules, Rule 4.19.4; Milan Chamber of Arbitration Rules, Article 25; Commercial Arbitration Centre of the Portuguese Chamber of Commerce and Industry Rules of Arbitration, Article 31.1; Madrid Court of Arbitration Rules of Arbitration, Article 29.3; DIFC–LCIA Rules, Article 22.1(vi); HKIAC Rules, Article 22.2; ICDR Rules, Article 20.6; NAI Rules, Article 26.1.. Interestingly, the ICC Rules do not contain a specific provision to the same effect. Article 25(1) of the ICC Rules simply provides that 'The arbitral tribunal shall proceed within as short a time as possible to establish the facts of the case by all appropriate means'.

evidence.'[6] Similar provision may be found in the Belgian Judicial Code[7] and the Netherlands Code of Civil Procedure.[8] The United States Courts have uniformly held that arbitrators possess broad powers to determine arbitral procedures, including the assessment of evidence,[9] and national courts consistently affirm a tribunal's inherently broad discretion over evidentiary issues.[10] Section 34 of the English Arbitration Act contains a statement of the same principle.[11]

Thus, there is wide recognition of a tribunal's discretion to admit evidence, to determine its relevance and probative value, as well as to reject evidence that it regards as being of little or no assistance.[12] To that extent, the wide powers granted to a tribunal under the IBA Rules are broadly consistent with the position likely to exist under any applicable arbitration rules, and as a matter of accepted practice in international arbitration. 12.10

However, a tribunal's discretion around evidentiary matters is not entirely without constraints, as it must take care to observe due process and respect the right of each party to have a fair opportunity to present its case as required by the IBA Rules,[13] and in applicable institutional rules, or mandatory national laws or procedural norms at the seat of arbitration.[14] In particular, during the course of the proceedings each party should be given an opportunity to respond to and comment on the relevance, materiality, admissibility, or probative value of the evidence that has been presented.[15] 12.11

What distinguishes the IBA Rules from the majority of other arbitration rules is that they contain clear benchmarks to determine what evidence has value in the proceedings, and the categories of evidence that may be excluded from consideration by the tribunal.[16] 12.12

[6] German Code of Civil Procedure (Zivilprozessordnung) 2013, s 1042.

[7] Belgium Judicial Code 2016, Article 1700, para 3 states that 'Unless the parties have agreed otherwise, the arbitral tribunal shall have discretion in the rules of evidence to be applied'.

[8] Netherlands Code of Civil Procedure 2011, Article 1039(5).

[9] See Gary B Born, *International Commercial Arbitration* (2nd edn, Kluwer Law Arbitration 2014) 2146–49 (hereafter 'Born'). Born cites *U.S. Turnkey Exploration, Inc. v PSI, Inc.* 577 So2d 1131, 1135 (La App 1991), in which it was said that: 'Unless a mode of conducting the proceedings has been prescribed by the arbitration agreement or submissions, or regulated by statute, arbitrators have a general discretion as to the mode of conducting the proceedings and are not bound by formal rules of procedure and evidence and the standard of review of arbitration procedures is merely whether a party to an arbitration has been denied a fundamentally fair hearing'.

[10] Born (n 9) 2306–13. Born cites decisions of the United States Courts in which it has been said that '[a]rbitrators have broad discretion to make evidentiary decisions' and that 'arbitrators are not bound by rules of evidence'; see *Int'l Chem. Workers Union v Columbian Chem. Co.* 331 F3d 491, 497 (5th Cir. 2003); and *Generica Ltd v Pharm. Basics, Inc.* 125 F3d 1123, 1130 (7th Cir. 1997).

[11] English Arbitration Act 1996, s 34.

[12] Jeffrey Waincymer, *Procedure and Evidence in International Arbitration* (Kluwer Law International 2012) 750–51 (hereafter 'Waincymer').

[13] IBA Rules (n 3) Preamble 1 and 3. See Chapter 2.

[14] See further Waincymer (n 12). See also Chapter 4 paras 4.10–4.60.

[15] Konstantin Pilkov, 'Evidence in International Arbitration: Criteria for Admission and Evaluation' (2014) *Arbitration* 147, 154 (hereafter 'Pilkov').

[16] These are set out in IBA Rules (n 13) Article 9.2 and are addressed at 12.57– 12.316. See also Chapter 6 paras 6.76–6.146 on the meaning of 'relevant to the case and material to its outcome' for the purposes of Article 9.2(a).

12.13 The next sections address matters covered by Article 9.1—determination of the relevance and materiality of evidence, the admissibility of evidence, and the weight to be attached to individual pieces of evidence.

3. Relevance and Materiality

12.14 Article 9.1 refers expressly to the power of the tribunal to determine relevance and materiality of evidence. As mentioned, these benchmarks have a special significance within the IBA Rules.

12.15 The concepts of relevance and materiality are expressed in the IBA Rules by reference to two yardsticks—'*relevant to the case*' and '*material to its outcome*'. These benchmarks permeate the whole of the infrastructure of the IBA Rules and are the standards by which the introduction, use, and value of evidence is managed.

12.16 For example, as noted elsewhere, a request to produce under Article 3.3 must include a statement explaining why the documents requested are relevant to the case and material to its outcome.[17] Under Article 3.5, a party may object to a request to produce on the basis that the documents requested lack 'sufficient relevance to the case or materiality to its outcome'.[18] Under Article 3.7, the tribunal may make an order for production only if it determines that 'the issues that the requesting party wishes to prove are relevant to the case and material to its outcome'. At the evidentiary hearing, pursuant to its powers under Article 8.2, the tribunal may exclude evidence it considers to be 'irrelevant' or 'immaterial' or if it lacks 'sufficient relevance to the case or materiality to its outcome'. Under Article 8.5, the tribunal may ask any person to give evidence on any issue that the tribunal considers to be 'relevant to the case or material to its outcome'.

12.17 Thus, the tribunal has the power to both exclude evidence that is not sufficiently relevant and material *and* to actively seek evidence that is. The combined effect of Article 9.1 and the other provisions mentioned is that the tribunal is the final arbiter of whether or not evidence presented to it for use in the arbitration is relevant and material. If it is the view of the tribunal that evidence *is* relevant and material, then that evidence has a place in the proceedings.

12.18 The meaning of relevance and materiality as used in the IBA Rules, and Chapter 6 paras 6.76–6.146 discuss related factors that may influence a determination of relevance and materiality by the tribunal. In practice, the way in which these two tests are applied will depend on the context in which the particular piece of evidence is being considered.

[17] IBA Rules (n 3) Article 3.3(b). See Chapter 6 paras 6.76–6.159.
[18] IBA Rules (n 3) Articles 3.5 and 9.2(a).

4. Admissibility

Article 9.1 makes clear that the tribunal is to determine questions of admissibility of evidence. 12.19

a. General approach

Article 9.2 sets out express limitations on admissible evidence. However, it is for the tribunal to decide if a piece of evidence falls outside or inside those parameters. 12.20

Admissibility is a topic on which most national courts will have a body of practice and rules. These will lay down what evidence is inadmissible in that particular forum and may vary between jurisdictions. For example, in England, the 'parole evidence rule' bars the introduction of pre-contract communications as an aid to contractual interpretation, whereas in many civil law countries pre-contractual documents are taken into account in determining the terms of a contractual relationship.[19] 12.21

In international arbitration, where tribunals will nearly always have an express power to determine issues of admissibility, the rules of national courts will not generally apply. In consequence, where an issue of admissibility arises, tribunals will have a much wider discretion as to whether to admit or exclude the evidence in question and, in practice, the tendency of many arbitrators will be to permit the introduction of evidence, rather than to exclude it. This position has been confirmed by one experienced arbitrator in the following terms: 12.22

> [T]echnical rules of evidence are usually not observed in arbitration, and the tribunal will err substantially on the side of permitting presentation of the facts that a party desires. Consistent with this, international arbitrators have repeatedly declared that they are not bound by national evidentiary rules or formalities [. . .] On questions of admissibility, arbitrators ordinarily err in the direction of permitting introduction of irrelevant or duplicative materials [even though permitted under Article 9.2 of the IBA Rules] to exclude evidence on a number of grounds . . .[20]

Under Article 9.1 of the IBA Rules, the question of what evidence may be admitted into the proceedings is left entirely to the discretion of the tribunal. However, the tribunal 12.23

19 See further Julian Lew, 'Chapter 1. Document Disclosure, Evidentiary Value of Documents and Burden of Evidence' in Teresa Giovannini and Alexis Mourre (eds), *Written Evidence and Discovery in International Arbitration: New Issues and Tendencies* (Kluwer Law International 2009). For a discussion of how this issue is treated in international arbitration, see Carol Mulcahy, 'What Does it Mean? Contractual Interpretation in International Commercial Arbitration' (2015) Dispute Resolution International 15. The standard of admissibility in civil law traditions is said to be lower than in common law jurisdictions; see Anna Kubalczyk, 'Evidentiary Rules in International Arbitration: A Comparative Analysis of Approaches and the Need for Regulation' (2015) 3(1) Groningen Journal of International Law 85, s IV (hereafter 'Kubalczyk'). There are dangers in such generalizations, but certainly the common law approach may derive in part from a concern that certain types of evidence should be excluded because those who decide on the facts (traditionally, in those jurisdictions, a jury of lay people) should not be permitted to consider certain types of evidence for fear that they may attach undue weight to it (for example, hearsay evidence) or because certain interests need to be protected (for example, documents that are confidential in nature or protected by legal privilege).

20 Born (n 9) 2306–13.

is assisted by other provisions of the IBA Rules—in particular, by the theme prevalent throughout the rules that the evidence that merits admission is that which is relevant to the case and material to its outcome, subject to the exceptions to that principle stated in Article 9.2. Those exceptions are relatively limited and this reflects the view that a tribunal, like a judge (but unlike a jury),[21] is considered sufficiently skilled to evaluate evidence without the need to be 'protected' from questionable evidence that might otherwise distort its findings.[22]

12.24 This liberal approach to admissibility of evidence is facilitated to a significant extent by the ability of a tribunal operating under the IBA Rules to evaluate the evidence presented to it. Article 9.1 makes express provision for the power of a tribunal to determine the 'weight' of evidence.[23] Adopting a pragmatic approach, rather than having to decide if the evidence should be admitted or excluded, the tribunal may deal with any shortcomings in the character of evidence that is admitted by means of the weight that the tribunal attributes to it. This approach is illustrated by a statement made by one ICC tribunal in its final award:

> The Arbitral Tribunal also points out that, pursuant to § 22 of Procedural Order No. 2 and Article 9 § 1 of the IBA Rules (2010) which the Tribunal may take into consideration, it is within its discretion to assess the weight to be given to each piece of evidence submitted in the present case. *For this reason, the Tribunal has not deemed it appropriate to discard any specific testimony or document on the basis of one Party's criticisms thereof.*[24]

12.25 Another reason justifying a liberal approach to admissibility of evidence in international arbitration is that tribunals may wish to avoid any suggestion that due process has not been followed—in particular, that a party has been prevented from presenting its case by the exclusion of evidence on which it wishes to rely.[25]

12.26 Tribunals will generally deal with issues of admissibility as and when they arise. The wide discretion afforded to them under Article 9.1 is a valuable resource in tailoring decisions to the individual circumstances of the case and dealing pragmatically with issues of admissibility that might otherwise distract resources from more important aspects of the case.

b. 'Stolen' evidence

12.27 There does not appear to be any accepted prevailing practice with respect to admission into evidence of illegally obtained documents, or documents that have been leaked

[21] ibid.

[22] See further Pilkov (n 15) 150–51.

[23] This topic is addressed at 12.31– 12.56.

[24] 'Extracts from ICC Case Materials on the Taking of Evidence with References to the IBA Rules' (2016) 1 ICC Dispute Resolution Bulleting 127 (emphasis added). Waincymer (n 12) 792–800 notes that: 'International adjudicatory bodies generally consider questions of weight in relation to all submitted evidence and do not wish to hear separate clams as to admissibility'.

[25] ibid. The same point is made by other commentators. See, for example, Kubalczyk (n 19).

into the public domain by a third party. Much may depend on the facts of an individual case and the attitude of the tribunal. In one ICSID case, the respondent raised an objection to the introduction into evidence by the claimant of an audio recording of a conversation in which a bribe was allegedly sought by the respondent from the claimant. The tribunal rejected the claimant's application to introduce the evidence (in part) on the grounds that (a) given the ease with which technology permitted manipulation of audio recordings, proven authenticity was an essential condition for the admissibility of this type of evidence (the claimant being unable to discharge that burden in the face of objection from the respondent); and (b) because the recording had been made without the knowledge of the respondent's representative (and was therefore illegal under the applicable national law) to admit the evidence would be contrary to the principles of good faith and fair dealing required in international arbitration.[26] In contrast, in another reported case, the tribunal chose to admit an unlawfully obtained video recording.[27]

There are many ways of looking at such situations. Once documents are in the public domain—for example, where they have been 'hacked' by a third party—there may be strong arguments for saying that they should be permitted on to the record if one party wishes to introduce them. On the other hand, issues of fairness may arise in relation to unlawfully obtained documents, particularly if one of the other parties to the arbitration is responsible for the 'theft'. As one author explains, there may be nothing in principle to prevent such evidence being introduced on to the record, but the tribunal may decline to admit it on the basis that it would be unfair to the party from whom the documents have been stolen: **12.28**

> [N]othing prevents a tribunal from admitting into evidence documents that may have been stolen or otherwise unlawfully obtained. However, tribunals will most likely refuse to admit such documents on the grounds of procedural fairness and equality of parties. As regards documents obtained from a public source such as Wikileaks, tribunals are guarded in their approach with respect to documents covered by attorney–client privilege, but as regards any other documents available in the public domain, a tribunal may be willing to admit such documents since ignoring them would lead to an unreasonable conclusion, which could make the award subject to challenge.[28]

[26] *EDF (Services) Limited v Romania* (Procedural Order No. 3, 29 August 2008) ICSID Case No. ARB/05/13 [29]–[38] (hereafter '*EDF v Romania PO3*').

[27] Anne Schlaepfer and Philippe Bärtsch, 'A Few Reflections on the Assessment of Evidence by International Arbitrators' (2010) International Business Law Journal 217 (hereafter 'Schlaepfer and Bärtsch'), which references decisions 4A_362/2013 and 4A_448/2013 of the Swiss Supreme Court. For an example of a case where documents leaked online were admitted into evidence, see *Caratube International Oil Company LLP and Devincci Salah Hourani v Republic of Kazakhstan* ICSID Case No. ARB/13/13. This case is discussed at 12.30.

[28] Brigitta John, 'Admissibility of Improperly Obtained Data as Evidence in International Arbitration Proceedings' (*Kluwer Arbitration Blog*, 28 September 2016) <http://arbitrationblog.kluwerarbitration.com/2016/09/28/admissibility-of-improperly-obtained-data-as-evidence-in-international-arbitration-proceedings/> accessed 4 December 2018.

12.29 Another commentator has proposed that the question of who benefits from the wrongdoing is a factor to be taken into account in relation to their admissibility, but that documents subject to certain types of privilege, such as attorney–client privilege, should always be inadmissible.[29] A further relevant factor may be whether the documents fall within a category of documents that had previously been requested by an opponent party, but which, in breach of an order for production, had not been produced.

12.30 International arbitration tribunals have sometimes admitted into evidence documents leaked online. For example, in a recent case involving the Kazakhstan government,[30] the claimant applied to admit into evidence leaked emails published on a WikiLeaks-type website. The tribunal acknowledged the need to protect against computer and cybercrime and the potential unfairness of allowing confidential evidence obtained through hacking to be admitted against the legitimate expectations of the parties. However, it also recognized that there was a need for the tribunal to have access to information that is in the public domain, accessible to all, and allegedly relevant and material to the dispute—there was an interest in upholding a party's right to prove its case. Importantly, however, although the tribunal admitted the leaked material into evidence, it excluded from admission documents that were privileged.[31]

5. The Weight of Evidence

12.31 Article 9.1 of the IBA Rules provides that the tribunal is to determine the weight of the evidence presented to it. In other words, the tribunal is to decide what reliance it places upon each individual piece of evidence.

12.32 Determination of the weight of evidence is an evaluative exercise, separate to that of deciding whether evidence is admissible. A piece of evidence may be admissible but given little or no weight by the tribunal when it comes to evaluating the body of evidence that has been presented.

12.33 In theory, in an arbitration conducted under the IBA Rules, a large part of the evidence admitted to the record should be given some weight when the tribunal comes to carry out its evaluation. In addition to fact and documentary evidence that the parties volunteer in support of matters relied on in written submissions, and expert evidence directed at specific issues germane to the dispute, any other evidence obtained by document production under those rules should be demonstrated to be relevant and material

[29] This view was expressed by Cherie Blair QC; see Alison Ross, 'Blair's Two-Step Test for Illegally Obtained Evidence' (*Global Arbitration Review*, 27 April 2017) <https://globalarbitrationreview.com/article/1140718/blair%E2%80%99s-two-step-test-for-illegally-obtained-evidence>accessed on 4 December 2018.

[30] Unpublished decision of the tribunal in *Caratube International Oil Company LLP v The Republic of Kazakhstan* ICSID Case No. ARB/13/13.

[31] See, also Alison Ross, 'Tribunal Rules on Admissibility of Hacked Kazakh emails' (*Global Arbitration Review*, 22 September 2015) <https://globalarbitrationreview.com/article/1034787/tribunal-rules-on-admissibility-of-hacked-kazakh-emails> accessed on 4 December 2018.

to the outcome of the case.[32] However, experienced practitioners of international arbitration will know that this is not always the case. Much documentary evidence that finds its way into the record is never looked at again, either by the parties or by the tribunal; either the parties are not sufficiently discriminating in what they choose to introduce, or the requirements of relevance and materiality are not strictly applied by participants in the arbitration. Even in the face of arguments around the admissibility of a peripheral piece of evidence, the tribunal may take a relaxed approach and permit its introduction. However, whatever the attitude of a tribunal to issues of admissibility, a tribunal is likely to be much more discriminating when it comes to weighing the evidence.

The question of what weight should be given to a particular piece of evidence is an obscure and imprecise exercise, whether carried out in a court room or by a tribunal. In general terms, a tribunal will consider the evidence it has and decide, on an essentially subjective basis, what it believes are the correct facts or conclusions. The weight of the evidence is the persuasive effect of the evidence on the arbitrator's mind. There are no detailed rules—nor should there be—about how that exercise is to be carried out. That said, there are a number of common factors taken into account when a tribunal is considering how far it should rely on the evidence submitted. **12.34**

a. Reliability

An important factor for the tribunal will be the reliability of the evidence, ie if it constitutes genuine and reliable proof of what it is offered to prove. Case-specific factors are likely to determine the view the tribunal ultimately takes on this question, but a number of general considerations are also likely to be taken into account. **12.35**

i. Witness evidence

For example, in relation to witness evidence: **12.36**

- was the witness tendered for/did the witness decline to attend for cross-examination;
- is the tribunal being asked to rely only on a witness statement prepared with the assistance of counsel;
- how credible is the witness under cross-examination;
- is the witness evidence contradicted by another credible witness;
- whether the witness had a direct or only an indirect role in the events to which the evidence relates;
- the period of time that has elapsed since the events described by the witness took place;
- whether the witness is a former employee of the 'other' party and may hold a grudge that may taint the evidence given against that party;

[32] IBA Rules (n 3) Articles 3.3 and 9.

- whether the witness is an employee who is supporting without questioning the argument of his or her employer;
- whether a witness is independent of the parties at the time the witness offers evidence; or
- whether the answer given by a witness was in reality suggested by counsel asking the question.

In relation to expert evidence, a tribunal may temper the reliance it places on written evidence in a number of different circumstances. For example, the assumed facts on which the expert evidence is based may not be proven or shown to be justified on the fact evidence, or during cross-examination of the expert it may become apparent that his or her real expertise relates to a different, albeit related, body of knowledge. When opposing experts have very different opinions, the tribunal may lean in favour of the evidence given by the expert who performs better under cross-examination or in questioning during 'hot-tubbing'[33] of the experts.

- *ii. Documents*

12.37 In relation to documents, the tribunal may consider:

- When and in what circumstances the document was prepared;
- Whether the document is signed and whether any handwriting or signature present is consistent with that available elsewhere;
- Whether there are documents later in time that contradict its content;
- Whether there is a compelling body of evidence that contradicts what the document appears to say;
- Whether the author of the document was sufficiently well informed about the relevant events to justify reliance being placed on the document;
- Whether the purpose for which the document was created may have affected the manner in which it was drafted, including omissions and emphasis; and
- Whether the document or correspondence was written in the period leading up to a formal dispute when the parties were merely trying to position themselves for an impending arbitration with a self-serving document trail.

As mentioned, another factor is the authenticity of a document relied on. Logically, it is difficult to see how a document that is not authentic can have any useful part to play in the proceedings.[34] If there are issues around the authenticity of a document or other evidence, it is likely that these will have been raised when the evidence is first introduced.

[33] 'Hot-tubbing', or witness conferencing, is a technique in which two or more fact or expert witnesses presented by one or more of the parties are questioned together on particular topics by the arbitral tribunal and possibly by counsel. See further *ICC Arbitration Commission Report on Controlling Time and Costs in Arbitration* (International Chamber of Commerce 2018) para 79. See Chapter 11 paras 11.72–11.74. See also Guidelines for Witness Conferencing in International Arbitration (Chartered Institute of Arbitrators, 2019).

[34] See, for example, the statement by the tribunal in *EDF v Romania PO3* (n 26) [35] that 'An obvious condition for the admissibility of evidence is its reliability and authenticity. It would be a waste of time and money to admit evidence that is not and cannot be authenticated'.

It will be a matter for the tribunal to decide whether or not to admit the document, and the decision made will depend very much on the individual circumstances.[35] However, even if the evidence is admitted, the tribunal may nonetheless attribute less (or no) weight to it as a result of the allegations of forgery or lack of authenticity.

iii. Indirect evidence

12.38 Parties to international arbitration are typically permitted to present indirect evidence (for example, hearsay evidence from a witness who has heard second-hand what has been said on a relevant matter)[36] but the tribunal may consider as more reliable (and place greater weight on) direct evidence. For example, a tribunal may place more reliance on the content of a relevant document than it will on oral testimony about what the document says. However, if a party can demonstrate that there are reasons for non-production of direct evidence, this may have a mitigating effect on the tribunal's assessment (ie it may place more weight on the indirect evidence than might otherwise be the case), eg where a party can provide credible evidence about the prior destruction of a document.[37]

b. Difference in approach to issues of admissibility and weight

12.39 Rules and practice on the admissibility of evidence—whether framed by the legal tradition of the tribunal and/or counsel, or by reference to guidelines on exclusion of evidence as set out in the IBA Rules or other applicable rules—are sufficiently tangible that the parties will be able to actively engage with them.

12.40 The position in relation to the weighing of evidence by a tribunal is very different. As mentioned, the weighing of evidence is a nebulous and essentially subjective task. Where the majority of the evidence favours one of the parties it is probable that different tribunals would arrive at the same outcome. In less clear-cut cases, different tribunals might arrive at different conclusions on the same evidence. This is because there is no obviously right or wrong answer in relation to such assessment—the individual tribunal must be persuaded on the evidence that the facts support the case being advanced.[38]

12.41 The consequence of these different considerations is that it will be far easier to advance an argument that a tribunal has improperly excluded evidence than it will be to argue that the tribunal has not properly evaluated the evidence once admitted. For example, if a tribunal makes a decision to exclude evidence on grounds other than those set out in Article 9.2 of the IBA Rules, a party whose evidence has been excluded may argue

[35] Waincymer (n 12) 797. See also IBA Rules (n 3) Article 3.12(a). See Chapter 6 paras 6.361–6.365.

[36] Hearsay evidence is a written or oral statement made otherwise than by a witness giving their own first-hand evidence in proceedings, which is tendered as evidence of the matters stated and which is relied on to prove the truth of those matters.

[37] Born (n 9) 2306–13. For discussion about destruction of documents see 12.258– 12.274 for more detail.

[38] See further Pilkov (n 15) 152 and citing Audun Jøsang and Viggo Bondi, 'Legal Reasoning with Subjective Logic' (2000) Artificial Intelligence and Law 289.

that this was unfair by reference to the terms of that provision. It is far more difficult to analyse and attack the subjective approach a tribunal has taken to assessment of the evidence.

12.42 The distinction that exists is reflected in the approach taken by national courts when dealing with challenges to awards brought on the basis that a tribunal has not weighed the evidence correctly. For example, the English Court has made clear that, while a failure to give proper consideration to a piece of key evidence could be grounds for challenging an award, such circumstances should not include a situation where the tribunal had evaluated the evidence but simply reached a conclusion that the challenging party does not like. In *Arduina Holdings BV v Celtic Resources Holding plc*, the Court said that:

> The assertion in the claim form that the decision was contrary to the weight of the evidence does not begin to meet the requirements of section 68 [of the English Arbitration Act 1996].
>
> [...]
>
> The assertion that the arbitrator failed to take any or proper consider[ation] of the evidence could, in an exceptional case, give rise to a challenge under section 68, based on the general duty of an arbitrator under section 33 if, for example, an arbitrator genuinely overlooked evidence that really mattered, or got the wrong end of the stick in misunderstanding it. But there is all the difference in the world between such cases and an arbitrator evaluating evidence but reaching factual conclusions on it (as will happen in most arbitrations) which one party does not like. That cannot be the basis of a complaint under section 68.[39]

This perspective should provide comfort to a tribunal when exercising the broad discretion to determine the weight of evidence afforded to it under Article 9.1.

6. Other Considerations

12.43 When evaluating evidence, the tribunal will need to consider related matters, such as the burden and standard of proof, as well as any inferences or presumptions that the tribunal may feel able to make. The IBA Rules do not contain any provisions relating to burden of proof and only limited provision in relation to the drawing of inferences.[40] The following general principles will nonetheless apply in connection with the evaluation of evidence under Article 9.1.

[39] *Arduina Holdings BV v Celtic Resources Holding plc* [2006] EWHC 3155 (Comm) [45]–[46]. See also *London Underground Limited v Citylink Telecommunications Limited* [2007] EWHC 1749 (TCC) [37], and *Sonatrach v Statoil* [2014] EWHC 875 (Comm) [44]–[45].

[40] IBA Rules (n 3) Articles 9.5 and 9.6; see also Article 9.1.

a. Burden of proof

It is widely accepted that a party to arbitration has the burden of proving the facts relied on to support its claim/counterclaim, defence, or right of set-off.[41] **12.44**

A number of institutional rules contain an express statement that each party bears the burden of proving the facts necessary to its claims and defences (see, for example, Article 41.1 of the CIETAC Rules,[42] Article 29 of the CAM Rules,[43] Article 27.1 of the PCA Rules,[44] and Article 27.1 of the PRIME Finance Arbitration Rules).[45] **12.45**

The IBA Rules contain no such provision. However, the position described is consistent with commentary on the issue and accepted practice.[46] **12.46**

However, it is worth bearing in mind that there is a divergent approach between and among civil and common law legal systems with respect to classification of the burden of proof.[47] If a question does arise about how a burden of proof should be allocated, the answer may have an impact on how evidence is to be produced and evaluated.[48] Associated conflict of laws questions may arise. For example, should a tribunal apply the law of the seat (on the basis that the burden of proof is a procedural matter), the law **12.47**

[41] Waincymer (n 12) 762–66; Courtney Lotfi, 'Documentary Evidence and Document Production in International Arbitration' (2014) 4 Transnational Dispute Management 6 <www.transnational-dispute-management.com/article.asp?key=2136> accessed on 29 November 2018, s II (hereafter 'Lotfi'); see also Kubalczyk (n 19) s IV.3.

[42] 'Each party shall bear the burden of proving the facts on which it relies to support its claim, defense or counterclaim and provide the basis for its opinions, arguments and counter-arguments'.

[43] 'Each party shall have the burden of proving the facts relied on to support its claim or defence'.

[44] 'Each party shall have the burden of proving the facts relied on to support its claim or defence'.

[45] 'Each party shall have the burden of proving the facts relied on to support its claim or defence'.

[46] See further Born (n 9) 2313–15.

[47] The issue of burden of proof was not dealt with in the UNCITRAL Model Law on International Commercial Arbitration (as adopted by UNCITRAL on 21 June 1985 and as amended by UNCITRAL on 7 July 2006) (hereafter 'UNCITRAL Model Law') in part because of differences in view between legal families as to whether burden of proof is procedural or substantive. Waincymer (n 12) 762–65. See also Anne Véronique Schläpfer, 'The Burden of Proof in International Arbitration' in Albert Jan van den Berg (ed), *Legitimacy: Myths, Realities, Challenges* (Kluwer Law International 2015). The position is complex. For example, Lord Collins of Mapesbury and others (eds), *Dicey, Morris and Collins on The Conflict of Laws* (15th edn, Sweet & Maxwell 2012) para 7-034 notes that, 'Although there is some authority for the proposition that at common law, questions relating to the burden of proof are matters for the *lex fori*, there is much to be said for treating them as substantive' (footnote omitted). See further Lotfi (n 41) s II.

[48] For example, as a matter of English law, unless otherwise provided by statute, questions of evidence are generally determined by the *lex fori* and not by the law governing the substantive issue selected by English rules as to conflict of laws. See Hodge Malek and others (eds), *Phipson on Evidence* (19th edn, Sweet & Maxwell 2013) para 1-26. Under German law, the burden of proof appears to be primarily dealt with as part of substantive law, although procedural law may also have an impact. For example, in relation to the former position, German Civil Code (Bürgerliches Gesetzbuch) 2013, s 363 provides that: 'Burden of proof in the case of acceptance as performance of contract: If the obligee has accepted performance offered to him as performance of contract, he bears the burden of proof if he does not wish to have the performance considered as performance of contract because it was different from the performance owed or because it was incomplete'. However, with reference to the second category, German Code of Civil Procedure, s 287 provides that the court may 'estimate the amount of damages on the basis of the court's discretion, *based on its evaluation of all circumstances*' (emphasis added), an approach that is said to relax the burden of proof. Annette Keilmann, 'How to Prove Your Case: Conflict between Substantive and Procedural Law in International arbitration?' (*Global Arbitration News*, 31 March 2016) <https://globalarbitrationnews.com/how-to-prove-your-case-conflict-between-substantive-and-procedural-law-in-international-arbitration-20160324/> accessed 4 December 2018. The author also draws attention to the potential consequences of adopting the substantive provisions of a national system without also taking account of the procedural corollary that may exist in that jurisdiction.

governing the underlying substantive issue, or some international standard?[49] A pragmatic solution to such questions is that advocated by Born, who suggests that the strict distribution of the burden of proof applied by national courts does not arise in international arbitration and that the tribunal should adopt a more flexible approach designed to meet the needs of the particular issues in the case:

> [T]he tribunal need not apply the burden of proof rules of any specific jurisdiction, but can instead fashion specialized rules in light of the particular substantive issues and procedures at issue in a specific instance.[50]

12.48 We agree that a pragmatic approach to burden of proof is desirable and a strict analysis of where it rests may not always be helpful or wanted. An obvious case is where a claim and counterclaim relate to the same factual issue. One cited example of this is the case of a construction dispute where a builder delivers an account to the owner to receive payment. The owner seeks a declaration that the money is not owed. The builder counterclaims for the money due. From a technical perspective each has a burden of proof in relation to its contention but, from a practical perspective, the tribunal will simply consider all of the evidence and decide which position is to be preferred.[51]

12.49 As arbitration proceedings progress, evidence will be presented by different parties at different times. It is therefore very common for the 'balance' of evidence to change backwards and forward between the parties. A claimant with the burden of proof may present a prima facie case that satisfies the standard of proof required at that stage, only to find that the respondent subsequently presents a preponderant body of evidence leading to a decision in favour of the respondent.

12.50 In common law legal systems the party with the burden of proof may be required to initially establish a prima facie case (ie one that should succeed in the absence of rebuttal by its opponent), failing which the responding party has the right to seek a determination that there is no case to answer before being called on to present any of its own evidence. The process of 'no case to answer' does not have a significant role to play in international arbitration. Tribunals tend to defer decisions on whether the burden of proof has been discharged to the end of the proceedings and respondents tend to present evidence even if they believe that the respondent has no case to answer.[52] That said, in recent years there appears to have been some limited erosion of that position.

[49] Born (n 9) 2313–15.

[50] Born (n 9) 2315. See also Sigvard Jarvin, 'The Sources and Limits of the Arbitrator's Powers' (1986) Arbitration International 140, 151, who suggests that where parties and counsel come from different legal traditions the tribunal should adopt an approach that is fair to all sides: 'The arbitrators, faced with parties and counsel from different legal systems, used to different principles with regard to the burden of proof, and presentation of evidence, should try to find a middle way which can be applied by both sides and thus achieve fairness for both of them. The strict distribution of the burden of proof applied by national courts does not apply in international arbitration.'

[51] See further Waincymer (n 12) 762–66.

[52] See ibid 771–72.

For example, Article 39 of the SCC Rules (Summary Procedure) makes some provision for a party to request early determination of an issue of fact, including on grounds that an allegation of fact is 'manifestly unsustainable'. Similar summary procedures for early dismissal of claims have been introduced under other arbitration rules, but on the basis of the language used, these appear to be limited to an assessment of the legal merits of the claim[53] and on the assumption that the supporting facts are as stated. There is some suggestion that an exception to this may arise where the factual allegations underlying the legal arguments are regarded by the tribunal as being (manifestly) incredible, frivolous, vexatious, inaccurate or made in bad faith.[54] Of course, if the claimant cannot even present a prima facie case, the claim will not succeed in any event.

b. Standard of proof

The burden of proof deals with the question of which party has responsibility for presenting evidence on a particular issue. It does not indicate the level of proof required. **12.51**

In relation to the sufficiency of evidence needed to discharge the burden of proof, it is widely accepted that the standard in international arbitration is the 'balance of probabilities' or a 'more likely than not' standard.[55] It is often pointed out that this is the standard formulated in common law systems and that civil law systems speak of 'the satisfaction of, or the inner conviction of the adjudicator'.[56] However, when it comes to practical application, there does not appear to be any difference of substance between the two formulations. **12.52**

c. Inferences and presumptions

In arriving at conclusions on the facts in issue in the proceedings, arbitral tribunals are permitted to rely on presumptions or inferences regarding evidence. **12.53**

i. Positive and negative inferences

An example of a positive inference would be that contemporaneous documentation is more likely to be reliable than documents prepared for the purpose of the **12.54**

[53] See, for example, SIAC Rules, Rule 29.1: 'A Party may apply to the Tribunal for the early dismissal of a claim or defence on the basis that: (a) a claim or defence is manifestly without legal merit; or (b) a claim or defence is manifestly outside the jurisdiction of the Tribunal'. See also (well-established) ICSID Arbitration Rules 2006, Rule 41(5) in similar terms.

[54] A recent analysis and commentary on tribunal practice in relation to ICSID Arbitration Rules, Rule 41(5) contains an interesting discussion on the extent to which tribunals should and do assume that the facts underlying the legal claim are as stated and (in summary) the circumstances in which it might be permissible to dismiss on the basis that the facts as stated are plainly unsustainable and the benchmark to be applied to reach that conclusion. See Michele Potestà, 'Chapter 9: Preliminary Objections to Dismiss Claims that Are Manifestly Without Legal Merit under Rule 41(5) of the ICSID Arbitration Rules' in Crina Baltag (ed), *ICSID Convention after 50 Years: Unsettled Issues* (Kluwer Law International 2016).

[55] Born (n 9) 2313–15.

[56] Waincymer (n 12) 766–71 concludes that, despite some comments to the contrary, there is unlikely to be any difference between the two formulations—the real test in each case must be a test of preponderance of evidence. No system allows a party to succeed if their opponent's contentions are preferred. See also Lotfi (n 41) s II. See also Pilkov (n 15) 153, who opines that, in assessing the sufficiency of the evidence, the tribunal must 'determine whether there is a valid line of reasoning and permissible inferences which could lead a rational person to the conclusion reached by the arbitrator on the basis of the evidence'.

arbitration. Absent a statement to the contrary in the first procedural order, an arbitral tribunal may also presume that documents introduced on to the record are authentic unless an allegation is made to the contrary.[57] Of course, such presumptions may not be appropriate in all cases. For example, there may be few contemporaneous documents and those that exist may be contradictory, or the volume of documents may be so great that, in the absence of positive collaborative assistance from the parties in finding those that are material, primary reliance by the tribunal on those documents may be difficult.[58]

12.55 Examples of adverse inferences include negative inferences drawn from a party's failure to produce material documents or witnesses in its control, or the failure of a witness to answer certain questions put to them.[59] Absent a valid excuse, it is natural (if not logical) to assume that the withheld information is adverse to the interests of the party controlling it and the tribunal may wish to form a view on the kind of information or evidence that is being withheld.[60] A tribunal may also draw inferences from circumstantial evidence.[61] As with other indirect evidence a tribunal may place more or less weight on such evidence depending on what direct evidence is available.

ii. The use of adverse inferences under Articles 9.5 and 9.6 of the IBA Rules

12.56 The IBA Rules make express provision for the drawing of adverse inferences by reason of a party's failure to produce witness or other evidence. Articles 9.5 and 9.6 provide for the right of the tribunal to infer that the withheld evidence would be adverse to the interests of the party that has failed to produce it. These provisions are addressed at 12.357-12.386. The possible use of adverse inferences in relation to bad-faith conduct by a party to arbitration in breach of Preamble 3 of the IBA Rules is also considered briefly in Chapter 2.[62]

C. Exclusion of Evidence

9.2. The Arbitral Tribunal shall, at the request of a Party or on its own motion, exclude from evidence or production any Document, statement, oral testimony or inspection for any of the following reasons.

[57] Waincymer (n 12) 774–75. IBA Rules (n 3) Article 3.12(a). See Chapter 6 paras 6.351–6.365.

[58] Schlaepfer and Bärtsch (n 27) 217.

[59] See further Born (n 9) 2306–15 and Waincymer (n 12) 775–78.

[60] The difficulties associated with this exercise are addressed at 12.368– 12.374.

[61] In an international law context, circumstantial evidence has been described in a dissenting judgment of the International Court of Justice as: 'facts which, while not supplying immediate proof of the charge, yet make the charge probable with the assistance of reasoning'; Waincymer (n 12) 793–94, citing the dissenting opinion of Judge Badawi Pash in the Corfu Channel Case, *United Kingdom of Great Britain v People's Republic of Albania* (Merits) (1949) ICJ Reports 4, 18.

[62] See Chapter 2 paras 2.95–2.97.

1. Introduction

Article 9.2 sets boundaries for the evidence (oral or written) that a party may be asked to provide or produce under the IBA Rules, and the evidence that a tribunal may exclude. It is an extremely important provision and the grounds of objection set out in Article 9.2 are adopted by reference into various other provisions of the IBA Rules.[63] **12.57**

The provision states that the tribunal 'shall' (either upon request by a party or on its own motion) exclude from evidence or production, a document, statement, oral testimony, or inspection, if that evidence falls within one of the limitations listed in Article 9.2(a)–(g). Thus, if a tribunal is satisfied that one or more of those grounds is established, the evidence should be excluded. However, it is for the tribunal to determine whether an objection under Article 9.2 (a)–(g) has been made out, thereby retaining control of the decision to exclude evidence.[64] The Commentary on the IBA Rules explains that the limitations contained in Article 9.2 are important because they 'preserve the lines of distinction between the rights of the parties and the authority of the arbitral tribunal'. **12.58**

The grounds for exclusion of evidence set out in Article 9.2 constitute important protections for the parties and, in relation to document production, they provide a necessary counterbalance to the right of a party to request production of documents from its opponent.[65] **12.59**

2. Grounds for Exclusion

Article 9.2 lists the grounds on which (a) the production of documents or (b) the admission of evidence, can be resisted. **12.60**

A disputed request for document production is one of the most common situations in which the provisions of Article 9.2 (a)–(g) will come into play. Under Article 3.5 of the IBA Rules, those provisions contain the grounds upon which a party may raise an objection to production, and under Article 3.7(ii), those which the tribunal must consider when it has to decide whether an order for production should be made. **12.61**

While Article 9.2 appears to provide an exhaustive list of limitations, it has been suggested that the provision omits reference to one other ground that is available to a party **12.62**

[63] See IBA Rules (n 3) Articles 3.5, 3.9, 3.10, 4.10, 6.3, 7, 8.2, and 8.5.

[64] 1999 IBA Working Party and 2010 IBA Rules of Evidence Review Subcommittee, 'Commentary on the Revised Text of the 2010 IBA Rules on the Taking of Evidence in International Arbitration' (International Bar Association, 2014) 25 <www.ibanet.org/Document/Default.aspx?DocumentUid=DD240932-0E08-40D4-9866-309A635487C0> accessed 27 November 2018 (hereafter 'Commentary on the IBA Rules') confirms the discretion of the tribunal to determine the objections: 'While the provision states that the arbitral tribunal "shall" exclude evidence meeting one of the specified exceptions (including relevance and materiality) the arbitral tribunal obviously retains its discretion to determine whether one of the specified criteria has been met'.

[65] See Hilmar Raeschke-Kessler, 'The Production of Documents in International Arbitration: Commentary on Article 3 of the New IBA Rules of Evidence' (2002) *Arbitration International* 411 (hereafter 'Raeschke-Kessler').

to raise in connection with a disputed document production request—that the document that has been requested does not exist:

> One important substantive objection is not included in the catalogue of Article 9, section 2: the non-existing document; that is, a document which has never existed and leads only a virtual life in the mind of the requesting party. A non-existing document does not come within the scope of Article 9, section 2(d), which is only concerned with the loss or destruction of documents.[66]

12.63 The point is made elsewhere[67] that, although Article 3.3 does not expressly require a party to state in a request to produce the grounds on which it believes the requested documents to exist, it should be read as containing an implied requirement in those terms. In any event, it would be prudent for the requesting party to mention the grounds for such belief, particularly where this is not obvious from the nature of the documents requested. The absence of an express requirement for a statement in these terms may explain why there is no corresponding right of objection under Article 9.2. Clearly, if documents do not exist, they cannot be produced, although an allegation of their non-existence will not prevent an order for production being made if the tribunal is persuaded that the documents do, in fact, exist.

12.64 Each of the grounds for exclusion of evidence expressed in Article 9.2 is addressed in the sections that follow.

D. Relevance and Materiality

9.2(a) lack of sufficient relevance to the case or materiality to its outcome

1. Introduction

12.65 The power to exclude evidence on the basis of relevance and materiality extends to all types of evidence—whether a document, oral or written fact evidence, or expert evidence—and may be exercised at any stage of the proceedings.

12.66 The tribunal is to exclude evidence that it determines does not have 'sufficient relevance to the case or materiality to its outcome'.[68]

12.67 The requirement of 'sufficient' relevance suggests that there are gradations of relevance and a tipping point (sufficiency) where the test is met. On this basis, it is suggested

[66] ibid 422.

[67] See Chapter 6 para 6.65.

[68] As mentioned, IBA Rules (n 3) Article 9.2 provides that the tribunal 'shall' exclude evidence on this basis, either on its own motion, or following an application by one of the parties.

that the sufficiency requirement at Article 9.2(a) bites only on the relevance limb of the benchmark, presumably on the basis that a piece of evidence either is or is not material to the outcome.[69] We agree with that view.

In relation to document production, it should be remembered that the requirement of relevance and materiality at Article 9.2(a) is expressly restated at Article 3.3(b) as a requirement of a request to produce documents. **12.68**

12.69 A failure to include in the request an explanation of how the documents requested are relevant and material is a standalone basis for rejection or dismissal of the request. These matters are discussed further in Chapter 6 paras 6.76–6.146.

2. Exclusion of Documentary Evidence

In general terms, there are two situations where a tribunal's assessment of a document as not being relevant and material will result in that document being blocked from appearance on the record. The first is where the tribunal declines to order production of a requested document under Article 3.7.[70] The second is where it excludes a document already on the record. **12.70**

The factors described[71] as being relevant to an assessment of relevance and materiality for the purposes of a document production request or order have similar application to the exercise of the tribunal's more general discretion to exclude documentary evidence under Article 9.2(a) for 'lack of sufficient relevance to the case or materiality to its outcome'. **12.71**

Situations not related to document production requests where a tribunal may, in theory, decide to exercise its power under Article 9.2(a) will be case specific. For example, a party may have introduced a document with its written submissions that the other party contends should be removed from the record for lack of relevance and materiality,[72] or a party may, late in the day—after written submissions and voluntary production have been completed—indicate that it wishes to introduce a document on to the record against the wishes of the other party. **12.72**

Although relatively rare in our experience, also possible is a situation where, of its own initiative, the tribunal decides that a document is not sufficiently relevant and material to justify its retention or inclusion on the record. For example, when an issue between the parties has been conceded by one side, a tribunal may decide pursuant to Article 9.2(a) **12.73**

[69] Reto Marghitola, *Document Production in International Arbitration* (Kluwer Law International 2015) 47 (hereafter 'Marghitola').
[70] This will involve indirect consideration of the circumstances listed at IBA Rules (n 3) Article 9.2(a)–(g). See IBA Rules (n 3) Article 3.7, where the tribunal may order production if 'none of the reasons for objection set forth in Article 9.2 applies' and the other requirements of that provision are met.
[71] Chapter 6 paras 6.76–6.146.
[72] In practice, such occurrences are extremely rare.

that no further evidence should be permitted because it will serve no purpose. In *Abaclat*, a tribunal excluded from the record legal opinions that had been filed in prior arbitration proceedings by expert witnesses providing testimony in the matter before them. The respondent wanted to introduce the opinions in order to embarrass the claimant's experts by reference to allegedly inconsistent testimony contained in the opinions. In deciding to exclude the opinions, the tribunal considered the assistance that the opinions would provide on the issues in the case. It took the view that 'these [opinions] would be used in the first place for impeachment purposes' and 'not to shed more light on the legal issues at stake'. The tribunal went on to say that that there was sufficient material available upon which the experts' evidence could be challenged so as to render admission of the opinions 'excessive'.[73]

3. Exclusion of Witness Evidence

12.74 The factors described[74] as being relevant to an assessment of relevance and materiality for the purposes of document production will also have application in relation to an assessment by the tribunal of the relevance and materiality of witness evidence.

12.75 If exclusion of witness evidence is being considered at the time of the evidentiary hearing, a tribunal is much more likely to be fully up to speed on the issues in the case and may find a determination of what is relevant and material (and what is not) much easier than at an earlier stage of the proceedings, when contested document production requests are being ruled on, or the intended scope of witness evidence is being discussed.[75]

12.76 One example cited elsewhere of tribunal intervention at an evidentiary hearing is that of an ICC arbitration conducted in Paris presided over by a sole arbitrator. During the hearing a witness had been called to give evidence concerning a licence to produce pharmaceutical products. In the course of oral testimony, after cross-examination had continued for a reasonable period, the question turned to matters that the arbitrator understood as relating to the witness' own liability. As the witness was not a party (or an employee of a party), the tribunal ruled that further questioning would be inadmissible.[76] In practice, many tribunals will permit counsel to have a degree of latitude in relation to questions put to witnesses during cross-examination. However, if there is a tight timetable and it is clear that counsel is wasting time on unimportant points, it may well step in to move matters along.[77]

[73] *Abaclat and Others v Argentine Republic* (Procedural Order No. 3, 27 January 2010) ICSID Case No. ARB/07/5 [136]–[151]. See also Chapter 6 paras 6.106–6.108.

[74] Chapter 6 paras 6.76–6.146.

[75] See Chapter 7 paras 7.189–7.192.

[76] Nathan O'Malley, *Rules of Evidence in International Arbitration: An Annotated Guide* (Informa Law 2012) paras 9.10–9.11 (hereafter 'O'Malley Rules of Evidence').

[77] Chapter 11 paras 11.25, 11.39–11.42.

E. Legal Impediment and Privilege

9.2(b) legal impediment or privilege under the legal or ethical rules determined by the Arbitral Tribunal to be applicable.

[...]

9.3 In considering issues of legal impediment or privilege under Article 9.2(b), and insofar as permitted by any mandatory legal or ethical rules that are determined by it to be applicable, the Arbitral Tribunal may take into account:

(a) any need to protect the confidentiality of a Document created or statement or oral communication made in connection with and for the purpose of providing or obtaining legal advice;

(b) any need to protect the confidentiality of a Document created or statement or oral communication made in connection with and for the purpose of settlement negotiations;

(c) the expectations of the Parties and their advisors at the time the legal impediment or privilege is said to have arisen;

(d) any possible waiver of any applicable legal impediment or privilege by virtue of consent, earlier disclosure, affirmative use of the Document, statement, oral communication or advice contained therein, or otherwise; and

(e) the need to maintain fairness and equality as between the Parties, particularly if they are subject to different legal or ethical rules.

1. Introduction

Article 9.2(b) and Article 9.3 address the important subject of legal impediment and privilege as a bar to the use of evidence. **12.77**

As the Commentary to the IBA Rules makes clear, those responsible for drafting Article 9.2(b) felt it important that certain privileges that may apply under the appropriate applicable law should be recognized in international arbitration.[78] The Commentary on the IBA Rules refers to three examples of such privileges—attorney–client privilege, professional secrecy, and without prejudice privilege. There is potential for misunderstanding in relation to the use of such terms, as different national jurisdictions may have different labels for the same category of privilege, and the nature and scope of particular privileges may not be the same across jurisdictions. However, there are two broad categories of privilege that are widely used in international arbitration. **12.78**

The first category is privilege protecting certain types of communications between a party and its lawyer (and sometimes extending to communications with third parties) **12.79**

[78] Commentary on the IBA Rules (n 64) 25.

relating to legal advice and/or litigation. In England, this category of privilege is broken down into 'legal advice' privilege and 'litigation' privilege, while in the United States, the equivalent privileges are (in broad terms) 'attorney–client' privilege and 'attorney–work product' privilege. In a number of civil law jurisdictions, such protections as exist in respect of these matters are often covered by a single privilege known as professional secrecy.

12.80 The second category of widely used privilege is a protection that attaches to communications between disputing parties relating to efforts to settle their dispute—often referred to in England as 'without prejudice' privilege. These and other privileges are discussed in more detail at 12.88 – 12.101.

12.81 Evidentiary privileges play a significant role in legal proceedings across the world. However, legal privileges and other legal impediments to production or introduction of evidence generally arise out of a provision of law or practice within a national jurisdiction and, while there may be common themes across jurisdictions, complex issues of conflicts of laws can arise in relation to the application of such privileges in an international forum.

12.82 Article 9.2 provides that the tribunal may exclude from evidence or production evidence to which legal privilege or legal impediment attaches. Article 9.3 describes a number of factors that a tribunal may take into account when considering issues of privilege and/or legal impediment—in substance, the need to protect a document or oral statement made for the purpose of obtaining/providing legal advice; in connection with settlement negotiation; the parties' expectations when the legal privilege or impediment is said to have arisen; any waiver of the privilege/impediment; and the need to maintain fairness between the parties, particularly where those parties may be subject to different rules.

12.83 It is convenient to consider Article 9.2(b) and Article 9.3 together. In doing so it is important to note that, under those provisions:

(a) The basis of exclusion from production or evidence is the existence of a legal impediment or privilege *under the legal or ethical rules that are determined by the tribunal to be applicable*;[79] and
(b) In considering issues of legal impediment/privilege, and to the extent permitted by any *mandatory* legal or ethical rules that the tribunal determines to be applicable, the tribunal may take into account the factors described in Article 9.3.[80]

12.84 Although the 1999 IBA Rules contained a provision in identical terms to Article 9.2(b), there was no guidance on the application of its terms. When preparing the 2010 IBA Rules, those responsible for drafting the rules felt it appropriate to provide the additional

[79] See IBA Rules (n 3) Article 9.2 (b).
[80] ibid opening paragraph, Article 9.3.

non-binding guidance that is now found at Article 9.3. The approach taken by the IBA Committee when formulating these guidelines has been described in these terms:

> In tackling the issue of privileges, the IBA Working Group had to strike a delicate balance. The new rules had to be specific enough to provide international arbitrators with more practical and workable guidance as to how to handle privilege issues in international arbitration than the 1999 edition of the Rules. At the same time, however, the new provision had to be generic enough to avoid the impression of over-emphasising the issue of privilege and any interference with the complex conflict of laws problems related to privileges as well as any conflict with mandatory, public-policy nature of domestic privilege rules. Such a conflict would have been inconsistent with the soft-law nature of the IBA Rules, which constitute a restatement of best practice standards but cannot and do not intend to override applicable domestic law of a mandatory nature.[81]

Despite these objectives, the provisions that appear in the IBA Rules have nonetheless been criticised for being too general and not providing more precision around how potentially applicable privilege rules are to be sorted and applied. One commentator puts it this way: **12.85**

> [A]rt. 9.2(b) refrains from providing a specific conflict rule for the application of privileges in international arbitration. At the same time, the rule is not specific enough to provide international arbitrators with concrete guidance as to the practical handling of privilege issues.[82]

However, the view has also been expressed that the discretion afforded to a tribunal by application of the relatively 'high level' guidance given in the IBA Rules is a good thing: **12.86**

> There may be competing privilege claims, and the decision as to which privilege rule or rules to apply falls into the general category of procedural matters left to the arbitrators' discretion.[83]

Our view is that the combination of Article 9.2(b) and Article 9.3 provides useful practical guidance for a tribunal asked to rule on issues of legal impediment or privilege. While avoiding expression of a fixed rule that might trespass on mandatory provisions of applicable law (and thereby create more problems than would be solved), the rules provide a decision-making framework that provides assistance to the tribunal as it navigates its way through these complex issues. Express provision on this topic in institutional rules is scarce.[84] National laws vary considerably in the substance of legal **12.87**

[81] Klaus Peter Berger, 'Evidentiary Privileges under the Revised IBA Rules on the Taking of Evidence in International Arbitration' (2010) International Arbitration Law Review 171, 171 (hereafter 'Berger'; footnotes omitted).

[82] ibid.

[83] James H Carter, 'Privilege Gets a New Framework' (2010) International Arbitration Law Review 177, 177.

[84] The majority of institutional rules simply provide that the tribunal may determine questions of admissibility. The ICDR Rules, Article 22, is one of very few arbitration rules dealing specifically with the privilege: 'The arbitral tribunal shall take into account applicable principles of privilege, such as those involving the confidentiality of communications between a lawyer and client. When the parties, their counsel, or their documents would be subject under applicable law to different rules, the tribunal should, to the extent possible, apply the same rule to all parties, giving preference to the rule that provides the highest level of protection'.

and ethical rules that may apply. The IBA Rules rightly grant the tribunal considerable discretion and, while tending to suggest that the laws of the home jurisdictions of the parties are the appropriate ones to take into account on issues of privilege (and thereby downplaying the potential relevance of other possibilities),[85] the additional considerations expressed in Article 9.3 allow the tribunal take into account factors relevant to the broader conduct of the arbitration.

2. Different Types of Legal Impediment or Privilege

12.88 In international arbitration, the term 'privilege' is very often used to refer to what in English practice is known as legal advice privilege, litigation privilege, or 'without prejudice' privilege. However, Articles 9.2(b) and 9.3 are not confined to these categories of privilege. In addition, those provisions make express reference to a 'legal impediment'. In consequence, tribunals may have to consider a wide range of privileges and legal obstacles to production asserted by the parties. The next few sections describe some categories of privilege or legal impediment that may arise.

a. Professional privileges

12.89 Professional privileges are those that attach to documents, knowledge, or information that comes into existence or that are shared between parties in the context of a professional relationship. An individual may obtain access to such privileged information by reason of belonging to a particular profession and may be bound by legal or ethical rules to keep that information secret from other parties. Professional privileges often exist within industries where one party may wish or need to reveal sensitive or confidential information to a member of that profession and public policy dictates that such communications should be protected. Examples of professional privileges include the following:[86]

- **Legal advice privilege** (*widely recognized in many common law jurisdictions and referred to in some as attorney-client privilege or professional secrecy*)—designed to protect the confidentiality of communications between a client and a lawyer in connection with the taking and providing of legal advice. This type of privilege is dealt with in more detail at 12.139-12.196.
- **Litigation Privilege** (*again, widely recognised across a number of jurisdictions and having broad equivalents (for example, 'attorney work product') in others)*—protects communications with third parties where the dominant purpose of the communication is to further litigation which is pending, reasonably

[85] For example, the law of the seat, or the substantive law of the dispute. See further Marghitola (n 69) 74–90. See also 12.102-12.134 in relation to choice of applicable law.

[86] See, for more detail about these privileges, Richard M Mosk and Tom Ginsburg, 'Evidentiary Privileges in International Arbitration' (2001) 50 International and Comparative Law Quarterly 345, 353–55 (hereafter 'Mosk and Ginsburg').

contemplated or existing. This type of privilege is dealt with in more detail at 12.149-12.151 and 12.169.

- **Medical privilege**—this prevents doctors and medical staff from revealing information about the health of their patient without the patient's consent.[87]
- **Accountant-client privilege**—some US states treat certain types of communication between an accountant and a client as privileged (either on the basis of an extension to the accountant of litigation and legal advice privilege or as a standalone privilege). In Europe, the position is rather different and accountants cannot normally claim legal advice privilege although, in some instances, they can rely on litigation privilege.

b. Other privileges

- Other privileges not connected to a particular profession also exist. As with professional privileges, many of these have their provenance in considerations of public policy. One of the most important of such privileges is that which attaches to settlement discussions (also known as 'without prejudice privilege'). This type of privilege is dealt with in more detail at 12.174-12.186. Other examples include business secrets privilege (historically an American concept, the privilege may apply to a secret formula, patent, device, or compilation if it is used in the owner's business and enables the owner to obtain a competitive business advantage), and other privileges such as those attaching to bank records, political votes, tax returns, etc.[88]

A further important privilege is that of privilege attaching to government information or matters of national interest. In some cases, this privilege exists as a general principle of law and in others it is embodied in legislation. For example, in Nigeria, Section 243(1) of the Evidence Act 2011 provides that: 'A Minister, or in respect of matters to which the executive authority of a State extends, the Governor or any person nominated by him, may in any proceedings object to the production or request the exclusion of oral evidence, when, after consideration, he is satisfied that *the production of such document or the giving of such oral evidence is against public interest*'.[89] 'Cabinet privilege' exists under Section 38 of the Canada Evidence Act 1985.[90] According to this provision, the production of documents prepared for or used by Ministers of the Crown in executive policy-making deliberations is to be refused.[91] In England 'public interest immunity' has replaced 'Crown Privilege' and is similar in scope to that found in the Nigerian provision mentioned above. Halsbury's Laws describe it thus: 12.90

[87] For the position under English law, see: *W v Egdell* [1990] Ch 359; *L v UK* [1999] 9 WLUK 63; *R v Derby Magistrates Court ex parte B* [1996] AC 487.

[88] See, for more detail, Mosk and Ginsburg (n 86) 358–62.

[89] Emphasis added.

[90] Canada Evidence Act, RSC 1985, c C-5.

[91] Meg Kinnear, Andrea Bjorklund, and John Hannaford, *Investment Disputes Under NAFTA: An Annotated Guide to NAFTA Chapter 11* (Kluwer Law International 2006) 1120–45.

> It is a general rule of law founded on public policy and recognised by Parliament that any documentary evidence may be withheld or an answer to any question may be refused on the ground that the disclosure of the document or the answering of the question would be injurious to the public interest. The rule is a rule of substantive law and may be described as a principle of constitutional law; it is not a mere matter of practice or procedure.[92]

12.91 A similar type of privilege known as 'executive privilege' exists in the United States. This allows the President and other state officials to withhold certain communications within the executive department from the courts and from Congress. In addition, some US states courts recognize a privilege protecting the deliberative process of government.[93]

12.92 In some jurisdictions, certain of these protections may be classified as legal impediments rather than privileges.

12.93 It should be noted that, even if appropriate to raise under Article 9.2(b), some of these privileges may also give rise to a ground for exclusion under one of the other provisions of Article 9.2. For example, rather than relying on a privilege that protects government information, reference might also be had to Article 9.2(f): 'grounds of special political or institutional sensitivity (including evidence that has been classified as secret by a government . . .)'.

c. Legal impediment

12.94 As with evidentiary privileges, a 'legal impediment' may take many forms. As mentioned, what is classified as an evidentiary privilege in some jurisdictions may have a different status in others and perhaps fall more readily under the description 'legal impediment'. In addition, there may be particular types of 'legal impediment' that are peculiar to an individual jurisdiction or region. Such impediments may cover a broad range of subject matter and it is therefore much more difficult to provide an illustrative list. However, what follows are some examples of provisions that have been relied upon/considered as legal impediments.

i. Risk of prosecution/blocking statutes

12.95 National courts have in some cases found that a threat of foreign prosecution is a reasonable excuse for non-production of evidence.[94] In essence, the argument is that if the relevant party were to comply with an order for discovery of documents, such conduct would breach the laws of another state and render that party liable to sanctions. The laws of the foreign state constitute the legal impediment.

[92] Adrian Zuckerman, *Halsbury's Laws* (vol 12, LexisNexis 2015) para 665.
[93] For more detail and references, see Mosk and Ginsburg (n 86) 364.
[94] ibid 373–74.

However, there have also been cases—in England and in the United States—where national courts have refused to bar disclosure of documents by reason of foreign 'blocking statutes' existing in some civil law jurisdictions. The latter jurisdictions—generally with a tradition of very limited document production—have sometimes viewed pre-trial discovery requests made to one of its nationals in proceedings before a foreign court as interference with the sovereignty, customs, and national interests of that jurisdiction. In order to prevent the discovery procedures from being executed in their territories, those jurisdictions have therefore enacted what are known as 'blocking statutes', under which a party complying with the discovery order of a foreign court becomes liable to a penalty.[95] 12.96

ii. Banking secrecy

Another commonly raised legal impediment to production of evidence, particularly in disputes involving banks, is the banking secrecy regime. National legislation may provide that a bank cannot disclose information and documents about bank accounts held by clients of the bank. This may put the bank at a genuine risk of sanctions if it were to breach that legislation. Breach of a banking secrecy regime may, in some jurisdictions, even trigger a criminal prosecution and conviction. For example, under the Criminal Code of the Russian Federation, unauthorized receiving, disclosure, or usage of information covered by commercial, tax, or bank secrecy, made without the permission of its owner, by a person to whom it was entrusted or who has obtained the information in the course of business, constitutes a crime.[96] The information may, in certain circumstances, be provided to certain third parties (for example, state officials), but the list does not include arbitral tribunals.[97] As a result, if a bank employee were to disclose to a tribunal any document or information that is subject to bank secrecy without first obtaining the permission of the bank's client, the employee may face criminal prosecution in Russia. In addition, the client whose rights have been violated by the disclosure can seek damages from the bank.[98] 12.97

A balancing of interests approach has been adopted by American courts when considering an application for production of documents from a bank subject to application of 12.98

[95] See *In re Anschuetz & Co.*, 754 F 3d 602, 614 n. 29 (5th Cir. 1985), where a blocking statute was described as 'a law passed by the foreign government imposing a penalty upon a national for complying with a foreign court's discovery request'. In some such cases, it has been argued that, in order to avoid contravention of the blocking statute, any discovery or document production requests should be made in strict compliance with international treaties, such as the 1970 Hague Convention on the Taking of Evidence Abroad in Civil or Commercial Matters. This would clearly delay production of the documents by some significant time. For cases indicating the approach taken by some national courts when considering such impediments, see *Secretary of State for Health v Servier Laboratories Ltd* [2013] EWCA Civ 1234, paras 99, 107, and 118; *In re Air Cargo Shipping Services Antitrust Litigation* 2010 WL 1189341 (E.D.N.Y. Mar. 29, 2010); *Societé Nationale Industrielle Aerospatiale v United States Dist. Court for S. Dist. Of Iowa* 482 US 522, 546 (1987), cited in *In re Vivendi Universal, S.A. Securities Litigation*, 2006 WL 3378115 (S.D.N.Y. Nov. 16, 2006); and *United States of America and Earl Tripplett, Revenue Officer, IRS, Petitioners-Appellees v The First National Bank of Chicago, Respondent-Appellant*, 699 F2d 341 (US 7th Circuit, CA) [1].

[96] Russian Federation Criminal Code, Article 183.

[97] Federal Law of the Russian Federation 'On Banks and Banking' (enacted on 2 December 1990 and revised on 13 July 2015), Article 26.

[98] Russian Federation Civil Code, Article 867(2).

foreign law prohibiting production. In one case concerning enforcement of an Internal Revenue Service summons directed to the First National Bank of Chicago seeking disclosure of certain records in First Chicago's branch bank in Athens, Greece, the Court found that:

> First Chicago has adequately demonstrated that compliance will subject its employees to the risk of substantial criminal penalties under Greek law, and that a balancing of relevant competing interests weighs against compelling disclosure at this time. We therefore reverse the judgment of the district court, but remand for consideration of an order requiring First Chicago to make a good faith effort to secure permission to make the information available.[99]

iii. Data protection/privacy laws

12.99 Production of evidence may also be resisted by reference to data protection or privacy laws. A number of jurisdictions have in place legislation that prevents the holding, use, or disclosure of personal information.[100]

12.100 Under the rules of the Swedish Code of Judicial Procedure, purely personal notes are not subject to disclosure unless there are exceptional circumstances justifying this.[101] Russia and the Ukraine also have a high level of protection in relation to personal correspondence and communications. For example, under Article 23.2 of the Constitution of the Russian Federation, 'Everyone has the right to privacy of correspondence, or telephone conversations and of postal, telegraph and other messages. Limitation of this right shall be allowed only on the basis of a court decision'.[102]

12.101 Under Article 138 of the Russian Federation Criminal Code, violation of the secrecy of correspondence, telephone calls, and postal, telegraph, and other communications of individuals is a criminal offence punishable with a fine, compulsory community

[99] *United States of America and Earl Tripplett, Revenue Officer, IRS, Petitioners-Appellees v The First National Bank of Chicago, Respondent-Appellant*, 699 F2d 341 (US 7th Circuit, CA) [1].

[100] For example, EU Member States: The General Data Protection Regulation (Regulation (EU) 2016/679 of the European Parliament and of the Council of 27 April 2016 on the protection of natural persons with regard to the processing of personal data and on the free movement of such data, and repealing Directive 95/46/EC [2016] OJ L119/1 (hereafter 'GDPR') is a European Union law that entered into force in 2016 and, following a two-year transition period, became directly applicable law in all Member States of the European Union on 25 May 2018, without requiring implementation by the EU Member States through national law; United Kingdom: Alongside the GDPR, the United Kingdom has a national data protection law, the Data Protection Act 2018 ('DPA'), that entered into force on 25 May 2018; United States: The United States has about twenty sector-specific or medium-specific national privacy or data security laws, and hundreds of such laws among its fifty states and its territories (California alone has more than twenty-five state privacy and data security laws); Hong Kong: The Personal Data (Privacy) Ordinance (Cap. 486) ('PDPO') regulates the collection and handling of personal data. The PDPO has been in force since 1996 but was significantly amended (notably as regards direct marketing) in 2012/13.

[101] Swedish Code of Judicial Procedure, ch 38 s 2: 'The obligation to produce written documents does not extend to jottings or any other like personal notes prepared exclusively for one's private use unless extraordinary reason exists for their production'.

[102] Constitution of the Russian Federation, art 23.2. This provision is treated as containing an absolute right to privacy that may only be interfered with by order of the court. There is no express exception based on consent, although in civil proceedings the court may read documents that are subject to the protection in open court if all parties so agree. Without such agreement the court still can review the document but only in camera. Labour Code of the Russian Federation, Article 88.

service, or, if committed by a person who abused his or her occupational status, by imprisonment of up to four years. Based on this provision, it has been argued in some cases that a corporate respondent cannot produce the business emails of its employees without putting him/herself and company officers in danger of criminal prosecution. Certain Russian data protection laws—for example, Article 88 of the Labour Code of the Russian Federation—do permit employers, in certain circumstances, to disclose personal data of employees, provided they first obtain the written consent of the employee.[103]

3. Applicable Law—Legal or Ethical Rules Determined by the Tribunal to Be Applicable

a. Introduction

Article 9.2(b) makes provision for evidence to be excluded on the basis of a legal impediment or privilege 'under the legal or ethical rules determined by the Arbitral Tribunal to be applicable'. This invites the question of how a tribunal should go about determining that applicable law in cases where this is disputed. **12.102**

Although objections of legal impediment are likely to be directly linked to application of a national system of law, more complex questions may arise in relation to evidentiary privileges. The parties to international arbitration will very often come from different countries, may sometimes instruct counsel based in a different jurisdiction to their own, and the arbitration in which they are involved may be seated in yet another jurisdiction. When a party claims the protection of a privilege, that party, or its legal counsel, will generally have in mind a specific domestic or internationally recognized protection that it believes should apply. However, where parties are in dispute—and, in particular, where one of them is trying to obtain production of evidence and another is resisting this—disputes may arise as to what standard of protection (if any) should apply. For example, if a party from the United States is in dispute with a French party and the seat of the arbitration is in London, which jurisdiction's laws should determine the question of legal privilege? **12.103**

[103] Russian data protection laws were considered by the US Courts in *Okean B.V. and Logistic Solution International*, where the US District Court addressed an application for discovery made pursuant to 28 U.S.C. § 1782. In several decisions, District Judge Engelmayer refused to grant the requested subpoena because of the existence of Russian and Ukrainian data protection laws. In a 2013 order Engelmayer J suggested that the Courts should be more sympathetic to difficulties created by the existence of such protections than they were in relation to 'blocking statutes' deliberately targeted at preventing compliance with foreign court discovery order. *Re: Application Pursuant to 28 U.S.C. 1782 of Okean B.V. and Logistic Solution International To Take Discovery of Chadbourne & Parke LLP* 12 Misc 104 (PAE) (SDNY, 10 October 2014). In a 2014 Order, the District Judge affirmed again that no discovery should be allowed due to the operation of Russian privacy laws and the potential consequences for parties involved in giving discovery in breach of those protections. The Court recognized that 'the burden and intrusiveness of compelling production of these documents would be substantial . . . production of such materials, in violation of foreign advocate secrecy and data privacy laws, could expose its lawyers to sanctions'.

12.104 The most straightforward solution to this issue would be an express agreement between the parties on the law or rules that should apply to questions of privilege. As in other contexts, the principle of party autonomy means that parties are free to agree the law or rules that are to govern questions of privilege and may even themselves define the scope of privilege that is to apply. Party agreements on such matters will generally be binding on the tribunal.[104] In practice, however, such agreements are rare.

12.105 Another pragmatic approach used by some tribunals is to address the issue of privilege at an early case management conference in order to expose any likely complexities or disagreements in relation to issues of privilege, and whether an agreed approach can be found. It may be sensible to include this topic on a list of possible agenda items for discussion under Article 2 of the IBA Rules.

12.106 In the absence of party agreement, the position remains difficult. Institutional rules and national laws seldom make express provision for issues of privilege.[105] Most institutional rules,[106] and many national arbitration[107] laws, simply contain general provisions granting a tribunal wide powers in relation to the conduct of the proceedings, including the admissibility of evidence. Even where privilege is mentioned, it is usually only to make clear that the tribunal has the power to determine the matter.[108]

12.107 The IBA Rules start from the same standpoint of granting the tribunal wide powers to determine all issues related to evidence, including the question of admissibility.[109] The IBA Rules go on to state expressly in Article 9.2(b) that a tribunal may exclude evidence for reason of legal impediment or privilege but, as mentioned, also indicate that the tribunal must first establish the applicable rules to determine if that ground of relief is available.[110]

b. Possible tribunal approaches to determination of applicable rules

12.108 It is suggested that, faced with the question of which rules apply to an issue of privilege, there are four approaches a tribunal might take:[111]

(a) The application of general principles of law;
(b) The application of a single national law determined through a choice-of-law approach;

[104] See Annabelle Möckesch, *Attorney-Client Privilege in International Arbitration* (OUP 2017) paras 8.06–8.11 (hereafter 'Möckesch').
[105] One rare exception is Article 22 of the International Arbitration Rules of the International Centre for Dispute Resolution, which does address the issue head-on by giving relatively firm guidance on the approach to be taken.
[106] See 12.8..
[107] For example, see UNCITRAL Model Law (n 47); German Code of Civil Procedure, s1042; Swiss Private International Law Act, Article 182; English Arbitration Act 1996, s 34; Hong Kong Arbitration Ordinance CAP 609, s 47(2).
[108] For example, see SIAC Rules, Article 27(o).
[109] IBA Rules (n 3) Article 9.1 states that 'The arbitral tribunal shall determine the admissibility, relevance, materiality and weight of evidence'.
[110] IBA Rules (n 3) Article 9.2 states that evidence may be excluded on grounds of legal impediment or privilege 'under the legal or ethical rules determined by the Arbitral Tribunal to be applicable.'
[111] See Möckesch (n 104) para 8.83 et seq.

(c) The cumulative application of two or more potentially relevant national laws or rules; or
(d) The creation of an autonomous standard defining the scope of the privilege.

These different approaches are briefly considered below. 12.109

i. Application of general principles

One possible approach is simply to apply general principles to the question of whether the asserted protection exists. The difficulty with this approach is that it may be difficult to identify a set of such principles in relation to each type of privilege or impediment that may be raised. The position may be easier in relation to some categories of privilege than it is in respect of others. One example of the former category is that of legal advice (attorney–client) privilege. 12.110

However, even if the existence of legal advice privilege can be treated as an internationally accepted norm, it is still the case that the scope and application of such privilege varies considerably between jurisdictions. In addition, while there is no doubt that legal advice privilege is internationally recognized and understood, the same cannot be said for the wide variety of lesser-known privileges that may be available or which operate within national boundaries. Without constant and uniform application, a rule cannot be treated as a general principle of law. Accordingly, as attractive as it sounds, application of 'general principles' may be of limited practical assistance in relation to issues of legal impediment/privilege. 12.111

ii. Application of a single system of law

Where there are competing systems of law potentially applicable to resolution of an issue, application of a single system of law determined by conflict-of-laws principles is the traditional approach to take. In some cases, the discretion afforded to a tribunal may be sufficiently wide to enable it to make a direct choice of an appropriate system of law. Both of these routes will result in application of a single system of law. This introduces simplicity, but comes with a certain level of rigidity. Domestic law on privilege is rarely designed to deal with international disputes. 12.112

In relation to identification of a single applicable law, a number of possibilities are generally available to a tribunal. 12.113

Lex arbitri *(the law of the seat of arbitration)* Arguments for application of the *lex arbitri* are based on the premise that the operation of legal privilege as a restriction on the production or admission of evidence is procedural in nature and should be governed by the law of the seat of arbitration in the same way as other procedural matters not expressly addressed in applicable institutional or arbitration rules. However, this approach is criticized for not upholding the legitimate expectations of the parties who may have assumed the applicability of certain privileges that exist in their home jurisdiction. In addition, given that national laws on arbitration do not generally contain any detailed rules dealing with privilege in arbitration, the tribunal may have no choice 12.114

but to resort to procedural rules applicable in state courts. This may be said to be inconsistent with the expectations of the parties who have opted to have their disputes settled through arbitration and not by reference to national court rules.[112] Members of the tribunal may also come from a jurisdiction different to that of the seat and have no appetite or experience of local procedural rules.[113]

12.115 The potential advantages of applying the *lex arbitri* is that it will often be neutral territory for the parties and will put both on an equal footing. A further advantage may be that counsel for the parties are often based at the seat and will therefore be familiar with the applicable rules.

12.116 **Lex causae** Another possibility is to apply the *lex causae*—the law that applies to the substantive relationship between the parties. For example, if the claim is founded on a contract, the proper law of the contract. The *lex causae* is applied on the premise that evidentiary privileges are substantive in their nature (rather than procedural).[114] As mentioned, this premise is not accepted in all jurisdictions and party expectations may be undermined by adoption of this approach.

12.117 *The law most closely connected* The 'closest connection' approach involves taking account of a number of factors linking the evidence in dispute to the potentially applicable privilege laws. These may include the country where the document/information was created; the country where the document is held/the communication took place; the domicile of the party seeking to rely on the privilege; and where the evidence in question is a communication with a legal adviser, the law of the jurisdiction where the lawyer is registered. Berger suggests that the law of the jurisdiction where the party has its place of business at the moment the relevant communication took place, and where (in the case of legal advice privilege) the lawyer–client contact took place, may also be applied.[115]

12.118 The 'most closely connected' approach has benefits and drawbacks. On the one hand, it may come reasonably close to reflecting the parties' expectations. On the other hand, the appropriate applicable law is not obvious and can lead to uncertainty as to what law is to be applied.[116] At a practical level, in a truly international case with parties and counsel all being located in different countries, it may not be that easy to find a 'centre of gravity' or place of the closest connection.[117] Perhaps more troubling is the possibility

[112] Peter Rosher, 'The Application and Scope of Attorney-Client Privilege in International Arbitration' (2007) 2 Stockholm International Arbitration Review 1, 17–18 (hereafter 'Rosher'); see also Evgenia Rubinina, 'Evidentiary Privileges in International Arbitration Involving Russian Parties' in Anton Asoskov, Nina Vilkova, and Roman Khodykin (eds), *New Horizons of the International Arbitration* (Infotropic Media 2013) 179–80 (hereafter 'Rubinina').

[113] See Möckesch (n 104) para 8.117.

[114] Rubinina (n 112) 178–79.

[115] Berger (n 81) 172.

[116] Rosher (n 112) 20; Rubinina (n 112) 178–79; See also: Möckesch (n 104) paras 8.124–8.146.

[117] For more detail, see Caroline Cavassin Klamas, 'Finding a Balance Between Different Standards of Privilege to Enable Predictability, Fairness and Equality in International Arbitration' (2015) 45 Revista Brasilieira de Arbitragem 159, 173 (hereafter 'Klamas').

that there may be a number of different documents that have different 'closest connections' to different laws. This in turn may lead to different parties being found subject to different national systems of law with the potential for allegations of unfairness or inequality.

The 'most-favoured-nation' regime This approach involves selecting, from the pool of conflicting laws and principles available, the law of the country which gives the highest level of protection. This approach is one that puts the parties on an equal footing and is popular with a number of arbitrators. It is criticized for (a) the lack of a satisfactory analytical basis—privileges only apply because they are created by national laws and, if they do not exist or operate in relation to a given situation, they should not be applied;[118] (b) the fact that routine application of such standards across the board in an arbitration may lead to the creation of a 'super privilege', which is undesirable; and (c) because the search for material evidence may be hindered by application of this standard.[119] **12.119**

The 'least-favoured-nation' regime This approach is the mirror image of the most-favoured nation approach described above. In essence it also treats the parties equally in that the same regime is applied across the board. However, it may have draconian consequences. Under this approach a tribunal can order production of a document if it is not considered to be privileged in any one of the potentially relevant jurisdictions. The advantage of this approach is that it permits wider scope for production of documents or other evidence. The disadvantage is that, against party expectations, it may deprive a party of the greater protection provided for in its domestic law.[120] **12.120**

iii. The cumulative approach

The cumulative approach is one in which a tribunal applies two or more relevant laws simultaneously. For example, the tribunal applies the *lex arbitri* to all issues of privilege but also takes into account domestic legal or ethical rules that bind individual counsel acting in the case. Cumulative application of laws is not an extraordinary feature in international arbitration. **12.121**

However, this approach is criticized on the basis that it really only works when application of all of the chosen legal systems yield the same outcome.[121] **12.122**

iv. Autonomous approach

Using the autonomous approach a tribunal may approach a difficult privilege issue by applying its own independent standard to the claimed privilege—subject always to the tribunal's overriding duty to act fairly and treat the parties equally. Adopting this approach, the tribunal does not need to apply the precise rules of any particular national system of law. For example, in *Bank for International Settlements* the tribunal **12.123**

[118] Born (n 9) 2386.
[119] An overview of different views can be found in Möckesch (n 104) paras 8.202–8.203.
[120] Rosher (n 112) 23; Rubinina (n 112) 181.
[121] Möckesch (n 104) para 8.164.

applied an autonomous international standard for legal advice privilege and waivers and held that a waiver of privilege occurred if the communications are disclosed 'beyond the circle of those who are authorized to or make or participate in making of the decision' in respect of which legal advice was sought. Applying this standard, the tribunal ordered the bank to produce a document that had been disclosed at a press conference as a result of which all confidentiality in the document had been lost.[122] The same approach has also been used in international commercial arbitration from time to time.[123]

v. Conclusion

12.124 While the approaches described above (and others) are available and used by tribunals there is no universally accepted approach to identify the appropriate rules to apply to issues of privilege. Nor is there any universal standard of what constitutes privilege for the purpose of excluding material from evidence or production in international arbitration, or therefore any acknowledged 'best practice'.[124]

4. Identification of Applicable Rules under Article 9.2 and the Relationship between Article 9.2 and Article 9.3

12.125 Article 9.2 provides that the tribunal may exclude material from evidence or production where legal impediment or privilege exists under the legal or ethical rules that the tribunal deems applicable to the issue.

12.126 Use of the phrase 'legal or ethical *rules*' (emphasis added) suggests that the standard to be applied under Article 9.2(b) is derived from a pre-existing set of rules available under a national system rather than a standard laid down by the tribunal[125] (although the latter cannot be ruled out). In addition, the Commentary on the IBA Rules (as well as Article 9.3(e); see 12.228-12.241) refers to a situation in which the parties are subject to different legal or ethical rules, which again suggests a national standard is engaged—namely, that of a party's home jurisdiction.

12.127 However, superimposed on Article 9.2(b) are the guidelines set out in Article 9.3 that a tribunal 'may' take into account when 'considering' issues of legal impediment or privilege. It may do so subject to any mandatory provisions of the applicable legal or ethical rules.[126]

[122] *Bank for International Settlements* (Procedural Order No. 6, 11 June 2002) PCA Case No. 2000-04. For more detail see: Möckesch (n 104) paras 8.162–8.163.

[123] See, for more detail: Möckesch (n 104) paras 8.165–8.176.

[124] See further VV Veeder, 'Chapter 6. Are the IBA Rules "Perfectible"?' in Teresa Giovannini and Alexis Mourre (eds), *Written Evidence and Discovery in International Arbitration: New Issues and Tendencies* (Kluwer Law International 2009) 325 (footnotes omitted).

[125] For example, following the autonomous approach mentioned at 12.123.

[126] See IBA Rules (n 3) Article 9.3.

It has been suggested that this checklist of guideline factors should be a primary and straightforward source of reference for tribunals operating under the IBA Rules when deciding issues of privilege. For example, Berger says that: 12.128

> Arbitral tribunals that are faced with privilege issues in the future no longer have to enter into a time-consuming review of applicable laws. Instead, they can consult the checklist contained in the new Article 9(3). At the same time, the new provision leaves enough room for a flexible approach and does not interfere with the substance of domestic privilege rules or with complex conflict of laws issues which prevail in the area of privileges.[127]

Klamas puts it this way: 12.129

> [A]lthough the IBA Rules leave the door open for the tribunal to decide which law (or laws) they will apply, they do set out some basic and important principles to guide its decision.[128]

However, although Article 9.3 is an innovative and helpful addition to the IBA Rules, the precise status of that provision, and its relationship to Article 9.2(b), is not altogether clear. For example, it is not possible to consider the Article 9.3 guidelines in isolation, as they are made expressly subject to any mandatory provisions of the legal or ethical rules referred to in Article 9.2(b). In addition, it is possible to see that the considerations expressed in several of the Article 9.3 guidelines may be at odds with the substance of potentially applicable laws. For example, a need to protect the confidentiality of a document created for the purpose of providing legal advice may be recognized pursuant to the guideline expressed in Article 9.3(a), but privilege in the relevant document may not be recognized under the applicable law (for example, French law)[129] because the document was prepared by in-house, rather than external, counsel. If the applicable law, and its effect, is determined in isolation under Article 9.2(b), the tribunal's flexibility to have regard in any meaningful way to the considerations in Article 9.3 may be significantly hindered. 12.130

One way of reconciling this tension is to interpret the Article 9.3 factors as matters that the tribunal should take into account when deciding what the applicable standard under Article 9.2(b) should be. For example, if there are two possible sets of rules in contention and one provides appropriate protections contemplated by one or more of 12.131

[127] Berger (n 81) 176. An almost identical view is expressed in Peter Ashford, *The IBA Rules on the Taking of Evidence in International Arbitration. A Guide* (CUP 2013) para 9-59 (hereafter 'Ashford').

[128] Klamas (n 117) 169.

[129] In France, the concept of legal professional privilege (LPP) does not exist for communications between an in-house counsel and her/his employer. In-house counsel in France may not be members of a French bar and, as mere employees, the protective rules governing French lawyers' day-to-day activities, including LPP, cannot be applied to them. There have been several attempts at changing the status of in-house counsel in France, the latest of which was earlier this year ('Projet de loi Macron'), in order to extend some form of LPP to them, but all such attempts have failed in the face of the French Bar's opposition. See Bryan Cave, 'Crossing the River: The Law on Legal Professional Privilege' (*The Law Society Gazette*, 12 August 2016) <https://www.lawgazette.co.uk/practice-points/crossing-the-river--the-law-on-legal-professional-privilege/5057114.article> accessed on 4 December 2018.

the Article 9.3 guidelines, and the other does not, the tribunal could favour the former over the latter. Möckesch describes the secondary nature of the Article 9.3 provisions in the following terms:

> They [the Article 9.3 considerations] are mere guidelines regarding the most relevant factors that may influence a tribunal's decision, which should be tailored on a case-by-case approach.
>
> So, Article 9.3 of the [IBA Rules] does not include a rule on how the applicable standard should be determined. It does not solve the conflict-of-laws problem; rather, it merely reminds arbitrators of certain factors they may keep in mind when determining the applicable standard.[130]

12.132 An alternative approach would be for the tribunal to take account of the Article 9.3 factors in the exercise of its wider discretion on the admissibility of evidence under Article 9.2. For example, if it is found that the law determined to be applicable to the issue of privilege does not provide adequate (or any) protection to meet the considerations identified in Article 9.3, then the tribunal may nonetheless decide to exclude the evidence to which the privilege is said to attach.

12.133 In practice, a tribunal may be able to avoid this type of analysis by simply choosing the approach to identification of the applicable rules (see 12.108-12.124) that provides the outcome the tribunal considers to be fair in all of the circumstances, taking account of the factors identified in Article 9.3 where relevant.

12.134 While noting the importance of the factors outlined in Article 9.3, the Commentary on the IBA Rules appears to confirm that the standard that is ultimately applied to determine an issue of legal impediment/privilege is a matter for the tribunal's discretion, whatever route it uses to arrive at that result:

> Although *the standard to be applied is left to the discretion of the arbitral tribunal*, it is desirable that the tribunal take account of the elements set forth in Article 9.3, in particular if the parties are subject to different legal or ethical rules.[131]

5. Factors to Be Considered by the Tribunal under Article 9.3

12.135 Article 9.3 of the IBA Rules lists five different factors that the tribunal may wish to consider when resolving issues of legal impediment or privilege. The relationship between these factors and the terms of Article 9.2(b) is discussed at 12.125-12.134.

12.136 The Commentary to the IBA Rules makes clear that the factors listed at Article 9.3 are 'non-binding guidelines'. This position is reinforced by the fact that the introductory words of Article 9.3 state that the tribunal *may*, rather than *shall*, take the listed factors

[130] Möckesch (n 104) para 8.42.
[131] Commentary on the IBA Rules (n 64) 25 (emphasis added).

into account. Nonetheless, in all cases, it would be sensible for the tribunal to invite submissions from the parties on the matters covered by Article 9.3.

The considerations listed at Article 9.3 comprise the following: **12.137**

(a) any need to protect the confidentiality of a Document created or statement or oral communication made in connection with and for the purpose of providing or obtaining *legal advice*;
(b) any need to protect the confidentiality of a Document created or statement or oral communication made in connection with and for the purpose of *settlement negotiations*;
(c) the *expectations of the Parties* and their advisors at the time the legal impediment or privilege is said to have arisen;
(d) any possible *waiver* of any applicable legal impediment or privilege by virtue of consent, earlier disclosure, affirmative use of the document, statement, oral communication, or advice contained therein, or otherwise; and
(e) the need to maintain *fairness and equality* as between the Parties, particularly if they are subject to different legal or ethical rules.

Before considering these factors in more detail it is useful to note a number of general points. **12.138**

The first is that factors (a) and (b) are directed at particular types of privilege—namely, the protection that is commonly afforded to communications between a lawyer and client in connection with the taking and giving of legal advice, and the protection afforded to disputing parties in connection with efforts to negotiate a settlement of their differences. The Commentary to the IBA Rules describes (a) as encompassing both the common law understanding of legal advice/attorney–client privilege and the civil law understanding of the duty of professional secrecy. It describes (b) as expressing a generalized understanding of the so-called 'without prejudice' or 'settlement' privilege that exists in certain jurisdictions. Consideration of factors (a) and (b) will be relevant only in relation to claimed protections falling broadly into these two categories of privilege. **12.139**

Factors (c), (d), and (e) are of more general application. As explained in the Commentary on the IBA Rules, factor (c) highlights for the tribunal that it should take into account the expectations of the parties at the time that the legal impediment or privilege—whatever its nature—is said to have arisen. As also explained in the Commentary, factor (e) emphasizes the need for any outcome to maintain fairness and equality between the parties. Factor (d) reflects a widely accepted exception to the operation of an evidentiary privilege—namely, the waiver of that protection. **12.140**

The second general point to note is the potential for tension between the different considerations described in Article 9.3. For example, in a dispute between French and English companies, the tribunal could take note of the fact that privilege does not attach **12.141** to communications between a French in-house lawyer and his employer, whereas similar communications between an English in-house lawyer and his employer will attract privilege. If the tribunal were to treat the two situations as being subject to different rules, this would be consistent with the parties' expectations as contemplated by paragraph (c), but would arguably result in a lack of equality or fairness between the parties as contemplated by paragraph (e).

12.142 In any case where tension between different considerations arises the tribunal will need to consider how best to balance those competing factors and/or which consideration should have priority. We suggest that the overriding consideration must always be to maintain fairness and equality between the parties. This is an express obligation of the tribunal under many national arbitration laws and the majority of institutional rules, as well as being one of the principles of the IBA rules.[132] We suggest that this principle should guide the tribunal in its application of other considerations. For example, in the situation described in12.141, the tribunal could adopt the 'most-favoured nation' approach described at 12.119 so that the more favourable English rules would apply to all parties.

a. The need to protect confidentiality of legal advice

> **9.3(a) any need to protect the confidentiality of a Document created or statement or oral communication made in connection with and for the purpose of providing or obtaining legal advice.**

12.143 Guideline 9.3(a) is concerned with the need to protect the confidentiality of legal advice received by a lay client from a lawyer or professional adviser. In one form or another, such privilege is widely recognized across jurisdictions.[133] As mentioned, it is referred to as 'legal advice privilege' in the UK, 'attorney-client privilege' in the United States and falls within the protection of 'professional secrecy' in many civil law jurisdictions. Article 9.3(a) does not give the privilege a label, but rather describes it by reference to the nature of the communication. This makes sense. National labels carry specific meanings based on domestic law and practice. A generic description of the material to be protected creates a more even playing field devoid of the 'baggage' that comes with localized terms.

12.144 As with most other privileges, the burden of proof is on the party claiming the privilege.[134]

[132] IBA Rules (n 3) Preamble 1. See Chapter 2 paras 2.7–2.24.

[133] Klamas (n 117) 161 et seq.

[134] *West London Pipeline and Storage v Total UK* [2008] EWHC 1729 (Comm). Hamilton refers to one ICC decision where the tribunal made plain that '[t]he burden is on the party opposing disclosure to establish the factual support for the work product exemption'. See Virginia Hamilton, 'Document Production in ICC Arbitration' in *Special Supplement 2006: Document Production in International Arbitration* (International Chamber of Commerce 2006) 77 (hereafter 'Hamilton').

i. The policy behind legal advice privilege

As a matter of principle, legal advice privilege is designed to protect open and frank communications between lawyer and client by providing a protection against any obligation or instruction to disclose such communications to a third party.[135] If the rule did not exist, lay clients might be reluctant to disclose relevant facts to their lawyers and the lawyers, in turn, would not then be able to give the advice that the lay client may need. This would have negative consequences for the administration of justice and settlement of disputes. In common law countries, legal advice privilege exists for the benefit of the client and can be waived by the client if s/he chooses. **12.145**

In one report in which reference was made to a number of decisions made by the English House of Lords (now the Supreme Court), the foundations of legal advice privilege in that jurisdiction were very efficiently summarized: **12.146**

> Legal professional privilege is a substantive right founded on public policy, and not merely a rule of evidence determining which documents are admissible or inadmissible in court proceedings. The courts have regarded the client's right to communicate confidentially with his or her legal adviser under the seal of legal professional privilege, as a necessary corollary of the fundamental right of access to legal advice.[136]

As mentioned, a number of civil law countries regard communications between lawyer and client as a 'professional secret', a concept that provides a broad umbrella of protection. The concept of 'professional secrecy' has developed in order to protect information and communications passing between a lawyer and a client, but the precise nature of the professional secrecy, and the ways in which it may be waived or lifted, varies.[137] Some civil law jurisdictions impose penal sanctions on counsel who violate the duty to safeguard privileged information.[138] **12.147**

Generally speaking, professional secrecy attaches to *all* information the lawyer gains in the exercise of his or her professional practice. This includes information the attorney receives from third parties, as long as this occurs in the exercise of his or her professional work. As a result, the rules regarding professional secrecy do not contain the distinctions between legal advice privilege and 'litigation privilege' that exist in some common law jurisdictions. **12.148**

[135] See Möckesch (n 104) para 1.01.

[136] Council of the Bars and Law Societies of the European Union, *The Professional Secret, Confidentiality and Legal Professional Privilege in Europe (An Update on the Report by D.A.O. Edward QC.)* (Council of the Bars and Law Societies of the European Union 2003) <http://www.europarl.europa.eu/meetdocs/2009_2014/documents/libe/dv/ccbeedward_report_update_/ccbeedward_report_update_en.pdf> accessed 4 December 2018. See also *R. v Derby Magistrates Court, Ex p. B.* [1996] AC 487; *R v Secretary of State for Home Department, Ex p. Daly* [2001] UKHL 26; and *Special Commissioner and Another, Ex p. Morgan Grenfell and Co Ltd* [2002] UKHL 21.

[137] See, eg the country reports on privilege set out in *Report of the ICCA-Queen Mary Task Force on Third Party Funding in International Arbitration* (International Council for Commercial Arbitration 2018) Annex A.

[138] For example, in France, a counsel who divulges privileged information may be subject to criminal sanctions of one year's imprisonment and a fine of Euro 15,000. In Brazil, the penalty is of one to three years in prison or a fine to be established by the magistrate. See Klamas (n 117) 163.

12.149 In common law jurisdictions, legal advice privilege does not generally extend to communications with third parties or other professionals. However, where a communication relates to arbitration or court proceedings it may nonetheless be protected by a separate head of 'litigation privilege'.[139] In broad terms, litigation privilege arises from the principle that a litigant or potential litigant should be free to seek evidence without being obliged to disclose the result of their enquiries to their opponent. For example, in England, the protected communication may be between a lawyer (acting in a professional capacity) and the client, or between either of them and a third party (or be a document created by or on behalf of the client or the client's lawyer). The communication must be for the dominant purpose of litigation, and the litigation (or arbitration) must be existing or reasonably contemplated.

12.150 Litigation privilege is therefore generally wider than legal advice privilege in that it extends to communications with non-lawyers. It is narrower in that it attaches only to documents and communications made for the purpose of litigation or arbitration. If there is no litigation or arbitration in existence or in contemplation, the right to assert litigation privilege may not arise.

12.151 A further but related head of privilege existing in some common law jurisdictions is 'common interest privilege'. Two or more parties (for example, two respondents to an arbitration claim) may have a common interest in the subject matter of the proceedings and a common interest in keeping confidential communications between them on those matters. In those circumstances, common interest privilege may apply to protect the communications.[140]

ii. The general scope of legal advice privilege

12.152 When considering Article 9.3(a) it is useful to bear in mind a number of different factors that may operate at a national level to determine whether a particular communication falls within the scope of any protection afforded to the taking and giving of legal advice. Such factors generally relate to issues around such matters as:

(a) Who the parties are receiving and giving the legal advice in question; and
(b) The nature of the communication.

12.153 *The person giving the advice* A factor that can be relevant to the existence and nature of legal advice privilege is the status of the person giving the advice.

[139] See Colin Passmore, *Privilege* (3rd edn, Sweet & Maxwell 2013) (hereafter 'Passmore')—one of the leading texts on privilege—which contains, at paragraph 1-002, a broad statement of the scope of two subheads of legal professional privilege in England, namely, legal advice privilege and litigation privilege.

[140] It used to be the case in England that the two parties had to be represented by the same lawyer but that requirement no longer applies. See *The Good Luck* [1988] 10 WLUK 197, and more recently, *Martin Penny v Montagu Private Equity LLP & Ors* [2010] EWHC 2354 [12]–[13]. Common interest privilege has been held to apply between companies in the same group; a reinsurer and the reinsured; principal and agent and communications between a party and its third-party funder. For more detail, see Meriam N Alrashid, Jane Wessel, and John Laird, 'Impact of Third Party Funding on Privilege in Litigation and International Arbitration' (2012) Dispute Resolution International 99, 101–29.

Lawyers

Legal advice is generally thought of as being given by a 'lawyer' or 'attorney', but what does this actually mean? In broad terms, the requirement is generally satisfied if the advice is given by a lawyer admitted to a local bar/roll of solicitors or another legal professional regulatory body. However, the position is less clear with respect to other types of professionals who are not so admitted. In such a case, a factual enquiry to assess the true position may be necessary.[141] **12.154**

The question may be more acute in relation to professionals from jurisdictions where the giving of legal advice is not restricted to a lawyer admitted to the bar or other professional body. For example, in Russia the legal profession is only partially regulated.[142] In particular, it is only in criminal cases that a lawyer appearing in court must be an 'advocate', ie a person admitted to the local bar. There is no similar requirement with respect to civil proceedings. As a result, there are a substantial number of 'lawyers' who are practising law without being formally admitted to the bar.[143] The scope of legal advice privilege afforded to those distinct categories of professional is also different. Advocates in Russia enjoy the protection of 'Advocate's secrecy', which is similar to the concept of professional secrecy in France. Advocates cannot be interrogated about facts they learned from their clients, their premises cannot be searched, and the law is clear that any related documents obtained during any searches or seizures are inadmissible in court.[144] In contrast, the privilege applicable to legal representatives who are not members of the Russian bar permits those representatives to refuse to testify about matters they have learned from their clients when representing them in legal proceedings underway or contemplated,[145] but there are no express provisions providing for the inadmissibility of lawyer/client correspondence or any prohibition on search and seizure of files.[146] If a tribunal is faced with an assertion of privilege in relation to correspondence between a client and a Russian lawyer, it may be necessary to establish whether the lawyer in question is a member of the bar and what is the regime of legal advice privilege applicable to that particular counsel. **12.155**

In England, privilege may exist in relation to communications with legal executives and licensed conveyancers who are employed to give advice on English law by a licensed body. Section 190 of the Legal Services Act 2007 provides that communications and documents relating to services provided by a person who is an 'authorised person' in relation to rights of audience, the conduct of litigation, or conveyancing or probate services are privileged from disclosure as if the provider had been a solicitor. An authorized **12.156**

[141] Ashford (n 127) para 9-25.

[142] This is the present position. The Ministry of Justice is currently considering changes to the rules regulating the provision of legal services.

[143] See: Roman Khodykin, *Arbitration Law of Russia: Practice & Procedure* (Juris Publishing 2013) 117.

[144] Russian Federal Law No. 63-FZ 'On the Bar and Advocacy', Article 8.

[145] Russian Federation Civil Procedure Code, Article 69.3(1).

[146] Although in *ZAO "RaiffeisenBank" v Kalinin E. and Rybinsky P. V.* Case No. 2-17/2015 (Pervomayskiy District Court of Novosibirsk, 17 September 2014), the court excluded witness evidence of a representative from the records as inadmissible.

person is one who is authorized to carry on the relevant activity by an approved regulator. Approved regulators include the Chartered Institute of Legal Executives (CILEX) and the Council of Licensed Conveyancers.

In-house lawyers

12.157 Another important factor is the distinction that is sometimes drawn between in-house counsel and external counsel. The relevance of this distinction can vary significantly between jurisdictions.

12.158 In England, as well as in the majority of the common law countries, both in-house and external legal advice is covered by privilege. This is also the case in some civil law countries, eg in Portugal, subject to the requirement that counsel is a member of the Portuguese Bar Association.[147]

12.159 In Germany, legal privilege does not apply to in-house counsel who are regarded as ordinary employees of a company.[148] A similar position prevails in France.[149] Decisions of the Court of Justice of the European Union have also given rise to debate. In *Akzo Nobel Chemicals Ltd and Akcros Chemicals Ltd v Commission*,[150] the CJEU held that in European competition investigations communications with in-house counsel are not privileged. The rationale for this decision was a finding by the court that in-house counsel do not enjoy the same degree of independence from their employer as external counsel.[151]

Other professionals

12.160 There are a number of non-legal professionals who provide legal or quasi-legal advice—for example, tax advisors, customs clearance specialists, accountants, etc. To take the example of a tax adviser—although the purpose of the advice given by the tax advisor may be to find the jurisdiction with the lowest, yet legal, tax rate, the tax advisor will sometimes find themselves in the domain of legal advice because that is an inextricable part of the strategy on which s/he is advising. The question then arises as to whether protection should attach only to legal advice given by a qualified lawyer admitted to practise law, or should it also attach to advice given by a professional from another discipline, provided that they are permitted under the relevant domestic law to give such advice and where the advice given concerns matters of law?

[147] Article 68 of the Statutes of the Portuguese Bar Association and Opinion No. 14/PP/2008-G of the General Council of the Portuguese Bar Association.
[148] For more detail, see Raeschke-Kessler (n 65) 428–29.
[149] See (n 129).
[150] Case C-550/07 P *Akzo Nobel Chemicals Ltd and Akcros Chemicals Ltd v Commission* [2010] ECR I-8301.
[151] For more detail, see Möckesch (n 104) paras 5.26–5.28. There is some evidence of a shift in approach so as to widen the scope of protection afforded to communications with in-house counsel. For example, in Belgium, in-house counsel's advice traditionally did not attract privilege. However, from 1 March 2000 privilege was extended to advice given by members of the Institut des Juristes d'Enterprise (Institute of In-house Legal Counsel) for the benefit of their employer and where such advice was given in the course of their activity as in-house legal counsel. See Klamas (n 117) 164.

This issue has generated much debate and the position varies widely across jurisdictions. One of the arguments for extending legal advice privilege to other professionals is that, irrespective of the status of the person who is giving legal advice, there exists a special relationship between the client and the professional adviser in which the client should feel secure disclosing confidential information. If the privilege did not attach to such communications this would hinder frank and open discussions between client and adviser. However, there is also a considerable body of opinion in favour of limiting privilege to advice that is given by lawyers who are members of a regulated profession and bound by professional rules and standards. It is said that it is only by the observance of such rules and standards that the proper administration of justice be achieved.[152] **12.161**

Conclusions

In summary, the question of whether advice given by in-house lawyers, by non-legal professionals or by quasi-lawyers will attract legal advice privilege may be treated differently in different jurisdictions and by different tribunals. A tribunal operating under the IBA Rules will have to consider whether, as a matter of the applicable law referred to in Article 9.3(a), legal advice privilege is engaged, as well as the factors described in Article 9.3. **12.162**

The person receiving the advice There is generally no requirement concerning the attributes of the party receiving the legal advice. Access to legal advice is a universal fundamental right. **12.163**

However, issues may arise where the party seeking advice is not an individual, but a corporate entity or other organization or collective. Communications may take place between the lawyer and several individuals at the relevant entity, and those individuals may perform different functions and be based in different parts of the organization. Does privilege attach to all of the communications? The definition of 'client' in this context may vary across jurisdictions. For example, the English courts have laid down a restrictive definition of client. In *Three Rivers District Council and Others*, the Court of Appeal held that privilege would attach only to communications between the bank's lawyers and a small group of the bank's employees actually charged with instructing those lawyers.[153] In contrast, the United States Supreme Court has adopted a broader approach and has recognized the privilege existing in relation to all employees of the corporation, provided that the communications concern matters within the scope of the employees' corporate duties.[154] **12.164**

The content of the advice As mentioned, the rationale underlying legal advice privilege is the need to protect communications between a client and a professional adviser in **12.165**

[152] See decision of the English Employments Appeals Tribunal in *New Victoria Hospital v Ryan* [1992] 12 WLUK 90; [1993] ICR 201, 203–04.
[153] *Three Rivers District Council and Others v Governor and Company of the Bank of England* [2003] EWCA Civ 474.
[154] *Upjohn Co v US* (1981) 449 US 383, 384.

relation to the seeking and giving of legal advice. To attract privilege, the substance of the communication should therefore concern the matters to which the required legal advice relates. Where this is not the case, the communication may not be privileged, even though it takes place between lawyer and client.

12.166 This is an issue that most commonly arises in respect of communications between in-house counsel and their internal client. In-house counsel sometimes perform several functions, not all of which will necessarily be concerned with the giving of legal advice. As alluded to in an English House of Lords case:

> It does sometimes happen that such a legal advisor does work for his employer in another capacity, perhaps of an executive nature. Their communications in that capacity would not be the subject of legal professional privilege. So the legal advisor must be scrupulous to make that distinction. [155]

12.167 Examples of written materials that may attract legal advice privilege include correspondence relating to the advice given, meeting notes (taken by client or lawyer) recording oral discussions between them on the same subject, and notes of advice on possible legal strategies. Letters sent by the client for the purposes of receiving legal advice will generally have the same status. The way the client has formulated the questions, and the background facts provided by the client, can give away the position of that party in any pending or contemplated proceedings.

iii. Exceptions to the normal application of available privileges

12.168 When considering what are the applicable rules for the privilege being asserted, a tribunal may also have to consider possible exceptions to the general rule that are said to apply.

12.169 For example, if English law were to apply, both legal advice privilege and litigation privilege are lost *if* it can be shown that the communication or document in question came into being for the purpose of furthering a criminal or fraudulent purpose.[156] In the United States there exists the fiduciary exception. For example, in derivative shareholder litigation, courts have been reluctant to allow the management of a company to assert attorney–client information as a basis for a refusal to disclose information to the company's shareholders. The justification for the exception is that the management owes fiduciary duties to both the company and its shareholders.[157]

iv. Scope of application of Article 9.3(a)

12.170 Article 9.3(a) refers to a need to protect the confidentiality of a document or statement or oral communication made for the purpose of providing or obtaining legal advice.

[155] *Alfred Crompton Amusement Machines Ltd. v Customs and Excise Commissioners (No. 2)* [1972] 2 QB 102, 129.

[156] *Kuwait Airways Corporation v Iraqi Airways Company* [2005] EWCA Civ 286. German law contains a substantially similar exception. For more detail, see Möckesch (n 104) para 2.675.

[157] *Garner v Wolfinbarger* 430 F2d 1093 (5th Cir 1970). For more detail, see Möckesch (n 104) paras 2.68–2.69.

Given the distinctions between types of legal privilege that exist in some common law jurisdictions, the terms of Article 9.3(a) might be seen as aligning more closely with (say) English legal advice privilege than litigation privilege (see 12.145-12.151). However, Article 9.3(a) is concerned with communications 'in connection with' as well as 'for the purpose of providing or obtaining' legal advice. In our view, the consideration described in Article 9.3(a) should be interpreted broadly and we see no reason why it should not be taken into account in relation to claims of privilege that are broader than a direct communication between lawyer and client containing legal advice—thus including, for example, English litigation privilege or appropriate categories of professional secrecy.

Similarly, the text of Article 9.3(a) does not mention in-house lawyers or quasi-lawyers. **12.171** It draws no distinction between advice given by different types of lawyers. It simply says that the tribunal should take into account the need to protect confidentiality of communications 'made in connection with and for the purpose of providing or obtaining legal advice'. It is in the discretion of the tribunal to interpret that provision as it thinks appropriate.

Article 9.3(a) confirms that the need for confidentiality in the context of privilege **12.172** claims may arise in relation to a wide range of potential evidence. It refers to a

> *Document created or statement or oral communication made* in connection with and for the purpose of providing or obtaining legal advice.[158]

Taking into account the wide Definition of 'Document' contained in the IBA Rules,[159] this encompasses all types of evidence likely to be submitted or sought under the IBA Rules and is consistent with the wide scope of material capable of attracting legal privilege.

In the case of legal advice privilege, and some communications covered by professional **12.173** secrecy, the confidential nature of the material may be plain. In relation to litigation privilege, or some other communications covered by professional secrecy, the position may be less clear, particularly where the communication takes place with a third party such as a potential witness. It will be for the parties to make submissions on these matters. In any case, and subject to consideration of the applicable rules determined under Article 9.2(b), the tribunal is likely to pay heed to the broad policy considerations underpinning the particular privilege and the confidential information that it is designed to protect. Obviously, if the confidentiality has never existed,[160] or has been lost for reasons of waiver (as discussed at 12.202-12.227), the need to take such matters into account may not arise.

[158] Emphasis added.

[159] See Chapter 3 paras 3.5–3.6.

[160] For example, as is the case in respect of communications between parties to the arbitration or litigation. For a more complex example of where the English court found that there could never have been a reasonable expectation of privacy, see *Simpkin v The Berkeley Group Holdings plc* [2017] EWHC 1472 (QB).

b. The need to protect the confidentiality of settlement discussions

9.3(b) any need to protect the confidentiality of a Document created or statement or oral communication made in connection with and for the purpose of settlement negotiations.

12.174 As is explained in the Commentary to the IBA Rules, Article 9.3(b) expresses a generalized understanding of what is known in England as the 'without prejudice privilege' and in the United States as the 'settlement privilege'. Both concepts protect from disclosure communications and documents generated in connection with and for the purposes of settlement negotiations. Historically, such communications were regarded as being created by the parties pursuant to an implied agreement of confidentiality and in recognition of a public interest in protecting that confidentiality as an aid to dispute resolution.[161]

i. Background to the 'without prejudice' rule

12.175 'Without prejudice' privilege is an important tool in the conduct of disputes. In an effort to reach an amicable resolution of a dispute the parties may, during negotiations, make admissions or statements adverse to their 'open' position, or offer a compromise or terms of settlement that may carry an implicit acknowledgment that they are not wholly confident in all parts of their case. If such admissions or settlement proposals were admitted onto the record in the dispute, they might be exploited by the opponent party, or influence the tribunal's view of the strength of a claim or defence and/or the appropriate measure of damages.

12.176 Communications between parties directed at a settlement of a dispute are frequently labelled 'without prejudice', but provided the necessary characteristics of a without prejudice communication are met, the omission of this express tag will not necessarily be fatal to a claim of privilege.[162]

12.177 Not all civil law jurisdictions recognize without prejudice privilege. For example, as a matter of Russian law, the substance of settlement negotiations may be admitted as evidence.

[161] See further Carol Mulcahy, 'Lifting the Veil on Without Prejudice Negotiations' (2000) 144 Solicitors' Journal 444, 444–45. The English Court has confirmed both the underlying public policy and the quasi-contractual basis for the confidentiality of without prejudice communications. See *Alan Ramsay Sales & Marketing Ltd v Typhoo Tea Ltd* [2016] EWHC 486 (Comm). See also *Cutts v Head* [1984] Ch 290, 306. Courts in the United States have expressed similar views. See *Goodyear Tire & Rubber Co v Chiles Power Supply Inc.*, 332 F. 3rd 976, 981 (6th Cir. 2003)

[162] This is the position under English law. See *Rush and Tomkins Ltd v GLC* [1989] A.C. 1280, 1299–1300: 'The ["without prejudice"] rule applies to exclude all negotiations genuinely aimed at settlement whether oral or in writing from being given in evidence. A competent solicitor will always head any negotiating correspondence "without prejudice" to make clear beyond doubt that in the event of the negotiations being unsuccessful they are not referred to at the subsequent trial. However the application of the rule is not dependent upon the use of the phrase "without prejudice" and if it is clear from the surrounding circumstances that the parties were seeking to compromise the action, evidence of the content of those negotiations will, as a general rule, not be admissible at the trail and cannot be used to establish an admission or partial admission'.

ii. Recognition of the 'without prejudice' rule in international arbitration

The notion that communications aimed at reaching a settlement should not be admitted into evidence has now been generally recognized in international arbitration. As Berger explains with reference to Article 9.3(b): 12.178

> That provision acknowledges that there is a transnational privilege principle with respect to written or oral statements made in good faith by the parties to an arbitration during previous settlement negotiations between them.[163]

Furthermore, the without prejudice rule is not always applied by reference to what might be considered to be the applicable law of the privilege. For example, in ICC Case No. 13176, a tribunal seated in Paris considered the issue of 'without prejudice' privilege by reference to the 'case law and practice of international commercial arbitration and the Iran–US Tribunal' and the UNCITRAL Model Law.[164] Berger articulated this in the following terms: 12.179

> There is a unanimous view today in international ADR and arbitration practice that a general mediation privilege exists which renders all evidence, whether written or oral, stemming from mediation, conciliation and similar ADR processes between the parties, inadmissible as evidence in subsequent arbitration proceedings. [. . .] The underlying rationale of the mediation privilege is derived from the special nature and character of these negotiations conducted in good faith between the parties. Such policy considerations apply irrespective of whether one is dealing with formalised ADR proceedings, or with private, informal settlement negotiations conducted between the parties without the presence of a third, neutral party. [. . .] This view has been confirmed repeatedly in the case law of the Iran–United States claims tribunal.[165]

iii. Application of Article 9.3(b)

A claim of without prejudice privilege may be asserted by reference to domestic law principles, or in reliance on accepted practice in international arbitration. In either case, pursuant to Article 9.2(b) the tribunal may have to consider if any particular rules are applicable to the circumstances relied on. However, the terms of Article 9.3(b) appear to acknowledge the desirability of preserving the confidentiality of information generated for the purposes of reaching the settlement of a dispute. In our view, the absence of privilege attaching to settlement discussions under the appropriate applicable law should not be a bar to the tribunal's determination that protection of the confidentiality of those settlement discussions is desirable. 12.180

In considering the need to protect the confidentiality of material over which settlement privilege is claimed, the tribunal may find it helpful to consider some of the 12.181

[163] Berger (n 81) 173 (footnotes omitted).

[164] 'Procedural Order of May 2006 in ICC Case 13176 (Extract)' in *Special Supplement 2014: Procedural Decisions in ICC Arbitration* (International Chamber of Commerce 2014) 16.

[165] Berger (n 81) 173 and 174.

matters taken into account in those jurisdictions where the concept of this protection is well-developed.

12.182 First, it should be clear that the parties are seeking to protect communications or documents created in good faith with a genuine desire to explore possible ways of resolving the dispute. A party cannot invoke the settlement privilege if the document or communication was generated under a 'without prejudice' tag solely for the purpose of being able to hide this information from the tribunal.[166] Indiscriminate labelling of correspondence as 'without prejudice' in an attempt to take advantage of the privilege should not be accepted.

12.183 Second, it is the character of the discussions, not the character of the participants, that should lead to application of the settlement privilege. For example, from the tribunal's perspective, it should be irrelevant whether the parties are conducting negotiations either through or with the advice of lawyers, or by use of a mediator, etc. It is not uncommon for the without prejudice rule to be recognized as covering third-party communications commissioned to facilitate a settlement.[167]

12.184 Third, the tribunal should take into account the parties' expectations pursuant to Article 9.3(c) as discussed at 12.87-12.201. In particular, if a document or communication is in good faith marked 'without prejudice' this may be a strong signal for the tribunal that the parties, or at least the sender, regarded the communication as privileged. It is very common for conduct of the dispute and without prejudice communications to take place in tandem. Clear marking of the two associated streams of correspondence as 'open' or 'without prejudice correspondence' may create a similar presumption. If settlement negotiations took place orally, a relevant consideration in deciding whether evidence on those discussions is to be admitted may be whether one or both of the parties expressly stated that they wanted to speak on a without prejudice basis. However, application of the without prejudice rule should be a question of substance not form and its application should not be dependent on use of the phrase 'without prejudice'.[168]

12.185 Fourth, settlement offers may have some significance when it comes to cost assessment. For example, a party may wish to argue that its opponent should not have all of its costs, even though it was successful in the arbitration, because the winning party recovered less that it had been offered by its opponent as part of a settlement proposal. In order to preserve its right to make such an argument, a party may mark a settlement proposal 'without prejudice save as to costs' so as to preserve its right to show the offer to the tribunal after its determination on the merits but prior to a decision on allocation of costs. The use of this device has wide acceptance in the practice of arbitration and supports

[166] Berger (n 81) 174.

[167] See, eg *Rabin v Mendoza & Co* [1954] 1 WLR 271. In this case, for example, surveyors were commissioned to investigate whether an insurance policy could be obtained, which would avoid the need for the parties to proceed with a dispute.

[168] See further *Avonwick Holdings Limited v Webinvest Limited and another* [2014] EWHC 3322 (Ch).

the policy behind the use of without prejudice communications as a means of encouraging settlement.[169]

As is the case with legal advice privilege,[170] without prejudice privilege may be lost if the information in question is no longer confidential in nature, eg if it has been waived by the parties or has come into the public domain. 12.186

c. The expectations of the parties and their advisors

> **9.3(c) the expectations of the Parties and their advisors at the time the legal impediment or privilege is said to have arisen.**

Article 9.3(c) invites the tribunal to take into account 'the expectations of the parties and their advisors' when resolving issues related to claims of legal impediment or privilege. The Commentary to the IBA rules reiterates that 'Article 9.3(c) expresses the guiding principle that expectations of the parties and their advisers at the time the legal impediment or privilege is said to have arisen should be taken into consideration'. 12.187

There is a serious timing consideration—Article 9.3(c) states expressly that the expectations to be considered are those existing at the time the legal impediment or privilege is said to have arisen. If taken literally, the tribunal may disregard any expectations that have arisen after the relevant document/communication was made. 12.188

The importance of the expectations of the parties vis-à-vis the legal advice privilege have been explained as follows. Although this statement refers to legal advice privilege it is equally applicable to other privileges: 12.189

> [A]ttorney–client privilege will encourage communications between attorney and client only if both parties know at the time of the communications whether the privilege will apply. If they are uncertain, their communications will be chilled, and the purpose of the privilege will be entirely defeated.[171]

i. *Defining 'expectations'*

Expectations very often play an important part in a decision by a party to do or refrain from doing something, and the manner in which it is done. However, not every expectation merits legal protection. This is why legal documents sometimes contain reference to party expectations qualified by such words as 'justified', 'legitimate', or 'reasonable'. 12.190

In English law, the doctrine of 'legitimate expectation' was first developed as a basis for judicial review in administrative law to protect a procedural or substantive interest 12.191

[169] Sometimes dealt with by use of a 'sealed offer' lodged with the arbitrator and only opened after a determination on the merits.

[170] See 12.202– 12.227 for more detail.

[171] Steven Bradford, 'Conflict of Laws and the Attorney-Client Privilege: A Territorial Solution' (1991) University of Pittsburgh Law Review 909, 943.

when a public authority seeks to withdraw from a representation made to another party.[172] The United States Restatement (Second) of Conflict of Laws makes express reference to 'the protection of justified expectations' as a relevant consideration in relation to choice of applicable law.[173] The commentary to that provision explains that protection of justified expectations is an important value in all fields of law, including in choice of law situations where a party may be adversely affected by the application of a law that is unfamiliar to him.[174]

ii. Party expectations regarding home jurisdiction protections

12.192 Consistent with these considerations, there exists a body of opinion that the expectations of individual parties in relation to available legal protections should be assessed by reference to their 'home' jurisdiction (the place of incorporation or domicile) and that they should expect no more and no less than the protection that is available to them under the relevant domestic law.[175]

12.193 Of course, in international arbitration, difficulties arise when parties from different jurisdictions—particularly those without prior experience of international arbitration—have different expectations as to the procedural and evidentiary protections that will be afforded to them.[176] One of the raisons d'etre for the IBA Rules was to create a set of rules on evidence that would meet, or at least accommodate, the expectations of parties from different sides of the common/civil law divide.

12.194 In the context of legal impediment or privilege, differences in expectation are illustrated by the example given at 12.141 of a dispute between a French company and an English company. What are the expectations of the parties with respect to communications with in-house lawyers? Under French law, such communications do not attract legal advice privilege, while under the laws of England, they do. Ignoring the considerations expressed in Article 9.3(e), and looking at these circumstances exclusively from the perspective of the parties' expectation, it might be said that the French party expects to have to produce communications with its in-house lawyer, while the English party does not.

iii. Expectations regarding the law of the seat of arbitration

12.195 Although application of the law of the seat of arbitration might be considered to fall within the reasonable expectations of the parties, there is a considerable body of opinion opposed to this idea. For example, it is said that there is often no obvious or conclusive link between the rules of the seat and the communications or documents over which

[172] A substantive legitimate expectation arises where an authority makes a lawful representation that an individual will receive or continue to receive some kind of substantive benefit.

[173] Restatement (Second) of Conflict of Laws (Am Law Instit), s 6(2)(d).

[174] ibid, comment on s 6(2), para (g).

[175] For discussion, see Möckesch (n 104) para 8.190.

[176] ibid para 1.12.

privilege is claimed, and that application of the rules of the seat cannot therefore be consistent with the expectations of the parties.[177] Möckesch expresses the position that:

> [T]he application of the national privilege rules of the seat of arbitration is presumably inconsistent with the legitimate expectations of the parties. The parties and their counsel most likely do not have the privilege rules of the seat of arbitration in mind when communicating with each other. Moreover, the parties are free to agree on any seat. Therefore, the seat of arbitration may have no connection to the parties, their counsel or the dispute. In fact, the seat of arbitration is regularly chosen due to its neutrality in relation to the parties, convenience, the seat's mandatory rules, and the provisions for setting aside an award. The parties most likely do not consider the privilege rules of the seat of arbitration when selecting it.[178]

Others concur in this view.[179] The point has also been made that a party is unlikely in practice to adjust its behaviour in connection with lawyer/client communications based on an expectation that it might at some later date become a party to this or that arbitration or litigation.[180] **12.196**

In our view, it may be possible to draw a distinction between situations where the seat of arbitration is selected by the parties, and circumstances in which the seat is determined by the tribunal or arbitral institution[181] or pursuant to a default provision in institutional rules.[182] While it may be correct that, in the latter cases, parties could not reasonably expect the law of the seat to apply to issues of privilege (or at least not in relation to communications/documents generated prior to determination of the seat), in the former case we do not see why, as a matter of principle, a party could not have an expectation to that effect when concluding an arbitration agreement with an express choice of seat. **12.197**

iv. Weighing considerations of party expectations under Article 9.3(c)

Other than the temporal restriction mentioned at 12.188, Article 9.3(c) does not qualify the nature of the expectations that a tribunal may take into consideration. However, even without such qualification, it would (in our view) be inappropriate for the tribunal to protect any illegitimate or unreasonable expectation any party may have had. For example, other than on the basis of an agreement or representation, if a corporate party expected that its opponent party would not seek production of internal communications **12.198**

[177] See 12.114.

[178] See Möckesch (n 104) para 8.118.

[179] Fabian von Schlabrendorff and Audley Sheppard, 'Conflict of Legal Privileges in International Arbitration: An Attempt to Find a Holistic Solution' in Gerald Aksen and Robert Briner (eds), *Global Reflections on International Law, Commerce and Dispute Resolution: Liber Amicorum in Honour of Robert Briner* (International Chamber of Commerce 2005) 769.

[180] For discussion, see Möckesch (n 104) para 8.190.

[181] For example, see ICC Rules, Article 18.1 pursuant to which the seat of arbitration is fixed by the ICC court in the absence of agreement between the parties.

[182] For an example of a default position expressed in institutional rules, see LCIA Rules, Article 16.2, which provides that, in the absence of agreement between the parties, the seat of arbitration shall be London.

held by that corporate party, it is unlikely that the tribunal would place any weight on that expectation because there was no reasonable basis for the expectation to arise.

12.199 In the context of privilege, there exists a strong case that consideration of a party's expectations must encompass a recognition of the desirability of ensuring that the protection afforded to 'privileged' documents should generally not be a lower level of protection than a party enjoys under its local laws. However, the tribunal will then need to consider the interaction between Article 9.3(c) and the need to maintain fairness and equality as contemplated by Article 9.3(e).

12.200 As mentioned, it has been suggested that application of the 'most-favoured nation' approach will ensure that party expectations are met (even if the protection afforded to one party is greater than anticipated), as well as preserving equality between the parties. In the example given earlier concerning French and English parties, if the tribunal were to apply English law to both parties and thus extend the legal advice privilege communications between the French party and its in-house counsel, this would be squarely within the expectations of the English party and would exceed (rather than frustrate) the expectations of the French party. Conversely, if the tribunal were to apply French law and order production of the correspondence between the parties and their respective in-house counsel, that would be inconsistent with the expectations of the English party, as well as with Article 9.3(e).[183] However, there is no hard rule requiring a tribunal to grant a party protection beyond that available under the law determined to be applicable to the privilege.

12.201 It may not always be an easy task to balance party expectations. If a party is forced to disclose documents that at the time of their preparation were reasonably considered to be privileged in their home jurisdiction, that party may well feel that it has been treated unfairly. On the other hand, parties whose requests for document production are denied because a generous basis of privilege has been applied may argue that they have been denied access to essential evidence to prove their case.[184] In both instances, the parties may try to attack the award on the grounds of serious irregularity or a breach of due process, leading to delay and additional costs even if the claims are ultimately found to have no merit.

d. Waiver of privilege or legal impediment

9.3(d) any possible waiver of any applicable legal impediment or privilege by virtue of consent, earlier disclosure, affirmative use of the Document, statement, oral communication or advice contained therein, or otherwise.

[183] Support for application of the 'most-favoured nation' approach can be found in *ICDR Guidelines for Arbitrators Concerning Exchanges of Information* (International Centre for Dispute Resolution 2008) Guideline 7.

[184] See, eg Guido Santiago Tawil and Ignacio J Mirorini Lima, 'Chapter 2. Privilege-Related Issues in International Arbitration' in Teresa Giovannini and Alexis Mourre (eds), *Written Evidence and Discovery in International Arbitration: New Issues and Tendencies* (Kluwer Law International 2009) 37.

Article 9.3(d) invites the tribunal to consider whether the legal impediment or privilege that is relied on has been waived. The Commentary to the IBA Rules indicates that this express reference to waiver encapsulates an important exception to the existence of privilege common to many jurisdictions. 12.202

i. Introduction

The precise manner in which a privilege may be lost will vary considerably according to the nature of the privilege and the applicable rules that operate on it. Therefore, it would be difficult to draft a provision including express reference to all of the possibilities. 12.203

For example, the nature of the privilege under its applicable law may affect the basis on which it can be lost—in particular, who may waive the privilege. Under English law, legal advice privilege belongs to the client and may be waived by the client.[185] In contrast, in some civil law jurisdictions the protection afforded by the relevant privilege may be both a right and a duty that is not so easily waived. For example, in Germany only the lawyer has an explicit right to refuse to testify or to produce documents, the scope of the privilege being tied to the lawyer's obligation of professional secrecy and ethical rules.[186] As a result, documents in the hands of the client are not expressly protected by the privilege, but the court may take into account the interest of the party in the confidentiality of communications with its lawyer when exercising its discretion in relation to use of the documents.[187] 12.204

It should also be borne in mind that in some cases, an apparent waiver by one party to the communications may leave unaffected a mandatory prohibition against disclosure supported by penal sanctions in the event of a breach of the prohibition. In some circumstances this may give rise to a separate legal impediment for the purposes of Article 9.2(b). As Klamas expressed it by reference to civil law practice: 12.205

> As opposed to most common law systems, under civil law privilege is not considered to be an individual right that could be waived by the parties under party autonomy. It is both a right and a duty. Also, one may argue that the penal rules that protect it are mandatory rules based on public order. So, it becomes questionable whether a tribunal would have the power to (or should) order the disclosure of privileged information in disregard of such mandatory rules of protection.[188]

No doubt in recognition of the difficulty of identifying and expressing all possibilities, Article 9.3(d) contains a non-exhaustive list of actions which may constitute a waiver—namely, 'consent', 'earlier disclosure', or 'affirmative use' of the privileged material—as 12.206

[185] See, for example, the comments of Mr Justice Blackburne in *Nationwide Building Society v Various Solicitors* that: '... whether or not the client has any recognisable interest in continuing to assert privilege in the confidential communications, the privilege is absolute in nature and the lawyer's mouth is "shut for ever"'. *Nationwide Building Society v Various Solicitors* [1999] PNLR 52 [69].

[186] See Möckesch (n 104) para 1.03.

[187] German Code of Civil Procedure, s 142(1). See also Möckesch (n 104) para 6.05.

[188] Klamas (n 117) 164.

well as a catch-all description 'or otherwise'. It can be seen from these descriptions that some effort has been made to capture the substance of laws and practice relating to waiver of privilege from a number of jurisdictions. As a result, it is not surprising that there may exist some overlap of concepts. For example, in some instances, the voluntary prior disclosure of a privileged document may be treated as carrying the consent of the disclosing party to waive privilege. The important question is whether any one of the described grounds of waiver can be identified.

12.207 There are a number of other factors that may need to be considered, but in general, the tribunal will have to establish whether a party asserting privilege or legal impediment has behaved in a way inconsistent with the (normally confidential) nature of the privilege, or whether that privilege remains in place. Subject to mandatory provisions of applicable law, it appears that Article 9.3(d) invites the tribunal to consider events that may give rise to 'any possible' waiver of privilege, even if the law otherwise applicable to the privilege does not recognize those events as a waiver, or treats the consequences of them differently.

12.208 We discuss further, by reference to the different labels listed at Article 9.3(d), some instances of how a waiver may occur in practice, and how such events have been treated at a national level in jurisdictions where the waiver of privilege is a recognized and developed concept.

ii. Waiver by consent

12.209 Consent may manifest itself in various forms but, in the majority of cases, it arises by reason of a voluntary waiver by which the client, or the client's lawyer, makes a deliberate choice to waive privilege over a document or other evidence.[189]

12.210 A client may decide to consent to waiver of privilege for various reasons, eg if s/he has obtained independent legal advice and wants this advice to be made known to the other party in order to persuade it to reconsider its position or admit the claim. By disclosing the advice, the client is consenting to the waiver of privilege that might have otherwise attached to it.

12.211 A common issue associated with an express waiver of privilege in relation to materials to be admitted to the record in an arbitration is the question of how far the consent extends. Where privilege is waived voluntarily over a document, it is necessary to bear in mind the 'collateral waiver' rule. The effect of this rule is that, when a party waives privilege in a document because it wants to use it in evidence, it may be taken to have waived privilege in relation to the whole of the material relevant to the issue in question. If this were not the case, the court or tribunal might otherwise be presented with a misleading picture of the material.[190] As a result, even if the consent was only directed towards

[189] A solicitor in England has implied authority to waive privilege. See *Great Atlantic Insurance Company v Home Insurance Company* [1981] 1 WLR 529.

[190] Under English law, defining the 'issue in question' is a matter of fact in each case that falls to be determined by reference to the purpose for which the disclosure of privileged material was made. See the discussion in *Fulham*

disclosing a confidential legal opinion or another privileged document, depending on the rules applied, consent may be deemed to have extended to all collateral materials in relation to that opinion/document. For example, all correspondence with the lawyer for the purposes of obtaining the legal opinion may be found to fall within the waiver by consent.

In the United States, a failure to object to a request for disclosure may constitute an implied waiver of privilege, even where the right to claim privilege may have existed.[191] **12.212**

iii. Earlier disclosure

Privilege may be waived by an earlier disclosure of the relevant document or other evidence to the opponent party, whether such disclosure is made by the client or the client's lawyer (provided the lawyer had the necessary authority to waive the privilege). Once disclosure has been given, the general rule is that it cannot be reclaimed at a later date. **12.213**

Issues may arise around inadvertent or involuntary disclosure of privileged material. For example, in the United States, there is no waiver if the confidential communication is involuntarily disclosed—for example, if the opponent party steals a document or breaches reasonable protections put in place in order to eavesdrop on communications with the lawyer.[192] **12.214**

In Germany, in some circumstances, even involuntary disclosure of privileged documents can result in a loss of privilege. Documents that were lost or stolen can still be admitted into the record. Furthermore, if a lawyer consciously or subconsciously breaches the duty of professional secrecy by testifying in relation to protected matters, that testimony is nevertheless considered admissible evidence.[193] **12.215**

Ashford suggests that the following five factors may assist in deciding how to deal with an inadvertent disclosure: **12.216**

(i) The reasonableness of the precautions taken to prevent inadvertent disclosure in view of the extent of the document production;
(ii) The number of inadvertent disclosures;
(iii) The extent of the disclosure;
(iv) Any delay and measures taken to rectify the disclosure; and
(v) Whether the overriding interests of justice would or would not be served by relieving the party of its error.[194]

Leisure Holdings Ltd v Nicholson Graham & Jones [2006] EWHC 158 (Ch) on how to identify the issue in question. The principle behind the collateral waiver rule is described in *Brennan v Sunderland City Council* [2008] 12 WLUK 468; [2009] ICR 479 [63].

191 For more detail, see Möckesch (n 104) para 2.71.
192 ibid para 2.72.
193 For more detail, see ibid paras 4.79–4.81.
194 Ashford (n 127) paras 9–47.

12.217 Under English law, where a disclosed document has been redacted in order to conceal the parts of the document that are privileged, this will not amount to a waiver of privilege.[195] However, if the redactions result in the remaining content of the document that has been disclosed being read in a misleading way, arguments that the 'collateral waiver' rule[196] applies may be engaged.

12.218 It may also be necessary to consider whether the waiver of privilege can be limited to a particular party to whom a party has given earlier disclosure. This issue is illustrated by the facts of the English case of *Gotha City*[197] where Sotheby's was in possession of some legal advice that had been given to it by a co-defendant. The lower court had made a disclosure order against its co-defendant, on the grounds that sharing the advice with Sotheby's had amounted to a waiver of privilege over the legal advice as against the whole world. The English Court of Appeal, however, disagreed, finding that the key issue was whether the advice was disclosed to Sotheby's in confidence. If it was, then privilege had been waived as against Sotheby's, but not as against the whole world.[198] Thus, in some jurisdictions, and in some circumstances, it may be possible to disclose a privileged document, or an extract or paraphrase of a privileged document, to a third party without waiving privilege as against other parties.[199] However, this may not be the case everywhere.

12.219 In each case, a tribunal may have to consider whether a waiver has occurred under the applicable regime, what mandatory requirements of that regime may apply, and the other considerations contained in Article 9.3.

iv. Affirmative use of the document/statement/oral communication or advice contained therein

12.220 Another possible instance of waiver identified in Article 9.3(d) is 'affirmative use' of a privileged document, statement, oral communication, or advice contained in any of those things. Affirmative use is not defined, but it is likely to be interpreted as positive reliance on the evidence, or use of it in such a way that there is no doubt about the intention to rely on it.

[195] See speech of Lord Justice Hoffman in *GE Capital Corporate Finance Group v Bankers Trust Co* [1995] 1 WLR 172, 176 where he quoted Mr Justice Savile in *The Good Luck* [1988] 10 WLUK 197 saying 'disclosure of the unprivileged part of a document was not a waiver of privilege for the rest, even though both dealt with the same subject matter'.

[196] See Möckesch (n 104) para 6.29, who explains: 'Neither US nor English law allows for partial disclosure if it is misleading. In a similar vein, if the client waives the privilege with respect to a document, the waiver extends to other documents that concern the same subject matter. Partial as well subject-matter waiver are guided by considerations of fairness'.

[197] *Gotha City v Sotheby's (No.1)* [1998] 1 WLR 114.

[198] It is worth noting that in this case, the disclosure to Sotheby's had not been made on an expressly confidential basis, but the court nevertheless found that the circumstances of the case were such that 'in the ordinary way, one would expect confidentiality to be assumed by all present rather than expressly agreed upon' and that there was a 'plain inference that those communications were intended to be confidential'.

[199] In this situation, the party making the disclosure would do well to make it clear that privilege is *not* being waived.

An obvious example of affirmative use is where a document or other evidence is expressly referenced and relied upon by a party in submissions or witness/expert evidence. Such reliance may be found to be inconsistent with an assertion of privilege. In addition, there may be instances where an act or event of waiver falling under one of the other headings described in Article 9.3(d) may also be regarded as affirmative use, eg a voluntary prior disclosure of a document in connection with the proceedings. 12.221

Some other, less-obvious circumstances that may give rise to an argument of affirmative use include making reference to a privileged communication during discussions with an opponent party. Article 9.3(d) makes explicit reference to a 'statement' and 'oral communication'. In this respect, the English courts draw a sensible distinction between a reference in oral communication to the fact or effect of legal advice received (which is unlikely to result in a waiver of privilege) and a reference to the actual advice tendered, which may do so.[200] 12.222

Another possible circumstance is where a party makes reference to a privileged document/communication in evidence (for example, during cross-examination). Legal privilege may have been asserted in relation to correspondence between one of the parties and their legal advisers on a matter in issue between the parties. The privilege may have been upheld and the relevant documents excluded from production. However, the party who requested the correspondence may try to trespass on that privilege by asking questions about the correspondence during cross-examination of one of the witnesses and the witness may respond in positive terms. If the reference is to a document, there is a risk that privilege in that document may be irretrievably waived by that responding witness. 12.223

v. Otherwise

Article 9.3(d) describes three instances in which privilege may have been waived (consent, earlier disclosure, and affirmative use), but the list is not exhaustive. Article 9.3(d) also refers to waiver having occurred 'otherwise' than in the instances described. It goes without saying that 'otherwise' is very broad and will encompass all instances where a waiver can be established. In each case, the tribunal will have to consider the arguments and evidence put forward on the point. 12.224

The circumstances that may fall under the 'otherwise' umbrella are likely to be varied and case specific. For example, in Germany a client may impliedly waive privilege by nominating his lawyer as a witness.[201] If the lawyer reveals the content of legal advice, it may be said that the waiver is lost because of the affirmative use of the advice. However, it appears that a mere nomination of the lawyer, even in the absence of the affirmative use, may amount to a waiver. 12.225

[200] For more detail, see Passmore (n 139) para 7-204 et seq. See also 12.149– 12.150.
[201] Möckesch (n 104) para 4.77.

12.226 The 'otherwise' category may also capture circumstances in which the material covered by privilege has ceased to be confidential.[202] For example, this may happen if a party has made reference to privileged legal advice in a non-confidential application to a public authority, or where documents have come into the public domain through carelessness on the part of the party to whom the privilege attaches. If the loss of confidentiality has been involuntary, it cannot be regarded as consent. The documents were not introduced as evidence by way of affirmative use and the 'earlier disclosure' ground might not be applicable to inadvertent release of the documents into the public domain. The loss of confidentiality has nonetheless occurred as a result of conduct by the party who might otherwise have been able to claim privilege.

12.227 More complex questions may arise where loss of confidentiality is not the result of action by the party to whom the privilege attaches. Privileged documents may have been hacked or stolen and then released into the public domain. There will have been a loss of confidentiality, but the cause of this will not be conduct or 'waiver' on the part of the party holding the privilege.[203]

e. Need to maintain fairness and equality between the parties

9.3(e) the need to maintain fairness and equality as between the Parties, particularly if they are subject to different legal or ethical rules.

12.228 Article 9.3(e) is the last (but nonetheless very important) factor that the tribunal is invited to consider in relation to issues of legal impediment and privilege. It refers expressly to the need to treat the parties with fairness and equality. As highlighted elsewhere, tribunals are in nearly all cases bound to observe these principles, whether pursuant to provisions of applicable national arbitration law, institutional rules, and/or Preamble 1 of the IBA Rules.[204]

i. Introduction

12.229 The Commentary to the IBA Rules explains that the need to safeguard fairness and equality between the parties may arise when the approach to privilege existing in the disputing parties' home jurisdictions differ. This issue has already been discussed at 12.187-12.201 in relation to considerations of party expectations under Article 9.3(c), and the differences in approach to privilege that exist between jurisdictions has also been illustrated in discussion of the other considerations listed in Article 9.3.[205]

12.230 As explained in the Commentary on the IBA Rules, applying different rules to individual parties to arbitration could create unfairness by shielding the documents of one

[202] Confidentiality is at the heart of most forms of privilege. See, eg 12.89.
[203] See 12.27–12.30.
[204] See Chapter 2 paras 2.7–2.24.
[205] See 12.145–12.162.

party from production but not those of another party. For example, in the example given at 12.141 of a dispute between French and English companies, ordering production of correspondence between the French party and its in-house counsel, but not ordering production of the equivalent correspondence from the English party, is likely to lead to an inequality of access to evidence.

Tribunals are generally reluctant to subject the parties to different treatment. It may create an inequality in access to evidence and for that reason be unfair to the party subject to the less restrictive privilege regime. 12.231

ii. Fair and equal treatment

One obvious approach to avoiding such a situation is to apply the same set of rules to all parties. The chosen rules could be the least favourable rules applicable to any of the parties, or the most favourable, or another set of rules altogether. The 'most-favoured nation', 'least-favoured nation', and the 'autonomous' approaches are discussed at 12.102-12.124. 12.232

Application of the 'most-favoured' approach meets the parties' expectations and provides the necessary level of parity between them. There is evidence of support for this approach in tribunal practice. For example, in one unpublished ICC decision, the tribunal indicated that international arbitration practice was to apply to all parties only the privilege law that awards the broadest protection to privileged information so as to maintain fairness and equality between the parties.[206] 12.233

Of course, if one party has already produced documents not subject to privilege in its home jurisdiction, but which are privileged under the laws of the adverse party, then it might be thought fair to order the other party to produce the same category of documents in order to offset the imbalance that would otherwise arise.[207] 12.234

Another factor to be borne in mind is that application of the law giving the highest level of privilege protection will not always mean application of a single national law. For example, the national law of one party may provide greater protection in relation to a certain category of material (eg correspondence with in-house counsel), but the national law of the other party may offer broader protections with respect to other matters (eg waiver). If the most-favoured nation approach were to be applied uniformly, the applicable national rule might vary depending on the issue at stake.[208] While this may be correct as a matter of principle, in our view, it will necessarily add an additional layer of complexity. If circumstances warrant this approach, it would be sensible for the various rules decided upon to be noted for the record in case of future issues of privilege arising in the case. 12.235

[206] For more detail, see Möckesch (n 104) paras 8.110, 8.144, and 8.200.

[207] See *Poštová banka, a.s. and ISTROKAPITAL SE v Hellenic Republic* (Procedural Order No. 6, 20 July 2014) ICSID Case No. ARB/13/8 [16].

[208] Möckesch (n 104) para 8.197.

f. Assessment of whether privilege exists

12.236 Assessment of whether privilege attaches to any type of evidence is, in the first instance, a matter for counsel representing the producing party. Counsel will also generally draft the objections to a request for documents in which a claim to privilege is asserted.

12.237 A party relying on legal impediment or privilege by way of response to a document production request delivered under Article 3.2 of the IBA Rules will have to explain the nature of the privilege relied on and why it attaches to the particular documents requested. If the requesting party has doubts about the veracity or reliability of the statements made then it should be permitted to raise them.[209]

12.238 Tribunals will sometimes order parties to produce what is called a 'privilege log'—a document containing sufficient details of each and every document the parties are withholding on grounds of privilege so that the opponent party and the tribunal are able to understand why privilege is said to apply. For example, the log may record the date of a communication, the sender, and recipient, and the reason for asserting privilege (eg 'contains legal advice').

12.239 Although the level of detail contained in a privilege log is not always sufficient to enable the other party to reach a firm conclusion on whether or not the relevant documents contain privileged material, in some cases it may do so. For example, the date of the document may show that it came into existence at a time when the dispute was not in contemplation and that the claim of litigation privilege may be incorrect, or an email may be shown as having been circulated to a third party, thereby potentially waiving the privilege.

12.240 However, the use of privilege logs is not without problems, nor are they universally employed by tribunals. For example, there is some evidence to suggest that the use of privilege logs in ICC arbitration has, in the past, generally only occurred where a party has requested it.[210] A disadvantage of the privilege log is that it can be very time-consuming and costly to prepare. In addition, to be of value to the receiving party in relation to its assessment of the claim to privilege, the withholding party may have to disclose so much detail that the confidential information sought to be protected is revealed to a greater or lesser extent. For example, even the names of the lawyers with whom correspondence has taken place may provide information as to a particular course of action or area of expertise in which advice has been sought.

[209] By way of example, in one ICSID case, the tribunal asked the party alleging privilege to justify document-by-document the reasons why they should remain protected. The other party then had an opportunity to ask for additional explanation. Having considered the objections and responses, the tribunal issued its decision. See *Glamis Gold, Ltd. v The United States of America* (Decision on Parties' Request for Production of Documents Withheld on Grounds of Privilege, 17 November 2005) NAFTA.

[210] Hamilton (n 134) 77.

It is clearly not appropriate for a copy of the document over which privilege is claimed to be provided to the other party in advance of a dispute as to its privileged status being resolved. If the tribunal believes that it needs to review the document before making a decision on a disputed claim of privilege, then it may do so.[211] However, as the Commentary on the IBA Rules makes clear,[212] such review is generally undesirable because the document may contain information that, once seen by the tribunal, cannot be unseen, and which may taint the tribunal's view of the case.[213] It may also constitute an improper delegation of the tribunal's powers. **12.241**

F. Unreasonable Burden to Produce

9.2 (c) unreasonable burden to produce the requested evidence

Article 9.2(c) permits the exclusion from evidence or production of material that it would be an unreasonable burden to produce. The 1999 IBA Rules contained an identical provision. **12.242**

1. Introduction

The concept of unreasonable burden is mentioned three times in the IBA Rules. The first is in Article 3.3(c)(i), which allows a requesting party to seek production of a document that it already has in its possession, custody, or control where it would be 'unreasonably burdensome' for the requesting party to produce it.[214] The second is Article 8.2, which gives the tribunal power to limit or exclude any question to, or answer or appearance by, a witness at an evidentiary hearing where such question, answer, or appearance is unreasonably burdensome.[215] The third reference appears in Article 9.2(c), and is discussed below. **12.243**

Article 9.2 allows the tribunal to exclude material from evidence or production. However, Article 9.2(c) refers expressly to an 'unreasonable burden *to produce*'.[216] This raises the question of whether this ground of objection is intended to be available only by way of response to a request for production made by another party under Article 3.2 of the IBA Rules, and is not to be relied upon in support of a request to/decision by the tribunal to exclude documents or other evidence from the record. **12.244**

211 IBA Rules, Article 3.8.
212 Commentary on the IBA Rules (n 64) 10–11 states that 'It is generally preferable that the arbitral tribunal not review any . . . documents itself because (i) if after reviewing the document the arbitral tribunal upholds the objection, it could not eliminate its knowledge of the document . . . '.
213 See Chapter 6 paras 6.266–6.279.
214 See ibid paras 6.156–6.159.
215 See Chapter 11 paras 11.32–11.34.
216 Emphasis added.

12.245 It is certainly the case that the examples for application of Article 9.2(c) described in the Commentary to the IBA Rules refer only to situations involving document production.[217]

12.246 However, the Commentary also states that 'Article 9.2(c) permits the arbitral tribunal *to exclude* from production or *from evidence any documents or evidence* which would be an unreasonable burden to produce',[218] thereby indicating that the provision has a wider application than document production. This makes sense. Many of the considerations discussed below have the potential to apply equally to documents and other evidence introduced pursuant to other provisions of the rules as they do to production of documents pursuant to the provisions of Articles 3.2–3.8 of the IBA Rules.[219]

12.247 For example, under Article 4.10 of the IBA Rules, a tribunal is permitted to ask a party to make arrangements for the appearance of a witness identified by the tribunal. In some cases, it may be extremely burdensome for the party to have to approach the witness and make those arrangements. The circumstances in which such a situation may arise will be fact specific. However, for example, in a dispute relating to the performance of a power plant, the project manager responsible for managing the site on behalf of the employer may have left the employer company and moved on to another project in a remote location. If the project manager's evidence on a particular point becomes relevant in a dispute between the employer and a third party responsible for commissioning the plant, the employer may have to first trace the former employee, then persuade him to testify, negotiate an appropriate leave of absence from his present employer, and support applications for a visa and travel, etc. Much may depend on the perceived relative value of the evidence sought, but a tribunal might be persuaded that these steps are unreasonably burdensome.

12.248 Such examples aside, it is undoubtedly true that an objection of 'unreasonable burden' comes most into play in the management of document production in international arbitration. If a tribunal is satisfied that it would be unreasonably burdensome for a party to produce a particular document or (more likely) one or more categories of document, the tribunal will be entitled to dismiss a document production request for those documents. Given the volume of electronic documents potentially in play in most arbitrations it is right that some consideration of the burden of production, whether in time or costs (or both), should be taken into account.

12.249 Where relied upon in other circumstances, the claim of unreasonable burden is most likely to be engaged in advance of the evidence in question being introduced

[217] Commentary on the IBA Rules (n 64) 26.
[218] Emphasis added.
[219] A number of provisions in IBA Rules (n 3) make express reference to Article 9.2. For example, Article 8.4 states expressly that a party to whom such a request is addressed may object for 'any of the reasons set forth in Article 9.2'. Similar considerations arise in relation to other provisions of the IBA Rules (n 3). See IBA Rules (n 3) Articles 3.5, 3.7, 3.9, 3.10, 4.10, 6.3, 7, 8.2, and 8.5.

on to the record. If the evidence is already available, the burden of maintaining that evidence on the record is likely to be negligible or non-existent. That said, there may be some circumstances where, in cases of disagreement between the parties, the operation of this provision may be useful. For example, if one party is insisting that a large volume of documents, introduced into evidence, but which has later become redundant because of changes in case, be included in the hearing bundles at considerable cost, the other party might wish to rely on Article 9.2 to have the material excluded.[220]

No guidance is given as to how a tribunal should decide whether the action necessary to provide the evidence is reasonable action to be expected of a party, or if it presents an unreasonable burden. This gives the tribunal considerable flexibility as to how to interpret the provision, and whether the relevant standard has been met on the facts of a particular case. This flexibility is intentional. As stated in the Commentary on the IBA Rules: 'This unreasonable burden can take many forms, and the nature of the burden is purposely left to the discretion of the arbitral tribunal'. **12.250**

To make out an objection of 'unreasonable burden', we suggest that something additional to the ordinary burden of conducting proceedings that is specific to the facts of the case should generally be established. This may include objections based on serious practical difficulties in providing a witness, or making available for inspection a site or other property or materials. A party wishing to raise an objection should explain as fully as possible why provision of the document or other evidence is unreasonably burdensome to them and, if possible, why that burden is out of the ordinary. **12.251**

Document production is inevitably a time-consuming and costly exercise. In large commercial disputes, it may involve interrogation of thousands, sometimes hundreds of thousands, of electronic documents. Even with the assistance of data review software, the burden of undertaking this exercise can be considerable. The Commentary on the IBA Rules notes that even where a request for documents properly identifies why the requested documents are relevant and material this may not be sufficient to warrant an order for production where 'their sheer quantity creates an unreasonable burden on the receiving party to produce'. Of course, the sheer volume of the documents and/or the costs involved, cannot be decisive factors or there would be very limited production given in a large number of cases. In this vein, it has been reported that one ICC tribunal pointed out to the parties involved that the costs incurred by a party in complying with a request for the production of documents is a reimbursable arbitration cost and that it is open to the parties to claim such costs with supporting evidence at the end of the proceedings.[221] **12.252**

[220] Of course, in these circumstances, the party wishing to exclude the material could also rely on IBA Rules (n 3) Article 9.2(a): *lack of sufficient relevance to the case or materiality to its outcome.*

[221] Hamilton (n 134) 74.

12.253 In assessing whether a particular proposed step is unreasonably burdensome, a tribunal may consider the proportionality of the request. This is a separate ground of objection under Article 9.2(g) and is discussed in more detail at 12.308-12.316. However, it is suggested that an assessment of whether a particular step is unreasonably burdensome must involve considerations of proportionality. Thus, in addition to assessing arguments on the time, cost, or other difficulty associated with provision of the particular documents or other evidence under discussion, the tribunal may wish to consider whether the alleged burden is (or is not) disproportionate to the likely evidential value of the requested evidence and/or the value of the dispute.

2. Practical Examples

12.254 This section provides examples of decisions by tribunals following an argument raised by one of the parties that production would be unreasonably burdensome.

12.255 In one case, the documents requested by the claimant had already been collated and analysed by the respondent when preparing its own evidence. In these circumstances the tribunal was not persuaded by the respondent's argument that the burden of producing them was too great.[222]

12.256 In another case, the arbitral tribunal considered as unduly burdensome a request for documents that should already have been in the requesting party's possession. There was therefore no reason to compel the other party to engage in a broad search of its files for those documents.[223]

12.257 In an unreported LCIA case, a sole arbitrator expressed the view that it would be unreasonably burdensome to require the claimant to search email inboxes of all of its employees. In that case, the claimant was a large bank with over 30 offices in different jurisdictions and having around 30,000 employees.

G. Loss or Destruction of the Documents

9.2(d) loss or destruction of the Document that has been shown with reasonable likelihood to have occurred.

12.258 Article 9.2(d) permits the exclusion of a document from evidence or production on the grounds that it has been lost or destroyed. The 1999 IBA Rules contained an identical provision. 'Document' is widely defined in the IBA Rules.

[222] ibid 73.
[223] ibid.

1. Introduction

Unlike other provisions of Article 9.2, Article 9.2(d) refers expressly to a 'Document', thus limiting the application of this provision to that category of evidence. The reference to 'Document' makes sense as it has a physical existence and may be lost or destroyed in a way that eg witness evidence yet to be given cannot be. 12.259

The 1999 IBA Rules provided that loss or destruction should be 'reasonably shown to have occurred'. The current IBA Rules mention loss or destruction that has been shown 'with reasonable likelihood to have occurred'. It appears to have been recognized that the provision was imprecisely phrased and that a more specific wording of the 1999 IBA Rules was desirable. 12.260

Article 9.2(d) appears to be relatively straightforward. In practice, there may be a number of considerations that require attention. 12.261

2. Reasonable Likelihood of Loss/Destruction

Article 9.2(d) does not require incontestable evidence that a document has been lost or destroyed. Rather, it sets a benchmark. A party is required to show that it is 'reasonably likely' that the document is no longer available. 12.262

For example, if a party demonstrates that a document was sent three months ago to a company specializing in paper shredding and document destruction, and that such company normally destroys the documents received within one or two weeks, this may satisfy the benchmark in Article 9.2(d). In fact, the document may still await its fate at the storage premises of the shredding company, but the tribunal might well conclude that it is inappropriate to order that the party should try to find that document. 12.263

A frequent starting point for the raising of an objection under Article 9.2(d) is the document retention policy of a relevant party. If a party has a document retention policy that requires it to destroy a particular type of document after, say, three years, and that period expired before the commencement of arbitration, the tribunal may accept that it can reasonably be inferred that the document is likely to have been destroyed. 12.264

The position is rarely as clear cut with regard to documents that are said to have been lost. A tribunal is unlikely to accept a bare assertion that a document has disappeared. The party seeking to rely on this ground may want to produce evidence confirming that a reasonable search has been undertaken in the files/locations where the document is likely to have been stored or archived, but that the document cannot be found. If the party knows how the document has been lost—for example, because it was taken by an employee who has moved to a foreign jurisdiction with no forwarding address—then an explanation of those events should be included. 12.265

12.266 In some cases, the requesting party may demand an affidavit or witness statement confirming that proper searches have been carried out to find the document. If the tribunal has concerns about what it is being told it may be prepared to order this.

3. Loss or Destruction of Documents during the Arbitration

12.267 Additional considerations may arise when the document is said to have been lost or destroyed after the arbitration was commenced.

12.268 Many jurisdictions impose an obligation on locally qualified lawyers to advise their client, on commencement of a litigation or arbitration, that they should preserve potentially relevant and disclosable documents.[224] Although not universal, this practice has been incorporated into the IBA Guidelines on Party Representation in International Arbitration:

> When the arbitral proceedings involve or are likely to involve Document production, a Party Representative should inform the client of the need to preserve, so far as reasonably possible, Documents, including electronic Documents that would otherwise be deleted in accordance with a Document retention policy or in the ordinary course of business, which are potentially relevant to the arbitration.[225]

12.269 Upon receipt of such advice a party is expected to take steps to ensure that potentially relevant documents are identified and ring-fenced in such a way that they are not destroyed and that any routine document destruction policies are suspended. Deliberate destruction of evidence is sometimes referred to as spoliation of evidence.

12.270 If it is demonstrated that a party has destroyed potentially relevant documents after the arbitration has commenced, a tribunal may be asked to draw adverse inferences as to the reasons for the destruction, ie it may be asked to conclude that the content of the documents was adverse to the interests of the destroying party in relation to the subject matter that it addressed.[226] It is debatable as to whether a document that no longer exists could fall within the provisions of Article 9.5 of the IBA Rules[227] but, even if it does not, a tribunal may feel it is justified in drawing an adverse inference pursuant to its general powers in relation to the assessment of evidence. If satisfied that the

[224] Examples include England and Wales, Australia, and the United States.

[225] *IBA Guidelines on Party Representation in International Arbitration* (International Bar Association 2013) Guideline 12.

[226] For more detail about the appropriate test for drawing adverse inferences, see Jeremy K Sharpe, 'Drawing Adverse Inferences from Non-Production of Evidence' (2006) Arbitration International 549, 558 (hereafter 'Sharpe').

[227] Article 9.5 makes express provision for the drawing of adverse inferences in cases of non-production of a document.

document was destroyed deliberately in order to prevent it having to be produced, the tribunal might also impose a cost sanction under Article 9.7 on the basis that the party responsible for destroying the document has failed to conduct itself in good faith in the taking of evidence, as required by Preamble 3 to the IBA Rules.[228] Before taking such a step, the tribunal may wish to be satisfied that the appropriate warning about preservation of evidence was given to the party.

4. Destruction of Electronic Records

The loss of electronic files can occur through various events. One possibility is the destruction of data by computer viruses or other malware. Another possibility is a loss of hardware containing relevant files. In the latter case, the loss should only be relied upon if there are no other available copies of the documents on other hardware. **12.271**

Destruction of electronic files is another phenomenon. In recent years, the volume of electronic documents has grown exponentially. In an organization with thousands of employees, the number of documents held may grow by hundreds of thousands every week. As a result, large organizations often require off-site storage for archived material. However, even with this facility, an organization may need to have destruction policies in place to enable data and cost management. Many organizations have introduced email retention policies that provide for the mandatory deletion of all emails after a certain period of time. Shorter email retention policies are cheaper to implement, but in some instances local laws require certain types of information to be retained for a longer minimum period of time. To comply with these requirements businesses may be required to keep the data on backup tapes. **12.272**

An issue that sometimes arises in relation to document production is whether a document that has been deleted but is still retrievable from a backup tape should be considered as 'destroyed'. Although backup tapes contain information, they are not normally easily searchable. Objection to production of such documents may be better made under Article 9.2(c) although it has been suggested that backup tapes, as well as electronic data that has been 'fragmented' or 'damaged', may fall within Article 9.2(d).[229] **12.273**

Clearly, there may be cases where, even taking account of issues of proportionality, a fair determination of the case requires that a party be asked to go through backup tapes to find a document or category of document. However, we suggest that such approach should be limited to cases in which the evidential value of the document sought is likely to be significant. **12.274**

[228] See Chapter 2 paras 2.43–2.99.
[229] Ashford (n 127) para 3-47.

H. Commercial or Technical Confidentiality

9.2(e) grounds of commercial or technical confidentiality that the Arbitral Tribunal determines to be compelling.

12.275 Under Article 9.2(e), the tribunal may *exclude* evidence, including by the rejection of a document production application, on compelling grounds of commercial or technical confidentiality. The attaching of *protections* to confidential information is dealt with at Article 9.4. It is up to the party invoking confidentiality as a ground for exclusion to prove its existence.[230]

1. Introduction

12.276 As a general rule, it is customary within international arbitration for consideration to be given to any legitimate need to keep sensitive business or technical information secret. Article 9.2(e) expressly reserves the right to object to production or introduction of evidence on this basis. A request for production of 'confidential' material should not be permitted to be used by one party to gain unwarranted insight into the business secrets of the other party.

12.277 The evidence requiring confidentiality can take many forms, but it is most likely to apply to confidential business records or models, technical formulae, know-how, trade secrets, and other forms of proprietary information or commercial know-how.

12.278 Determining what may be considered a compelling commercial or technical reason for denying or excluding evidence under Article 9.2(e) is largely a question of fact in each case.[231] The word 'compelling' is not defined in the IBA Rules, but it appears clear that circumstances justifying the complete exclusion of evidence will be the exception, rather than the rule.

12.279 There may be cases where the information requested is not relevant to the case or material to its outcome. In these cases, it should be possible for the requested party to resist production under Article 9.2(a), but it may additionally wish to rely on Article 9.2(e).

12.280 In considering an objection under Article 9.2(e) to deny a request for production or to exclude a piece of evidence from the record, a tribunal will have to consider whether the document or other evidence requires special consideration. This is what one commentator describes as '[t]he threshold question'. It is said that an Article 9.2(e) objection is a form of objection applicable to 'evidence which a party would

[230] See further Yves Derains, 'Evidence and Confidentiality' in *Special Supplement 2009: Confidentiality in Arbitration: Commentaries on Rules, Statutes, Case Law and Practice* (International Chamber of Commerce 2009) para 13 (hereafter 'Derains').

[231] O'Malley Rules of Evidence (n 76) para 9.83.

normally go to great lengths to keep from disclosure to business contacts or the public more generally'. One ICC tribunal denied a request for production on this basis because it regarded the relevant request as constituting an 'unacceptable invasion of [business] privacy'.[232] We agree that adoption of such a threshold test is a useful starting point.

The complete exclusion of evidence may be justified if the confidential information has a high economic value and its production is likely to cause significant damage to the party holding the document. However, much will depend on the attitude of the tribunal and the facts of the case. Examples given elsewhere of where evidence has been excluded include:[233] **12.281**

- A company specializing in credit card security in dispute with a credit card company regarding the quality of its services cannot be expected to disclose its highly secret security mechanisms, even to its client.
- A chocolate manufacturer in a dispute with a distributer regarding the quality of the chocolate cannot be expected to disclose a secret recipe.
- A pharmaceutical company in a dispute with a supplier will not be required to disclose know-how about the development of a drug not yet protected by a patent.

None of the respondents to a recent survey on use of the IBA Rules[234] was aware of any national court decisions laying down a test for commercial or technical confidentiality under Article 9.2(e), although respondents from China reported that the Intermediate People's Court has held that technical confidentiality can be defined as 'technical information with a commercial value that can generate wealth for its owner'.[235] **12.282**

Each argument for special treatment preventing or restricting introduction of the evidence will need to be considered against the particular facts of the case and the precise issues to be determined. The tribunal must balance the interests of one party in maintaining confidentiality against the interests of other parties in being able to obtain access to the evidence. By way of illustration, in one case, a tribunal made up of continental European lawyers considered that the claimant's right to prove its case or advance arguments outweighed the respondent's obligation towards a third party to keep a document confidential.[236] **12.283**

232 O'Malley Rules of Evidence (n 76) para 9.84. This cites ICC Case No. 1000, Procedural Order No. 8 (2006) (unpublished). The documentation requested in that case concerned financial information about a corporate party to the arbitration, including bank statements and tax returns.

233 Marghitola (n 69) 92.

234 BCLP Survey on the use of the IBA Rules.

235 *Xi'an People's Procuratorate v Pei Guoliang* (2005)西刑二初字第93号；(2006)陕刑二终字第50号 (Xi'an Intermediate People's Court).

236 Hamilton (n 134).

2. Third-Party Confidentiality

12.284 The confidentiality sought to be protected will, in most cases, attach to one of the parties to the arbitration and will often concern a document created by that party for internal circulation only, but this will not always be the case. One example known to the authors concerned a request by one party for proprietary information relating to the software by which the other party's expert had produced models relating to a technical issue in the case.

12.285 There may be good commercial reasons why third-party confidentiality rights have been put in place and a relevant factor for the tribunal to consider when asked to impose restrictions is whether a confidentiality agreement with a third party will be breached if the evidence is disclosed. Generally speaking, a tribunal will be reluctant to require a party to the arbitration to breach its agreement with a third party if this can be avoided.[237] In *Dongwoo*, the tribunal accepted the existence of confidentiality arrangements in place between Mann+Hummel and a third party as justification for the non-production of documents.[238]

12.286 A related factor may be the potential consequences that could follow from the breach—for example, whether a breach of the contractual provision constitutes a ground for the third party to terminate a contract or not to conclude a new contract.[239] In some cases, the party ordered to produce the document may feel more comfortable if it does so under compulsion pursuant to an order of the tribunal.

12.287 On the other hand, a party should not be permitted to obstruct production of a document by contriving in bad faith to make it subject to a confidentiality undertaking with a third party.[240] Where a tribunal finds that a confidentiality undertaking to a third party has been entered into for purposes other than legitimate business needs (eg in order to avoid the production of documents), the tribunal may consider the restriction as posing no real obstacle to the production of the requested evidence.[241] In such circumstances there is no genuine commercial sensitivity or relationship of confidentiality to be protected.

[237] Although not an arbitration decision, the English Patents Court had to consider such a situation where a party to litigation had a right to call for documents held by a third party under an agreement with that third party, but subject to an obligation of confidentiality. The Court took the view that disclosure of documents obtained under that agreement in the litigation would be a breach of the confidentiality agreement and refused to order disclosure of the documents in the litigation. *Unilever plc v Gillette (UK) Ltd* [1988] RPC 416.

[238] *Dongwoo Mann & Hummel Co Ltd v Mann & Hummel GmbH* [2008] SGHC 67.

[239] Marghitola (n 69) 93.

[240] See further ibid 92.

[241] O'Malley Rules of Evidence (n 76) para 9.90.

3. General Considerations

Irrespective of the exact nature of the evidence over which confidentiality is claimed, where a party wishes to rely on Article 9.2(e), a clear statement of the nature of the confidentiality relied on together with an explanation of the potential adverse consequences for anyone who may be affected by disclosure or production must be the proper starting point for submissions to the tribunal. The tribunal's decision as to whether the grounds relied on are 'compelling' as required by Article 9.2(e) will always depend on the facts and circumstances of each case. A tribunal is unlikely to place much weight upon an objection that relies on a general claim to 'business secrecy' unsupported by evidence as to why this is so.[242] 12.288

Where the party seeking confidentiality protection is simply concerned about the use to which its opponent might put the information, it may be possible for the other party and the tribunal to review a hard copy of the evidence and for arguments to be made on exclusion of the evidence in the same way as happens with any other form of contested application. Where the 'protecting' party does not wish its opponent to see the evidence, the position becomes more difficult. In such circumstances it may be thought appropriate for access to the document to be restricted to the tribunal so that it can consider the need for confidentiality. However, this may pose a problem if either party contends that the tribunal would be unable to treat the parties fairly and in an even-handed way after viewing the evidence, even if it were to uphold the objection under Article 9.2(e).[243] 12.289

As mentioned, an alternative approach to tribunal review of documentary evidence is the appointment by the tribunal of a 'confidentiality expert' under Article 3.8 of the IBA Rules who will be tasked with reviewing the document/s and reporting to the tribunal who will then decide whether to accept or reject the objection.[244] 12.290

In circumstances where a tribunal determines that a 'compelling' reason of commercial or technical confidentiality has *not* been made out, it may nonetheless feel that the evidence in question should be made subject to some form of confidentiality protection under Article 9.4 of the IBA Rules.[245] For example, it may be clear that the evidence in 12.291

[242] A view expressed by the English Court on a similar point is a useful expression of this position: 'Simple assertions of confidentiality and of the damage that will be done by publication, even if supported by both parties, should not prevail. The court will require specific reasons why the party would be damaged by the publication of the document'; see *Patokh Chodiev, Alexander Machkevitch, Alijan Ibragimov v Kirill Stein* [2016] EWHC 1210 [19]-[22] (quoting from *Lilly Icos Ltd v Pfizer (No. 2)* [2002] WLR 2253). Although in the *Stein* case the Court was examining what factors would justify the making of a confidentiality order in respect of documents that had already been referred to in open Court—and therefore in the context of the principle of open justice and transparency—the point being made holds good for present purposes.

[243] It has been suggested that where both parties consent to the tribunal seeing the evidence this should constitute a waiver of the disclosing party's right to contest the award on those grounds. Waincymer (n 12) 825–84. See also Marghitola (n 69) 94.

[244] See Chapter 6 paras 6.263–6.280.

[245] See 12.317–12.356.

question is commercially sensitive, but because it also has significant probative value, the tribunal may determine that the reasons to refuse production or exclude the evidence from the record are not compelling on the facts of the particular case.

4. Practical Examples

12.292 In a survey of use of the IBA Rules,[246] several respondents had direct experience of evidence being excluded for reasons of commercial or technical confidentiality.[247] Respondents in France gave examples of several cases where a decision to exclude was made: in one case, the excluded evidence was a report which included specific know-how on uranium; in another, it was accounting documentation containing the calculation of margin in maritime transport documents (the margin being the main element for price setting). Spanish respondents reported that, in a dispute concerning a claim to damages for a failure to deliver goods under a commodity contract, the tribunal denied a request for production of a contract of resale between the claimant and a third party on grounds of commercial confidentiality. This last case is interesting because the terms of the contract of resale might in some cases be relevant to the measure of damages for non-delivery. In another case, the tribunal denied a request to produce a document issued by a third party that contained the third party's know-how on running and operation of an energy installation.

I. Political or Institutional Sensitivity

9.2(f) grounds of special political or institutional sensitivity (including evidence that has been classified as secret by a government or a public international institution) that the Arbitral Tribunal determines to be compelling.

12.293 Article 9.2(f) allows tribunals to exclude from the evidentiary record, or from production, evidence that has political or institutional sensitivity. The tribunal must find the reasons advanced in support of reliance on Article 9.2(e) to be compelling.

1. Introduction

12.294 In some jurisdictions, political sensitivity is treated as a type of privilege. However, even in those countries where it is not regarded as an evidentiary privilege, there are often specific national laws or regulations governing the treatment of state, diplomatic or military secrets. Article 9.2(f) allows the tribunal to exclude documents or evidence on

[246] BCLP Survey on the use of the IBA Rules.
[247] These included respondents from France, the United States, Italy, Spain, Sweden, and Argentina.

grounds of political or institutional sensitivity, even if that type of confidentiality is not considered to be an evidentiary privilege for which protection might be available under Article 9.2(b).

The Commentary on the IBA Rules explains that Article 9.2(f) was added because certain international political organizations pointed out that 'commercial and technical confidentiality' as covered by Article 9.2(e) might not include confidentiality within such organizations. Article 9.2(f) was added to put such political or institutional sensitivity on an equal footing with commercial or technical confidentiality. **12.295**

Article 9.2(f) gives only one example of a situation falling within the category of political or institutional sensitivity—namely, 'evidence that has been classified as secret by a government or a public international institution'. However, this example is preceded by the work 'including' thereby making clear that Article 9.2(f) can also embrace other confidential communications meeting the description set out in that provision. **12.296**

2. Political Sensitivity

In some jurisdictions, local law may provide a benchmark for the kinds of evidence that are not disclosable in any court or arbitration proceedings because of their political nature. A party may rely on these rules as evidence of the political sensitivity of the material for the purposes of Article 9.2(f) in addition to raising a claim of legal impediment or privilege under Article 9.2(b). In *Merill & Ring Forestry LP*,[248] the tribunal found that Cabinet privilege, as defined by s. 9(3) of the British Columbia Crown Proceedings Act, can fall within the definition of 'special political or institutional sensitivity' and therefore could be a valid ground for exclusion of evidence on that basis.[249] **12.297**

Examples of public interest or national security privileges available under national systems of law may be found at 12.90-12.93. Any of those matters might be relied upon under Article 9.2(f). **12.298**

It has been suggested that national security privileges (also referred to as 'public interest immunity') are widely acknowledged by international arbitration tribunals.[250] The argument has also been advanced that public interest immunity is, in fact, a general principle of law or an identified tenet of public international law. However, that argument has not been universally accepted. For example, it was raised but rejected in *Biwater Gauff (Tanzania) Ltd.*[251] **12.299**

[248] *Merrill and Ring Forestry L.P. v The Government of Canada* (Decision on Production of Documents in Respect of Which Cabinet Privilege Has Been Invoked, 3 September 2009) ICSID Case No. UNCT/07/1.

[249] For discussion, see Möckesch (n 104) paras 9.24–9.25.

[250] See, eg Tobias Zuberbühler and others, *IBA Rules of Evidence: Commentary on the IBA Rules on the Taking of Evidence in International Arbitration* (Schulthess 2012) paras 45–46 (hereafter 'Zuberbühler').

[251] *Biwater Gauff (Tanzania) Ltd. v United Republic of Tanzania* (Procedural Order No. 2, 24 May 2006) ICSID Case No. ARB/05/22 8.

12.300 Waincymer[252] cites the following two examples of circumstances connected to security considerations where political sensitivity was regarded by the ICJ as being a bar to production of evidence. The first concerned acceptance by the ICJ of an assertion of naval secrecy as a reason for refusing to produce naval orders in *Corfu Channel*.[253] In the former Yugoslavia *Genocide* case, the ICJ declined to make an order in relation to redacted material on the (claimed) basis of military secrets.[254]

12.301 Political sensitivity may arise in many different situations and in relation to varied subject matter. For example, the document may relate to development of a new governmental policy on immigration, or contain information about suspected terrorist activities or set out details of a military strategy to be employed in respect of a hostile state. The possibilities are numerous. However, Article 9.2(f) has obvious application in cases where there are national security considerations in play.

12.302 Under Article 9.2(f), even in situations where the local law does not explicitly say that the politically sensitive documents are protected from document production, the tribunal is entitled to exclude them from production if the tribunal is satisfied that there are compelling reasons for doing so.

3. Institutional Sensitivity

12.303 Article 9.2(f) expressly mentions 'institutional sensitivity'. Some international organizations—for example, the United Nations, the International Monetary Fund (IMF)—may not be political organizations, but may nonetheless be working in the interests of the public or communities at large. The reference to 'institutional sensitivity' provides an umbrella for sensitive documents generated by such organizations.

12.304 It is not clear whether 'institutional' or 'political' sensitivity can be extended to companies that are involved with projects of national importance. For example, can a large bank that funds military enterprises, or holds their accounts, claim exclusion of evidence by reference to these matters? As far as state secrets are concerned, the United States courts have taken the view that the protection afforded to that type of information belongs to the government and cannot be waived by a private party.[255]

[252] See Waincymer (n 12) 869–70.
[253] *Corfu Channel (United Kingdom v Albania)* [1949] ICJ 4, 32.
[254] *Application of the Convention on the Prevention and Punishment of the Crime of Genocide (Bosnia and Herzegovina v Serbia and Montenegro)* [2007] ICJ 75 [204].
[255] *U.S. v Reynolds*, 345 US 1, 7-8 (1953). For more detail see: Mosk and Ginsburg (n 86) 363.

4. Tribunal's Approach to Claims of Political or Institutional Sensitivity

Although tribunals are bound to consider an objection raised under Article 9.2(f) very seriously, a mere reliance on Article 9.2(f) is not enough. The provision clearly states that the reasons advanced in support of reliance on Article 9.2(e) must be determined by the tribunal to be 'compelling'. As the Commentary on the IBA Rules makes clear, the tribunal retains the final discretion to determine whether the considerations of sensitivity are sufficient to warrant the exclusion from evidence or production of the relevant documents or other evidence. 12.305

The fact that private tribunals, comprising arbitrators from various jurisdictions, may be deciding on matters of state importance has triggered some concerns. For example, in response to a recent survey by the IBA on the use of soft law products, it was suggested that those responsible for drafting the IBA Rules should consider whether these tribunals are best placed to decide disputes about the production of documents relating to political or institutional matters.[256] 12.306

Practical difficulties can arise in relation to discussions about the content of the document in question or, in exceptional cases, the need for a review of the document by the tribunal in order to make a determination on the objection. If the document contains highly sensitive information for which special security clearance is required, the tribunal may have to take on trust submissions made by counsel about the generic content of the document. In some cases, tribunals have ordered that a log of politically sensitive documents be produced in the same fashion as privilege logs are sometimes produced.[257] However, such logs have similar shortcomings as privilege logs.[258] 12.307

J. Economy, Proportionality, and Fairness

9.2(g) considerations of procedural economy, proportionality, fairness or equality of the Parties that the Arbitral Tribunal determines to be compelling.

Article 9.2(g) of the IBA Rules states expressly that the Tribunal may exclude evidence from the record or production for reasons of 'procedural economy, proportionality, fairness or equality of the Parties' that the tribunal determines to be 'compelling'. 12.308

Achieving an 'efficient, economical and fair' process is one of the principles underpinning the IBA Rules and is expressly stated in Preamble 1 to the IBA Rules.[259] Consistent 12.309

[256] 2016 IBA Report (n 1) para 88.
[257] *Vito G. Gallo v The Government of Canada* (Procedural Order No. 2, 10 February 2009) PCA Case No. 55798 [4]-[5].
[258] See 12.238–12.40 for more detail.
[259] See Chapter 2 paras 2.6–2.27.

with this, Article 9.2(g) provides express grounds for excluding evidence from the record or production on this basis, as well as for considerations of proportionality. It is described in the Commentary on the IBA Rules as a 'catch-all provision' intended to assure procedural economy, proportionality, fairness, and equality in the case. Although reflected in the principle stated in Preamble 1, the provision at Article 9.2(g) adds teeth by making these considerations an express basis for the exclusion of evidence from the record or production. The same principle is emphasized again at Article 9.3(e) in relation to considerations of privilege.

1. Economy and Proportionality

12.310 Procedural economy and proportionality are, in reality, two sides of the same coin. Both of these considerations are directed at ensuring an efficient and economic arbitration, taking into account both the financial or commercial value of the matters in dispute and its complexity.[260] The value of a piece of evidence—in terms of its relevance and materiality to outcome—may be weighed by a tribunal against the cost, delay, and burden associated with its provision or production.[261]

12.311 The amount at stake is normally a good starting point to assess the proportionality of costs likely to be incurred. If the tribunal is dealing with a claim for $1 million, it may well be disproportionate to order substantial production of documents if the costs of production would be a significant percentage of the claimed amount. However, although the amount in question is a good starting point, it is not always conclusive. For example, it may be a 'bet the company case', in which the entire business of one of the parties rests on the outcome of the dispute, or there may be a series of similar contracts between the same parties and the outcome of the arbitration will be regarded as a precedent by reference to which the parties may be able to address the same issue on those other contracts. As mentioned, the potential probative value of the evidence sought must also be considered.

12.312 Georg von Segesser, one of the members of the committee responsible for drafting the IBA Rules, notes that different tribunals may have different perspectives on an assessment of proportionality and economy. In relation to issues of document production he states that:

> Proportionality and economy will be factors that most likely will be applied differently by arbitrator panels depending on their backgrounds and practice, e.g. a tribunal with arbitrators practising as lawyers in the U.S. may be less restrictive than a Swiss panel, and common law practitioners' perception of procedural economy in the context of document production may differ from that of practitioners in civil law jurisdictions.[262]

[260] See Chapter 2 paras 2.6 *et seq.*
[261] Born (n 9) 2319–2423, 2362.
[262] Georg von Segesser, 'The IBA Rules on the Taking of Evidence in International Arbitration: Revised version, adopted by the International Bar Association on 29 May 2010' (2010) 28 ASA Bulletin 735, 743.

In our experience this is correct. Depending on the facts, assessment of what is considered to be reasonable and proportionate may vary significantly between tribunals made up of different arbitrators with varying backgrounds and viewpoints.

The ICC Task Force on E-Discovery contains an express recommendation that proportionality be taken into account in determining the scope of document production,[263] the object being to achieve a balance between the benefits of production and the burdens associated with it. The report produced by that Task Force states: 12.313

> If the arbitrators are satisfied that the document or category of documents sought is sufficiently identified, relevant and material and all other applicable criteria for the production of documents are met (in particular, pursuant to the IBA Rules of Evidence or generally accepted 'best practices'), they should then consider whether the requested production would be likely to impose an unreasonable burden on the producing party.
>
> This process requires arbitrators to consider the balance between the likely benefits of production to parties and arbitrators and the potential costs, delay and other burdens that the production exercise may entail. It requires consideration of the specific circumstances of the case at hand. Parties and arbitral tribunals therefore require a degree of flexibility in this respect.[264]

However, in no case should the objectives of proportionality and procedural economy be used by the tribunal as an excuse not to review a large volume of documents where this is required in order to make a proper determination on the dispute.[265] Thus, in deciding whether to exclude a body of evidence from the arbitration—whether part of requested document production or otherwise—the tribunal must consider the issues to which the documents relate, weigh the arguments on production, and balance the competing considerations as best it can. 12.314

2. Fairness and Due Process

Considerations of fairness and equality are concerned with issues of due process. In addition to the principle of fairness stated at Preamble 1 of the IBA Rules, a tribunal will be required by the majority of national arbitration laws and institutional rules to ensure that the arbitration process is fair to both parties. This topic is discussed further in Chapter 2 paras 2.7–2.24. 12.315

The Commentary on the IBA Rules makes clear that considerations of fairness under Article 9.2(g) (or indeed any of the other matters mentioned in that provision) may 12.316

[263] *ICC Arbitration Commission Report on Managing E-Document Production* (International Chamber of Commerce 2012) paras 3.12–3.13.

[264] ibid.

[265] Waincymer (n 12) 858–60.

have direct application to objections arising under any of the grounds listed at Article 9.2(a)–(f).[266] Article 9.3 is addressed in tandem with Article 9.2 (b) at paras 12.125–12.241.

K. Confidentiality Protection

9.4. The Arbitral Tribunal may, where appropriate, make necessary arrangements to permit evidence to be presented or considered subject to suitable confidentiality protection.

1. Introduction

12.317 Article 9.4 allows a tribunal to arrange matters so that evidence of a confidential nature may be introduced into the arbitration subject to protections designed to prevent unnecessary disclosure or dissemination. The discretion granted to the tribunal is a wide one. The tribunal may make such arrangements where it considers it 'appropriate' to do so. The nature of the arrangements contemplated by this provision is also unrestricted—the only requirements being that they be 'necessary' to permit the evidence to be used.

12.318 Article 9.4 should be considered in conjunction with Article 3.13 of the IBA Rules, which states a general principle providing for the confidentiality of documents introduced into the arbitration. The parties may also wish to consider any general obligation of confidentiality that may exist in the underlying arbitration agreement or in applicable institutional rules[267] or national arbitration laws.[268]

[266] Commentary on the IBA Rules (n 64) 25 gives an example of such application by reference to issues of privilege arising in the first instance under IBA Rules (n 3) Article 9.2(b) and Article 9.3(e).

[267] Institutional rules are broadly consistent in stating the obligation of parties to arbitration to keep arbitration proceedings confidential. By agreeing to application of those institutional rules the parties adopt those provisions into their agreement to arbitrate. In some cases, the relevant provision may contain express reference to the duty of confidentiality extending to evidence that is produced in the arbitration proceedings. For example, see WIPO Arbitration Rules, Article 74(a), and LCIA Rules, Article 30.1. Other institutional rules contain a more general provision without express reference to evidence introduced into the arbitration. For example, SIAC Rules, Rule 39.1.

[268] The national laws of a number of jurisdictions impose a duty of confidentiality on parties to arbitration, but this is not always the case. Under English Law, the parties to arbitration and the tribunal are under implied duties to maintain the confidentiality of the hearing, documents generated and disclosed during the arbitral proceedings, and the award. The duty of confidentiality is subject to a number of exceptions: (i) The parties may dispense with, or modify, the obligation of confidentiality by agreement or consent; (ii) The duty of confidentiality will not preclude disclosure of documents where such disclosure is ordered or permitted by the court; (iii) Disclosure may be permitted where it is reasonably necessary for the establishment or protection of a party's legal rights; and (iv) Disclosure may be permitted where it is necessary in the interests of justice. Duties of confidentiality are also found in other jurisdictions. For example, the Spanish Arbitration Act, Article 24.2 imposes express duties of confidentiality on the parties and the arbitral tribunal, unless otherwise agreed by the parties; the Australian International Arbitration Act 1974 provides for a confidentiality regime which (as a result of amendments in 2015) applies by default unless the parties agree to opt-out; the New Zealand Arbitration Act 1996, s14 provides that the tribunal must conduct proceedings in private and that every arbitration agreement carries an implied term that parties and the tribunal will not disclose confidential information; in Singapore there is an implied duty of confidentiality at

Article 3.13 states that: 12.319

> Any Document submitted or produced by a Party or non-Party in the arbitration and not otherwise in the public domain shall be kept confidential by the Arbitral Tribunal and the other Parties, and shall be used only in connection with the arbitration. This requirement shall apply except and to the extent that disclosure may be required of a Party to fulfil a legal duty, protect or pursue a legal right, or enforce or challenge an award in bona fide legal proceedings before a state court or other judicial authority . . . [269]

It goes on to provide that 'The Arbitral Tribunal may issue orders to set forth the terms of this confidentiality'. Thus, for example, a tribunal may issue an order—perhaps included in its first procedural order— setting out a protocol by which any confidential materials are to be identified or processed. If the subject matter of the dispute or the industry sector in which the parties operate is one where sensitive or highly valuable commercial information is likely to be generated, there may be good reason to anticipate issues of confidentiality. If the tribunal does make such an order, application of Article 9.4 must be considered in tandem with whatever arrangements have already been agreed or ordered. Article 3.13 is dealt with in greater detail in Chapter 6 paras 6.386–6.394. 12.320

Whatever general provisions may apply to an arbitration, where extremely confidential or sensitive evidence is in issue, parties will very often wish to secure additional targeted safeguards to reduce the risk of that evidence being disclosed outside of the arbitration proceedings. All of the major institutional rules confer a wide discretion on the tribunal in relation to the conduct of the proceedings which would cover the imposition of confidentiality protections on evidence presented were the tribunal to consider such protections to be necessary.[270] The ICC Rules include an express provision to this effect, as do (unsurprisingly) the World Intellectual Property Organization (WIPO) Arbitration Rules.[271] 12.321

common law in all arbitrations seated in Singapore—see *AAY and others v AAZ* [2009] SGHC 142 [55]. In contrast, it is reported that in Sweden parties are not bound by any implied obligation of confidentiality, although general rules on trade secrets can sometimes apply.

[269] IBA Rules (n 3) Article 3.13.

[270] For example, SCC Rules, Article 23(1); HKIAC Rules, Article 13.1; SIAC Rules, Rule 19.1; LCIA Rules, Article 14.5. See also ICSID Arbitration Rules, Rules 19 and 39(1) and the comments of the tribunal in *Abaclat and Others v Argentine Republic* (Procedural Order No. 3, 27 January 2010) ICSID Case No. ARB/07/5 [61]–[62].

[271] ICC Rules, Article 22 (3) states that: 'Upon the request of any party, *the arbitral tribunal may make orders concerning the confidentiality of the arbitration proceedings* or of any other matters in connection with the arbitration and may take measures for protecting trade secrets and confidential information' (emphasis added). WIPO Arbitration Rules, Article 52 (Disclosure of Trade Secrets and Other Confidential Information).

2. When Will an Arbitral Tribunal Make a Confidentiality Order under Article 9.4 of the IBA Rules?

12.322 The circumstances in which a confidentiality order may be made under Article 9.4 is a matter for the discretion of the tribunal. The tribunal can make such an order whenever it considers it 'appropriate' to do so.[272]

12.323 Parties to an arbitration tend to face confidentiality issues in one of two situations. The first is when they are requested to produce documents by their opponent. The second is in connection with evidence they wish to submit in support of their case (whether documentary, witness, or expert evidence).

12.324 Under Article 3.5 and Article 9.2(e) of the IBA Rules, a party may object to a request for production on grounds of commercial or technical confidentiality. Where it finds that there are compelling grounds to do so—a question of fact in each case—the tribunal is permitted under Article 9.2 to *exclude* that evidence or production altogether. Where the tribunal is *not* satisfied that the necessary threshold to justify exclusion has been met, it may nonetheless feel, or be sympathetic to an application by the relevant party, that measures should be implemented to protect the confidentiality of the relevant evidence.[273]

12.325 However, the power given to the tribunal under Article 9.4 is not limited to situations where confidentiality concerns have been raised as part of document production under Article 9.2. The tribunal may propose or agree to confidentiality safeguards whenever it considers it appropriate to do so. The material attracting such safeguards can include documents produced by one of the parties, written and/or oral witness evidence, proprietary materials used or relied on by experts in preparing their evidence, or premises and technology inspected during the course of the proceedings.

12.326 The nature of the content that may attract protection will include commercial confidences, confidential business records or models, samples, recipes, technical formulas, other forms of know-how, price calculations, sources of supply, distribution channels, agreements with suppliers and customers, trade secrets or proprietary information, and all forms of intellectual property.[274] The nature of the relationships may also be

[272] It has been suggested that the requirement of relevance and materiality of evidence that permeates the IBA Rules should be regarded as a threshold test for considerations of confidentiality (presumably on the basis that the evidence can be excluded under IBA Rules (n 3) Article 9.2(a)). If the evidence is not relevant and material it is not needed to resolve the dispute and the issue of confidentiality does not arise; see Derains (n 230) para 11. There appears to be general acceptance that establishing relevance is an appropriate starting point. For example, in relation to a request for disclosure of commercially sensitive documents, our Irish law firm respondents reported that in *Flogas Ireland Limited v Tru Gas* [2012] IEHC 259, the Irish High Court held that the requesting party must take particular care to explain why the documents wanted are relevant and necessary to the matters in dispute: 'Where contested documentation is confidential, then the courts should exercise special care to ensure that a party is not given free access to such information without having satisfied the court that there is some basis on which the information is likely to be relevant and necessary'.

[273] Marghitola (n 69) 93 describes such evidence as 'confidential, but not highly confidential'.

[274] See further Born (n 9) 2319–2423, 2387; O'Malley Rules of Evidence (n 76) para 9.84; Zuberbühler (n 250) para 43.

relevant. For example, if parties to the arbitration are competitors or one supplies goods or services to the other, such factors may heighten the need to protect confidential information if there is a risk of market advantage being undermined by the disclosure of confidential information. Examples of evidence potentially justifying confidentiality protection extend to politically sensitive material or confidential information of institutions such as the World Bank or the IMF.[275] Specific examples that have been reported to us include (in a dispute between competitors in the insurance business) contracts between one of the parties and its customers[276] and business models or drawings or software customized to handle the trading and logistics of commodities.[277]

3. The Nature of the Measures

The tribunal is empowered to make 'necessary' arrangements to permit evidence to be used with the benefit of 'suitable' confidentiality protection. At the heart of this provision is the wide discretion granted to the tribunal to tailor measures to the facts of an individual case: what is necessary—no more and no less. **12.327**

a. General approach

Each situation will be different. However, in each case, the tribunal must find the right balance between ensuring due process—in particular, that the restrictions around the evidence do not hamper the ability of the parties to prepare and present their cases, and to test the evidence of their opponent—and the need to accommodate legitimate confidentiality concerns. The point has been made elsewhere that, because claims to protection based on confidentiality alone will not engage application of a legal principle (for example, legal privilege), a tribunal has considerable flexibility as to the manner in which the issue can be resolved. As a result, the spectrum of measures adopted to deal with confidentiality is very broad and generally restricted only by the facts of the case. **12.328**

For this reason, a tribunal will be very keen to establish as much consensus as possible when considering and formulating appropriate protection measures. The more that can be done with agreement of the parties—or even better, by encouraging direct agreement between the parties—the smaller will be the risk of a challenge based on the arrangements ordered to be made. **12.329**

The power to attach safeguards is directed at permitting evidence to be both 'presented or considered'. A tribunal will wish to consider and encourage measures facilitating party review or assessment of the evidence, and the presentation of that evidence at any evidential hearing that may take place. **12.330**

[275] See further Zuberbühler (n 250) paras 45–46.
[276] The tribunal found that the documents were confidential in nature.
[277] ibid.

12.331 The arrangements that a tribunal will consider necessary to protect confidentiality will vary depending upon the facts of the case and the attitude of the parties and of the tribunal. Relevant factors will include the nature and form of the evidence; who among the parties, witnesses, experts, and legal teams will need access to the evidence in order to provide all parties with a reasonable opportunity to assess its nature and relevance; and how can the evidence be used or presented so as to best protect its confidential or sensitive character. Basic questions to be considered at the outset are:

- the nature of the concern or risk;
- at what stages in the arbitration the need to assess the evidence will arise;
- what form of protection is most appropriate to address the problem while ensuring due process; and
- how long the measures should remain in place.

12.332 The tribunal may, as a first step, invite or direct the parties to consult to see if agreement can be reached on a mutually acceptable form of confidentiality protection. Where a third party is involved, the tribunal may ask the party holding the evidence (or having the relationship with the third party) to engage in good-faith negotiations to obtain the third party's consent to the evidence being used. A form of order mentioned elsewhere provides that the respondent should 'negotiate production of the document with the third party. Should the third party not agree to production, the respondent is ordered to produce a letter from the third party to this effect'.[278]

12.333 Whether confidentiality concerns are dealt with by way of confidentiality agreements between the parties or protective orders issued by the tribunal, individual confidentiality undertakings are likely to be required from any individual permitted to see the confidential information, whether it be an employee, fact witness, technical expert, or counsel. This in itself may call for some form of negotiation or request by the parties to secure these undertakings.

b. Possible measures

12.334 Possible confidentiality measures that may be agreed or directed are diverse in nature limited only by the ingenuity of the tribunal and the parties. Even where the same mechanism is chosen in different cases, the drafting of the agreement or order will need to be carefully tailored to the particular circumstances of the dispute.

12.335 Commonly used mechanisms include the following:

- Redaction
- Synopsis
- Single location review

[278] This example of a procedural order in an ICC arbitration is referred to in O'Malley Rules of Evidence (n 76) para 3.168.

- Confidentiality circles
- Confidentiality adviser

i. Redaction

Redaction of documents is a straightforward means of protecting confidential material and its use is commonplace in arbitration. The confidential parts of a document are simply excised from the copy of the document produced. An obvious example is minutes of board meetings containing confidential material on different topics, only one of which is relevant to the arbitration. Redacting material related to the other topics may very often be appropriate. 12.336

As has been noted elsewhere, redaction of truly irrelevant material does not intrude on due process since neither party is being denied access to material that may affect the case. However, where the broad subject matter of a document is known but there is a dispute as to its relevance and materiality, redaction may not be appropriate—to deny a party access to potentially material evidence engages issues around the ability of each party to present its case. Such circumstances may give rise to a need to review proposed redactions against the originals so as to assess whether redaction is an appropriate measure to adopt. This review might be done by the tribunal, and possibly 'counsel only' for each party, subject to provision by counsel of confidentiality undertakings. Another option is for the tribunal to delegate the selection of those parts to be redacted to a 'confidentiality' expert (see 6.263-6.280).[279] 12.337

ii. Synopsis

Provision of a synopsis of key elements of the content of a document is a variation on redaction and can be useful in appropriate circumstances. In one ICC arbitration in which the parties had agreed that the arbitral tribunal could take into account relevant provisions of the IBA Rules, the claimant requested production of contracts that the respondent had concluded directly or indirectly with designated customers. The contracts formed the basis of the claimant's claim for commission from the respondent. The respondent objected to production on grounds that 'disclosure as requested . . . would violate confidentiality of Respondent's contracts with third Parties and legitimate interest of Respondent for "non-disclosure and secrecy" of its commercial and contractual practices'. In order to protect the respondent's concerns over confidentiality of its commercial interests and practices, the tribunal decided not to compel the respondent to produce a copy of the contracts, but only a list containing the date of the contract, the subject matter of the contract, the original contract price (and any variation), payments received, and payments pending or anticipated.[280] 12.338

[279] Domitille Baizea and Juliette Richard, 'Chapter 4. Addressing the Issue of Confidentiality in Arbitration Proceedings: How Is This Done in Practice?' in Elliott Geisinger (ed), *Confidential and Restricted Access Information in International Arbitration* (Juris Publishing 2016) 56–57 (hereafter 'Baizea and Richard').

[280] Final award in ICC Case 15583 (Extract), (2016) 1 ICC Dispute Resolution Bulletin 139 [274].

iii. Single location review

12.339 Another possibility is to restrict inspection of documents to a single location with no right to take copies, notes, photographs, or other form of record.[281] It is suggested that this solution may be used where the primary goal is to reduce the risk of dissipation of the information. It is often combined with the use of a confidentiality 'club'. An example mentioned elsewhere concerns a dispute involving the review of industrial designs. The tribunal ordered the setting up of a data room for inspection of the relevant information under the supervision of an expert.[282]

iv. Confidentiality club

12.340 Another measure frequently used in arbitration is to restrict access to the confidential material to selected individuals. The narrower the 'club', the greater the risk of infringing due process. The wider the club, the weaker the protection afforded in respect of the confidential material.[283]

12.341 In theory, it would be possible for the confidential material to be disclosed only to the tribunal.[284] However, it is difficult to see how such a step would be consistent with due process. Both the tribunal and the producing party would have the opportunity to see the material while the other party would be denied such access. It would be difficult for the other party to challenge or test the evidence effectively.

v. Counsel- or expert-'only' review

12.342 Restricting access to legal counsel and the tribunal may be appropriate depending upon the facts of the case. Under this arrangement, outside counsel will sign a confidentiality agreement by which they agree not to disclose the relevant material to third parties, including their own clients.[285]

12.343 The potential advantage of this approach is that, despite its confidentiality, the relevant material can still be included in the development of a case strategy. The disadvantage is that, in many cases, without counsel being able to seek instructions on the material, the evidence cannot be usefully challenged.[286] For example, the evidence in question may be technical evidence that does not lend itself to proper assessment without input from the client or expert, thereby hampering preparation of the case. Other commentators highlight similar shortcomings in this approach.[287]

12.344 Another possibility in appropriate circumstances is for the confidential information to be shared only with the experts for each the parties. However, similar difficulties to

[281] See further Born (n 9) 2319–2423, 2387.

[282] Reported in Baizea and Richard (n 279) 63.

[283] Born (n 9) 2319–2423, 2387. Baizea and Richard (n 279) 57–60. See further Marghitola (n 69) 95–96.

[284] Baizea and Richard (n 279) 57, fn 14 note that they were unable to find any examples of this approach in practice.

[285] See further Born (n 9) 2319–2423, 2387; Marghitola (n 69) 95.

[286] See further Waincymer (n 12) 877–79.

[287] Baizea and Richard (n 279) 57–58.

those identified above in relation to 'counsel-only' review may arise when access is limited to the tribunal and the relevant discipline of expert on each side. The experts may have the knowledge to assess technical evidence but the use that can be made of that assessment is hindered if the expert cannot consult with counsel to facilitate challenge to the evidence thereby (arguably) hindering a party's right to be heard. A possible solution may be to extend access to both counsel and the appropriate discipline of expert. This approach may be appropriate where the disputing parties are competitors who have concerns about providing their rival with access to sensitive commercial material.

A further possibility, where necessary, is to extend the confidentiality 'club' to key party representatives—for example, in-house counsel, an employee with 'hands on' knowledge of the facts in issue, or a client technical specialist. Who should be included in the club will depend very heavily on the nature of the dispute. **12.345**

With only one exception, all respondents to a recent survey on use of the IBA Rules[288] had direct experience of protective measures being used in arbitration. Redaction and the use of confidentiality clubs appear to be widely used regardless of nationality or jurisdiction. Respondents from France reported one example of redaction where the tribunal had given the claimant a week to make proposals about paragraphs to be redacted for reasons of business secrecy and/or proprietary information before ruling on the objection. Spanish respondents reported another case in which the tribunal reviewed the original documents against the proposed redactions and then issued a ruling confirming the appropriateness of certain redactions and requiring the deletion of others. **12.346**

Spanish respondents also cited a number of examples of single location examination of confidential documents—one arrangement permitted documents to be inspected by counsel at the arbitration room during a fixed two-hour window; another involved the setting up of a special data room with attached secrecy and access conditions. Respondents from Spain and Argentina reported orders by an arbitral tribunal permitting tribunal-only review of documents. **12.347**

4. Confidentiality 'Expert'

There may be circumstances where, despite concerns around due process, the tribunal accepts that it would not be appropriate to allow any member of the tribunal or anyone in the parties' teams (including counsel) to have access to confidential or sensitive information. One possible approach in these circumstances is to appoint a confidentiality 'expert'.[289] Depending on the nature of the issue to be addressed, the expert may be appointed under Article 3.8 or Article 6 of the IBA Rules.[290] However, because of the danger of challenge to the process on the basis that the tribunal has improperly **12.348**

[288] BCLP Survey on the use of the IBA Rules.
[289] Raeschke-Kessler (n 65) 411 and 430.
[290] See Chapter 6 paras 6.263–6.280 and Chapter 9.

delegated its powers, it is important that such arrangements are formulated with care. For obvious reasons, it will become even more desirable for the tribunal to try to obtain agreement from the parties on the precise arrangements to be put in place.

12.349 In one ICC arbitration concerning a technology licence agreement in the defence and security industry, reliance was placed by both parties on extremely sensitive evidence that each party refused to disclose to the other party. The solution proposed by the tribunal, and accepted by the parties, was the appointment of a 'third-party neutral' to collect the evidence, review the sensitive information, and answer factual questions from each party, and from the tribunal. As with a tribunal-appointed expert, the parties (and the tribunal) had the opportunity to comment on the third-party neutral's report, but any questions over access to sensitive information were to be referred to the tribunal for decision.[291] Where parties have expressly agreed to such an approach and it is therefore—in essence—a 'carve-out' from the matters put before the tribunal for determination, we see no problem (in principle) with such an arrangement.

5. Ancillary Matters

12.350 Even when a primary protection mechanism has been devised there are a number of ancillary questions that may need to be addressed. For example, these may include defining the nature and scope of the material subject to the protective measures, deciding how confidential materials are to be referred to in submissions and witness/expert evidence and award, how oral evidence relating to those matters is to be presented and challenged, and how confidential or sensitive documents are to be provided for in hearing bundles or for cross-examination. These are practical matters that need to be considered in order to ensure that the arbitration runs smoothly.

12.351 One approach to redacted documents prepared for the arbitration is to file two versions of the documents—a redacted and a non-redacted version—with the latter being made available only to the confidentiality 'club'. As to hearing bundles, in our experience, confidential documents will often be placed in a separate bundle with each page marked 'confidential' and made available only to members of the relevant confidentiality 'club'. If a witness or expert is to be cross-examined on that material, special directions may have to be given as to who may remain in the hearing room during the examination and a redacted version only of the transcript provided to those not in the confidentiality club. An order made in one ICC arbitration provided that:[292]

> Whenever any Particularly Sensitive Material [previously defined] or the information contained therein is to be used in connection with the giving of testimony before

[291] This case is referenced in Baizea and Richard (n 279) 69–70.
[292] Baizea and Richard (n 279) 70–71 quoting from Confidentiality Order of 12 July 1994 in ICC Case No.7893.

the Tribunal (a) only persons who are authorised under paragraph 3 of this Order to have access to Particularly Sensitive Material shall be in attendance, and (b) no witness shall be permitted to review the portions of an transcripts or Documents containing Particularly Sensitive Material without first executing a copy of [an agreement to be bound by a confidentiality order].

In another case under the 1998 ICC Rules, the arbitral tribunal ordered that no one outside the hearing room should be allowed simultaneous access to the hearing transcript. In another matter, the arbitral tribunal issued an order relating to the confidentiality of oral testimony.[293] **12.352**

Special arrangements may also be necessary in the more unusual situation where the identity of the witness, as well as the content of her or his testimony, needs to be kept confidential.[294] **12.353**

A further issue is the question of how long any confidentiality obligation should remain in place and what should happen to confidential evidence, and any copies or related working notes made, after the arbitration proceedings are closed. Applicable data protection regulations may also be relevant.[295] When formulating confidentiality protections the tribunal and the parties should give consideration to these matters. The provision made will generally provide either for return or destruction of the material but the point of contention between the parties may be the timing of such steps. For example, the party required to return or destroy may wish to keep the materials for a certain period after the arbitration is completed for reasons connected to potential enforcement or challenge proceedings.[296] Given the uncertainty that may exist about the nature of timing and forum for such action, drafting to take account of such matters can be complex. Where fixed deadlines for return or destruction are imposed it is suggested that a useful approach may be to stipulate different periods of time for different categories of recipient of the confidential information – for example, that the parties should return/destroy the confidential information more or less immediately but counsel should be permitted to retain it for a longer period.[297] **12.354**

[293] The Secretariat's Guide to ICC Arbitration (n 275) para 3-808.

[294] For example, where the witness may suffer reprisals for giving evidence. Baizea and Richard (n 279) note that in one investor–state arbitration conducted under the UNCITRAL Rules the tribunal ordered that the identity and evidence of a former employee of the investor, who agreed to testify only if his name was kept confidential, could be disclosed only to an agreed confidentiality club. For the hearing it was agreed that only one designated party representative could remain in the hearing room with counsel during the examination and the name of the witness could not be mentioned in case it was recorded on the transcript. Baizea and Richard (n 279) 71.

[295] For example, GDPR (n 100) which forms part of the data protection regime in the UK, together with the new Data Protection Act 2018.

[296] See further Baizea and Richard (n 279) 60–61.

[297] Practice on this issue appears to vary greatly. See further Baizea and Richard (n 279) 62. The authors give the example of an ICC arbitration where all confidential documents were ordered to be destroyed 'upon termination of the proceedings' but counsel were entitled to retain the confidential documents for ten years. They refer also to an order in another ICC arbitration that simply provided that the confidentiality agreement 'remain in full force and effect after the conclusion of the arbitral proceedings'. Another case provided for the obligation to continue for ten years and in yet another for five years.

12.355 Securing enforcement of confidentiality obligations can also raise difficult issues in themselves, but those issues can, to some extent, be addressed by including enforcement provisions in the relevant confidentiality orders.[298]

12.356 Michael Hwang has developed a model confidentiality order (the 'Hwang Model Procedural Order on Confidentiality'). Among other matters, this includes a draft definition of the 'confidential information' to be protected, the confidentiality obligation itself, exceptions to the obligation and a detailed procedure for giving notice of an intention to rely on an exception, an express statement as to duration, and provision for the Court of the seat of arbitration to perform the role of tribunal under the order in the event of the arbitrator/s becoming *functus officio*.[299]

L. Adverse Inferences

9.5. If a Party fails without satisfactory explanation to produce any Document requested in a Request to Produce to which it has not objected in due time or fails to produce any Document ordered to be produced by the Arbitral Tribunal, the Arbitral Tribunal may infer that such document would be adverse to the interests of that Party.

9.6. If a Party fails without satisfactory explanation to make available any other relevant evidence, including testimony, sought by one Party to which the Party to whom the request was addressed has not objected in due time or fails to make available any evidence, including testimony, ordered by the Arbitral Tribunal to be produced, the Arbitral Tribunal may infer that such evidence would be adverse to the interests of that Party.

1. Introduction

12.357 Articles 9.5 and 9.6 make express provision for the drawing of adverse (also known as negative) inferences by a tribunal in circumstances where evidence has been withheld by a party to the arbitration. The mechanism of adverse inference is considered at 12.53-12.56 in the broader context of assessment by the tribunal of the weight of available evidence pursuant to its powers under Article 9.1 of the IBA Rules.

[298] Born (n 9) 2319–2423 and fn 314. See also Baizea and Richard (n 279) 75–77.

[299] Michael Hwang and Nicholas Thio, 'A Proposed Model Procedural Order on Confidentiality in International Arbitration: A Comprehensive and Self-Governing Code' (2012) Journal of International Arbitration 137. See also examples of Procedural Orders, Confidentiality Agreements and Undertakings compiled by Lalive and published in Elliott Geisinger (ed), *Confidential and Restricted Access Information in International Arbitration* (Juris Publishing 2016).

When considering the use of adverse inference by a tribunal, it is important to bear in mind that, even with the assistance of the local courts,[300] it is not always possible to guarantee compliance with a tribunal order for the production of evidence. This is in contrast to the position prevailing in relation to national courts, who have coercive powers to compel performance of court orders. Given these practical limitations, it is suggested that the use of adverse inferences is an essential part of the arbitrator's toolbox.[301] 12.358

Each of Article 9.5 (documents) and Article 9.6 (other relevant evidence, including testimony) empower the tribunal to 'infer that such [document or other relevant evidence, including testimony] would be adverse to the interests of [the non-producing] Party'.[302] 12.359

Absent a valid excuse, it may be reasonable (if not logical) to assume that the withheld information is adverse to the interests of the party controlling it and the tribunal may form a view on the kind of information or evidence that is being withheld.[303] However, the mechanism of adverse inference must be used appropriately and cautiously. Articles 9.5 and Article 9.6 understandably contain no guidance on the nature of the adverse inference to be drawn. As mentioned, they merely state that the tribunal may 'infer that such [document/evidence] is adverse to the interests of the [defaulting] Party'. The appropriate adverse inference (if any) to be drawn will be case specific—the drawing of a conclusion from known or assumed facts. Those facts must be identified and the precise inference that can be drawn from them must be carefully formulated. We suggest that it is up to the requesting party to explain to the tribunal the precise nature of the adverse inference it asks to be drawn and why such an inference is a reasonable one. 12.360

2. Conditions for Adverse Inferences

Articles 9.5 and 9.6 set conditions for the drawing of adverse inferences by the tribunal: 12.361

(a) The document or evidence in question was requested by a party or ordered by a tribunal;
(b) No objection to production has been raised or, if it has, the objection has been overruled by the tribunal and an order for production made;
(c) The producing party has failed to produce the document or other evidence requested or ordered; and
(d) There has been no satisfactory explanation for the failure to produce by the party in default.

300 IBA Rules (n 3), Articles 3.9, 3.10, and 4.9.
301 Sharpe (n 226) 550–51;
302 Commentary on the IBA Rules (n 64) 26 indicates that the use of adverse inferences under IBA Rules (n 3) Articles 9.5 and 9.6 may be an appropriate sanction for violation of the requirement of good faith.
303 Waincymer (n 12) 775–78.

12.362 The first three factors are straightforward matters of fact that should not be controversial. The last factor may require more detailed consideration.

12.363 It will be a matter for the tribunal's discretion as to whether any explanation provided by the defaulting party for the non-production is considered satisfactory. The reasons given will be case specific and will have to be assessed by a tribunal on their merits, and sometimes taking into account prior issues of default or conduct by that party.

12.364 One obvious possible explanation for non-production is that the party said to be in default does not have the relevant document or other evidence. It is suggested that tribunals should only resort to use of adverse inferences if they are confident that the party in default has the evidence but is refusing to produce it.[304]

12.365 Similar issues may arise where the evidence in question is held by an associated company of the party in default and there is a dispute as to whether or not the party has access to it. The question of whether, in such circumstances, a document is in the possession, custody, or control of a party to the arbitration is addressed at Chapter 6 paras 6.165–6.198. However, if the tribunal concludes that the document is available to the defaulting party, if it is not produced, then there seems to be no reason why a tribunal should not consider drawing an adverse inference. Sharpe supports this view:

> Occasionally, however, a party's purported inability to produce evidence is pretextual, as the evidence sought might well be in the hands of a parent, subsidiary or related company. In such cases, the arbitral tribunal may determine that the requested documents are in fact accessible to the requested party, and may draw appropriate inferences from their non-production.[305]

12.366 Of course, regardless of what the tribunal's initial conclusion may have been on the issue of 'possession, custody or control', if (for whatever reason) the third party proves uncooperative in permitting access to the document, and this can be demonstrated to the satisfaction of the tribunal, the pre-conditions for use of adverse inferences set out in Article 9.6 are unlikely to be met.[306]

12.367 Furthermore, while it may be appropriate to draw adverse inferences where it is established that the party had a document but deliberately destroyed it to avoid production,[307] some tribunals may require that it first be established that the defaulting party had an obligation to preserve evidence and/or was aware of that obligation.[308]

[304] Waincymer (n 12) 864. A similar view was expressed in: Vera van Houtte, 'Adverse Inferences in International Arbitration' in Teresa Giovannini and Alexis Mourre (eds), *Written Evidence and Discovery in International Arbitration: New Issues and Tendencies* (Kluwer Law International 2009) 202 (hereafter 'van Houtte').

[305] Sharpe (n 226) 558.

[306] See further ibid 557–58;

[307] For more detail about the US Courts test for drawing these inferences, see ibid 558.

[308] ibid. For more detail about the loss and destruction of documents, see 12.258– 12.274.

3. The Nature of the Inference to Be Drawn

Even if a tribunal is persuaded that, as a matter of principle, the drawing of adverse inferences is justified, it is not an easy task to identify what particular inference can or should be made. The content of the document or other evidence withheld may not be known and the precise subject matter in relation to which an adverse inference might be drawn not readily apparent. Even where, in a case of withheld oral testimony, the witness has previously provided a witness statement, the position is difficult. In certain circumstances it might be inferred that the witness has failed to attend an evidential hearing to give oral testimony because, under cross-examination, that evidence will be different to that contained in the witness statement, but in what respects? **12.368**

One helpful illustration of the difficulty of formulating an appropriate adverse inference is a dispute involving a construction delay claim where the contractor refuses to produce all construction schedules. Is it reasonable for the tribunal to draw an adverse inference that the contractor breached the requirement to maintain scheduling records or, alternatively, would it be fair for the tribunal to infer that the contractor concealed from the owner the fact that the project would be delayed?[309] A further illustration is that described below: **12.369**

> [W]hen a requesting party pretends that its opponent has an internal document (e.g. board minutes) that contains an acknowledgement of its debt to the requesting party, what adverse inference can a tribunal draw from the debtor's refusal to produce the document? It will probably infer that the debtor acknowledged that it owed something to the requesting party. But it will be unable to infer whether the acknowledgement was for the total amount of the debt or only a part thereof, whether it was an unconditional acknowledgement and whether any modalities were linked to the acknowledgement.[310]

There is a dearth of guidance as to how a tribunal should approach the formulation of adverse inferences, most likely because of the necessity for such inferences to be case specific. One of few statutory provisions that explicitly authorizes arbitrators to draw negative inferences is the English Arbitration Act 1996, s 41(7)(b), which states that if a party fails to comply with a peremptory order,[311] the tribunal may 'draw *such adverse inferences* from the act of non-compliance *as the circumstances justify*'.[312] However, that provision is also very general in terms and simply ties the inferences to be drawn to the circumstances of the case. **12.370**

[309] See Nadia Darwazeh, 'Document Discovery and the IBA Rules on Evidence: A Practitioner's View' (2002) International Arbitration Law Review 101, 107–08. The example is also mentioned at para 2.97.

[310] Van Houtte (n 304) 204–05.

[311] English Arbitration Act 1996, s 41(5) empowers the tribunal to make a peremptory order, which sets a final deadline for the defaulting party to comply with a previous order. If a party fails to comply with that peremptory order the English Court may make an order under English Arbitration Act 1996, s 42 requiring compliance with the tribunal's peremptory order.

[312] Emphasis added.

12.371 As a matter of practice, the drawing of adverse inferences can be problematic for a tribunal even in relation to fact evidence. In relation to expert evidence, the position is even more difficult because the issues upon which experts are asked to opine are rarely binary in nature. On the rare occasions when expert evidence is withheld, it may be impossible to define the appropriate inference that might be drawn from the withholding of that evidence.

12.372 It is been suggested that any inferences drawn must be reasonable,[313] but other authors suggest that 'reasonableness' is not a helpful guide to determining precisely what inferences may be justified.[314]

12.373 Of course, there are circumstances where it is possible to make a reasonable case for the drawing of a particular inference. For example, in a minority shareholder dispute, the majority shareholder may claim that the terms of a particular related-party transaction, which the majority shareholder caused the company to enter into without approval of the minority shareholders, was beneficial for the company to which the dispute relates, but refuses to produce a category of documents that might verify this. In such a case, the tribunal might infer that the transaction was not beneficial for the company and, therefore, that it had a negative effect on the company's value. This conclusion is justified and reasonable because the evidence can only produce a binary result—the transaction is either beneficial, or it is not. Had it been beneficial, the document would have been produced. As it has not been produced, the tribunal is entitled to infer that the documents would prove that the transaction was not beneficial to the company. What the tribunal cannot do, in the absence of other evidence, is to make any inference as to the *measure* of financial damage caused to the company as a result of the transaction.

12.374 It is right that a tribunal should consider very carefully what inferences it is possible to draw from the non-production of a particular piece of evidence. However, it is also important for the tribunal to have in mind the prejudice that may be caused to a party to the dispute where its opponent deliberately withholds material evidence helpful to that party's case. The point has been made that the more reluctant tribunals are to draw negative inference in appropriate cases, the more incentive there may be for parties to act in bad faith.[315]

4. The Weight to Be Attached to Adverse Inferences

12.375 Adverse inferences do not remove the need for other evidence relating to the same subject matter. The appropriate adverse inference (if any) is the drawing of a conclusion from known or assumed facts. Those facts must be identified and the precise inference

[313] Van Houtte (n 304) 207; and Sharpe (n 226) 558.

[314] See, eg Frédéric G Sourgens, Kabir Duggal, and Ian A Laird, *Evidence in International Investment Arbitration* (OUP 2018) paras 8.11–8.21 (hereafter 'Sourgens, Duggal, and Laird').

[315] ibid paras 8.43–8.45.

that can be drawn from them must be carefully formulated. A failure to produce documents or other evidence does not shift the burden of proof on to the defaulting party[316] and any resulting adverse inference is likely to carry less weight than other direct evidence.[317] Vera van Houtte describes the position this way:

> An adverse inference belongs to the category of indirect evidence. It is in fact a presumption that a party that presumably has control over certain evidence does not produce it because it is harmful to its case. An arbitrator who, as a fact-finder, makes an unfavourable deduction based on a party's failure to produce evidence that is favourable to it accepts indirect evidence and cannot as such give it the same weight as direct evidence.
>
> Because of its reduced evidential weight, the adverse inference in itself is insufficient evidence to justify an *intime conviction* or to create a 'preponderance of evidence'. Its value is relative and depends on the existence and weight of other evidence and its consistency with that other evidence.[318]

Other authors have expressed similar views: **12.376**

> To the extent that a point is proved through the submission of an inference, the tribunal still must determine whether the direct evidence used as a foundation for the inference is probative and credible—i.e., it must determine whether the evidence states what the party relying upon it submits it does and must further determine whether the evidence is credible. This part of a party's submission remains subject to the same standard of proof as before.[319]

However, while it is correct that adverse inferences belong to the category of indirect evidence, and may therefore have less weight than direct evidence, they still have evidential value. There are many examples of facts being established on the basis of indirect evidence, particularly where there is a large body of such evidence pointing in the same direction. **12.377**

That said, the tribunal will still have to decide the case on the basis of the totality of evidence before it. If the inference sought is inconsistent with the available documentary record, the tribunal should refuse to draw the inference.[320] In addition, a tribunal may **12.378**

[316] Although in some cases, if assessed in combination with an established prima facie case, it may be sufficient. As one commentator has put it: '. . . the sanction for an opponent who fails to bring evidence that rebuts the prima facie case is not the same as for a party that has not discharged its burden of proof. The arbitral tribunal can (in certain circumstances or under certain conditions . . .) but need not draw an adverse inference from the non-production that, together with the prima facie case established by the claimant, will be part of the total evidence to be assessed by the tribunal when forming its in time conviction'; van Houtte (n 304) 196.

[317] See further: Sharpe (n 226) 552; van Houtte (n 304) 195–96; Sourgens, Duggal, and Laird (n 314) paras 2.15–2.18.

[318] Van Houtte (n 304) 197.

[319] Sourgens, Duggal, and Laird (n 314) para 8.28.

[320] See, eg '*Frederica Lincoln Riahi v The Islamic Republic of Iran*, Award, IUSCT Case No. 485 (600-485-1), 27 February 2003' in Albert Jan van den Berg (ed), *Yearbook Commercial Arbitration* (vol *XXVIII*, Kluwer Law International 2003) 464, 208–10 (hereafter '*Riahi*') although this conclusion was questioned by Charles N. Brower in his dissenting opinion. See ibid 533–34.

refuse to draw negative inferences when the non-defaulting party has itself not done its best to produce corroborative evidence of the inference sought.[321]

12.379 In addition, tribunals are generally reluctant to hold that a fact is proven by negative inferences alone, without being corroborated by other (even if indirect) evidence.

5. Due Process

12.380 Attempts are sometimes made to set aside an award in circumstances where it is alleged that a tribunal has either drawn negative inferences it should have not drawn, or has not drawn inferences where it was appropriate to do so. Courts are generally averse to setting aside an award on this basis because findings of fact and the weighing of evidence are matters for the tribunal.[322]

12.381 However, in some circumstances, there may be justified criticism of procedural steps relating to a tribunal's decision on the use of adverse inferences. It is important that due process is followed, and that the parties—in particular, any party threatened with adverse inferences—has a fair opportunity to make submissions on that point to the tribunal. In order to ensure due process, it is suggested that a tribunal should make clear the consequences of non-compliance with an order for production of documents or other evidence, including the fact that the adverse inferences may be drawn if the evidence is not produced.[323] The defaulting party may not otherwise fully appreciate the need to produce the document or other evidence in order to remove the grounds for an adverse inference being drawn. The unsatisfactory nature of such a situation will be heightened when a document in question actually contains evidence that disproves the inference that is later requested to be drawn. For example, in the example described in 12.369, the mere production of a complete set of scheduling records will answer an allegation (and inference sought to be drawn) that the producing party was in breach of an obligation to maintain such records.[324]

12.382 Consistent with these considerations, the risk of adverse inferences being drawn is highlighted by some tribunals in document production orders. A number of such orders in ICC cases have been found to include such warning.[325] In other cases, the

[321] For more detail, see Sharpe (n 226) 554–57.

[322] See, eg '*United Mexican States v The Attorney General of Canada*, Marvin Roy Feldman Karpa (US), Superior Court of Justice of Ontario, 03-CV-23500, 3 December 2003' in Albert Jan van den Berg (ed), *Yearbook Commercial Arbitration* (vol *XXIX*, Kluwer Law International 2004) 167; *Dongwoo Mann + Hummel Co Ltd. v Mann+Hummel GmbH* [2008] SGHC 67; *Bhandari v Satish Jassal* OMP No. 257/2007 (High Court of Delhi, 3 August 2007); *Tribunal Fédéral Suisse* Case 4 A.450/2007 (9 January 2008). For more detail, see van Houtte (n 304) 210–12.

[323] Van Houtte (n 304) 208; Sharpe (n 226) 569–70.

[324] See further Sharpe (n 226) 551.

[325] Hamilton (n 134) 80–81, author of a review of such orders, notes that: 'A nother way of inciting compliance with document production orders is for the arbitral tribunal to state that it will draw appropriate or negative inferences in the event that the documents are not produced by the party requested to produce them. In eight of the procedural orders examined reference was made to such practice. In five cases the arbitral tribunal warned that it would or could draw appropriate conclusions from a party's refusal to produce the documents requested.'

warning may be given by way of a peremptory order making clear the consequences of default. Where the tribunal has invited the non-defaulting party to make submissions on the nature of the inference that it is said can be drawn from the default, the defaulting party should also be given an opportunity to respond. Whether a failure to warn the relevant party will provide grounds on which to challenge the tribunal or the award will depend very much on the facts of the case and the significance of any inferences drawn to the outcome of the case. We think the cases in which such a challenge is warranted will be relatively rare.[326]

6. Examples of Adverse Inferences

Sourgens, Duggal, and Laird suggest that tribunals frequently make findings of facts by means of inferences, particularly when documents are scarce and witness evidence is self-serving.[327] In our experience, tribunals are cautious about drawing an adverse inference and, when they are prepared to draw one, they will often avoid placing significant reliance on it in the award. Unsurprisingly, it is difficult to find published awards where the nature and effect of adverse inferences is considered in any detail. This does not mean tribunals do not regularly draw adverse conclusions when weighing the evidence;[328] rather, simply that they prefer not to say so explicitly and tend to rely on such inferences in conjunction with other supporting evidence.[329] **12.383**

A helpful example of adverse inferences can be found in NAFTA arbitration case *Feldman*,[330] where the claimant alleged that Mexico improperly refused to rebate excise taxes applied to his company while extending these benefits to Mexican companies in the same position. The tribunal held that the claimant 'established a presumption and a prima facie case that the claimant had been treated in a different and less favourable manner than several Mexican-owned cigarette retailers, and the respondent had failed to introduce any credible evidence into the record to rebut that presumption.'[331] The tribunal concluded that, had evidence withheld by Mexico been favourable to its case, Mexico would have produced it. On that basis the tribunal drew a negative inference that the claimant had been discriminated against (although one arbitrator dissented). **12.384**

[326] For example, in a case decided by the Swiss Supreme Court the award was upheld even though the tribunal drew adverse inferences without first warning the parties of this possibility. *Tribunal Fédéral Suisse* Case 4 A.450/2007 (9 January 2008). For more detail, see van Houtte (n 304) 210–12.

[327] Sourgens, Duggal, and Laird (n 314) para 8.01.

[328] See 12.31–12.56.

[329] Van Houtte (n 304) 208; Laurence Craig, William Park, and Jan Paulsson, *International Chamber of Commerce Arbitration* (3rd edn, Dobbs Ferry 2000) 456; Andrew de Iotbiniere McDougall and Nicholas Bouchardie, 'L'arbitre international et la prevue documentaire: How International Tribunals Establish the Facts of a Case Through Documentary Evidence' (2018) International Business Law Journal 517.

[330] *Marvin Roy Feldman Karpa v United Mexican States* (Award, 16 December 2002) ICSID Case No. ARB(AF)/99/1, (2003) 42 ILM 625.

[331] ibid 662.

12.385 In *Riahi*, the claimant struggled to prove ownership of 510 bearer shares in a company involved in trading steel. The claimant invited the tribunal to draw adverse inferences from the failure of the respondent to submit any corporate records of the company to contradict the claimant's ownership of shares. The claimant invited the tribunal to infer that the records, if produced, would correspond to a list of shareholders filed by the claimant. Although the tribunal noted the possible difficulties that an owner of bearer shares can face in proving ownership of shares without a share certificates, the tribunal in this case found that the inference that it was asked to draw was not an appropriate one on the facts of the case. It found that:

> With respect to the Claimant's request that the Tribunal draw an adverse inference from the Respondent's failure to produce Khoshkeh's share register, the Tribunal notes that the matter in respect of 510 shares concerns bearer shares and that Iranian law does not require that transfers of bearer shares be entered into share registers of the companies. In addition, Article 10 of the Articles of Association of Khoshkeh provides that only the transfer of registered shares requires the approval of the board of directors and recording in the share register. The Tribunal therefore is not convinced that the share register or other requested corporate records of Khoshkeh would show that the Claimant owned these 510 bearer shares and that the transfer of those shares from her spouse took place before his shares were expropriated. Accordingly, the Tribunal finds no need to consider the issue of whether the Respondent has complied with the relevant Tribunal Orders as far as Khoshkeh is concerned.[332]

12.386 However, a dissenting arbitrator questioned this conclusion against the background of a repeated failure by the respondent to produce the relevant documents and suggested that a failure to draw negative inferences left the claimant with no effective remedy:

> [T]he Award arbitrarily denies the Claimant any ability to have satisfied this extraordinary burden of proof. Correctly, the Tribunal ordered the Respondent, not once, but twice, on 18 November 1994 and again on 18 May 1995 (five years and more prior to the Hearing), to produce, inter alia, the share registers (and some related documents) of each of the six corporate entities it had expropriated in which the Claimant alleged an interest, as well as financial statements and audit reports of five of those six entities. (Footnote omitted) [. . .]
>
> The Respondent never denied possession of the requested records; indeed, such possession was confirmed by its selective inclusion in later written submissions of an outdated portion of the share register of one company (Tarvandan) and certain financial records of others (Khoshkeh and Iran Bohler). The twice-ordered production,

[332] *Riahi* (n 320) [90]–[104].

however, was never made. When the Tribunal by Order of 10 July 1995 deferred until an unspecified 'later stage of the proceedings' any decision on 'the question whether the Respondent has complied with the Tribunal's [production] Orders' (which it clearly had not), the Claimant requested that the Tribunal draw the usual inferences against the Respondent and in her favor establishing her claimed ownership interests, (footnote omitted) a request repeated thereafter with both frequency and force. Quite evidently, the Claimant, though able to make out a prima facie case, was in no position to prove her case 'beyond a reasonable doubt' without such inferences, for the drawing of which she had satisfied all applicable criteria.[333]

M. Costs Sanctions for Lack of Good Faith

9.7. If the Arbitral Tribunal determines that a Party has failed to conduct itself in good faith in the taking of evidence, the Arbitral Tribunal may, in addition to any other measures available under these Rules, take such failure into account in its assignment of the costs of the arbitration, including costs arising out of or in connection with the taking of evidence.

1. Introduction

Article 9.7 enables a tribunal to take a party's failure to act in good faith into account when allocating costs of the arbitration. **12.387**

Preamble 3 states that the taking of evidence shall be conducted on the principle that each party shall act in good faith.[334] That statement might be read as merely aspirational were it not for Article 9.7 of the IBA Rules,[335] which makes clear that a party's failure to act in good faith may attract a financial sanction, thereby confirming the existence of an obligation to act in good faith.[336] **12.388**

[333] Described by the dissenting arbitrator in these terms: 'According to precedent, the Tribunal may appropriately draw adverse inferences when: (1) the requested documents are relevant and material to the proceedings; (2) the Tribunal is convinced that the requested documents are at the disposal of the requested party; (3) the requesting party has made out a prima facie case; (4) the party failing to produce the requested documents has offered no satisfactory explanation for its failure; and (5) the requested party has been given sufficient time and opportunity to produce the requested documents, but has failed to do so . . .'.

[334] See Chapter 2 paras 2.43–2.99.

[335] Introduced in 2010 at the same time as the principle of good faith was introduced into the Preamble.

[336] This analysis is consistent with the view taken by other commentators. For example, Ashford (n 127) 13 states that 'Whilst there is . . . no express reference to a duty of good faith, any doubt that such a duty arises is removed by the new provision at Article 9.7'. Newmark makes a similar point; Christopher Newmark, '"Efficient, Economical and Fair": The Mantra of the New IBA Rules' (2010) International Arbitration Law Review 165, 166 (hereafter 'Newmark').

2. Assignment of Costs

12.389 Article 9.7 of the IBA Rules makes express provision for a tribunal to impose costs sanctions where a party fails to conduct itself in good faith in the taking of evidence. That provision states:

> If the Arbitral Tribunal determines that a Party has failed to conduct itself in good faith *in the taking of evidence*, the Arbitral Tribunal may, in addition to any other measures available under these Rules, *take such failure into account in its assignment of the costs of the arbitration, including* costs arising out of or in connection with the taking of evidence'.[337]

3. The Scope of the Power to Assign Costs

12.390 The emphasized words in the above extract require close attention.

12.391 The costs sanction provided by Article 9.7 relates only to a failure to act in good faith 'in the taking of evidence'. This is consistent with the nature and scope of the IBA Rules—namely, the management of conduct relating to the taking of evidence.

12.392 However, the power to assign costs relates to the entire 'costs of the arbitration'—ie the costs that may be assigned against a party that has failed to act in good faith are not limited to costs incurred in connection with the taking of evidence. This adds greater weight to the sanction and makes its practical application more straightforward.[338]

12.393 Martinez-Fraga has argued that giving a tribunal the express power to impose costs penalties for lack of good faith conduct ascribes to the arbitration process a public policy objective that it does not have.[339] It has also been suggested that extending the potential costs sanctions to costs not arising out of the taking of evidence goes beyond the mandate of the IBA Rules.[340] However, while these are valid points to make, these views may give insufficient weight to the internationally recognized duty of a tribunal to ensure a fair and efficient process, a principle that is widely reflected in domestic arbitration laws and institutional rules,[341] and importantly, is enshrined in the IBA Rules themselves.[342] Bad or obstructive conduct will nearly always involve wasted time and increased costs.

337 Emphasis added.

338 Ignoring any general discretion to allocate costs that may exist under applicable arbitration rules or arbitration laws, if the costs to be allocated were limited to costs relating to the taking of evidence it might be very difficult to isolate those costs from other costs incurred on other aspects of the arbitration.

339 Pedro J Martinez-Fraga, 'King or Arbitrator: Exploring the Inherent Authority of Arbitrators to Impose Sanctions within the Framework of the 2010 IBA Rules on the Taking of Evidence in International Arbitration' (2011) 12 Spain Arbitration Review 57, 58–59 and 62.

340 Newmark (n 336) 166; Ashford (n 127) 15.

341 See Chapter 2 paras 2.7–2.24.

342 See IBA Rules (n 3) Preamble 1.

Before imposing a cost sanction, the tribunal should satisfy itself that a party has indeed acted in bad faith.[343] Issues may arise around whether counsel, or the party instructing them, is primarily responsible for the conduct in question.[344] However, in each case, counsel will still be acting as agent or representative of his or her instructing party and the question of whether the conduct was driven by the client or by counsel will be irrelevant to the issue of whether a breach has arisen. However, the tribunal may consider it a relevant factor in deciding whether and how to sanction the conduct. 12.394

4. Practical Examples

Whether a tribunal will impose a costs sanction in response to a failure by a party to act in good faith will depend upon the facts of the case, the nature of the conduct complained about, the history of the proceedings to date, and the views and attitudes of the particular tribunal. Each case will be different. Nonetheless, it is helpful for both parties and tribunals to consider what approaches and responses have been proposed and adopted in other cases. 12.395

We are aware of cases where a party has been penalized in costs in relation to the taking of evidence—in particular, in relation to document production. For example, in one LCIA case the tribunal felt it appropriate to increase the percentage of costs payable by a respondent by approximately 50 per cent to take account of that party's poor conduct in relation to production of documents. The Commentary on the IBA Rules refers expressly to a failure to comply with an order to produce documents as rendering a party susceptible to an order under Article 9.7.[345] 12.396

Published ICC cases provide many examples of costs sanctions imposed for reasons of party conduct. Although the corresponding provision in the ICC Rules does not contain an express reference to a party's failure to act in good faith, it does permit the tribunal to take into account all relevant circumstances and the extent to which each party has conducted the arbitration in an expeditious and cost-effective manner.[346] The provision provides a basis for argument that a party has acted in bad faith and should be penalized in costs. 12.397

In one such case involving a dispute over the sale of manufacturing plant, although neither party had been completely successful in its claims, the tribunal ordered that the whole of the costs of the arbitration should be borne by one party. The tribunal's decision was based on its view that the paying party had failed to act in good faith and 12.398

343 See discussion at 2.81–2.86.
344 ibid.
345 Commentary on the IBA Rules (n 64).
346 ICC Rules, Article 37.5. Earlier iterations of the ICC Rules did not include a reference to party conduct, but nonetheless afforded the tribunal a general discretion in relation to allocation of costs. See ICC Rules 1988, Article 20 and ICC Rules 1998, Article 31.

should be penalized in costs.[347] The tribunal listed the cumulative instances of default it had taken into account:

> The defendant made none of the advance payments on costs which are required for the proceedings. Further, *not only did it file its counterclaim belatedly*, that is, only after the first draft of the terms of reference; *it also refused to sign the terms of reference*, which had been modified according to its wishes, notwithstanding a detailed explanation by the arbitral tribunal of the terms' meaning and legal consequences, and *it did not participate in the oral hearings* although it had been given sufficient notice to appear. Further, *it also contributed to unnecessary delay and confusion in the proceedings by appointing counsel at the last moment*, that is, after the closing of the oral hearings and shortly before the expiry of the latest time limit for a statement concerning the minutes of the hearings; compounded by counsel's renunciation to the mandate only a few days afterwards.[348]

12.399 Although in this case the incidents of delay and obstruction did not relate to collection and presentation of evidence, a similar approach might properly be taken when a party obstructs progress in the arbitration by persistent conduct undermining the effective presentation of evidence. For example, this may include the failure to identify all expert witnesses on whose testimony the party intends to rely with the intention to ambush or surprise the other party at a later date, raising objections to production of documents under Article 3.5 without a reasonable and good faith basis for doing so, and deliberately withholding production of documents that are known to exist and that fall within an order for production by a tribunal.[349]

12.400 On a wider interpretation, the obligation of good faith might also extend to the prohibition of conduct that *undermines* effective operation of the IBA Rules in achieving the provision of an 'efficient, economical and fair process', as required by Preamble 1. For example, this may include where a party, with the intention of causing delay or of increasing the other party's costs, submits document requests that are intentionally burdensome, or produces a significant volume of documents with only peripheral relevance to the matters in dispute but which an under-resourced receiving party will have to review in order to establish this fact.[350]

12.401 In an ICC case under the IBA Rules, the losing respondent sought to obtain an award of costs based on alleged improper conduct relating to document production requests.

[347] '*Manufacturer v Buyer*, Final Award, ICC Case No. 8486, 1996' in Albert Jan van den Berg (ed), *Yearbook of Commercial Arbitration* (vol *XXIV*, Kluwer Law International 1999) 26: 'According to the general principles of international arbitration law, the arbitral tribunal must take into account for its decision on costs not only the results of the proceedings but also the behaviour of the parties during the proceedings . . . *According to good faith, the parties to an international arbitration must in particular facilitate the proceedings and abstain from all delaying tactics . . . The behaviour of the defendant during the entire proceedings did not comply with these requirements in any way*' (emphasis added).

[348] ibid (emphasis added). See also '*Consultant v Contractor*, Final Award, ICC Case No. 6248, 1990' in Albert Jan van den Berg (ed), *Yearbook Commercial Arbitration* (vol *XIX*, Kluwer Law International 1994).

[349] See 2.71.

[350] For further discussion see 2.70–2.76.

The respondent argued that the claimant had submitted improper requests that did not comply with the IBA Rules—including some that had already been rejected by the tribunal; that the claimant had made assertions concerning the deficiency of the respondent's document production that had necessitated a search by the respondent to demonstrate that available material had already been produced; that the claimant refused to provide un-redacted copies of key documents; and the necessity for the respondent to seek the tribunal's intervention in order to obtain an adequate level of detail about the claimant's claims of privilege.

The tribunal rejected the respondent's claim. It said that, as the claimant had been the winning party, the starting point must be that the claimant should have its costs, thereby placing the onus on the respondent to demonstrate that there were facts justifying a departure from this position. On the facts of this case, the respondent had failed to do so. The tribunal appears to have concluded that the conduct relied upon was not unusual and that, where the claimant's conduct was questionable, the respondent had not suffered any prejudice because the tribunal had taken steps to prevent this happening.[351] **12.402**

The ICC Commission Report (Decisions on Costs in International Arbitration) provides further examples of conduct relevant to the taking of evidence that tribunals have taken into account when allocating costs, including, in some cases, an assessment of whether the parties acted in good faith. Cited examples of conduct giving rise to cost-shifting include a failure to reply to document production requests; withholding of evidence needed by another party; and obscuring factual and legal matters.[352] **12.403**

[351] Final Award dated October 2015 as cited in 'Extracts from ICC Case Materials on the Taking of Evidence with References to the IBA Rules' (2016) 1 ICC Dispute Resolution Bulletin 127, 13.

[352] *ICC Arbitration Commission Report on Decisions on Costs in International Arbitration* (International Chamber of Commerce 2015) 23.

APPENDIX 1

Commentary on the Revised Text of the 2010 IBA Rules on the Taking of Evidence in International Arbitration*

1999 IBA Working Party[1] *& 2010 IBA Rules of Evidence Review Subcommittee*[2]

In every arbitration, a key issue the parties and their counsel—as well as the arbitral tribunal—must face is the determination of the procedures for that arbitration. The principal institutional and ad hoc rules provide the framework for the arbitration and add detailed provisions concerning matters such as initial statements of the case, appointment of arbitrators and challenges, and the nature of the award and costs—but they are purposely silent about how evidence should be gathered and presented in any arbitration pursuant to those rules.

Quite properly, the principal institutional and ad hoc rules do not require that every arbitration be conducted in the same manner and so allow parties flexibility in devising the procedures best suited for each arbitration. Party autonomy and flexibility are among the significant advantages of international arbitration.

However, in many cases this intentional gap in the rules can cause problems if the parties have conflicting views as to how the case should proceed. This is particularly so when the parties come from different legal backgrounds and cultures. Problems can also occur when one or both of the parties are inexperienced in international arbitration.

* This article is a revised and expanded version of the commentary to the previous text of the IBA Rules, 'Commentary on the New IBA Rules of Evidence in International Commercial Arbitration', published in 2 B.L.I., pp. 16–36 (2000).

1 The *IBA Rules on the Taking of Evidence in International Commercial Arbitration* were drafted by a Working Party appointed by the Committee on Arbitration and ADR of the International Bar Association (Committee D). The Working Party was led by Giovanni Ughi of Italy, and its members were Hans Bagner, Sweden; John Beechey, England; Jacques Buhart, France; Peter Caldwell, Hong Kong; Bernardo M. Cremades, Spain; Otto De Witt Wijnen, The Netherlands; Emmanuel Gaillard, France; Paul A. Gelinas, France; Pierre A. Karrer, Switzerland; Wolfgang Kilhn, Germany (former Chair of Committee D); Jan Paulsson, France; Hilmar Raeschke-Kessler, Germany; David W. Rivkin, United States (Chairman of Committee D); Hans van Houtte, Belgium; and Johnny Veeder, England.

2 On 29 May 2010, the IBA Council approved the revised version of the IBA Rules on the Taking of Evidence in International Arbitration. In 2008, the Arbitration Committee of the International Bar Association tasked the IBA Rules of Evidence Review Subcommittee with the review of the 1999 IBA Rules. The Subcommittee was led by Richard Kreindler of United States/Germany, and its members were David Arias, Spain; C. Mark Baker, United States; Pierre Bienvenu, Canada (former co-chair of the Arbitration Committee); Antonias Dimolitsa, Greece; Paul Friedland, United States; Nicolas Gamboa, Colombia; Judith Gill, Q.C., United Kingdom (co-chair of the Arbitration Committee); Peter Heckel, Germany; Stephen Jagusch, New Zealand; Xiang Ji, China; Kap-You (Kevin) Kim, Korea; Amy Cohen Klasener, Review Subcommittee Secretary, United States/Germany; Toby T. Landau, QC, United Kingdom; Alexis Mourre, France; Hilmar Raeschke-Kessler, Germany; David W. Rivkin, (former chair of the Arbitration Committee and of the Legal Practice Division), United States; Georg von Segesser, Switzerland; Essam al Tamimi, United Arab Emirates; Guido S. Tawil, Argentina (co-chair of the Arbitration Committee); Hiroyuki Tezuka, Japan; Ariel Ye, China.

Some three decades ago, the International Bar Association set out to assist parties by providing a mechanism to fill in the gap. The IBA is uniquely suited to provide such guidance, as its Arbitration Committee now has more than 2,500 arbitration practitioners from 90 countries around the world.

In 1983, the IBA adopted the *Supplementary Rules Governing the Presentation of Evidence in International Commercial Arbitration* (the '1983 Rules'). The 1983 Rules were generally well received and were frequently discussed at arbitration conferences as an example of the harmonisation procedures that can occur in international arbitrations.

By 1999, the nature of international arbitration had changed significantly. New procedures had developed; different norms as to appropriate procedures had taken root; and the scope of international arbitration had grown considerably, as many regions of the world formerly inhospitable to international arbitration embraced it.

As a result, the 1983 Rules needed to be updated and revised, and in 1997 Committee D of the IBA (now called the 'Arbitration Committee') formed a new Working Party, chaired by Giovanni Ughi of Italy, to do this. The Working Party consisted of 16 members (*see* fn 1). It held many meetings and discussed the Rules at public meetings of the IBA in Delhi in November 1997 and in Vancouver in September 1998. Drafts were also circulated for public comment to Committee D members and others, and were discussed at numerous arbitration conferences. The Working Party considered comments received throughout this process in drafting the final IBA Rules on the Taking of Evidence in International Commercial Arbitration, which were adopted by the IBA Council on 1 June 1999 (also referred to herein as the 'previous text of the IBA Rules').

The IBA Rules on the Taking of Evidence in International Commercial Arbitration were well received as a useful harmonisation of the procedures commonly used in international arbitration and were widely used in international arbitrations. In 2008, the IBA's Arbitration Committee (formerly called 'Committee D') established the IBA Rules of Evidence Review Subcommittee and tasked it to review and, as needed, update the 1999 IBA Rules on the Taking of Evidence in International Commercial Arbitration. It held many meetings and discussed the Rules at open fora of the IBA in Buenos Aires in October 2008, in Dubai in February 2009, and in Madrid in October 2009. It conducted an online survey of Arbitration Committee members and others in 2008. In early 2010, the Arbitration Committee circulated a draft for public comment. The contemplated revisions were discussed at numerous arbitration conferences, and the comments received were duly considered throughout this process. The revised IBA Rules on the Taking of Evidence in International Arbitration were adopted by the IBA Council on 29 May 2010 (referred to herein as the 'IBA Rules of Evidence' or the 'revised IBA Rules of Evidence').

The resulting text of the 2010 revised IBA Rules of Evidence reflects the Arbitration Committee's wish to change and update only as necessary to reflect new developments and best practices in international arbitration since 1999. Users of the IBA Rules of Evidence will recognise the same structure, mechanisms and successful balance in the 2010 revised text of the IBA Rules of Evidence. The word 'commercial' was deleted from the title of the Rules to acknowledge the fact that the IBA Rules of Evidence may be and are used both in commercial and investment arbitration.

The IBA Rules of Evidence contain procedures initially developed in civil law systems, in common law systems and even in international arbitration processes themselves. Designed to assist parties in determining what procedures to use in their particular case, they present some (but not all) of the methods for conducting international arbitration proceedings. Parties and arbitral tribunals may adopt the IBA Rules of Evidence in whole or in part—at the time of drafting the arbitration clause in a contract or once an arbitration commences—or they may use them as guidelines. Parties are free to adapt them to the particular circumstances of each matter.

This article describes the essential provisions of the IBA Rules, as revised in 2010, and provides some background on their drafting and the revision process. The Working Party and IBA Rules of Evidence Subcommittee hope this commentary will be helpful to parties in determining whether or not to use the IBA Rules of Evidence and how best to apply them in their particular arbitration. The IBA Rules of Evidence and translations of the Rules into various languages are available for download at www.ibanet.org.

Preamble

It was considered important to identify certain general principles which governed the IBA Rules of Evidence, so that parties and arbitral tribunals could best understand how to apply them. The Preamble is also important in illustrating both what the IBA Rules of Evidence hope to accomplish and what they do not intend to do.

i. The Preamble notes that the IBA Rules of Evidence are 'designed to supplement the legal provisions and the institutional, ad hoc or other rules that apply to the conduct of the arbitration'. The IBA Rules of Evidence are not intended to provide a complete mechanism for the conduct of an international arbitration (whether commercial or investment). Parties must still select a set of institutional or ad hoc rules, such as those of the ICC, AAA, LCIA, UNCITRAL or ICSID, or design their own rules, to establish the overall procedural framework for their arbitration. The IBA Rules of Evidence fill in gaps intentionally left in those procedural framework rules with respect to the taking of evidence.
ii. As the very first sentence of the Preamble notes, the IBA Rules of Evidence are intended to provide an 'efficient, economical and fair process' for the taking of evidence in international arbitration. This principle informs all of the IBA Rules of Evidence. The Working Party considered that as international arbitration grows more complex and the size of cases increases, it is important for parties and arbitral tribunals to find methods to resolve their disputes in the most effective and least costly manner. The Review Subcommittee revised this sentence to include expressly the principle of fairness. This change goes hand in hand with the revision to paragraph 3 of the Preamble, which now includes a requirement that each Party shall act 'in good faith' in the taking of evidence pursuant to the IBA Rules. At the discretion of the arbitral tribunal, violation of the good faith requirement can result in the consequences set forth in Articles 9.5, 9.6 and 9.7.
iii. It was recognised that there is not a single best way to conduct all international arbitrations, and that the flexibility inherent in international arbitration procedures is an advantage. Therefore, it was considered important to note specifically, in paragraph 2 of the Preamble, that the IBA Rules of Evidence are not intended to limit this flexibility. Indeed, as noted in that paragraph, the IBA Rules of Evidence should be used by parties and arbitral tribunals in the manner that best suits them.
iv. The Preamble notes the overriding principle of the IBA Rules of Evidence that the taking of evidence shall be conducted on the principle that each party shall be 'entitled to know, reasonably in advance of any Evidentiary Hearing or any fact or merits determination, the evidence on which the other Parties rely'. This principle infuses all of the provisions of the IBA Rules of Evidence. Accordingly, the provisions for the exchange of documentary evidence, witness statements, and expert reports, among others, provide each party and the arbitral tribunal with significant information about each side's evidence.

Definitions

The Definitions section of the IBA Rules of Evidence (no longer a numbered Article) sets forth basic definitions to be applied in the IBA Rules of Evidence. The definitions are generally straightforward, with commonly understood meanings. The definitions themselves do not provide any substantive rules of conduct or evidence.

One definition that is not so commonly used is that for 'General Rules'. This term refers in the IBA Rules of Evidence to the institutional or ad hoc rules according to which the parties are conducting their arbitration, such as those of the ICC, AAA, LCIA, UNCITRAL and ICSID. The term is used in Articles 1.3 and 1.5, which discuss among other things conflicts between the IBA Rules of Evidence and other rules that govern the arbitration proceeding.

The definition of 'Document' in the previous text of the IBA Rules was broad enough to include most forms of electronic evidence. The Review Subcommittee introduced minor changes intended to ensure that all forms of evidence, including electronic evidence, are subject to the IBA Rules and may be requested, subject to (i) the requirements of Article 3.3, including satisfaction of the relevance and materiality standard, and (ii) the reasons for objection set forth in Article 9.

Article 1—Scope of Application

International arbitrations are subject to general rules establishing the procedural framework for the arbitration and to mandatory law relating to arbitration procedure at the seat of the arbitration. Therefore, while the IBA Rules of Evidence have been drafted to conform with the principal institutional and ad hoc rules generally used by parties, conflicts may nevertheless arise with the other set of rules chosen by the parties (the 'General Rules' in the parlance of the IBA Rules of Evidence) or any mandatory legal provisions. Article 1 (formerly Article 2) sets forth several basic principles as to how arbitral tribunals should apply the IBA Rules of Evidence in the event of a conflict with any of these other provisions:

1. In a conflict between the IBA Rules of Evidence and mandatory legal provisions, the mandatory legal provisions shall govern.
2. In a conflict between the IBA Rules of Evidence and the General Rules (*i.e.*, the institutional or ad hoc rules chosen by the parties), the parties have a right, in keeping with the principle of party autonomy which is central to any international arbitration, to resolve this conflict in the manner they choose, as long as both parties agree. In the absence of such agreement, the arbitral tribunal shall try to harmonise the two sets of rules to the greatest extent possible.
3. If a conflict exists regarding the meaning of the IBA Rules of Evidence, or if both the IBA Rules of Evidence and the General Rules are silent on a particular issue, then the IBA Rules of Evidence instruct the arbitral tribunal to apply the general principles of the IBA Rules of Evidence, such as those set forth in the Preamble, to the greatest extent possible.

As mentioned above, the IBA Rules may be used in commercial or investment arbitration. However, the IBA Rules do not contain any specialised rules for investment arbitrations such as rules pertaining to the participation of *amici curiae*.

Article 1.2 provides that parties who have agreed to the application of the IBA Rules prior to 29 May 2010, the date of adoption of the 2010 revisions, shall be deemed to have agreed to the previous version of the IBA Rules in the absence of a contrary indication. As the IBA Rules could be potentially subject to further updates, parties wishing to apply the version of the IBA Rules current at the time of the arbitration should consider including this in the arbitration clause (*see* suggested arbitration clause in the Foreword to the IBA Rules).

Article 2—Consultation on Evidentiary Issues

The 2010 revisions include the addition of a new Article 2. The Subcommittee carefully considered whether and how the IBA Rules should be adapted or expanded in response to the increased size and complexity of arbitrations and the evidentiary issues associated with them. After review of various sets of domestic and international arbitration rules and procedures, the Subcommittee agreed on a 'meet and consult' approach.

Article 2.1 provides for a mandatory consultation between the arbitral tribunal and the parties 'at the earliest appropriate time in the proceedings'. Under normal circumstances, this consultation would coincide with a procedural conference or exchange of views early in the proceedings. Early timing allows the participants to organise the taking of evidence in an efficient, economical and fair manner. Where the evidentiary issues are not considered to be sufficiently clear at an early stage in the arbitration, the arbitral tribunal might postpone such conference or exchange.

The issues which may be appropriate for discussion at the Article 2.1 consultation include, but are not limited to, those enumerated in Article 2.2. While Article 2 provides a framework for discussing evidentiary issues, it is not intended to prescribe how evidence should be taken in any particular arbitration. For example, in any given arbitration the arbitral tribunal and the parties may determine not to require disclosure of electronic evidence. On the other hand, if they determine that taking evidence in electronic form would be conducive to the efficient, economical and fair taking of evidence, it may be advisable to discuss the related details at an early stage, such as the form of production (Article 3.12(b)) and the formulating of requests to produce by identifying specific files, search terms, individuals or other means for searching for documents in an efficient and economical manner (Article 3.3(a)(ii)).

Article 2.2(e) encourages discussion of means to save time and costs in the arbitration. It also refers to the conservation of resources in connection of the taking of evidence, which could include, by way of example, the economic and environmental costs of travel or document reproduction (including by submitting documents using web-based platforms such as NetCase, the platform of the ICC).

Article 2.3 (formerly paragraph 3 of the Preamble) encourages arbitral tribunals to identify to the parties, as early as possible, the issues that they may regard as relevant to the case and material to its outcome. That paragraph also notes that a preliminary determination of certain issues may be appropriate. While the Working Party did not want to encourage litigation-style motion practice, the Working Party recognised that in some cases certain issues may resolve all or part of a case. In such circumstances, the IBA Rules of Evidence make clear that the arbitral tribunal has the authority to address such matters first, so as to avoid potentially unnecessary work.

Article 3—Production of Documents

Article 3 deals with documents that the parties wish to introduce as evidence into the arbitral proceedings.

Article 3 refers to three groups of documents:

(1) documents that are at the party's own disposal; (2) documents that the party wants to use as evidence for its submissions but cannot produce on its own, because they are either in the possession of the other party in the arbitral proceedings or in the possession of a third party outside of the arbitration; and (3) documents that neither party has introduced or wants to introduce as evidence into the arbitral proceedings, but which are seen as relevant and material by the arbitral tribunal. In addition, Article 3 contains several general principles for the treatment of documents as evidence by the parties and by the arbitral tribunal.

Production of Documents Available to One Party

The IBA Rules of Evidence begin with the principle that each party shall introduce those documents available to it and on which it wants to rely as evidence.[3] This provision reflects the principle, generally accepted in both civil law and common law countries, that parties have a burden to come forward with the evidence that supports their case.

Article 3.1 contains the phrase 'within the time ordered by the arbitral tribunal'. This phrase is repeated throughout the IBA Rules of Evidence when a submission is to be made or an action to be taken by the parties. The Working Party believed that the best course is to maintain maximum schedule flexibility for the parties and arbitral tribunals. Therefore, throughout the IBA Rules of Evidence, as here, time frames are left to be determined by the arbitral tribunal in each case, presumably in consultation with the parties. For example, with respect to the initial production of documents on which each party intends to rely, the specific time when such documents are to be submitted may vary depending upon how well framed are the issues in the initial pleadings. Time frames will also, of course, vary depending upon the complexity of the matter, the resources and locations of the parties and the particular circumstances of each case.

[3] *See* UNCITRAL Model Law, Article 23; HKIAC Rules, Article 23.2; ICC Rules, Article 20(2); ICDR Arbitration Rules, Article 19.2; ICSID Arbitration Rules, Rule 33; LCIA Rules, Article 15.6; SCC Arbitration Rules, Article 26(2); WIPO Arbitration Rules, Articles 35–36.

Following such an initial production of documents on which each party intends to rely, later submissions in the case, such as witness statements or expert reports, may make it necessary for parties to submit additional documents to rebut statements contained in such submissions. Article 3.11 (formerly Article 3.10) provides for such a second round of submission of documents within each party's possession. Again, the arbitral tribunal is to determine when such a second round of production may take place.

Documents in the Possession of an Opposing Party

The issue of whether and under what conditions one party should be able to request production of documents from another party occupied much of the Working Party's discussions in 1999. The vigour with which this issue was debated demonstrated that the question of document production was the key area in which practitioners from common law countries and civil law countries differ. The debate produced a balanced approach that became a central aspect of the IBA Rules of Evidence and has become widely accepted by both common law and civil law practitioners. The current revision of the IBA Rules of Evidence preserves this balance.

Principles

The Working Party was able to reach agreement on certain principles governing document production because practices in international arbitration can be, and have been, harmonised to a large extent. The Working Party was guided by several principles:

1. Expansive American- or English-style discovery is generally inappropriate in international arbitration. Rather, requests for documents to be produced should be carefully tailored to issues that are relevant and material to the determination of the case.
2. At the same time, however, it was believed that there is a general consensus, even among practitioners from civil law countries, that some level of document production is appropriate in international arbitration. According to some of the most frequently used general rules, arbitral tribunals are to establish the facts of the case 'by all appropriate means'.[4] This includes the competence of the arbitral tribunal to order one party to introduce certain documents, including internal documents, into the arbitral proceedings upon request of the other party. Even in some civil law countries, a State court is entitled to order the production of internal documents, either upon request of one party or because it sees the need for these documents itself.
3. The revised text of the IBA Rules provides that requests to produce are to be directed both to the arbitral tribunal and to the other parties. In the first instance, a party is to produce all documents requested in its possession, custody or control as to which it makes no objection (Article 3.4). However, the decision on the scope of document production—whether or not a party must introduce internal documents into the arbitral proceedings against its will—shall lie solely with the arbitral tribunal. Therefore, only the arbitral tribunal has the competence to make a decision on the request if the receiving party refuses to produce the requested documents voluntarily.
4. The scope of the permissible document request is also limited by certain objections described in Article 9.2 (*see* the discussion of these objections below) or the failure to satisfy the requirements set forth in Article 3.3. A party may raise any of the reasons for objection in opposing the document request. If it does so, the arbitral tribunal may first invite the relevant parties to consult with each other with a view to resolving the objection (Article 3.6).
5. If the objection is not resolved by means of such consultation, either party may request the arbitral tribunal to make a decision as to whether or not any of these objections apply as well as a decision on the propriety of the request for production itself (Article 3.7, formerly Article 3.6).

[4] Eg ICC Rules, Article 20(1); LCIA Rules, Article 22.l(c).

> The arbitral tribunal shall order the production if it is convinced, first, that the issues that the requesting party wishes to prove are relevant to the case and material to its outcome; second, that none of the reasons for objection set forth in Article 9.2 applies; and, third, that the requirements of Article 3.3 have been satisfied.

The rules set forth in Articles 3.2—3.8 follow from the principles described above. These rules concerning requests for production of documents from other parties represent a balanced compromise between the broader view generally taken in common law countries and the more narrow view generally held in civil law countries. The IBA Rules of Evidence may be particularly useful, therefore, when an arbitration involves parties coming from these different legal backgrounds. A Continental European party may, for example, find that these Rules are useful in seeking to restrict an overly broad request from a common law party, while a common lawyer may be able to use the IBA Rules of Evidence to obtain documents from a Continental European party that the latter may not otherwise wish to provide.

Procedures

Usually following the initial submission of documents on which each party intends to rely pursuant to Article 3.1, any party may submit a request to produce documents to the arbitral tribunal and the other parties. This request must be submitted within the time ordered by the arbitral tribunal, as provided in Article 3.2. Article 3.3 provides certain requirements regarding the content of a request to produce, which are generally designed to have the request specifically describe the documents being sought. Article 3.3 is designed to prevent a broad 'fishing expedition', while at the same time permitting parties to request documents that can be identified with reasonable specificity and which can be shown to be relevant to the case and material to its outcome. This specificity of the information required by Article 3.3 is also designed to help the receiving party decide whether it wants to comply with the request voluntarily (as provided in Article 3.4), or if it wants to raise objections (Article 3.5). The specificity of the request is also designed to make it possible for the arbitral tribunal to decide, if there is an objection to the request to produce, whether or not to grant the request pursuant to the standards set forth in Article 3.7.

The request to produce must (i) identify the document or documents sought, described in sufficient detail; (ii) state *why* the documents requested are relevant to the case and material to its outcome; and (iii) state that the documents requested are not in the possession of the requesting party (with one exception) and the reasons *why* that party assumes the documents requested to be in the possession of the other party. In a compromise between the common law and civil law systems, the request to produce can identify documents either by describing an individual document (Article 3.3(a)(i)) or by describing 'in sufficient detail (including subject-matter) . . . a narrow and specific requested category of Documents that are reasonably believed to exist11 (Article 3.3(a)(ii)). The description of an individual document is reasonably straightforward. The IBA Rules of Evidence simply require that the description be 'sufficient to identify' the document.

Permitting parties to ask for documents by category, however, prompted more discussion. The Working Party and the Subcommittee did not want to open the door to 'fishing expeditions'. However, it was understood that some documents would be relevant and material and properly produced to the other side, but that they may not be capable of specific identification. Indeed, all members of the Working Party and of the Subcommittee, from common law and civil law countries alike, recognised that arbitrators would generally accept such requests if they were carefully tailored to produce relevant and material documents. For example, if an arbitration involves the termination by one party of a joint venture agreement, the other party may know that the notice of the termination was given on a certain date, that the Board of the other party must have made the decision to terminate at a meeting shortly before that notice, that certain documents must have been prepared for the Board's consideration of that decision and that minutes must have been taken concerning the decision. The requesting party cannot identify the dates or the authors of such documents, but nevertheless can identify with some particularity the nature of the documents sought and the general time frame in which they would have been prepared. Such a request may qualify as a 'narrow and specific category of Documents', as permitted under Article 3.3(a)(ii).

As documents in electronic form have become more important in international commerce and hence in dispute resolution, and since their production may be burdensome to the requesting party, the Subcommittee introduced in Article 3.3(a)(ii) the means for parties to identify more precisely a narrow and specific requested category of documents maintained in electronic form. Either at a party's own behest or upon order of the arbitral tribunal, electronic documents may additionally be identified by file name, specified search terms, individuals (for example, specific custodians or authors) or other means of searching for such documents in an efficient and economic manner (Article 3.3(a)(ii)). The revised Rules are neutral regarding whether electronic documents should be produced in any given arbitration; they simply provide a framework for doing so where the parties agree or the arbitral tribunal orders production of such documents.

As noted above, the provisions of Articles 3.3(b) and (c) also serve as checks on the scope of any request to produce. The content of the requested document needs to relate to issues in the case, and the relationship between the documents and the issues must be set forth with sufficient specificity so that the arbitral tribunal can understand the purpose for which the requesting party needs the requested documents. By requiring the requesting party to state that the documents sought are not in its own possession, the IBA Rules of Evidence seek to prevent unnecessary harassment of the opposing party by the requesting party. Article 3.3(c)(i) of the revised IBA Rules recognises one exception to this principle. In the age of electronic documents, it will become increasingly less likely that a particular document has been entirely deleted from a party's records, as it may continue to exist electronically, such as on back-up tapes or in electronic archives. Where a document is no longer easily accessible, for example because it is not in a server's active data, it may be less burdensome and costly for another party to produce it.

Under the previous text of the IBA Rules, documents produced pursuant to a request to produce were to be sent not only to the other parties in the arbitration but also to the arbitral tribunal. The rationale had been that because any documents produced would automatically become a part of the record, the self-interest of parties should cause them thereby to limit the scope of their request. This rule was revised in 2010 in light of the observation that it is often not efficient for arbitrators to review all of the documents at the stage of their production. Accordingly, the default has been changed such that documents are to be produced to the other parties and only to the arbitral tribunal if it so requests.

The specificity required in the request to produce makes it likely that such a request will be made only after the issues have become sufficiently clear in the case. The precise timing of such a request will be determined by the arbitral tribunal. It will naturally depend upon the specificity of the initial pleadings and any Terms of Reference or other documents identifying the issues.

A party seeking to oppose entirely or to limit a request to produce must raise its objections in writing within the time ordered by the arbitral tribunal. As noted, the reasons for objection shall be those set forth in Article 9.2 of the IBA Rules of Evidence (discussed below) or a failure to satisfy any of the requirements of Article 3.3. If a party raises such objections, the arbitral tribunal must decide on the propriety of the request to produce. The revised text of the IBA Rules provides that the arbitral tribunal may, before making such decision, give the parties an opportunity to consult with each other with a view to resolving the objection themselves (Article 3.6). Party to party consultation may in some circumstances be the more effective means of resolving objections, including those based on insufficient descriptions and other deficiencies in the form of the request to produce.

If the arbitral tribunal deems such consultation to be unnecessary or if it takes place but objections remain following it, the arbitral tribunal shall consult the parties regarding the request to produce and the objections, and shall 'in timely fashion' decide whether to accept some or all of the objections. The arbitral tribunal may order production of the documents sought in the request to produce only if it is convinced that (i) 'the issues that the requesting party wishes to prove are relevant to the case and material to its outcome', (ii) 'none of the reasons for objection set forth in Article 9.2 applies' and (iii) 'the requirements of Article 3.3 have been satisfied'. This third requirement was added in the 2010 revision.

Occasionally, an objection—such as on the grounds of privilege, commercial confidentiality or special political or institutional sensitivity (*see* Article 9.2(b), (e) and (f))—may require the arbitral tribunal first to review the document itself without review by the requesting party. It is generally preferable that the arbitral tribunal not review any such documents itself because (i) if after reviewing the document the arbitral tribunal upholds the objection, it could not eliminate its knowledge of the document once it had been reviewed, or (ii) there may be confidentiality concerns. For such cases, Article 3.8 (formerly Article 3.7) provides that in such 'exceptional circumstances', when the arbitral tribunal determines that it should not review the document, it may appoint an independent and impartial expert, who is bound to confidentiality, to review any such document and report on the objection. In other circumstances, such as where time and cost factors are considered to be compelling, the arbitral tribunal may, nonetheless, decide to review the document itself.

The expert, who need not necessarily be appointed pursuant to the terms of Article 6 of the IBA Rules of Evidence, would provide a report on the objection, but the arbitral tribunal is to make the final ruling as to its validity. If the objection is upheld, then the document is to be returned by the expert to the producing party, and it does not become a part of the arbitral proceedings. If, on the other hand, the objection is denied, then the requested party should produce the document to the other parties pursuant to the request to produce. In either event, the expert would, of course, also keep confidential the information learned in reviewing the document.

Requests to Produce by the Arbitral Tribunal

The IBA Rules of Evidence also permit the arbitral tribunal to seek certain documents that it considers to be relevant to the case and material to its outcome or to allow or request parties to use their best efforts to obtain them.

First, a party may request production of documents from a person or organisation that is not a party to the arbitration. Some arbitration laws permit arbitral tribunals to take or to apply for certain steps, such as a subpoena, to obtain documents from non-parties. Therefore, Article 3.9 (formerly Article 3.8) permits parties to ask an arbitral tribunal 'to take whatever steps are legally available to obtain the requested Documents, or seek leave from the arbitral tribunal to take such steps itself'', as long as the arbitral tribunal determines that such documents would be 'relevant to the case and material to its outcome', the requirements of Article 3.3 have been satisfied and none of the reasons for objection set forth in Article 9.2 applies.

In addition, since the arbitral tribunal may be required under certain arbitral rules to establish the facts of the case by all appropriate means,[5] it should be entitled to order a party to produce documents so far not introduced as evidence into the proceedings (*see* Article 3.10, formerly Article 3.9) or to request any party to use its best efforts to take, or itself take, any step that it considers appropriate to obtain documents from any person or organisation. Ultimate oversight and control over this process should remain with the arbitral tribunal. However, there may be circumstances under which a party is better positioned to undertake such steps, including, for example, due to presence in the country in question. A party receiving such a request from an arbitral tribunal, however, has the same right to raise objections, pursuant to Article 9.2, as if the documents had been sought in a request to produce by another party. If such objections are raised, the arbitral tribunal makes a decision based upon the considerations described above.

General Issues Regarding Documents

Copies

The IBA Rules of Evidence permit the production and submission into evidence of copies of documents, rather than originals. Of course, the copies must fully conform to the originals (Article 3.12 (a),

[5] ICC Rules, Article 20(1); LCIA Rules, Article 22.l(c).

formerly Article 3.11). The arbitral tribunal may request the production of an original document at any time, so that if a party believes that the copy does not fully conform to the original document, it may ask the arbitral tribunal to require the production of that original.

As electronic transmission and storage of documents often leads to the existence of multiple copies of the same document, the revised text of the IBA Rules of Evidence provides that a party is not obligated to produce multiple copies of documents that are 'essentially identical' unless the arbitral tribunal decides otherwise (Article 3.12 (c)). In some cases, multiple copies may be individually relevant to the dispute. In other cases, the production of multiple copies of the same document may unduly increase the cost of reviewing the documents for the other party and even be at odds with the parties' obligation to conduct themselves in good faith in the taking of evidence (Preamble 3).

Form of production for electronic documents

The cost of the taking of evidence in electronic form can vary widely depending on the form in which documents are to be submitted. Thus, absent agreement by the parties or determination by the arbitral tribunal to another form, the revised text of the IBA Rules of Evidence provides that the default form of production for electronic documents shall be the form most convenient or economical to the producing party that is reasonably usable by the recipient (Article 3.12(b)). This format will generally not be the native format with full metadata, as submission in this format can be unduly expensive and inconvenient. Where electronic disclosure is likely to play a role in an arbitration, the question of the form of production should be addressed early in the Article 2.1 consultation (*see* Article 2.2(c)).

Translations

Article 3.12(d) requires that if translations of documents are to be submitted, they are to be submitted together with the originals, marked as translations and identify the original language. The IBA Rules do not govern whether translations are required in particular arbitral proceedings, whether particular documents may be translated in part only, the resolution of disputes regarding translations or the timing of submission of translations.

Confidentiality

Both the Working Party and the Subcommittee discussed at length what confidentiality ought to be accorded to documents produced pursuant to the IBA Rules of Evidence. The issue of the extent of confidentiality that should attach to arbitration proceedings continues to be a controversial topic, in particular with respect to intellectual property and investment treaty-based arbitrations. The Working Party decided in 1999 that the IBA Rules of Evidence should not seek to change the evolving standards with respect to confidentiality and distinguished between documents submitted by a party in support of its own case and documents produced pursuant to a request to produce or other procedural order of the arbitral tribunal. When reconsidering the issue, the Subcommittee decided to expand Article 3.13 (formerly Article 3.12) to cover the former category as well as documents submitted by non-parties.

Article 3.13 now provides that any document submitted or produced by either parties or non-parties in the arbitration is to be kept confidential by the arbitral tribunal and by the other parties. Such a document may be used only in connection with the arbitration. This requirement does not apply to documents that are already in the public domain or are made public by the parties prior to production in the arbitration. Of course, parties remain free to make their own documents public at any time.

The IBA Rules of Evidence take no position with respect to the confidentiality of non-documentary evidence such as oral testimony (although a transcript recording oral testimony would be subject to confidentiality protection as a document submitted or produced by a non-party). Furthermore, the 'General Rules' applicable to the arbitration may also impose requirements relevant to confidentiality, or the parties or the arbitral tribunal may agree or determine additional rules relating to confidentiality (*see* Article 9.4, which applies to all types of evidence). For this reason, the IBA Rules state simply, 'this requirement shall be without prejudice to all other obligations of confidentiality in the arbitration'. Therefore, parties must look to the institutional or ad hoc rules pursuant to which they are conducting the arbitration, or to the parties' agreement or the legal regime governing the arbitration, to determine what level of confidentiality would apply to such documents.

Finally, the revised IBA Rules of Evidence also include certain exceptions to this obligation, namely where disclosure is required of a party to fulfil a legal duty, protect or pursue a legal right or enforce or challenge an award in *bonafide* legal proceedings before a state court or other judicial authority. To prevent inadvertent disclosure of documents, tribunals and parties are well-advised to discuss procedures for consideration of confidentiality in any consultation under Article 2.1 (*e.g.*, proper retention or deletion of evidence following conclusion of arbitral proceedings and any challenge or enforcement proceedings).

Inferences

Article 9.5 (formerly Article 9.4) of the IBA Rules of Evidence provides that if a party fails to comply with a procedural order of an arbitral tribunal concerning the production of documents, then the arbitral tribunal may infer from this failure to comply that the content of the document would be adverse to the interests of that party. This inference also applies when an opposing party does not make a proper objection to a request to produce within the time-limit set by the arbitral tribunal, but nevertheless fails to produce requested documents. As an additional deterrent, new Article 9.7 provides that in assigning costs, the arbitral tribunal may also consider the failure of a party to conduct itself in good faith in the taking of evidence. Such failure may include a failure to comply with orders to produce.

Stages

New Article 3.14 provides that the taking of documentary evidence may also be scheduled in phases. This procedure was already contemplated by the previous text of the IBA Rules with reference to witness testimony (Article 4.4), and has now been expanded to encompass documentary evidence as well. This mechanism can be an important means to manage time and control costs in particular circumstances and may be proposed by the parties or introduced by the tribunal of its own accord.

Article 4—Witnesses of Fact

In arbitration, the facts of the case are often established through witnesses, who testify about events of which they have personal knowledge. This personal knowledge distinguishes the witnesses of fact from experts, who provide opinions based on their expertise in a particular field. Witnesses of fact are addressed in Article 4 of the IBA Rules of Evidence; experts are addressed in Articles 5 and 6.

While witness testimony is less frequently used as evidence in civil law courts, where documentary evidence is preponderant, than in common law courts, arbitration proceedings in both the civil law and common law traditions often rely on witnesses. In the common law tradition, witnesses are questioned by the parties. In the civil law tradition, they are questioned by the court; parties may at most suggest to the court questions to be asked. In transnational arbitrations, the arbitral tribunal and the parties need to establish how to handle witnesses of fact.

Arbitration rules and statutes are usually silent on witness testimony. The IBA Rules of Evidence thus fill in a substantial gap: Article 8 of the IBA Rules of Evidence, discussed later, addresses how witnesses are examined at the hearing; Article 4, to be discussed here, organises the stages before this hearing.

Information on Witnesses

Article 4.1 requires each party to identify the witnesses on whose testimony it intends to rely, as well as the subject matter of that testimony. As a result of this requirement, which is common practice and explicitly confirmed in various sets of arbitration rules,[6] the opposing party cannot be surprised by unannounced witnesses or facts and can select its own evidence in response well in advance of the hearing.

The revised text of the IBA Rules of Evidence requires that each witness statement contain a statement as to the language in which it was originally prepared and the language in which the witness anticipates giving testimony at the evidentiary hearing (Article 4.5(c)). If no witness statement is prepared for a witness, each party should inform the arbitral tribunal and the other parties in the event the witness intends to testify in a language other than the language of the arbitration proceedings. If the witness cannot present evidence in the language of the arbitration proceedings, translation has to be provided.

The 1983 IBA Rules imposed a fixed time period for submitting this information on witnesses if parties did not agree or if the tribunal did not impose another time frame.[7] The UNCITRAL and ICDR Arbitration Rules require that the information must be given at least some time before the hearing.[8] The IBA Rules of Evidence leave it entirely to the tribunal to impose the time within which the information must be given.

Affiliated Persons as Witnesses

Differences exist among legal systems as to whether an executive employee, agent or other person affiliated with one of the parties in dispute can be heard as a witness. This status as a witness may have important consequences. For instance, in some legal systems, a party may be a witness in its own case, whereas in others only third parties may testify as witnesses. In such systems, a party providing information would not be considered a 'witness', and the information would not be provided under oath or a similar commitment to tell the truth.

Article 4.2 of the IBA Rules of Evidence, however, provides that the party's officers, employees and other representatives may be witnesses for the purpose of the IBA Rules of Evidence. Therefore, under Article 8.4, the arbitral tribunal may ask a party witness to affirm, 'in a manner determined by the Arbitral Tribunal to be appropriate', some commitment to tell the truth. The arbitral tribunal may also consider the identity of a witness, and his or her affiliation with any party, as one of many factors that may or may not affect the weight to be given to such evidence (*see* Article 9.1).

Preliminary Contacts Between Party and Witness

Another important difference between legal systems is the extent to which parties may have contacts with the witnesses they offer.[9] In some systems, parties may discuss with their own witnesses the facts on which they will submit testimony. The degree of 'witness preparation' may vary from a general overview of the issues at stake to an extensive rehearsal of the witness' answers to questions expected to be asked. On the other hand, in some systems it may be impermissible for a lawyer to discuss the case with a witness prior to his testimony in court.

[6] *See*, e.g., HKIAC Rules, Article 23.5; ICDR Arbitration Rules, Article 20.2; LCIA Rules, Article 20.1; SCC Arbitration Rules, Article 28(1); UNCITRAL Arbitration Rules, Article 25.2; WIPO Arbitration Rules, Article 54.

[7] 1983 IBA Rules, Article 5: 'Within 60 days of the delivery of the last introductory submission made by the defendant or by the date agreed between the parties or determined by the arbitration . . .'.

[8] *See*, e.g., HKIAC Rules, Article 23.5; ICDR Arbitration Rules, Article 20.2—at least 15 days; UNCITRAL Arbitration Rules, Article 25.2.

[9] UNCITRAL Notes on Organizing Arbitral Proceedings, para 67.

In transnational arbitration, it is now generally well established 'that a party and its counsel are, as a general rule, permitted to contact a potential witness on its behalf and question him or her about the facts of the dispute'.[10]

Reflecting the generally accepted practice, the IBA Rules of Evidence, in Article 4.3, confirm that it is not 'improper' for a party or its lawyers to interview its own witnesses. The revised text of the IBA Rules further clarifies that such an interview need not remain general, but may indeed relate to the subject-matter of the prospective testimony. At the same time, of course, the arbitral tribunal may consider the scope of any such interview in assessing the weight it accords the witness's testimony (*see* Article 9.1). Of course, the drafting of a witness statement presupposes contact between the witness and the party that is presenting him or her.

Witness Statements

Pursuant to the IBA Rules of Evidence, the arbitral tribunal may order the parties to submit to the arbitral tribunal and the other parties a written 'witness statement' (*see* Article 4.4). The arbitral tribunal, in consultation with the parties, should determine whether or not to require such witness statements, depending on the circumstances of each case.

If witness statements are used, the evidence that a witness plans to give orally at the hearing is known in advance. The other party can thereby better prepare its own examination of the witness and select the issues and witnesses it will present. The tribunal is also in a better position to appreciate the testimony and put its own questions to these witnesses. Witness statements may in this way contribute to a shortening of the length of oral hearings. For instance, they may be considered as the 'evidence in chief' ('direct evidence'), so that extensive explanation by the witness becomes superfluous and examination by the other party can start almost immediately.

In order to save on hearing time and expense, witnesses need not appear unless their presence is requested by a party or the arbitral tribunal (Article 8.1). Often the arbitral tribunal and the parties may agree that a witness whose statement is either not contested or not considered material by the opposing party need not be present at the oral hearing.[11]

Article 4.5 of the IBA Rules of Evidence specifies that a witness statement shall contain:

- the name and address of a witness; any present and past relationship with any of the parties; his or her background and qualifications;
- a full and detailed description of the facts and the source of the witness's information, as well as any documents on which the witness relies that have not already been submitted;
- a statement as to the language in which the witness statement was originally prepared and the language in which the witness anticipates giving testimony at the evidentiary hearing; and
- an affirmation of the truth of the statement confirmed by the witness's signature.

The IBA Rules of Evidence do not require that the statement be made under oath. Arbitration practice and legal systems differ too much on this point. In many civil law systems, sworn declarations can be made only before the state court authorities, or a *notaire,* which makes sworn affidavits too cumbersome. Consequently, sworn affidavits cannot be the required form for witness statements in transnational arbitration proceedings.[12] The IBA Rules of Evidence simply require a witness of fact to affirm that he or she commits to tell the truth (Article 8.4). This wording was revised in 2010 for purposes of greater clarity and precision.

[10] M. Schneider, 'Witnesses in International Arbitration', *ASA Bulletin,* 1993, 302, at 306. However, attorneys from certain civil law countries may deem it a violation of their ethical rules to contact witnesses. Consequently, LCIA Article 20.6 allows such contracts 'subject to the mandatory provisions of any applicable law . . . '.

[11] The possibility that uncontested witnesses can limit their testimony to the written statement and do not have to attend the oral evidentiary hearing is provided for in ICDR Arbitration Rules, Article 20.5; LCIA Rules, Article 20.3; SCC Rules, Article 28(3); WIPO Arbitration Rules, Article 54(d).

[12] Under LCIA Rules, Article 20.3, and WIPO Arbitration Rules, Article 54(d), the parties for instance, have the choice between mere signed statements or sworn affidavits, unless the tribunal has ordered otherwise.

Article 4.4 of the IBA Rules of Evidence leaves it to the arbitral tribunal to specify when the written statements have to be submitted. There is a basic choice to be made in this respect: the parties may exchange their statements simultaneously or consecutively. The second round of witness statements should address only information contained in witness statements, expert reports or submissions submitted by another party in the first round or otherwise not previously presented in the arbitration (*see* Article 4.6).

Appearance of Witnesses for Testimony in an Evidentiary Hearing

Revised Article 8.1 requires each party to inform the arbitral tribunal and the other parties of the witnesses whose appearance at the hearing it requests. This aligns the IBA Rules to current best practice, according to which witnesses appear only if cross-examination has been requested or the party presenting the testimony wishes to do so by means of live testimony rather than written statements alone.

Any witness whose appearance has been so requested by any party, or from whom the arbitral tribunal wishes to hear, shall attend the hearing. If a witness whose appearance has been requested fails to attend without a valid reason, the arbitral tribunal shall disregard the witness statement unless exceptional circumstances justify this failure to attend (Article 4.7).[13]

If the parties and the arbitral tribunal agree that a fact witness need not appear, the progress of the arbitration may be enhanced. Article 4.8 states that such an agreement does not reflect agreement on the content of the witness statement. Article 5.6 contains a similar rule for expert reports.

The revised text of the IBA Rules of Evidence provides that a witness's 'appearance' shall be in person, unless the arbitral tribunal allows the use of videoconference or similar technology (Article 8.1). An application for permission for a particular witness to appear by videoconference should state the reasons why that particular witness is unable to appear in person and propose a protocol. The tribunal's decision should depend, among other things, on the sufficiency of the reasons given and the ability of the proposed protocol to maintain equality and fairness among the parties and approximate live testimony. The technology used should ensure sufficient quality of transmission and include a fall-back plan should the quality become insufficient. The ability to share exhibits between the witness and the hearing room is desirable. Additionally, the protocol should ensure that the witness testifies under the same conditions as he or she would have in the hearing, *i.e.* without conferring with anyone else during testimony or referring to any documents to which the other participants do not have access.

Recalcitrant Witnesses

If a witness whose testimony is requested by a party refuses to cooperate, that party may ask the arbitral tribunal to take whatever steps are available to obtain that testimony, or seek leave from the arbitral tribunal to take such steps itself (*see* the discussion of Article 3.9 above relating to document production from third parties). The arbitral tribunal, however, may exercise its discretion to refuse this request if it considers the potential testimony of the witness not to be relevant to the case or material to its outcome (*see* Article 4.9).

Under most arbitration laws, either the arbitral tribunal or a party with the approval of the arbitral tribunal may ask the State courts to compel the witness to appear or to examine the witness itself.[14] As a general rule, it shall be the State courts at the seat of arbitration which may help the arbitral tribunal to obtain testimony from a recalcitrant witness. In transnational proceedings, however, witnesses often are not domiciled in the country where the arbitration has its seat. The arbitral tribunal may then have to request help from foreign courts, directly or indirectly. The power of an arbitral tribunal

[13] *See also* LCIA Rules, Article 20.4, and WIPO Arbitration Rules, Article 54(d).
[14] *See*, e.g., UNCITRAL Arbitration Model Law, Article 27.

in such circumstances is, of course, limited to 'whatever steps are legally available' to it (*see* Article 4.9). In some cases, however, the tribunal may elect instead to authorise a party to take such steps and approach the foreign courts itself. Proceeding in this manner might be more practical or efficient if, for instance, the party requesting the evidence was located in that country, spoke the local language or already had local legal counsel.

Witnesses Requested by Tribunal

Witnesses of fact are the responsibility of the parties. The parties have to select the witnesses they will present and the issues on which they will testify. However, the revised text of the IBA Rules provides that the arbitral tribunal may request the appearance of a particular witness even if neither party requests that witness's appearance (Article 8.1). As a general matter, the arbitral tribunal may order any party to provide for, or to use its best efforts to provide for, the appearance for testimony of any person, including one whose testimony has not yet been offered (Article 4.10). However, a party also has the right to object to any such request addressed to it for the reasons set forth in Article 9.2.

Article 5—Party-Appointed Experts

Modern arbitration rules specifically refer to party-appointed experts.[15] In particular, most of these rules codify the well-established notion that a party can present its own expert witnesses to testify on the points at issue.

Early Disclosure of Expert Evidence

In accordance with the last paragraph of the Preamble and Article 5.1, a party intending to rely on expert testimony must so notify the other party. As with other provisions of the IBA Rules of Evidence, the arbitral tribunal shall determine when such notification and the submission of expert reports shall occur (*see* Article 5.1). In scheduling the reports, the arbitral tribunal should consider the interaction of this provision with other submissions made by the parties, such as the supplemental witness statements provided for in Article 4.6.

Content of the Expert Report

Article 5.2 sets forth the requirements for expert reports. Most importantly, the expert report must describe 'the methods, evidence and information used in arriving at the conclusions' (*see* Article 5.2(e)). This information is required in order to place the other party in a position meaningfully to evaluate the expert report. If the expert has relied on any documents not already submitted in the arbitration, these must be provided as well (Article 5.2(e)).

Article 5.2(g) commits the expert to his or her report. The wording of this subsection differs slightly from the wording found in Article 4.5(d) addressing fact witnesses, as the contents of the expert report will contain opinions and expert views. Nevertheless, the expert should be prepared to take responsibility for the contents of his or her report.

Article 5.2(a) requires disclosure with respect to any and all relationships the expert may have with the parties, their legal advisors and the arbitral tribunal. Article 5.2(c) then requires a statement of the expert's 'independence'. While the former requirement requires disclosure, satisfaction of the latter requirement requires the expert to evaluate any such relationships and attest that he or she is

[15] *See*, e.g., HKIAC Rules, Article 23.5; 1998 ICC Rules, Article 20(3); 1997 ICDR Rules, Article 22(4); 1998 LCIA Rules, Article 21(2); SCC Rules, Article 28; 1994 WIPO Rules, Article 55(c); UNCITRAL Rules, Article 27(4).

'independent', for example in the sense that he or she has no financial interest in the outcome or otherwise has relationships that would prevent the expert from providing his or her honest and frank opinion. Receiving payment for services as an expert does not preclude 'independence'. Article 5.2(c) is intended to emphasise the duty of each party appointed expert to evaluate the case in an independent and neutral fashion rather than to exclude experts with some connection to the participants or the subject-matter of the case.

Article 5.2(i) requires that where multiple persons sign an expert report, as is sometimes the case when an organisation is hired as an expert, the report must indicate whether the report is attributable as a whole to a single author or, if not, which specific parts thereof may be attributed to each co-author. This requirement is intended to aid parties in determining which experts they wish to attend the evidentiary hearing (Article 8.1) as well as in preparing for questioning one or more of the co-authors.

Pursuant to Article 8.3, parties may submit a second round of rebuttal expert reports. However, these rebuttal reports are limited to responses to matters contained in another party's witness statements, expert reports or other submissions that have not been previously presented in the arbitration. Considerations of efficiency and good faith weigh in favour of giving a party a single opportunity to present its arguments and allowing additional opportunities only when it was not possible to make those arguments at the time. This procedure helps to prevent parties from attempting to surprise other parties with evidence or to derail the procedural timetable late in the proceedings.

Pre-hearing Conference among Experts

Article 5.4 permits the arbitral tribunal to order the party-appointed experts to meet and to discuss the issues considered or to be considered in their expert reports either in advance of their preparation or in advance of the hearing. Article 8.3(f) provides for conferencing of experts or fact witnesses during an evidentiary hearing. If they can reach agreement on any issues, they shall record that agreement in writing as well as any remaining areas of disagreement and the reasons therefor.

The practices suggested here, when deemed appropriate by the arbitral tribunal, can make the proceeding more economical. Experts from the same discipline, who are likely to know each other, can identify relatively quickly the reasons for their diverging conclusions and work towards finding areas of agreement. The revised Rules provide additionally for consultation before the reports are drafted, which may be an effective means to produce reports that identify the areas where the experts agree and are narrowly focused on the remaining areas of disagreement. Where the experts succeed in reaching agreement on their findings, the parties and the arbitral tribunal will likely accept those findings, so that the hearing may focus on the truly disputed aspects of the case.

Appearance of Experts at Evidentiary Hearings

Article 8.1 of the revised IBA Rules foresees the same mechanism for determining whether experts or fact witnesses must appear for testimony at an evidentiary hearing, namely on the request of any party or the arbitral tribunal. As with fact witnesses, the expert report of a non appearing party-appointed expert may nevertheless be accepted 'in exceptional circumstances' if the arbitral tribunal so determines (*see* Article 5.5), and agreement not to require attendance of an expert witness at hearing does not reflect agreement on the content of the expert report (*see* Article 5.6).

Finally, it is worth noting that the IBA Rules of Evidence do not address how to deal with the testimony of an expert called upon to testify when such expert had previously been appointed by a national court in connection with the same issues. European parties frequently apply to their local courts, immediately upon the occurrence of an injury and long before arbitration is commenced, for the appointment of an expert to determine the cause of the damage and possible remedies or to preserve evidence. It is often difficult for an Anglo-American lawyer to be convinced that such a judicially appointed expert is by definition independent, as such an appointment has first been sought by the other party. In such circumstances, an arbitral tribunal will therefore have to determine how such an expert should be considered—as a party-appointed expert, a tribunal-appointed expert, or otherwise—and to issue directions with respect to the production in evidence of his or her report or with respect to his or her appearance at an evidentiary hearing.

Article 6—Tribunal-Appointed Experts

Article 6 regulates the appointment of independent experts by the arbitral tribunal. A general principle underlying Article 6 is the substantial involvement of the parties in the process, even though the expert is being appointed by the arbitral tribunal itself. Article 6.1 makes clear that the arbitral tribunal is to consult with the parties before appointing such an expert and also with respect to the terms of reference for such an expert. The parties also have an opportunity, pursuant to Article 6.2, to identify any potential conflicts of interest and to state any objections (*e.g.*, lack of independence, insufficient qualification, lack of availability, cost) on such basis. Most importantly, parties have an opportunity to be involved in the information-gathering process by the tribunal-appointed expert and to respond to any report by that expert. However, to avoid delays, Article 6.2 now provides that later objections may be made only if they relate to reasons of which the party becomes aware after the appointment has been made.

Article 6.3 provides the parties and their representatives with the right to receive any information obtained by the tribunal-appointed expert and to attend any inspection conducted by the expert.

Article 6.4 sets forth the required contents of the expert report. These requirements are the same as those in Article 5.2 with the exception of the statement of independence required of party appointed experts (which the tribunal-appointed expert had already submitted before accepting the appointment (Article 6.2)).

Article 6.5 permits the parties to examine any documents that the tribunal-appointed expert has examined and any correspondence between the arbitral tribunal and the tribunal-appointed expert. That Article also provides any party with the opportunity to respond to a report by a tribunal-appointed expert, within the time ordered by the arbitral tribunal. The Working Party and the Subcommittee believed strongly that parties should know what the arbitral tribunal is being told by a tribunal-appointed expert and should have an opportunity to rebut his or her conclusions. A party may respond either by making its own submission or by submitting a witness statement or an expert report by its party-appointed expert.

The tribunal-appointed expert shall be present at an evidentiary hearing and available for questioning at that hearing, so long as any party or the arbitral tribunal requests such presence. Article 6.6 permits the parties or their party-appointed experts to question the tribunal-appointed expert at the hearing. However, the scope of this questioning is limited to the issues covered in his or her expert report and the responses provided pursuant to Article 6.5: namely, a party's submission, witness statement or an expert report by a party-appointed expert that is provided in response to the tribunal-appointed expert's report. This provision is included to assure that the tribunal-appointed expert knows in advance the subjects on which he or she might be questioned, in order to prepare his or her responses. The Working Party wanted to avoid situations where issues were raised involving the tribunal-appointed expert's report for the first time at the hearing, which would inevitably require an adjournment for the party-appointed expert to consider that issue before the hearing could resume.

Article 6.3 makes certain that the tribunal-appointed expert shall have access to whatever information he or she needs to respond to the issues posed in his or her terms of reference. The tribunal-appointed expert may request the party to provide any relevant and material information, which includes relevant documents, goods, samples, property, machinery, systems, processes or access to a site for inspection. Parties have the right to object to such requests, based upon the provisions of Article 9.2. If such an objection is raised, the arbitral tribunal shall make a determination as to the materiality and the appropriateness of the tribunal-appointed expert's request in the manner provided in Articles 3.5–3.8, which concern requests to produce.

Finally, in Article 6.7, the IBA Rules of Evidence make clear that it is the arbitral tribunal, not the tribunal-appointed expert, who is to determine the issues in the case. That Article provides that a tribunal-appointed expert's report 'and its conclusions shall be assessed by the Arbitral Tribunal with due regard to all circumstances of the case'.

Article 7—Inspection

Article 7 is a simple provision, making possible inspections of relevant site, property, machinery or any other goods, samples, systems, processes or documents that may help the decision-making process, wherever they may be located. Such inspections most frequently occur in construction arbitrations, in which the arbitral tribunal visits the construction site in dispute.

Article 8—Evidentiary hearing

Article 8 deals with the evidentiary hearing, a term defined in the Definitions section. The evidentiary hearing may be held in person, by teleconference or other method, and it involves the presentation of oral or other evidence to the arbitral tribunal. In most international arbitrations, this hearing is preceded by substantial preparation, on the principle that each party shall be entitled to know reasonably in advance the evidence on which the other parties rely (*see* Preamble, paragraph 3). There may have been a Terms of Reference or other type of preliminary or preparatory hearing.[16] There will have been an exchange of extensive written submissions containing allegations of fact and often discussions of law. Documents will have been submitted (*see* above, Article 3). Witnesses of fact may have submitted written witness statements (*see* above, Article 4). Party-appointed experts or tribunal-appointed experts may have submitted written expert reports (*see* above, Articles 5 and 6). The parties must have adequate notice of the evidentiary hearing.[17]

As a result of all this preparation, by the time the evidentiary hearing is conducted the various participants in the arbitral process are likely to know each other better, and they will also know the case better than at the outset of the arbitration.

Article 8 of the IBA Rules of Evidence is the most general of all the provisions. The Article provides a general framework for the procedure to be followed at the evidentiary hearing. This is necessary because the variety of procedures and order to be followed at an evidentiary hearing is enormous. Ordinarily, parties and the arbitral tribunal will be able to devise the procedures best suited to the circumstances of the case. While some of the special features described in Article 8 will be seen in many evidentiary hearings, an evidentiary hearing incorporating them all should be rare.

Managing the Hearing

Article 8.2 makes clear that the power to manage the evidentiary hearing rests with the arbitral tribunal, not the parties, an idea which originally came from civil law procedure but which has been widely adopted.[18] The arbitral tribunal may limit or exclude questioning, or even the appearance of a witness, if it is irrelevant, immaterial, unreasonably burdensome, duplicative or otherwise covered by a reason for objection set forth in Article 9.2. While some counsel are accustomed to raising objections, the arbitral tribunal may also apply these standards on their own. This Article also finds objectionable unreasonably leading questions, which may render direct and re-direct testimony worthless. These provisions are all designed to give the arbitral tribunal the ability to focus the hearing on issues material to the outcome of the case and thereby make hearings more efficient.

[16] *See*, ICC Rules, Article 18; ICSID Arbitration Rules, Rule 21; UNCITRAL Notes on Organising Arbitral Proceedings, paragraph 17; WIPO Arbitration Rules, Article 47.

[17] *See*, e.g., HKIAC Rules, Article 23.3; ICC Rules, Article 21(1); ICDR Arbitration Rules, Article 20.1 (30 days); LCIA Arbitration Rules, Article 19.2; SCC Arbitration Rules, Article 27.2; UNCITRAL Arbitration Rules, Article 25(1); WIPO Arbitration Rules, Article 53(b). The 15 days in Article 25 of the UNCITRAL Arbitration Rules are usually too short.

[18] *See*, e.g., ICC Rules, Article 21(3); ICDR Arbitration Rules, Article 16.1; LCIA Arbitration Rules, Article 14.2 (to the extent no party agreement to the contrary); SCC Rules, Article 19; UNCITRAL Arbitration Rules, Article 15.1.

Order of Witnesses

Articles 8.3 (a), (b) and (c) set out the basic order of witnesses followed in many cases: claimant's witnesses, followed by respondent's witnesses, and experts. For each witness, testimony is first presented by the party offering that witness, followed by examination by the opposing party and then an opportunity for re-examination by the presenting party. Usually, any re-examination is limited to new matters raised in the previous oral testimony. Many arbitral tribunals ask their questions only towards the end, except for questions designed to help the process along or to make a witness feel comfortable.

However, arbitral tribunals, particularly in more complex cases, are increasingly adapting these procedures to provide for better examination of the issues in dispute. Article 8.3(g) confirms the arbitral tribunal's ability to pose questions at any time. Arbitral tribunals often hear oral argument by counsel for the parties, which may be a part of, or may be separate from, the evidentiary hearing. Therefore, Article 8.3(f) confirms the discretion of arbitral tribunals to vary this order of proceeding in the manner best suited for the circumstances of that case. For example, the provision allows the arrangement of testimony by particular issues or that witnesses be questioned at the same time and in confrontation with each other about particular issues (witness conferencing). Such techniques may enable arbitral tribunals better to understand the contradictions in testimony and to be able to determine the weight and credibility to be given to the testimony. Ultimately, the IBA Rules of Evidence leave it to the arbitral tribunal and the parties to determine how best to proceed.

The IBA Rules of Evidence do not address whether witnesses who have not yet testified may be in the hearing room or whether witnesses who have testified may remain. This is left for the arbitral tribunal to decide, because it depends on the circumstances of the case, the nature of the dispute and the persons involved.

The affirmation by a witness that he or she commits to telling the truth, as described in Article 8.4, is widely observed. Often, the arbitral tribunal will also simply admonish the witness to tell the truth, and sometimes it will additionally advise the witness of criminal sanctions applying at the seat of the arbitration or at the physical place of the hearing. Arbitral tribunals, at least in some countries, rarely swear in the witness themselves.

Where witnesses and experts have provided written witness statements or expert reports, they are first confirmed at the beginning of the testimony. The third sentence of Article 8.4 states the rule applied in many arbitrations where witness statements are used, that such statements may serve in lieu of the witness's direct testimony. Having the witness statement stand entirely in lieu of direct testimony provides an incentive for witness statements to be comprehensive.

Nothing in the IBA Rules of Evidence, however, prevents an arbitral tribunal from hearing witnesses in another manner, such as the traditional method in certain civil law countries where witnesses are initially questioned by the arbitral tribunal, followed by questioning by the parties. This is a technique which presupposes a thorough knowledge of the case and a full study of the law by the arbitral tribunal.

Tribunal Witnesses

Inquisitorial powers of the arbitral tribunal follow from the *lex arbitri* of the seat of the arbitration.[19] Inquisitorial powers may also follow from the arbitration rules agreed by the parties.[20] The IBA Rules of Evidence do not provide for similarly sweeping inquisitorial powers of the arbitral tribunal, but Article 8.5 covers the main case where inquisitorial powers may be exercised: the hearing of a key witness who typically had an earlier association with both parties but whom the parties for some reason failed to persuade to appear, perhaps because they no longer have close ties with the witness. Such a

[19] *See*, e.g., Article 34, subs. 2 lit. g, English Arbitration Act 1996; Article 184 Swiss Private international Law Act.

[20] *See*, e.g., ICC Rules, Article 20; LCIA Rules, Article 22.l(c).

tribunal witness will often be questioned in the inquisitorial fashion described above. To proceed in this fashion is not mandated, but is contemplated by the second sentence of Article 8.5.

At the close of an evidentiary hearing, the parties are sometimes invited to comment on the assessment of the evidence and on the law. Such comments may also be made in post-hearing briefs or at a separate 'final' or 'pleading' hearing, or in both. The IBA Rules of Evidence do not address this phase of the proceeding.

Article 9—Admissibility and Assessment of the Evidence

Articles 1–8 of the IBA Rules of Evidence provide the mechanisms for the gathering and presentation of evidence to the arbitral tribunal. Article 9 provides the principles by which the arbitral tribunal should determine what evidence it should properly consider and how it should assess the evidence that is properly before it.

Article 9.1 states the general principle, also found in many institutional and ad hoc arbitration rules, that the arbitral tribunal shall determine the admissibility, relevance, materiality and weight of evidence. Obviously, the arbitral tribunal shall exercise its discretion in making such determinations, which are central to its role.

Article 9.2 provides the limitations on admissible evidence, whether oral or written. These limitations also apply to the production of documents pursuant to Article 3 and inspections pursuant to Article 7. These limitations are important, for they preserve the lines of distinction between the rights of the parties and the authority of the arbitral tribunal. While the provision states that the arbitral tribunal 'shall' exclude evidence meeting one of the specified exceptions, the arbitral tribunal obviously retains its discretion to determine whether one of the specified criteria has been met.

Article 9.2(a) states the simple proposition that the arbitral tribunal shall exclude evidence that is not sufficiently relevant to the case or material to its outcome.

Article 9.2(b) provides protection for documents and other evidence that may be covered by certain privileges, under the appropriate applicable law, such as the attorney–client privilege, professional secrecy or the without prejudice privilege. The Working Party felt that it was important that such privileges be recognised in international arbitration.

The Subcommittee provided additional non-binding guidance on determining the applicable privileges in Article 9.3. Although the standard to be applied is left to the discretion of the arbitral tribunal, it is desirable that the tribunal take account of the elements set forth in Article 9.3, in particular if the parties are subject to different legal or ethical rules. Article 9.3(a) seeks to encompass both the common law understanding of attorney–client privilege and the civil law understanding of the duty of professional secrecy. Article 9.3(b) expresses a generalised understanding of the so-called 'without prejudice' or 'settlement' privilege, which is recognised in certain jurisdictions and relates to the contents of settlement negotiations. Article 9.3(c) expresses the guiding principle that expectations of the parties and their advisors at the time the legal impediment or privilege is said to have arisen should be taken into consideration. Often, these expectations will be formed by the approach to privilege prevailing in the home jurisdiction of such persons. Article 9.3(d) encapsulates an important exception to privilege in many countries, namely waiver. Finally, Article 9.3(e) emphasises the need to maintain fairness and equality among the parties. The need to protect fairness and equality among the parties may arise when the approach to privilege prevailing in the parties' home jurisdictions differs. For example, one jurisdiction may recognize the settlement privilege, whereas another may not, or one jurisdiction may extend the attorney–client privilege to in-house counsel, whereas another may not. In such cases, applying different rules to the parties could create unfairness by shielding the documents of one party from production but not those of the other.

Article 9.2(c) permits the arbitral tribunal to exclude from production or from evidence any documents or evidence which would be an unreasonable burden to produce. This unreasonable burden can take many forms, and the nature of the burden is purposely left to the discretion of the arbitral tribunal. For example, it may involve the production of documents pursuant to a request to produce which, although properly identified pursuant to Article 3.3(a)(i) and relevant to the case and material to its outcome, would because of their sheer quantity create an unreasonable burden on the receiving party to produce. Similarly, Article 9.2(c) could cover a situation where a certain document exists and may even be considered to be within the 'possession, custody or control' of another party (*see* Article 3.3(c)(ii)), but which nevertheless could be unreasonably difficult for the party to obtain. Article 9.2(d) is also straightforward, as a document that has been lost or destroyed cannot reasonably be produced. As it may be impossible to prove a negative (loss of the document), Article 9.2(d) provides that such loss shall be shown with a reasonable likelihood to have occurred.

Articles 9.2(e) and (f) involve special and related concerns. Article 3 reflects the belief that some internal documents are properly subject to production in international arbitration, even documents that may not be producible in a state court in certain jurisdictions. However, the IBA Rules also recognise that some documents may be subject to such commercial or technical confidentiality concerns that they should not be required to be produced or introduced into evidence. When an early draft of the IBA Rules of Evidence referred only to such confidentiality, certain international political organisations pointed out that 'commercial and technical confidentiality' might not include confidentiality within such organisations. Therefore, Article 9.2(f) was added to put such special political or institutional sensitivity on an equal footing with commercial or technical confidentiality. In the case of both provisions, the arbitral tribunal retains the discretion to determine whether the considerations of confidentiality or sensitivity are sufficient to warrant the exclusion from evidence or production of those documents or other evidence. As noted in the IBA Rules, the arbitral tribunal must find the concerns to be 'compelling' in order to exclude the evidence. Article 9.4 also makes clear that the arbitral tribunal may make certain arrangements, such as entering a confidentiality agreement or order, to permit evidence to be considered subject to suitable confidentiality protection.

Article 9.2(g) is a catch-all provision, intended to assure procedural economy, proportionality, fairness and equality in the case. For example, documents that might be considered to be privileged within one national legal system may not be considered to be privileged within another. If this situation were to create an unfairness, the arbitral tribunal may exclude production of the technically non-privileged documents pursuant to this provision. In general, it is hoped that this provision will help ensure that the arbitral tribunal provides the parties with a fair, as well as an effective and efficient, hearing.

Finally, as noted above in the discussion of Article 3, Articles 9.5 and 9.6 create inferences where a party has failed to produce a document or make available other evidence required by the arbitral tribunal. The arbitral tribunal may then conclude that such document or evidence would be adverse to the interests of that party. New Article 9.7 specifically grants the arbitral tribunal the discretion to sanction parties for breaches of good faith (*see* Preamble paragraph 3) by way of the apportionment of costs or any other means available under the IBA Rules.

The IBA Arbitration Committee and its Rules of Evidence Subcommittee believe that the revised IBA Rules preserve the careful balance achieved by the 1999 IBA Rules of Evidence. They are also confident that the revisions will further promote the use and success of the IBA Rules as an effective mechanism to assist parties in the conduct of international arbitrations.

APPENDIX 2

Article 1 Roadmap: Scope of Application (and How to Deal with Conflicting Provisions)

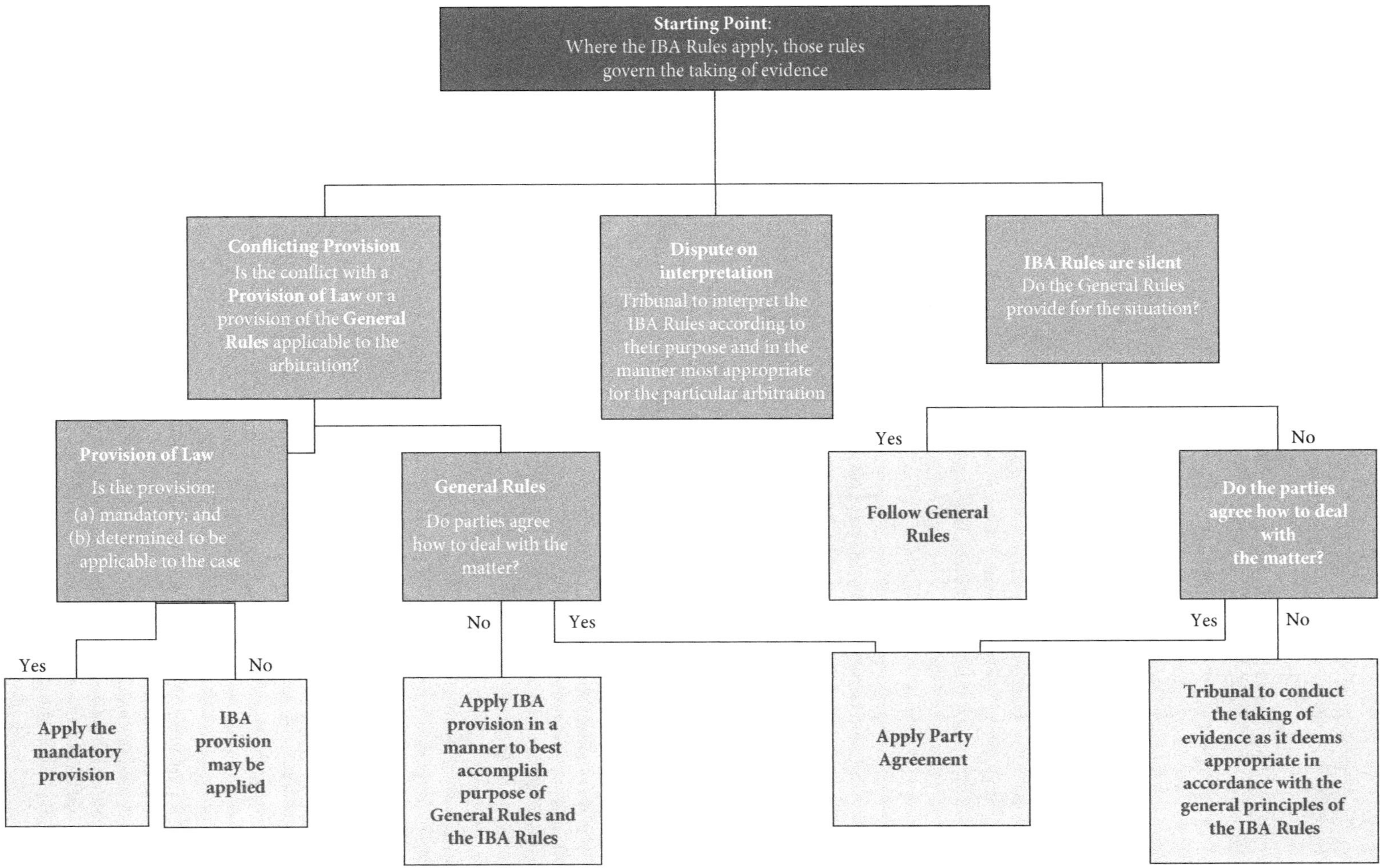
Starting Point:
Where the IBA Rules apply, those rules govern the taking of evidence
Conflicting Provision
Is the conflict with a Provision of Law or a provision of the General Rules applicable to the arbitration?
Dispute on interpretation
Tribunal to interpret the IBA Rules according to their purpose and in the manner most appropriate for the particular arbitration
IBA Rules are silent
Do the General Rules provide for the situation?
Provision of Law
Is the provision:
(a) mandatory; and
(b) determined to be applicable to the case
General Rules
Do parties agree how to deal with the matter?
Yes
Follow General Rules
No
Do the parties agree how to deal with the matter?
Yes
No
No
Yes
Yes
No
Apply the mandatory provision
IBA provision may be applied
Apply IBA provision in a manner to best accomplish purpose of General Rules and the IBA Rules
Apply Party Agreement
Tribunal to conduct the taking of evidence as it deems appropriate in accordance with the general principles of the IBA Rules

APPENDIX 3

Checklist of Points to Consider at the First Procedural Conference (and/or Subsequently) in Relation to the Process for the Taking of Evidence

IBA Rules

Have the IBA rules been formally adopted as binding on the parties or are they to be used as guidelines only?

Issues for which the Tribunal Considers Preliminary Determination May Be Appropriate

Are there any issues which might be suitable for preliminary determination?

Issues the Tribunal Regards as Relevant to the Case and Material to Its Outcome

Should the parties prepare for the tribunal an (agreed) draft list of issues between them and identify (with reasons) why the determination of those issues is relevant to the case and material to outcome? At what stage should they do this?

Submissions

Do the parties wish to use common law style pleadings or memorial form submissions?

Documents and the Production of Documents (Article 3 of the IBA Rules)

- Should the parties produce all documents relied on with their submissions?
- Is document production (other than the production of documents relied on by each of the parties) necessary?
- Should there be a limit on the number of document production requests that each party is permitted to make?
- Should document production take place before or after the exchange of written submissions? Should there be provision for a second round of document production?
- Should documents be produced in hard copy or electronically and by what method?
- Should documents produced electronically be produced in native format?

- Should all metadata be produced with electronic documents (and, if so, as a matter of course or only if requested (with reasons) in relation to specific documents)?
- Is it desirable for the parties to agree a date range and list of custodians from which soft copy documents should be collected by each party preparatory to meeting document production requests from other parties? This may be important if one of the parties is already starting to collect documents for loading onto a database.
- Do any of the parties intend to use predictive coding to either collect documents or to identify documents responsive to document production requests?
- Should document production requests be in the form of a Redfern Schedule or other format?
- Should document production requests for electronic documents be accompanied by proposed date range/custodians and search terms? Should there be provision for consultation between the parties on the search terms?
- Should the parties be invited to consult with each other in relation to objections to document production requests with a view to resolving such objections?
- Should foreign language documents be accompanied by a translation of the whole document or relevant part(s) and which party should provide the translation?
- Is legal privilege likely to be an issue in the case? Have the parties considered what rules of privilege should apply in relation to documents falling within document production requests? Is it appropriate to use a privilege log?

Fact Witness Evidence (Article 4 of the IBA Rules)

- Are there issues of fact requiring witness evidence?
- On which issues should fact witness evidence be permitted?
- Should there be a limit on the number of fact witnesses?
- Will fact witness evidence be served simultaneously with written submissions or afterwards?
- What form will fact witness evidence take? Possibilities include:
  - witness summaries;
  - witness statements; or
  - only oral testimony at the evidentiary hearing (ie no written statements).
- If using witness summaries (as opposed to full witness statements), include directions to the effect that there will be evidence in chief at the hearing.
- If using witness statements, consider whether to include directions to the effect that they will serve as direct examination at the hearing.
- If witness statements or summaries are to be prepared:
  - should there be a limit on the length?
  - will the statement be organised chronologically, by reference to issue/topic or by reference to a particular phase of the arbitration?
  - will they be submitted simultaneously by the parties or consecutively?
- how many rounds should there be and will subsequent rounds be limited to rebuttal evidence?
- Consider including the requirements on the form and content of witness statements contained in Article 4.5 of the IBA Rules.[1]
- Is there a clear understanding as to what level of witness preparation is considered acceptable?
- By what date must the parties identify the witness(es) (and subject matter of testimony) upon whose evidence they wish to rely? See Article 4.1 of the IBA Rules.

[1] If the IBA Rules have been formally adopted these requirements will apply in any event, but the Tribunal may find it useful to set them out.

- By what date must the parties identify the witness(es)/experts whose presence is required at the hearing? See Article 8.1 of the IBA Rules.
- Is the physical appearance of the witness(es)/expert(s) necessary or can oral testimony be given by telephone, videoconference or some other technology?
- How will the tribunal deal with the witness statement of a witness who is asked to attend the evidentiary hearing but fails to do so? In particular, consider Article 4.7 of the IBA Rules.
- Are counsel able to reach agreement on whether all parts of the evidence of a witness that an 'opposing' party intends to challenge in submissions are to be put to that witness during cross-examination?[2]
- Will there be witness conferencing (hot-tubbing) at the hearing and what procedure is to be followed?
- If there will there be witness conferencing (hot-tubbing) at the hearing, should there be an opportunity for cross-examination?

Expert Evidence (Articles 5 and 6 of the IBA Rules)

- Are there technical issues requiring expert evidence?
- On which issues should expert evidence be permitted?
- How many disciplines of expert are required and should there be a limit on the number of experts?
- Does the Tribunal wish to appoint an expert under Article 6?
- Do the parties wish to appoint experts under Article 5?
- Will the submission of expert reports be organised by reference to issue or phase?
- Will expert evidence be served simultaneously with written submissions or afterwards?
- Will the parties deliver each discipline of expert evidence simultaneously or consecutively?
- Will the parties have the opportunity to submit rebuttal expert evidence?
- Should rebuttal evidence be added to first round reports or submitted in a separate report?
- Should there be a meeting of the experts to explore issues that can be agreed in a joint report?
- Consider including in directions the requirements on the form and content of expert reports contained in Article 5.2 of the IBA Rules.[3]
- By what date must the parties identify the experts (and subject matter of testimony) upon whose opinion evidence they wish to rely? See Article 5.1 of the IBA Rules.
- By what date must the parties identify the experts whose presence is required at the hearing? See Article 8.1 of the IBA Rules.
- Will there be expert conferencing (hot-tubbing) at the hearing and what procedure is to be followed? Will cross-examination be permitted?
- How will the tribunal deal with the expert report of an expert who is asked to attend the evidentiary hearing but fails to do so? In particular, consider Article 5.5 of the IBA Rules.

Foreign Law Issues

Do the parties wish to present expert evidence to prove applicable foreign law or will the parties address any issues of foreign law by means of submissions?

[2] See Chapter 7 for discussion on this issue.

[3] If the IBA Rules have been formally adopted these requirements will apply in any event, but the Tribunal may find it useful to set them out.

Good Faith Conduct

Are the parties clear about the standard of conduct expected in the arbitration, and the tribunal's powers under Article 9.7 of the IBA Rules to impose costs sanctions in appropriate circumstances?

Adverse Inferences

Are the parties aware that the tribunal may draw adverse inferences in the event a party fails to produce documents or other evidence when ordered to do so? See Articles 9.5 and 9.6 of the IBA Rules.

Inspections (Article 7 of the IBA Rules)

Do any of the parties, or the tribunal, require an inspection of any site, goods, documents, or anything else?

Evidentiary Hearing (Article 8 of the IBA Rules)

- Is an evidentiary hearing necessary?
- How much time is required for the evidentiary hearing?
- Is it possible to fix a date when the evidentiary hearing will take place?
- Does there need to be any time held in reserve if the length of the hearing is uncertain?
- Will witnesses give their evidence under oath or affirmation and, if so, in what form?
- In what language(s) will evidence be given at hearings?
- Are interpreters required?
- If interpreters are required, will there be simultaneous or consecutive interpretation and what impact will this have on the allocation of time between the parties?
- What arrangements should be put in place if video conferencing or other technology is to be used at the evidentiary hearing to ensure that the technology and connections are adequate? Provision for a protocol to be agreed between the parties concerning materials to be available to the witness and other arrangements to ensure fairness and due process?
- Is any form of electronic case management and trial presentation platform (for example, Opus 2 Magnum) to be used by the parties? Do the parties need to reach early agreement on how to prepare and present submissions and evidence in order to facilitate this?
- Will a chess clock timing arrangement be used? Parties to agree provisional timetable and split of time for approval by the tribunal.

Confidentiality (Articles 3.13 and 9.4 of the IBA Rules)

- Are specific directions required regarding the confidentiality of the fact of the arbitration and the conduct of proceedings?
- Are specific directions required regarding documents produced during the course of the arbitration that a party regards as having some special commercial or technical confidentiality?
- Are special directions required regarding the confidentiality and security of evidence and other material exchanged electronically and who can have access to this information?
- Consider steps necessary to comply with any applicable data protection legislation (eg the EU General Data Protection Regulation).

Points to Consider to Promote Efficiency, Economy, and Conservation of Resources in Connection with the Taking of Evidence

- Can the number of witnesses/experts be reduced further?
- Page limits for fact witness statements and expert reports?
- Is it possible to use electronic documents and electronic hearing bundles exclusively?
- Can video and telephone conferencing be used instead of in-person hearings?

APPENDIX 4

Sample Redfern Schedule Delivered by Claimant

This invented dispute concerns a contract for the design and installation of bespoke software and related work giving rise to a claim to damages for breach of contract and delay damages, with a counter-claim for the cost of additional out-of-scope work.

	Description of Document/Category of Document[1]	Relevance and Materiality		Response/Objections to Request	Tribunal's Ruling on Disputed Requests
		Explanation	Reference to issue in submissions		
1	Communications between Mr A (Respondent's Project Manager) and Mr B (Team leader of Respondent's sub-contractor) over the period 1 January 2016 to 31 July 2016 relating to the additional work alleged to have been requested by the Claimant to be undertaken by the Respondent during that period as described in paragraphs [•] of the Respondent's Defence Submissions. The claimant suggests the following search parameters: Email folders of Mr A: emails to, from or copied to Mr B having a date between 1 January 2016 to 31 July 2016 and containing the words [**name of claimant**] or [**Respondent's contract reference for the claimant's contract**] or [**Respondent's contract reference for the Sub-contract**] OR [**name of site where work is being conducted**]. The documents requested are not and never have been in the possession custody or control of the Claimant. The Claimant was not copied on correspondence between the Respondent and its sub-contractor.[2]	By way of defence and counterclaim to the Claimant's delay claim the Respondent alleges that (a) the Claimant caused the Respondent's delay in completion of the project works by the contractual deadline by making demands for performance of additional work at short notice to be carried out in priority to the project works and (b) such works were outside of the contract scope and the Claimant agreed to pay for those works on an *ad valorum* basis. This allegation is denied by the Claimant. The requested correspondence will contain evidence touching on the true reasons for the delay, and the nature of/reasons for any out of scope works that the Respondent asked its sub-contractor to carry out. The documents will help the Claimant show that no such additional works were requested and will be material to outcome of the respondent's defence and counterclaim to payment for the out-of-scope items	Respondent's Defence Submissions ¶[•] and Claimant's Reply Submissions ¶[•].	V[4] B The request is too vague. The Claimant has failed to provide a description of a narrow and specific category of document as required under IBA Rule 3.3(a)(ii). The correspondence between the Respondent and its sub-contractor over the relevant period is voluminous. Furthermore, the Claimant is permitted by IBA Rule 3.3(a) to request documents that it reasonably believes to exist. The Claimant has no such belief. The Claimant's case is that it did not request the additional work relied on by the Respondent. It is for the Respondent to prove its case in this respect and it is not open to the Claimant to make this request.	

	As the Respondent is a party to the correspondence it will have a copy of the documents within its possession, custody or control.[3]			
2	A copy of Mr A's diary entry for 1 to 7 February 2016 or notes made by Mr A during that period relating to or referring to the meeting described at Defence ¶[•]. Mr A remains an employee of the Respondent and it is assumed that his diary and notes of professional engagements will be accessible to the Respondent and within its possession, custody or control. The Claimant does not have a copy of the diary or any related notes.	The Respondent asserts that at a meeting between Mr A of the Respondent and Mr C of the Claimant that took place around 4 or 5 February 2016, Mr C agreed that certain items of out-of-scope work were requested by the Claimant and further agreed that those works be undertaken in advance of the balance of in scope work. The Claimant denies that such a meeting took place. The document will help the Claimant show that no additional works could have been requested by the Claimant at a meeting on 4 or 5 February and will be material to outcome of the Respondent's defence and counterclaim to payment for the alleged out-of-scope items	Respondent's Defence Submissions ¶[•] and Claimant's Reply Submissions ¶[•].	L U F The Respondent raises an objection to this Request under to **IBA Rule 9(2)(d), (c), and (g).** Mr A does not keep a hard copy diary. Mr A's electronic diary for the period in question has been deleted. Furthermore, it would place an unreasonable burden on the Respondent to have to search and reinstate data from back-up tapes. The costs of doing so (estimated to be in the order of USD$[•]) would be disproportionate and not in keeping with considerations of procedural economy.

	Description of Document/Category of Document[1]	Relevance and Materiality		Response/Objections to Request	Tribunal's Ruling on Disputed Requests
		Explanation	Reference to issue in submissions		
3	A copy of all internal communications and other documents created by the Respondent in connection with the project during the period 1 September 2015 to 30 September 2016. Given the nature of the documents requested it is assumed that they will be in the possession, custody or control of the Respondent. While the Claimant may have been copied on a small number of communications sent internally within the Respondent it does not possess the totality of documents. It would be unreasonably burdensome for the Claimant to find and identify the limited number of documents that it may have.	These documents are likely to contain evidence relating to the real reasons for the Respondent's delay in completing the project and will be relevant to the Claimant's claim for delay damages and material to its outcome.	Respondent's Defence Submissions ¶[•] and Claimant's Reply Submissions ¶[•].	B F R/M U P The Claimant has failed to provide a description of a narrow and specific category of document as required under **IBA Rule 3.3(a)(ii).** Without prejudice to the above position, the Respondent raises an objection to this Request **under IBA Rule 9(2)(a), (b), (c), and (g).** As drafted, the request is too wide and too vague. The Claimant has failed to identify specific categories of document that are relevant to the case and material to its outcome. A large proportion of the requested documents have nothing to do with the issues in the case and will not assist the tribunal. Should the Claimant wish to pursue this request it is invited to reformulate the request and to identity document custodians, date ranges and subject matter. The request is burdensome given that it could potentially involve collecting and harvesting all of the Respondent's documents relating to the project. It is estimated that the costs of collecting and reviewing all of the documents to identify those relating to delay would be in the order of USD [•]. These costs are disproportionate to the potential value of the evidence obtained. Furthermore, some of the communications will be between members of the Respondent's project team and the Respondent's in-house counsel. The respondent claims legal privilege and objects to production of this category of document on that basis.	

4	A copy of all documents created between 1 September 2015 and 31 December 2015 relating to design and testing by the Respondent, and its subsidiary ZCo, of the bespoke software installed at the Claimant's offices in January 2016. The documents requested are not and never have been in the possession custody or control of the Claimant. The Claimant was not copied on correspondence between the Respondent and its subsidiary, or document relating to the said design and testing. As the Respondent or its subsidiary is the author or recipient of the documents requested it will have a copy of the documents within its possession, custody or control. ZCo is a wholly-owned subsidiary of the Respondent incorporated to undertake part of the work on the Claimant's project.	The Claimant's case is that the real reason for the Respondent's delay in completing the project was that the software designed and installed by it was unfit for purpose, caused substantial delay in the project and required numerous patches and updates before it could support ongoing work necessary to complete the project. The Claimant believes that the problems with the software would have been apparent to the Respondent during testing and that they were sufficiently serious that the Respondent should have called a halt to further work on the project and requested an extension of time in accordance with the procedure set out in the contract between the Claimant and Respondent. Evidence on these matters likely to be contained in the requested documents is relevant to the issues described above and material to outcome of the Claimant's claim for delay damages.	Claimant's Claim Submissions ¶[•], Respondent's Defence Submissions ¶[•] and Claimant's Reply Submissions ¶[•].	C	PCC The Respondent raises an objection to this Request under **IBA Rule 9(2)(e) and 3.3(c)(ii)**. The documents requested contain technical material that is confidential to the Respondent and its affiliates. In its design of bespoke software, the Respondent employs certain techniques, coding, and approaches that are unique to the Respondent. This material has a commercial value and the Respondent's business may be adversely affected if this information was shared externally. Without prejudice to the above position, if the tribunal is minded to make an order for production of the requested documents, the Respondent will seek confidentiality protection pursuant to IBA Rule 9.4. Furthermore, documents held only by ZCo are not within the possession, custody or power of the respondent. ZCo is an independent legal entity not a party to the arbitration and subject to the tribunal's jurisdiction.

	Description of Document/Category of Document[1]	Relevance and Materiality		Response/Objections to Request	Tribunal's Ruling on Disputed Requests
		Explanation	Reference to issue in submissions		
5	A copy of communications between the Respondent and the Ministry of Defence of State X during the period 1 August 2015 to 31 October 2015 relating to the allocation of software designers by the Respondent to a new contract between Respondent and State X. The Claimant was not a party to these communications and does not have them in its possession, custody or power. As the Respondent is a party to the correspondence it will have a copy of the documents within its possession, custody or control.	The Claimant contends that, in breach of contract, the Respondent redeployed specialist software designers who it had been agreed would work on the Claimant's project to another project with State X prior to the Claimant's work being completed. The lack of expertise devoted to the Claimant's project contributed to the faults in the software and delay in the project. This is denied by the Respondent. The communications requested will contain evidence of the redeployment of specialist resources in breach of the Respondent's obligations. This is relevant and material to outcome of the Claimant's case on breach of contract and the Claimant's claim for delay damages.	Claimant's Claim Submissions ¶[•] and Respondent's Defence Submissions ¶[•]	S The Respondent raises an objection to this Request under **IBA Rule 9(2)(f)**. The Respondent's contract with the Ministry of Defence of State X is highly confidential and not in the public domain. Its existence was mentioned to the Claimant by a disgruntled employee of the Respondent. Had it not been the Claimant would not have known of its existence. The Claimant is bound by the Official Secrets Act 1989 and may not disclose any information relating to the contract. Should the tribunal wish to see extracts of the confidentiality obligations to which the Respondent is subject the Respondent is willing to provide sight of these (to the tribunal only).	

[1] Sufficient detail must be provided to enable the document or category of documents to be identified with sufficient specificity. See Article 3.3(a).
[2] A statement that the documents requested are not in the possession, custody, or control of the requesting party, or that it would be too burdensome to produce them, is a requirement of Article 3.3(c)(i).
[3] A statement of the reasons why the requesting party believes that the party to whom the request is addressed is in possession of the requested documents is a requirement of Article 3.3(c)(ii).
[4] This Redfern Schedule incorporates a row for the producing party to insert a 'Veeder Code' where objection to production is raised. Veeder Codes for Objections to Requests under the IBA Rules are sometimes used as a form of shorthand to indicate a basis for objection to production under the IBA Rules. Inclusion of Veeder Codes is not required and, in our experience, the codes are used relatively infrequently. Some parties may agree to use a customised form of shorthand—for example flagging privileged or confidential documents that may require special protections or be subject to a privilege log, etc. A copy of the Veeder Codes can be found at Appendix 6.

APPENDIX 5

Template Redfern Schedule

	Request	Basis for Request		Response/Objections to Request	Tribunal's Ruling on Disputed Requests
1	**[Description of document sufficient to identify it/ narrow and specific description of category of document][1]** **[Proposed custodians, files, search terms, or other parameters by reference to which a search for electronic documents should be conducted][2]**	<u>Relevance and Materiality</u> **[Explanation of why the document is/ documents are relevant to the case and material to outcome][3]** **[A statement of why the category of documents is believed to exist][4]**	<u>Reference to issue in submissions</u> Claimant's Claim Submissions ¶[•], Respondent's Defence Submissions ¶[•] and Claimant's Reply Submissions ¶[•]. ¶[•]	[The Respondent confirms that it will produce the requested documents] **OR** [**Name of party**] raises an objection to this Request on the basis that [**name of requesting party**] has failed to satisfy the requirements of Article 3.3. **AND/OR** [**Name of party**] raises an objection to this Request under to IBA Rule 9(2)[•] and [•][5]	
		[A statement that the document/documents are not in the possession custody or power of the requesting party or, if they are, why it would be unreasonably burdensome for that party to have to produce them][6] **[A statement of the reasons why the requesting party assumes that the documents requested are in the possession, custody or control of the other party].[7]** <u>Response to Objections to Production</u> **[Insert answer to any points of objection to the Request raised by the other party][8]**		**[Provide further details of basis of reliance on the grounds mentioned above]**	

[1] If a single document is requested, the description given must be sufficient to identify it. See Article 3.3(a)(i). If a category of documents is requested, the description must provide sufficient detail (including subject matter) of a narrow and specific category of documents. See Article 3.3(a)(ii).

[2] Where the documents requested exist in electronic form, the tribunal may order provision of this information under Article 3.3(a)(i). Where the requesting party has an informed view on the best way of carrying out a search for electronic documents, it may be sensible to provide these details before the other party wastes time and costs in approaching the search in a different way. It may also facilitate a discussion or negotiation on the scope of search/search parameters.

[3] See Article 3.3(b).

[4] The inclusion of a statement to this effect is not an express requirement of Article 3.3(a)(ii). However, if the request is contested by the other party and the requesting party has to seek an order for production from the tribunal, as contemplated by the wording of Article 3.3(a)(ii) the tribunal will have to be satisfied that there is a reasonable basis for belief in the existence of the documents. Accordingly, we suggest that it would be prudent for the requesting party to mention the grounds for belief in the request, particularly where this is not obvious from the nature of the documents requested.

[5] Identify which grounds of objection are relied on. In substance, the available grounds comprise a failure by the requesting party to meet the requirements of Article 3.3 and the grounds set out in Article 9.2(a)–(g).

[6] See Article 3.3(c)(i).

[7] See Article 3.3(c)(ii).

[8] Practice varies in relation to the inclusion of a rebuttal to points of objection raised after those objections have been received. Where an opportunity is given for rebuttal points, these are sometimes added in an additional column or included in this column.

APPENDIX 6

Veeder Codes for Objections to Requests for Production under the IBA Rules

Code	Articles of the IBA Rules	Ground for the decision made by the Arbitration Tribunal
V	3(3)(a)(i)	The description given is insufficient to identify the requested documentation. The request is too **vague**.
B	3(3)(a)(ii)	The category of documentation requested is insufficiently narrow and specific. The request is excessively **broad**.
E		The requested documentation does not **exist**.
M	3(3)(b); 9(2)(a)	The requested documentation is not **material** to the outcome of the case.
R	3(3)(b); 9(2)(a)	The requested documentation is not sufficiently **relevant** to the outcome of the case.
PCC	3(3)(c)	The requested documentation is in the **possession, custody, or control** of the requesting party and/or there is no basis to assume the requested documentation is the **possession, custody, or control** of the party to whom the request is addressed.
P	9(2)(b)	The requested documentation is protected from disclosure by legal impediment or **privilege**.
U	9(2)(c)	It would be an **unreasonable** burden for the respondent to the application to produce the requested documentation or it would otherwise be disproportionate to do so.
L	9(2)(d)	The requested documentation is **lost** or destroyed.
C	9(2)(e)	There are compelling grounds of commercial or technical **confidentiality** against the disclosure of the requested documentation.
S	9(2)(f)	The requested documentation is protected from disclosure by reason of special political or institutional **sensitivity**.
F	9(2)(g)	The requested documentation is protected from disclosure by reason of compelling considerations of **fairness or equality**.

APPENDIX 7

Checklist for Production of Documents

A. Voluntary Production of Documents

- By a date ordered by the tribunal, a party shall produce all documents on which it relies [Article 3.1 of the IBA Rules].
- By a date ordered by the tribunal, a party may produce documents that have become relevant to the case and material to its outcome by reason of issues raised in documents, witness statements, or expert reports [Article 3.11 of the IBA Rules].
- A party may provide with a witness statement or expert report documents on which the witness/expert relies that have not already been produced (Article 4.5 and 5.2 of the IBA Rules).

B. Requests to Produce Documents: From Another Party

1. Requesting Party: Content of the Request to Produce

- Document/category of documents requested [IBA Rules 3.3 (a)]:
  - has the document/category of documents requested been described in sufficient detail to meet the specificity requirements of Article 3.3(a)?
  - does the explanation for why the documents are 'relevant to the case and material to its outcome' (see below) relate to all of the documents described or does the explanation need to be tailored by reference to individual documents/categories?
  - is it possible to narrow the description of documents by reference to a date range, subject matter, or custodian? If the documents are electronic documents, is it possible to specify particular files/custodians, search terms (that is, words that are likely to appear in the documents being sought but not in other documents—for example, a name, reference number, project name, etc.), or other search parameters that may be used to retrieve the documents?
- Why the requested documents are 'relevant to the case and material to its outcome' [Article 3.3(b) of the IBA Rules]:
  - explain why the documents requested are both (a) relevant to the issues in the case *and* (b) will be material to the tribunal's determination on the merits of the dispute;
  - provide supporting paragraph references indicating the relevant parts of the written submissions that deal with the issues to which the documents are said to relate.
- State why the documents are believed to exist.
- State that the documents are not in the possession, custody, or control of the requesting party <u>or</u> that it would be unreasonably burdensome for the requesting party to have to produce them. [Article 3.3(c)(i) of the IBA Rules]. In particular:
  - if it may appear odd that the documents are not held by the requesting party explain why this is so;
  - if the 'unreasonably burdensome' ground is relied on explain why it would be burdensome to produce the documents and why it will be easier for the other party to produce them.
- Provide reasons why the requesting party believes that the other party has the documents [Article 3.3(c)(ii) of the IBA Rules].

2. Objecting Party: Response to Request to Produce

- Has the requesting party met the requirements for a valid request[Article 3.3 (a) to (c) of the IBA Rules] In particular:
- Has the requesting party described the documents in sufficiently specific terms? Is the description too vague? Consider offering to produce a narrower category of documents. Propose search parameters for electronic documents that the requesting party may be prepared to agree [Article 3.3(a) of the IBA Rules].
  - Has the requesting party explained why the documents requested are relevant and material [Article 3.3(b) of the IBA Rules]?
- Does the requesting party already have the documents [Article 3.3(c)(i) of the IBA Rules]?
- If the requesting party says it would be burdensome to have to produce the documents itself, is this in fact the case and how does it compare with the burden on the producing party? Are there ways in which the production might be more effectively managed to make it less burdensome [Article 3.3(c)(i) of the IBA Rules]?
- Does the producing party have the documents [Article 3.3(c)(ii) of the IBA Rules]?
- Are any grounds of objection under Article 9.2 applicable? For example:
  - the documents requested are (a) not relevant to the case and/or (b) not material to its outcome. The documents should be on the critical path to a determination of the dispute by the tribunal. Check that the documents requested really do relate to an issue in the arbitration and that the determination of that issue is material. [Article 9.2(a) of the IBA Rules];
  - a legal impediment or privilege is attached to the document—for example, legal advice privilege or litigation privilege [Articles 9.2(b) and 9.3 of the IBA Rules];
  - production of the documents would create an unreasonable burden—for example, electronic documents have been deleted and it would require back-up data to be identified and restored in order to provide the documents, or the documents are held in hard copy only and it would take several weeks to review files and identify the documents requested. If possible, attach a cost to the steps necessary to produce the documents [Article 9.2(c) of the IBA Rules];
  - the documents requested have been lost or destroyed. This must be shown with reasonable likelihood to have occurred. Provide details of the circumstances in which this has occurred with a statement or letter from someone who can speak directly to these events. If it has been done in accordance with a document retention policy, attach the policy [Article 9.2(d) of the IBA Rules];
  - the documents requested contain commercial or technical content of a confidential nature and there are compelling reasons why it would not be appropriate to order production. An indication of the nature of the confidential material will have to be provided, why it may damage the producing party if it is disclosed—for example, the requesting party is a business competitor and the documents contain trade secrets; a third party has an interest in the documents and there is a confidentiality agreement in place with that party. Consider, in the alternative to an objection to production, requesting protective measures under Article 9.4. [Articles 9.2(e) and 9.4 of the IBA Rules];
  - the documents have some special political or institutional sensitivity, for example, they contain information relating to matters of national security such as as projects being undertaken in the defence sector [Article 9.2(f) of the IBA Rules];
  - it would be disproportionate, unfair, or inefficient/wasteful of costs to order production, for example, evidence on the same issue is available from several other sources, the cost of production is extremely high, and the value of the claim to which the evidence relates is very small [Article 9.2(g) of the IBA Rules].

3. Tribunal

- The tribunal may make an order for production where:
  - the requesting party has satisfied the requirements of Article 3.3 (that is, it has provided specificity of description; relevance and materiality of the documents; documents not in the

requesting party's possession or burdensome to produce; and requesting party has provided reasons why the documents are held by the other party); and
- the issues that the requesting party wishes to prove by use of the documents are relevant to the case and material to its outcome; and
- none of the reasons for objection in Article 9.2 apply.

C. Requests to Produce Documents: From a Third Party [Article 3.9 of the IBA Rules]

- Article 3.9 contemplates two possible forms of application by a party seeking production of documents held by a third party:
  - where a party wishes the tribunal to take active steps to obtain production of documents from a non-party;
  - where, under the relevant national law, a party requires the permission of the tribunal to take active steps itself.
- In order for a party to make an application to the tribunal under Article 3.9, and for the tribunal to grant relief in the terms provided for in Article 3.9,[1] the following requirements must be met:
  - The documents to which the application relates (i) must be documents held by a person or organisation who is not a party to the arbitration and (ii) must be documents that the requesting party '*cannot obtain on its own*'.
  - The documents to which the application relates are documents that the tribunal determines to be '*relevant to the case and material to its outcome*'.
  - The requirements of Article 3.3 'as applicable' have been satisfied:
    - provision of a sufficiently detailed description of the documents;
    - provision of an explanation as to why the documents are relevant to the case and material to its outcome;
    - statement that the documents are not in the possession of the requesting party *or* why it would be unreasonably burdensome to have to produce them;
    - why the requesting party believes that the documents are in the possession of the third party.
- None of the reasons for objection set out in Article 9.2 applies.

See Chapter 6 for further explanation of these matters.

[1] The tribunal is not limited to an order in the terms of the application. It may order the taking of appropriate action by any of the parties to the arbitration, decide to take appropriate action itself, or dismiss the application.

APPENDIX 8

Checklist for Witnesses of Fact

A. Matters to Consider during Consultation on Procedure and Timetabling/Submissions for the First Procedural Order

- Is witness evidence necessary?
- Is there is a jurisdictional challenge, bifurcation into liability, and quantum, or a preliminary issue to be determined? If so, should the witness evidence be limited to a particular issue or phase until that matter is determined?
- Consider an appropriate date for notification of the identity of witnesses relied on by the parties [Article 4.1 of the IBA Rules].
- What form of procedure will best facilitate the taking of witness evidence—in particular, will a memorial style approach where witness statements are delivered with submissions work best, or is the common law approach of pleadings followed by witness evidence more appropriate for this case?
- Which party holds the majority of the documents, and is it desirable that document production take place prior to delivery of witness evidence?
- How many rounds of witness evidence should there be, and should delivery of each party's fact evidence take place simultaneously or should delivery be sequential?
- Consider an appropriate date for delivery of witness statements?
- Consider an appropriate date in the procedural order for party notification of witnesses required to attend the evidentiary hearing [Article 8.1 of the IBA Rules]?
- If likely to be needed, is it desirable to include express provision in a first procedural order for a possible application to use video-conferencing [Article 87.1 of the IBA Rules]?
- What is the legal tradition of counsel for each of the parties, and is it desirable, in order to establish an agreed common approach, that the first procedural order contain an express statement of what the tribunal expects in terms of counsel meetings with witnesses and preparation for the giving of evidence [Article 4.3 of the IBA Rules]?
- Should it be proposed that Article 4.7 of the IBA Rules should not apply, and to have this recorded in the first procedural order?

B. Matters to Consider When Drawing Up a List of Potential Witnesses and in the Preparation of Witness Statements

- If already filed, review pleadings/submissions to identify issues of fact to be addressed in witness evidence. Consider identity of appropriate witnesses and subject matter scope of evidence. Notification of this information may have to be given under Article 4.1 of the IBA Rules.
- Bearing in mind the terms of Article 4.7 of the IBA Rules, check that each of the witnesses is willing and available to attend the evidentiary hearing on the dates proposed. Consider including a statement to this effect in the witness statement/s.
- Check witness statements prior to filing to ensure they comply with the requirements of the IBA Rules [Article 4.5 of the IBA Rules]:
  - full name and address of witness;
  - statement of present and past relationship (if any) with any of the parties (or any of the tribunal);
  - description of qualifications, training, and experience to the extent relevant to the dispute;

- a complete statement of the witness' evidence on the facts *together with the source of the witness's knowledge* as to those facts;
- any additional requirements/directions of the tribunal as to structure and content;
- documents on which the witness relies that have not already been provided to the tribunal;
- a statement as to the language in which the statement was prepared;
- a statement of the language in which the witness anticipates giving testimony at the evidentiary hearing;
- an affirmation of the truth of the statement;
- the signature of the witness, and the date and place of signature.

- If the witness statement is a reply statement, check that its content is responsive to evidence delivered by another party. If it strays beyond responsive evidence, consider the justification for this in case of challenge [Article 4.6 of the IBA Rules].
- If the statement has been taken in one language and the statement translated into another language for filing, consider filing both the original and translated statement.
- Consider which witnesses to call for examination at the evidentiary hearing (and ensure that a notice to this effect is delivered within the time indicated by the tribunal [Article 8.1 of the IBA Rules]).

C. The Reluctant Witness

- If there is an important witness who is unwilling to present evidence, consider in good time an application to the tribunal under Article 4.9 and, in connection with such an application:
  - whether and on what basis the evidence of the witness is relevant to the case and material to its outcome;
  - where the witness is resident and whether it will be more effective to request assistance from the courts of the seat of arbitration or the courts in some other place;
  - whether the courts able to offer assistance permit a party and/or the tribunal to make an application to that court;
  - if an application to a court may be made by a party to the arbitration, whether that court requires that application to have the approval of the tribunal;
  - if there are steps other than a court order that might induce the witness to present evidence, consider raising these possibilities with the tribunal. For example, if a witness is within the 'control' or 'influence' of one of the other parties, or if a letter from the tribunal might assist in enabling the witness to take time from work to attend the hearing.

D. Tribunal Witnesses

If the tribunal indicates to you (a party) that you should try to arrange the attendance of a tribunal identified witness, consider whether you wish to object to this and, if so, whether any of the available grounds of objection under Article 9.2 apply [Article 4.10 of the IBA Rules].

E. Matters to Consider in Connection with the Evidentiary Hearing

- If a witness indicates that s/he is unable/unwilling, or simply fails, to attend the evidentiary hearing, consider:
  - if 'your' witness, whether there is a 'valid' reason, or 'exceptional circumstances' within the meaning of Article 4.7 of the IBA Rules, justifying the non-attendance that may be presented to the tribunal to avoid the consequences (disregard of the statement of that witness) set out in Article 4.7. If the IBA Rules are applied as guidelines only, consider proposing that the witness statement be admitted and appropriate adjustment be made to the weight attributed to it by the tribunal;

- if your opponent's witness, and in the absence of a valid reason for the non-attendance, consider an express request to the tribunal for application of Article 4.7.
- Are counsel able to reach agreement on (a) whether all parts of the evidence of a witness that an 'opposing' party intends to challenge in later submissions are to be put to that witness during cross-examination and (b) whether a witness may be cross-examined on matters not addressed in his or her witness statement? See Chapter 7 for commentary on Article 4.8.
- How is time for cross-examination of fact witnesses to be allocated between the parties? Matters to be taken into account include the number of witnesses for each party, the number of issues to which each witness speaks, and how time spent on tribunal questions is to be allocated.
- Are counsel able to agree whether sequestration of witnesses is desirable?

See also Appendix 2 containing a list of matters to consider during consultation on procedure and timetabling, and Chapter 7 on Witnesses of Fact.

APPENDIX 9

Checklist for Party-Appointed Experts

A. Matters to Consider during Negotiations on Procedure and Timetabling/Submissions on the First Procedural Order

- Are experts needed? Does a determination of the particular dispute require technical or other specialized knowledge?
- The issues on/disciplines in which expert evidence is required.
- Is expert evidence needed to prove applicable foreign law or will the parties address any issues of foreign law by means of submissions?
- Whether the evidence should be provided by party-appointed experts and/or tribunal-appointed experts.
- If there is a jurisdictional challenge or bifurcation into liability and quantum, should the expert evidence be limited to a particular issue or phase?
- Is simultaneous or consecutive exchange of evidence more appropriate? What form of procedure will best facilitate the taking of expert evidence—in particular, whether a memorial style approach or common law approach of pleadings followed by witness and expert evidence will work best?
- Are there dependencies between the disciplines of expert evidence or between fact and expert evidence that require adjustment to the timetable for delivery of expert evidence?
- Consider an appropriate date in the procedural order for party notification of expert evidence on which it intends to rely [Article 5.1 of the IBA Rules]?
- A date in the procedural order for delivery of expert's reports.
- A date for revised or additional expert reports responsive to matters contained in another party's witness statements, expert evidence, or submissions not yet filed when the expert report was prepared [Article 5.3 of the IBA Rules].
- Is it desirable to order the party-appointed experts to meet and seek to agree the issues on which they agree and the issues that remain in dispute? Is it better to require the experts to meet before or after the first round of expert reports?
- Should there be a meeting or telephone call between the experts and the tribunal to agree or discuss methodology (for example, in relation to critical path delay analysis) in order to ensure that the experts do not adopt irreconcilable approaches?
- Should the meeting between the experts be on a 'without prejudice' or 'open' basis?
- Is it desirable for the Tribunal to direct that the experts shall not accept instructions from their respective counsel and instructing party not to reach an agreement with an opposing expert on any particular issue?
- A date on which notice requesting attendance of experts at an evidentiary hearing should be served [Article 8.1 of the IBA Rules].
- Whether, if likely to be needed, there should be express provision in the first procedural order for a possible application to use video-conferencing [Article 8.1 of the IBA Rules].
- Should it be proposed that Article 5.5 of the IBA Rules should not apply and that this be recorded in the first procedural order?

B. Matters to Consider When Drawing Up a List of Potential Experts and Drafting Instructions to the Expert

- On what issues, and in which disciplines, is expert evidence required?
- If already filed, review pleadings/submissions to identify facts relevant to the expert evidence required and whether any of those facts are in issue between the parties.
- If a choice exists, and taking into account the background of tribunal members, consider which expert may carry more weight with some or all tribunal members in light of the legal tradition/background from which they come. In particular, consider whether the tribunal may be more receptive to expert evidence from an academic or somebody who practises in a particular industry.
- Check if there is any relationship between the potential expert and any of the parties (or their legal advisers) or the tribunal.
- Check that each of the experts is willing and available to attend the evidentiary hearing on the dates proposed.
- Do any of the experts require access to property or evidence held by another party? Consider an application for an inspection under Article 7 of the IBA Rules.
- Check expert reports prior to filing to ensure they comply with the requirements of Article 5.2 of the IBA Rules:[1]
  - the name and address of the party-appointed expert;
  - details of his or her relationship/s with any of the parties, their legal advisors, and the tribunal;
  - a description of the background, qualifications, training, and experience of the expert;
  - a description of the instructions pursuant to which s/he is providing his or her opinions and conclusions;
  - a statement of the expert's independence from the parties, their legal advisors, and the tribunal;
  - the facts that the expert has relied upon in reaching the opinion and conclusions;
  - the expert opinion/conclusions together with details of methodology and evidence relied upon. An expert report must be accompanied by any documents on which the expert relies that are not already on the record;
  - if the expert report has been translated, a statement as to the language in which it was originally prepared, and the language in which the expert anticipates giving testimony at the hearing. Consider filing both the original and translation;
  - an affirmation of the expert's genuine belief in the opinions expressed in the expert report;
  - signature, date, and place; and
  - where the report is signed by more than one person, a statement explaining which which parts of the report have been prepared by which author/s.
- If the expert report is a reply report, check that its content is responsive; if it strays beyond the responsive, consider justification for this in case of challenge. If the other party were to raise a legitimate objection on this basis to part of the 'responsive' evidence submitted, it might be necessary to obtain permission from the tribunal for the introduction of that evidence [Article 5.3 of the IBA Rules]. Note that reply evidence from a 'new' expert is permitted under Article 5.3.
- Is it better to serve an additional expert report or a revised expert report?
- Consider which experts to call for examination at the evidentiary hearing and ensure that a notice to this effect is delivered within the time indicated by the tribunal [Article 8.1 of the IBA Rules].

[1] The requirements are different for tribunal-appointed experts. See Appendix 11 and Chapter 9.

C. Expert Not Required/Unable to Attend the Evidentiary Hearing

- Are all disciplines of expert evidence contested? Is it possible for the parties to agree that experts whose evidence is not contested do not have to attend the hearing?
- Has any expert indicated that s/he is unable/unwilling, or simply fails, to attend the evidentiary hearing? If so, the provisions of Article 5.5 of the IBA Rules will need to be considered:
  - If it is 'your' expert, consider whether there is a 'valid' reason, or exceptional circumstances, justifying the non-attendance that may be presented to the tribunal to avoid the consequences (disregard of the report of that expert) set out in Article 5.5.
  - If it is an adverse party expert who is unable to attend, consider the justification given for the non-attendance provided by the relevant party are exceptional. Unlike witnesses of fact, party-appointed experts are retained by the parties to whom they owe a contractual obligation. The expert retainer will usually include an obligation to appear at the evidentiary hearing if so required. For that reason, a tribunal is likely to apply a very high standard to the question of whether a valid reason or exceptional circumstance exists which justify the non-attendance of an expert.
- Subject to considerations of procedural efficiency, if the unavailability of the expert is temporary, can the hearing be deferred? If a physical condition renders the expert immobile but capable of giving evidence, can the expert attend by video conference? If the expert report was prepared with assistance from a wider team, is it possible for someone else on the team to attend the evidentiary hearing in place of the original expert?
- If the IBA Rules are applied as guidelines only, consider proposing that the consequences set out in Article 5.5 should not apply, and that the expert report be admitted and appropriate adjustment be made to the weight attributed to it by the tribunal.

See also Appendix 2 containing a list of matters to consider during consultation on procedure and timetabling, and Chapter 8 on Party-Appointed Experts.

APPENDIX 10

Table for Joint Statement from Party-Appointed Experts on Areas of Agreement and Disagreement

Details of Claimant's Expert
Name:
Area of Expertise:

Details of Respondent's Expert
Name:
Area of Expertise:

Issue	Opinion of Claimant's Expert[1]	Opinion of Respondent's Expert[2]	Points of Agreement	Points of Disagreement and Reasons
1				
2				
3				
4				

[1] The contents of this column are not agreed or endorsed by the Respondent's expert.
[2] The contents of this column are not agreed or endorsed by the Claimant's expert.

Date:

Signature of Claimant's Expert:

....

Date:

Signature of Respondent's Expert:

....

APPENDIX 11

Checklist and Guidance on Use of Tribunal-Appointed Experts

A. Matters to Consider during Negotiations on Procedure and Timetabling/Submissions on the First Procedural Order (PO1)

- Are experts needed? Does a determination of the particular dispute require technical or other specialized knowledge?
- What are the issues on which expert evidence is required?
- Is expert evidence needed to prove applicable foreign law or will the parties address any issues of foreign law by means of submissions?
- Should the evidence be provided by party-appointed and/or tribunal-appointed experts?
- If the tribunal does appoint an expert, do the parties also wish to instruct party-appointed experts on the same issue?

B. Procedure for Appointment of Tribunal-Appointed Expert and Subsequent Steps

- Possible points for discussion during Article 6.1 consultation between tribunal and the parties:[1]
  - the advantages and disadvantages of a tribunal-appointed expert in the case;
  - the complexity of the issue for which expert evidence is required;
- whether a party has already instructed, or will be instructing, an expert on the issue in question;
- whether the instruction of a single tribunal-appointed expert is likely to assist the parties to resolve the issue more speedily and in a more cost-effective way than separately instructed experts;
- whether the expert evidence falls within a substantially established area of knowledge which is unlikely to be in dispute or there is unlikely to be a range of expert opinion;
- the fees of the tribunal-appointed expert and how are those fees to be funded during the arbitration;
- the scope of the mandate and issues it is proposed be put to the expert
- Potential candidates—there are three general approaches to identifying candidates:
  - the tribunal may invite the parties to suggest a suitable expert, with a suggested default appointment mechanism in the event that the parties are unable to agree;
  - the tribunal may identify an expert using their own contacts; and/or
  - the tribunal may approach a specialist institution for assistance in identifying a suitable expert.
- Under Article 6.2, if, following consultation with the parties, the tribunal decides to appoint an expert, the tribunal should ask the identified expert whether he or she is willing and able to take

[1] In accordance with Article 6.1 of the IBA Rules, before appointing a tribunal-appointed expert the tribunal must consult with the parties.

on the assignment and also to submit description of his or her qualifications and a statement of independence from the parties, their legal advisors and the tribunal.

All of this information should be sent to the parties.

- The tribunal must set a deadline by which the parties may raise objections to the expert's qualifications or independence.
- Article 6.2 does not require the expert to provide a statement of availability. However, during initial contact with a potential expert it is sensible for the tribunal to establish that the expert has sufficient time to devote to the proceedings and is available to attend any hearing dates that have been fixed. The parties may wish to seek confirmation that this has been done.
- If any of the parties raise an objection to the proposed expert, the tribunal must decide in a timely fashion whether to accept the objection and forego the expert (in which case the tribunal will have to find another expert and start the procedure over again); or (b) not to accept the objection and proceed with the appointment. See Article 6.2.
- The tribunal will generally indicate a date by which the tribunal-appointed expert evidence will be delivered. The report must contain the information set out in Article 6.4 of the IBA rules.
- The tribunal should set a deadline for each party to respond to the expert report by means of submissions, a witness statement or an expert report prepared by an expert instructed by the party [Article 6.5].
- Although not provided for in Article 6.5, the tribunal may consider whether it is appropriate to have a further round of expert evidence.
- The tribunal should set a date by which the parties must give notice of a request that the tribunal-appointed expert attends the evidentiary hearing to be cross-examined [Article 6.6].

C. Matters to Consider When Drawing Up Terms of Reference for the Tribunal-Appointed Expert

- It is desirable that the tribunal consult with the parties on the terms of reference for the tribunal-appointed expert. While always tailoring terms of reference to the circumstances of the individual dispute the following housekeeping points and general topics may be considered for discussion and/or inclusion:
  - Identification of the arbitration proceedings (parties to the proceedings and any institution number, etc.).
  - Name and address of the expert. Where a professional partnership or other body is retained, the individual assuming the role of expert should be identified.
  - Any other aspects of the desired organization, preparation, and presentation of the evidence. For example, the format in which the expert report should be presented.
  - A timetable for preparation and delivery of the expert evidence.
  - Definition of the expert's tasks and the questions/issues that the expert must address in the expert report.
  - The tribunal and the parties may also wish to include instructions on what is to happen should the expert identify an issue that has not been specifically addressed in the terms of reference. Options are to deal with those issues as the expert considers appropriate or to ask the tribunal as to whether the expert should address the additional issues.
  - An express statement of the power of the tribunal to adjust the expert's terms of reference, if so required, by the expert's findings (normally exercised after consulting the parties).
  - Identification of information (documents, specimens, etc.) that are to be provided to the expert and on which the expert should base his or her report. The right of the parties to see all material provided to the expert [Article 6.5].
  - A procedure by which the expert may collect further information that the expert may require in order to prepare the report. For example, the rules under which the expert can contact the parties to request information or hold interviews with them [Article 6.3 of the IBA Rules].
  - Rules for communications between the expert, the parties, and the tribunal designed to ensure transparency around the process by which the evidence is prepared. In particular, whether the

expert can communicate *ex parte* with the tribunal and whether s/he can be present during the tribunal's deliberations.

- An express statement of the parties' right to comment on the expert's report and, upon request, to question the expert at an oral hearing [Article 6.6].
- A statement of the expert's related obligations, for example, the duty to maintain confidentiality; the obligation to be truthful and impartial; the duty to disclose the expert's contacts with the parties and potential conflicts of interests prior to and during the arbitration proceedings.
- An explanation that the expert shall include in his/her report a description of the effect of the non-compliance with his document production/interview/inspection request on the determination of the specific issue to which it relates [Article 6.3 of the IBA Rules].
- Other optional items: scope of the expert's liability; grounds for termination of the retainer.
- A statement of the expert's rights in relation to the role for which the expert has been retained, and what the expert expects from the tribunal/parties.
- A statement of agreed arrangements in relation to remuneration and reimbursement of expenses (including fees for the expert's employees and charges for travel and accommodation, if appropriate). Any advance payment should be recorded.
- Basic rules for monitoring costs and readjusting the advance on expert's costs. In general, the tribunal will need to ensure that arrangements are in place to ensure that the fees and expenses of the expert will be paid by the parties as and when they are incurred.
- Expert's obligation to attend the hearing if it is requested by the tribunal or any of the parties.
- A statement that the expert shall be guided by the IBA Rules. In particular, the expert shall ensure that the expert report is compliant with Article 6.4 of the IBA Rules.

- It is common practice for draft terms of reference to be circulated to the parties for comment before being finalised. Another approach is for the tribunal to invite the parties to try to agree terms of reference. Whatever measure of agreement they are able to reach is then produced and any points of disagreement are resolved by a decision of the tribunal.

D. Matters to Consider in Connection with the Evidentiary Hearing

- If the parties accept the evidence of the tribunal-appointed expert it may be possible for the parties to agree that the tribunal-appointed expert need not attend the hearing for cross-examination. In this case, the tribunal may dispense with cross-examination of the expert unless the tribunal may need the expert's assistance during the hearing.
- At the hearing the tribunal-appointed expert may be questioned by the tribunal, or by the parties or their appointed experts [Article 6.6].
- What further role (if any) the expert may play at the hearing. For example, should members of the tribunal be permitted to have the expert sit with them as an adviser during questioning of any experts of the same discipline appointed by the parties, or when counsel for the parties are making submissions on the evidence of the tribunal expert? It is prudent for a tribunal considering such a step to first canvass it with the parties or, at the very least, to make known the intended scope of the expert's intended involvement so as to address as far as possible any concerns that the parties may have about the expert assuming a decision-making role (which is clearly prohibited).

APPENDIX 12

Checklist for Inspection

A. Is an Inspection Necessary or Desirable?

- Does the subject matter of the dispute concern goods/property or work product that may deteriorate, be altered, damaged or transferred to parties outside of the arbitration?
- Will the expert/s instructed in the case need to inspect goods/property or work product in order to provide expert evidence or to challenge that of their opponent?
- Will the tribunal's understanding of a material issue in the case benefit from an inspection of the relevant goods/property, process, etc.?
- Are there disputed issues around the content of computer hardware/a database that can only be addressed by an inspection?
- Is it desirable to obtain samples for analysis and do such samples need to be collected under jointly supervised conditions?

B. Objections to Inspection

There may exist grounds to object under Article 9.2 of the IBA Rules. Those grounds are set out here. Possible grounds of objection include:

- the information to be gleaned from the proposed inspection is not sufficiently relevant or material to outcome [Article 9.2(a)].
- that some legal impediment or privilege applies to the carrying out of an inspection [9.2(b)].
- that the carrying out of the inspection would be burdensome or disproportionate [9.2(c) and (g)].
- that the subject matter of the proposed inspection has been lost or destroyed [9.2(d)].
- that there are compelling grounds of commercial or technical confidentiality, or special political or institutional sensitivity, that make an inspection inappropriate [9.2(e) and (f)].
- that there exist considerations of procedural economy, proportionality, fairness, or equality of the Parties that militate against an inspection (and which the tribunal finds to be compelling) [9.2(g)].

An example of circumstances potentially meeting each of these grounds of objection is provided at paragraph 10.19 of Chapter 10 on Article 7.

C. Arrangements for the Inspection

Arrangements for an inspection will need to be tailored to meet the individual circumstances of the case. Matters to consider include:

- When should the inspection take place? Are there seasonal or other time factors that will affect the value of the inspection? Are there particular times/dates that will cause less disruption to a site/plant in commercial operation?

- What is the purpose of the inspection? What is it intended to achieve? This will inform other aspects of the arrangements.
- Who should attend the inspection? The tribunal? Party representatives? Experts? In what language is the inspection to be conducted? Will an interpreter be required?
- What is to be inspected? Is there a clear understanding of what is to be made available for inspection? Where participants may go?
- What are inspection participants permitted to do and say? Is there an agreed neutral commentary for any part of the inspection that requires explanation? Is there agreement on who may answer questions that the tribunal/experts have? Is there an express agreement that participants may not advocate a particular position?
- What record is to be made of the inspection? Notes, audio/video recording, transcript? Is that material to be admitted to the record in the arbitration?
- If samples are to be taken, is there an agreement on the conditions under which this is to be done? Are all parties to retain a portion of the sample? To whom are the test results on the sample to be distributed?
- Are there security or confidentiality issues or agreements that need to be addressed or put in place prior to the inspection taking place? Are there any limitations on who may attend, and how are these to be addressed to observe due process?
- Is any form of prior safety training/induction or special clothing/footwear necessary for inspection participants?
- Are the proposed inspection arrangements fair to all parties? Is the inspection being conducted in the most efficient and cost-effective manner?

See example of an inspection protocol provided at Chapter 10 on Article 7.

Index

Boxes are indicated by *b* following the page number

www.ingramcontent.com/pod-product-compliance
Lightning Source LLC
Chambersburg PA
CBHW081605021026
52493CB00005B/312
9780198818342